Collaborative Social Work

Strengths-Based
Generalist Practice

Collaborative Social Work

Strengths-Based Generalist Practice

John Poulin
Widener University

and Contributors

F. E. Peacock Publishers, Inc.
Itasca, Illinois

To Anne, my wife, for her love, support, and encouragement, and to Katherine, Jessica, and Claire, my daughters, for keeping me honest, humble, and feeling blessed.

Advisory Editor in Social Work
Donald Brieland

Cover illustration: Bob Commander/SIS

Photo credits:
Page xii Bob Daemmrich Photography
        2 © Syracuse Newspapers/C. W. McKeen/The Image Works
       32 Susie Fitzhugh/Stock, Boston
       54 Bob Daemmrich Photography
       80 Bob Daemmrich Photography
      102 David Wells/The Image Works
      134 Bob Daemmrich Photography
      182 Gale Zucker/Stock, Boston
      208 © Joel Gordon
      234 Alan Carey/The Image Works
      264 David Wells/The Image Works
      294 Rhoda Sidney/Stock, Boston
      326 Nubar Alexanian/Stock, Boston
      356 Reuters/Jeff Christensen/Archive Photos
      384 John Griffin/The Image Works
      414 Bob Daemmrich Photography

Contents

Preface

Collaborative Social Work: Strengths-Based Generalist Practice grew out of my inability to find a textbook consistent with my approach to teaching. Although there are a number of excellent books available, none provided what I needed in an introductory text. Some were too general to be of practical use to beginning students; others were too focused on problems and deficits; and still others were too focused on the direct service aspect of generalist practice. They all seemed to pay only minimal attention to the evaluative component of social work practice. Another factor influencing the development of this book was my increasingly stronger conviction that, regardless of the client population, the type of intervention, or the type of client system, the key to effective generalist social work practice is the helping relationship.

Collaborative Social Work: Strengths-Based Generalist Practice differs from other generalist practice texts in several ways. It integrates the strengths-based collaborative approach to working with client systems and empirical practice methods. The book operationally defines the helping relationship and emphasizes its use throughout the helping process. It provides detailed coverage of at-risk special populations. And it is one of the few introductory texts that incorporates the strengths or empowerment model of generalist practice with individual, family, group, organization, and community client systems.

Collaborative Social Work: Strengths-Based Generalist Practice is suitable for use in senior BSW generalist practice courses and for the first foundation practice course in an MSW curriculum. It presents concepts in an accessible manner, using straightforward language that is relatively free of jargon. There are case examples throughout, and each chapter concludes with a detailed case study and discussion questions.

ORGANIZATION

The seven chapters that make up Part I of the book provide students with a model of generalist practice with individuals, families, groups, organizations, and communities. Chapters 1 and 2 focus on the principles and concepts on which the stengths-based model is based. Chapter 1 presents the two theoretical frameworks of collaborative social work—logical positivism and postmodernism—as well as a review of the ecosystems and strengths perspectives. It introduces students to client systems and the experience of being a client, and it concludes with a discussion of core social work values and decision-making models for resolving ethical dilemmas. Chapter 2 presents the heart of the collaborative model of practice. It describes the practice principles of collaboration, empowerment, and evaluation, and it presents a conceptualization of the helping relationship that focuses on the structural and interpersonal aspects of the helping process.

Chapters 3, 4, and 5 focus on assessment of client systems. Chapter 3 approaches individual and family assessment from the perspective of the helping relationship within the context of the person-in-environment. It emphasizes client system strengths as well as challenges. Chapter 4 focuses on group, organization, and community client system assessment from the same perspective. Chapter 5 introduces tools and instruments for conducting traditional and strengths-based client system assessments.

Chapter 6 covers the contracting stage of the helping process. It provides guidelines for constructing goals and objectives, measuring client system change, designing an evaluation plan, evaluating change, and developing an intervention plan. Chapter 7 focuses on micro and macro generalist social work practice interventions and client system change activities. The chapter also presents information on the termination process. Together, the first seven chapters take the student through all aspects of the helping process while providing a framework for a strengths-based approach to generalist social work practice.

Part II of the book consists of eight chapters on practice with special populations. Each chapter was written by an expert in the area covered. Generalist social workers in agency-based practice often encounter economically disadvantaged people and communities (Chapter 8), persons with serious and persistent mental illness (Chapter 9), older people (Chapter 10), people of color (Chapter 11), abused and neglected children and their families (Chapter 12), gay and lesbian clients (Chapter 13), people with HIV and AIDS (Chapter 14), and survivors of natural disasters (Chapter 15). Each chapter provides the context for generalist practice with the specific at-risk population, including background information on the population, human behavior and social environment issues associated with it, relevant policy issues, micro and macro practice issues, and other considerations that need to be taken into account in working with the population. These chapters provide students with the information they need to be effective generalist social workers with each population group.

ACKNOWLEDGMENTS

Many people contributed to this book. My colleague, Tom Young, contributed immensely to the conceptualization of the helping relationship presented in Chapter 2. His understanding of the helping process and his insights into the interpersonal connection between social workers and their clients helped make this book possible. I want to especially thank my other colleagues at Widener University—Frann Anderson, Stephen Kauffman, Brent Satterly, Hussein Soliman, and Norma Thomas—as well as Martha Dore and Nancy Feldman, Columbia University, and Pat Sullivan, Indiana University, for their authorship of the special population chapters. These chapters enrich the book and make generalist practice come alive for students.

I would like to express my gratitude to Sybil Sosin, who edited the manuscript with care and enthusiasm and made wonderful suggestions for improving it, and to Kim Vander Steen, who coordinated the production of the book. Special thanks go to Dick Welna, Vice President and Publisher at F.E. Peacock Publishers, for supporting the project and working with me as it evolved. His patience, good humor, and support are greatly appreciated. Donald Brieland, Peacock's Social

Work Series Consultant, Peter Lehmann, John Ronnau, and Susan J. Rose reviewed the manuscript and made numerous suggestions that improved its organization, clarity of presentation, and content. I also thank my students for allowing me to try out my ideas, for their constructive feedback, and for their support. In particular, I am grateful to Denise Bubel, Jennifer Francella, Leslie Freas, Susan Getty, Dan Lafferty, and Kathleen McCabe for contributing the case examples used in Part I of the book. Finally, I thank my wife, Anne, for her love, support, and encouragement, and my daughters, Katherine, Jess, and Claire, for keeping me honest, humble, and feeling blessed.

About the Authors

Frann S. Anderson is a Senior Quality Assurance Operations Specialist for the State of Delaware and a commissioner on the Governor's Human Relations Commission, where she represents the gay and lesbian community. She received a BA in art and art therapy and a BA in psychology from Carlow College, an MA in art therapy from Vermont College, and an MSW from Widener University. She is a licensed social worker in Pennsylvania, is certified as an alcohol and drug counselor in Delaware, and is registered by the American Art Therapy Association as an art therapist. She has dedicated her private practice to the treatment of adult survivors of childhood sexual abuse and to work with sexual minorities.

Martha Morrison Dore is an Associate Professor of Social Work at Columbia University, where she teaches in the master's and doctoral programs. She received a BA from DePauw University, an MSW from the Atlanta University (now Clarke-Atlanta University) School of Social Work, and a PhD from the University of Chicago School of Social Service Administration. Her clinical experience has included work as an individual and family therapist, director of a therapeutic foster care program for children with special emotional and physical needs, and director of a group home program for emotionally disturbed adolescent girls. Her research and writing have focused on high-risk families presenting issues of substance abuse, domestic violence, mental illness, and child maltreatment.

Nancy Feldman is a doctoral candidate at the Columbia University School of Social Work. She received a BA from Tulane University, an MA in creative arts therapy from Hahnemann University, an MSW from Fordham University, and postgraduate training in family therapy and short-term psychotherapy. She has taught social work courses and trained city and contract agency child welfare workers, and she has worked with children, adolescents, and adults in an acute care psychiatric hospital, a mental health clinic, and a battered women's shelter, among other settings. Her research and teaching interests include creating developmental environments, performance-based social therapy, and abuse and violence prevention.

Stephen E. Kauffman is an Associate Professor at Widener University's Center for Social Work Education, where he has taught social policy, community practice, program evaluation, and research. He received a BA from University of the South, an MSW from the George Warren Brown School of Social Work at Washington University, and a PhD from the Graduate School of Social Work and Social Research at Bryn Mawr College. He works with community organizations to evaluate the effectiveness of their education, housing, substance abuse, and teenage pregnancy prevention programs. His research and writing interests are citizen participation and the role of ideology in policy development and implementation.

John Poulin is a Professor at Widener University's Center for Social Work Education, where he teaches foundation generalist practice and research. He received a BA from the University of Southern Maine, an MSW from the University of Michigan School of Social Work, and a PhD from the University of Chicago School of Social Service Administration. The former director of the BSW program at Widener, he began its MSW program and served as director and as Associate Dean of the School of Human Service Professions. His research and writing have focused on the helping relationship, the effective delivery of social work services, and social worker job satisfaction and burnout.

Brent Satterly is an Adjunct Assistant Professor of Human Sexuality and Social Work at Widener University's Center for Social Work Education, a clinical social worker with Family and Community Services of Delaware County, Pennsylvania, and a doctoral candidate at the University of Pennsylvania. He received a BA from Eastern College and an MSW from the Graduate School of Social Work and Social Research at Bryn Mawr College. He specializes in social work sexuality education.

Hussein Soliman is an Associate Professor at the Center for Social Work Education at Widener University. He received a BA from the University of Helwan (Cairo), Egypt, an MSW from the University of Southern Mississippi, and a PhD in social work from the University of Tennessee. He is Chair of the Disaster and Traumatic Stress Symposium at annual program meetings of the Council on Social Work Education. His research interests are community responses to disasters, evaluation of mental health services in disasters, cross-cultural studies of mental health services, and social policies on AIDS and the environment.

W. Patrick Sullivan is a Professor at the Indiana University School of Social Work in Indianapolis where he teaches master's and doctoral courses in mental health policies and services. He received his BSW, MSW, and PhD from the University of Kansas, School of Social Work. He previously served as director of the Indiana Division of Mental Health. His research interests are the strengths perspective, serious mental illness, addictions, spirituality, and rural practice.

Norma D. Thomas is an Associate Professor and the Assistant Director of the Center for Social Work Education at Widener University, where she teaches undergraduate and graduate courses. She received a BA in social work from Penn State University, an MSW from the Temple University School of Social Administration, and a DSW from the University of Pennsylvania School of Social Work. She has worked as a direct practitioner, administrator, and consultant and sits on a number of boards and advisory groups. Her primary research interests are issues related to people of color and aging.

Collaborative Social Work

Strengths-Based Generalist Practice

PART I Generalist Social Work Practice

CHAPTER 1

Principles and Concepts of Generalist Practice

Karen L. was a first-year MSW student who had recently graduated from college. She had had no prior social work experience when she reported to her first day of field placement in a drug and alcohol treatment program. Karen was excited about beginning her social work career and nervous about having to begin placement immediately.

After giving her a brief tour of the facility and introducing her to the staff, Karen's field instructor told her that he thought the best way to begin was to jump right in. He handed her three case files and copies of the agency's assessment form and told her that she was scheduled to conduct three assessments of new residents that morning. Karen felt stunned and overwhelmed as she went to meet her first client.

During the assessment interviews, Karen felt completely lost. She was unfamiliar with many of the terms on the form, and she was not sure how to proceed with the interviews. The assessment used open-ended questions, and it required her to describe the client's ecosystem, target systems, client system strengths and challenges, and factors that might influence the client's capacity to engage in a helping relationship. Karen did not see her field instructor again that day, and she left feeling discouraged and confused.

Karen's experience is every beginning social work student's worst nightmare. It raises a number of questions and issues. Generalist social work practice involves a wide variety of problems in a variety of practice settings (Pinderhughes, 1995). Generalist social workers define client issues, collect and assess data, and plan the intervention. Once the concern has been identified and the intervention planned, the generalist social worker selects and implements appropriate courses of action, monitors and evaluates outcomes, and plans termination (Baker, 1995).

This chapter provides an introduction to generalist social work practice. The chapter begins by defining the concept of strengths-based generalist social work practice. The theoretical foundations of generalist practice are then discussed, followed by discussions of clients and client systems and social work values and ethics. By the end of this chapter, you should be able to help Karen

1. Describe the ecosystem perspective and its role in generalist social work practice
2. Interpret the major principles of strengths-based generalist social work practice and understand how strengths-based practice differs from the traditional problem-solving model of practice
3. Clarify the differences among the terms *client system level, client system,* and *target system*
4. Classify clients by type and identify factors that might affect their willingness to develop a helping relationship and engage in the helping process
5. Describe the core values of the social work profession
6. Assess and resolve any ethical dilemmas that occurred when Karen had to jump right in.

STRENGTHS-BASED GENERALIST SOCIAL WORK PRACTICE

Traditional agency-based social work practice is problem-focused. Clients tend to be viewed as having deficits and pathology that need to be overcome to improve functioning (Saleebey, 1997). The strengths-based approach, on the other hand, focuses on inherent client strengths, resources, and coping abilities. Clients are viewed as being capable of change. They are partners and activie participants in the change process. The social worker is not the problem-solver; the client is the problem-solver. The generalist social worker's primary function is to help clients recognize, strengthen, and marshal their inherent strengths and abilities (Weick, Rapp, Sullivan, & Kisthardt, 1989). In the strengths-based approach, the client is the expert with the knowledge and ability to create the needed changes. Social work practice focuses on empowering clients and establishing collaborative helping relationships.

Strengths-based generalist social work practice is a collaborative process that employs a professional helping relatiohship directed toward individual, family, group, organizational, and/or community empowerment and the promotion of social and economic justice. It entails direct work with client systems of all sizes as well as indirect work on behalf of client systems. Work with and on behalf of clients is approached through the use of a collaborative helping process that focuses on client strengths and resources within an ecosystem framework.

Ecosystems Perspective

The ecosystems perspective has been widely adopted as one of the primary conceptual bases of social work practice (Compton & Galaway, 1994; Meyer, 1988). Indeed, one could easily argue that it has been the dominant framework of social work practice since the mid-1970s. The ecosystems perspective fits well with social work's longstanding mission to address the situational and environmental factors that negatively affect disadvantaged persons.

The heart of the ecosystems perspective is the *person-in-environment* concept, which views individuals and their environments as an interrelated whole

(Germain & Gitterman, 1980). "Individuals are perceived as a system composed of biological, psychological (including cognitive), and emotional dimensions. Also, individuals are perceived as interacting with a variety of external systems, such as immediate family, extended family, peers, work or school, and community" (Jordan & Franklin, 1995, p. 5).

The person-in-environment perspective in social work recognizes the interdependence of these various systems. The relationship between individuals and their social environment is reciprocal, with each component in the client's system affecting and being affected by the others. The social environment influences individuals' perceptions of themselves and their interactions with others. Individuals, in turn, influence their social environment (Sullivan, 1992).

In the ecosystems perspective, "understanding the nature of the ecological *level of fit* between a person's needs, capacities, and aspirations, on the one hand, and environmental resources and expectations, on the other, is the core task in assessing individuals' and collectives' life situations" (Gitterman, 1996, p. 475). The ecosystem perspective "helps the practitioner to see that all aspects of an individual's problem involve circular connections between the individual and environment, leading to a "transactional focus" for practice that is consistent with social work's dual concern with person and environment" (Wakefield, 1996, p. 6).

A defining characteristic of social work practice, which sets it apart from most other helping professions, is the importance given to improving clients' person-in-environment transactions to facilitate their growth, health, and social functioning (Gordon, 1981):

> In attempting to understand a problem in social functioning, you cannot achieve understanding by adding together, as separate entities, the assessment of the individual and the assessment of the environment. Rather you must strive for a full understanding of the complex interactions between client and all levels of social systems as well as the meaning the client assigns to these interactions. (Compton & Galaway, 1994, p. 118)

The ecosystems perspective recognizes the role of the worker in the client's environmental system (Germain & Gitterman, 1980). Worker-client transactions are viewed as a component of the client's ecological system (see Figure 1.1). The interactions between the worker and the client and between the worker and the client's social environment become part of the client's dynamic person-in-environment system. Shulman (1991 portrayed the social worker as "in the middle," between the client and the systems he or she must negotiate. However, this puts the client in "a reactive, secondary role *vis-à-vis* the worker" (Petr, 1988, p. 624) and portrays the worker as intervening on behalf of the client and responsible for affecting change in the client. In this respect, mutuality and reciprocity do not characterize the worker-client relationship. The interaction is, instead, unidirectional, flowing from worker to client. This is not the case in strengths-based generalist practice.

Strengths Perspective

The idea of building on clients' strengths has received a lot of attention during the 1990s, and it is fashionable to claim adherence to *"the strengths perspective."* However, as Saleebey put it:

> Many of these calls to attend to the capacities and competencies of clients are little more than professional cant. So let us be clear: The strengths perspective is a dramatic

FIGURE 1.1. The Ecosystems Model

departure from conventional social work practice. Practicing from a strengths orientation means this—*everything* you do as a social worker will be predicated, in some way, on helping to discover and embellish, explore and exploit clients' strengths and resources. (1997, p. 3)*

The strengths perspective is a dramatic departure from the traditional approach, which focuses primarily on pathology and dysfunction (Hepworth & Larsen, 1993). Social work has a long history of helping disadvantaged clients overcome individual problems and problem situations. Clients come to us with problems, and there is a natural tendency to attempt to resolve the problems and to view the clients from a deficit perspective. Maluccio (1979) found that social workers' perceptions were in stark contrast to their clients' self-perceptions. The clients' viewed themselves as proactive, autonomous human beings who were using counseling services to enhance their functioning and competence. In contrast, social workers tended to underestimate clients' strengths, focusing on their problems, underlying weaknesses, and limited potential.

Focusing on problems leads social workers to perceive clients in essentially negative terms, as a collection of problems and diagnostic labels. This negative perception may lower expectations for positive change. More likely than not, clients are seen as diagnostic categories and/or their presenting problems. These perceptions distance the "helper from the lifeworld of the client" (Saleebey, 1997, p. 5). They also create pessimism in both the social worker and the client. Negative labels and expectations obscure the unique capabilities of clients (Pray, 1991). The social worker's ability to recognize and promote a client's potential for

*From D. Saleebey, *The Strengths Perspective in Social Work* (2nd ed.). Copyright © 1997 by Allyn & Bacon. Reprinted/adapted by permission.

change is markedly reduced. The focus is on what is wrong and the client's inability to cope with his or her life situation. Saleebey (1997) suggests that instead of focusing on problems we should focus on *possibilities.*

The pathology approach searches the past for causes. How did the client get into this situation? Why is the client experiencing these difficulties? The search for causes and rational explanations assumes a direct link between cause, disease, and cure (Saleebey, 1997). Human experience is rarely that simple. More often than not, it is filled with uncertainty and tremendous complexity. In addition, looking to the past diverts attention away from exploring the present. The shift from problems to strengths moves the focus from the past to the present and future. Strengths-oriented social workers seek to discover the resources clients currently have that can be used to change their future. The past cannot be completely dismissed: it provides a context for the present. Nevertheless, in strengths-based practice, the focus is on the present and the future.

Social work has a long tradition of dealing with problems as ordinary aspects of human life. The profession's early efforts in charity organizations and settlement houses developed "family-oriented and community-oriented strategies to help those who were caught in the tide of major social upheaval" (Weick & Chamberlain, 1997, p. 40). However, during the 1940s, social problems and problems of everyday life were redefined as complex intrapsychic pathology. "Psychological and psychiatric theories made human actions mysterious, complex, and rarely what they seemed" (Weick & Chamberlain, 1997, p. 41). Psychological definitions of problems and the shift toward focusing on why pathology occurred have become the dominant perspective in social work, diverting attention from the "profession's historic commitment to working with people in the midst of their daily lives" (Weick & Chamberlain, 1997, p. 42).

Rather than focusing on why clients are having problems, social workers adopting a strengths perspective ask:

> What do clients want? What do they need? How do they think they can get it? How do they see their situation—problems as well as possibilities? What values do they want to maximize? How have they managed to survive thus far? (Saleebey, 1997, p. 7)

These and similar questions will help you and your clients identify, use, build, and reinforce their strengths, resources, and abilities.

Principles of Strengths-Based Practice

Five principles central to the strengths perspective guide the application of strengths-based generalist practice (Saleebey, 1997). They also link the model to the core values of the profession.

Principle 1: *Every individual, group, family, and community has strengths.* Regardless of the situation, every person, family, and community possesses assets, resources, wisdom, and knowledge that you need to discover (Saleebey, 1997). To become aware of these strengths, you need to be genuinely interested in your clients and respectful of their perceptions of their own experiences:

> In the end, clients want to know that you actually care about them, that how they fare makes a difference to you, that you will listen to them, that you will respect them no matter what their history, and that you believe that they can build something of value with the resources within and around them. But most of all, clients want to know that

you believe they can surmount adversity and begin the climb toward transformation and growth. (Saleebey, 1997, p. 12)

The ultimate key to identifying client strengths is your belief in the clients and their possibilities. Adopting a strengths perspective requires you to view your clients as underutilized sources of knowledge and as untapped resources.

Principle 2: *Trauma, abuse, illness and struggle may be injurious, but they may also be sources of challenge and opportunity.* Dwelling on clients' pasts and hardships promotes "an image of themselves as helpless in the past, which then [becomes] the basis for fault-finding and continued helplessness in the present" (Wolin & Wolin, 1993, p. 14). Focusing on past hurts and deficits leads to discouragement, pessimism, and what Wolin and Wolin (1993) call the "victim trap." What is more extraordinary is that your clients have survived and that they are working with you to bring about changes in their lives. There is dignity and affirmation in having prevailed over trauma, abuse, illness, and other difficult situations. The strength of having survived and coped with numerous obstacles is often lost on clients who are struggling to meet life's daily challenges. A strengths approach recognizes clients' inherent competencies, resilience, and resourcefulness in having survived past difficulties as well as their current motivation for growth and development.

Principle 3: *Assume that you do not know the upper limits of the capacity to grow and change, and take individual, group, and community aspirations seriously.* Simply put, this means that you should set high expectations for your clients and help expand their hopes, visions, and aspirations. The strengths perspective is the perspective of hope and possibilities. Believe in clients' capacities for change, growth, and self-actualization. If you do not believe in their abilities and motivation, you really do not believe in the possibility of change. Creating hope where there is little, strengthening belief when there is little to believe in, and creating aspirations where there are none is the essence of social work practice from a strengths perspective.

Principle 4: *We best serve clients by collaborating with them.* The strengths perspective calls for a partnership characterized by reciprocity and mutual respect between you and your clients. There should be a sharing of knowledge and resources. You are not the sole expert or the only one with specialized information; your client is the expert who knows more about coping with his or her situation than you:

> A helper may best be defined as a collaborator or consultant: an individual clearly presumed, because of specialized education and experience, to know some things and to have some tools at the ready but definitely not the only one in the situation to have relevant, even esoteric, knowledge and understanding. (Saleebey, 1997, p. 14)

Take advantage of the wisdom, insights, and understanding your clients bring to the helping process by entering into a collaborative partnership with them. The strengths approach to social work practice requires it. Work *with* your clients in partnership. Do not presume to work on your clients or to do the work for them.

Principle 5: *Every environment is full of resources.* No matter how deprived a client's community, neighborhood, and/or family system is there is an abundance of untapped resources. "In every environment, there are individuals, associations, groups, and institutions who have something to give, something that others may desperately need: knowledge, succor, an actual resource or talent, or simply time and place" (Saleebey, 1997, p. 15). Looking to these untapped resources does not negate our responsibility to work for social and economic justice, and it does not mean that we accept the notion that the disadvantaged should assume sole responsibility for their situation and its amelioration. It does mean, however, that the possibilities for identifying and arranging needed resources for clients from within their own environment is greater than you would expect. The following case illustrates how Dawn W., a first-year social work student, built on her client's strengths to further his treatment goals.

No Time for Me

John R. is an eleven-year-old with behavior management problems. He has attention deficit hyperactivity disorder and has a great deal of difficulty controlling his impulses. He is socially immature. His peers usually make fun of him and are rejecting. He usually plays with much younger children. In addition to his behavior problems, he has a very difficult family situation. His mother lives out of state. He lives with his father, his stepmother, and an eighteen-month-old stepsister. His stepmother resents his presence in the family and the difficulties he causes her.

John is a student at an alternative school, where he is in a special behavior modification program. Dawn is John's social worker at the school and is also assigned to work with the family. The behavior management program is working well, but John's relationship with his stepmother is undermining his progress at home. The stepmother refuses to follow the treatment plan and is very rejecting. In fact, she openly tells John that he is bad and that she does not want him anywhere near his stepsister. While at home, John is generally either being punished or is alone in his room.

One of the treatment goals is to improve the relationship between John and his stepmother. Dawn recognized that one of John's strengths is that he is very good with young children. He is thoughtful and caring and has a nice way of engaging them in play. Dawn suggested to John's stepmother that she allow him to take care of his little sister for one hour a day. The plan was to have Dawn supervise John for the first week or until the stepmother was comfortable with John's ability to care for his sister.

The intervention was successful. John took care of his little sister well, and his appreciation of being allowed to play with and care for her was evident. His stepmother's confidence in and patience with him improved. John's self-esteem appeared to improve, as did his overall relationship with his stepmother. By recognizing one of John's strengths and enlisting that strength in the case plan, Dawn ensured progress on a critical treatment goal.

THEORETICAL AND CONCEPTUAL FRAMEWORKS

Philosophical and theoretical frameworks form the basis of theories, assumptions, and generalizations in all academic disciplines. These frameworks provide the structure for the application of practice models. The model of strengths-based generalist practice presented here integrates two very different conceptual frameworks: logical positivism and postmodernism.

Logical Positivism

Logical positivism, or the scientific approach, has dominated the social work profession (Reid, 1994; Weick & Saleebey, 1995): "the history of the social work profession has been consistently marked by both its adherence to and its attempt to maximize its linkage to a scientific model of knowledge" (Weick, 1993, p. 15). Logical positivism calls for empiricism, objectivity, and neutrality (Allen, 1993). Within this tradition, the social worker is an expert who helps clients resolve their problems. The social worker is expected to be a neutral, value-free participant, and the relationship is expected to be hierarchial. There is a power differential between the social worker and the client. Client assessment and diagnosis are based on the superior knowledge of the social worker:

> It was the social worker who determined what the problem was, giving rise to sophisticated and widely varied diagnostic catalogs. It was the social worker who orchestrated the course of treatment, presumably based on the diagnosis. The social worker took the role of actor and organizer; the client took the role of obedient recipient. (Weick, 1993, p. 16).

Social work's adherence to the scientific method began with the publication of Mary Richmond's *Social Diagnosis* in 1917. Richmond viewed "social diagnosis" as a scientific process of gathering facts and testing hypotheses about clients' social functioning. The psychoanalytical-oriented casework movement that began in the 1920s also adhered to scientific principles of study, diagnosis, and treatment (Reid, 1994). The psychosocial and psychodynamic approaches that evolved out of the psychoanalytic tradition have dominated social work practice theory from the 1940s to the present.

The 1960s marked the beginning of the empirical practice movement in social work (Reid, 1994). The empirical practice movement stresses the application of research methods to practice with individuals, families, and groups. The distinguishing characteristic of empirical social work is the use of the scientific method in assessing client situations, specifying goals, formulating solution-focused interventions, and evaluating effectiveness (Reid, 1994). Empirical social workers focus on the assessment of relevant facts, the specification of the problem in measurable terms, and the objective assessment of outcomes (Fischer, 1981; Hudson, 1982; Reid, 1994). Logical positivism and empirical practice

- Assume the existence of an objective reality that can be measured
- Emphasize the expertise of the helping professional and attribute less importance to the client's own knowledge and experience
- Place knowledge and power in the hands of the objective expert social worker
- Stress the application of research methods in practice
- Require clear specification of client problems
- Involve developing measurable goals and objectives
- Require measuring client progress and outcomes.

Postmodernism

Logical positivism's dominance in social work has been challenged by postmodernism, which is also called social constructivism (Dean, 1993; Weick, 1987).

Postmodernism is based on the assumption that language is used to construct our perceptions of reality (Greene, Jensen, & Jones, 1996). "Constructivism is the belief that we cannot know an objective reality apart from our views of it. . . . Knowledge is not so much discovered as created" (Dean, 1993, p. 58). With postmodernism, the emphasis is on the experiences of individuals and their perceptions of that experience, as well as on the social aspects of knowing and the influence of cultural, historical, political, and economic conditions (Dean, 1993). The interpersonal and interactional aspects of an individual's experiences are stressed. Individuals' perceptions are influenced by their communities and social environment. The individual cannot be separated from his or her interactions with others.

In sharp contrast to logical positivists, postmodernists argue that it is impossible to distinguish facts from values. "Reality is invented, constructed largely out of meanings and values of the observer" (Allen, 1993, p. 32). The constructivist perspective is not value-free; it is value-based (Murphy, 1989). Values, not objective facts, become the central issue of treatment (Allen, 1993; Dean, 1992). The values and attitudes of both the client and the social worker determine what facts are relevant and how they are interpreted. This perspective explicitly recognizes the importance of values in the helping process and encourages their exploration.

Social workers operating under postmodernist perspective recognize that understanding comes through dialogue and communication with the client. The client is the expert who is most knowledgeable about his or her life situation. The social worker also recognizes that he or she is a coparticipant in the quest for meaning. Worker-client interactions are characterized as collaborative conversations designed to create mutual understanding of the client's life events and issues. The exploration of each participant's values and beliefs and the process of hearing the client's story are the basis on which the worker-client relationship is developed. Postmodernism

- Highlights the importance of clients' subjective perceptions of their experiences
- Places clients in the role of expert about their life experiences and potential solutions
- Recognizes that clients' perceptions of their experiences are shaped by their culture and social environment
- Views the ongoing dialogue between the social worker and the client as fundamental to the change process
- Requires an open discussion of the social worker's and client's values and beliefs
- Recognizes that meaning is developed through the process of interaction between the worker and the client
- Stresses the collaborative aspects of the worker-client relationship.

SOCIAL WORK CLIENTS

Generalist practice involves work with client systems of all sizes. The *primary client system* could be an individual, a family, a small group, an organization, and/or a community. The primary client system is unlikely to be the only client system involved in the helping relationship or the only target of change. Typically, generalist practice involves working with multiple interrelated client systems.

As discussed earlier, strengths-based generalist social work practice utilizes an ecosystems perspective. This perspective focuses assessment and intervention on problematic transactions between individuals and their environment. These problematic transactions become the *target systems* that the client and worker seek to change (Pincus & Minahan, 1973). A target system can be an individual client and/or another individual, family, group, organization, or community system within the client's person-in-environment system. Any and all systems within a client's environment are potential target systems in the helping process. The following example illustrates the use of the person-in-environment perspective, client systems, and target systems in generalist social work practice.

I Can't Tell My Parents

Alice C. is seventeen. She has been pregnant with her first child for two months. She is unmarried and very committed to her relationship with the teenage father of the child. They are both seniors in high school and plan to attend college in the fall. Alice's parents are strict Catholics who follow the teachings of the church. Although quite strict, they have always been loving and have always encouraged and supported their only adopted daughter. Alice is afraid to talk to her parents about her situation. She is concerned about disappointing them and about the shame she will bring to the family. She has not told her boyfriend about the pregnancy either. She is unsure how he will react.

Alice does not know what to do. Unwilling to confide in her family and friends, she contacted the school social worker for help.

In this example, if Alice agrees to work with the social worker, she will be the primary client system. She needs help assessing her options and making a decision about a course of action. Depending on what she decides to do, her parents, the boyfriend, and the school are all possible target systems.

If Alice decides, for instance, that she wants to keep the baby and ask her parents to help her care for the child, the transaction between Alice and her parents becomes the focus of the intervention and the target system. In this situation, the key to successfully assisting Alice is to help her parents respond supportively to her situation. The social worker would probably help Alice prepare for the meeting with her parents, possibly attend the meeting with her, and offer to help the parents adjust to and cope with their daughters' pregnancy and the pending birth. In this case, Alice is the client system and her parents are a target system.

It is also possible for the school to become a target system. If, for example, the school had a policy prohibiting students in their third trimester from attending classes, Alice and her social worker might ask the school to develop an alternative plan for Alice to complete high school or to change the policy. The school system would become a target system again in the process of helping Alice carry out her plan to keep the baby.

It is also possible that none of the systems within Alice's environment would become target systems. If Alice decides, for example, to have an abortion and not tell anyone about her decision, her parents, the boyfriend, and the school do not become target systems. Alice would be both the client system and the target system.

In any given client situation, all the systems within the client's person-in-environment system are potential target systems. Whether a system becomes a target system for intervention depends on the specifics of the case and the focus of the work.

Types of Clients

A potential client becomes a client only if and when there is an explicit agreement with you about the purpose of your work together. Clients are those who agree to work with you to achieve some specified outcome. There are three types of clients: voluntary, nonvoluntary, and involuntary (Garvin & Seabury, 1997).

Voluntary clients seek out the services of a social worker or social agency. They want help with some aspect of their lives. A young mother who recognizes that she has a drinking problem and who seeks help from a professional social worker is an example of a voluntary client. She has made a decision to get professional help and she is voluntarily entering into a helping relationship with the social worker.

Nonvoluntary clients are not mandated by law or society to receive help but are nevertheless being pressured to do so. Other people see them as having problems; they themselves may or may not agree. Even if they acknowledge the existence of problems, they are not seeking help on their own volition. Someone in their life is forcing them to seek help. They come to you because "they may suffer unpleasant consequences if they refuse" (Garvin & Seabury, 1997, p. 132).* A young mother who is being pressured by her husband to get help for her drinking problem is an example of an nonvoluntary client. She is meeting with the social worker only because her husband has threatened to leave her and to seek custody of their child. She is essentially being forced by her husband to get professional help with her drinking problem and she is complying with his wishes to prevent his leaving and possibly losing custody of her child.

Involuntary clients are legally mandated to receive services. These clients have no choice in the matter. If the young mother with a drinking problem was arrested for drunken driving, part of her sentence might be a court order requiring her to participate in a twenty-week counseling program. She has no choice in the matter, and in this situation she is an involuntary client.

Regardless of whether clients are voluntary, nonvoluntary, or involuntary, to become clients, they must make some sort of contract or agreement with the social worker. They must knowingly and willingly participate in the helping process. Clearly, it is easier to reach an agreement with voluntary clients than with nonvoluntary or involuntary clients. Voluntary clients are motivated to seek help. The others, at the point of initial contact, have probably not made a decision to seek help and engage in a collaborative helping process.

---

*From Charles D. Garvin & Brett A. Seabury, *Interpersonal Practice in Social Work: Promoting Competence and Social Justice.* Copyright © 1997 by Allyn & Bacon. Reprinted/adapted by permission.

Clients progress through five stages in self-initiated, professionally assisted change. The stages are precontemplation, contemplation, preparation, action, and maintenance. "*Precontemplation* is the stage at which there is no intention to change in the foreseeable future" (Prochaska, DiClemente, & Norcross, 1992, p. 1103). Clients at this stage are often unaware of their problems and are not seriously considering getting help. They are reluctant participants in the helping process. They have not chosen to seek help and probably are unhappy about the prospects of being helped. "*Contemplation* is the stage in which clients are aware that a problem exists and are seriously thinking about overcoming it but have not yet made a commitment to take action" (Prochaska, DiClemente, & Norcross, 1992, p. 1103). The key here is the lack of commitment to change. Many clients recognize the need to address concerns or problems but need help in making a genuine commitment to bring the change about. "*Preparation* is the stage that combines intention and behavioral criteria" (p. 1104). Clients at this stage have started to address the problem and are motivated to make the necessary changes. *Action* is the stage in which individuals modify their behavior, experiences, or environment in order to overcome their problems" (p. 1104). During the action stage, clients are engaged in the helping process and are taking the necessary steps to achieve the desired changes. "*Maintenance* is the stage in which people work to prevent relapse and consolidate the gains attained during action" (p. 1104). In a way, maintenance is a continuation of the action phase. The client is actively trying to prevent a relapse.

The five stages of change highlight client differences in readiness to engage in the helping process and the importance of recognizing individual differences. Not all potential clients are at the contemplation or action stages. Many clients who are referred or mandated for service are in the precontemplation or contemplation stage. To become clients, they must make a commitment to change. In the end, only those who willingly agree to work with you to achieve some specified outcome can engage in a collaborative helping relationship. Nonvoluntary and involuntary clients might go through the motions because they are required to do so, but they will not truly become clients until they decide to engage in a helping relationship.

The Experience of Being a Client

A number of factors associated with clienthood affect the helping process. Understanding these factors and the way a person feels about being a client can facilitate the helping process and the development of a collaborative helping relationship. Understanding your client's feelings about needing and asking for help as well as his or her perceptions of what it means to be a client can facilitate the process of reaching an explicit agreement about the purpose of your work together. Whether the individual arrives on a voluntary, nonvoluntary, or involuntary basis, being sensitive to his or her feelings about clienthood is a critical first step in the process of having that individual become a client.

Beliefs and feelings about receiving help from a professional are related to culture. The dominant culture in American society is based on a strong tradition of individualism (Billups, 1992). Individuals who need psychological and/or social services are stigmatized and viewed negatively in American society because they are perceived as not living up to the cultural mandates of individual responsibility and self-reliance. This keeps many who need the services provided by social workers from seeking their assistance. Only after everything else has failed are they willing to get professional help.

Most clients approach getting help with mixed feelings (Maluccio, 1979). People are uncomfortable about admitting to a stranger that they have failed or are unable to resolve their difficulties on their own. Clients may feel shame and embarrassment. They are concerned about what you will think of them and what friends and family will think. Asking for help also raises negative feelings for them about themselves. They may view receiving professional help as some sort of personal failure. Obviously, the degree to which this occurs will vary greatly. However, it is probably safe to assume that each client has some degree of difficulty in asking for your help and in being a client.

On the other hand, positive and motivating feelings are also associated with clienthood. People hope that something can be done, that things will get better, and that help is on the way. Clients feel good about the possibilities of change. Even the most reluctant nonvoluntary or involuntary client will have some degree of hopefulness and expectation for positive outcomes. At some level, all clients may have positive feelings and expectations about getting help with difficult life situations. However, these expectations are often overshadowed by feelings of failure and stigma.

It is realistic to expect clients to have ambivalent feelings about working with you and receiving professional help. Your first interactions with them will probably determine if they engage in the helping process or drop out. Decreasing negative feelings and increasing positive feelings about seeking help and becoming a client are critical aspects of your initial meetings.

Prior Experiences with Helping Professionals

Chances are that most clients who come to you will have received social services in the past and will have had numerous prior contacts with helping professionals. Ignoring the possibility of prior negative experiences or assuming that all prior experiences with helping professionals were positive is a mistake. Clients' expectations about receiving help from a professional are influenced by their past experiences (Gambrill, 1997). Were they treated with respect? Were they given a voice in the decision-making process? Were the services helpful? Were their prior experiences with helping professionals satisfactory or unsatisfactory? Clients whose prior experiences were negative may expect more of the same and approach your work together with reservations, while those who enjoyed more positive experiences might be much more willing to engage in the helping process.

Early in your work together, preferably during your initial meeting, explore your clients' perceptions of their prior experiences. You may not change these perceptions, but recognizing them and learning what clients liked and did not like about earlier experiences is an important step in the helping process.

Clients' perceptions of the agency may also influence their approach to service (Garvin & Seabury, 1997). Does the agency have a negative or positive reputation in the community? Does the agency communicate respect for clients and their cultures in its physical appearance and decor? Are the clients greeted at the agency in a courteous and respectful manner? Is the waiting area pleasant and comfortable? Negative agency perceptions can impede the development of a helping relationship and the client's receptiveness to the helping process.

Understanding clients' perceptions of their prior experiences with helping professionals and their expectations for upcoming experiences with your agency is a critical step in the engagement process. Being sensitive to the possibilities of both positive and negative prior experiences enables you to directly address possible concerns. Communicating empathy about negative experiences and perceptions validates clients' experiences and perceptions. This validation begins the process of coconstructing a more positive mindset regarding the helping process and a willingness to engage in a collaborative helping relationship.

Expectations About the Helping Experience

Social workers also need to be sensitive to clients' expectations about the helping process and their role as client. "Ignoring or misunderstanding client expectations may result in premature drop out" (Gambrill, 1997, p. 22). Research findings show that clarification of the client role is associated with better outcomes (Orlinsky, Grawe, & Parks, 1994; Yalom, 1995). Client expectations about what will happen and what to expect in terms of change or outcomes should match those of their helpers. Different expectations will affect outcome and client retention.

Clients come to the helping process with varied expectations. Some may have little or no hope of making any meaningful change in their lives, while others may expect a miracle. Some might be aware of the collaborative nature of the helping process, and others might expect you to fix the problem. Early in your work together, although not necessarily during your first meeting, you need to discuss how you will work together and your respective roles. Clients need to clearly understand the helping process as well as their roles and responsibilities within it. Inappropriate expectations and misunderstandings about how the work will proceed can lead to disillusionment and dissatisfaction. It is important to share your vision of the helping process. It is probably wise to assume that you and your clients have different visions and expectations. These differences need to be reconciled before meaningful work can begin.

Cultural and Ethnic Diversity

American society is characterized by cultural and racial diversity, so it is no surprise that social work clients are diverse in terms of cultural backgrounds and beliefs. Values and beliefs of clients from different cultural groups might conflict with the dominant cultural values and/or with your own values and beliefs. Although social workers and clients often have a great deal in common, the expectation should be one of diversity and heterogeneity. Expect your clients to be unique individuals with different beliefs and values, and expect them to have a belief system that differs from yours in important ways.

The cultural and ethnic background of individuals may influence whether they become clients. Perceived similarities lead to understanding, empathy, and trust. Perceived differences may hinder the development of mutual understanding and trust (Miley, O'Melia, & DuBois, 1998). Perceived differences are barriers to clients' willingness to develop helping relationships. Most people seek out others with whom they feel a connection, a sameness, a likeness. Individuals tend to trust those they perceive as similar and distrust those they perceive as different.

The tendency to distrust those who are different makes the task of overcoming cultural and ethnic differences a challenge for all social workers.

Potential differences between you and your clients are infinite. Differences in values, perspectives, and experiences create communication and trust barriers. It is your responsibility, as the professional helper, to acknowledge differences directly and to communicate respect for your clients' values and beliefs. Rather than viewing cultural differences as threatening, view them as a resource that enhances the relationship with additional perspectives and options (Miley, O'Melia, & DuBois, 1998). Overcoming client-worker differences requires that you acknowledge the differences as well as communicate understanding of the clients' values, perceptions, and beliefs. Value your clients' differences. Show respect and appreciation of diversity. The differences will remain; what will change is the perception that they are barriers to communication and trust. Directly acknowledging differences early in the helping process will increase the likelihood that the individual will become a client. Ignoring cultural and ethnic differences will tend to exacerbate the magnitude of the differences and hinder the development of trust.

In working with people of color, women, gays and lesbians, and other oppressed populations, it is important to acknowledge that their perceptions and experiences have been subjugated by the dominant culture (Collins, 1990). To understand the experiences of clients, ask questions from a position of not knowing. Be curious, and show a genuine interest in what the client has to say. The client, not the worker, is the expert on his or her perceptions and experiences (Pray, 1991). Client expertise also encompasses cultural, ethnic, and racial experiences and perceptions.

Hartman points out that "in our attempt to become more skilled and more sensitive in our work with people of color, we have sought to gather information about cultures, to learn about difference, to become experts" (1994, p. 29). This approach leads to stereotyping and to assuming that all members of oppressed groups are alike. A better approach is to "abandon our expert role and really listen to our clients and believe and trust their experience" (Hartman, 1994, p. 29). If we listen to our clients, are open to their experiences, and take the position of curiosity and of not knowing, the chances of overcoming our differences are greatly improved.

Another important factor in cross-cultural practice is awareness of self and one's own cultural and ethnic heritage (Greene, Jensen, & Jones, 1996). Being aware of your own ethnic and cultural identity will increase your comfort in working with clients from different ethnic and cultural background (Pinderhughes, 1983). A culturally self-aware person is capable of recognizing and acknowledging differences. Social workers who are not aware of their own cultural beliefs and values are more likely to impose their values and beliefs on their clients and to feel threatened by their clients' differences. The more you know about yourself, the more likely you will be open to learning about your clients.

Client Skills and Knowledge

Clients often seek professional help only after attempting to resolve problems on their own, with assistance from friends, family, informal community organizations, and/or other helping professionals. First meetings with new clients usually occur after they have made numerous attempts to cope with their situations. They have a wealth of experience in dealing their problem situation. They know what has worked and what has not worked. They probably have ideas about what makes the issue difficult to resolve and what they need to do to successfully resolve it. Be open to and use this knowledge.

Clients also bring unique skills to the relationship. Each client comes with inter-personal skills and competencies. Clients have developed coping strategies and have found ways to get by in spite of pressing life demands and circumstances. They have developed unique ways of adapting to their life experiences. They have been successful, at some level, in coping with their difficulties. They are struggling and they need help, but they have managed to survive and cope with challenging situations. All clients bring strengths and skills to the helping relationship.

Acknowledging clients' strengths, knowledge, and skills is empowering. It is also encouraging. Clients are given hope when they are viewed as capable and com-petent individuals. Miley, O'Melia, and DuBois point out that clients' ability to "articulate thoughts and feelings; skills in thinking, planning, and organizing; com-petencies in giving and receiving support—all are general skills for living that may have relevance for overcoming any challenging situation" (1998, p. 127). Regardless of their level of functioning, irrespective of the severity of their life circumstances, and in spite of the magnitude of the problems that need to be overcome, clients, knowledge and skills can contribute to the resolution of their problem situations. Look for strengths and abilities and expect to find them. It is your job to help clients identify and articulate the knowledge and skills that they bring to the helping process. Recognizing these strengths helps foster collaborative worker-client rela-tionships by increasing clients' willingness to engage in the helping process.

SOCIAL WORK VALUES AND ETHICS

The practice of social work is based on a number of value positions and principles that guide the work with clients irrespective of the approach used, the presenting client problem(s), the client population, or the setting in which services are pro-vided. These values and principles apply to all forms of social work practice.

Core Social Work Values

Social work is a value-based profession (Reamer, 1990). Values provide the basis for professional social work practice (Loewenberg & Dolgoff, 1992). They guide the actions we take and what we evaluate as "good" (DuBois & Miley, 1996). Values represent "a constellation of preferences concerning what merits doing and how it should be done" (Levy, 1976, p. 234).

Social work has a rich tradition of principles and beliefs. The heart of these traditions and beliefs is reflected in the 1997 National Association of Social Workers (NASW) *Code of Ethics*, which is reprinted in the Appendix. The *Code of Ethics* identifies core social work values and associated ethical principles. Four of these values—service to others, social justice, dignity and worth of the person, and importance of human relationships—play a critical role in generalist practice.

Service to Others.   The first ethical principle states that "social workers' primary goal is to help people in need and to address social problems" (NASW, 1997, p. 5). Service to others is placed above self-interest.

Social work is a service profession dedicated to providing help to individuals, families, and groups in need and to improving community and social conditions. This commitment to service is reflected in the goals of the profession:

- To enhance social functioning of individuals, families, groups, organizations, and communities
- To link client systems with needed resources
- To improve the operation of social service programs and service delivery systems
- To promote social and economic justice through advocacy and policy development (DuBois & Miley, 1996, p. 11).

Inherent in each of these goals is *service to others.* All four goals focus on helping others directly by enhancing their capacities to resolve problems and indirectly by linking clients with resources, improving service delivery systems, and developing social programs and policies.

Social Justice.   The value of social justice has had a long tradition in social work. Concern with social justice and inequality in the profession goes back to the advocacy efforts of Jane Addams and the settlement house movement of the early 1900s (Mickelson, 1995).

The *Code of Ethics* identifies *social justice* as a core social work value and states that challenging social injustice is an ethical principle of the profession:

> Social workers pursue social change, particularly with and on behalf of vulnerable and oppressed individuals and groups of people. Social workers' social change efforts are focused primarily on issues of poverty, unemployment, discrimination and other forms of social injustice. . . . Social workers strive to ensure access to needed information, services, and resources; equality of opportunity; and meaningful participation in decision making for all people. (NASW, 1997, p. 5)

Beverly and McSweeney define *"justice* as fairness in the relationships between people as these relate to the possession and/or acquisition of resources" (1987, p. 6). Social workers traditionally work with people who are victims of discrimination and prejudice. Many of our clients are unemployed or underemployed, have limited access to resources, received inadequate education and training, and are among the most disadvantaged members of society. They often face prejudicial attitudes and are "identified as 'lesser'—less capable, less productive, and less normal" (DuBois & Miley, 1996, p. 151). Social injustice is manifested in discrimination on the basis of race, gender, social class, sexual orientation, age, and disability. Prejudicial attitudes provide justifications for "social structures that provide fewer prospects—fewer opportunities, fewer possibilities, and fewer resources—for those with lower status" (DuBois & Miley, 1996, p. 150).

Social workers' commitment to social justice is based on concern about the negative effect of discrimination and prejudice on disadvantaged populations. We often work with clients who have been denied basic rights and opportunities. We are called on to *challenge social injustice* and to increase the opportunities, possibilities, and resources of our clients. We have an ethical responsibility to address the social, physical, and economic needs of our clients as well as their psychological needs.

Human Dignity and Self-Worth.   A third core value is to treat our clients in a caring and respectful fashion, being mindful of individual differences and cultural and ethnic diversity. The underlying assumption of this value is that "all human beings have intrinsic worth, irrespective of their past or present behavior, beliefs, lifestyle, race, or status in life" (Hepworth & Larsen, 1993, p. 55). As a social worker, you are expected to treat your clients with respect and dignity. They deserve respect by virtue of their humanness. This does not mean that you have to agree with your clients' life choices or decisions. It does mean that you should strive to affirm their dignity and self-worth. Not doing so can have profound negative effects on the helping process.

Hepworth and Larsen point out that "before people will risk sharing personal problems and expressing deep emotions, they must first feel fully accepted and experience the good-will and helpful intent of practitioners" (1993, p. 56). This takes on greater urgency when clients' problematic behaviors involve moral, social, or legal infractions. There is little likelihood that a client whose behavior has violated social and cultural norms will engage in a collaborative helping relationship with a professional who communicates disapproval and condemnation.

Closely associated with the value of respecting the individual is the concept of adopting nonjudgmental attitudes. Being nonjudgmental means adopting non-blaming attitudes and behaviors (Biestek, 1957). You should focus on understanding your clients and their difficulties and on helping them find solutions or alternative ways of behaving. If you blame them for their difficulties and assign pejorative labels, most will become defensive and unwilling to trust you. The more you understand the life experience of your clients, no matter how personally distressing their behavior or beliefs may be, the more likely you will be able to accept them as human beings who may have "suffered various forms of deprivation and have themselves been victims of harsh, abusive, rejecting, or exploitative behavior" (Hepworth & Larsen, 1993, p. 56).

Being nonjudgmental does not mean that you have to approve of or accept your clients' behaviors or attitudes. Many of our clients' behaviors are in conflict with our own personal values and beliefs. More often than not, there will be a clash of values between you and your clients. These value differences should be viewed as a normal part of generalist social work practice. Expect them and accept them. There are going to be differences—in fact, there are going to be major differences. If you focus on your values and on assigning blame to clients for adopting behaviors or attitudes with which you disagree, you will not be able to help your clients.

Adopting nonjudgmental attitudes is a prerequisite for developing effective working relationships (Perlman, 1979). The challenge is to maintain your own values without imposing them on others and without judging those whose behavior and beliefs are in conflict with your belief system. To accomplish this, you need to be open to others and to treat everyone with respect and dignity. This is difficult when you have negative feelings about your client. You are human, and you will have negative feelings about some clients. Pretending that you do not have these feelings will not work; your clients will pick up on your insincerity and negative reactions. The best approach is to try to *understand* your client and to communicate that understanding back to him or her in a caring and nonjudgmental manner. Clients are not seeking your approval; they are seeking your help. What they need to feel is that they have been heard and that you have an understanding of them and their situations. They need to feel that you care and that you want to work with them. Communicating care and concern facilitates the helping process. If your client perceives you as judging and blaming, help is unlikely.

Importance of Human Relationships.   A fourth core value of social work concerns the importance of human relationships. "Positive social exchanges may be the strongest elements shaping and enriching human life; adverse and coercive social exchanges are among the deepest sources of human pain" (Mattaini, 1997, p. 120). The *Code of Ethics* states that "social workers seek to strengthen relationships among people in a purposeful effort to promote, restore, maintain, and enhance the well-being of individuals, families, social groups, organizations, and communities" (NASW, 1997, p. 6). Focusing on the relationship issues of clients is common in generalist social work. Many clients need help improving their human relationships and interpersonal interactions. "Deficits and excesses in social behavior often result in severe isolation (and loneliness), and many clients seen individually identify improvements in relationships among their most important goals" (Mattaini, 1997, p. 120).

Historically, the helping relationship has been given a central role in the helping process (Biestek, 1957; Perlman, 1979). The *Code of Ethics* states that "social workers engage people as partners in the helping process" (NASW, 1997, p. 6). *Relationship* implies a reciprocal interactive process between two people. In social work, the helping relationship is a partnership. Both you and the client have input and make decisions together. You are joint participants. Social workers do not solve problems for their clients; they work with their clients and help them solve their own problems.

Beginning social workers often feel that unless they are doing something specific and concrete for their clients, they are not being helpful. You will be tempted to do things for your clients, to use your skills and abilities to get the task done and hand over the results to the client. It will make you feel useful and productive. Avoid the temptation—it is a trap. More often than not, your clients will not appreciate your generous efforts on their behalf. By doing it for them, you will have put them in a dependent position, which only highlights their inability to manage their own lives. No one likes feeling incompetent and dependent. Rather than making your clients dependent on you, empower them. Help them help themselves. Help them do what ever they need to do to manage their own lives as best they can. Ultimately, your clients must gain the confidence and abilities to do the tasks for themselves. The helping relationship in social work is a collaborative partnership. Social workers do not work *for* clients; they work *with* clients.

Ethical Standards

The core social work values and ethical principles set forth the ideals to which all social workers should aspire. The *Code of Ethics* also specifies ethical standards that describe in greater detail how these core values and principles apply to the activities of professional social workers. "Values are concerned with what is *good* and *desirable,* while ethics deal with what is *right* and *correct*" (Loewenberg & Dolgoff, 1992, p. 21). The standards spell out social workers' ethical responsibilities to clients, to colleagues, in practice settings, as professionals, to the social work profession, and to the broader society (NASW, 1997, p. 7). They provide detailed and comprehensive guidelines for professional conduct. For example, the standards for ethical responsibilities to clients cover sixteen areas, including commitment to clients, self-determination, informed consent, and competence

---

FIGURE 1.2. Outline of Ethical Standards

Social Workers' Ethical Responsibilities to Clients

Commitment to Clients	Self-Determination	Informed Consent
Competence	Cultural Competence	Conflicts of Interest
Confidentiality	Access to Records	Sexual Relationships
Physical Contact	Sexual Harassment	Derogatory Language
Payment for Services	Decision-Making Capacity	Interruption of Services
Termination of Services		

Social Workers' Ethical Responsibilities to Colleagues

Respect	Confidentiality	Interdisciplinary Collaboration
Disputes Involving Colleagues	Consultation	Referral for Services
Sexual Relationships	Sexual Harassment	Impairment of Colleagues
Incompetence of Colleagues	Unethical Conduct of Colleagues	

Social Workers' Ethical Responsibilities in Practice Settings

Supervision and Consultation	Education and Training	Performance Evaluation
Client Records	Billing	Client Transfer
Administration	Staff Development	Commitments to Employers
Labor-Management Disputes		

Social Workers' Ethical Responsibilities as Professionals

Competence	Discrimination	Private Conduct
Dishonesty, Fraud, and Deception	Impairment	Misrepresentation
Solicitations	Acknowledging Credit	

Social Workers' Ethical Responsibilities to the Social Work Profession

Integrity of the Profession
Evaluation and Research

Social Workers' Ethical Responsibilities to the Broader Society

Social Welfare	Public Participation
Social and Political Action	Public Emergencies

(see Figure 1.2). A detailed discussion of each ethical standard in the six professional practice areas may be found in the Appendix.

The guidelines in the ethical standards section of the *Code of Ethics* provide a basis for formulating judgments regarding unethical behavior and help resolve value conflicts. It is your responsibility as a professional social worker to be familiar with the *Code of Ethics* and to follow it in your professional practice.

Ethical Dilemmas

Social workers frequently have simultaneous ethical obligations to several parties. For example, we have ethical obligations to both our clients and our employing organizations. This creates the possibility of conflict, or ethical dilemmas. "An ethical dilemma occurs when you cannot simultaneously meet your obligations to two different parties in the role set without violating your ethical commitment

---

FIGURE 1.3. Ethical Guidelines

---

1. "The right to life, health, well-being, and necessities of life are superordinal and take precedence over rights to confidentiality and opportunities for additive 'goods' such as wealth, education, and recreation."
2. "An individual's basic right to well-being takes precedence over another person's right to privacy, freedom, or self-determination."
3. "People's right to self-determination takes precedence over their right to basic well-being providing they are competent to make informed and voluntary decisions with consideration of relevant knowledge and so long as the consequences of their decisions do not threaten the well-being of others."
4. "Person's rights to well-being may override laws, policies, and arrangements of organizations" (Hepworth & Larsen, 1993, pp. 85–86, based on Reamer, 1990).

---

to one or the other" (Compton & Galaway, 1994, p. 240). In these situations, you are forced to "choose between two apparent goods or to avoid two equally undesirable courses of action" (McGowan, 1995, p. 35). Since we have ethical responsibilities to our clients, our colleagues, our practice settings, the profession, and the broader society, value conflicts and ethical dilemmas occur often within and between these six areas of professional responsibilities.

Resolving ethical dilemmas is never easy or straightforward. Rarely is there a clear-cut right or wrong choice. The choice is between two seeming "rights"; the task is to determine which "right" is more so given the circumstances. If this is not the case, there is no dilemma.

The first step in addressing ethical dilemmas is to refer to the *Code of Ethics* for clarification of the standards of practice. The *Code*, however, does not offer any basis for choosing between two or more conflicting ethical standards. A number of guidelines have been developed to help resolve ethical dilemmas by providing a hierarchy of value assumptions as the basis for decision making (Loewenberg & Dolgoff, 1992; Reamer, 1990; Rhodes, 1991). One such hierarchy is shown in Figure 1.3.

The first guideline in Figure 1.3 proposes that a person's right to health and well-being takes precedence over rights to confidentiality. If you had to choose between protecting a person's health and well-being and violating a client's confidentiality, you would choose health and well-being. For example, the right of neglected and abused children to protection takes precedence over their parents' rights to confidentiality.

The second guideline proposes that a person's right to health and well-being takes precedence over another person's right to privacy, freedom, or self-determination. When faced with choosing between protecting a person's freedom and protecting another person from harm, the choice is to protect the person from harm. For example, if a client reveals plans to seek physical revenge on his or her former spouse, you should warn the former spouse.

The third guideline states that a person's right to self-determination takes precedence over his or her own right to well-being. That is, an individual's self-determination supersedes that person's well-being. The principle promotes freedom to choose and possibly fail or make mistakes. It protects the right of people to carry out actions that do not appear to be in their own best interests, as long as they are competent to make informed and voluntary decisions. However, the first guideline takes precedence if the individual's decision might result in death or serious harm. For example, you must take action to protect a client who is at risk of committing suicide.

The final guideline proposes that the right to well-being may override agency policies and procedural rules. Social workers are obligated to follow the policies and procedures of social work agencies, voluntary associations, and organizations. When agency policy has a negative effect on a client's well-being, however, violating the policy or procedure may be justified. "It would be permissible, for example, for a social worker who is prohibited from treating clients outside of the agency to counsel a suicidal client who has called from home to request assistance" (Reamer, 1983, pp. 34–35).

The guidelines described above—or any other guidelines—will not provide "unambiguous and commonly accepted solutions to ethical dilemmas" (Reamer, 1983, p. 35). Guidelines provide a framework for ordering values to help clarify your thinking about ethical issues. Resolving ethical dilemmas almost always entails making value judgments and subjective interpretations. For example, the third guideline states that a person's right to self-determination takes precedence over his or her right to basic well-being, provided he or she is competent to make an informed decision. Apply this guideline to a typical situation with a person who is mentally ill and homeless, who prefers to remain on the street, and who has little or no interest in participating in a treatment program. Does this person have the right to refuse treatment as well as the right to live wherever he or she wants? The complicating factor in this situation is interpreting the person's competence and the degree of physical or mental harm likely to ensue. Can a person who is mentally ill, delusional, and exhibiting psychotic behavior make informed decisions? At what point does refusing shelter and/or treatment create a serious risk of physical and mental harm? Clearly, the answers to these questions are subjective and subject to value judgments.

In attempting to resolve ethical dilemmas, always invoke the concept of shared responsibility and decision making. Do not make the decision on your own; enlist others in the process. Get your supervisor's or administrator's advice and approval before you take action on an ethical dilemma. The following case example illustrates the difficult decisions involved in resolving ethical dilemmas.

Don't Rock the Boat

Jill C. is a first-year MSW student placed in an after-school program for emotionally disturbed children. The program is run by a comprehensive mental health agency that offers a wide range of services for children and adults. The agency is a subsidiary of a larger organization that owns and operates numerous inpatient and outpatient mental health facilities. The after-school program has two full-time social workers, a case aide, a half-time supervisor, and a quarter-time program administrator. Approximately twenty children with emotional and behavioral problems are provided on-site services five days a week and in-home services once a week.

Because of a technicality, the program lost its primary source of funding and was slated to close. Jill learned about the pending closing from her supervisor, and she was told not to tell the other staff or the children. The program administrator had decided that it was best for the children and their parents, as well as the staff, not to know in advance that the program was closing.

Jill was concerned about the children's need to have an appropriate amount of time to deal with their feelings about leaving the program and also about the parents' needs for time to make alternative arrangements for the treatment and after-school care of their children. She was also concerned about the effects the lack of time to process the closing of the program would have on the staff and their morale.

Jill believed that the well-being of the children was being subjugated to the perceived needs of the agency. She suspected that the agency adminis-trator felt that telling the children and their parents would be upsetting and would result in the children's acting out more than usual during the remain-der of the program. She also suspected that the administrator wanted to avoid having the parents put pressure on the agency to continue the pro-gram. It appeared to Jill that the secrecy was designed to protect the agency from disruption at the expense of the children and their parents.

Jill was faced with an ethical dilemma. She was told by her supervisor to fol-low an agency policy that she believed was not in the best interest of her clients. What are Jill's options? Is it advisable for her to apply guideline 4 and to disre-gard the agency policy? What might be the consequences of such action? How should she attempt to resolve her dilemma?

SUMMARY

The ecosystems perspective is one of two primary frameworks guiding the model of generalist social work practice presented in this book. The heart of the ecosys-tems perspective is the person-in-environment concept. Clients are not viewed in isolation but rather within the context of their environments. The focus is on the level of fit between the client system and the environment and on improving per-son-in-environment transactions to facilitate growth, empowerment, health, and social and economic justice.

The strengths perspective is the second framework or philosophical perspec-tive guiding the model of generalist social work practice presented in this book. The strengths perspective provides a lens for viewing client situations that is very different from the traditional problem-focused approaches to social work prac-tice. The helping process utilizing this perspective emphasizes client strengths and resources as opposed to limitations and deficits. The client rather than the social worker is recognized as the expert. The focus of strengths-based generalist practice is on developing partnerships, empowerment, and collaboration.

The application of the ecosystem and strengths perspectives in generalist practice takes place with individual, family, small group, organization, and com-munity client systems. Thus, generalist social workers are prepared to address both micro-level and macro-level concerns. In addition to working with various sized client systems, generalist social work often entails working with multiple client systems. Typically, the generalist social worker will be working with a number of different client systems simultaneously. For example, generalist social work with individual clients often entails work with the family system as well as work with organizations and community groups within the individual's environmental system. The target systems are those within the client system's environment that are targeted for change or intervention.

Clients can be voluntary, nonvoluntary, or involuntary. Regardless of the circumstances that brings a client into contact with a generalist social worker, the client has to choose to participate in the helping process. For this to occur, the client has to have progressed at least to the preparation stage of change. The challenge for generalist social workers is to help clients move beyond the precontemplation and contemplation stages so that clients do not drop out or go through the motions without engaging in the helping process.

A number of factors influence clients' ability to engage in helping relationships. One factor is their feelings about getting help and the stigma they feel about needing to go to a stranger for assistance. Cultural values and beliefs as well as prior experiences with helping professionals influence these feelings. At best, most clients have mixed feelings about working with a social worker. Communicating understanding of these feelings and creating an expectation that change is possible are critical to having clients engage in the helping process. Being sensitive to clients' expectations and their role in the helping process and clarifying the collaborative nature of your work together also help promote client participation.

Strengths-based generalist practice is consistent with the core values of social work. The social work profession and strengths-based generalist practice both emphasize service to others, social justice, human dignity and self-worth, and the importance of human relationships. Generalist social workers incorporate these core values in their work with clients and utilize the ethical principles described in the profession's *Code of Ethics* to help resolve issues related to clients, colleagues, agencies, the profession, and the broader society. Ethical dilemmas occur when an individual has to choose between two or more conflicting ethical standards. Ethical dilemmas can be resolved by using a hierarchical decision-making approach. This approach is useful when faced with a choice between two apparent goods or equally undesirable courses of action.

CASE EXAMPLE

The final case in this chapter was written by Daniel Lafferty when he was a first-year MSW student. It is based on one of the clients with whom he worked in his first-year field placement. The case illustrates the differences between a strengths-based approach and the traditional deficit approach.

Under a Cloud   *Daniel Lafferty*

Practice Setting
The Parents and Children Together (PACT) program functions as a family preservation agency. It's main mission is to support family well-being, prevent child abuse and neglect, and promote optimal child development. It provides

parenting skills training and family needs assessments, and it helps clients assess needed resources. Clients are referred to the program by Children and Youth Services (CYS), the county child-welfare agency. The referral objectives are to prepare parents to be reunited with children who have been placed in foster care due to abuse or neglect and to prevent the removal of children who are at risk for placement by means of a parenting program. PACT clients are expected to participate in agency-based parent skills training every other week. Home visits are scheduled for nonprogram weeks, during which clients are able to demonstrate learned parenting skills in the family's natural environment.

Problem Situation

Patrick J. is a thirty-four-year-old, single, Caucasian male who works part-time as a construction worker. He was referred to the PACT program by CYS following his daughter's placement in foster care due to neglect. Patrick's daughter was three years old and living with her mother at the time of placement. Since then, Patrick has made it known that he intends to seek custody of his daughter. He has been attending parenting classes at PACT and meeting with his daughter for one-hour supervised home visits every two weeks in preparation for achieving this goal. Because of Patrick's separation from his daughter during the years prior to her placement in foster care, he is interested in building a father-daughter relationship that can be parlayed into being awarded full custody of his daughter.

History of Problem Situation

Patrick states that in 1992 he became involved in an intimate relationship, after a few months together, his paramour informed him that she was pregnant. Three months after the birth of their daughter, Patrick's paramour left and took the daughter to live with her parents because Patrick "refused to become a born-again Christian." Following this separation, Patrick had only sporadic involvement with his daughter for the first three years of her life. Throughout this period, the girl's mother reportedly denied him contact with his daughter for religious reasons.

Patrick states that while he was attempting to have contact with his daughter, he noticed signs that she was being neglected by her mother. He claims that on several occasions he made reports to CYS about his concerns, but none of the investigations established a case of neglect until the last one. At that time, his daughter was found to be extremely developmentally delayed and showed signs of emotional and medical neglect. She was placed in foster care as a result of these findings. Since that placement, she has made remarkable progress. The mother is described as suffering from a serious mental illness. She has not made any attempts to regain custody of her daughter.

Following his daughter's placement in foster care, Patrick began working with CYS and the PACT program in an attempt to gain custody. Due to the early and lengthy separation of Patrick and his daughter, it was decided that they need time to form a parent-child relationship before custody could be considered. Although progress has been made, Patrick believes the process has been moving slower than necessary as a result of the restrictive handling of his case by CYS.

There are several reasons that the CYS staff is reluctant for Patrick to gain custody of his daughter. He has a significant substance abuse history (about twenty years of marijuana abuse), and questions have been raised about his mental health. Over six months ago, Patrick decided to seek treatment for marijuana use. Recently, he completed a residential rehabilitation program followed by outpatient substance abuse treatment. Since entering rehab, he claims to have abstained from all substances.

At the present time, questions about Patrick's mental health status remain unanswered. Psychiatric assessment results have been conflicting. Patrick's substance use at the time of some of these evaluations may have contributed to the findings. The CYS worker assigned to the case has serious concerns about his mental health. The general opinion of the PACT staff is that Patrick does not suffer from a major mental disorder, but at times he exhibits character traits consistent with a dependent personality disorder. The CYS worker is also concerned about his employment situation and his ability to provide full-time care for his daughter.

Current Situation

Patrick has been consistent in visiting his daughter. He has attended all the scheduled parent training classes, and he has met with his PACT social worker weekly. He is motivated to establish a strong parent-child relationship and obtain custody of his daughter. He is looking for a full-time job, but the parenting classes and visitation schedule make it difficult for him.

Patrick's interactions with his daughter at the PACT program and during their visits are appropriate. His daughter appears to be comfortable with him, and their relationship is strengthening. She seems to enjoy the visits and talks positively about going to live with her father.

The CYS worker continues to have concerns about Patrick's suitability as a full-time parent and is reluctant to increase his visitation privileges. The foster mother has become attached to the daughter and has indicated that she wants to adopt her if possible. The foster mother also appears to be against Patrick's visits with his daughter. She claims that it upsets the child, and that the girl has no interest in visiting with her father. The foster mother frequently finds excuses to cancel the scheduled visits.

Client System Obstacles and Strengths

The effects of certain obstacles are evident in the problem situation for this client. Patrick's substance abuse history complicates the custody issues. If the client relapses, the child may be at risk for further neglect. The extent of Patrick's marijuana use appears to have created a negative impression of him among some of the staff in the child protection system. Another potential obstacle is the recent revelation that the foster mother may wish to adopt Patrick's daughter. This has put a strain on the visits (she brings the daughter to the visits), and it seems that she has the support of the CYS worker assigned to the case.

Patrick's use of marijuana on an almost daily basis since he was eleven may have had serious implications for his developmental life stages. It is not surprising that he appears immature in certain life domains. Addressing this issue will be important if Patrick is to gain insight into the source of some of his difficulties, especially with interpersonal relationships.

Patrick's strengths include his decision to discontinue his substance use; the recent establishment of a healthier support system, and weekly drug, alcohol, and mental health counseling; a Narcotics Anonymous sponsor; PACT staff who are helping to increase the quality and quantity of visits with his daughter; and his supportive parents, who assist with these visits. In addition, Patrick's expressed commitment to be reunited with his daughter is a real strength. He has been cooperative with the demands of CYS in the interest of this goal.

DISCUSSION QUESTIONS

1. Identify the various system levels associated with the case example. How do the various systems affect Patrick's attempts to obtain custody of his daughter?
2. Assess Patrick's person-in-environment system. What systems in his environment have relevance for his situation? What transactions are problematic, and what transactions are resources? What are the potential target systems in this case example?
3. Apply the five principles of strengths-based practice to the case. How does viewing the case from a strengths perspective differ from the child protective worker's perspective?
4. What factors in Patrick's background potentially influence his relationship with the PACT social worker? How might the social worker strengthen the helping relationship?
5. What additional information would you want to obtain if you were the social worker assigned to this case. What unanswered questions do you have about the case?
6. What social work values appear to bear on this case? Are there any ethical dilemmas that you would want to address? If so, how would you resolve the ethical dilemmas?

REFERENCES

Allen, J. A. (1993). The constructivist paradigm: Values and ethics. In Joan Laird (Ed.), *Revisioning social work education: A social constructionist approach* (pp. 31–54). New York: Haworth.

Baker, R. L. (1995). *The social work dictionary* (3rd ed.). Washington, DC: NASW Press.

Beverly, D. P., & McSweeney, E. A. (1987). *Social welfare and social justice.* Englewood Cliffs, NJ: Prentice-Hall.

Biestek, F. (1957). *The casework relationship.* Chicago: Loyola University Press.

Billups, J. O. (1992). The moral basis for a radical reconstruction of social work. In P. N. Reid and P. R. Popple (Eds.), *The moral purposes of social work: The character and intentions of a profession* (pp. 100–119). Chicago: Nelson-Hall.

Collins, P. H. (1990). *Black feminist thought.* New York: Routledge.

Compton, B. R., & Galaway, B. (1994). *Social work processes* (5th ed.). Pacific Grove, CA: Brooks/Cole.

Dean, R. G. (1992). Constructivism: An approach to clinical practice. *Smith College Studies in Social Work, 63,* 405–414.

Dean, R. G. (1993). Teaching a constructivist approach to clinical practice. In Joan Laird (Ed.), *Revisioning social work education: A social constructionist approach* (pp. 55–75). New York: Haworth.

DuBois, B., & Miley, K. K. (1996). *Social work an empowering profession* (2nd ed.). Boston: Allyn and Bacon.

Fischer, J. (1981). The social work revolution. *Social Work, 26,* 199–207.

Gambrill, E. (1997). *Social work practice: A critical thinker's guide.* New York: Oxford University Press.

Garvin, C. D., & Seabury, B. A. (1997). *Interpersonal practice in social work: Promoting competence and social justice* (2nd ed.). Boston: Allyn and Bacon.

Germain, C. B., & Gitterman, A. (1980). *The life model of social work practice.* New York: Columbia University Press.

Gitterman, A. (1996). Ecological perspective: Response to Professor Jerry Wakefield. *Social Service Review, 70,* 472–476.

Gordon, W. E. (1981). A natural classification system for social work literature and knowledge. *Social Work, 26,* 134–136.

Greene, G. J., Jensen, C., & Jones, D. H. (1996). A constructivist perspective on clinical social work practice with ethnically diverse clients. *Social Work, 41,* 172–180.

Hartman, A. (1994). Social work practice. In F. G. Reamer (Ed.), *The foundations of social work knowledge* (pp. 13–50). New York: Columbia University Press.

Hepworth, D. H., & Larsen, J. A. (1993). *Direct social work practice: Theory and skills* (4th ed.). Pacific Grove, CA: Brooks/Cole.

Hudson, W. (1982). Scientific imperatives in social work research and practice. *Social Service Review, 56,* 246–258.

Jordan, C., & Franklin, C. (1995). *Clinical assessment for social workers: Quantitative and qualitative methods.* Chicago: Lyceum.

Levy, C. (1976). *Social work ethics.* New York: Human Sciences Press.

Loewenberg, F. M., & Dolgoff, R. (1992). *Ethical decisions for social work practice* (4th ed.). Itasca, IL: Peacock.

Maluccio, A. (1979). Perspectives of social workers and clients on treatment outcome. *Social Casework, 60,* 394–401.

Mattaini, M. A. (1997). *Clinical practice with individuals.* Washington, DC: NASW Press.

McGowan, B. (1995). Values and ethics. In C. H. Meyer and M. A. Mattaini (Eds.), *The foundations of social work practice: A graduate text* (pp. 28–41). Washington, DC: NASW Press.

Meyer, C. H. (1988). The ecosystems perspective. In R. A. Dorfman (Ed.), *Paradigms of clinical social work* (pp. 275–294). New York: Brunner/Mazel.

Mickelson, J. S. (1995). Advocacy. *Encyclopedia of social work.* Washington, DC: NASW Press.

Miley, K., O'Melia, M., & DuBois, B. L. (1995). *Generalist social work practice: An empowering approach.* Boston: Allyn and Bacon.

Miley, K., O'Melia, M., & DuBois, B. L. (1998). *Generalist social work practice: An empowering approach* (2nd ed.). Boston: Allyn and Bacon.

Murphy, J. W. (1989). Clinical intervention in the postmodern world. *International Journal of Adolescence and Youth, 2,* 61–69.

National Association of Social Workers (1997). *Code of Ethics.* Washington, DC: Author. Copyright 1999, National Association of Social Workers, Inc.

Orlinsky, D., Grawe, K., & Parks, B. (1994). Process and outcome in psychotherapy—noch einmal. In A. Bergen & S. Garfield (Eds.), *Handbook of psychotherapy and behavior change* (4th ed., pp. 270–376). New York: John Wiley.

Perlman, H. (1979). *Relationship: The heart of helping people.* Chicago: University of Chicago Press.

Petr, C. (1988). The worker-client relationship: A general systems perspective. *Social Casework, 69,* 620–626.

Pincus, A., & Minahan, A. (1973). *Social work practice: Model and method.* Itasca, IL: Peacock.

Pinderhughes, E. (1983). Empowerment for our clients and for ourselves. *Social Casework, 64,* 331–338.

Pinderhughes, E. (1995). Direct practice overview. *Encyclopedia of social work.* Washington: DC: NASW Press.

Pray, J. (1991). Respecting the uniqueness of the individual: Social work practice within a reflective model. *Social Work, 36,* 80–85.

Prochaska, J. O., DiClemente, C. C., & Norcross, J. C. (1992). In search of how people change: Applications to addictive behaviors. *American Psychologist, 47,* 1102–1114.

Reamer, F. G. (1983). Ethical dilemmas in social work practice. *Social Work, 32,* 31–35.

Reamer, F. G. (1990). *Ethical dilemmas in social services: A guide for social workers* (2nd ed.). New York: Columbia University Press.

Reid, W. (1994). The empirical practice movement. *Social Service Review, 68,* 165–184.

Rhodes, M. L. (1991). *Ethical dilemmas in social work practice.* Milwaukee: Family Service America.

Richmond, M. (1917). *Social diagnosis.* New York: Russell Sage.

Saleebey, D. (1997). *The strengths perspective in social work practice* (2nd ed.). New York: Longman.

Shulman, L. (1991). *Interactional social work practice: Toward an empirical theory.* Itasca, IL: Peacock.

Sullivan, W. P. (1992). Reconsidering the environment as a helping resource. In D. Saleebey (Ed.), *The strengths perspective in social work practice* (pp. 148–157). New York: Longman.

Wakefield, J. C. (1996). Does social work need the ecosystems perspective? Part 1. Is the perspective clinically useful? *Social Service Review, 70,* 1–32.

Weick, A. (1987). Beyond empiricism: Toward a holistic conception of social work. *Social Thought, 13,* 36–46.

Weick, A. (1993). Reconstructing social work education. In Joan Laird (Ed.), *Revisioning social work education: A social constructionist approach* (pp. 11–30). New York: Haworth.

Weick, A., & Chamberlain, R. (1997). Putting problems in their place: Further explorations in the strengths perspective. In D. Saleebey (Ed.), *The strengths perspective in social work practice* (2nd ed., pp. 39–48). New York: Longman.

Weick, A., & Saleebey, D. (1995). A post modern approach to social work practice. The 1995 Richard Lodge Memorial Lecture, Adolphi University School of Social Work, Garden City, NY, October 20.

Weick, A., Rapp, C., Sullivan, W., & Kisthardt, S. (1989). A strengths perspective for social work practice. *Social Work, 34,* 350–354.

Wolin, S. J., & Wolin, S. (1993). *The resilient self: How survivors of troubled families rise above adversity.* New York: Villard.

Yalom, I. D. (1995). *Theory and practice of group psychotherapy* (4th ed.). New York: Basic Books.

CHAPTER 2

The Helping Relationship and the Collaborative Model

Julie V. was a first-year MSW student placed in a unit of a drug and alcohol rehabilitation center. Her unit provided discharge planning for patients who were leaving the facility. Typically, Julie had one or two contacts with her clients before they were discharged.

Before she entered the MSW program, Julie worked for two years in a foster-care agency that served children who were in long-term placement. She spent a lot of time with her clients, and she felt that she got to know them and developed strong helping relationships with them. In contrast, her work at the rehabilitation center was fast-paced and short-term. She had to complete the assessment and discharge plans after one or two brief client contacts.

By the end of her first week of placement, Julie was concerned about the effectiveness of her work. She felt that her approach was too task-focused and that she was not making any connection with her clients. Instead, she was getting information as quickly as possibly, filling out a form, and telling the clients about the plan. It felt rote and dehumanizing to her. She wondered what she could do to make the experience more positive for her clients and for herself. Was it possible, desirable, and important for her to engage her clients in the discharge-planning process? Was it realistic to expect a positive helping relationship to develop in one or two brief contacts? How would the helping relationship in a short-term setting differ from one that developed over a longer period of time?

It is through the helping relationship and associated practice principles that social workers provide help and facilitate the change process. The helping relationship is the mechanism through which the client and the worker address the client's identified concerns. The helping relationship supports and structures clients' change efforts. This chapter presents a model of generalist practice that focuses on the helping relationship. It begins with a review of the practice principles of collaboration, empowerment, and evaluation. This is followed by the presentation of the collaborative model of generalist practice, including a discussion of the structure, development, and evaluation of the helping relationship between clients and their social workers. The chapter concludes with a review of the Helping Relationship Inventory, a rapid assessment instrument that measures the strength of the helping relationship. By the end of this chapter, you should be able to help Julie

1. Conceptualize the helping relationship
2. Understand the importance of the helping relationship to the helping process
3. Describe what is entailed in a collaborative approach to generalist practice
4. Identify ways to empower clients
5. Conceptualize the role of evaluation in the helping process
6. Develop a rationale for using the Helping Relationship Inventory in work with clients.

THE HELPING RELATIONSHIP

The helping relationship is the heart of the helping process. Its use in strengths-based generalist practice is built on the practice principles of collaboration, empowerment, and evaluation. These three practice principles are what make the helping relationship the medium through which client change occurs.

Historically, the profession of social work has recognized that the success of the helping process is dependent on the quality of the worker-client relationship (Biestek, 1957; Hollis, 1970; Perlman, 1979; Richmond, 1917). Biestek (1954) characterized the helping relationship as the "soul" of the helping process, a dynamic interaction of feelings and attitudes between the worker and the client. Perlman (1979) defined the professional helping relationship as a supportive, compassionate working alliance between the worker and client. Drawing on Rogers' (1957) work, Perlman named five worker attributes necessary for the development of a therapeutic relationship: warmth, acceptance, empathy, caring-concern, and genuineness. Clients who experience their interactions with social workers as caring, empathic, nonjudgmental, and genuine are more likely to engage in the helping process and to develop a sense of trust than those who do not.

Perlman's worker attributes have been widely accepted by the social work profession, and the importance of the worker-client relationship is a common assumption of social work practice. As with all assumptions, the importance of the helping relationship has been taken as a given rather than critically examined (Perlman, 1979). As early as 1979, Perlman noted that less and less attention was being paid to the helping relationship in social work research and practice literature. More recently, Coady observed "the continued neglect of relationship factors" in social work research (1993, p. 292). While social work has consistently accorded the relationship between worker and client a central role in treatment, "the precise nature of this relationship and the manner in which it contributes to treatment has not been spelled out" (Proctor, 1982, p. 430).

Instead, social work research has for the most part focused on developing and testing models of intervention and on measuring outcomes (Reid, 1994). Much of the research conducted between 1970 and 1988 attempted to establish a scientific basis for clinical social work interventions (Russell, 1990). Social work practice research has consisted of outcome-oriented investigations testing the efficacy of structured interventions. There have been few direct studies of the helping relationship.

Most conceptual work and research on the helping relationship during the past twenty years has taken place in psychology (Dore & Alexander, 1996). It has been stimulated by the seminal ideas of Bordin (1979), who defined the construct of a therapeutic or working alliance. In social work, the focus has tended to be on the feeling dimension and on worker characteristics that promote positive feelings. In clinical psychology, on the other hand, the concept of the helping relationship has been expanded to include treatment goals and tasks (Hartley & Strupp, 1983; Horvath & Greenberg, 1986; Luborsky, Crits-Christoph, Alexander, Margolis, & Cohen, 1983). These investigators view "the working alliance as a collaboration between the client and the therapist on the work of therapy" (Tichenor & Hill, 1989, p. 196). The relationship between therapist and client includes the specification of goals and agreed-on tasks for both the therapist and client, as well as the emotional bond between them.

Several studies have examined the correlation between the client's ratings of the relationship and outcome of the therapy. In a meta-analysis of twenty-four of these studies, Horvath and Symonds (1991) found that client ratings were positively associated with positive therapeutic outcome. Others have verified that the correlation appears to hold across at least three types of therapy: behavioral, cognitive-behavioral, and interpersonal (Dore & Alexander, 1996; Marziali & Alexander, 1991). A large study funded by the National Institute of Mental Health found strong correlations between relationship and outcome regardless of the type of treatment provided (Krupnick et al., 1996). Thus, social work and psychology research consistently and convincingly support the association between development of a positive helping relationship and successful treatment outcomes.

Collaboration

Collaboration—a partnership between the client and the worker—has been a pivotal practice ideal since the beginning of the social work profession (Richmond, 1917). Collaboration "requires helpers to be open to negotiation, to appreciate the authenticity of the views and aspirations of those with whom they collaborate, and to be willing to subdue their own voices in the interest of bespeaking those of their clients" (Saleebey, 1992, p. 12).

Collaboration is closely tied to self-determination (Weick, Rapp, Sullivan, & Kisthardt, 1989). The NASW *Code of Ethics* states that "the social worker should make every effort to foster maximum self-determination on the part of clients" (NASW, 1997, p. 3). Self-determination is achieved when "the client is fully involved and participating in all of the decisions and...the social worker is working with the client rather than doing things to the client" (Compton & Galaway, 1994, p. 11). Self-determination is fostered by client participation in the decision-making process. The worker and the client form a partnership to help the client resolve his or her own problems or concerns. Social workers cannot promote collaboration or foster self-determination if they see their role as reforming or changing clients. Similarly, collaboration and client self-determination are not achieved if the social worker tries to fix the problem for the client. Social work is based on the premise that clients must ultimately help themselves. Self-determination requires workers and clients to collaborate in all decisions and all aspects of their work together.

Self-determination is, for the most part, a "grand illusion" in actual practice (Perlman, 1965, p. 410). Achieving it is difficult at best. "The challenge for every practicing social worker is that of balancing the act of offering expert help while respecting the client's autonomy" (Bisman, 1994, p. 49). Problems arise when a client makes choices that are self-destructive or inconsistent with prevailing societal norms. In these situations, the dilemma for the social worker is how to resolve the conflict between his or her values and the value choices of the client while still honoring client self-determination. Levy (1972) suggests that the worker and the client openly discuss the value conflicts. Differences in value positions should be aired and the right to have different views respected.

Strengths-based generalist practice is based on the belief that clients are the experts and that they ultimately know what is best for themselves. The emphasis is on the collaborative process between the worker and the client. Engaging clients in a collaborative helping relationship increases clients' ownership of their decisions and ultimately their level of self-determination. In a collaborative partnership, the worker helps the client expand his or her repertoire of choices and behaviors. Ideally, this involves helping the client identify the range of alternatives and the pros and cons associated with each choice. With this approach, balancing the offering of expert help while respecting the client's autonomy becomes less problematic.

Empowerment

Collaboration requires the social worker to relinquish power, expertise, and control to the client. This does not mean that the worker has no expertise or role in the helping process. It does mean, however, that the balance of power and authority is distributed more equitably between the social worker and the client.

The use of empowerment in social work has grown out of the work of Solomon (1976), Rappaport (1981), and Pinderhughes (1983). It has evolved as a method for working with women, people of color, and other oppressed groups (Gutiérrez & Nurius, 1994). Empowerment is defined as the "process of increasing personal, interpersonal or political power so that individuals can take action to improve their life situations" (Gutiérrez, 1990, p. 149). The process of empowerment emphasizes the acquisition of power, which is "the capacity to influence the forces which affect one's life space for one's own benefit" (Pinderhughes, 1982, p. 332).

The focus of social work practice with individuals should be on the "reduction of the power imbalance between workers and clients—specifically on increasing the client's power resources" (Hasenfeld, 1987, p. 478). The balance of power between the social worker and the client is inherently unequal. Theories of social work practice do not adequately address this power differential and tend to understate the effect of power on the helping relationship (Hasenfeld, 1987).

Social workers have three types of power: *expertise* power derived from their access to and command of specialized knowledge, *referent* power or persuasion derived from their interpersonal skills, and *legitimate* power derived from their sanctioned position. In other words, social workers derive power from their expertise, their interpersonal skills, and the fact that they control resources needed by the client (Hasenfeld, 1987). Strengths-based generalist practice requires social workers to recognize the power they bring to the helping relationship and to engage clients in an open discussion of the various sources of power in their relationship. Acknowledging the inherent power differential is the first step in shifting the balance of power to the client. Although they rarely mention it, clients are acutely aware of the power differential between themselves and their social workers. Opening up the topic for discussion is in itself empowering (Gutiérrez, 1990). It gives the social worker and the client an opportunity to evaluate the resources available to address the client's areas of concern. The client is given a voice in defining the resources and in determining how they will be utilized in the helping relationship. As Hasenfeld states: "if we view social work practice as an exchange of resources, social work effectiveness, then, is predicated on the reduction of the power imbalance between workers and clients—specifically on increasing the client's power resources" (1987, p. 478).

Although strengths-based generalist practice acknowledges the client's expertise regarding his or her life situation, the social worker does not ignore his or her access to and command of specialized knowledge. This knowledge can help the client. But the social worker's view of the situation is not imposed on the client. The client is empowered by increasing his or her feelings of self-efficacy (Evans, 1992).

The helping relationship is the basis of empowerment (Gutiérrez, 1990; Weick & Pope, 1988). The helping relationship begins with an open discussion of each participant's interpersonal styles, preferences, and abilities. Giving clients a voice in determining what works for them is empowering. The social worker communicates willingness to be responsive to the client's interpersonal preferences. Involving the client in the definition and evaluation of the relationship empowers the client and shifts the balance of power toward the client. The social worker's referent power becomes a resource that the client has some control over.

Empowerment also entails an analysis of the agency resources controlled by the social worker and an analysis of the client's resources (Hasenfeld, 1987). In discussing agency resources, the worker needs to lay out the options available and the conditions required to access them. The worker and client explore the possibilities and costs associated with each option. The client is empowered by being involved in the analysis and by being an active participant in the decision-making process.

The worker and client should also analyze the client's potential resources. Gutiérrez suggests that part of assessing the client's potential resources or strengths "involves analyzing how conditions of powerlessness are affecting the client's situation" (1990, p. 152). After exploring the factors that might contribute to the client's perception of powerlessness, the worker and client can examine the client's potential sources of power: "Clients and workers should be encouraged to think creatively about sources of potential power, such as forgotten skills, personal qualities that could increase social influence, members of past social support networks, and organizations in their communities" (Gutiérrez, 1990, p. 152).

The worker has to adopt an empowering mind-set, which involves giving up control and essentially abandoning the role of expert diagnostician and provider of expert advice. The worker has to become a team member with the client. The client must be willing to take responsibility for all aspects of the work together. The social worker can help the client take responsibility by believing in the client's right to self-determination, by expecting the client to assume responsibility for himself or herself and the planned interventions, and by giving up the need to be in control of the helping process. The social worker can also empower the client by listening. To be listened to and heard is empowering. It validates the client's perceptions of his or her life experiences.

The client is unlikely to immediately move from a position of powerlessness to one of power. Individual empowerment is a process and should be viewed as a long-term goal of the helping relationship. Strengths-based generalist practice recognizes the shared responsibilities of the worker and the client. Ultimately, the success of the helping process depends on the client's assuming responsibility. "Clients who do not feel responsible for their problems may not invest their efforts in developing solutions unless they assume some personal responsibility for future change" (Gutiérrez, 1990, p. 150).

Evaluation

In strengths-based generalist social work practice, *evaluation* means ongoing assessment throughout the helping relationship. This involves specifying problems and goals in measurable terms, developing solution-focused interventions, and using "evaluation methods in practice" (Reid, 1994, p. 176). Evaluation involves informal feedback from the client as well as the use of formal standardized measures and rating scales. It is a joint and collaborative effort. Both the worker and the client are involved in all aspects of evaluation.

Informal Evaluation. In keeping with the principles of collaboration and empowerment, in which the client is the expert about his or her progress, subjective assessments play a prominent role in strengths-based generalist practice. Clients' subjective assessments of their situations are the primary basis for evaluating the effectiveness of the helping process. The critical factor whether the issues or concerns they are seeking help for have improved.

Informal evaluation is an ongoing process. The client and worker begin their work together by exploring the client's person-in-environment system and life experiences in order to identify concerns and the factors that potentially affect them. During this and later stages, the social worker makes sure that his or her interpretations of the client's experiences are consistent with the client's perceptions. Strengths-based generalist practice places the emphasis on listening to the client's story and understanding the client's perceptions of his or her experiences. The worker needs to continually evaluate the extent to which his or her understanding of the client's experiences is consistent with the client's.

As the client and the social worker continue to work together, informal evaluation techniques identical to the process described above play a role. The social worker has to make a conscious effort to ensure that there is agreement about the identified goals and the specifics of the helping contract. The worker and client need to evaluate the client's commitment to the plan. Is it genuine? How strong is it? What can the social worker do to help the client maintain or strengthen his or her commitment to change? Strengths-based generalist practice assumes client commitment to the helping process and stresses client responsibility. Unfortunately, clients are not always committed to addressing their concerns. A client's commitment should not be taken for granted or assumed. To address this, strengths-based generalist practice emphasizes an open dialogue between the worker and client about commitment and responsibility.

Formal Evaluation. Formal evaluation refers to the development of measurable goals and objectives and the use of standardized measures and single-item rating scales to evaluate progress on the goals. Strengths-based generalist practice incorporates formal evaluation techniques at various stages of the helping relationship.

In recent years, the number of rapid assessment instruments appropriate for social work practice has increased. Such instruments are readily available and easily accessible (Fischer & Corcoran, 1994), and the range of problem areas covered is extensive. Thus, it is often possible to find a standardized scale that measures the problem area being addressed. Standardized measures provide an excellent basis on which to evaluate client progress. They are easily incorporated in generalist social work practice. Reviewing the results of standardized measures provides opportunities for the worker and client to discuss the identified area of concern. The standardized measures are first administered as part of the goal and contracting process and are readministered periodically throughout the helping relationship. They provide the worker and client with evaluative information on client progress and open the door for a discussion of why progress is or is not being made.

Individual rating scales are the second type of formal evaluation measures used in strengths-based generalist practice. These scales are easily constructed by the worker and client. Their purpose is to assess the worker's and client's perceptions of progress on the identified areas of concern. Incorporating rating scales into the helping process is a way to evaluate progress and to obtain information on the client's perceptions of the effectiveness of the work. The primary value of this type of evaluation is that it provides a basis for the worker and client to discuss progress or the lack of it. It helps keep the work focused on the identified goals and opens up an opportunity to reevaluate priorities. Formal evaluation is covered in detail in Chapter 6, "Developing Goals, Objectives, and the Intervention and Evaluation Plan."

THE COLLABORATIVE MODEL

According to the collaborative model of generalist practice the helping process is composed of two components that influence each other: a structural component and an interpersonal component (Poulin & Young, 1997). The *structural component* is composed of tasks that are undertaken as part of the assessment and planning and action phases of the helping process (see Figure 2.1). The assessment and planning phase includes

- Identifying client concerns and strengths
- Discussing the helping process
- Clarifying worker and client roles
- Establishing priorities.

The action phase includes

- Developing goals
- Developing an action and evaluation plan
- Implementing the action and evaluation plan
- Terminating the helping relationship.

The order in which structural activities are carried out is not nearly as important as the way in which they are approached. Whatever the identified tasks, the job of the generalist social worker is to engage the client in a collaborative process

FIGURE 2.1. The Structural Component of the Collaborative Model

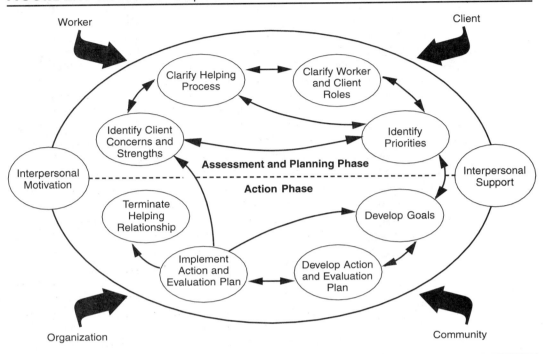

that is client-centered, evaluative, and empowering. The collaborative process used in addressing the structural aspects of the helping process influences the development of the interpersonal relationship as well as the accomplishment of the identified tasks. The structural component draws from the task-centered model of social work practice (Reid & Epstein, 1972; Tolson, Reid, & Garvin, 1994) and from research on the therapeutic alliance, especially the work of Horvath and Greenberg (1986). Conceptually, the structural component is viewed as a dynamic process, rather than a linear one (Perlman, 1979)—that is, helping relationships develop through collaborative efforts and shared experiences. The structural component comprises the agreed-on purposes of the work, and it provides the worker and client with the means, context, and experiences through which the interpersonal aspects of their relationship develop and strengthen.

The *interpersonal component* of the collaborative model refers to the psychological bond that develops between client and worker as a result of their interactions. It is based on a variety of cognitive and emotional responses, such as appreciation, respect, trust, comfort, hope, and understanding. The interpersonal component focuses on the client's subjective perceptions of his or her experience with the social worker and on the worker's subjective perceptions of his or her experiences with the client. As shown in Figure 2.2, the interpersonal component is composed of two interrelated factors: motivation and support.

Motivation refers to the client's perception that the helping relationship with the social worker has caused the client to want to take action. Enhancing a client's

FIGURE 2.2. The Interpersonal Component of the Collaborative Model

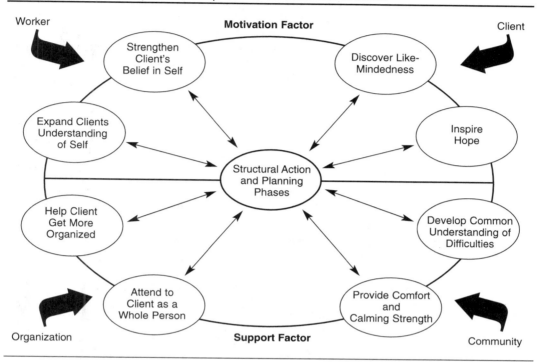

motivation is a collaborative process; the social worker taps into the client's existing motivation to help him or her sustain and heighten that motivation.

There are a number of ways social workers can help motivate clients, including inspiring hope, being perceived as like-minded, inspiring clients to believe in themselves, and helping clients think clearly about themselves and their difficulties (Poulin & Young, 1997). Workers who are perceived as understanding, competent, comforting, and inspiring tend to develop stronger relationships with their clients than those who are not (Poulin & Young, 1997). These positive client perceptions strengthen the psychological bond between workers and clients, which in turn helps motivate both to sustain their commitment to the helping relationship.

For so-called involuntary or mandated clients, experiencing the relationship with the worker as motivating is more complex. Most mandated clients have as their primary motivation the desire to protest the mandate. This protest and its supporting stories must be listened to as well. Doing so can help the involuntary client feel that the worker is committed to finding a way to make the relationship helpful and meaningful. Believing that the worker is committed to the relationship's being meaningful to the client can be the first step to finding a basis for motivation in the mandated client.

Strengths-based generalist practice views the client's perception that the relationship with the social worker is providing emotional support as a critical factor in developing and sustaining the helping relationship. The social worker's ability to communicate support not only contributes to the psychological bond that develops between the client and worker; it also influences the client's perception of the helping relationship as collaborative and empowering and reinforces the client's commitment to the intervention strategies.

Social workers who pay attention to their clients, demonstrate an understanding of their difficulties, help them get more organized, and have a calming or soothing effect develop stronger interpersonal connections than those who do not. Similarly, clients who perceive that their social workers share a common understanding of their difficulties and who become more organized as a result of interactions with their workers tend to develop stronger relationships than those who do not (Poulin & Young, 1997).

The Assessment and Planning Phase

The four major structural tasks that need to be accomplished during the assessment and planning phase of the helping relationship are

1. Identifying client concerns and strengths
2. Discussing the nature of the helping process
3. Clarifying worker and client roles
4. Establishing the client's priorities for the work to be undertaken.

These activities are described in detail in Chapter 3, "Individual and Family Assessment."

The activities associated with this phase of the helping relationship usually take place at the beginning of the helping process, but they can be revisited in response to changing client concerns and priorities. Client concerns and priorities often change as the work progresses and as the helping relationship develops (Gambrill, 1983; Northen, 1995). A focus that was initially agreed on may no longer be a primary concern. Rigidly following the initial agenda without periodic reassessment and verification is unwise and most likely will lead to weakening the helping relationship and/or unplanned termination. Thus, workers and clients need to reevaluate various aspects of the assessment and planning phase periodically during their work together.

During the assessment and planning phase, the motivating and supporting aspects of the interpersonal component of the helping relationship continue to influence and be influenced by the structured activities. The client and worker talk together about concerns, problems, and resources (including personal strengths) in a way that allows them to co-construct an understanding of the client and his or her situation.

At the point of seeking or being mandated to seek help, many clients have mixed emotional reactions. Vulnerability, fear of being criticized or judged, hurt pride, anger, and shame are common feelings that clients bring to the initial relationship. Strong emotional reactions of this nature can interfere with cognitive processes. Thus, the worker's ability to accept emotional distress and provide some comfort merely through talking often allows the client to move forward more productively in thinking about his or her difficulties. Then, as the worker puts forth a tentative statement of understanding to be clarified and verified, both client and worker move toward a similar understanding of the client's difficulties. As the worker validates the oppressive and upsetting aspects of the client's difficulties, the client often regains some self-confidence and begins to feel hopeful that their common understanding will lead to change.

Strengths-based generalist practice views these shifts in feeling and thinking as motivating in the sense that they move clients forward in the process of understanding the manifestations, contexts, and histories of their difficulties. This process includes consideration of efforts that have already been made to resolve difficulties, thus providing additional information about the client's personal strengths and resources as well as previous failures, frustrations, and disappointments. The worker's appreciation of these is often experienced by the client as both supportive and empowering.

The Action Phase

The four major structural tasks that need to be accomplished during the action phase of the helping relationship are

1. Articulating goals
2. Developing the action and evaluation plan
3. Implementing the action and evaluation plan
4. Terminating the relationship.

Chapter 6, "Developing Goals, Objectives, and the Intervention and Evaluation Plan," and Chapter 7, "Intervention and Termination," cover these steps in detail.

The order of accomplishing these tasks is relatively fixed. The social worker and client need to identify the goals they hope to achieve before they develop an action and evaluation plan. The action plan has to be developed before it can be implemented. Although the order of the tasks is fixed, the process is not static. It is dynamic and evolves and changes over time.

During the action phase of the helping relationship, the motivating and supporting aspects of the interpersonal component continue to influence and interact with the structured activities. As the social worker and the client co-create the plan for addressing the client's difficulties, the worker encourages and supports the client's imagination, which in turn further stimulates the worker's. This process includes consideration of how the plan's success will be measured when it is implemented.

Implementing the plan brings forth another form of motivation and support, a willingness to experiment. The creativity of the planning process typically culminates in a plan that includes actions unfamiliar to the client. The worker's role is to encourage the client to experiment, to provide support for trying the unknown, and to deal with the fear of failure.

One way the worker enhances motivation is by engaging the client in the process of thinking and talking about how progress will be assessed. Doing so emphasizes that the worker is supporting the client's desire and efforts. As the client experiences the worker's calming effect and efforts to help him or her become more organized and stay focused, the motivational effect is enhanced.

Integrating the Structural and Interpersonal Components in Practice

Strengths-based generalist practice views the helping relationship as a dynamic process involving structural activities and interpersonal interactions between the client and the social worker. The structural and interpersonal components both need to develop for the helping relationship to be effective. They tend to develop concurrently. The process of collaborating on the structural activities builds and strengthens the interpersonal connection or psychological bond between the worker and the client. It takes time and shared experiences for a strong interpersonal connection to develop. The structural activities provide the interactions on which the interpersonal relationship is built. Through verbal and nonverbal interactions and collaborative efforts, the client experiences the worker as motivating and supportive.

While accomplishing the structural activities, the worker should engage the client in an empowering collaborative process that is client-centered. For example, during the initial sessions, the primary structural task is identifying concerns and strengths. The way the worker interacts with the client during this process profoundly influences the development of their interpersonal relationship. The worker should strive to motivate and support the clients as they tell their stories. If the worker communicates understanding of the client's concerns and difficulties, provides comfort and calming strength, and pays attention to the client as a whole person, the client will probably experience the worker as supportive. This will in turn strengthen the client's interpersonal connection with the worker. Similarly, if the worker helps the client expand his or her self-understanding, strengthen his or her self-belief, and find hope and inspiration, the client will probably experience the worker as motivating. These experiences will also strengthen the psychological bond between the worker and the client.

ASSESSING THE HELPING RELATIONSHIP

The Helping Relationship Inventory (HRI) is a rapid assessment instrument designed to assess the strength of the structural and interpersonal components of the helping relationship (Poulin & Young, 1997). There are client (HRI:C) and worker (HRI:W) versions that are sensitive to important differences in client and worker concerns (Poulin & Young, 1997). Both are reliable and valid measures of the helping relationship.

The client version, HRI:C, measures the strength of the helping relationship in social work practice from the perspective of the client (see Figure 2.3). It is composed of ten structural and ten interpersonal items that capture those aspects of the helping relationship most important to clients. The worker version, HRI:W, measures the relationship from the perspective of the worker (see Figure 2.4). It is composed of ten structural and ten interpersonal items that capture those aspects of the helping relationship that are most important to workers providing help.

The worker and client versions of the HRI complement and strengthen social work practice with a variety of client populations. They evolved from a conception of social work practice that focuses on a collaborative process of assessment, goal specification, intervention, and evaluation within which the social worker motivates and supports the client's efforts to achieve his or her goals. Thus, the HRI:C and HRI:W are compatible with the strengths-based generalist practice conceptualization of the helping relationship.

FIGURE 2.3. Helping Relationship Inventory—Client HRI:C

1. How much input have you had in determining how the two of you will work together?

2. How much have you and your social worker discussed the specific problem(s) with which you want help?

3. How much input have you had in determining the specific problem(s) you are addressing in your work together?

4. To what extent have you and your social worker discussed the specific goal(s) you hope to accomplish in your work together?

5. How much input have you had in determining the goals you are working on?

6. To what extent have you and your social worker discussed the specific actions you will take to address your difficulties?

7. To what extent have you and your social worker discussed the specific actions your social worker will take to address your difficulties?

8. How much have you and your social worker discussed how your progress is going to be assessed?

9. How much input do you have in determining how you and your social worker will assess your progress?

10. To what extent have you and your social worker discussed your progress?

11. Do you feel your social worker pays attention to you?

12. Is your social worker's understanding of your difficulties similar to your own?

13. Does talking with your social worker help you get more organized about resolving your difficulties?

14. Does talking with your social worker have a calming, soothing effect on you?

15. Does talking with your social worker give you hope?

16. Does your social worker help you think more clearly about your difficulties?

17. Does talking with your social worker help you to believe more in yourself?

18. In general, do you feel you and your social worker see things in similar ways?

19. Does your social worker help you think more clearly about yourself?

20. Do you feel that you and your social worker are alike in some ways?

Note: All of the items are measured with Likert-type scales ranging from (1) *not at all* to (5) *a great deal.* The HRI:C structural index has a reliability coefficient of .91, and the interpersonal index has a reliability coefficient of .96. Overall, the HRI:C has a reliability coefficient of .96. It demonstrates concurrent and discriminant validity. Originally published in "Development of a Helping Relationship for Social Work Practice," by J. Poulin and T. Young, 1997, *Research on Social Work Practice, 7,* pp. 463–489.

Scoring the HRI

The worker and client versions of the HRI both contain ten structural and ten interpersonal items that are rated on five-point Likert-type scales. Scores for the structural component are calculated by summing items 1 through 10. Scores for the interpersonal component are calculated by summing items 11 through 20. The total HRI score is calculated by summing the structural and interpersonal scores.

Since the reliability and validity estimates of the structural and interpersonal subscales of the HRI are strong, social workers and their clients should calculate scores for the structural and interpersonal subscales as well as the overall HRI scores. Although scoring norms have not been developed for the HRI, a score of 30 or lower on either component should be considered indicative of a problematic relationship. If either the worker and/or client rates the structural or interpersonal component of their work together at or below this level, there is a strong likelihood that a satisfactory relationship is not developing or that there has been a rupture in the relationship. Workers and clients should compare both sets of scores to identify the areas of difficulty and/or disagreement and discuss ways to strengthen the relationship.

FIGURE 2.4. Helping Relationship Inventory—Worker HRI:W

---

1. How much input does your client have in determining how your work together will be approached?

2. How much have you and your client discussed the specific problem(s) with which he/she wants help?

3. How clear are you about the specific problem(s) that you and your client are addressing?

4. To what extent have you and your client discussed the specific goal(s) you hope to accomplish in your work together?

5. How much input does your client have in determining the goals he/she is working on?

6. How clear are you about your client's goals?

7. To what extent have you and your client discussed the specific actions he/she will take to address his/her difficulties?

8. How clear are you about the actions you are taking?

9. How much input does your client have in determining how you and your client will assess his/her progress?

10. How clear are you about how you and your client are assessing his/her progress?

11. Do you explain to your client your understanding of his/her difficulties?

12. Is your client's understanding of his/her difficulties similar to your own?

13. Is your client more organized about resolving his/her difficulties as a result of talking to you?

14. Does talking with you have a calming, soothing, effect on your client?

15. Does talking with you give your client hope?

16. Are you able to handle the emotional aspects of your client's difficulties?

17. Do you enjoy meeting and talking with your client?

18. In general, do you feel you and your client see things in similar ways?

19. Do you help your client think more clearly about him/herself?

20. Do you feel that you and your client are alike in some ways?

Note: All of the items are measured with Likert-type scales ranging from (1) *not at all* to (5) *a great deal.* The HRI:W structural index has a reliability coefficient of .86, and the interpersonal index has a reliability coefficient of .91. Overall, the HRI:W has a reliability coefficient of .93. It demonstrates concurrent and discriminant validity. Originally published in "Development of a Helping Relationship for Social Work Practice," by J. Poulin and T. Young, 1997, *Research on Social Work Practice, 7,* pp. 463–489.

The scores are rough benchmarks the worker can use to assess the need to address relationship issues with the client. There are no clinically established cut-off scores. For example, a combined score of 61 should not automatically be viewed as problem-free or a score of 59 as problematic. Worker and client scores on the HRI have to be viewed within the context of the helping relationship and the unique circumstances of the case.

Applications for Social Work Practice

The HRI is designed to help social workers and clients examine their perceptions of the helping relationship. Early in the helping process, no later than after the third session, the worker and client should complete the HRI and compare and discuss the results. Comparing the worker and client ratings of the individual items can lead to fruitful discussions about working together and what does and does not work in the helping relationship (Young & Poulin, 1998). Comparing the worker and client versions of the HRI facilitates the important process of collaboration and empowerment of the client early in the helping process.

Using the HRI:C and HRI:W as part of the helping process can provide both worker and client with important information on key elements of their work together. Clients and workers often have significantly different perceptions of the helping relationship (Horvath & Greenberg, 1994). For social workers to assume that their clients share their view of their work together is risky and could impede progress.

The relationship between the worker and client is the strongest predictor of both client change and client satisfaction (Horvath & Symonds, 1991). A solid helping relationship is a prerequisite for successful outcomes. Given the demonstrated differences in perceptions of shared experiences and the importance of the helping relationship in the change process, early and ongoing examinations of the client's and worker's perceptions of the relationship are critical.

If the client and worker do not develop a strong collaborative relationship that the client perceives as helpful, the client most likely will terminate. Failure to develop a helping relationship is a common reason for termination (Levine & Herron, 1990). Using the HRI early in the helping process might increase client collaboration and reduce the likelihood that the client will prematurely discontinue treatment. Administering the HRI and discussing the adequacy of the relationship will in itself help strengthen the helping relationship.

The HRI should be administered periodically throughout the helping process to obtain feedback on the strength of the relationship as the work evolves. This is particularly critical if clients and/or workers become discouraged about the possibilities of meaningful change or frustrated over what needs to be done to bring change about. Administering the HRI during the middle phase of treatment can provide the worker and client with important information on the strength of the relationship and open discussion about what they are working on and how they are doing so together.

Finally, the HRI should be administered as part of planned termination. An important aspect of termination is reviewing the helping relationship. This review helps clients become better consumers of social work services. It helps them articulate what has and has not worked for them, how they have changed themselves or their situation, and how they brought change about. Reviewing the structural and interpersonal components of the HRI draws attention to specific aspects of the helping relationship. It can enhance the worker's and client's review of how they worked together. Completing the HRI during termination also allows the worker and client to compare their ratings with ratings made earlier in the process. This provides a basis for a review of progress and experiences.

SUMMARY

The collaborative model of generalist social work practice emphasizes the importance of the helping relationship. The helping relationship is composed of a structural and an interpersonal dimension. The structural component focuses on tasks, while the interpersonal component focuses on the psychological bond between the client and the worker. For the work to proceed, both aspects of the helping relationship must be developed.

Three practice principles contribute to the development of the helping relationship. The first is collaboration. The premise is that workers and clients develop a partnership in their work together. They are equal partners in the helping process. Clients are viewed as experts about their situations, they ultimately know what is best for themselves. Engaging clients in a collaborative helping relationship increases clients' ownership of the change process.

The second practice principle is empowerment. Empowerment is the process of increasing personal, interpersonal, or political power so that individuals can take action to improve their life situations. In generalist practice, social workers give up control of the helping process. They actively work to shift control and power to their clients. Clients are encouraged to take an active role in defining resources and in determining how they will utilize the helping relationship. Ultimately, the success of the helping process depends on clients' assuming responsibility and control.

The third practice principle is evaluation. Evaluation means on-going assessment throughout the helping relationship. It involves informal feedback from clients as well as the use of formal standardized measures and rating scales. Evaluation is a joint and collaborative effort. The worker and the client take active roles in evaluating progress and the helping process.

The HRI is a tool for both the worker and the client to assess progress in the development of the helping relationship. The HRI measures the strength of the structural and interpersonal components of the helping relationship from the client's and worker's perspectives. Since the helping relationship is vital to the helping process, social workers should make a conscious effort to evaluate its development. Doing so can provide important information on differences between worker and client perceptions of how things are progressing as well as validation of what is working well. In addition to providing important feedback on the helping relationship, use of the HRI helps promote client empowerment and the development of a collaborative approach to the helping process.

CASE EXAMPLE

The final case example in this chapter was written by Denise Bubel when she was a first-year MSW student. It is based on her work with a client at her field placement in a partial hospitalization program for elderly persons with serious and persistent mental illness. The case illustrates the importance of developing both the structural and interpersonal aspects of the helping relationship. It also is an excellent example of how listening to clients empowers them and promotes the development of the helping relationship.

No One Ever Asked Before   *Denise Bubel*

Practice Setting

Terra Firma, a partial hospitalization program for elderly mentally ill clients, serves as a temporary oasis to aid transition from crisis to regaining maximum function. The agency employs specialists to enable the clients to benefit from cognitive, behavioral, individual, group, and family therapy. A client experiences an intense structured program of five therapy sessions daily, from three to five days a week, until the treatment team agrees on the proper time of discharge.

Problem Situation

Alfred C. is a fifty-nine-year-old African-American male who lives with his eighty-year-old mother. Two weeks ago, his mother brought him to the emergency crisis center at the hospital. She was concerned that he was extremely depressed and that he had secluded himself inside the house. She reported to the doctor that he was not taking care of his personal hygiene and general health and that his condition was declining.

At the crisis center, Mr. C. told the doctor that he had a poor appetite and that he had lost approximately fifty pounds over the last six months. He talked about being unable to sleep and his feeling of being watched, which forced him to stay secluded in his house. Mr. C. also complained to the doctor about chronic auditory hallucinations. He denied having a history of substance abuse. Mr. C. was admitted into the locked psychiatric unit at the hospital.

The doctor reported that Mr. C. was "preoccupied, dysphoric, and was a relatively limited historian. He complained of depression and was ruminating about finances and appeared preoccupied and somewhat psychotic. He was very thin, disheveled, and pacing." When the doctor left the room, the client apparently had an episode of an undetermined cause that was either a seizure or a syncope. When the doctor returned, the client was "unresponsive and his pulse was not palpable and his breathing was shallow. At that point, a CODE was called and the client was brought into the medical part of the hospital." The doctor reported that the client "came around nicely." Medications were prescribed, and Mr. C. was returned to the psychiatric unit after a few days. The results of the tests to determine the nature of the seizure or syncope were not available at the time of the initial interview for admittance to the partial program.

Initial Contact

As a social work intern, I was assigned to be Mr. C.'s case manager. When I first sat down to talk with him, he would not talk or make eye contact with me. He stared at one spot and seemed preoccupied with his thoughts or hallucinations. I felt *very* uncomfortable at first. I understood that I should not be aggressive, offer help, or be overly intrusive. Since I had a brief history from the initial intake, I decided that I would just focus on trying to establish some sort of connection with Mr. C.

I introduced myself in a quiet voice and sat a comfortable distance away from the client. I explained to Mr. C. that I was going to ask him some questions so I would be able to better assess his situation. Then he and I would make some goals for him to reach while he was in the program. I asked him if that was OK, and he did not respond. I gave it a few minutes and asked again. He looked at me and said "OK." I asked him questions about his circumstances and his situation. During the first fifteen minutes,

I collected very little information about his life. He was basically unresponsive to my inquires.

I asked him about his delusions and hallucinations and gave him ample time to respond. He opened up and said that he was not able to tell if the voices were male or female, adult or child. He told me that many voices were whispering to him today, and that they had been yelling at him on the days before he was admitted to the hospital. He went on to explain that the voices upset his stomach so he could not eat, and it made him depressed. The voices told him not to let the doctor look at the lump in his side, to stay in the house, to stay away from others, and not to go near any steps. The voices were telling him to leave Terra Firma and go home.

I told Mr. C. that he did well and that we were happy to have him aboard. I told him that he did not have to participate in any activities, that he was safe and secure, and that no one would bother him. I felt I was able to convey empathy without being intrusive. Lastly, I asked him what he wanted to change in his life that Terra Firma could help him work toward. I was floored when he unexpectedly responded, "Get people to like me and get me to talk to people."

Second Contact

During our second meeting, Mr. C. opened up to me, and I was able to collect some pertinent information about his life. Five years prior, as a result of mental illness, Mr. C. moved back in with his mother after he had lost his job packing goods at a dairy. Approximately ten months prior to this episode, he lost his job as a janitor at a bus station as a result of his mental illness. He was divorced twenty years ago and has one adult son and one adult daughter with whom he has no contact. He denied any past or present history of physical, sexual, emotional, or substance abuse. Mr. C. reported that he is still hearing voices, but not as often as before he came to the hospital.

During the session, I tried to focus all my attention on Mr. C. Rather than thinking about asking the questions, I concentrated on listening to his answers. It seemed to work. He told me about his life and his experiences. It was a very satisfying experience for both of us. I believe that he felt he was heard and that I was interested in him and what he had to say.

Third Contact

I was able to collect extensive information from Mr. C. during the third interview. He seems to be stabilizing, which I attribute to his compliance with his medication, specifically the injection of Haldol Decanoate. He showed a major difference in his cognitive abilities. Mr. C.'s mood and affect still remain blunted and depressed, but he is less withdrawn and internalized.

During this session, Mr. C. did most of the talking. I tried to appear to be empathic and supportive. I told him I was happy with his progress and the strides he had made. I also told him how pleased I was with how well we seemed to get along and that I enjoyed working with him. He seemed to respond favorably to my comments.

Current Situation

After three weeks, Mr. C. continues to show marked improvement. He has recovered from the hernia repair without incident. He is compliant about taking his medication and attends the Terra Firma program as scheduled. The client has not missed a day or been late since he began the program. He approaches me on the days I am there, says "Good morning," and is willing to hold extensive conversations with me and with the other clients attending the program. His spirits are up, and he appears to be adjusting well. The client has not yet attended any activities outside his home or returned to church. He has implemented a walking program in his neighborhood, but is not yet socializing with his neighbors. He has not yet made contact with his son or daughter. At this time, returning to work has not been suggested until further improvement is made.

Client System Obstacles and Strengths

The client is a very likable and cooperative person. He is willing to try to improve his life situation. He is hindered by his mental illness and needs to stay on his medication and visit his doctor regularly so that the medicine can be monitored. This client is preoccupied with finances and needs to return to work to alleviate the major stress of this concern. Even though the client does not have a formal education, he has been able to hold down jobs. The biggest obstacle to employment is the employer's lack of understanding of the client's mental illness.

The client needs to work on interpersonal skills to be able to communicate his concerns and disagreements with others. In the active phase of his illness, he becomes withdrawn and internalized, shutting out the world. The client has the will to achieve a self-sufficient status. He reports that he wants to be liked and to be able to communicate with others.

Though the client cannot drive, he is able to get a ride if needed. Also, he will eventually be able to take public transportation once he comes out of the active phase of his illness.

Even though he lacks relationships, friendships, and acquaintances, his mother and neighbor offer him support. Mr. C. needs to successfully return to a functioning capacity and return to work. He lives in an area close to public transportation and is in an area where he is able to find employment.

The major obstacle in his environment is people who do not understand his mental illness. With some understanding and minimal accommodations, this client can function in society and be productive.

DISCUSSION QUESTIONS

1. What contributed to the development of a helping relationship between Denise and Mr. C.? What did Denise do to facilitate the development of a relationship? What would you have done differently?
2. The case example focused only on Mr. C. What other client systems need to be taken into consideration in this case? What unanswered questions do you have about the other client systems? If this was your case how would you proceed?

3. Discuss the interrelationship between the structural and interpersonal components of the helping relationship. How is the process of developing a helping relationship with a client different than and similar to that of developing a relationship with a peer?

4. Contrast the collaborative approach to social work practice with the traditional diagnostic model of practice. Describe the approach used in your field placement agency. How might you adopt a more collaborative approach in a setting that adheres to the diagnostic model?

5. Brainstorm about all the possible ways a social worker could promote client empowerment. Examine a specific case from an empowerment perspective. What needs to happen in the helping relationship for client empowerment to occur? What do social workers need to do to empower clients?

6. How does informal evaluation differ from formal evaluation in generalist social work practice? How do you currently evaluate progress with your clients? What are the reasons for and against the use of informal and formal evaluation?

7. Discuss the use of the HRI in your practice. How might it enhance or inhibit the helping process? How would your clients react to being asked to evaluate the helping relationship? How would you feel about having your clients rate your relationship?

8. How do the concepts of collaboration, empowerment, and evaluation apply to working with people with serious and persistent mental illness? In what ways is developing a helping relationship different with this client population? In what ways is it the same?

REFERENCES

Biestek, F. (1954). An analysis of the casework relationship. *Social Casework, 35,* 57–61.

Biestek, F. (1957). *The casework relationship.* Chicago: Loyola University Press.

Bisman, C. (1994). *Social work practice: Cases and principles.* Pacific Grove, CA: Brooks/Cole.

Bordin, E. (1979). The generalizability of the psychoanalytic concept of the working alliance. *Psychotherapy: Theory, Research, and Practice, 16,* 252–260.

Coady, N. (1993). The worker-client relationship revisited. *Families in Society, 74,* 291–300.

Compton, B., & Galaway, B. (1994). *Social work processes* (5th ed.). Pacific Grove, CA: Brooks/Cole.

Dore, M., & Alexander, L. (1996). Preserving families at risk of child abuse and neglect: The role of the helping alliance. *Child Abuse and Neglect, 20,* 349–361.

Evans, E. (1992). Liberation theology, empowerment theory and social work practice with the oppressed. *International Social Work, 35,* 135–147.

Fischer, J., & Corcoran, K. (1994). Measures for clinical practice: A sourcebook (Vols. 1–2, 2nd ed.). New York: Free Press.

Gambrill, E. (1983). *Casework: A competency-based approach.* Englewood Cliffs, NJ: Prentice-Hall.

Gutiérrez, L. (1990). Working with women of color: A empowerment perspective. *Social Work, 35,* 149–153.

Gutiérrez, L., & Nurius, P. (1994). *Education and research for empowerment practice* (Monograph No. 7). Seattle, WA: University of Washington, School of Social Work, Center for Policy and Practice Research.

Hartley, D., & Strupp, H. (1983). The therapeutic alliance: Its relationship to outcome in brief psychotherapy. In J. Masling (Ed.), *Empirical studies of psychoanalytic theories* (Vol. 1, pp. 1–38). Hillsdale, NJ: Analytical Press.

Hasenfeld, Y. (1987). Power in social work practice. *Social Service Review, 61,* 469–483. Quotations reprinted by permission of the University of Chicago Press.

Hollis, F. (1970). The psychosocial approach to the practice of casework. In R. Roberts & R. Nee (Eds.), *Theories of social casework* (pp. 33–76). Chicago: University of Chicago Press.

Horvath, A., & Greenberg, L. (1986). The development of the working alliance inventory. In L. Greenberg & W. Pinsof (Eds.), *The psychotherapeutic process: A research handbook* (pp. 529–556). New York: Guilford.

Horvath, A., & Greenberg, L. (Eds.). (1994). *The working alliance: Theory, research, and practice.* New York: Wiley.

Horvath, A., & Symonds, B. (1991). Relation between working alliance and outcome in psychotherapy: A meta-analysis. *Journal of Counseling Psychology, 38,* 139–149.

Krupnick, J., Sotsky, S., Simmens, S., Moyer, J., Elkin, I., Watkins, J., & Pilkonis, P. (1996). The role of the therapeutic alliance in psychotherapy and pharmacotherapy outcome: Findings in the National Institute of Mental Health treatment of depression collaborative research program. *Journal of Consulting and Clinical Psychology, 64,* 532–539.

Levine, S., & Herron, W. (1990). Changes during the course of the psychotherapeutic relationship. *Psychological Reports, 66,* 883–897.

Levy, C. (1972). Values and planned change. *Social Casework, 53*(8), 488–493.

Luborsky, L., Crits-Christoph, P., Alexander, L., Margolis, M., & Cohen, M. (1983). Two helping alliance methods for predicting outcome of psychotherapy. *Journal of Nervous and Mental Disease, 171,* 480–91.

Marziali, E., & Alexander, L. (1991). The power of the therapeutic relationship. *American Journal of Orthopsychiatry, 61,* 383–391.

National Association of Social Workers (1997). *Code of Ethics,* Washington, DC.

Northen, H. (1995). *Clinical social work* (2nd ed.). New York: Columbia University Press.

Perlman, H. (1965). Self-determination: Reality or illusion? *Social Service Review, 39*(4), 410–421.

Perlman, H. (1979). *Relationship: The heart of helping people.* Chicago: University of Chicago Press.

Pinderhughes, E. (1983). Empowerment for our clients and for ourselves. *Social Casework, 64,* 331–338.

Poulin, J., & Young, T. (1997). Development of a helping relationship for social work practice. *Research on Social Work Practice, 7,* 463–489.

Proctor, E. (1982). Defining the worker-client relationship. *Social Work, 27,* 430–435.

Rappaport, J. (1981). In praise of paradox: A social policy of empowerment over prevention. *American Journal of Community Psychology, 9,* 1–15.

Reid, W. (1994). The empirical practice movement. *Social Service Review, 68,* 165–84.

Reid, W., & Epstein, L. (1972). *Task-centered casework.* New York: Columbia University Press.

Richmond, M. (1917). *Social diagnosis.* New York: Russell Sage.

Rogers, C. (1957). The necessary and sufficient conditions of therapeutic personality change. *Journal of Consulting Psychology, 21,* 95–103.

Russell, M. (1990). *Clinical social work: Research and practice.* Newbury Park, CA: Sage.

Saleebey, D. (1992). *The strengths perspective in social work practice.* New York: Longman.

Solomon, B. (1976). *Black empowerment.* New York: Columbia University Press.

Tichenor, V., & Hill, C. (1989). A comparison of six measures of working alliance. *Psychotherapy, 26,* 195–199.

Tolson, E., Reid, W., & Garvin, C. (1994). *Generalist practice: A task-centered approach.* New York: Columbia University Press.

Weick, A., & Pope, L. (1988). Knowing what's best: A new look at self-determination. *Social Casework, 69,* 10–16.

Weick, A., Rapp, C., Sullivan, W., & Kisthardt, S. (1989). A strengths perspective for social work practice. *Social Work, 34,* 350–354.

Young, T., & Poulin, J. (1998). The helping relationship inventory: A clinical appraisal. *Families in Society, 79,* 123–133.

CHAPTER 3

Individual and Family Assessment

om B. was a first-year MSW student placed in an in-patient psychiatric unit of a metropolitan hospital. The unit was designed to provide short-term treatment to stabilize patients who were experiencing mental health crises, to conduct comprehensive assessments, and to develop care plans for discharge.

The unit followed the traditional medical model of patient care. The treatment team placed a great deal of emphasis and time on diagnosing and identifying the patients' particular mental illnesses. There was a heavy emphasis on psychopharmacology and on fine-tuning patients' medications. The treatment team set the patients' goals and treatment objectives, and they developed the discharge care plans. Tom was impressed by the professionalism of the staff and by how much they seemed to know about various mental illnesses. Everyone seemed very committed to the job and worked hard to make diagnoses and to complete their parts of the treatment and discharge plans.

Over the course of the semester, Tom noticed that a high percentage of the patients had been placed in the unit before. Most had multiple in-patient psychiatric hospitalizations. Tom began to question the effectiveness of the approach used to treat mental illness. Why didn't the patients have any voice in the treatment process? What was the value of diagnosis beyond affixing a label to the patient? How did focusing on patients' problems help them develop effective coping strategies after they were discharged? Why weren't the families involved in the assessment process and in the discharge care plans?

Assessment is the exploration and analysis of the client's situation. In collaborative social work, it is a process in which you and the client explore the client's perceptions and experiences. Major goals of the assessment process are to help the client identify and clarify problem areas and to begin to understand characteristics of the client and the environment that influence the identified problems. It is from this beginning understanding that plans to address the client's concerns are formulated. Assessment is the key to effective social work practice (Jordan & Franklin, 1995; Meyer, 1993).

This chapter begins with a general discussion of assessment and diagnosis, followed by a review of the strengths perspective and the helping relationship as they relate to assessment. The remainder of the chapter presents information on assessing individual and family client systems. Key content areas for each client system are reviewed. By the end of the chapter, you should be able to help Tom

1. Understand the role diagnosis plays in the assessment process
2. Describe the structural and interpersonal aspects of the assessment process
3. Plot personal and environmental client systems strengths and obstacles
4. Conduct a strengths-based assessment of individual and family client systems.

ASSESSMENT AND DIAGNOSIS

Assessment is more than diagnosing the client's presenting symptoms and coming up with a diagnostic label. Typically, insurance companies require a diagnosis using the *Diagnostic and Statistical Manual of Mental Disorders*, or *DSM-IV* (American Psychiatric Association, 1994) for reimbursement of services. While useful in communicating symptom types, diagnostic labels do not tell you anything about the unique circumstances of your clients, nor do they tell you anything about how to approach your work with clients.

Diagnostic labeling can also have negative consequences (Gambrill, 1997; Kinney, Haapala, & Booth, 1991; Kirk & Kutchins, 1992; Levy, 1972). Psychiatric labels tend to create negative expectations. They focus attention on deficits and away from the potential to change. "Labeling makes it harder for us to be warm and supportive, if we're thinking about coping with the negative traits we've assigned to our clients" (Kinney, Haapala, & Booth, 1991, p. 84).

Another negative consequence of labeling is that it reduces feelings of hopefulness. Labeling is all-inclusive. For example, a client is psychotic, or a client has a personality disorder. Labels imply that what clients are is what they will always be (Kinney, Haapala, & Booth, 1991). These negative expectations discourage a sense of hopefulness, reduce client motivation, and minimize possibilities for change (Rapp, 1998).

Additionally, reliance on *DSM-IV* labels places the social worker in the role of expert about clients' problems. Clients' understanding and knowledge about themselves and their situations are minimized. The labeling process takes power away from clients and places it in the hands of the expert diagnostic social worker.

Many beginning social workers like to use the DSM-*IV*. Referring to clients by their diagnostic labels makes a new social worker feel and sound professional and gives the illusion of understanding and expertise. Avoid the temptation and the trap. Beyond the requirements of managed care, using diagnostic labels probably hinders the helping process more than it helps. Most labels create negative expectations for both you and the client, focus on a condition or trait rather than the context in which the problem occurs, offer little in the way of understanding the unique circumstances of the client, and do not provide any information about how to resolve the problem.

Assessment and Client Strengths

Focusing on client pathology promotes homogenization, (Rapp, 1998). Clients are viewed as a collection of generalized problems that are finite and shared by many clients. This results in a generic case plan that sees all clients as essentially exhibiting the same groups of symptoms. Clients are not seen as unique individuals with unique circumstances and problem situations.

Strengths-based assessments enhance the individualization of clients. The focus is on what is unique about each client in terms of interests, abilities, and how they have coped with their problem situation. "The work should focus on what the client has achieved so far, what resources have been or are currently available to the client, what the client knows and talents possessed, and what aspirations and dreams the client may hold" (Rapp, 1998, p. 45). Cowger outlined the following guidelines for a strengths assessment:

1. Give preeminence to the client's understanding of the facts
2. Believe the client
3. Discover what the client wants
4. Move the assessment toward personal and environmental strengths
5. Make the assessment of strengths multidimensional
6. Use the assessment to discover uniqueness
7. Use language the client can understand
8. Make the assessment a joint activity between worker and client
9. Reach a mutual agreement on the assessment
10. Avoid blame and blaming
11. Assess, do not diagnose (1997, pp. 63–66).

Adherence to these guidelines will ensure that your assessment interviews are collaborative and that the process will identify client strengths. The tendency to focus on pathology and dysfunction will be minimized.

Identifying client strengths is not always easy. Clients are often unable to identify specific strengths related to how they have coped with the problem situation. They often indicate that they do not have any strengths, or they respond in very general terms, such as "I am a nice person" (McQuaide & Ehrenreich, 1997). The challenge is to help clients recognize how they have "taken steps, summoned up resources, and coped" (Saleebey, 1997, p. 239). However, "whether a given client's characteristic represents a strength or a weakness depends on subtleties of personal history, the immediate social environment, the larger societal matrix, the mix of client characteristics, challenges, and the meanings the client ascribes to his or her experience and situation" (McQuaide & Ehrenreich, 1997, p. 211).

Assessment and Client Problems

Utilizing a strengths perspective does not negate the very real problems clients face. The problems that cause clients to seek professional help cannot be disregarded or ignored. The assessment process must attend to both the obstacles and the strengths that potentially affect the resolution of the problem and the helping process. Much of the assessment that takes place in social work is focused on client problems and deficits (Saleebey, 1997). The strengths approach seeks to provide a balance between client obstacles and strengths.

Cowger (1997) proposed an assessment axis to help attain this balance. As shown in Figure 3.1, it is composed of two axes. The first axis is the environmental-personal continuum, and the second is a strengths-obstacles continuum, resulting in four quadrants: environmental strengths, personal strengths, environmental

FIGURE 3.1. Assessment Axis

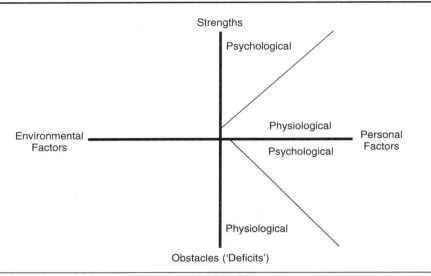

From C. Cowger, "Assessing Client Strengths: Assessment for Client Empowerment" in *The Strengths Perspective in Social Work* (2nd ed.). Copyright © 1997 by Allyn & Bacon. Reprinted/adapted by permission.

obstacles, and personal obstacles. The quadrants for personal strengths and obstacles include both psychological and physiological components. Attention to all four quadrants helps ensure a comprehensive assessment that is balanced in terms of individual and environmental strengths and obstacles.

ASSESSMENT AND THE HELPING RELATIONSHIP

The helping relationship begins to take shape during the assessment process. It involves structural aspects, or tasks that need to be accomplished, and interpersonal aspects, the interactions between the worker and the client that facilitate the exploration of the client's story. Attention to the structural aspects of assessment provides a collaborative activity that helps build the trust needed for the client to fully participate in the helping process. Effective use of interpersonal skills helps the client open up and engage in the structural activities.

Four major tasks are associated with the initial assessment process: (1) to identify and clarify the client's concerns; (2) to analyze the person-in-environment factors (strengths and obstacles) that affect the identified problem situation; (3) to clarify the helping process; and (4) to establish priorities and the target problem.

Identify Client Concerns

The first order of business is to listen to your client's story. What are the areas of concern? How does the client perceive the problem situation? What are the indications or manifestations of the problem? Where, when, and how often does the problem occur? How severe is the problem? How does it affect the client? What are the client's emotional reactions to the problem? What other systems within the client's environment affect the problem situation? How has the client coped with the problem? Answers to these questions provide an understanding of the problem situation from the client's perspective. The way you go about developing this understanding is as critical as the answers themselves.

Ideally the answers will emerge as the client tells his or her story. Focus on listening and on communicating your understanding of the story. Be curious. Your goal is to obtain a detailed picture of the client's concerns. The client's perception of feeling heard is going to motivate him or her to open up to you and engage in a helping process. It will set a solid foundation for the development of the helping relationship. If your client does not feel heard, your work together will probably not continue.

Asking a battery of questions without really listening to the client's responses puts the focus on you, the worker, rather than where it needs to be, on the client. A common mistake by beginning social workers is to assume that their job is to ask brilliant questions. Many are preoccupied with *their* own responses to the client, with saying the right thing. Rather than focusing on what you are going to say or on the questions you need to ask, you should focus on what the client is saying. Do you understand what he or she is attempting to communicate? Are you listening to the client? Are you hearing what he or she is saying? Have you communicated your understanding back to the client? If you focus on listening and ask questions that help you understand what the client is saying, the information you need will be forthcoming. The client will feel heard and empowered. You will have conveyed respect, caring-concern, and a willingness to let the client be the expert on his or her problem situation.

Identify and Analyze Person-in-Environment Factors

The second major task in assessment is based on the ecosystems perspective (see Chapter 1). It entails exploring and analyzing the client's person-in-environment context—the personal and environmental strengths and obstacles that potentially affect the target problem. The model, shown in Figure 3.2, examines the effect of the worker, organization, community, and client system on the target problem. It identifies the relevant internal and external factors that positively and negatively affect the resolution of the identified area of concern.

The model recognizes the influence the worker has in the client's environmental system. Worker-client transactions are viewed as a component of the client's ecological system (Germain & Gitterman, 1980). Interactions between the worker and the client and between the worker and the client's social environment become part of the client's dynamic person-in-environment system. In this respect, mutuality and reciprocity characterize the worker-client relationship. The model recognizes the mutual effect the worker and client have on one another and on the helping relationship (Petr, 1988).

The interrelationships of the systems shown in Figure 3.2 differ from the traditional ecological systems model in which the worker is seen as a mediator operating between the individual and his or her environment. In the conceptualization presented here, the social worker is a major component of the client's person-in-environment system—a component that affects the system and is affected by the other system components.

FIGURE 3.2. Person-in-Environment Assessment

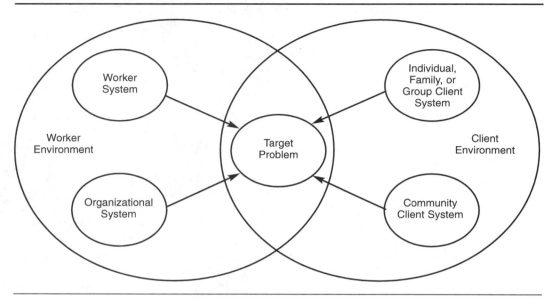

This model also emphasizes the worker's role as a partner in the helping process. The critical issue for social workers and their clients is how the various systems in the client's person-in-environment system affect the concerns the client is attempting to resolve. Factors that affect the client system but do not affect the helping relationship system are not relevant to their work together. Focusing on the helping relationship system provides the worker and client with a framework that guides assessment and intervention decisions.

Social workers need to understand clients by "tapping into their unique perspective and personal realities" (Jordan & Franklin, 1995, p. 98). In exploring the client's reality, it is important for social workers to be aware of their own biases and beliefs, which may influence their clinical perceptions. Social workers need to be able to differentiate between their interpretations and those of the client (Gilgun, Daly, & Handel, 1992). They also need to recognize that by exploring a client's subjective reality, they become part of that reality. On entering into a helping relationship, the worker becomes part of the client's person-in-environment system. Thus, the worker can influence a client's subjective perceptions of self and of experiences. Care must be taken to allow the client's subjective reality to emerge. The social worker's job is to understand the client's experiences and perceptions and to engage the client in a discussion of how those experiences influence their work together. The worker needs to incorporate his or her understanding of the client's experiences into the helping relationship system.

Conducting a person-in-environment assessment is immensely complex and difficult. It is, however, critical to the success of the work. Assessment is an ongoing task in the helping process and should not be limited to the beginning assessment phase. It requires mutual exploration and evaluation of the client's person-in-environment system throughout the helping process.

Clarify Roles and the Helping Process

At some point during the initial assessment phase, you and your client need to discuss his or her expectations of the helping process as well as how you hope your work together will proceed. Clarifying expectations and agreeing on general guidelines about what will take place during the helping relationship sets the framework for a collaborative process. Clients often have little understanding of the helping process or perceptions that differ widely from yours. Perlman (1968) found that fewer clients dropped out during intake when client expectations were clarified and worker-client discrepancies addressed. Zwick and Atkinson (1985) found similar results for clients who viewed an orientation video prior to psychological counseling.

Hepworth, Rooney, and Larsen (1997) suggest that you should determine your client's expectations and briefly explain the nature of the helping process when you begin working together. Unacknowledged discrepancies between your and your client's expectations about what is going to happen and how it is going to happen may jeopardize the helping process.

Clients may make it very clear what they expect you to do or what they think will happen. If they have not, ask them at an appropriate time during the interview. This applies to both voluntary and nonvoluntary clients. For nonvoluntary clients, review the mandated aspects of service provision, and then ask what they hope to get out of the experience. What would they like to have happen? How would they like the work to proceed?

The second component of clarifying the helping process is communicating your expectations about what you will do and not do, as well as what you expect your client to do and not do. Your job as social worker is to structure the helping process and help support and motivate the client throughout the process. The client's job is to make a commitment to engage in the helping process, to be the decision maker about choices that emerge as the process unfolds, and to follow through on those choices. Be respectful of the client's expectations, especially if they are at variance with yours. Acknowledge the client's expectations even if they are unrealistic. Be empathic regarding his or her feelings. Clients typically want help and answers to problems that they have struggled with and have been unable to resolve on their own. They are looking to you to provide expert advice and guidance. Acknowledge these feelings while emphasizing your partnership and how you will work together to address concerns. The helping relationship is a collaborative process.

It is also helpful to discuss the kind of relationship you hope to develop. A truly collaborative relationship requires openness. Your client has to be willing to share feelings, and you have to be willing to communicate openly. This requires the development of trust. Trust is built on actions and shared experiences. It is not created through words alone, and it does not happen instantaneously. You need to communicate concern, understanding, and empathy, both verbally and nonverbally, to provide opportunities for trust to develop. Share your feelings about the kind of open and collaborative relationship you hope to have with your client, and acknowledge that you must earn his or her trust. An open discussion of your feelings will model for your client the type of interactions you hope to have and will communicate the reciprocal nature of the helping relationship and your client's role as a partner.

Establish Priorities and Identify the Target Problem

The final aspect of the assessment process is to have the client prioritize the various areas of concern and identify a target problem that will be the initial focus of your work together. The task is to move from general areas of concern to a target on which you and the client agree to work (Bloom, Fischer, & Orme, 1995).

The first step is to review the areas of concern expressed by the client. Writing them down and making a list for the client to review is often helpful. It forces you and the client to clearly articulate the concerns, and it ensures that both of you have a common understanding of the problem situation. It also forces you to break down the problem area into specific concerns.

The next step is to prioritize the identified concerns and select a target problem. Failure to focus on a limited set of concerns is one of the greatest obstacles to effective practice (Bloom, Fischer, & Orme, 1995). The client needs to decide on a beginning or starting point. A number of considerations influence this decision. Bloom, Fischer, and Orme recommend selecting a problem that meets as many of the following criteria as possible:

"**1.** It is one that clients prefer to start with or about which they are most concerned;
"**2.** It has the greatest likelihood of being changed;
"**3.** It is relatively concrete and specific;
"**4.** It can be readily worked with by you given your resources;
"**5.** It has the greatest chance of producing the most negative consequences if not handled;
"**6.** It has to be handled before other problems can be tackled; and
"**7.** Changes in the problem will result in tangible, observable changes for those involved, thereby perhaps increasing the participants' motivation to work on other problems." (1995, p. 68)

Selecting the target problem is a critical component of the assessment process. It sets the stage for your work together, and it is the base from which other decisions are made. The guidelines will help you and the client analyze and assess his or her areas of concern. You can help the client analyze the options and explore his or her feelings about the possible choices. It is also important to help motivate the client to make a commitment to work on the target problem. Communicate a sense of hopefulness about the possibilities of change. You and the client are at the beginning of a journey. Your optimism about the process will strengthen the client's commitment and motivation to undertake the journey. Focusing on possibilities and the client's strengths will help create hopefulness and belief that change is indeed possible.

ASSESSMENT OF INDIVIDUAL CLIENT SYSTEMS

An individual client system consists of four major subsystems: demographic characteristics, ethnicity and culture, personal characteristics, and life experiences. These four subsystems and the specific characteristics associated with each of them are shown in Figure 3.3.

FIGURE 3.3. Subsystems of Individual Client Systems

Demographics
Gender
Race
Age
Socioeconomic Status

Ethnicity and Culture
Values and Beliefs
Spirituality/Religion

Personal Characteristics
Responsibility
Commitment
Motivation
Coping Skills
Resourcefulness

Life Experiences
Relationships
Support Networks
Life-Cycle Stage
Mental Health Status
Health Status

Demographic Characteristics

Demographic characteristics, such as gender, race, age, and socioeconomic status, potentially affect the helping relationship and the identified target problem. Although demographic characteristics might directly influence the helping relationship, their primary influence is through transactions with the worker system. You and your clients need to explore the effects of their demographic characteristics on your work together. For example, there are often significant age discrepancies between workers and their clients. Social workers who are significantly younger than their clients should raise the issue for discussion. If it is not a concern for the client, no harm has been done, and it opens the door for a discussion of other factors. If it is a concern, it can be addressed.

Another sensitive demographic factor is race. In our society, race is a highly charged issue for all people. Race may be an issue when there are racial differences between workers and clients. It may also be an issue when the worker and client have minority status. Being willing to explore the potential effect of race on the helping relationship communicates sensitivity and a willingness to enter into a partnership.

Ethnicity and Culture

The second group of client characteristics that affect the helping relationship is ethnicity and culture. This is a broad category of factors that includes personal ideology and cultural values and beliefs. Assessment of this group of factors requires introspection. You have to understand your value system and how values influence your perceptions of yourself and others. Only after developing an awareness of your own value system can you explore value differences with clients.

You need to be sensitive to areas of disagreement and agreement when exploring personal beliefs, cultural traditions, and value positions with clients. It is important to explicitly recognize both. Identifying differences in values and beliefs allows recognition and acceptance of the differences and development of strategies for dealing with them. Identifying areas of agreement strengthens the connection between you and the client. It is important to limit mutual exploration of values and beliefs to areas that potentially affect the helping relationship and your work together. It is not possible or appropriate to explore all aspects of your and client belief systems. However, the more that each understands what the other holds dear, the more likely that a strong helping relationship will develop.

Personal Characteristics

Three primary characteristics influence a client's ability to benefit from a helping relationship: responsibility, commitment, and motivation. A number of factors influence a person's ability or willingness to make a commitment and assume responsibility for creating change. Nevertheless, responsibility and commitment profoundly affect the helping relationship and are critical to the success of the helping process. Social workers help clients help themselves. Success requires a commitment to the change process.

It is unrealistic to expect all clients to assume responsibility for change and to be committed to the helping process at the outset. Clients need to develop commitment to the helping process and self-help through the ongoing helping relationship.

Many clients seeking social work services have difficulty taking responsibility for their actions and sustaining their commitment to improve their life situations. Thus, the interaction between you and the client is critical. You must use your interpersonal qualities and clinical skills to address the client's level of commitment and responsibility. You and the client need to explore experiences and feelings related to taking responsibility and making a commitment to change. You have to motivate clients to take responsibility for their actions and support their commitment to the process.

Two additional personal characteristics that should be assessed are the client's coping skills and resourcefulness. Identifying past ways of coping with problem situations is an important aspect of the assessment. The strengths perspective emphasizes client capacity and previous success in coping with the target problem. Clients often are unaware of their resourcefulness and past successes. Exploring past experiences and providing ideas about additional ways of coping empowers the client and enhances the helping relationship.

Life Experiences

The broad category of life experiences refers to the client's prior history. Included are experiences with family and interpersonal relationships, support networks, developmental life stage, and mental health and health status. This subsystem consists of the traditional topics of biopsychosocial assessments. You need to explore the client's life story. You need to understand the client's self-perceptions, world view, prior experiences, and the way that experiences potentially influence the helping relationship.

ASSESSMENT OF FAMILY CLIENT SYSTEMS

Generalist social workers often provide services to families. Social work has a long tradition of viewing individual functioning within the context of families. Janzen and Harris point out that even though "family treatment as a mode of practice was formally introduced in the 1950s, some of the underlying ideas and observations that support this process appeared in the social work literature as early as the first quarter of the century" (1997, p. 4). An individual's problems and concerns usually include difficulties with transactions with others. Since the family is the primary social unit for most people, assessment of an individual's person-in-environment system often results in the identification of the family as a target system in the helping process. Consequently, assessment of family systems is a critical aspect of generalist social work practice. Generalist social workers need to understand family functioning and become skilled in conducting family assessments.

Family Systems Problems

It is important to help the family view a problem as a family systems issue and not just the result of the behavior of the identified patient (Freeman, 1981). The worker needs to encourage the family to adopt a different way of viewing the problem situation (Watzlawick, Weakland, & Fisch, 1974). Often a single member of a family is considered to be the problem. This individual is the *identified patient* (Shulman, 1992). For example, a difficult child may be the identified patient, and the family seeks help in controlling the child. The worker will encourage the family to redefine the situation as a family system problem, not one caused simply by the child's difficult behavior. The task is to delabel the identified patient and help family members assume ownership for the roles they play in the problem (Hepworth, Rooney, & Larsen, 1997).

Hepworth, Rooney, and Larsen outline two strategies for delabeling the identified patient. One strategy is to "explore relationships *between* family members in lieu of focusing on the behavior of individual members" (1997, p. 485). For example, you may first focus on the interactions between the mother and the difficult child, then the father and the child, then the mother and the father, and finally the interactions among all three together. Your goal is to help family members see that the difficulties with the child do not take place in isolation and that the problems are in the functioning of the family system. This takes the blame off the identified patient and allows the problem to be viewed as belonging to the family.

The second strategy is to "focus initially on the role of blamers (or plaintiffs) in the difficulties about which they complain" (Hepworth, Rooney, & Larsen, 1997, p. 485). Instead of focusing on the difficult child, focus on the mother's and/or father's role in the problem behaviors exhibited by the child. Doing so shifts the family away from blaming to focusing on interactions between the parents and the child. It also helps family members take responsibility for changing their own behavior to improve family functioning. As Hepworth, Rooney, and Larsen point out, "it is critical to emphasize that members cannot change each other and that each individual can alleviate problems only by concentrating on changing his or her own behavior" (1997, p. 486).

Helping families change the way they view problem situations is not easy. More likely than not, you are asking them to give up long-held beliefs. They are likely to resist assuming responsibility for a difficult and painful situation, it is more comfortable to hold on to the belief that the problem belongs to the identified patient.

You need to be sensitive about how difficult it is for other family members to change their view of the problem. Avoid blaming as you explore the interactions among family members. Reframe problematic interactions. For example, if a mother is controlling and the child rebels, you might reframe the mother's controlling behavior as a positive expression of concern for the child's well-being that is not achieving the desired result. Empathize with the mother about how difficult the problem situation has been for her and the whole family. She is more likely to be receptive to this message than to one that blames her for being too controlling.

Despite your efforts, some family members may persist, in blaming the identified patient. Your task is to support the entire family, not collude with some members in labeling the problem-bearer (Hepworth, Rooney, & Larsen, 1997). You must continue to try to help the family view itself as a system in which all members influence one another and all interactions are reciprocal. Ask family members to identify ways they might be contributing to the problem situation. What could they do to improve? How do their reactions affect the situation? What would they like to change to help cope with the problem situation?

Family-in-Environment Assessment

The major family assessment subsystems are structure, life-cycle stage, emotional climate, communication patterns, boundaries, and ethnicity and culture. These subsystems for understanding and assessing families, which are shown in Figure 3.4, are highly interrelated. It is difficult and may be misleading to separate them because they are so intertwined. Taken as a whole, they provide a comprehensive picture of the internal structure and functioning of a family system. For a thorough assessment, it is important to develop an overall picture of how the family relates and functions as a unit. This goal can be accomplished by using the family characteristics as a general frame of reference to guide the assessment process.

Structure.   Family structure is the way family members organize themselves into interactional patterns (Minuchin & Fishman, 1982). "Repeated transactions establish patterns of how, when, and to whom to relate and these patterns underpin the system" (Minuchin, 1974, p. 51). Closely associated with the interaction patterns are the rules that govern them (Janzen & Harris, 1997). Families develop informal rules about family behavior and interactions. Issues of authority and power as well as other areas of family life are defined by those informal rules. Assessment of family systems requires an exploration and understanding of the unique rules that govern family interactions.

FIGURE 3.4. Subsystems of Family Client Systems

Structure
Number of People
Ages of Family Members
Relationship Subsystems

Life-Cycle
Development Stage
Transitions

Emotional Climate
Affect
Range of Feelings
Closeness
Conflict

Communication Patterns
Verbal
Nonverbal
Contextual

Boundaries
Open/Closed
Ridged/Diffuse
Enmeshed/Detached

Ethnicity and Culture
Values and Beliefs
Rules
Myths

Another structural aspect of families is the subsystems in which they are organized (Aponte & Van Duesen, 1981). Most families have couple, parental, sibling, and parent-child subsystems (Janzen & Harris, 1997). Each subsystem needs to be evaluated. Figure 3.5 displays the four primary subsystems and some of the important roles they fulfill (Jordan & Franklin, 1995). Understanding how the various subsystems interact and the roles they play is critical to understanding the overall functioning of the family and the effect of family structure on the target problem.

Life-Cycle. Families pass through developmental life-cycle stages much the same way as individuals. Carter and McGoldrick (1989) developed a conceptual life-cycle framework that characterizes the developmental stages of the traditional two-parent family with children (see Figure 3.6). Each stage has tasks that need to be accomplished for the family to make a successful transition to the next developmental stage (Jordan & Franklin, 1995). Although Carter and McGoldrick's family life-cycle stages have been widely accepted, their conceptualization is based on a middle-class American family model. As such it "has important weaknesses, especially when the family is not a 'traditional' family, has

FIGURE 3.5. Family Subsystems and Normative Roles

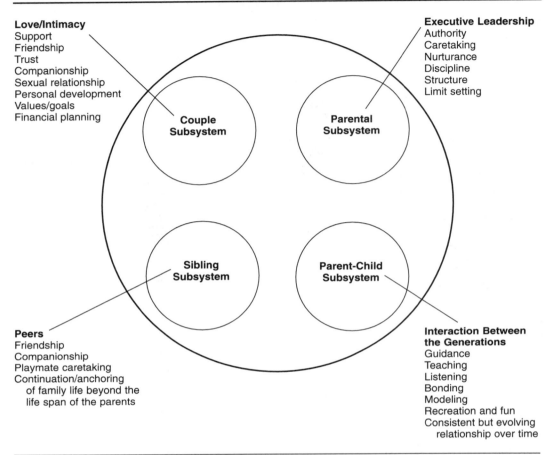

Love/Intimacy
Support
Friendship
Trust
Companionship
Sexual relationship
Personal development
Values/goals
Financial planning

Executive Leadership
Authority
Caretaking
Nurturance
Discipline
Structure
Limit setting

Couple Subsystem

Parental Subsystem

Sibling Subsystem

Parent-Child Subsystem

Peers
Friendship
Companionship
Playmate caretaking
Continuation/anchoring
  of family life beyond the
  life span of the parents

Interaction Between the Generations
Guidance
Teaching
Listening
Bonding
Modeling
Recreation and fun
Consistent but evolving
  relationship over time

Reprinted from *Clinical Assessment for Social Workers: Quantitative and Qualitative Methods* by Catheleen Jordan and Cynthia Franklin, Copyright 1995 by Lyceum Books, Inc.

no children, or is in some other way different from the view of the family as composed of a married couple and their children" (Garvin & Seabury, 1997, p. 218).

Family life-cycle stages all involve additions or losses to family membership (Janzen & Harris, 1997), They require adapting to change, and they necessitate changes in family roles and rules. The transitions between stages often cause family difficulties and are the points at which families are most likely to be in need of help (Janzen & Harris, 1997; Jordan & Franklin, 1995). A comprehensive assessment requires attention to important life-cycle transitions and the family's adjustment to them.

Carter and McGoldrick's family life-cycle stages provide a framework for identifying the stage and appropriate developmental tasks of a traditional two-parent family. The first step is to identify the family's stage of development. If you are working with a nontraditional family, and the life-cycle stages do not appear to fit, the first task is to identify any transitions the family may be experiencing.

FIGURE 3.6. Family Life-Cycle Stages and Associated Developmental Tasks

Leaving Home: Single Young Adults
Differentiating Self in Relation to Family of Origin
Developing Intimate Peer Relationships
Establishing Self Through Work and Financial Independence

The Joining of Families Through Marriage: The New Couple
Forming Marital System
Realigning Relationships with Extended Families and Friends to Include Spouse

Families with Young Children
Adjusting Marital System to Make Space for Child(ren)
Joining in Child-rearing, Financial, and Household tasks
Realigning Relationships with Extended Family to Include Parenting and
    Grandparenting Roles

Families with Adolescents
Shifting Parent-Child Relationships to Permit Adolescent to Move in and
    out of System
Refocusing on Midlife Marital and Career Issues
Beginning Shift Toward Joint Caring for Older Generation

Launching Children and Moving On
Renegotiating Marital System as a Dyad
Developing Adult-to-Adult Relationships Between Grown Children and Parents
Realigning Relationships to Include In-laws and Grandchildren
Dealing with Disabilities and Death of Great-Grandparents

Families in Later Life
Maintaining Own and Couple Functioning and Interests in face of
    Physiological Decline
Supporting a More Central Role of Middle Generation
Making Room in the System for the Wisdom and Experience of the Elderly,
    Supporting the Older Generation Without Overfunctioning for Them
Dealing with Loss of Spouse, Siblings, and Peers, and Preparation for Own Death;
    Life Review and Integration

From Betty Carter & Monica McGoldrick (Eds.), *The Expanded Family Life Cycle: Individual, Family and Social Perspectives*
3/E. Copyright © 1999 by Allyn and Bacon. Reprinted/adapted by permission.

Are there additions or losses to family membership? The second step is to assess
family members' adaptation to the transition from one stage to another. Are there
specific tasks that are more problematic than others? How are the various family
members adjusting to their new roles and responsibilities? Are family members
mourning the loss of tasks associated with the prior life-cycle stage?

Emotional Climate.   Like individuals, families exhibit emotions. "When people
are in close interaction (as in families or groups), the emotions of some individuals tend to be 'contagious,' and others begin to express similar feelings" (Garvin
& Seabury, 1997, p. 218). Although the expression of individual affect within the
family may vary, family patterns of emotions develop (Lewis, Beavers, Gossett, &
Phillips, 1976).

FIGURE 3.7. Family Emotional Climate Matrix

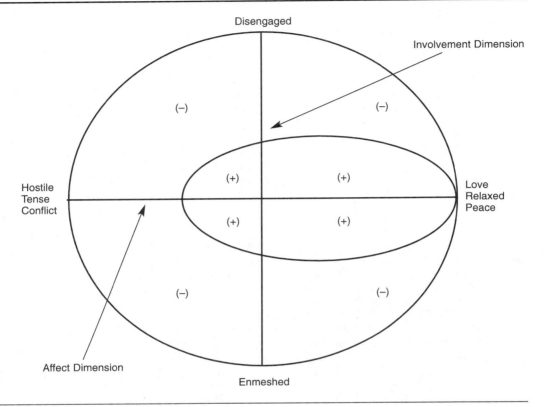

An affect dimension and an involvement dimension influence a family's emotional climate. The *affect dimension* is the mode tone of the family system. There are family environments that are hostile, tense, and conflicted, while others are more relaxed and peaceful, characterized by love, warmth, and harmony.

The second dimension of the family emotional climate is the extent to which the family members are involved with one another. This dimension encompasses the concepts of *enmeshment* and *disengagement* (Minuchin, 1974). In families that are disengaged, members have little emotional involvement with each other. In enmeshed families, on the other hand, members are overly involved with one another. There is "excessive closeness in which family members think and feel alike; there is little opportunity for independent functioning and what happens to one family member immediately affects others" (Gambrill, 1997, p. 575). The disengagement-enmeshment dimension has also been referred to as *family cohesion* (Olson, Sprenkle, & Russel, 1979). Families that fall at the extremes of this continuum are at risk of dysfunction. Those that fall between the extremes are considered to have a more balanced emotional climate and less risk of family dysfunction (Thomas & Olson, 1993). Members in more balanced families are supportive, help one another, and are committed to each other, but not to the extent that the individuality of the members is lost or subsumed by the family system.

The interaction between the affect and involvement dimensions of family emotional climate is shown in Figure 3.7. Families with healthy emotional climates (+) are those in which the family mode tone is rated more toward the positive side of the affect dimension (love, relaxed, peace) and in the middle of the involvement dimension. Families with dysfunctional emotional climates (–) are those rated on the negative side of the affect dimension (hostile, tense, conflict) and at the top or bottom of the involvement dimension (disengaged, enmeshed).

The inner circle of Figure 3.7 represents a healthy or acceptable range of the affective and involvement dimensions within families. It is assumed that within normal families there will be some conflict, tension, and hostility and that a normal family will fall approximately in the middle of the disengagement-enmeshment continuum. It is also assumed that there cannot be too much love within a family as long as the family is centered on the involvement dimension. Problems occur for families that are characterized by the extremes of the two dimensions.

Communication Patterns.   A family's ability to communicate effectively and to deal with problems in communication can enhance its relationship and problem-solving ability (Satir, 1983). "Communication is important to competent functioning of family systems. For communication to be effective between family members, it must be open, direct, clear and congruent at different levels, such as one's tone and the content of the message" (Jordan & Franklin, 1995, p. 209). Communication problems are common when family members are having difficulty getting along and in families that show other signs of dysfunction (Satir, 1983). Janzen and Harris point out that communication modes and problems are intertwined with family structure and role divisions: "Family rules and structure are evident in the freedom or lack of it in expressing doubt or difference, and in who can say what to whom and when. Communication conveys how much each family member is valued and who has power in the system" (1997, p. 15).

Cultural beliefs and norms can influence family communication style and the degree of openness. Many cultural groups discourage the open expression of feelings (Ho, 1987). In assessing family communication patterns, be aware of possible cultural differences, and respect the communication styles practiced within the family's cultural system. Do not assume that open, direct, and honest communication is desirable for ethnically and culturally diverse families.

There are three basic levels of communication: verbal, nonverbal, and contextual (Satir, 1983). *Verbal communication* refers to the words and the content of the message. *Nonverbal communication* refers to the body language that accompanies the verbal message, including gestures, facial expressions, posture, and eye contact. *Contextual communication* refers to context or situation in which the message is delivered, such as the tone of voice, the timing of the message, and the circumstances in which the message is delivered. Nonverbal and contextual levels of communication can reinforce or contradict the verbal message.

Effective communication requires congruency among the three levels of communication, and in dysfunctional families congruency is often lacking. Thus, an important aspect in assessing family communication patterns is to determine "the extent to which there is congruence between the *verbal, nonverbal,* and *contextual* levels of messages on the part of individuals in a family system" (Hepworth, Rooney, & Larsen, 1997, p. 311). Is there congruence among the three levels of communication? Is the verbal message supported by nonverbal messages and the situation in which the messages are delivered?

In addition to problems related to the congruence of messages, problems may be related to sender skills, such as expressing and owning feelings, and/or to receiver skills, such as openness to hearing feelings, listening, and validating (Gambrill, 1997). Hepworth, Rooney, and Larsen point out that

> when comparing processes of optimally functioning families with those of troubled families, it becomes evident that the former possess several categories of verbal and non-verbal responses that are noticeably absent in the latter. Included in these responses are messages that convey understanding, demonstrate respect for the uniqueness of the sender's experience, and invite further expression and exploration. (1997, p. 313)

In assessing sender and receiver skills of family members, ask how receptive or open they appear to be to the thoughts and feelings of other family members. Do they listen to each other? Do they acknowledge the sender's message? Do they encourage the sharing of feelings and the expression of thoughts? How open are the individual members to sharing their thoughts and feelings? Do they express how they are feeling or what they think? Do they take responsibility for their own feelings and thoughts? Are the messages expressed as *I* statements or as *you* statements?

Boundaries.   Family system boundaries are the demarcations that define the sub-systems within a family (internal) and its interactions with larger systems (external). Nichols (1984) defined boundaries as invisible barriers between individual family members, family subsystems, and larger systems that regulate interactions. "The function of boundaries is to safeguard the differentiation and autonomy of the family and its subsystems" (Janzen & Harris, 1997, p. 37). Boundaries can be rigid or diffuse (Minuchin, 1974). Rigid boundaries allow little interaction between systems, while diffuse boundaries are loose and blurred, providing little differentiation between the family subsystems or the family and other systems.

Families are part of larger systems, such as neighborhoods and communities. They interact with these other systems on a daily basis. "They differ widely, however, in the degree to which they are open to transactions with other systems and in the flexibility of their outer boundaries" (Hepworth, Rooney, & Larsen, 1997, p. 291). The extent to which people who are not family members are allowed to interact with the family varies. Kantor and Lehr (1975) identified three family boundary types: open, closed, and random.

Open family systems are those in which the family has a great deal of interaction with people outside the family. Members of open families have friends over frequently, are active in the community, and participate in outside activities. *Closed family systems*, on the other hand, are characterized by a lack of interaction with the external environment. The family restricts and limits involvement with others. Guests are not welcomed; family members are not involved in outside activities; and transactions with others are guarded. *Random family systems* have no boundary patterns. Each member of the family develops his or her own type of interaction pattern with the external environment.

Knowledge of the three boundary patterns can help you assess how a family interacts with its external environment. The patterns are prototypes, and any family's boundary pattern will probably include characteristics of all three. There are benefits and liabilities associated with each boundary type. Your task is to identify the boundary transactions of the family and, in collaboration with family members, assess how these transactions affect the identified target problem. This includes an assessment of strengths as well as obstacles associated with the family's external transactions.

Internal family boundaries relate to the transactions among the various subsystems within the family. As with external boundaries, internal boundaries can be characterized as rigid or diffuse. Families with rigid internal boundaries have a disengaged emotional climate, and those with loose or diffuse boundaries have an enmeshed climate, as discussed earlier in this chapter. Disengagement and enmeshment are not always problematic. "According to Minuchin, every family experiences some enmeshment or disengagement in its subsystems as a family goes through developmental phases" (Hepworth, Rooney, & Larsen, 1997, p. 294). Most families fall somewhere between the extremes. Assessment of internal boundaries requires an understanding of the developmental phase of the family, a description of the various interaction styles among the family's subsystems, and identification of the benefits as well as liabilities of the internal boundary patterns in relation to the identified target problem. It is also important to keep in mind cultural variations in family relationships. Family interactions and boundaries should be assessed from the perspective of the family's ethnic and cultural background.

Ethnicity and Culture.   Families possess sets of beliefs that are drawn from their ethnic and cultural heritage. A family's cultural beliefs affect all aspects of family functioning and need to be taken into consideration when assessing structure, life-cycle stages, emotional climate, communication patterns and boundaries. Assessment of the family's *rules* of behavior also needs to be culturally based. "Families have rules about who can do what to whom and what may or may not be discussed by whom in what context" (Gambrill, 1997, p. 574). Some rules are explicit and clearly stated (*children don't talk back to parents*), and other are implicit and not openly verbalized (*be careful not to hurt mother's feelings*). Implicit rules must be inferred from the interactions of family members; they are unwritten and unspoken and may be beyond family members' conscious level of awareness. Explicit and implicit family rules govern family members' behavior toward one another. The rules that emerge in families are influenced by the family's values and beliefs. "Although rules govern the processes of families from any cultural origin, they differ drastically from one culture to another" (Hepworth, Rooney, & Larsen, 1997, p. 279).

In considering family rules, you need to understand and respect the values and beliefs of the family. Understanding the cultural basis of the norms governing family members' behavior provides the context for assessing the effect of family rules on the identified target problem. Family rules can potentially have positive or negative effects on family functioning. The cultural context of a rule determines whether it enhances functioning or contributes to dysfunction. Assessment of ethnicity and culture takes into consideration values and beliefs and how they affect the functioning of the family system.

Assessment and Family Strengths

Creating an empowering assessment process with families is similar to creating the process with individual clients. The main difference and the biggest challenge is to focus your attention and efforts on both the family as a whole and on each individual member. Assessment must be a collaborative process in which concerns are heard, strengths are recognized, and understanding, empathy, and hope are communicated. Together you explore the family members' perceptions of the problem situation.

Assessment emphasizes the identification of family strengths as well as strengths of each individual family member. "Social workers should help families build on their strengths, gain access to resources, learn how to negotiate the many systems their members contact (school, neighborhood, social services), and overcome problems that affect healthy family development" (Hodges, Burwell, & Ortega, 1998, p. 146). Families have power from within to bring about positive change. The strengths perspective, however, must come from you. Although all families have strengths, family members may not always recognize or be aware of them. By adopting the attitude that strengths exist and that they can be used to help the family resolve the problem situation, you can help the family recognize their individual and collective strengths. Focus on strengths. Look for the ways the family and its members have coped with problem situations and concerns. Help them recognize past successes as well as resources and abilities they can draw on in the helping process.

A collaborative approach to family assessment empowers families by allowing their expertise in functioning and their concerns to emerge. Strive to empower the family as well as each individual member. The perceptions of the problem situation by the family and its members are where you should begin. Do not force your analysis and assessment of their problems, interpersonal relationships, or individual dysfunction on them, even if you believe that numerous problems exist. Engage in a collaborative exchange, sharing your insights and perceptions and exploring those of family members. "To engage in a truly collaborative relationship, *each party* must stay open to discussing and resolving differences in an honest and respectful manner" (Hodges, Burwell, & Ortega, 1998, p. 150). Become a partner with the family by sharing responsibility and decision making.

Assessment is the key to the helping process. To be able to effectively help clients, you need to understand their concerns, their strengths, potential resources, and the challenges they face. The assessment process provides an opportunity for clients to tell their stories. It is more about listening than asking questions. Strengths-based assessments focus on clients' perceptions rather than on diagnostic labels. A comprehensive assessment takes into consideration the effect of the person's environment on the problem situation. The strengths and challenges associated with all relevant systems are reviewed with the client. Ideally, the process should empower the client and create a sense of hopefulness. Focusing on strengths rather than deficits helps create expectations about the possibilities of change.

SUMMARY

Diagnosis is only a small part of the assessment process. It is useful in communicating symptom types. However, diagnostic labels do not tell you anything about the unique circumstances of clients or how to approach your work together. Psychiatric labels tend to create negative expectations, and they focus attention on client deficits. They focus on the condition or trait rather than on the context in which difficulties occur. They also offer little in the way of understanding the unique circumstances of the client, and they do not provide any information about how to resolve the problem.

Strengths-based assessments enhance the individualization of clients. A strengths-based assessment focuses on what is unique about each client in terms of interests, abilities, and the way they have coped with their problem situation. Clients often need help identifying their strengths. The challenge is to help them recognize how they have taken steps to resolve problem situations and how they have managed to cope with difficult circumstances.

The assessment process must attend to both the challenges and strengths that potentially affect the resolution of the problem and the helping process. A strengths approach seeks to provide a balance between client obstacles and strengths. Cowger's assessment axis can help you maintain a balanced assessment by identifying personal and environmental client strengths and obstacles.

The helping relationship begins to take shape during the assessment process. It involves structural tasks that need to be accomplished and interpersonal aspects that facilitate the exploration of the client's story. The four structural tasks to identify and clarify the client's concerns, to analyze the person-in-environment strengths and obstacles, to clarify the helping process, and to establish priorities and the target problem.

An individual client system consists of demographic characteristics, ethnicity and culture, personal characteristics, and life experiences. These four subsystems all potentially affect the helping process and work on the target problem. The assessment process must explore with the client the ways these subsystems interact with the worker, community, and organizational systems in the client's environment.

Assessment of family systems also involves examination of a number of subsystems. The major family subsystems are structure, life-cycle stage, emotional climate, communication patterns, boundaries, and ethnicity and culture. The assessment process is an exploration of the ways these subsystems affect and interact with the target problem.

CASE EXAMPLE

The final case example in this chapter was written by Susan Getty when she was a first-year MSW student in field placement at an alternative school for emotionally troubled children and adolescents. This assessment of a teenage client is an excellent example of the value of a comprehensive strengths-based assessment. In addition to providing both Susan and her client with a better understanding of the situation and the client's strengths and challenges, the assessment process strengthened their relationship, enabling Susan and her client to develop meaningful goals for their work together.

At Least I Can Fight   *Susan Getty*

Erica W. is a twelve-year-old African-American female. She was referred to Community School for assessment, and ultimately placement, because of severe behavioral problems she exhibited in her district school. She continually got into fights with other students; she was both physically and verbally aggressive. Recently, she had to go to court concerning a fight she had been in. When she is questioned about the cause of these fights, she blames the other children for starting them. Erica reports that the other children pick on her and that she has a reputation for being a fighter. She has said that she likes it when children she doesn't know come up to her to talk about fights she has been in.

It is reported by her aunt that the fights started when other children were teasing her about her weight. Erica is quite overweight, and this is definitely a sensitive issue for her. Her weight concerned her primary care physician, who recommended that she be evaluated for an eating disorder. It appears to me, though, that her obesity stems from poor nutrition and bad eating habits of the family. Her aunt is also very overweight, and Erica doesn't appear to exhibit the signs of a true eating disorder.

She does seem to have very low self-esteem, as evidenced by several comments she has made, her intense wish for approval from others, and her inability to discuss positive aspects of herself. I see her pride in her ability to fight as another sign of low self-esteem. She sees fighting as a positive quality, and she uses it to gain approval and attention. She feels that the way for her to gain acceptance and respect from her peers is to fight them—that she is not worthy otherwise.

In addition to the immediate problem of fighting in school, this client has academic difficulties. These difficulties are partly a result of the problem behaviors that continually got her in trouble, but prior reports indicate that there is a suspicion of a learning disability of some sort. Erica has trouble understanding much of her schoolwork, and this is a source of frustration for her. She repeated fifth grade because of poor academic performance.

Another aspect of this client's problem situation is that she has a stressful family life. For the past two years, she has lived in her aunt and uncle's home with her mother, younger sister, and two older cousins. Erica's father is uninvolved with her and her sister; he reportedly promises to spend time with them, but he never shows up. Erica claims that this does not bother her in the least, but I believe it is a source of great disappointment to her. She has made remarks to her teacher that her father doesn't come to see her because he is upset about her performance in school. This is very telling with regard to her self-esteem because she has, in fact, been doing very well at Community School. The fact that she feels she isn't doing well enough for him, although she has been earning almost all of her points (behavior points on the system that the school uses), is indicative of how much value she places on his opinion.

Her relationship with her mother seems to be very up and down. She doesn't discuss it much, but from all indications, her aunt is the primary caretaker. Her aunt is the one who came in for intake, and her aunt is the one who takes all phone calls about Erica. The mother has custody, though. Recently, the mother disappeared for several days, and no one knew where she was. This was having an obvious effect on Erica's behavior; she became very irritable and wouldn't talk about what was bothering her. I had to call the aunt to discover what was wrong. Erica maintains that this wasn't what was bothering her at all—that she was perfectly fine, and everyone was assuming that her mother's disappearance was upsetting her. She told me that it was "no big deal," that her mother did this a lot, and that she always came back (she came back this time as well, the day after I called the aunt).

Even though her relationship with her mother has obvious problems, it is equally obvious that Erica craves her mother's attention. For example, she was so happy and proud a few weeks ago when her mother braided her hair for her. She basked in the compliments everyone gave her, and she was eager to say that her mother had done it for her.

Erica's relationship with her younger sister is problematic. She has reported that they fight all the time. I think this may be a result of normal sibling arguments. However, I have heard hints (from my supervisor) that the younger sister is the "perfect" child of the family, so maybe some jealousy is underlying the fighting between the sisters.

To summarize, my client's problem situation, on the surface, centers around the physical and verbal aggression that she uses to deal with her peers' teasing. When we look a bit deeper, though, we find a young girl struggling with poor self-esteem stemming from a weight problem, a rough family life, and a potential learning disability. This client knows no other way of dealing with her anger and frustration than fighting.

Erica has many strengths. First of all, she has begun to establish a relationship with me. She is starting to feel more comfortable talking to me and seems to look forward to our individual sessions. This is an important step; she needs to be able to talk about her concerns and have someone she trusts to help support her as she develops and works on goals. She also has the support of her aunt. She seems to have a good relationship with her aunt, and her aunt seems to be a very caring person who will help Erica as she tries to change. Another strength that I haven't delved into much yet is her religious affiliation. Erica told me that she is a Jehovah's Witness. I am not sure how much she identifies with this aspect of herself, but it could be another source of support for her. Also, her religious affiliation may help her see how important it is to try to change. A final source of support is the Community School environment. Erica's behavior has definitely been less severe since she has been attending our program. This is an indication that she feels more comfortable here (a fact she has expressed to me) and that the supportive environment is helpful to her.

Other strengths I see in Erica are that she is intellectually capable of making changes in her behavior, has no major physical or mental health issues impeding her progress, and has several friends from her district school who may be a source of support for her. These friends could just as easily be a problem, though. They could perpetuate her old behaviors by egging her on in fight situations. On the positive side, my client is definitely capable of making friends, and she could always make new ones.

Some strong obstacles face Erica in trying to work on her goals. As I have already mentioned, she is fixated on fighting as a solution to problems; she is proud of her fighting capabilities and sees fighting as necessary. A factor tied into this may be stereotypes of African-Americans: she may feel that she is expected to be "tough" because that is the image she sees of African-Americans.

An additional obstacle is her weight problem. She may need some help setting up an appropriate dieting plan, or if it turns out to be a true eating disorder, she may need extra counseling. This is not only an issue for her self-esteem; it is a health issue as well.

Another major obstacle is that Erica has problems with family support. While she does have the support of her aunt, she craves the attention, recognition, and love of her mother and father. This could really affect her work on goals. She may feel that she has no reason to try to change if the people she wants to notice her the most don't pay attention.

DISCUSSION QUESTIONS

1. Erica, the client in the final case study, was diagnosed as having oppositional defiant disorder, dysthymic disorder, and an eating disorder. Compare your image of Erica based on the strengths assessment with the image you develop based on these diagnostic categories. How are the two images alike, and how are they different? Are there differences in your expectations for Erica? What do you gain from the diagnosis? How does the diagnosis influence how you would proceed with the case?

2. Discuss Erica's person-in-environment system and its effect on the target problems of fighting and self-esteem. Discuss whether and how the transactions within the person-in-environment system change depending on the target problem.

3. What effect did the worker system have on the helping process with Erica? What are the advantages of assessing the transactions between the worker and client systems? What are the disadvantages?

4. Describe the process of conducting a strengths-based assessment. How is it different from the assessments made at your field placement? How is it similar? Which of the strengths guidelines are followed in your field placement agency?

5. What are the structural tasks that need to be accomplished during an initial assessment? What needs to be accomplished interpersonally? What is the interrelationship between the structural and interpersonal aspects of the helping relationship during the assessment process?

6. Describe the individual and family subsystems that can potentially affect the helping relationship and a target problem. How would a social worker use a strengths approach to assessment of the subsystems with an individual client? How would a social worker assesses family subsystems?

REFERENCES

American Psychiatric Association (1994). *Diagnostic and statistical manual of mental disorders* (4th ed.). Washington, DC: American Psychiatric Association.

Aponte, H., & Van Duesen, J. (1981). Structural family therapy. In A. S. Gurman & D. P, Knirsken (Eds.), *Handbook of family therapy* (pp. 45–72). New York: Brunner/Mazel.

Bloom, M., Fischer, J., & Orme, J. (1995). *Evaluating practice: Guidelines for the accountable professional* (2nd ed.). Boston: Allyn and Bacon.

Carter, B., & McGoldrick, M. (1989). *The changing family life cycle: A framework for family therapy* (2nd ed.). Boston: Allyn and Bacon.

Cowger, C. (1997). Assessing client strengths: Assessment for client empowerment. In D. Saleebey (Ed.), *The strengths perspective in social work practice* (2nd ed., pp. 59–73). New York: Longman. From C. Cowger, "Assessing Client Strengths: Assessment for Client Empowerment." In *The Strengths Perspective in Social Work* (2nd ed.). Copyright © 1997 by Allyn & Bacon. Reprinted/adapted by permission.

Freeman, D. (1981). *Techniques of family therapy*. New York: Aronson.

Gambrill, E. (1997). *Social work practice: A critical thinker's guide.* New York: Oxford University Press.

Garvin, C., & Seabury, B. (1997). *Interpersonal practice in social work: Promoting competence and social justice* (2nd ed.). Boston: Allyn and Bacon.

Germain, C. B., & Gitterman, A. (1980). *The life model of social work practice.* New York: Columbia University Press.

Gilgun, J., Daly, D., & Handel, G. (Eds.). (1992). *Qualitative methods in family research.* Newbury Park, CA: Sage.

Hepworth, D., Rooney, R., & Larsen, J. (1997). *Direct social work practice: Theory and skills* (5th ed.). Pacific Grove, CA: Brooks/Cole.

Ho, M. (1987). *Family therapy with ethnic minorities.* Newbury Park: CA: Sage.

Hodges, V., Burwell, Y., & Ortega, D. (1998). Empowering families. In L. Gutiérrez, R. Parsons, and E. Cox (Eds.), *Empowerment in social work practice* (pp. 146–162). Pacific Grove, CA: Brooks/Cole.

Janzen, C., & Harris, O. (1997). *Family treatment in social work practice* (3rd ed.). Itasca, IL: Peacock.

Jordan, C., & Franklin, C. (1995). *Clinical assessment for social workers: Quantitative and qualitative methods.* Chicago: Lyceum.

Kantor, D., & Lehr, W. (1975). *Inside the family: Toward a theory of family process.* San Francisco: Jossey-Bass.

Kinney, J., Haapala, D., & Booth, C. (1991). *Keeping families together: The homebuilders model.* New York: Aldine de Gruyter.

Kirk, S., & Kutchins, H. (1992). *The selling of DSM: The rhetoric of science in psychiatry.* New York: Aldine de Gruyter.

Levy, C. (1972). Values and planned change. *Social Casework, 53,* 488–493.

Lewis, J., Beavers, W., Gossett, J., & Phillips, V. (1976). *No single thread: Psychological health in family systems.* New York: Brunner/Mazel.

McQuaide, S., & Ehrenreich, J. (1997). Assessing client strengths. *Families in Society: The Journal of Contemporary Human Services, 78,* 201–212.

Meyer, C. (1993). *Assessment in social work practice.* New York: Columbia University Press.

Minuchin, S. (1974). *Families and family therapy.* Cambridge: Harvard University Press.

Minuchin, S., & Fishman, H. (1982). *Family therapy techniques.* Cambridge: Harvard University Press.

Nichols, M. (1984). *Family therapy: Concepts and methods.* New York: Gardner.

Olson, D., Sprenkle, D., & Russel, C. (1979). Circumplex model of marital and family systems: Cohesion and adaptability dimensions, family types and clinical applications. *Family Process, 18,* 3–28.

Perlman, H. (1968). *Persona: Social role and responsibility.* Chicago: University of Chicago Press.

Petr, C. (1988). The worker-client relationship: A general systems perspective. *Social Casework, 69,* 620–626.

Rapp, C. (1988). *The strengths model: Case management with people suffering from severe and persistent mental illness.* New York: Oxford University Press.

Saleebey, D. (1997). The strengths perspective: Possibilities and problems. In D. Saleebey (Ed.), *The strengths perspective in social work practice* (2nd ed., pp. 231–245). New York: Longman.

Satir, V. (1983). *Conjoint family therapy* (2nd ed.). Palo Alto, CA: Science and Behavior Books.

Shulman, L. (1992). *The skills of helping: Individuals, families and groups* (3rd ed.). Itasca, IL: Peacock.

Thomas, V., & Olson, D. (1993). Problem families and the circumplex model: Observational assessment using the clinical rating scale (CRS). *Journal of Marital and Family Therapy, 19,* 159–175.

Watzlawick, P., Weakland, J., & Fisch, R. (1974). *Change: Principles of problem formulation and problem resolution.* New York: Norton.

Zwick, R., & Atkinson, C. (1985). Effectiveness of a client pretherapy orientation videotape. *Journal of Counseling Psychology, 32,* 514–524.

CHAPTER 4

Assessment of Group, Organizational, and Community Client Systems

Karen A. is a first-year MSW student with a field placement at a private social service agency. The agency runs a life-skills and parenting program for teenage mothers and their children. Karen and Krystal W., a recent MSW who works at the agency, cofacilitate the weekly group session for the teenage mothers in the program. Karen is Caucasian and Krystal is African-American, as are most of the women in the program. Both Karen and Krystal are in their early twenties, and neither has children of her own.

Karen and Krystal had difficulty getting the young women to participate in the group sessions. During the first three sessions, most of them looked bored and rarely said anything. As a group, they were unresponsive and did not seem to be interested in the information that Karen and Krystal were presenting. Karen began to feel discouraged and a bit resentful about their lack of interest in child development and parenting skills. Karen and Krystal were unsure why the group was so unresponsive and what they should do to correct the situation. The one thing they were sure about was that what they were doing was not working.

Collaboration, client strengths, empowerment, and the helping relationship apply to the assessment of groups, organizations, and communities as well as to individuals and families. The common element among larger client systems is the assessment of groups and group process. Generalist social work with small groups of clients, organizations, and communities entails dealing with groups of individuals. Assessment with any type of group requires you to be sensitive to each individual member of the group as well as to the ongoing dynamics of the group as a whole (Reid, 1997). The assessment process involves individual assessments of each member's functioning as well as an assessment of the overall functioning of the group. "This requires an awareness of each member and an awareness of the themes and patterns of the group" (Reid, 1997, p. 14)

Working with groups has a long tradition in social work, dating back to the settlement house era (Popple & Leighninger, 1993). The use of groups in social work practice has increased in recent years, due in part to managed care and cost containment incentives (Magen, 1995). Today, group work is a major component of generalist social work practice. Consequently, the ability to effectively assess group functioning, whether a small treatment group of clients, an agency task force, or a community citizens' group, is a fundamental generalist social work skill.

This chapter presents information on assessment with small groups, organizations, and communities. By the end of the chapter, you should be able to help Karen and Krystal

1. Classify the type of group they are running
2. Assess the functioning of their group and identify problem areas
3. Assess the effect their agency and organizational factors have on the functioning of the group
4. Assess the effect of community factors on the group's participants and on the overall functioning of the group.

SMALL GROUP ASSESSMENT

As a generalist social worker, you may be involved in creating and implementing a new client or community group. More often than not, however, you will be assigned to work with an already existing group. Many social service agencies have established on-going groups. Regardless of whether it is a new group you help design and implement or an existing group you join, at some point you will need to assess the functioning of the group in relation to a problem or concern.

Types of Groups

Generalist social workers are involved with many different types of groups. At the broadest level, groups have been classified into two categories: treatment and task (Toseland & Rivas, 1995). Within these two categories, there are several subtypes. Toseland and Rivas (1995) identified four types of treatment groups (educational, growth, remedial, and socialization), while Garvin and Seabury (1997) identified five types of individual change groups (therapy, support, self-help, educational, and peer) and four types of task groups (community professional, community resident, agency task, and policy). Others have developed similar classifications (Corey & Corey, 1997; Jacobs, Harvill, & Masson, 1994).

The primary purposes of treatment groups are to increase members' coping abilities and help them resolve sociopsychological needs. The primary purposes of task groups, on the other hand, are to accomplish a specific undertaking, produce a product, or carry out a mandate (Hepworth, Rooney, & Larsen, 1997). The distinction between treatment and task groups, however, "should be used loosely rather than rigidly" (Garvin & Seabury, 1997, p. 231). In actual practice, groups often overlap in terms of function and objectives (Toseland & Rivas, 1995). For example, individuals who belong to a treatment group for substance abuse problems may become involved in a community education task group aimed at informing teenagers about the dangers of substance abuse.

Groups can also be categorized by client systems level. Generalist social workers typically work with client groups, agency groups, and community groups. Groups can be divided between formed and natural groups: "Formed groups are

---

FIGURE 4.1. Types of Groups

Client Groups

Therapy	Groups that focus on remediation or rehabilitation of members' intrapsychic or interpersonal problems, such as groups for depression, anger management, and substance abuse
Support	Groups established to help members cope with an issue common to all members of the group, such as a parent bereavement group
Educational	Groups that have an educational objective and use educational techniques, such as parent training groups and teen leadership groups
Growth	Groups that focus on self-improvement and personal growth of members, such as consciousness-raising groups and empowerment groups

Agency Groups

Project	Ad hoc groups or committees formed to accomplish specific tasks related to the functioning of the agency, such as an agency task force on working conditions
Administrative	Standing groups or committees formed to develop and administer agency policies and procedures, such as grievance committees

Community Groups

Professional	Groups composed primarily of professionals from different agencies that focus on community issues or intraagency coordination of services
Citizen	Groups composed primarily of community residents that seek to improve community conditions and/or services

---

Note: Based on *Interpersonal Practice in Social Work: Promoting Competence and Social Justice,* 2nd ed., by C. Garvin and B. Seabury, 1997, Boston: Allyn and Bacon; *Social Work Practice with Groups: A Clinical Perspective,* by K. Reid, Pacific Grove, CA: Brooks/Cole; *An Introduction to Group Work Practice,* 2nd ed., by R. Toseland and R. Rivas, 1995, Boston: Allyn and Bacon.

established through some outside influence, such as an agency, and are convened for a particular purpose . . . ." Natural groups, on the other hand, are those that develop in a spontaneous manner on the basis of friendship, location, or some naturally occurring event" (Reid, 1997, p. 10). Another way of classifying groups is by leadership. Some groups have a professional leader or group facilitator, while in others leadership functions are assumed by group members.

Figure 4.1 classifies groups by client system level and includes the types of groups that are usually formed and typically include a social work professional as leader or facilitator. These are the types of groups generalist social workers typically encounter in their work environments. The classification does not include self-help groups or natural groups, since most often they do not include professional leadership. Social work, however, has a tradition of involvement with these types of groups (Reid, 1997). As a generalist social worker, you may have the opportunity to help develop a self-help group or assist a natural group. The assessment skills and concepts used with formed, professionally led client, agency, and community groups can also be applied to these groups.

As with other classifications, the categories of groups are not mutually exclusive. In practice, few groups are purely one type or another. Most have more than one purpose or function. Furthermore, there is a great deal of variety within each category. The range of possibilities for groups is extensive. It is limited only by client, agency, and community need.

Group-in-Environment Assessment

Concerns about group functioning may arise from the group, or you may raise them. In this respect, group assessment is different from individual and family system assessment. Individuals and families usually seek professional help for a problem they are aware of and want to correct. Problems in group functioning, however, are not always apparent to individual members or to the group as a whole, and groups usually do not seek professional help. An important part of your job as the group leader is to identify potential issues and concerns and to bring them to the attention of the group.

As shown in Figure 4.2, there are six major subsystems within the group-in-environment system that have potential relevance for the assessment process: purpose, structure, life-cycle stage, culture, alliances, and tasks. Just as with family subsystems these group subsystems are highly interrelated. Taken as a whole, they provide a comprehensive picture of the internal structure and functioning of a group system. An ecosystems assessment requires the social worker and the group to mutually and continually assess the effect the various subsystems have on one another and on the functioning of the group.

Purpose.   Every formed group has a purpose. The purposes of groups vary by the type of group. Since in many respects, the type defines a group's purpose, assessment of purpose is an excellent first step in assessing group functioning. "The failure of many groups can be attributed to the lack of a consensus on the purpose of the group" (Magen, 1995, p. 162). The group's purpose should be clearly stated and agreed on by group members. It is from the purpose that all other aspects of a group evolve. Is the identified problem or concern related to confusion or disagreement about the purpose of the group? Is the purpose clear and unambiguous? Is there agreement about the purpose of the group? Does the group have more than one purpose? If so, are the different purposes in conflict?

Structure.   This subsystem deals with the composition of the group, its size, whether the group is time-limited or ongoing, and whether the group is open to new members or closed. Problems in group functioning can often be traced back to structural issues. An examination of a group's structure and the effect of the four structural dimensions on the area of concern is an important aspect of group assessment.

Composition.   Group composition refers to who is included in the group and who is excluded. It pertains to the vital issue of group homogeneity versus heterogeneity (Hepworth, Rooney, & Larsen, 1997). There are a number of issues associated with group composition, including gender, age, education, socioeconomic status, and racial composition of the membership (Garvin, 1997). Another consideration is the socioemotional capacity and intellectual functioning of the members (Levine, 1991).

FIGURE 4.2. Subsystems of Group Client Systems

Purpose (Type)
Therapy
Support
Education
Growth
Project
Administrative
Professional
Citizen

Structure
Membership Composition
Size
Duration
Open/Closed

Culture
Traditions
Values
Norms

Alliances
Communication Patterns
Interpersonal Attraction
Power
Leadership

Life Cycle
Developmental Stage

Tasks
Performance
Decision Making

"Conventional wisdom suggests that for a group to be viable, it should be both homogeneous and heterogeneous" (Reid, 1997, p. 176). There are advantages to highly homogeneous groups, such as increased identification and group cohesion, and disadvantages that stem from the lack of diversity, just as there are advantages (different points of view, different perspectives) and disadvantages (difficulty in relating, less bonding, longer to develop trust) associated with highly heterogeneous groups (Flapan & Fenchel, 1987). "The challenge is to attain a workable balance between homogeneity and heterogeneity" (Hepworth, Rooney, & Larsen, 1997, p. 323).

Issues associated with group composition are numerous and complex. What is ideal for one group is less so for another. There is no single correct prescription. It depends, among other things, on the purpose of the group, the unique characteristics of its members, the leader's style and personality, and the prior experiences of the members and the group. In assessing composition, ask whether something about the composition of the group is contributing to the target problem. Is the gender, age, race, or other composition of the group contributing to the identified concern? Is the homogeneity or heterogeneity of the group a contributing factor? What are the strengths of the group's composition? What are the weakness or obstacles associated with it?

Size.   Whether a group is too small, too large, or just right is relative (Reid, 1997). It depends on the group's purpose, the characteristics of the members, and the leader's level of comfort, among other factors. Generally, smaller groups of eight to twelve members allow everyone to participate and form close relationships. Client groups of four or fewer are problematic in that they often cease to function as a group because they lack the critical mass needed for sustained interaction among the members (Yalom, 1995). "Interaction among members diminishes, and the practitioner finds himself or herself engaged in individual therapy within a group situation" (Reid, 1997, p. 180). At the other end of the continuum, larger groups are generally recommended when the purpose is to convey information and a high level of interaction among the participants is not expected.

While group size is most directly related to purpose and expected level of participation, it can contribute to a number of other issues related to functioning. Does the size of the group have an effect on the identified problem situation? Is the group too large or too small to accomplish its purposes? What are the benefits of the group's size? What are the negatives associated with the number of participants in the group?

Duration.   Duration refers to how long the group stays together. Some groups are time-limited and meet for a fixed number of sessions. One advantage of time-limited groups is that having a fixed termination point encourages productive work (Magen, 1995; Reid, 1997). "The primary disadvantage of a time-limited group is that time allotted for the group may not be enough for the group to reach its goals" (Reid, 1997, p. 181).

There is no fixed rule regarding the optimal number of meetings for a time-limited group. It depends on the group's purpose and the participants. Reid (1997) suggests that twenty sessions are ideal for therapy groups. Corey (1995) suggests that the number of sessions for client groups should be sufficient for cohesion and trust to develop and for the work to be productive, but not so excessive that the group seems to drag on forever.

Open-ended groups have no fixed ending point (Magen, 1995). These groups continue meeting as long as the members desire. They too have advantages and disadvantages. The primary advantage of an ongoing group is that members have adequate time to accomplish the tasks at hand. Members of client groups vary in the amount of time they need to achieve individual change. On the negative side, open-ended groups foster dependency and are often less productive (Reid, 1997).

The decision regarding the duration of the group should be directly related to the group's purpose. However, duration can also effect a number of other issues associated with group functioning. What are the advantages and disadvantages associated with the number of sessions or meetings? Could limiting the number of meetings cause a problem? Has the group gone on for too long?

Open or Closed. Groups may be open or closed to new members. Membership of closed groups is fixed at the beginning of the group, and no new members are allowed to join once the group gets underway. The advantages of closed groups are greater group cohesion and bonding and identification among the members (Reid, 1997). There is also a greater likelihood of the development of trust and support. A disadvantage of closed groups is the possibility that the group will terminate because of member attrition.

Reid (1997) identified three types of open groups: drop-in, replacement, and re-formed. The drop-in group is very flexible in terms of membership. Entry criteria are broad, and members may continue with the group as long as they wish. The replacement group usually has a fixed upper limit of members. As members drop out, they are replaced with new members so that the size of the group remains relatively constant. In a re-formed group, members contract for a set time period. During this time period, no new members are added. At the end of the contracted time, the group is reconstituted. The new group contains the remaining original members and some new members (Reid, 1997).

The advantages of an open group are a constant flow of members into the group and the flexibility it allows members in joining, participating, and dropping out. The primary disadvantage of an open group is that changing membership hinders the development of group cohesion and bonding among members. In addition, frequent changes of membership disrupt the work of the group.

Open and closed group membership is most directly associated with the purpose of the group, the setting, and the population (Hepworth, Rooney, & Larsen, 1997). It also can be associated with a number of other issues related to group functioning. Group client system assessment should include an exploration of the effect of the membership format on an identified target problem. Is the target problem due in part to the group's having open or closed membership? Would a different membership policy improve the problem situation? What are the advantages and disadvantages of an open or closed membership for the group?

Culture. The traditions, beliefs, and norms developed by the group constitute the cultural components of group functioning. Traditions, beliefs, and norms are highly interrelated. An examination of a group's culture and the effect it has on an identified area of concern is an important aspect of group assessment.

Traditions. All groups develop traditions that become associated with the group. Traditions are ritualized activities, such as ceremonies, prayers, and songs, that are incorporated into group meetings. A group's traditions are influenced by members' ethnic, racial, and cultural backgrounds (Garvin & Seabury, 1997). They are important symbols for group members, strengthening group identification and helping members feel closer to the group. They also help define the uniqueness of a group. Individuals who violate group traditions are not viewed favorably by other members. Violations can lead to reprimand and rejection by the group. To avoid this, "workers who begin to work with groups after their formation should learn their traditions as quickly as possible" (Garvin & Seabury, 1997, p. 242).

Norms. Group norms are the understandings group members have about behaviors. They define what members should and should not do within the group (Garvin & Seabury, 1997; Hepworth, Rooney, & Larsen, 1997). All groups develop unwritten rules that govern the behavior of the members. Norms may have a positive or negative influence on group functioning. Regular attendance at meetings, treating one another with respect, and communicating concerns directly to the group are examples of norms that have a positive effect on groups. Norms that have a negative or dysfunctional effect on the group include encouraging discussion of topics not related to the purpose of the meeting, letting a few members dominate the group, and avoiding talking about group problems.

Group norms are not explicitly expressed. They are implicit rules of behavior. Norms are discerned by observing the behavior of members and the group's reactions to this behavior. Sanctions and social disapproval are given for violating a norm: praise and social approval are given for compliance (Toseland & Rivas, 1995).

Values.   Groups also develop values or beliefs that are held in common by all or most group members (Toseland & Rivas, 1995). Values are what group members believe to be true. They are the shared belief system of the members. The values held by a group can have a positive or functional influence on group functioning, or they can have a negative or dysfunctional influence. As with norms, values can only be inferred through observation. They are not written down, nor are they usually stated explicitly.

Assessment of a group's culture is an important function of the group leader. Cultural influences can have positive or negative effects on a concern or problem. To be able to effectively assess a group's culture you need to be aware of the traditions, values, and norms that have developed. This is an ongoing process. How does group culture affect the target problem? What are its positive influences? What are its negative influences?

Alliances.   There are four dimensions of alliance: the communication patterns of members, interpersonal attraction, power, and leadership. These four dimensions are highly interrelated. Taken together, they provide a comprehensive overview of the alliance component of group functioning.

Communication Patterns.   The communication pattern involves who talks to whom and about what (Garvin & Seabury, 1997). It is the structure of the interactions among members. An analysis of communication patterns indicates who dominates group discussions, whether some members are isolated, and who the informal leaders are. It also provides insight into subgroup formation and the effect of the various subgroups on the functioning of the group (Hartford, 1971). Subgroups do not necessarily adversely affect a group. In fact, the formation of subgroups helps members form closer attachments to other members and to the group as a whole. They negatively affect the group when they exclude the formation of relationships with other members or when power struggles between subgroups interfere with member support for the larger group (Hepworth, Rooney, & Larsen, 1997).

Interpersonal Attraction.   Closely associated with communication patterns and subgroup formation is the attraction of members to one another. As members get better acquaied, some members are attracted to others, while other members have the opposite reaction. Interpersonal attraction is influenced by race, culture, and gender as well as physical appearance, personality, and interests, among other factors (Garvin & Seabury, 1997). Members with similar backgrounds and interests are more likely to be attracted to each other than those who are very different from one another.

Power. *Power* is the ability of one individual to cause another to act in some specified way. There are five types of power:

> *Reward power*—the ability to influence others by providing them something that they value. A group member may use reward power by offering friendship, support, praise or other goods and services.

> *Coercive power*—the ability to influence others by the use of punishment. A group member may use coercive power by criticizing, insulting or physically threatening another group member.

> *Legitimate power*—the ability to influence others by virtue of the person's position in the group. The social work leader may exercise legitimate power based upon his or her assigned role.

> *Referent power*—the ability to influence others by being liked or respected. A group member may have referent power based upon his or her personality or attractiveness.

> *Expert power*—the ability to influence others because of specialized knowledge or skills. A member may exercise expert power by virtue of his or her special training. (Garvin & Seabury, 1997, p. 235; based on French & Raven, 1959)

Both the sources of power and the locus of power within the group may vary. Power does not itself negatively affect group functioning. Problems arise when there are power struggles within the group. "Groups, in fact, are sometimes torn apart and meet their demise because of unresolved power issues that prevent the group from meeting the needs of some members" (Hepworth, Rooney, & Larsen, 1997, p. 338). The issue in group assessment is not so much who has the power but rather the group's ability to share power and to find resolutions to power conflicts that do not result in some members' feeling they have been forced to give up too much.

Leadership. *Leadership* is more difficult to define than power. In simple terms, it is the capacity to mobilize group members into action. Garvin and Seabury (1997) view leadership as a process that grows out of interactions among group members related to the attainment of goals. They further break leadership into two types of group processes: task and social-emotional. "Task leadership occurs when the individual helps the group move toward defining and achieving group goals. Social-emotional leadership occurs when the member positively affects the interaction among group members by such things as reducing conflicts and facilitating the expression of positive feelings" (Garvin & Seabury, 1997, p. 239).

The alliance component has powerful influences on group functioning. A comprehensive assessment needs to carefully evaluate the effect of these processes on an identified problem area or concern. As the social worker involved with the group, part of your leadership task is to become aware of the alliance structure of the group. This requires ongoing observation of group behavior. Before you can assess the effect the processes have on the group, you need to understand how the group functions. Once you have a clear understanding of the communication patterns, interpersonal alliances, power, and leadership within the group, you can assess their effect on a specific area of concern.

Life-Cycle.   This aspect of group functioning deals with group development. Groups go through a number of developmental stages. They change and evolve as they mature. Like humans, groups have a pattern of development. "While theorists and clinicians agree that groups go through various stages, there is no agreement as to how many stages exist and what the stages actually look like" (Reid, 1997, p. 56). Magen (1995) reports that the various typologies of group development range from three stages (Schwartz, 1986) to nine (Beck, 1983) and that there is considerable overlap in the labels applied to the stages and in their conceptualization. One widely used conceptualization is Tuckman's (1965) four stage model of group development: forming, storming, norming, and performing. Magen (1995) added a fifth stage, adjourning, to Tuckman's model. Tuckman's model as modified by Magen provides the framework for the following discussion of group development.

Group development is not as tidy a process as the various conceptualizations suggest. Reid points out that

Groups do not move along in an orderly sequence;

Groups may revert to earlier stages;

Stages cannot be thought of in any *pure* form but in various blends and combinations; and

A group's life span and development can and will be influenced by the worker and by the members. (1997, p. 58)

Forming.   The initial stage of the group, *forming*, is when members come together for the first time. In most groups, especially client groups, this is an exciting and anxious time for both the members and the leader. "Group members generally experience anxiety about the new situation and what will be expected of them" (Reid, 1997, p. 63). They are anxious about what will happen, what their experience in the group will be, and how they will perform. At this point, the group is a collection of individuals with individual concerns. "Excessive dependency on the worker is common in the initial session" (Reid, 1997, p. 64). Group members look to the leader for answers to questions about "expectations, about rules, roles, limits, and about how the sessions will run" (Reid, 1997, p. 64). Interactions among members are superficial and guarded. Members do not have a strong commitment to the group and have not developed an identification with the group as a whole.

The length of time groups stay in the forming stage varies. "Open-ended groups with frequent and excessive turnover of members would not be expected to move beyond the 'forming' stage of group development" (Magen, 1995, p. 166). Closed groups that meet on a fairly frequent basis might move to the next stage after a few sessions. Other groups never get beyond the initial stage and may terminate prematurely.

Storming.   The second developmental stage, labeled *storming* by Tuckman (1965), is characterized by conflict among the members and with the leader. The emotional climate is characterized by tension. Members exhibit hostility toward one another and frustration with the group. The worker's leadership is challenged, and the purpose, structure, and operation of the group is often questioned. "Until this stage of development, the group has been the worker's group" (Reid, 1997, p. 68). Conflict is an expression of the group's emerging identity and group members' efforts to obtain power and control of the group. "Resistance may be directed at the subject matter, the group, or the leader, and may take the form of withdrawal, absence from the group, attacking others, or questioning the purpose of the group" (George & Dustin, 1988). Through this process, the group begins to develop a collective identity and a sense of togetherness.

Although this stage of group development is difficult for the worker, it presents an opportunity to model behavior for the group. In the face of often unpleasant challenges, you need to stay calm, nondefensive, and open to criticism, and you should demonstrate a willingness to share power and control with the group.

Norming.   The third stage, *norming*, is the period during which group identity is solidified and the various roles, norms, and boundaries of the group emerge. Guidelines for group functioning are agreed on during this stage of development; they are the product of the group's coming together and developing a sense of itself. Guidelines are not just the leader's vision of what the group should do and how they should do it; they are the group's guidelines. At this point, the group has established ownership, and a collective sense of purpose and expected behavior has emerged.

Performing.   This is the action phase of the group's life-cycle, the time when the group has worked out its leadership issues, structural concerns, and behavioral expectations. The *performing* stage is characterized by solidarity, cohesion, and commitment (Reid, 1997). Patterns of communication have become more predictable, and the members are more comfortable with one another. Exchanges are open and honest, and differences are less likely to lead to conflict. The group has worked out mechanisms for managing and resolving conflict. There is a sense of cohesiveness among the members. They are now a group, and they are ready to work on and accomplish the tasks at hand.

One potential problem during this stage is unwillingness of members to challenge one another. There is a fear of upsetting the feeling of closeness the group has achieved, and members may be unwilling to do anything that might jeopardize that closeness (George & Dustin, 1988).

Adjourning.   This is the ending phase or termination stage of the group's development. A wide range of feelings among the members often characterizes it. If the group has developed a sense of closeness characteristic of the performing stage, the *adjourning* phase can be difficult for group members and the leader. Feelings of loss and abandonment are common. There is often regression on the part of some members—they revert back to earlier stages in an attempt to keep the group going. Reasons for continuing are put forth. Groups may go through a grieving process similar to that of individuals: denial, rage and anger, bargaining, depression, and acceptance (Kübler-Ross, 1969). "Because the ending of a group may trigger so many different responses—including flight, denial, repression,

---

FIGURE 4.3. Group Performance Tasks

Generating Tasks
> *Planning Tasks:* Generating plans for how the group will undertake some activity.
> *Creativity Tasks:* Generating ideas, "brainstorming."

Choosing Tasks
> *Intellective Tasks:* Solving problems in which there exists an answer whose "correctness" will be clearly evident.
> *Decision-Making Tasks:* Solving problems about which some ambiguity exists about how members will agree upon the "correctness" of the answer.

Negotiating Tasks
> *Cognitive-Conflict Tasks: Resolving* conflicts of viewpoints; that is, members disagree on the definition of the issue to be resolved.
> *Mixed-Motive Tasks: Members* have a conflict of interests; that is, gains may be made by some members at the expense of others as the task is carried out.

Executing Tasks
> *Contests/Battles:* Activities in which members are pitted against one another as in competitive sports.
> *Performances:* Psychomotor tasks performed against objective or absolute standards of excellence, such as in producing a painting or a dance step.

Note: From Groups: *Interaction and Performance,* by J. McGrath, 1984, Englewood Cliffs, NJ: Prentice-Hall; quoted in *Interpersonal Practice in Social Work: Promoting Competence and Social Justice,* 2nd ed. (p. 240), by C. Garvin and B. Seabury, 1997, Boston: Allyn and Bacon.

---

clinging together, and anger—the worker needs to help each member examine his or her responses" (Reid, 1997, p. 72).

Assessment of the group's stage of development is an important aspect of understanding group functioning. Groups develop at different rates and progress in their development differently. What might seem like a problem in group functioning may be a normal stage of the group's development. To what extent is the behavior being exhibited by group members related to the group's developmental stage? How far has the group progressed developmentally?

Task Performance.   This subsystem is "related to the ways the group defines and carries out its purposes through enacting tasks" (Garvin & Seabury, 1997, p. 237). It is composed of two related dimensions: performance and decision making. Assessment of this subsystem provides information on how group processes are affecting the accomplishment of identified group tasks.

Performance.   *Performance* is the way group members carry out tasks to accomplish group purposes. Drawing on McGrath's (1984) typology of group tasks, Garvin and Seabury (1997) saw performance as composed of four categories of tasks—generating, choosing, negotiating, and executing tasks—and each category further divided, into two subcategories (see Figure 4.3).

If a group fails to accomplish the tasks at hand, the task performance classification helps determine the stage in the process the group is failing to accomplish. Once the problem is defined and located, solutions can be identified.

Decision Making.   "Effective deliberations and decision making are critical in determining the productivity and success of a group" (Hepworth, Rooney, & Larsen, 1997, p. 326). The way a group makes decisions is as important as the actual decisions made. Some groups allow a few members to make decisions. This excludes members from the decision-making process and can create conflict, unrest, and dissatisfaction. A common method of decision making in client groups is to adopt a decision-by-consensus approach. Everyone in the group is empowered and given an equal vote. The group encourages all members to express their opinions and to contribute to the deliberations.

Another factor in the decision-making process is the willingness of the group to make a decision. Some groups work hard to avoid making decisions. Groups with problems in making decisions find a variety of excuses not to make a decision. There are numerous legitimate reasons for not being ready to make a decision. But if it happens frequently or on a regular basis, it is probably a symptom of some other problem in the group.

Assessment of group functioning should include an assessment of the group's performance in relation to its purpose as well as an assessment of the group's decision making. Dysfunction in these areas can be related to problems in many other areas of group functioning. Is the target problem in part caused by the group's decision-making style and effectiveness? What role does the group's task performance play in the occurrence of the problem area? What are the strengths and weaknesses of the group's performance and decision making?

Strengths-Based Group Assessment

Group assessment is a collaborative process that you and members of the group undertake to change conditions that impede the group from achieving its purpose or improving its functioning. An empowering approach to group assessment involves the members in the analysis of group functioning and the problem situation. You may raise an issue or concern, but the entire group explores it and its effect on the group. The group decides whether it is a problem, what contributes to the concern, and what should be done to help correct the situation. The group and its members are the experts. Your starting point is their perceptions of the problem situation. Do not force your analysis and assessment of the group's problems, interpersonal relationships, or individual dysfunction on the group. Engage in a collaborative exchange with the group, share your insights and perceptions, and explore the perceptions of the members. You guide the assessment process, but the group members actually conduct the assessment. Ensure that each member's perception of the situation is acknowledged and validated. There is no single correct view. There are always multiple perceptions of reality. Each member's perception of the situation is accurate from his or her perspective. Seek consensus about the target problem. If that is not possible, seek agreement about the need to address the concern. The group has the power to set the agenda. It has ownership of the problem as well as the potential solutions.

A strengths-based assessment emphasizes the identification of group strengths as well as strengths of each individual member. Groups have individual and collective power to bring about positive change. Incorporating a strengths perspective in the assessment process, however, must come from you, the professional leader. Regardless of the type of group, emphasizing strengths requires a conscious effort on your part. All groups, regardless of the level of functioning of individual members, have strengths. Do not expect group members to recognize or be aware of their individual and collective strengths. Adopt the attitude that strengths exist and that they can be used to help the group resolve the problem situation.

ORGANIZATIONAL ASSESSMENT

The worker's organizational system is the agency and/or program through which services are provided to the client. As shown in Figure 4.4, this organizational client system has three major subsystems: organizational policies, organizational resources, and organizational culture. Assessing an organization's functioning is an important aspect of generalist social work practice. Social workers need to assess the effect of the organizational climate on their work with clients. A negative organizational climate can have serious indirect negative effects on clients and the quality of the services they receive. Awareness of how these intangible factors affect job satisfaction and feelings of burnout helps social workers deal with potentially negative effects on the helping relationship.

Organizational Policies

Organizational policies include external and internal policies and procedures. Both external and internal policies can profoundly influence the helping relationship. Agency-based social workers function within an organizational context. The types of services provided, the length of service, and the kinds of clients served are but a few of the agency influences that can affect the helping relationship. Agency policies have a strong influence on the worker, on the client, and on the helping relationship. The influence of the worker and client on the agency is most likely weaker. Nevertheless, all social workers have a responsibility to work to improve agency policies and procedures and the efficiency and effectiveness of service delivery.

Organizational Resources

This subsystem encompasses your workload and the adequacy of support staff and professional staff. These organizational factors tend to be interrelated and strongly affect your work with client systems. Underfunded agencies often are understaffed, and social workers have large caseloads and workloads that negatively affect their energy, commitment, and capacity to develop strong helping relationships with their clients. Numerous research studies have found significant associations between adequacy of organizational resources and social worker job satisfaction and burnout (Poulin, 1994; Poulin & Walter, 1993a; Silver, Poulin, & Manning, 1997).

Social workers need to assess the effect of organizational resources on their work with clients. A realistic assessment of organizational resources will enable the worker and client to develop an understanding of the constraints facing the worker and how these constraints influence their work together. This assessment can also provide the worker with information that can be used to advocate for organizational change.

FIGURE 4.4. Subsystems of Organizational Client Systems

Organizational Policies
Internal Policies and Procedures
External Policies and Procedures

Organizational Resources
Professional Staffing Patterns
Support Staffing Patterns
Workload

Organizational Culture
Support
Autonomy
Trust

Organizational Culture

The organizational culture subsystem deals with less tangible components of the agency environment. These factors have a profound effect on the provision of services and the helping relationship. For example, studies have consistently found that the level of supervisor support is positively associated with social worker's job satisfaction (Glisson & Durick, 1988; Poulin & Walter, 1992; Poulin & Walter, 1993b; Silver, Poulin, & Manning, 1997). Social workers who feel supported by their supervisors have significantly higher job satisfaction and lower burnout than those who do not feel supported. Similarly, job autonomy and levels of trust among the professional, supervisory, and administrative staff are strongly associated with social worker job satisfaction and negatively asociated with burnout (Poulin, 1994; Poulin & Walter, 1993a; Poulin & Walter, 1993b). These and other aspects of organizational culture have indirect effects on the helping relationship and the services provided to clients.

COMMUNITY ASSESSMENT

As shown in Figure 4.5, the community system has three major subsystems: ethnicity and culture, community conditions, and community resources. These subsystems are highly interrelated. An assessment of these subsystems provides a comprehensive picture of how community factors affect the identified target problem.

Ethnicity and Culture

This subsystem is composed of the community's values and beliefs. Cultural beliefs shape a community's value system the same way they shape an individual's value system. Community values play a major role in the helping relationship. They influence the client's and worker's values and beliefs. They also affect the agency's organizational policies and procedures. In assessing the client's concerns, you and your clients need to take prevailing community values and beliefs

---

FIGURE 4.5. Subsystems of Community Client Systems

Ethnicity and Culture
Values
Beliefs

Community Conditions
Employment
Housing
Transportation
Education
Recreation
Crime and Safety

Community Services and Resources
Social Services
Community Groups
Religious Organizations

---

into account. If there is a value clash between the client and the community values, the implications of the clash need to be explored from your, the client's, the agency's and the community's perspectives. Often, value positions are taken for granted and not directly addressed in the assessment process.

A problem may arise if the client's perceptions and/or actions are viewed as unlawful, unethical, or inappropriate by the prevailing community values and beliefs. Mutual exploration of values and beliefs does not mean value consensus or agreement. It does mean, however, that the client's and your beliefs are articulated. The emphasis should be on understanding the client and the client's perceptions. Working out differences is part of the helping process. It requires mutual understanding and recognition of the value positions of everyone involved. As Compton and Galaway put it: "when the values of a person conflict with the rights of others or get in the way of the client achieving agreed-upon goals, the values themselves become a topic for discussion and for consideration as an appropriate target of change" (1994, p. 232).

Community Conditions

Community conditions can have a significant effect on clients and on the helping relationship. Employment opportunities, housing quality and availability, accessibility and affordability of transportation, the quality of the educational system, the availability of leisure activities, and other conditions can profoundly affect clients, their life situations, and the helping relationship. You and your clients need to assess all the potential environmental factors that might influence the client's ability to resolve the identified target problem. Many interpersonal or social functioning problems have environmental components. The helping relationship might focus on environmental change or on overcoming the difficulties associated with the environmental problem (Young, 1994). In other instances, simply increasing awareness of environmental conditions helps you and the client understand the client's subjective reality.

Community Services and Resources

Community services and resources can also affect the helping relationship system. Community resources include social service organizations, community groups, and religious organizations. You and your clients need to review the client's past and current history with social service and community groups. This review can identify important sources of assistance in the client's life as well as the client's nonuse of available community services. It is also important to understand clients' perceptions of their experiences with other helping professionals and community groups. Helping clients think through and articulate what they liked and disliked about their previous interactions with helping professionals provides important clues about how to productively work together. The process also helps the client put this helping relationship into a perspective that differentiates it from previous experiences. If the client has not used other social or community services, you and the client need to explore the reasons the client did not use these available resources.

Understanding Community Functioning

Generalist social workers need to be skilled in community assessment. Understanding community functioning is vital to the provision of services to individuals, families, and groups as well as to the development of interventions aimed at community change. The ethnicity and culture, social and economic conditions, and services and resources of communities vary widely. Ignoring the effect of these factors on client systems results in an unbalanced assessment. Environmental conditions and concerns have a tremendous effect on everyday lives, especially the lives of those living in impoverished and disadvantaged communitiees. As members of a profession committed to social and economic justice, generalist social workers must make efforts to strengthen and empower disadvantaged communities and their residents.

SUMMARY

Generalist social workers are involved with many types of groups. Types of client groups include therapy, support, educational, and growth. Social workers also are frequently involved with agency or organizational groups. Some agency groups are formed to deal with specific projects, and others are established groups or committees within the organization. Generalist social workers often come into contact with two types of community groups: professional task forces and citizen groups. Both tend to focus on community conditions and/or issues.

Assessment of small groups is an important part of the social worker's job as group leader. It is your responsibility to identify potential issues and concerns and to bring them to the attention of the group. A number of subsystems related to group functioning need to be assessed. The primary subsystems are purpose, structure, culture, alliances, life-cycle, and tasks. These subsystems are interrelated and together provide a comprehensive assessment of the functioning of the group system.

Organizational assessment is also an important aspect of generalist social work practice. The functioning of the organization has an effect on the work that is carried out within the organization as well as on the workers. The three major organizational subsystems that have the greatest effect on service delivery are organizational policies, resources, and culture. Assessment of organizational policies focuses on both internal and external policies and procedures. Organizational resources of particular relevance to the delivery of services are adequacy of professional staffing, suport staff, and workload. The organizational climate subsystem focuses on support, autonomy, and trust issues within the organization, among the social workers, and between the workers and administrators.

Generalist social workers also need to be skilled in community assessment. Understanding community functioning is vital to the provision of services to individuals, families, and groups as well as to the development of interventions aimed at community change. Community systems have three major subsystems of particular relevance for generalist social work: ethnicity and culture, community conditions, and community resources.

CASE EXAMPLE

The final case example in this chapter is based on the experience of one of my first-year MSW students. The student was placed in a setting that provided individual and group treatment to elderly persons by means of a partial hospitalization program. The case example illustrates the process of assessing problematic group functioning.

Coming Together

Danielle A. was in the second semester of her first year as an MSW student when she was placed at Springton, a partial-day hospitalization program for elderly persons with mental health problems. As part of her placement responsibilities, Danielle was co-leader of an insight group for about one month. After a month, Danielle asked Anne Z., her field instructor and co-leader, to let her take the lead in running the group. Danielle had observed Anne running a similar group during the first semester, and she was eager to try her hand at running the group under Anne's supervision.

Insight groups at Springton have a therapeutic focus and are designed to help the members deal with interpersonal and intrapersonal issues associated with their mental health problems. Membership in the insight groups is relatively fixed, with between six and ten clients assigned to each group. The groups meet once a week for fifteen weeks, which is the usual length of time clients remain in the partial hospitalization program. Members occasionally leave the group early if they are discharged from the program, and every so often a new group member is added to a group after it has been formed. Insight groups are kept semiclosed in terms of membership so that the members can become comfortable enough with the social worker and with one another to share their personal stories and struggles.

Danielle was concerned that her group was not developing a sufficient level of trust. Discussions continued to be superficial even after one month of being together. She felt that the members were not using the group to truly work on their issues. Members seemed to enjoy the group and one another, but a level of openness and willingness to use the group to help deal with common problems had not developed. Danielle discussed her concerns with Anne and agreed to conduct a preliminary assessment of the group's functioning that they could go over during their next supervisory session. The plan was to assess the situation and develop a strategy to try to get the group on track.

Danielle decided to assess the group's purpose, structure, life-cycle stage, and culture. She concluded that the group's therapeutic purpose was clearly defined and appropriate for the participants. However, she was not sure that all members of the group were clear about the purpose of the group. She also concluded that having eight members in the group was an ideal size and that having it structured as a semiclosed group that met once a week for fifteen weeks was appropriate given its purpose.

Danielle placed the group at the forming stage in terms of its developmental life cycle. Superficial and guarded interactions among members are characteristic of the beginning stage of group development, as are member's lack of strong commitment to the group and lack of identification with the group as a whole. Danielle concluded that the group seemed to be stuck at the forming stage or, at the very least, had not progressed to the storming or norming stages.

Also related to the group's developmental stage was the absence of group norms. Danielle felt that the group had not developed appropriate norms regarding member behavior. The only norms appeared to be politeness and superficial discussion. Norms regarding behavior appropriate to the therapeutic purpose of the group were absent.

In assessing the group's communication patterns, Danielle realized that interactions were for the most part directed toward her. The group was a wheel, and she was the hub. When anyone spoke, they seemed to direct their comments to her, and Danielle likewise tended to direct her comments to individual members. There was very little member-to-member interaction. Communication was rarely expressed to the group as a whole.

Danielle shared her preliminary assessment with Anne. Anne concurred with the assessment, and together they identified lack of understanding about the group's purpose and the communication pattern as problem areas that could be contributing to the lack of appropriate norms and the developmental-stage problem. Anne also pointed out to Danielle that she might be exercising too much control over the group and its interactions. She recommended that Danielle try to give the members a greater voice in shaping group experiences. Anne encouraged Danielle to view her role more as facilitator than leader. Danielle agreed to try to change her style and to address her concerns with the group at their next meeting.

Danielle was anxious about the meeting and was not sure how the elderly participants were going to react. She wanted to be honest with the group. She decided that the best approach was to share her concerns, to express her feelings, hopes, and fears, and to see how the group responded. Since the prevailing norm was politeness, she figured that the worst that could happen was that she would be met with indifference.

At the next meeting of the group, Danielle began talking about her concerns. She said that the purpose of their group was clear to her, but she was afraid that it might not be clear to everyone else. At this point, her natural instinct was to explain what the purpose was supposed to be. However, she resisted and instead focused on finding out what the group members thought the purpose should be. It was not easy, but after a while some of the members opened up and expressed what they would like to have happen in the group. By the end of the session, almost everyone was participating, and a common understanding of the purpose had been reached. They agreed that the following week they would talk more about the purpose of the group and what they would like to have happen in the group.

Although the agreed-on purpose was not exactly what Danielle had in mind for the group, it was close enough. The important thing was that the purpose was stated in members' words and that members started to feel ownership of the group. Although they had not talked specifically about any of the members' issues, Danielle felt that the meeting had been productive. It felt like a good beginning. She was hopeful that the group might turn out all right after all.

DISCUSSION QUESTIONS

1. Critique Danielle's assessment of the insight group. What additional factors could have contributed to group functioning? In what other ways could Danielle have intervened with the group?
2. Discuss Danielle's use of the strengths perspective and empowerment with the group. In what ways did she empower group members? Are there other ways she might have empowered them? What would have happened to the group if she had not changed her approach?
3. Describe the types of client, organizational, and community groups in your field placement agency. In what ways are they similar? How are they different?
4. Using your class as a group, assess its life-cycle stage and development, the culture of the group, and alliance patterns. How do the dynamics of the group affect its functioning? What could be done to improve the functioning of the group?
5. Critique your field placement agency in terms of its organizational functioning. In what ways do internal and external policies and procedures affect your work with clients? Are the agency's organizational resources adequate? How do they affect service delivery? Describe the organizational climate of the agency and its effect on the professional staff? How does the organizational climate affect service delivery?
6. Create a hypothetical client who lives close to your school. Assess the client's community and its effect on his or her problem or concern. How does the ethnicity and culture of the community affect your client? What about community conditions and the availability of community services and resources? What do you need to know about the community to be able to understand your client's situation?

REFERENCES

Beck, A. (1983). A process analysis of group development. *Group, 7,* 19–28.

Compton, B. R., & Galaway, B. (1994). *Social work processes* (5th ed.). Pacific Grove, CA: Brooks/Cole.

Corey, G. (1995). *Theory and practice of group counseling* (4th ed.). Pacific Grove, CA: Brooks/Cole.

Corey, M., & Corey, G. (1997). *Groups: Process and practice* (5th ed.). Pacific Grove, CA: Brooks/Cole.

Flapan, D., & Fenchel, G. (1987). *The developing ego and the emerging self in group therapy.* Northvale, NJ: Aronson.

French, J., & Raven, B. (1959). The bases of social power. In D. Cartwright (Ed.), *Studies in social power* (pp. 150–167). Ann Arbor, MI: Institute for Social Research.

Garvin, C. (1997). *Contemporary group work* (3rd ed.). Boston: Allyn and Bacon.

Garvin, C., & Seabury, B. (1997). *Interpersonal practice in social work: Promoting competence and social justice* (2nd ed.). Boston: Allyn and Bacon.

George, R., & Dustin, D. (1988). *Group counseling: Theory and practice.* Englewood Cliffs, NJ: Prentice Hall.

Glisson, C., & Durick, M. (1988). Predictor of job satisfaction and organizational commitment in human service organizations. *Administrative Science Quarterly, 33,* 61–81.

Hartford, M. (1971). *Groups in social work.* New York: Columbia University Press.

Hepworth, D., Rooney, R., & Larsen, J. (1997). *Direct social work practice: Theory and skills* (5th ed.). Pacific Grove, CA: Brooks/Cole.

Jacobs, E., Harvill, R., & Masson, R. (1994). *Group counseling: Strategies and skills.* Pacific Grove, CA: Brooks/Cole.

Kübler-Ross, E. (1969). *On death and dying.* New York: Macmillan.

Levine, B. (1991). *Group psychotherapy.* Prospect Heights, IL: Waveland Press.

Magen, R. (1995). Practice with groups. In C. Meyer & M. Mattaini (Eds.), *The foundations of social work practice* (pp. 156–175). Washington, DC: NASW Press.

McGrath, J. (1984). *Groups: Interaction and performance.* Englewood Cliffs, NJ: Prentice-Hall.

Popple, P., & Leighninger, L. (1993). *Social work, social welfare, and American history.* Boston: Allyn and Bacon.

Poulin, J. (1994). Job task and organizational predictors of social worker job satisfaction change: A panel study. *Administration in Social Work, 18,* 21–38.

Poulin, J., & Walter, C. (1992). Retention plans and job satisfaction of gerontological social workers. *Journal of Gerontological Social Work, 19,* 99–114.

Poulin, J., & Walter, C. (1993a). Social worker burnout: A longitudinal study. *Social Work Research and Abstracts, 29,* 5–11.

Poulin, J., & Walter, C. (1993b). Burnout in gerontological social work. *Social Work, 38,* 305–316.

Reid, K. (1997). *Social work practice with groups: A clinical perspective.* Pacific Grove, CA: Brooks/Cole.

Schwartz, W. (1986). The group work tradition and social work practice. *Social Work with Groups, 8,* 7–27.

Silver, P., Poulin, J., & Manning, R. (1997). Surviving the bureaucracy: Predictors of job satisfaction of direct service supervisors in public human services. *The Clinical Supervisor, 15,* 1–20.

Toseland, R., & Rivas, R. (1995). *An introduction to group work practice* (2nd ed.). Boston: Allyn and Bacon.

Tuckman, B. (1965). Developmental sequence in small groups. *Psychological Bulletin, 63,* 384–399.

Yalom, I. (1995). *The theory and practice of group psychotherapy* (4th ed.). New York: Basic Books.

Young, T. (1994). Environmental modification in clinical social work: A self-psychological perspective. *Social Service Review, 68,* 202–218.

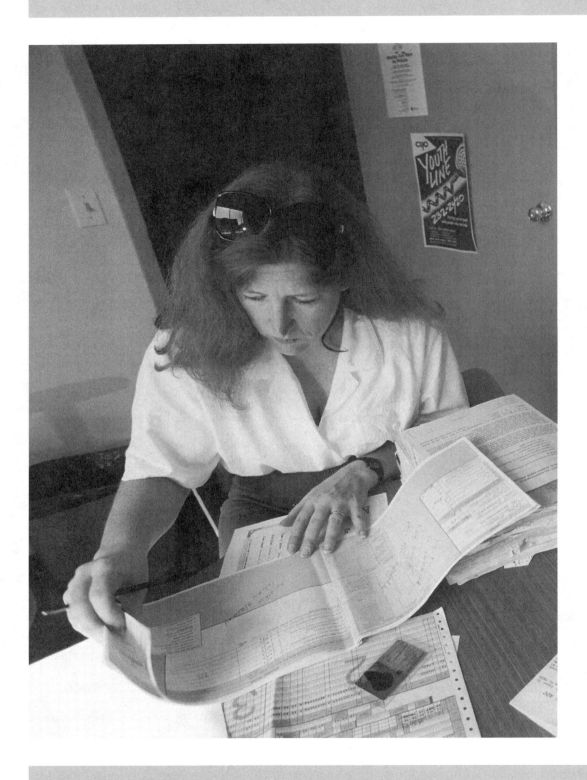

CHAPTER 5

Assessment Tools

Following completion of her BSW degree, Korrie A. took her first social work job with a small community-based program that helps teenage mothers obtain their GEDs and enter the job market. Korrie was hired to provide case management and supportive services to the program participants.

Korrie asked about the policies and procedures to follow in her work with the young women. The program coordinator told her that none had been developed for the social work position. All the intake and program functions focused on participant's educational achievement and job readiness.

Korrie realized that, to effectively provide supportive services, she would need to have some basic psychosocial information about each participant as well as some understanding of her unique circumstances. She decided that her first project would be to design an assessment form. Korrie was not sure what to include on the assessment form or how to proceed.

The use of assessment instuments is a means to an end, not the end itself. Assessment is a process that you and your client engage in, and together you articulate the target problem and analyze the relevant factors in the client's person-in-environment system that potentially affect it. Assessment tools can help you and the client identify and organize the assessment information.

Obtaining the necessary information to complete assessment instruments requires sensitivity, compassion, caring-concern, and curiosity. Keep the focus on listening and understanding rather than on obtaining answers to the questions on the assessment tools. Attention to the interpersonal aspects of the helping relationship are extremely critical during the initial assessment phase. Let the information flow from the interview; focus on the client's story and concerns. If the client does not feel heard or understood, he or she will probably not return to complete the assessment, or in the case of a nonvoluntary client, he or she will not engage in a collaborative helping relationship.

In recent years, a number of instuments have been developed to measure client problems and assess client functioning (Fischer & Corcoran, 1994; Nurius & Hudson, 1993; Reid, 1994). Most of the work in this area has focused on developing measures of specific client problems, such as self-esteem, anxiety, and marital satis-faction. These types of measures are important in the evaluation process and are discussed in Chapter 6. Quantitative measures designed to assess client outcomes are not presented here. The tools presented in this chapter aid in the collection and organization of assessment data, incorporate the ecosystems perspective, are rele-vant to generalist social work practice, and are easy to use.

A number of instruments can be used to collect and organize assessment data. Tools can help assess individual, family, group, organizational, and community client systems. This chapter presents strengths-based and traditional assessment forms and four graphical assessment tools. By the end of the chapter, you should be able to help Korrie

1. Develop a strengths-based assessment form
2. Construct a traditional biopsychosocial assessment form
3. Review the use of plot forms, ecomaps, and genograms for use in the assessment process
4. Evaluate the appropriateness of using a mental status examination for work with teenage mothers.

ASSESSMENT FORMS

Generalist social workers practice in a multitude of settings. The type of assess-ment tools used is as varied as the settings. Agencies adopt or develop assessment procedures based on the kinds of information they need and the types of services they provide. Most assessment tools are variations of the generic biopsychosocial assessment that has been taught in schools of social work for many years. Typically, these instuments collect information on client problems and past behaviors and experiences. Little or no attention is given to client strengths. Tools that focus on client strengths are now emerging, and strengths-based assessments are beginning to be incorporated into agency-based practice.

Strengths-Based Assessment Worksheets

Strengths-based worksheets were developed to help social workers and clients identify clients' strengths as well as the obstacles they face in resolving problem situations. There are four strengths worksheets, each of which focuses on a client system: individual/family, group, organization, and community. Together, the four worksheets provide a comprehensive assessment of the person-in-environ-ment system as it relates to the identified target problem. The worksheets help social workers and clients

- Summarize areas of concern and priorities
- Identify client strengths and obstacles
- Analyze the effect of the obstacles and strengths on the target problem.

The four strengths-based worksheets appear as Appendixes 5.1, 5.2, 5.3, and 5.4 at the end of this chapter.

Complete as much of the worksheets as possible between your first and sec-ond meetings with the client. During the second meeting, review your initial assessment findings and then together revise and finish the worksheets. Not all content areas will be related to the target problem. Explore only those areas that appear to have a major effect on the client's concerns. At this point in the helping relationship, your primary objectives are to

- Help your client select a priority area on which to focus
- Identify strengths that can be employed to help the client resolve the target problem
- Identify obstacles that will impede progress.

Biopsychosocial Assessment Form

Strengths-based worksheets integrate ecosystems and strengths perspectives. They focus on the present, on the here and now. To complete the picture, some understanding of past experiences is also needed (Sheafor, Horejsi, & Horejsi, 1997). Biopsychosocial assessments incorporate an ecosystems perspective and are widely used in agency settings (Jordan & Franklin, 1995). Typically, these assessments focus on the biological, psychological, and social functioning and histories of individual clients. They often include a psychiatric (*DSM-IV*) diagnosis. A comprehensive assessment requires an examination of these factors as well as the strengths and obstacles outlined on strengths-based worksheets. Appendix 5.5 is a generic biopsychosocial assessment form.

The following biopsychosocial assessment was written by Denise Bubel when she was a first-year MSW student and placed in an adult partial hospitalization program.

Biopsychosocial Assessment *Denise Bubel*

Identifying Information
Theodore J. is an eighty-two-year-old Caucasian. He is married and lives with his eighty-year-old wife in their own home in a suburban community.

Problem Situation
Mr. J. has been diagnosed with irreversible dementia. He suffers from memory loss and cognitive decline, and he feels a great deal of frustration and anxiety. Mr. J. has become depressed over his continuing physical decline and agreed to come to the partial hospitalization program for help with his depression and memory loss. He also stated that he wanted to work on issues of shame and embarrassment that are as a result of his medical condition. Mr. J. indicated that his wife has become "stressed out" from having to care for him and that he is worried about her ability to cope with his condition.

Background
In early January, Mr. J. was admitted to the hospital with severe dehydration and because of noncompliance with his medication. Apparently he was being treated for dementia and major depression with psychosis prior to being admitted to this hospital. Because his original psychiatrist left his practice abruptly, previous mental health records are unavailable and only the

diagnosis could be obtained. Therefore, the psychosis could not be further defined. The admitting psychiatrist reported that Mr. J.'s psychiatric history was limited to his wife's recollections, and she could not account for the "psychosis." However, the admitting psychiatrist stated that medical records revealed that Mr. J. was originally referred to a psychiatrist because of "vegetative symptoms of depression." Those symptoms were not described, nor were their duration or intensity.

The admitting psychiatrist reported a "complete remission of psychotic symptoms." He reported that Mr. J. denied any suicidal or homicidal ideation. The admitting psychiatrist noted that Mr. J.'s "thought process was impoverished with mild thought blocking" and that "there are definite problems with his memory." The admitting psychiatrist's report on Mr. J.'s initial assessment and evaluation was brief and limited:

Initial Diagnosis:

Axis I   Major depression with psychosis
Axis II Deferred
Axis III Dementia not otherwise specified and coronary artery
         disease
Axis IV None reported
Axis V   None reported

Medical and Psychiatric History

Approximately three years ago, Mr. J's prostate gland was removed, and he still experiences incontinence. Approximately two years ago, he had coronary artery bypass, he suffers from exhaustion at times. Approximately one year ago, he had a bowel resection and suffers from continuing intermittent constipation and diarrhea as well as fear of embarrassment.

Apparently, while Mr. J. was hospitalized for the bowel resection, he threw a fire extinguisher at a window in the hallway. His wife reported that he was hollering at the nurses and going "mad" and that he needed to be restrained and medicated. Mr. J. was put on the antidepressant drug Effexor, and the antipsychotic drug Risperdal while in the hospital. After discharge from the hospital, he began follow-up psychiatric treatment with a psychiatrist. Mr. J. remained on the medication for six months. His wife reported: "Within a month after he came home from the hospital, he began to decay and would just sit around the house like a zombie."

Six months ago, Mr. J. had to give up his license as a pilot because of the decline in his memory and eyesight. At that point, he abruptly stopped taking the Effexor and Risperdol. He said: "I know the medicine was making me like a zombie and making me forget things. I couldn't get an appointment with the psychiatrist, he only saw me once after the surgery, so I just stopped taking it." Following this, Mr. J. began to become severely depressed and stated: "I just couldn't drink anything, I stopped drinking, I just stopped drinking fluids." This resulted in his admission to the hospital two months ago for dehydration. This was the only change noted in his appetite and nutrition history. Prior to hospitalization in January, his weight had not fluctuated in many years.

Additional History

Mr. J. denied any past or present substance abuse and any past psychiatric problems other than those mentioned. He said that he noticed that his memory has been declining for the past three years, and his wife reported the same. He denied any family history of psychiatric or physical problems, any past or present physical, sexual, or emotional abuse, and any suicidal and homicidal ideation. No paranoid ideation was reported. He denied allergies to any medications or foods and denied any weight loss or gain other than a "few pounds" prior to admission to the hospital for dehydration. He denied any problems with sleep, any problems growing up, and any history of trauma.

Family Situation and History

Mr. J. lives with his wife of sixty-two years in a large house in an upper-class suburban neighborhood. The couple is financially well off. The couple has two daughters, aged thirty-nine and forty-five, who both live in a different part of the country. Both daughters sell real estate, and Mr. J. said that they are "very successful." He stated that the family is "very close." Before his medical problems began, he and his wife would visit his daughters four times a year for two weeks at a time. He has been avoiding social functions and travel because of the shame and embarrassment of having to wear adult incontinence protection. Also, he fears losing bladder and bowel control and not being able to "find a bathroom in time."

Mr. J.'s only brother passed away eleven years ago. Mr. J. stated that since his medical problems began, all his "friends have disappeared." He has no nieces or nephews, and the only support comes from his wife.

Mr. J. depends on his wife for everything, and this is how it has been for all sixty-two years of their marriage. She handles all the finances, shopping, and appointments and remembers all the birthdays and important dates. She picks out all his clothes, dispenses his medication, and takes care of all his "physical and emotional needs." He stated that he is concerned for his wife, and he feels all his problems have become an "enormous stressful burden" to her.

Education History

Mr. J. stated that he stopped attending school at the end of ninth grade.

Employment History

Mr. J. owned and operated his own printing business for "fifty very successful years." He said he was a typesetter, which required great precision and detail. He stated that he was very "eye-hand coordinated" and was proud of his work. He began working in a print shop after he dropped out of high school. "I would go to the corner print shop and help out with odd jobs. In a short time, I learned the business, and when the owner retired, he helped me get started with my own business."

Current Diagnosis

After reviewing the intake assessment, the consulting psychiatrist evaluated Mr. J. Copies of lab work and other tests from admission were reviewed. Reversible causes for dementia were ruled out. The follow-up diagnosis was:

Axis I   290.43 vascular dementia with depressed mood
Axis II   Deferred
Axis III Cerebrovascular disease, prostate cancer s/p resection of
          prostate, bowel symptoms of unclear etiology
Axis IV   Moderate, stress of chronic illness
Axis V   Global Assessment of Functioning Scale: 37 with
          difficulties with memory and confusion at times

The psychiatrist planned and recommended retrieval of all medical records, a discussion with the admitting psychiatrist, strict medication monitoring, consideration of an anti-Alzheimer agent, a family meeting, a discussion with the primary physician, and five days of group therapy to help Mr. J. cope with memory and loss.

Summary

After reviewing the initial assessment with the psychiatrist, it is clear that Mr. J's dementia is irreversible. It is organic, resulting in symptoms of memory loss, depression, and cognitive decline. The psychosis was isolated to a one-time occurrence in the hospital, a superimposed delirium. The medication prescribed in the hospital was the origin of the vegetative symptoms of depression.

Current Medication

Effexor (antidepressant), 75 mg at lunchtime
Nitro Transpatch (heart), on in the morning and off in the evening
Colace (bowels), 100 mg at 9 p.m.
Multivitamin (supplement to diet), 1 in the morning
Mineral oil (bowels), 1 ounce in the evening

Mental Status Evaluation

Another type of assessment frequently used in mental health and family service agencies is a mental status evaluation (Lukas, 1993). The mental status exam is designed to be used with individual clients. "The purpose of the mental status exam is to assess the quality and range of perception, thinking, feeling, and psychomotor activity so that the practitioner can understand how behavior is or is not symptomatic of mental disorders" (Jordan & Franklin, 1995, p. 180). The exam is usually organized around different categories of client functioning, including appearance, attitude, speech, emotions, thought process, sensory perceptions, and mental capacities (see Appendix 5.6).

Appearance. This category concerns the individual's physical appearance. It includes dress, posture, body movements, and attitude. What is the overall impression of the client's appearance? Are there any unusual aspects of the client's appearance, posture, movements, or demeanor? Is the "client overly flamboyant, meticulous, bizarre, exceedingly sloppy and dirty" (Jordan & Franklin, 1995, p. 180)?

Speech.   Is there anything unusual about individual's speech? Does he or she speak unusually fast or slow? Is the volume appropriate? How is the tone and pattern of the client's speech? Are there any noticeable speech problems?

Emotions.   Emotions or feelings encompass two dimensions: affect and mood. *Affect* "refers to the way the client *shows* his emotions while he is with you, and it may or may not coincide with the internal state the client describes himself as feeling over time" (Lukas, 1993, p. 19). Is the client's affect flat or blunted, expressing little emotion? Does the client experience rapid shift in affect? Is the affect appropriate given the subject matter?

   Mood refers to how the client is feeling most of the time (Lukas, 1993, p. 8). Is the client happy, sad, angry, or what? Do the client's feelings appear to be appropriate given his or her situation? Are they understandable given the topic and the context?

Thought Process.   This refers to the client's judgment about the content of speech and thought (Jordan & Franklin, 1995). *Process* concerns how the client thinks. Is there a logical flow? Are the client's thoughts all jumbled together? Is there a coherent flow of ideas? Does the client have difficulty getting to the point in responding to your questions? Does the client keep repeating certain words or phases? Does the client have difficulty connecting ideas?

   Content refers to what the client says. Do the client's thoughts appear to be delusional? Does the client have thoughts that he or she believes to be true that you know absolutely to be untrue? Does the client have reoccurring thoughts that have an obsessive or compulsive quality?

Sensory Perceptions.   Sensory perceptions concern indications of illusion or hallucinations. "Illusions refer to normal sensory events that are misperceived" (Lukas, 1993, p. 25). Hallucinations are sensory experiences unrelated to external stimuli (Lukas, 1993). Are there clear distortions in the client's view of reality? If so, when and under what conditions do they occur?

Mental Capacities.   *Mental capacity* refers to orientation, intelligence, concentration, and memory. Orientation concerns time, place, and person. Does the client know the approximate time of day, the day of the week, and the year? Does the client know where he or she is and what his or her name is?

   What is the client's overall level of intelligence? Does the client appear to possess average, above average, or below average intelligence (Lukas, 1993)? Can the client concentrate and focus on what you are discussing? Is the client easily distracted? Is the client able to remember recent events? How is the client's long term memory? Can the client remember events from his or her past?

Attitude.   What kind of attitude does the client project toward his or her problem, the interview, and you? Is the client cooperative and forthcoming or uncooperative and withholding? Is the client overly aggressive or submissive? "If disturbed, how aware is the individual of his or her disturbance (Jordan & Franklin, 1995, p. 181)?

   Denise Bubel wrote this mental status evaluation of Mr. J. at the same time she wrote the biopsychosocial assessment presented earlier in this chapter.

Mental Status Evaluation   *Denise Bubel*

Theodore J. is an eighty-two-year-old Caucasian male. He was well groomed and very well dressed in appropriate, immaculate, casual attire that had been carefully coordinated. He sat in a slouched position, legs crossed, leaning to the left of his chair. He had swollen eyes and a washed-out complexion. His attitude was one of concern, and he appeared to be worried as exhibited by his facial expression and verbal presentation.

The volume of Mr. J.'s speech was low. His pace of speech was slow, and he presented slight psychomotor retardation. Mr. J. had difficulty recalling words to finish his thoughts and sentences but was able to formulate complete sentences.

Mr. J. was engaging but appeared to lack a positive self-image. His mood and affect were depressed. His perception of his problem, content of thought, and associations were appropriate.

The patient denied any hearing deficits, and none were noted. He denied visual or auditory hallucinations. His eyesight has significantly declined over the last two years, and this appeared to be of major concern to him. He wears glasses.

Mr. Jones was oriented to person but could not recall the name of the program he was in, the floor he was on, or the date. There were apparent deficits in his immediate memory. He appeared to be of average intelligence and had the ability to concentrate on the subject being discussed. However, he was not able to count backward by threes. Mr. J.'s recent memory appeared somewhat intact in relation to recent events. He was able to recall facts from his past, but he was not able to recall or trace a timeline. He remembered that he had surgery but he could not remember if it was two or three years ago. His insight and judgment did not appear to be impaired.

Although depressed, Mr. J. was polite and cooperative. He was easy to relate to and appeared capable of developing a helping relationship. Mr. J. appeared motivated to participate in the partial hospitalization program and to get help with his depression and memory loss.

GRAPHIC DISPLAYS

Four types of graphical tools display information in a picture or graphic format. They condense what would take many words to describe into a single image. Graphic displays are an effective way to summarize assessment information and present it in a format that is readily understandable to a wide range of clients. The four graphic displays presented here are plot forms, ecomaps, genograms, and sociograms.

Strengths and Obstacles Plot Form

The strengths and obstacles plot form shown in Figure 5.1 is a modified version of a plot form developed by Cowger (1994). It is used in conjunction with the strengths worksheets. Brief descriptions of the strengths and obstacles identified

FIGURE 5.1. Strengths and Obstacles Plot Form

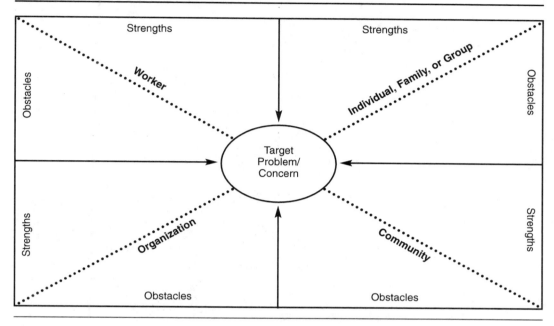

on the worksheets are written in the appropriate quadrants of the plot form. The completed form graphically summarizes the strengths and obstacles associated with the target problem. The value of this tool is that it succinctly summarizes all the identified strengths and obstacles on a single sheet of paper. It highlights in a concrete manner client strengths as well as obstacles that need to be overcome to resolve the identified target problem.

Ecomaps

Ecomaps graphically display the person-in-environment perspective. They show the ecological context of the client system (Hartman, 1995; Mattaini, 1993). Ecomaps focus on the relationships between the client and the major systems in the client's environment. The major systems vary by client. Typically, they include kin and friendship relationships, work, school, community and neighborhood organizations, the social worker, the agency, and other social service and health care organizations. An ecomap portrays the relevant systems, whether the relationships are positive or negative and strong or weak, and the direction or flow of energy and resources between the client and the other systems (Hartman, 1995).

Figure 5.2 illustrates a completed ecomap for an individual client system. The client system is a fifty-five-year-old African-American male named Harry M. He is divorced, has two adult children, lives alone, and is currently unemployed. He attends a partial hospitalization program for adults with mental health problems.

FIGURE 5.2. Ecomap of Individual Client System

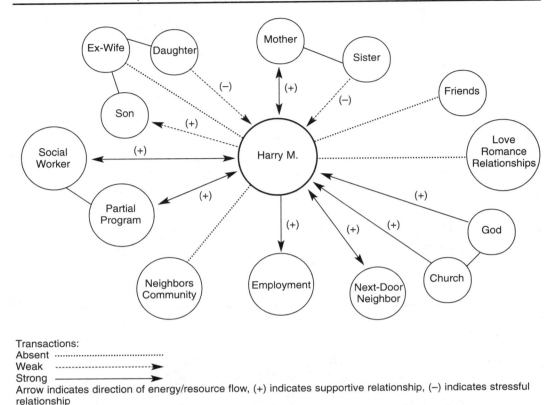

Transactions:
Absent ·····································
Weak ------------------------▶
Strong ——————————▶
Arrow indicates direction of energy/resource flow, (+) indicates supportive relationship, (−) indicates stressful relationship

The ecomap indicates that Mr. M. has strong mutually supportive relationships with the partial program, the social worker, his mother, and his next-door neighbor. He also receives support from his church, his belief in God, and his job. Mr. M. has a weak but supportive relationship with his son and weak stressful relationships with his sister and daughter. His relationship with his ex-wife is completely dissolved, and he does not have any romantic or friendship relationships or other connections with his neighbors and community.

Overall, Mr. M.'s person-in-environment shows a number of strengths or sources of support. He receives a great deal of support from formal associations, such as the partial program, his social worker, and his church. His informal support network appears to be limited to his mother and a next-door neighbor. His relationship with his ex-wife, his children, his sister, friends, and lovers are either weak or nonexistent.

Ideally, ecomaps are constructed in collaboration with the client. You begin by placing the client in the middle of the ecomap, and then identify the various personal and environmental systems with which the client interacts. After identifying all the relevant systems, discuss the nature of the transactions. The process encourages collaboration in the worker-client relationship (Hartman & Laird, 1983), and it helps you and the client describe the client's person-in-environment system to identify areas of strengths as well as sources of stress.

Ecomaps can also be used with family client systems. A family ecomap portrays the relevant systems within the family's environmental system. Like an individual ecomap, it indicates whether the relationships are positive or negative and strong or weak as well as the direction or flow of energy and resources between the family and the other systems. A family system ecomap is constructed the same way as an individual ecomap. The only difference is that the center of the map portrays the members of the family instead of an individual client.

Figure 5.3 illustrates a completed ecomap for a family client system. The family consists of a single mother and her two daughters, ages eleven and fifteen. The mother has requested help from a family service agency for problems she is having with the eleven-year-old daughter. She reports that the younger daughter is having problems in school and is acting out at home by not obeying her. She is disrespectful and defiant.

The ecomap shows that the mother has a stressful relationship with her younger daughter and a positive relationship with her older daughter, and that the two girls have a conflicted relationship. The father does not live with the family. He and the mother have no contact or ongoing relationship. The older daughter has a stressful relationship with her father, while the younger daughter feels close to him.

The identified patient is the eleven-year-old daughter. She is having problems in school and in her relationships with her mother and sister. Her mother is also concerned about the girl's friends. She feels that they are a negative influence on her daughter. On the positive side, the daughter is active in clubs and sports. She has a supportive relationship with her father.

The older sister is close to her mother, does well in school, and gets a great deal of satisfaction from her musical pursuits. On the negative side, she does not have any close friends, and her relationship with her father and sister is strained.

The mother has a supportive extended family network and derives a great deal of support from church-related activities. She also has a neighbor who is a source of support. Other than her neighbor, she does not have close friends, nor is she involved in the community beyond her church activities. Her relationship with the social worker and the family service agency at the time of the interview was weak but supportive, while her job was viewed as moderately stressful.

Genograms

Genograms graphically display information about family members over at least three generations (McGoldrick & Gerson, 1985). They are commonly used in assessments of family client systems. Basic types of information included in genograms are birth, gender, marriages, offspring, death, and household composition. "By highlighting

FIGURE 5.3. Ecomap of Family Client System

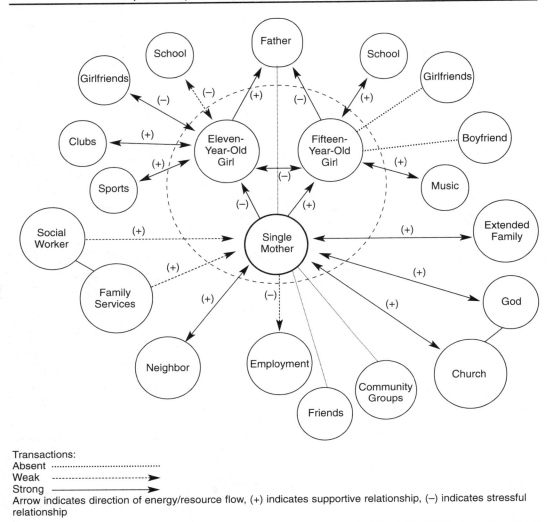

Transactions:
Absent ···
Weak -------------------------▶
Strong ───────────────────▶
Arrow indicates direction of energy/resource flow, (+) indicates supportive relationship, (−) indicates stressful relationship

contextual information, genograms aid our understanding of relationship patterns, transitional issues, and life cycle changes" (Miley, O'Melia, & DuBois, 1998, p. 242). Genograms are used to highlight cultural information about a family (Hardy & Laszloffy, 1995; McGill, 1992) and patterns of family strengths (Kuehle, 1995).

Genograms should be constructed in collaboration with family members. McGoldrick and Gerson (1985) recommend that gathering family information and constructing the genogram be part of the more general task of joining and helping the family. They suggest gathering information by casting the "information net" into wider and wider circles, moving from

- The presenting problem to the larger context of the problem
- The immediate household to the extended family and broader social systems

FIGURE 5.4. Genogram

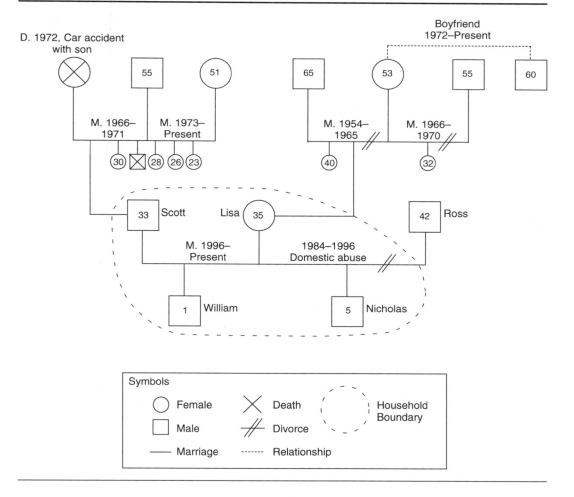

- The present family situation to a historical chronology of family events
- Easy, nonthreatening inquiries to difficult, anxiety-provoking questions
- Obvious facts to judgments about functioning
- Relationships to hypothesized family patterns.

The genogram in Figure 5.4 indicates that the family client system is composed of a husband and wife and two children. It is the second marriage for the wife, who has a five-year-old son from her first marriage, which ended in divorce because of domestic abuse. The couple's son is one year old.

The wife's mother divorced her first and second husbands and is currently in a longstanding relationship. The husband's mother died in a car accident, in which his younger brother also died. His father remarried and had three daughters with his second wife.

Sociograms

A group sociogram is similar to an ecomap. The ecomap describes a person-in-environment system; the sociogram describes the relationships among members of the group. Hartford's (1971) approach to sociogram construction examines attraction and repulsion between members of the group. It is a graphic representation of the alliances within a group. Usually, a worker constructs a sociogram based on observations of the group interactions. You include yourself in the sociogram. Doing so recognizes that you are part of the group-in-environment system and forces you to try to objectively analyze your relationships with each member of the group. Garvin and Seabury (1997) point out that discussion of alliances within groups creates anxiety and concerns about rejection. Therefore, sharing a sociogram with the group should be approached with caution. However, a sociogram can be an effective tool for helping group members understand the dynamics of the group and the effect of group alliances on a problem area or concern.

> The group shown in Figure 5.5 consists of six members—three males and three females—and the social worker. The sociogram shows that the social worker has strong positive relationships with members 3 and 5, weak positive relationships with members 1, 4, and 6, and a strong negative relationship with member 2. Members 3 and 6 are somewhat isolated. Each only has a strong relationship with one other member. Member 2 appears to be the informal leader of the group. He has strong positive relationships with members 1, 5, 3, and 4. He also appears to be in competition for leadership with the social worker, with whom he has a strong negative relationship.

SUMMARY

This chapter presented a number of tools that can be used to assess client systems. While traditional assessment tools focus on deficits and past history, most of the assessment tools presented here incorporate a strengths perspective. They are designed to help you and your clients organize relevant information in a way that promotes its integration and understanding. They are not designed as interview schedules in which the social worker asks structured questions. They complement the interview process and data gathering. The focus must remain on the client's telling his or her story, with the worker listening. Filling out the various types of forms should never be the focus of the assessment process.

The assessment tools provide the structure for a comprehensive assessment. The strengths-based assessment worksheets can be used to assess the strengths and obstacles of individual, family, group, organizational, and community client systems. The traditional biopsychosocial assessment form and mental status exam can be used for individual clients. Using a strengths-based approach in combination with a traditional biopsychosocial assessment provides a comprehensive picture of individual and family client systems.

FIGURE 5.5. Group Sociogram

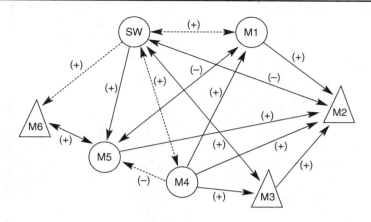

Transactions:

△ Male

◯ Female

Weak   - - - - - - - - - - - - - - - - ▸

Strong ───────────▸

Arrow indicates direction of energy/resource flow, (+) indicates supportive relationship, (−) indicates stressful relationship

The graphical tools can enhance the assessment process. Ecomaps and genograms are useful in obtaining information as well as in conveying the information back to clients in a form that is readily understandable. The plot form is an excellent tool for summarizing client system strengths and challenges from an ecosystem perspective. Finally, the sociogram is useful for assessing group communication problems and other aspects of group functioning.

CASE EXAMPLE

The following case example was written by Jennifer Francella when she was a first-year MSW student. Jennifer met with the family twice before completing the assessment. Together they completed the individual/family client systems–strengths-based assessment worksheet and the strengths and obstacles plot form. The case example illustrates a strengths-based family assessment.

Adjusting to Life Without Mom   *Jennifer Francella*

The K. family consists of the father, Bob, and three children, Sharon, Chad, and Jason. Ellen, Bob's wife and the children's mother, passed away eight months ago as a result of injuries she sustained in an automobile accident. Bob is forty-five years of age, Caucasian, and works in the banking industry.

Sharon is eighteen years old and a senior in high school. Chad is seventeen years of age and is currently a junior in high school. Jason is fifteen years of age and in the ninth grade. Chad has taken the death of his mother especially hard. This past year, he has been receiving failing grades in school and has been involved in numerous fights. He also has begun to experiment with drugs and alcohol. Ellen had been a constant source of support for Chad and the other children. However, the children describe Bob as not being supportive of them, and as having an especially stressful relationship with Chad.

In addition to the above problems, the family seems to not have allowed outsiders, even extended family members, help them deal with their grief and loss. Family traditions ended with Ellen's death, as did involvement with the church and other organizations. The family's emotional climate has become tense, and the family's communication patterns have been greatly altered since Ellen's death.

Bob and the children all recognize that, first and foremost, they need to deal with the sudden death of Ellen. They also acknowledge the need to deal with the strained relationship between Chad and his father and to strengthen Sharon's and Jason's relationships with their father. Chad has also agreed to receive help for his academic and behavioral problems at school.

The greatest obstacle facing the K. family is Ellen's absence. It is clear that she maintained the closest relationships with the children, led family traditions, was the mediator between Bob and the children, kept communication open, and allowed family boundaries to remain open to the outside world. Ellen was involved with the schools her children attended, the church she and the rest of the family attended weekly, and numerous community-wide events. Ellen also kept the lines of communication open between extended family members, including Bob's mother, siblings, and cousins.

Upon Ellen's death, the K. family seemed to completely "shut down." While Sharon's and Jason's performance at school has not changed as drastically as Chad's, the two children reported not feeling as good about themselves as they once did and also reported not wanting to continue participating in extracurricular activities.

Chad's sudden change in behavior and school performance is directly related to the death of his mother. His recent experimentation with drugs and alcohol is related to his mother's death and to the fact that alcoholism is prevalent in Ellen's family history. Ellen's father and brother are both recovering alcoholics. Chad, like the rest of his family, is dealing with Ellen's death in an unhealthy manner.

The weak relationships between Bob and his children had an effect before Ellen's death and now greatly affect the family's identified problem situation. Another obstacle the family faces is the fact that Bob never learned effective coping or parenting skills.

However, the K. family does have several strengths. All family members realize that there are definite obstacles and that no one has been dealing with Ellen's death in a healthy fashion. Chad appears to want to stop using drugs and alcohol and to change his recent behavior patterns at school. The children have expressed interest in maintaining strong and supportive relationships with their father. Bob has admitted that he never had a strong relationship with any of his children—or with his own father.

Another major strength is that the family wants to return to family traditions, change their emotional climate, open communication patterns, reset the family's boundaries, and utilize family resources. In addition, the children seem to have strong and supportive relationships among themselves, and extended family members have expressed an interest in being active participants in the lives of Bob, Sharon, Chad, and Jason. External strengths include a sincere desire by all family members to again become a part of their church, the community, and other associations.

DISCUSSION QUESTIONS

1. Critique the sample family assessment narrative on the K. family. What are the strengths of the assessment? Does it provide an adequate picture of the family situation? Is it comprehensive? Is there enough detail? What areas need to be strengthened? Is any critical information missing?
2. Discuss the use of assessment forms in the assessment process. In what ways can assessment forms facilitate the process? How might they hinder the process? In what ways are the pros and cons different for strengths-based forms and traditional problem-focused instruments? In what ways are they alike?
3. Discuss the use of ecomaps and genograms in the assessment process. In what ways can graphical tools facilitate the process? How might they hinder the process? How do assessment forms and graphical tools complement each other?
4. Review the family client system of the single mother and her two daughters portrayed in the sample ecomap. Develop at least two scenarios that describe the family dynamics of the case. Identify additional information that you need to complete the assessment. List specific questions about the case that you would like to have answered.
5. Critique the sample biopsychosocial assessment of Mr. J. What are its strengths? Does it provide an adequate picture of the case situation? Is it comprehensive? Is there enough detail? What areas need to be strengthened? Is there any critical information missing? What are the relevant client systems in this case? If you were assigned the case, what would you focus on? How would you proceed with the case?

REFERENCES

Cowger, C. (1994). Assessing client strengths: Clinical assessment for client empowerment. *Social Work, 39,* 262–267.

Fischer, J., & Corcoran, K. (1994). *Measures for clinical practice: A sourcebook* (Vols. 1–2, 2nd ed.). New York: Free Press.

Garvin, C., & Seabury, B. (1997). *Interpersonal practice in social work: Promoting competence and social justice* (2nd ed.). Boston: Allyn and Bacon.

Hardy, K., & Laszloffy, T. (1995). The cultural genogram: Key to training culturally competent family therapists. *Journal of Marriage and Family Therapy, 21,* 227–237.

Hartford, M. (1971). *Groups in social work.* New York: Columbia University Press.

Hartman, A. (1995). Diagrammatic assessment of family relationships. *Families in Society, 76,* 111–112.

Hartman, A., & Laird, J. (1983). *Family centered social work practice.* New York: Free Press.

Jordan, C., & Franklin, C. (1995). *Clinical assessment for social workers: Quantitative and qualitative methods.* Chicago: Lyceum.

Kuehle, B. (1995). The solution-oriented genogram: A collaborative approach. *Journal of Marital and Family Therapy, 21,* 239–250.

Lukas, S. (1993). *Where to start and what to ask: An assessment handbook.* New York: Norton.

Mattaini, M. (1993). *More than a thousand words: Graphics for clinical practice.* Washington, DC: NASW Press.

McGill, D. (1992). The cultural story in multicultural family therapy. *Families in Society, 73,* 339–349.

McGoldrick, M., & Gerson, R. (1985). *Genograms in family assessment.* New York: Norton.

Miley, K., O'Melia, M., & DuBois, B. (1998). *Generalist social work practice: An empowering approach* (2nd ed.). Boston: Allyn and Bacon.

Nurius, P., & Hudson, W. (1993). *Human service practice, evaluation, and computers.* Pacific Grove, CA: Brooks/Cole.

Reid, W. (1994). The empirical practice movement. *Social Service Review, 68,* 165–184.

Sheafor, B., Horejsi, C., & Horejsi, G. (1997). *Techniques and guidelines for social work practice* (4th ed.). Boston: Allyn and Bacon.

APPENDIX 5.1

Individual/Family Client Systems–Strengths-Based Assessment Worksheet

Client: _____ Worker: _____ Date: _____

> **INSTRUCTIONS:** Briefly describe to the best of your knowledge as many items on the worksheet as possible. Base your assessment on information you have obtained directly from your client and indirectly by your observations, case records, contacts with collaterals, and any other sources of information. The first page focuses on a description of the clients' concerns/problems situation. The remaining pages comprise an assessment of personal, family, and environmental factors. For each relevant factor, describe potential obstacles, strengths, and the effect on the problem situation.

Concerns/Problem Situation

Briefly summarize client concerns and/or problems that the client wants to address.

List concerns/problems in order of priority from highest to lowest.

Individual Factors

Subsystem	Obstacles	Strengths	Effect on Problem Situation
Motivation and Commitment			
Coping and Resourcefulness			
Values and Beliefs			
Developmental Life Stage			

Individual Factors, continued

Subsystem	Obstacles	Strengths	Effect on Problem Situation
Mental Health Status			
Health Status			
Employment/ Economic Status			
Interpersonal Relationships			

Family Factors

Subsystem	Obstacles	Strengths	Effect on Problem Situation
Structure and Subsystems			
Power and Authority			
Family Life-Cycle Stage			
Family Values and Beliefs			

Family Factors, continued

Subsystem	Obstacles	Strengths	Effect on Problem Situation
Family Rules and Myths			
Emotional Climate			
Communication Patterns			
Boundaries			

Environmental Factors

Subsystem	Obstacles	Strengths	Effect on Problem Situation
Work/School			
Clubs, Churches, and Associations			
Community/ Neighborhood			
Service Organization			

Environmental Factors, continued

Subsystem	Obstacles	Strengths	Effect on Problem Situation
Other Formal Services and Programs			
Other Factors and Considerations			

APPENDIX 5.2

Group Client Systems–Strengths-Based Assessment Worksheet

Group: _____ Worker: _____ Date: _____

INSTRUCTIONS: Briefly describe to the best of your knowledge as many items on the worksheet as possible. Base your assessment on information you have obtained directly from the group and indirectly by your observations. The first page focuses on a description of the areas of concern. The remaining pages comprise an assessment of internal and external group transactions. For each relevant factor, describe potential obstacles, strengths, and the effect on the problem situation.

Concerns/Problem Situation

Briefly summarize the problem areas or concerns.

List concerns/problems in order of priority from highest to lowest.

Subsystem	Obstacles	Strengths	Effect on Problem Situation
Purpose			
Structure (Size, Composition, Duration, Open or Closed)			
Life-Cycle Stage			

Subsystem	Obstacles	Strengths	Effect on Problem Situation
Culture (Values, Norms, Traditions)			
Alliances (Communication Patterns, Interpersonal Attractions, Power and Leadership)			
Tasks (Performance and Decision Making)			
Communication Patterns			

APPENDIX 5.3

Organizational Client Systems–Strengths-Based Assessment Worksheet

Organization: _____ Worker: _____ Date: _____

INSTRUCTIONS: Briefly describe to the best of your knowledge as many items on the worksheet as possible. Base your assessment on information you have obtained directly from key informants and indirectly by your observations. The first page focuses on a description of the areas of concern. The remaining pages comprise an assessment of organizational factors. For each relevant factor, describe potential obstacles, strengths, and the effect on the problem situation.

Concerns/Problem Situation

Briefly summarize the problem areas or concerns.

List concerns/problems in order of priority from highest to lowest.

Subsystem	Obstacles	Strengths	Effect on Problem Situation
Internal Policies and Procedures			
External Policies and Procedures			
Professional Staff Pattern			

Subsystem	Obstacles	Strengths	Effect on Problem Situation
Support Staff Pattern			
Workload			
Organizational Support			
Professional Autonomy			
Degree of Trust Among Administrators, Professional Staff and Support Staff			

APPENDIX 5.4
Community Client Systems—Strengths-Based Assessment Worksheet

Community: _____   Worker: _____   Date: _____

> **INSTRUCTIONS:** Briefly describe to the best of your knowledge as many items on the worksheet as possible. Base your assessment on information you have obtained directly from key informants and indirectly by your observations. The first page focuses on a description of the areas of concern. The remaining pages comprise an assessment of community factors. For each relevant factor, describe potential obstacles, strengths, and the effect on the problem situation.

Concerns/Problem Situation

Briefly summarize the problem areas or concerns.

List concerns/problems in order of priority from highest to lowest.

Subsystem	Obstacles	Strengths	Effect on Problem Situation
Ethnicity and Culture (Community Values and Beliefs)			
Employment			
Housing			

Subsystem	Obstacles	Strengths	Effect on Problem Situation
Transportation			
Education			
Recreation			
Crime and Safety			
Social Services			
Churches and Religious Organizations			

APPENDIX 5.5
Biopsychosocial Assessment Form

Client: _____ Worker: _____ Date: _____

(Indicate NA if problem does not exist or apply)

Problem Situation (Client's perception of the problem situation)

History of Problem Situation (Duration, intensity, stressors, coping methods, change)

Mental Health History (Sequence and description of past symptoms and treatment)

Substance Abuse History (Age of onset, specific drugs, extent of abuse, family history, treatment)

Physical Health and Developmental History (Current and prior medical problems, family history)

Current Medications (Medications, dosage, schedule, reason, length of time)

Nutrition/Appetite (Weight gain or loss, appetite, changes)

Current or Prior History of Physical, Sexual, and/or Emotional Abuse

Family Situation and History (Current living situation, family relationships)

Employment History

Education History (Highest level completed, academic and behavioral functioning)

Diagnosis

APPENDIX 5.6
Mental Status Exam

Client: _____ Worker: _____ Date: _____

(Be specific; if no problem exists in an area, indicate N/A)

_____

Appearance (Dress, posture, body movement, attitude)

_____

Speech (Speed, volume, pattern, tone)

_____

Emotions (Affect, mood)

_____

Thought Process (Content, perception, associations)

_____

Sensory Perceptions (Hearing, sight, hallucinations)

_____

Mental Capacities (Person, place, time, intelligence, concentration, memory)

_____

Attitude

CHAPTER 6

Developing Goals, Objectives, and the Intervention and Evaluation Plan

on A., who is in his second year of a three-year part-time MSW program, has a worksite field placement at an Area Agency on Aging. Ron had worked at the agency for three years before he began his graduate studies. He is a case manager for elderly clients. In this role, he oversees the delivery and coordination of the various services being provided to the clients. As part of his field placement duties, Ron visits the elderly person in his or her home and completes a comprehensive assessment that is the basis for the development of the client's case management plan.

Ron met with his first field placement client twice and completed the agency assessment form. He obtained all the necessary information and felt that he had a beginning relationship with his client and that he had a clear understanding of his client's concerns and service needs.

In his job as a case manager, Ron had worked with clients in implementing their case management plans, but he had never been involved in developing one with a client. He was unsure how to proceed. How much say did the client have in setting the goals and objectives? What goals should the client focus on? How should the goals be written? How should progress be evaluated? What action steps would need to be taken to achieve the client's goals?

The assessment and planning phase of the helping process focuses on identifying client concerns and strengths, clarifying roles and the helping process, and helping clients prioritize their concerns. The emphasis is on gaining an understanding of the client's situation, helping the client sort through and articulate his or her concerns, and strengthening or establishing a relationship. Although there is a logical progression to the assessment process, it rarely proceeds in a linear fashion. The order of accomplishing the various tasks associated with the assessment and planning stage is relatively unimportant. What is critical is accomplishing the tasks and gaining a clear understanding of the client's concerns and situation. This has to be accomplished before moving to the action phase of the helping process.

The action phase focuses on developing goals and objectives, developing the intervention and evaluation plan, implementing the plan, and ending the helping process. The development of goals and objectives naturally follows the identification of priorities. Selecting one or two goals to work on requires making a decision about priorities. The same applies to the subsequent steps in the action phase. A prior task must be completed before the next step in the process can be completed. Although the work in the action phase requires a sequential progression, the work usually moves back and forth between the various tasks.

This chapter focuses on the initial action phase of the helping relationship. In this phase, the worker and client develop a contract that specifies the target problem; the goals and objectives of the helping process; the intervention plan, which outlines the various activities and actions that will be undertaken; and how the effectiveness of the intervention will be evaluated (Maluccio & Marlow, 1974; Seabury, 1976). The chapter describes the process of developing measurable goals and objectives and creating an intervention and evaluation plan. Information on a range of interventions used by generalist social workers is provided in Chapter 7.

By the end of this chapter, you should be able to help Ron

1. Describe the difference between goals and objectives
2. Write measurable case objectives
3. Construct self-anchored rating scales and goal attainment scales
4. Adopt client logs and behavioral observation for use in measuring client progress
5. Locate standardized measures that are appropriate for use with social work clients
6. Interpret the reliability and validity of standardized measures
7. Design a single-system evaluation to monitor client progress
8. Plot single-system evaluation data on a line graph
9. Interpret the clinical, visual, and statistical significance of single-system evaluation data
10. Develop an intervention and evaluation plan for a client system.

DETERMINING GOALS

Client goals are derived directly from client problems and concerns. The assessment process focuses on identifying the areas of concern that clients want to address in the helping process. It also identifies client system strengths and resources. The contracting process follows this up by focusing on what the client system hopes to accomplish. Problems are negative statements about the client's current situation, while goals are positive statements about what the client's situation will be after the identified problem has been resolved or ameliorated (Bloom, Fischer, & Orme, 1995, p. 74).

Purpose of Goals

Goals serve multiple purposes. Reid (1970) found that social workers who were overly general in specifying goals were less effective than those who set clear and specific goals. Cases with vague and very general goals were characterized by frequent shifts in direction and focus. Thus, one of the major purposes of goals is to set the direction for the work.

Specifying goals ensures that the client and the worker are in agreement about what is expected. Without specific goals, the client and worker may have different expectations about what needs to be accomplished.

Goals help facilitate the development of the intervention and evaluation plan. They help determine appropriate tasks and activities that will be undertaken to address the identified target problems and concerns. Goals provide benchmarks for monitoring client progress and criteria for assessing outcomes. Without clear and specific goals, it is impossible for the worker or the client to determine whether progress is being made and whether a desired end has been attained. Without goals, you do not know where you are going, and consequently you cannot tell when or whether you have gotten there. "Goals provide the standard or frame of reference for evaluating whether or not the client is moving, and whether or not the destination is met" (Bloom, Fischer, & Orme, 1995, p. 74). In summary, goals

- Provide direction to the helping process
- Ensure agreement between the client and worker about the desired end state of the helping process
- Facilitate the development of the intervention and evaluation plan
- Provide benchmarks to judge progress
- Provide outcome criteria for evaluating the effectiveness of the intervention and the helping process.

Goals and Objectives

Goals are positive statements about desired ends. In fairly broad terms they describe the hoped-for end result of the helping process. They represent the client system's ultimate outcome for the resolution of the identified target problem. Goals have also been called *"ultimate goals"* (Rosen, 1993) and "long-term goals" (Goldstein, 1973; Jongsma & Peterson, 1995).

Goal statements do not need to be measurable (Jongsma & Peterson, 1995), but can be global statements of a desired positive outcome. Figure 6.1 provides examples of target problems and related goal statements for various client systems.

It is usually not possible to go directly from a problem to the accomplishment of broadly worded goals (Bloom, Fischer, & Orme, 1995). Instead, clients often must move through a series of measurable steps in order to reach the goal (Sheafor, Horejsi, & Horejsi, 1994).* These intermediate steps are commonly referred to as *objectives* (Kirst-Ashman & Hull, 1993). Objectives are subgoals that lead to the achievement of the long-term goal. They are the steps the client must take to arrive at the desired outcome or problem resolution. Well-written objectives answer the following questions:

"**1.** Who?
"**2.** Will do what?
"**3.** To what extent?
"**4.** Under what conditions?
"**5.** By when?" (Sheafor, Horejsi, & Horejsi, 1994, pp. 345–346)

*From B. W. Sheafor, C. R. Horejsi, & G. A. Horejsi, *Techniques and Guidelines for Social Work Practice* 3/E. Copyright © 1994 by Allyn & Bacon. Reprinted/adapted by permission.

FIGURE 6.1. Sample Goal Statements

Client System	Target Problem	Goal
Individual	I lose my temper with my teenage son	To be able to control my temper when dealing with my teenage son
Family	Family discussions always turn into shouting matches and arguments	To improve the family's ability to communicate without resorting to shouting and screaming
Group	Members of the support group do not trust one another	To have members of the support group develop a sense of trust
Organization	School system is unable to help children deal with family problems that affect school performance	To improve the school system's ability to help children with family problems
Community	Community and neighborhood groups are unwilling to work together to address community problems	To have community and neighborhood groups join together in addressing community problems

Objectives are specific and measurable. They describe in very concrete terms exactly what will be accomplished. Figure 6.2 presents examples of objectives that answer the above five questions. The examples illustrate the relationship between goals and objectives as well as their differences. The relationship between target problems, goals, and objectives is illustrated in Figure 6.3.

Selecting and Defining Objectives

Several factors should be kept in mind when selecting and formulating objectives (Hepworth, Rooney, Larsen, 1997; Siporin, 1975). First and foremost, objectives should be steps towards goals, and progress should be incremental. Objectives are the intermediate steps that clients need to accomplish to ultimately reach their goals.

Objectives also need to be feasible. Try to help clients set objectives that are realistic given the available resources and abilities. Make sure the objectives are obtainable.

Whenever possible, write objectives in positive language. State what will be accomplished rather than what will be eliminated (Bloom, Fischer, & Orme, 1995). Use words that describe specific behaviors. Describe what the client will actually do (or think or feel) to achieve the objective.

The activities should be measurable and, if possible, observable. In Figure 6.2, all the objectives describe behaviors that are measurable and observable. For example, in objective 1 for the individual client system, the father will wait ten seconds and take three deep breaths before responding to his son. This behavior is both observable and measurable. It would be relatively easy to measure the extent to which the father has been successful in achieving this objective.

FIGURE 6.2. Sample Objectives

Individual Client System Goal: *To be able to control my temper when dealing with my teenage son.*

- **Objective 1:** I (*who*) will wait ten seconds and take three deep breaths (*what*) 80 percent of the time (*to what extent*) that I have a conversation with my son that I find upsetting (*under what conditions*) by August 30 (*by when*).
- **Objective 2:** *I* (*who*) will express my feelings to my son (*what*) 80 percent of the time (*to what extent*) that I find our conversation upsetting (*under what conditions*) by August 30 (*by when*).

Community Client System Goal: *To have community and neighborhood groups join together in addressing community problems.*

- **Objective 1:** Representatives of the West End Neighborhood Association, the Community Action Association, the United Neighbors Block Club, and the Community Residents Coalition (*who*) will meet (*what*) at least twice (*to what extent*) to discuss the possibility of forming a Community Coordinating Council (*under what conditions*) before November 10 (*by when*).
- **Objective 2:** Representatives of the West End Neighborhood Association, the Community Action Association, the United Neighbors Block Club, and the Community Residents Coalition (*who*) will create a Community Coordinating Council (*what*) that will hold monthly community meetings (*to what extent*) devoted to sharing information and coordinating community improvement efforts (*under what conditions*) by February 28 (*by when*).

Another consideration in constructing objectives is to avoid confusing input with outcome (Sheafor, Horejsi, & Horejsi, 1994). A common mistake is to state objectives, especially direct service objectives, in terms of what the client will be receiving rather than in terms of a desired outcome. For example, stating that "the father will obtain counseling to help him deal with his temper problem" is both observable and measurable. However, the objective is not stated in performance terms and says nothing about the desired outcome. It is possible that the father could attend counseling and show no improvement in his temper problem. Or, on the other hand, he may make tremendous progress. However, the objective would not provide any basis for evaluating his progress. In this situation, obtaining counseling is a means to an end. It is not the desired end in itself. A desired outcome of the counseling needs to be specified for the objective to be used to help evaluate the father's progress in controlling his temper.

Another important consideration is for the objectives to be commensurate with your knowledge and skill level. "Certain problems and goals require higher levels of expertise that you may not yet have attained, and it is your responsibility to clients, the profession, and yourself not to undertake interventions for which you lack competence" (Hepworth, Rooney, & Larsen, 1997, pp. 348–349). Recognize your limitations, and when appropriate help your clients obtain the specialized services needed to address the identified target problems or concerns.

The final consideration concerns the mission and function of your agency. The objectives you and your clients develop should be consistent with the functions of

FIGURE 6.3. Relationship Between Target Problem, Goals, and Objectives

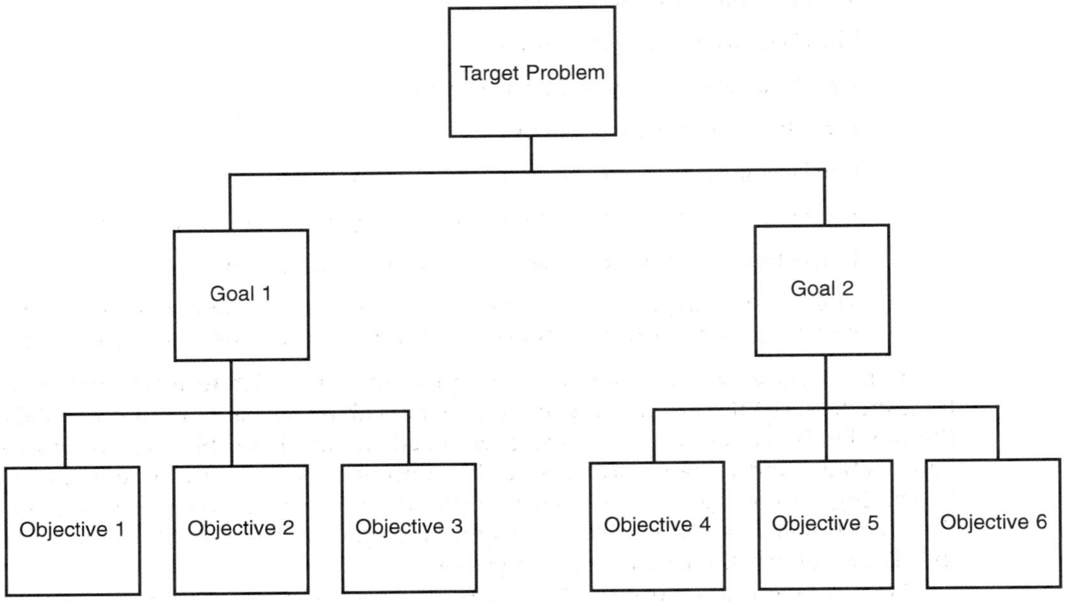

your agency. Are the client's service needs beyond the scope of activities and services provided by the agency? If so, referral to another agency or service provider for those services is the appropriate course of action.

In summary, effective objectives should be

1. Steps towards goals
2. Realistic and attainable
3. Observable and measurable
4. Stated in positive terms that emphasize outcomes
5. Acceptable to both clients and workers
6. Commensurate with the knowledge and skill of the practitioner
7. Consistent with the functions of the agency.

Goals, Objectives, and the Helping Relationship

Developing goals and objectives is a collaborative process. It is an extension of the assessment process. The first step is to help your client identify areas of concern that need to be addressed. A comprehensive assessment will identify a number of potential target problems. Review the list of concerns that you developed earlier with your client, and prioritize the list in terms of those that are most pressing and are most important to the client. Together determine which concern or problem has the highest priority. Bloom, Fischer, and Orme suggest negotiating with the client so as to work first on the problem that meets as many of the following criteria as possible:

The problem is one that:

The client prefers to start with;

The client has the greatest concern;

Has the greatest likelihood of being changed;

Is relatively concrete and specific;

Can be readily worked on given the available resources;

Has the greatest chance of producing the most negative consequences if not handled;

Has to be handled before other problems can be tackled; and

Will result in tangible, observable changes for those involved, thereby perhaps increasing the participants' motivation to work on other problems. (1995, p. 68)

It is critical to select only one or two problems on which to work. Failure to limit the focus of the work to one or two manageable areas is a common mistake (Bloom, Fischer, & Orme, 1995). The client needs to divide problems into component sections and to begin addressing the concerns one step at a time. It can be frustrating, discouraging, and disheartening to take on a number of problems at the same time or to take on one vaguely defined large problem. Either can make the client feel that the task is unmanageable.

Having selected the priority target problem, the next step is to write down at least one goal for each problem. Use the client's words, no matter how vague they are (Mager, 1972). It is important for the client to have ownership of the goals. The goal statements should reflect the client's expectations about the desired changes in the client's own words.

After developing one or two goals for each target problem, the next step is to construct specific objectives for each goal. Every effort should be made to construct objectives that satisfy the seven criteria presented earlier. Mager (1972) suggests brainstorming with the client and writing down all the things that the client could say or do to attain the goal. This process allows the client to contribute to the identification of possible solutions. Ideally, the client will identify the activities. Encourage your clients to put forth ideas. Give them the opportunity to express their opinions. Your job is to help them identify solutions, not to provide the solutions. At the very least, finding solutions should be a joint activity. At this point, you are focusing on the *what* component of the objective. Review all the possibilities. Is the potential solution realistic and obtainable? Is it observable and measurable? Is it a step toward the broader goal? Select the two or three activities that seem most promising and satisfy the criteria.

The next task is to determine a level of performance for each activity. This is the *to what extent* component of the objectives. The client should determine the level of performance. What does the client consider a reasonable level of success? What level of progress is satisfactory? Do not set the performance standards so high that achieving them seems unrealistic and improbable. It is better to have modest successes and to take small steps toward the desired result than to aim too high and fail.

After determining the performance level for each activity, discuss the timetable (*by when*) and the situations in which the changes are expected to occur (*under what conditions*). Make sure you and the client are clear about the specific conditions under which the expected changes are to occur. Are you and your client in agreement about the conditions under which the changes will take place? Are the specified conditions related to the target problem or concern? Is the timetable realistic?

You are now ready to craft specific objectives. Under each goal, write the objectives related to that goal. Use the client's words as much as possible. Make sure each objective states who will do what, to what extent, under what conditions, and by when. Review each objective. Revise as needed until both you and the client are comfortable with the objective and in complete agreement about what is expected.

EVALUATING PROGRESS

After developing goals and objectives, the next step is to develop a measurement plan. You and the client need to specify exactly how you will assess progress and evaluate the effectiveness of the interventions you will be implementing. Skill in designing and utilizing quantitative measures has become of critical importance in recent years (Franklin & Jordan, 1992). Funding sources, such as managed care companies, require social workers and other helping professionals to provide evidence of client problems and of the effectiveness of services provided. Skill in measurement is needed to comply with this requirement. The practice environment in which generalist social workers find themselves requires a higher level of accountability than at any other time in our professional history. It is no longer acceptable to rely solely on professional judgment in determining client service needs and in evaluating client progress.

There are also compelling ethical reasons to measure client progress. Social workers have an ethical responsibility to provide the best services available to their clients. You are responsible for making sure the services you are providing are helping your clients. To assume that what you are doing is working without systematically evaluating effectiveness is unethical. If the client is not making progress, both of you need to know so that you can address the lack of progress and, if appropriate, change the intervention (Berlin & Marsh, 1993).

Evaluation can also help motivate clients. If the client is making progress, having concrete evidence can strengthen his or her resolve to make further gains. Conversely, evidence of lack of progress can be a wake-up call, a challenge to renew commitment to change. Measuring progress forces you and the client to take stock. Are we making progress? Are the interventions working? Do we need to try another approach?

A common concern about measurement is that clients will react negatively and that it will disrupt the helping relationship (Witkin, 1991). Research has determined that this is not the case. Campbell (1988, 1990) found that clients prefer to systematically evaluate the effectiveness of the services they receive rather than to rely solely on practitioner opinion. Applegate (1992) also found that this concern was not justified. Indeed, Poulin and Young (1997) found that clients placed a higher value on evaluation procedures than did their social workers. Social workers tended to underestimate the importance clients placed on evaluating progress. They were much more interested in developing and implementing interventions than in evaluating effectiveness. Clients, on the other hand, were as interested in evaluating effectiveness as they were in developing and implementing interventions. A follow-up qualitative study obtained similar results (Young & Poulin, 1998), finding clients more concerned about evaluation than social workers. The message from these studies is clear: it is a mistake to assume that clients will resist measurement procedures and that they do not care about assessing and measuring progress. Clients of social work services, like other consumers, want to know that the services they are receiving are effective.

Measurement Guidelines

Jordan and Franklin state that "competence in measurement will improve social work's status, power base, and the profession's ability to function autonomously" (1995, p. 40). It will also improve the effectiveness of your practice and strengthen the helping relationship (Young & Poulin, 1998). Collaborative social work practice seeks to empower clients, and evaluation should be a collaborative activity. Having clients involved in the development of the measurement plan and in constructing measures is empowering. For this reason, it is best to use measures that involve the client in the data collection process.

Drawing on the work of Barlow, Hayes, and Nelson (1984), Berlin and Marsh developed guidelines for collecting client data. They suggest that the data collection effort will be enhanced if you:

Specify the client's problems and goals clearly;

Use multiple measures for each objective;

Collect information that is relevant rather than convenient;

Collect information early in the course of the work with the client;

Use good and accurate measures;

Organize the data; and

Obtain the client's cooperation and consent. (1993, p. 93)

Clearly Specify Problems and Goals. This guideline is fundamental to the measurement process. As noted earlier, client problems and expected outcomes must be specified and stated in clear, unambiguous terms. Measurable objectives related to each goal must be developed. The task of collecting client data is impossible to accomplish without specific and observable indicators attached to each objective (Berlin & Marsh, 1993).

Use Multiple Measures. The use of more than one measure to assess a single phenomenon is a basic research strategy referred to as "triangulation" (Royse & Thyer, 1996). The assumption behind this strategy is that all measures are to some extent flawed or imperfect. Since any one measure may not be adequate, it is necessary to use more than one measure to assess client progress. The reasoning is that if two or more imperfect measures indicate change, there is more reason to be confident that change has occurred than if only one imperfect measure is used. Relying on a single measure of client progress is risky. The problems addressed by generalist social workers and their clients are too complex to be assessed with a single imperfect measure.

Our inability to accurately measure client progress should not discourage you from attempting to utilize quantitative measures in your practice. Crude indicators of progress, are preferable to no indicators. What is important to keep in mind is the limitations of measurement tools. The data alone will not provide you and your clients with definitive answers. It will, however, provide you and your clients with helpful information that can be incorporated into your work together. Analyzing the data with your clients will facilitate the helping process and provide a basis for ongoing assessment of your work together.

Collect Relevant Information.   Berlin and Marsh warn that "one of the most frequent mistakes that clinicians make is to track something that is not very important" (1993, p. 94). Typically, the client's problem is reconceptualized to fit an existing measure or instrument. The convenience factor is high, but the relevance factor is low. "If the clinician is to collect useful information, he or she must look beyond the enticements of easily acquired, but barely relevant, assessment indices and focus on whether the aspects of the problem targeted for change are really changing" (Berlin & Marsh, 1993, p. 95). If you can not specify the expected changes, perhaps the problem has not been conceptualized accurately or in specific enough terms. Relevant measures should flow directly from well-conceptualized problems and objectives.

Collect Information Early.   There are a number of reasons to begin the process of collecting data early in the helping process. One is that measuring the target problem or objectives prior to implementing the intervention provides baseline data, which are a basis for comparison. Change must be evaluated comparatively. Without some sort of comparison, it is impossible to assess the extent to which the desired changes have occurred. Collecting assessment data early in the helping process will allow you to periodically evaluate the effectiveness of the work throughout the helping relationship.

A second reason to begin collecting data early in the helping process is to communicate to clients that you are interested in understanding their situation and that you are committed to helping them successfully address their concerns or problems. Measurement is an active and concrete process. Developing measures communicates that you are serious about their concerns and that their concerns are important enough to warrant the effort required to develop measures and collect data.

A third reason to start the measurement process early is that it engages the client in a collaborative activity. You and the client define the target problem, develop the objectives, and develop the measurement plan. You and your clients may even develop many of the measures used. The client becomes an active participant in the process. This communicates expectations about how you will work together as well as the idea that the client is the expert on his or her situation.

Use Good and Accurate Measures.   Every effort should be made to use the best measures available. According to Berlin and Marsh (1993) four criteria are useful in judging the adequacy of different measures: relevance, sensitivity to change, reliability, and validity.

Relevance refers to the extent the measure is directly related to the targeted outcomes. Is there a good fit between the measure and the expected changes? For example, one of the objectives for the father who was having trouble controlling his temper was to count to ten and take three deep breaths before responding to his son. In this situation, a measure of how many times the father counted to ten and took three deep breaths would be directly relevant and very appropriate. Measuring how often he refrained from yelling at his son might appear to be an appropriate measure, but it would in fact be less relevant given the change objective. If the treatment objective was to increase the father's self-control, then a self-control measure would be directly relevant. The relevance of any measure is a function of the identified target problem and/or the specific change objectives.

Sensitivity to change is the second criterion of a good measure. Not all measures are capable of capturing change. Some are more sensitive than others. It may be possible to use measures that have shown change in previous evaluations and have thus proved themselves. A measure's track record of detecting change is one of the best indicators of its sensitivity to change (Berlin & Marsh, 1993; Bloom, Fischer, & Orme, 1995). Often, however, information on a measure's sensitivity is not available.

It is not always possible to know in advance whether a measure will be sensitive to change (Bloom, Fischer, & Orme, 1995). Berlin and Marsh (1993) suggest that global measures are usually less sensitive to change than measures directly related to specific behaviors targeted for change. Bloom, Fischer, and Orme state that measures of behaviors that occur more frequently are more likely to be more sensitive than measures of behaviors that occur less frequently. "This is because a high-frequency behavior is likely to be more responsive to small changes and can both increase or decrease, while a low-frequency behavior can only increase and may be responsive only to major changes" (1995, p. 52).

Reliability refers to the consistency of measurements. "In testing for change, at least two and preferably more measurements are required" (Gabor, Unrau, & Grinnell, 1998, p. 165). When measuring for client change, you want to be reasonably confident that the differences between the first measurement and the subsequent ones are due to changes in the client and not to problems with the measure. "It is therefore important that a measuring instrument gives the same result with the same unchanged client every time it is administered. An instrument that can do this is said to be reliable" (Gabor, Unrau, & Grinnell, 1998, p. 165).

"Every type of measure involves some kind of error, and the measure is reliable to the extent that the error is minimal" (Berlin & Marsh, 1993, p. 97). The two most common ways of testing the reliability of a measure are to assess its internal consistency and test-retest characteristics. *Internal consistency reliability* is the extent to which the individual items that make up a scale or index are correlated with one another. *Test-retest reliability* refers to the extent to which the same result is obtained when the same measure is administered to the same client at two different points in time. Both types of reliability are important. However, in evaluating client change, test-retest reliability is critical. To the extent possible, use at least one measure that has been tested for reliability and has reliability coefficients of .80 or higher.

Validity refers to the extent to which an instrument measures what it is supposed to measure and not anything else (Kyte & Bostwick, 1997). For example, if you are assessing a client's self-confidence, the instrument should measure self-confidence, not a related concept such as self-esteem. "An instrument is said to be *valid* when it closely corresponds to the concept it was designed to measure" (Royse & Thyer,

1996, p. 188). Because concepts in social work tend to be complex, no measure will be entirely valid, only more or less so (Gabor, Unrau, & Grinnell, 1998).

There are various ways to determine the validity of an instrument. The least rigorous kind of validity is *face validity.* Does the instrument appear to measure the concept? A measure is said to have face validity if knowledgeable persons agree that it measures what it is intended to measure. "Do the items on the questionnaire appear to be 'getting at' what they should?" (Bloom, Fischer, & Orme, 1995, p. 187)

Another type of validity is *content validity.* This method also relies on expert opinion. In this case, "experts are asked to review it to see if the entire range of the concept is represented in the sample of items selected for the scale" (Royse & Thyer, 1996, p. 188). For example, a scale designed to measure stress should have items that represent the different components of stress, such as feeling tense, feeling pressured, having difficulty sleeping, and being shorted-tempered.

"Neither content nor face validity is sufficient for establishing that a scale has 'true' validity" (Royse & Thyer, 1996, p. 188). For this to occur, a measure must empirically demonstrate its validity. There are a number of methods to empirically demonstrate a measure's validity. *"Concurrent validity* is demonstrated by administering to the same subjects the new scale and another scale that has previously been determined (proven) to have validity" (Royse & Thyer, 1996, p. 188). If the two scales are highly correlated, at .80 or above, the new scale has demonstrated concurrent validity.

Predictive validity refers to the ability of a measure to predict future behavior or attitudes. "The simplest way to determine predictive validity would be to correlate results on a measure one time with the criterion information collected at a later time" (Bloom, Fischer, & Orme, 1995, p. 49). An example is correlating SAT scores with students' grade point averages.

Construct validity refers to the extent to which an instrument actually measures the concept in question. Construct validity is established by demonstrating convergent validity and discriminant validity. A measure is said to have *convergent validity* if it is correlated in a predicted manner with other measures with which it theoretically should correlate (Bloom, Fischer, & Orme, 1995). For example, a measure of the strength of a helping relationship should correlate positively with measures of trust and openness. Those who are more trusting and open are more likely to develop strong helping relationships with their social workers than those who are less trusting and open.

A measure's *discriminant validity* is demonstrated by a lack of correlation with measures with which it theoretically should not be correlated. This indicates that the measure can discriminate between concepts. For example, there is no theoretical basis for predicting a relationship between client problems and the development of a helping relationship with the social worker. Clients with high self-esteem are as likely to develop a strong helping relationship as those with low self-esteem. Similarly, a client's level of depression is not associated with the strength of the helping relationship.

Construct validity is demonstrated when a measure is correlated with other measures that it theoretically should be related to (convergent validity) and not correlated with measures with which it theoretically should not be correlated (discriminant validity). In selecting measures to evaluate client change, look for some evidence of the validity of the measure. At the very least, the measure should have face validity. Evidence of empirical verification of the measure's validity is preferable.

FIGURE 6.4. Client's Weekly Self-Esteem Scores

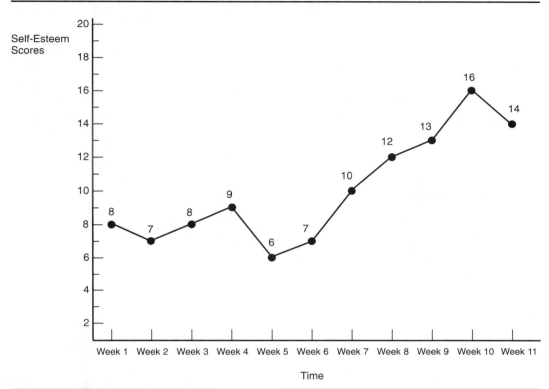

Organize the Data.   For data to be useful, they have to be organized in some systematic way. It is difficult to interpret or draw meaning from unorganized raw data. Data need to be presented in a way that makes sense to both you and your client. Typically, data obtained to evaluate client change can be easily computed and presented in simple graphs.

The basic graphic presentation of change data is a line graph on which the client's scores are plotted over time. A visual inspection of the data points provides feedback on client progress. Time is plotted on the horizontal (*x*) axis, and the scores on the measure of the target problem are plotted on the vertical (*y*) axis of the graph. The time dimension reflects the number of times the measure of the target problem is completed and the time period between measurements. The time unit selected depends on the nature of the target problem. Typically, measures of the target problem are completed on a daily or weekly basis. Figure 6.4 shows a sample line graph in which a client's level of self-esteem is plotted over an eleven-week period.

An important component of the helping process is to review the data that have been collected and organized in graphical displays with clients. In collaborative social work, the clients are actively involved in inspecting the organized data and interpreting the patterns and results. Most clients are interested in examining graphs of their progress and in providing interpretations of what is happening. Involving clients in this process can be a powerful tool. It keeps your work focused on the change objectives, and it provides an opportunity for you and the client to review progress, tasks, and effort as well as the appropriateness of goals and objectives. If strides are being made, it can motivate further efforts. If progress is not forthcoming, you and the client can assess the situation and make adjustments as needed.

Obtain Client Cooperation and Consent.   Naturally, the process of selecting and incorporating measurement strategies into your generalist practice requires the full cooperation of your clients. Collaborative social work is based on the assumption that clients are full partners in the helping process. Measuring client progress without their full cooperation is a waste of time. Clients need to have ownership of the measures and willingness to engage in a process of self-assessment. Their commitment to the data collection and evaluation process reflects their commitment to achieving the changes they are seeking.

Measurement Tools

There are a number of measurement methods that involve clients, are easy to construct and implement, and are appropriate for generalist social work practice. Among the more frequently used methods are

- Client logs
- Behavioral observation
- Rating scales
- Goal attainment scales
- Standardized measures.

Client Logs.   Having clients prepare narrative accounts of their activities, thoughts, and/or feelings is an effective method of monitoring progress. Client logs or journals help clarify the nature of client problems and the circumstances that contribute to the problem situation. Clients often find that keeping a log helps them increase their understanding and awareness of the factors that contribute to the identified problem situation. It enables them to "track the antecedents and consequences, or the feelings and thoughts, surrounding the occurrence of a specific event" (Berlin & Marsh, 1993, p. 99). Client logs allow a client to systematically take notes on the occurrence of a target problem and the events surrounding each occurrence. Doing so reduces the possibility of distortions and misperceptions due to faulty memory (Bloom, Fischer, & Orme, 1995).

Client logs also are an excellent source of baseline data on the frequency of the target problem. Baseline data obtained from logs serve as clinical measurement of client thoughts, feelings, and behaviors. "These recordings help the client and the practitioner to gain appropriate insights into the client's functioning, aid in structuring treatment tasks, facilitate client change, and monitor clinical progress during treatment" (Jordan & Franklin, 1995, p. 41).

Client logs are easy to construct. Most are divided into columns, with the types of information the client should record listed across the top of the form (see Figure 6.5). "At a minimum it involves recording whether some incident occurred, when it occurred, and how the client responded to it" (Bloom, Fischer, & Orme, 1995, p. 238). Information on circumstances just prior to and just after the problem event may also be included on client logs.

Two decisions need to be made regarding the completion of logs. The first is when to record the information, and the second is what to record. You can have a

FIGURE 6.5. Client Log

Date	Time	Event	Before Problem	After Problem	Reaction

From M. Bloom, J. Fischer, and J. Orme, *Evaluating Practice: Guidelines for the Accountable Professional* (2nd ed.). Copyright © 1995 by Allyn & Bacon. Reprinted/adapted by permission.

client use preset time periods or record immediately following the occurrence of the target event. Recording at preset time periods works if you have narrowed down the occurrence of a target event to a specific period—that is, if you know in advance approximately when the target problem is likely to occur. For example, a family might complain about sibling fights after school and during dinner. The client log then might cover the time period from three in the afternoon to seven in the evening. The client keeping the log would record all the sibling fights that occurred during this time period.

The second option is to use open time categories. This method is sometimes referred to as *critical incident recording* (Bloom, Fischer, & Orme, 1995). With this type of log, the client decides whether to record an event. The client decides if the event is related to the problem or target and then records it as soon as possible after it occurs. This method works best when you need information about events that are likely to be spread out over the entire day.

In addition to specifying when the recording will take place, you also need to clarify in advance what will be recorded. By design, client logs give the client control over the content. Clients choose which of the many thoughts, feelings, and behaviors they experience daily to include and exclude. They employ a great deal of subjective judgment in completing logs. Information recorded on the log should be limited to what the "client perceives as significantly related to the target" (Bloom, Fischer, & Orme, 1995, p. 240). Thus, you and the client need to be clear about what constitutes a critical incident. Discuss with the client the types of events that would be appropriate for inclusion in the log. In the beginning, encourage clients to be inclusive rather than exclusive in their recordings. Review the first logs together with an eye toward the appropriateness of the entries as well as events that the client did not record but should have.

Behavioral Observation. "Behavioral observations represent one of the most direct and effective measures of client behavior" (Jordan & Franklin, 1995, p. 46). The frequency and duration of specific client behaviors can be observed and recorded (Bloom, Fischer, & Orme, 1995). Behavioral observation can provide detailed information on the occurrence of client behaviors and the context of those behaviors. It represents one of the most reliable and valid methods of measuring client change.

Typically, the first step in using behavioral observation is to operationally define the target behavior. An example would be specifying the types of disruptive behaviors a child displays in the classroom, such as getting out of his or her seat, talking with classmates while the teacher is talking, and so forth. The target problem must be clearly defined in behavioral terms and must be observable. Observation cannot be used to measure target problems that focus on feelings or thoughts. It is limited to measuring the frequency, duration, and context of the client's behavior.

The second step is to select the observer or observers. Often, the observers are significant others, family members, or other professionals who have access to the client's person-in-environment interactions. For example, a young child having a problem controlling his or her temper can be observed at home by a parent and at school by a teacher or teacher's aide.

Ideally, at least two people should observe the same events. This makes it possible to establish interobserver agreement and determine the reliability of the observations. "Eighty percent or higher agreement is believed to be acceptable for most clinical situations" (Jordan & Franklin, 1995, pp. 46–47). However, not all practice situations lend themselves to direct observation. If obtaining two or more observers is impractical, you will have to settle for a single observer. "Behavioral observation using one observer lacks the scientific reliability of observation with two or more raters, but it remains an important measurement indicator in clinical assessments because it provides observations of the client's behavior in natural settings" (Jordan & Franklin, 1995, p. 47).

The third step is to train the observers. Observers must know in advance exactly what behavior to look for and how to recognize the behavior when it occurs (Jordan & Franklin, 1995). In addition, they have to be trained to conduct the observations. "Deciding how to sample the behaviors is the fundamental question in conducting a structured observation" (Berlin & Marsh, 1993, p. 107). You must decide whether to record all instances of the behavior or a sample. "Continuous recording involves recording every occurrence of a target behavior every time it occurs" (Bloom, Fischer, & Orme, 1995, p. 133). This requires the observer to be willing and available, and it works best when the target behavior does not occur with great frequency. Often, these conditions can not be satisfied, and a sampling strategy is used. Figure 6.6 is a form for continuous recording.

Time sampling is appropriate when events occur continuously or frequently. "Time sampling requires the selection of specific units of time, either intervals or discrete points, during which the occurrence or nonoccurrence of a specific behavior is recorded" (Berlin & Marsh, 1993, p. 107). The assumption is that the sample of behavior will accurately represent the occurrence of the behavior if all occurrences were recorded (Haynes, 1978). There are two types of time sampling: interval and discrete. Interval sampling involves selecting a time period and dividing it into equal blocks of time. The observer records the occurrence or nonoccurrence of the behavior during each interval. The behavior is recorded once for each interval regardless of how many times it occurs (Bloom, Fischer, & Orme, 1995). Figure 6.7 shows a form for interval recording.

Discrete time sampling involves selecting specific time periods and recording all instances of the target behavior that occur during the selected periods. The key issue in this type of recording is to select periods that are representative in terms of the target behavior. If the behaviors occur often and regularly, you would need fewer periods to obtain a representative sample of them (Bloom, Fischer, & Orme, 1995). If the behaviors occur during certain time periods, for example, during

FIGURE 6.6. Observation Form for Continuous Recording

Client's Name _____   Recorder's Name _____

Behavior to Be Observed _____

_____

Date _____   Location _____

Time	Description of Behavior and Context

FIGURE 6.7. Observation Form for Interval Time Sampling Recording

Client's Name _____   Recorder's Name _____

Behavior to Be Observed _____

_____

Date _____ Location _____ Time Period _____ Interval Length _____

Interval	Behavioral Occurrence		Context	Comments
1.	Yes	No			
2.	Yes	No			
3.	Yes	No			

meals, then the selected periods must correspond to the behavioral patterns of the client. Figure 6.8 shows a form for discrete time sampling recording.

Overall, direct observation is an excellent method for assessing client outcomes. It is one of the most effective tools we have for measuring behavior. When it is used with two or more observers, it can provide reliable and valid outcome data. It also has the potential to provide valuable clinical information on the context within which target problems occur. Direct observation should be seriously considered when a target problem is behavioral in nature, the situation allows for direct observation, and implementing direct observation is feasible.

FIGURE 6.8. Observation Form for Discrete Time Sampling Recording

Client's Name _____   Recorder's Name _____

Behavior to Be Observed _____

_____

Time Period _____   Location _____

Date	Number of Times Behavior Occurred	Comments

From Martin Bloom, Joel Fischer, & John G. Orme, *Evaluating Practice: Guidelines for the Accountable Professional* 2/E. Copyright © 1995 by Allyn & Bacon. Reprinted/adapted by permission.

Rating Scales.   Individualized rating scales are measures of client problems that are created by the client and the social worker together (Bloom, Fischer, & Orme, 1995). These types of measures are also referred to as self-anchored rating scales (Jordan & Franklin, 1995). The major advantage of an individualized rating scale is that it is constructed to measure the specific problem or concern that you and your client have identified as the focus of intervention. Thus, a rating scale is directly linked to the feeling, thought, or event that is being addressed in the helping process.

Another advantage of individualized rating scales is that they are based on the client's unique experiences and perceptions. The anchor points of the scale are defined by the client. Brief and explicit labels are provided for the low, middle, and high points of the scale. The labels or anchors provide examples of what the numbers represent. The anchors describe behaviors, thoughts, and feelings that the client would experience at various points along the scale. Having the client define the meaning of the anchor points on the scale means that the measure has great relevance for the client. It becomes a unique measure of the client's feelings, thoughts, or behaviors. It represents his or her perceptions and experiences.

Individualized rating scales usually have between 5 and 10 points. Scales that have more than 10 points are difficult for clients to score and are therefore not recommended (Bloom, Fischer, & Orme, 1995). For example, if a self-esteem scale ranged from 1 to 100, it would be very difficult to determine the difference between a rating of 70 and 75. Scales with 7 points are considered ideal, allowing "for some deviations that capture the client's varying experiences, but not creating so many deviations that they lose meaning" (Jordan & Franklin, 1995, p. 43).

Individualized rating scales are easy to construct. Identify with the client the behavior, thought, or feeling that is targeted for change. A wide range of characteristics of the target can be rated: "For example, the seriousness, intensity, importance, or frequency of the target might be rated" (Bloom, Fischer, & Orme, 1995, p. 165). It is important for the target to be clearly articulated and for each rating scale to measure only one aspect or dimension of the target (Gingerich, 1979). Bloom, Fischer, and Orme warn against using different dimensions at each end of the scale, such as happy at one end and sad at the other. People often experience contradictory feelings and can feel happy and sad at the same time. It is preferable to develop two measures, a sadness scale and a happiness scale, rather than to combine the two dimensions in a single measure. They also recommend that the target and its measurement be worded "in a way that emphasizes that the client is working toward something positive rather than just trying to eliminate something undesirable" (1995, p. 166). For example, if the problem is feeling sad, the goal might be to increase feelings of happiness, and the rating scale would measure level of happiness.

The next step is to decide on the number of scale points and develop anchor descriptions for the two end points and possibly the middle point. Scales with 7 or 9 points are popular since they have a clear midpoint. The numbers on the scale represent gradations for the target problem from low to high. The higher the score, the more frequent, serious, important, or problematic the target problem. The end points of the scale are defined by the client, as are the descriptions or examples of what the low, middle, and high numbers represent. These anchor descriptions define the meaning of the numbers on the rating scale. Begin by asking the client to describe what it would be like at one end of the scale for the given target problem. Repeat the process for the other end of the scale and for the midpoint. Anchors should describe the behaviors, thoughts, or feelings the client would experience along the continuum of the scale:

> The depressed client might characterize himself or herself as being most depressed (level 9 on the scale) when he or she can't sleep, can't work and has suicidal thoughts. Thus, when these conditions occur, the client would know to rate himself or herself at level 9. The depressed client may be least depressed, level 1, when he or she feels like going out, wants to eat a large meal, and really enjoys being with friends. (Bloom, Fischer, & Orme, 1995, p. 167)

After you and your client construct the scale, make sure that the anchors fit the client's perception of the situation and that both of you are clear about what constitutes a low and high score. This is best accomplished by practicing using the scale and asking the client to retrospectively complete a rating for different points in his or her life. This will increase the client's comfort in using the scale and provides an opportunity to determine whether the anchor points provide adequate differentiation of the target problem. Individualized rating scales are shown in Figure 6.9.

An important point to keep in mind in constructing individualized rating scales is that they must be *individualized*. The anchors reflect images and pictures of what the situation is like for the client. Your job is to help the client put those images into words. Make sure the words are the client's, not yours or someone else's. The strength of individualized rating scales is that they are client-defined and derived directly from the identified target problem.

An alternative to individually constructed anchors is to use general anchor descriptions. Rating scales with general anchors make it possible to use the same scale for different client situations. For example, a general rating scale measuring feelings of connectedness could be used to measure a client's relationships with

---

FIGURE 6.9. Individualized Rating Scales

Comfort in social situations

1	2	3	4	5	6	7	8	9

Terrified, overwhelmed,
completely unable to engage
in conversation with strangers

Somewhat anxious,
yet able to respond
when spoken to

Relaxed, confident,
able to initiate conversations
with strangers

Ability to control temper

1	2	3	4	5	6	7	8	9

Out of control,
completely unable
to control temper, flying
off the handle for the
slightest reason

Somewhat able to
control temper, only
losing temper when
provoked

In complete control, able
to control temper even in
the most trying conditions

---

various members of his or her family—the same scale could be used to measure the client's relationship with each family member. The disadvantage of general anchors is that they are more ambiguous and less precise than individually tailored anchors (Coulton & Solomon, 1977). Figure 6.10 contains rating scales with general anchors.

Individualized and general rating scales are excellent tools for measuring client progress and change on identified target problems. They have high face validity because they are derived directly from client problems or concerns. There is some evidence that the validity of single-item rating scales is comparable to that of standardized measures (Nugent, 1992). However, the validity and reliability of individualized rating scales cannot be readily established because they are designed for use with individual clients (Berlin & Marsh, 1993). In this sense, "these scales are not rigorous, scientifically valid, or reliable forms of measurement" (Jordan & Franklin, 1995, p. 46). Rating scales do, however, have high clinical applicability and are excellent tools for measuring client target problems and assessing progress.

Goal Attainment Scales.   Goal attainment scaling (GAS) was developed in the field of mental health during the 1960s (Royse & Thyer, 1996). It has been used in a large number of settings and with a wide range of client populations. GAS is similar to individualized rating scales in that the client develops and defines the scale anchors or descriptors. They differ, however, in that goal attainment scales are based directly on the client's goals, rather than on behaviors, thoughts, or feelings. A strength of GAS is that it can be used to monitor client progress toward the identified treatment goals (Jordan & Franklin, 1995). Thus, GAS has been found to be an effective method for assessing client change related to the identified goals (Corcoran, 1992).

To use GAS, you and your client need to have specified change goals. A question that arises is which goals or how many should be scaled (Seaburg & Gillespie, 1977). In general, the number of goals scaled should correspond to the number of goals being addressed in the helping relationship. The number of goals

---

FIGURE 6.10. General Rating Scales

Amount of anxiety

| 1 | 2 | 3 | 4 | 5 | 6 | 7 | 8 | 9 |

Little or no anxiety   Moderate anxiety   Extreme anxiety

Frequency of feeling lonely

| 1 | 2 | 3 | 4 | 5 | 6 | 7 | 8 | 9 |

Never   Sometimes   All the time

---

being addressed at any given time should be a limited number. As discussed earlier in this chapter, the goals selected should be those most significant to the client that intervention is most likely to change (Royse & Thyer, 1996).

In conjunction with the client, operationalize each goal on a five-point scale that ranges from -2 to +2. The scale categories are

(+2) most favorable outcome expected
(+1) more than expected outcome
(0)   expected outcome
(-1) less than expected outcome
(-2) most unfavorable outcome.

Work with the client to develop anchors for each scale point. The anchors should represent potential outcomes related to each category and should be as specific as possible. Avoid vague general outcome statements. Figure 6.11 shows a sample goal attainment scale that were developed with an eighty-year-old woman who was caring for her fifty-five-year-old mentally retarded son. The social worker was helping the women address her anxiety and concern about her son's future.

Instead of using the –2 to +2 scoring system, a modified format is more intuitive and easier to explain to clients. It uses the following scale categories:

(4) optimal progress
(3) major progress
(2) moderate progress
(1) some progress
(0) no progress.

These categories focus on desired progress to a greater extent than the traditional GAS scoring format and thus reflect a more positive orientation. Figure 6.12 contains the examples from Figure 6.11 using the modified scoring format.

GAS is a client-focused method of measuring progress. It is a direct extension of the goal-oriented approach to practice and is easily incorporated into generalist social work practice with a diverse range of client populations. GAS also empowers clients by placing responsibility for defining and monitoring progress with them. The client is viewed as the expert on what constitutes progress and on determining the extent to which progress is being made. In these respects, GAS is useful as a clinical measurement tool for engaging clients in the helping process.

FIGURE 6.11. Goal Attainment Scales

Level	Goal 1 Increase ability to deal with panic attacks	Goal 2 Make plans for son's future
Most unfavorable outcome (-2)	Unable to calm myself down, unable to catch breath, heart racing, extreme anxiety	Unable to discuss son's future needs and plans
Less than expected outcome (-1)	Limited ability to calm myself down, some difficulty breathing, pacing the floor, moderate anxiety	Discussed son's future with other members of the family
Expected outcome (0)	Able to calm down using breathing/relaxation techniques, maintain composure, low anxiety	Discussed future needs with son
More than expected outcome (+1)	Able to verbalize feelings, remain calm in stressful situations, almost no anxiety	Discussed future needs with son and involved family and outside agencies in assessing son's needs
Most favorable outcome (+2)	Able to deal with stressful situations without experiencing panic attacks, very low anxiety, calm and relaxed	Worked with son, family, and outside agencies and services to prepare son to care for himself in the future

FIGURE 6.12. Modified Goal Attainment Scales

Level	Goal 1 Increase ability to deal with panic attacks	Goal 2 Make plans for son's future
No progress (0)	Unable to calm myself down, unable to catch breath, heart racing, extreme anxiety	Unable to discuss son's future needs and plans
Some progress (1)	Limited ability to calm myself down, some difficulty breathing, pacing the floor, moderate anxiety	Discussed son's future with other members of the family
Moderate progress (2)	Able to calm down using breathing/relaxation techniques, maintain composure, low anxiety	Discussed future needs with son
Major progress (3)	Able to verbalize feelings, remain calm in stressful situations, almost no anxiety	Discussed future needs with son and involved family and outside agencies in assessing son's needs
Optimal progress (4)	Able to deal with stressful situations without experiencing panic attacks, very low anxiety, calm and relaxed	Worked with son, family, and outside agencies and services to prepare son to care for himself in the future

Standardized Measures. Standardized measures are instruments developed following empirical scale construction techniques with uniform administration and scoring procedures (Jordan & Franklin, 1995). Their reliability is known, and their validity has probably been empirically tested.

Standardized measures are available for a wide range of client behaviors, including martial satisfaction, self-esteem, anxiety, and family relations. Some standardized measures assess global behaviors, such as generalized contentment, while others assess specific behaviors and problems, such as fear, depression, and sexual satisfaction. Standardized measures are available in rapid assessment formats with twenty-five or fewer scale items as well as in lengthy, comprehensive formats with hundreds of scale items. Rapid assessment instruments are easy to use and to incorporate into generalist social work practice. Figure 6.13 reproduces a rapid assessment instrument designed to measure argumentativeness.

"Standardized measures represent the most useful quantitative clinical measurement tools that are available to practitioners" (Jordan & Franklin, 1995, p. 53). There are numerous sources of standardized measures. *Measures for Clinical Practice* by Fischer and Corcoran (1994) is an excellent two-volume collection of rapid assessment instruments. Volume 1 contains measures for use with couples, families, and children, while Volume 2 contains instruments for individual adults. The two-volume set contains more than three hundred different brief assessment instruments with supporting information on each instrument's purpose, scoring, reliability, and validity. Another excellent source of rapid assessment instruments is *Measures of Personality and Social Psychological Attitudes* (1991) by Robinson, Shaver, and Wrightsman. This sourcebook includes numerous measures organized by such clinical topics as self-esteem, depression, and anxiety.

An excellent list of commercially available measures can be found in *Clinical Assessment for Social Workers* by Jordan and Franklin (1995). The WALMYR Publishing Company is an excellent source for commercially available measurement instruments designed specifically for use in social work practice. Walter Hudson, the founder of WALMYR, pioneered the use of rapid assessment instruments in social work practice (Hudson, 1982). WALMYR sells a number of individual and family adjustment scales as well as comprehensive multidimensional assessment instruments.

Standardized measures, especially the rapid assessment variety, are well suited for use in generalist social work practice. If you can locate an instrument that closely corresponds to identified client problems or concerns, using standardized measures offers several advantages. They have known psychometric properties—that is, their reliability and validity have been established. They are also efficient, do not require extensive training, and are easy to administer and score (Fischer & Corcoran, 1994).

DESIGNING THE EVALUATION

Having established measurable goals and selected measurement strategies, the next step is to determine how you are going to implement the evaluation process. The term *evaluation design* is often used to describe how practitioners plan to evaluate progress and case outcomes (Bloom, Fischer & Orme, 1995). One of the most widely used ways to evaluate practice effectiveness in social work is the single-

---

FIGURE 6.13. Argumentativeness Scale (ARG)

AUTHORS: Dominic A. Infante and Andrew S. Rancer

PURPOSE: To measure argumentativeness.

DESCRIPTION: The ARG is a 20-item scale designed to measure the tendency to argue about controversial issues (or argumentativeness). Argumentativeness is viewed as a generally stable trait which predisposes the individual in communication situations to advocate positions on controversial issues and to attack verbally the positions other people take on those issues. Ten of the items indicate a tendency to approach argumentative situations and ten involve the tendency to avoid argumentative situations. The ARG is considered useful for examining communication and social conflict and dysfunctional communication. Both areas have implications for clinical practice in that high scores on the ARG may identify the incessant arguer whose behavior impairs interpersonal relations while very low scores may identify people who almost never dispute an issue and are compliant and/or easily manipulated. Thus, the ARG may prove useful particularly in couple and family counseling.

NORMS: A series of studies largely involving over 800 students in undergraduate communication courses formed the basis for much of the research on the ARG. No demographic data are reported nor are actual norms.

SCORING: Scores for each item ranging from I to 5 are totaled separately for the two dimensions. The total score for the tendency to avoid argumentative situations (items 1, 3, 5, 6, 8, 10, 12, 14, 16, 19) is subtracted from the total score for the tendency to approach argumentative situations (2, 4, 7, 9, 11, 13, 15, 17, 18, 20) to provide an overall score for the argumentativeness trait.

RELIABILITY: The ARG has good to excellent internal consistency, with the approach dimension (ARG ap) having a coefficient alpha of .91 and the avoidance dimension (ARG av) having an alpha of .86. The ARG also is a stable instrument with an overall ARG test-retest reliability (one week) of .91 and test-retest reliabilities of .87 for ARG ap and .86 for ARG av.

VALIDITY: The ARG has fairly good concurrent validity, correlating significantly and in the expected direction with three other measures of communication predispositions. In addition, the ARG significantly correlates with friends' ratings of argumentativeness. Further, the ARG has some degree of construct validity in accurately predicting a series of behavioral choices which should and should not correlate with argumentativeness.

---

system design (Miley, O'Melia, & DuBois, 1998). Single-system designs are sometimes also referred to as single-case designs, single-subject designs, N=1 designs, interrupted time-series designs, and subject-replication designs. "Whatever name is used, a formal case-level evaluation is a study of one entity—a single client, a single group, a single couple, a single family, a single organization, or a single community—involving repeated measurements over time in order to measure change" (Gabor, Unrau, & Grinnell, 1998, p. 175).

Single-subject designs hold great promise for generalist social workers. The requirements for using them fit well with generalist practice principles. Single-subject designs require clear specification of the target problem, development of measurable goals, selection and implementation of an intervention, and continued monitoring of the client's progress on the identified target problem. All

FIGURE 6.13. continued

PRIMARY REFERENCE: Infante, D. A. and Rancer, A. S. (1982). A conceptualization and measure of argumentativeness, *Journal of Personality Assessment, 46,* 72–80.

AVAILABILITY: Journal article.

ARG Index

This questionnaire contains statements about arguing controversial issues. Indicate how often each statement is true for you personally by placing the appropriate number in the blank to the left of the statement. If the statement is *almost never true* for you, place a "1" in the blank. If the statement is *rarely true* for you, place a "2" in the blank. If the statement is *occasionally true* for you, place a "3" in the blank. If the statement is *often true* for you, place a "4" in the blank. If the statement is *almost always true* for you, place a "5" in the blank.

_____ 1. While in an argument, I worry that the person I am arguing with will form a negative impression of me.
_____ 2. Arguing over controversial issues improves my intelligence.
_____ 3. I enjoy avoiding arguments.
_____ 4. I am energetic and enthusiastic when I argue.
_____ 5. Once I finish an argument I promise myself that I will not get into another.
_____ 6. Arguing with a person creates more problems for me than it solves.
_____ 7. I have a pleasant, good feeling when I win a point in an argument.
_____ 8. When I finish arguing with someone I feel nervous and upset.
_____ 9. I enjoy a good argument over a controversial issue.
_____ 10. I get an unpleasant feeling when I realize I am about to get into an argument.
_____ 11. I enjoy defending my point of view on an issue.
_____ 12. I am happy when I keep an argument from happening.
_____ 13. I do not like to miss the opportunity to argue a controversial issue.
_____ 14. I prefer being with people who rarely disagree with me.
_____ 15. I consider an argument an exciting intellectual challenge.
_____ 16. I find myself unable to think of effective points during an argument.
_____ 17. I feel refreshed and satisfied after an argument on a controversial issue.
_____ 18. I have the ability to do well in an argument.
_____ 19. I try to avoid getting into arguments.
_____ 20. I feel excitement when I expect that a conversation I am in is leading to an argument.

Note: From "A conceptualization and measure of argumentativeness," by D. A. Infante and D. S. Rancer, 1982, Journal of Personality Assessment, 46, 72–80. Copyright © 1982 by Lawrence Erlbaum Associates, Inc. Reprinted/adapted by permission.

these requirements are consistent with the requirements of sound generalist social work practice.

Bloom, Fischer, and Orme (1999) provide a comprehensive and detailed description of numerous types of single-subject designs (also see Tripodi, 1994). However, as Berlin and Marsh point out, "the types of designs that are likely to be used in an ongoing way in practice are more limited" (1993, p. 120). The single-subject design selected depends primarily on what questions you are attempting to answer (Berlin & Marsh, 1993). Two questions appropriate for generalist social work practice evaluations are Is the intervention working? and Is the intervention causing the change?

More complex experimental designs provide information on the causal effect of the intervention. Did the client system improve because of the intervention? What aspects of the intervention are most important in causing the change? Answers to such questions contribute to social work knowledge. They help document the effectiveness of various interventions with various types of clients and target problems. However, they are better addressed through research than through ongoing social work practice with clients. Answering questions about causality and implementing experiential type designs are beyond the level of evaluation expected for generalist social work practitioners.

As social workers, we have a responsibility to promote the well-being of our clients (NASW, 1997). This entails, in part, assessing the effectiveness of our interventions. Is the client making progress? Does the intervention appear to be working? Is the target problem improving, getting worse, or staying the same? This book focuses only on designs that provide information on client progress. Such designs best fit generalist social work practice. They are easy to implement with client systems, and they provide important information on the effectiveness of the work.

Components of Single-Subject Designs

There are a number of different single-subject evaluation designs. However, there are components common to all of them. The basic components of single subject designs are

- Specifying the target problem
- Developing quantitative measures of the target problem
- Establishing baseline measures of the target problem before intervention
- Measuring the target problem repeatedly throughout the intervention
- Graphically displaying the data
- Making comparisons across phases.

Specifying the target problem, developing measures, and graphically displaying the data were discussed earlier.

Establishing Baselines.   The baseline is the measure of the target problem before the worker provides service. Repeated measurement prior to the intervention is necessary to establish a baseline. The baseline allows you to compare the client's target problem before and after the intervention (Marlow, 1998).

There are two types of baselines. For the *concurrent* baseline, data are collected while other assessment activities are taking place. Repeated measures of the target problem are collected before you implement an intervention with the client system. For the *retrospective* baseline, the client reconstructs measures of the target problem from an earlier time period, using his or her memory. In many situations, delaying the intervention while a concurrent baseline is obtained is unacceptable. For example, it would be unethical to delay providing counseling services to people who experienced a traumatic event, such as a school shooting, in order to obtain baseline information on the victims' level of traumatic stress. In such cases, using a retrospective baseline is an acceptable alternative.

A common question is how many data points or measurements are needed for the baseline? The answer is that it depends. For meaningful comparisons to be made between the preintervention (baseline) and the intervention phases, the baseline has to be stable. That is, there has to be an observable pattern of measurement scores during the baseline period. "A stable baseline is one that does not contain obvious cycles or wide fluctuations in the data" (Bloom, Fischer, & Orme, 1995, p. 333). Fluctuations are acceptable only if they occur with some regularity (Marlow, 1998). Thus, ideally, the baseline phase does not end until you observe a stable baseline. How long this takes is influenced, in part, by the amount of variation between the data points. The greater the variation (range of scores), the more data points needed to achieve stability. Conversely, if the variation between points on the baseline is relatively small (similar scores), fewer data points are needed to achieve stability.

Using an unstable baseline is problematic. If the measures of the target problem fluctuate widely and no pattern exists, it is difficult to determine what factors are affecting changes in the target problem and whether change has occurred once the intervention starts (Bloom, Fischer, & Orme, 1995). In other words, it is unclear whether changes between the baseline and intervention phases are due to usual fluctuations in the target problem or if change has actually taken place.

Making Comparisons.   Assessing change requires making some sort of comparison. In traditional experimental evaluation designs, a treatment group is compared to a control group that does not receive treatment. In case evaluations using single-subject design methodologies, the client provides the basis for comparison. In essence, the client serves as his or her own control group. Is the client better after getting help than before the intervention? Without comparisons, it is impossible to assess change.

Work with clients can be divided into phases (Gabor, Unrau, & Grinnell, 1998). During the first few contacts, baseline data on the target problem may be collected; this is the assessment phase. The second phase is the next series of sessions, in which an intervention is implemented. If the first intervention did not achieve the desired results, a third phase may try a second intervention.

Single-subject evaluations use letters to label the different phases. The letter *A* is used to designate the baseline phase. "Successive intervention are represented by successive letters: *B* for the first, *C* for the second, *D* for the third, and so on" (Gabor, Unrau, & Grinnell, 1998, p. 180). A single-subject design that consists of a baseline phase followed by an intervention is called an *AB* design. An evaluation that does not have a baseline and only one intervention is called a *B* design. An *ABA* design is one in which a baseline (*A*) phase is followed by an intervention (*B*) phase and a second baseline (*A*) period. The various phases of a single subject design are usually labeled on the line graph and represented by dashed vertical lines. Figure 6.14 is a line graph of an *AB* design.

The *AB* design is the most frequently used single-subject design in service settings (Berlin & Marsh, 1993). In this design, repeated measurements of the target problem are taken during the baseline (*A*) and intervention (*B*) phases. Measures of the target problem are taken before the intervention is implemented and throughout the intervention. As with all single-subject evaluations, the findings are analyzed by plotting the data points on a chart.

The advantage of the *AB* design is its simplicity (Marlow, 1998). All that it requires is identifying and/or developing appropriate measures of the target problem and taking repeated measurements during the baseline phase one and intervention phase. Its simplicity allows it to be easily incorporated into generalist

FIGURE 6.14. *AB* Design

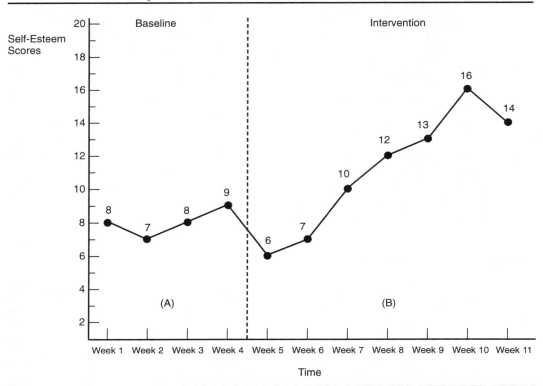

social work practice. It is consistent with normal practice procedures in that an assessment data-gathering phase is followed by an intervention phase (Berlin & Marsh, 1993). The design usually does not compromise or hinder the development of a helping relationship and the provision of service. It fits well into a collaborative model of generalist practice, and it provides evidence of whether the intervention is working.

The one area of potential difficulty with the *AB* design is obtaining a baseline. This is a problem with all single-subject designs used to evaluate ongoing practice with client systems. Delaying the intervention while baseline data is collected is problematic when the situation warrants immediate attention. Obtaining measures of the target problem over a prolonged period of time often is not feasible or desirable. In these situations, developing a retrospective baseline is the preferred alternative. You and the client construct a baseline based on the client's recollection of the target problem in the recent past. Although a compromise, a retrospective baseline does provide a basis of comparison before and after the implementation of the intervention. This comparison provides a basis to answer the fundamental question: Is the intervention working?

The *B* design is the preferred option when it is necessary to intervene immediately, as in a crisis situation, without collecting baseline information or retrospective baseline information (Berlin & Marsh, 1993). The *B* design is often referred to as a monitoring design (Miley, O'Melia, & DuBois, 1998) or a case study design (Bloom, Fischer, & Orme, 1999). It consists solely of an intervention (*B*) phase. Repeated measures of the target problem are taken throughout the intervention. This design is weaker than the *AB* design because of the lack of preintervention comparison data. It does, however, provide information on client progress, whether the target problem is improving, and whether the goals of the intervention have been achieved. Figure 6.4 earlier in this chapter illustrates the *B* design.

A third design that can be used to evaluate client progress is the *ABC* design, or the successive intervention design. This design is an extension of the *AB* design. It entails the introduction of a second intervention (*C*) phase. If additional interventions are added beyond the second (*C*), they are labeled *D, E,* and so on. The *ABC* design is used when the first (*B*) intervention is modified or if the first intervention does not appear to be working. It does not provide information on which intervention caused change in the target problem, nor does it allow for the separation of the effects of the successive interventions. It does, however, provide information on client progress.

Analyzing Single-Subject Data

Analysis of single-subject design data is derived from an examination of the data points on line graphs similar to Figures 6.4 and 6.14. Three types of significance can be used to judge change in the target problem: clinical, visual, and statistical.

Clinical Significance.   Clinical significance, also known as practical significance, is based on the idea "that somebody—especially the client—believes that there has been *meaningful change* in the problem" (Bloom, Fischer, & Orme, 1999, p. 506). Clinical significance is achieved when the specified goal of the intervention has been reached (Marlow, 1998). Determining clinical significance is generally a subjective process that requires discussion and negotiation among the involved parties (Bloom, Fischer, & Orme, 1999). If everyone involved concurs that the target problem has been resolved, clinical significance has been achieved.

Determining clinical significance in the case of less than full goal achievement is more difficult: How much change is clinically meaningful? There are no established criteria for establishing the clinical significance of partial change in the target problem. Client change can be considered clinically significant if those involved in the helping process agree that meaningful change has occurred.

Visual Significance.   Visual analysis takes place on data collected over time and focuses on the trend of the data and its direction (Krishef, 1991). A trend occurs when the data points move directionally in a relatively steady manner. Figure 6.15 shows three basic steady trends. "The 'a' line represents a steadily increasing pattern, the 'b' line displays steadiness of the data without either positive or negative direction, and the 'c' line depicts a steadily decreasing data pattern" (Krishef, 1991, p. 43).

Visual analysis also focus on changes in the level of the data (Berlin & Marsh, 1993, Marlow, 1998). *Level* refers to the magnitude of the data. For example, a change in level occurs when scores that were at 2 or 3 in the baseline stage jump to 8 or 9 during the intervention stage. Figure 6.16 shows a line graph in which there is a change in the level of the data.

FIGURE 6.15. Data Trends

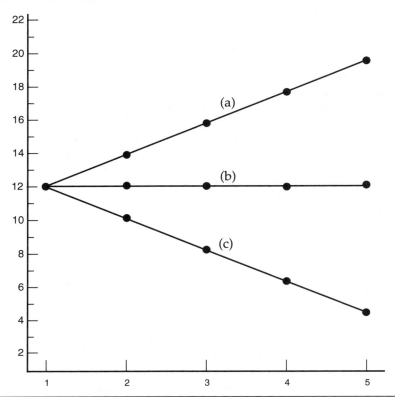

Note: From *Fundamental Approaches to Single Subject Design and Analysis* (p. 43), by C. H. Krishef, 1991, Malabar, FL: Krieger Publishing Company. Copyright © 1991 by Krieger Publishing Company. Reprinted/adapted by permission.

Data in which there are no discernible trends or patterns are considered unstable. Unstable data have wide fluctuations in the measurement of the target problem, as shown in Figure 6.17. Interpretation of unstable data is difficult. Little can be said beyond the fact that there is no pattern and the scores vary widely.

Visual analysis of single-subject data is based primarily on a comparison of the baseline and intervention phases. For meaningful comparisons to be made, the baseline data must be stable. If they are not, interpretation of the effect of the intervention is impossible. Interpretation is also difficult if the baseline data are moving steadily in a direction that would represent improvement on the target problem. For example, if a decrease on the target problem represents client improvement and the baseline trend shows a steady decline on the measure it would be difficult to attribute the improved scores to the effectiveness of the intervention, since the data were already moving in the desired direction (Krishef, 1991).

Figure 6.18 shows nine configurations of change in baseline and intervention phases. Determining change is unequivocal when the baseline is stable and the intervention has a sharply increasing or decreasing trend, as in panel a in Figure 6.18, or when the trend at the intervention phase is in the opposite direction of the

FIGURE 6.16. Change in Level

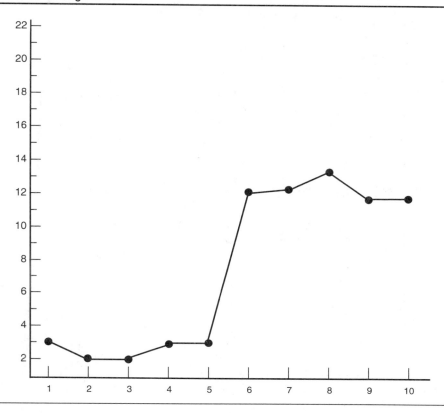

trend at baseline (panels b and c). The strongest change is when there is a shift in both trend and level in the improved direction (Berlin & Marsh, 1993).

Calculating a *celeration line* helps visually determine a trend in the data (Bloom, Fischer, & Orme, 1999). A celeration line connects the midpoints of the first and second halves of the baseline phase and extends into the intervention phase (see Figure 6.19). The basic idea is that the trend established during the baseline represents an estimate of what would happen if the baseline pattern were to continue and there were no intervention.

The steps involved in calculating a celeration line are as follows:

1. Plot the baseline and intervention data on a line graph.
2. Divide the baseline section of the line graph in half, drawing a vertical line. If there is an even number of data points in the baseline, draw the line between the data points; for odd numbers, draw the line through the midpoint number.
3. Divide each half into half by drawing dashed vertical lines on the chart.
4. Determine the mean score of the first half of the baseline by adding the scores in the half and dividing by the number of scores in the half. For baselines with an odd number of scores, omit the middle number.

FIGURE 6.17. Unstable Data

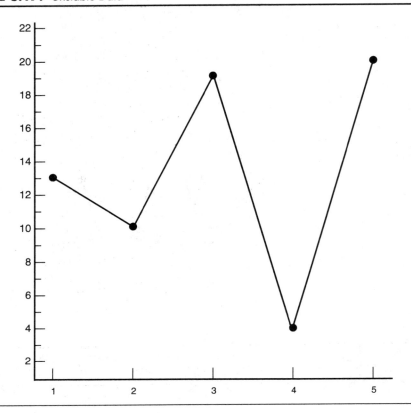

FIGURE 6.18. Possible Configurations of Change in Baseline and Intervention Phases

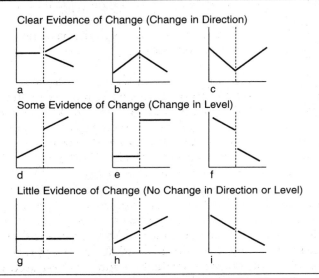

Clear Evidence of Change (Change in Direction)

a   b   c

Some Evidence of Change (Change in Level)

d   e   f

Little Evidence of Change (No Change in Direction or Level)

g   h   i

FIGURE 6.19. Line Graph with Celeration Line

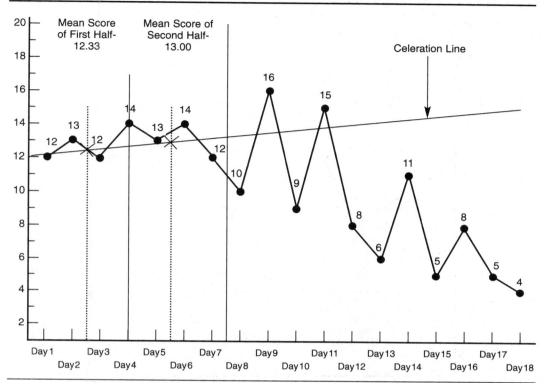

5. Determine the mean score of the second half of the baseline by adding the scores in the half and dividing by the number of scores in the half. For baselines with an odd number of scores, omit the middle number.
6. Mark the dashed vertical line at the mean point for each half.
7. Draw a solid line connecting the two marks in the baseline, and extend the line through the intervention phase.

Statistical Significance. Statistical analysis of single-subject data has become an accepted practice (Berlin & Marsh, 1993). There are a number of methods for determining statistical significance of time-series data (see Bloom, Fischer, & Orme, 1999, for a detailed discussion). One straightforward method for calculating statistical significance of single-subject data is the two standard deviation approach.

This approach, as its name suggests, is based on the standard deviation, which measures the dispersion of scores around the mean.

The basic idea is that ± 2 standard deviations represents about 95 percent of the scores, and the likelihood that two scores would fall outside of ± 2 standard deviations is less than five or fewer times in a hundred. Thus, if two or more scores fall outside the two standard deviation band, we assume that statistically significant change has occurred. The two standard deviation approach was developed by Shewart (1931) for industrial evaluation and was first used with single-subject data by Gottman and Leiblum (1974). The approach offers many advantages: "The procedure can be completed easily with a hand calculator, it can accommodate both independent and autocorrelated data series, and it can be completed even with 'short' baselines (i.e., when there are fewer than ten points in the baseline)" (Berlin & Marsh, 1993, p. 135).

The steps involved in calculating the two standard deviation approach are as follows:

"**1.** Record baseline observations.

"**2.** Sum (Σ) these scores.

x
6
6
5
4
3
4
4
5
5
4

"**3.** Calculate mean: divide sum by n where n is the number of scores in baseline phase.

$$\left(\text{Mean} = \bar{x} = \frac{\Sigma x_1}{n}\right)$$

$46/10 = 4.6 = \text{mean} = \bar{x}$

"**4.** Calculate standard deviation: find $(x - \bar{x})$ for all scores, then $(x - \bar{x})^2$, then sum and divide by $(n - 1)$. Find the square root.

x	$(x - \bar{x})$	$(x - \bar{x})^2$
6	1.4	1.96
6	1.4	1.96
5	.4	.16
4	−.6	.36
3	−1.6	2.56
4	−.6	.36
4	−.6	.36
5	−.4	.16
5	−.4	.16
4	−.6	.36
46	0	8.40/9 = .93

$$\left(\text{Standard Deviation} = \sqrt{\frac{\Sigma (x - \bar{x})^2}{n - 1}}\right)$$

$\sqrt{.93} = .96$

"**5.** Form the two standard deviation band by doubling the standard deviation, adding it to the mean for the upper band and subtracting it from the mean for the lower band.

$2 \times .96 = 1.92$
$4.6 + 1.92 = 6.5$
$4.6 − 1.92 = 2.7$

"**6.** Plot the upper and lower bands around the mean.

"**7.** If two consecutive data points during the intervention phase drift outside the standard deviation line, there is evidence for a statistically significant shift." (Berlin & Marsh, 1993)*

Interpretation of the two standard deviation approach is simple. Plot the bands representing two standard deviations above and below the baseline mean on a line graph that contains baseline and intervention scores. If two consecutive data points in the intervention phase go beyond the two standard deviation band, the results show change that is statistically significant at the .05 level. If two or more data points go beyond the band in the desired direction, the results show improvement that is statistically significant at the .05 level. If two or more data points go beyond the band in the undesired direction, the results show deterioration that is statistically significant at the .05 level (Bloom, Fischer, & Orme, 1999). Figure 6.20 is a line graph in which the two standard deviation approach is used.

Incorporating existing measures or developing your own instruments is a critical component of responsible generalist social work practice. In almost every practice setting, social workers are required to show effectiveness and to document client progress. Measurement and practice are becoming interdependent. No longer is an understanding of evaluation methods left to researchers. It is something that all social workers need to understand and master.

DEVELOPING THE INTERVENTION AND EVALUATION PLAN

The intervention and evaluation plan specifies what will be done by whom to achieve the identified goals as well as how progress on the goals will be evaluated. It is the plan of action for the helping relationship. This action plan is essentially a contract between you and the client about how you will collaboratively work toward the identified goals. The contract is connected with the "goal-setting process because goals without commitment and action plans are more difficult to realize" (Locke, Garrison, & Winship, 1998, p. 169).

Several considerations are involved in developing the intervention and evaluation plan. The contract is an evolving entity (Miley, O'Melia, & DuBois, 1998). "Contracting continues throughout the entire course of the helping venture" (Hepworth, Rooney, & Larsen, 1997, p. 360). The intervention and evaluation plan should not be viewed as fixed once it is developed. The nature of social work practice is such that priorities, goals, and plans change and are modified as the helping process unfolds. Consequently, the contract evolves and is modified to reflect the changing nature of the work.

The social worker and the client decide whether the contract will be oral or written (Locke, Garrison, & Winship, 1998). The disadvantage of oral contracts is that they rely on memory. It becomes increasingly difficult to keep the specifics of the contract clear and in focus as time passes. Another disadvantage of an oral contract is that there is a greater chance of miscommunication and misunderstanding between you and the client. Because of these potential problems, a written contract should be used whenever possible. The act of putting it on paper forces you and the client to come to terms about the specifics of the contract. It helps ensure agreement, and it can be easily retrieved and reviewed at a later time.

The contracting process should also clarify the roles of the participants involved in the helping relationship. At a minimum, you and the client should review your respective roles, expectations, and preferences. Clearing up possible misperceptions about the nature of the work and the way you will work together is critical to the development of a strong collaborative helping relationship and positive change of the identified target problem.

FIGURE 6.20. Line Graph with Two Standard Deviation Approach

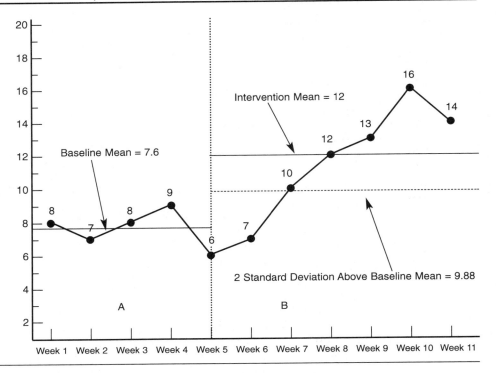

The intervention and evaluation plan developed by the social worker and the client is the integrated plan of action. Developing one is a collaborative undertaking. Your task as the social worker is to provide guidance and technical support. Your client's task is to create the substance of the plan. Obviously some clients can do this more easily than others. Regardless of the client's level of functioning, it is imperative that it be their action plan and not yours or someone else's.

The intervention and evaluation plan should specify who will do what and in what time frame to achieve each of the identified goals. For each goal, specify the tasks and activities that will be undertaken. This includes intervention as well as evaluation activities. The time frame for accomplishing each task also should be specified in the plan.

Appendix 6.1 is a sample intervention and evaluation planning form. The first page contains space for summarizing the problem situation or client concerns and listing the identified change goals. A separate worksheet is completed for each goal. The worksheet contains space to record the intervention activities that will be undertaken by the client, the worker, and other parties involved in the action plan. The worksheet also has space for recording the anticipated completion date for each activity as well as space to describe how progress on the goal will be evaluated.

SUMMARY

This chapter reviewed the process of developing goals and objectives that flow out of the client assessment. Goals are positive statements about what the client hopes to achieve. Objectives are measurable indicators of the identified goals. Together they specify the purpose of the helping relationship. All generalist social work practice should be purposeful, with clearly articulated goals and objectives. Strengths-based practice is client-centered and client-directed. Consequently, goals and objectives are based on the client's perceptions of need, not the social worker's.

Developing goals and objectives is a collaborative process. A comprehensive assessment will identify a number of potential target problems. Together you and the client determine one or two concerns that have the highest priority. The identified problem areas are then converted into statements that reflect the client's broad expectations about desired changes.

Objectives are steps towards goals. They are the intermediate steps that clients need to accomplish to reach their goals. Well-written objectives are specific and measurable. They specify who will do what, to what extent, under what conditions, and by when.

Evaluation is not separate from social work practice; it is an integrated part of generalist social work practice. The reasons for evaluating client progress are many. Social workers have an ethical responsibility to provide the best services available to their clients and to make sure that the services are helping. To assume that what you are doing is working without systematically evaluating effectiveness is unethical. If the client is not making progress, both of you need to know.

Guidelines for collecting evaluation data stress the importance of clearly specifying problems and goals. Multiple measures should be used to assess each goal; only relevant information should be collected; and measurement should begin as early as possible in the helping process. An important consideration in selecting measures is the reliability and validity of the instrument.

Five types of measures can easily be used in evaluating practice. Client logs have clients monitor their own behaviors, thoughts, or feelings. They can be a powerful tool not only in documenting the occurrence of specific behaviors but also in helping clients clarify the nature of problems and problem situations.

Behavioral observation is similar to client logs, except that someone other than the client does the recording. The other person, who may be a parent or a teacher, observes the client and records the frequency of specified behaviors. Behavioral observation can provide detailed information on the occurrence of client behaviors and the context of those behaviors.

Ratings scales are easy to construct and use. Individualized rating scales incorporate the client's own description of the desired changes. They are the client's own personal measure of progress. General rating scales are also created by the worker and client to measure desired changes. They are "general" in that the client does not describe in specific terms the lower and upper points of the scale. More general descriptors are used.

Goal attainment scales are similar to individualized rating scales in that the client develops and defines the scale anchors. They differ in that goal attainment scales are based directly on the client's goals rather than on behaviors, thoughts, or feelings. Their strength is that they can be used to directly monitor progress on the identified goals.

Standardized measures are instruments that have been developed following empirical scale construction techniques. The advantage of standardized measures is that they have established reliability and validity. There may or may not be standardized measures available that fit the identified target problem. If standardized measures are available that closely correspond to the identified client concerns, their use in evaluation is recommended.

Three single-subject evaluation designs are easily incorporated into generalist social work practice. The *AB* design is the most frequently used single-subject design in social service settings. In this design, repeated measurements of the target problem are taken during the baseline and intervention phases. Baseline data maybe collected concurrently or retrospectively. This design fits well with the collaborative model of generalist practice, and it provides evidence of client progress.

The case study or *B* design is the preferred option when it is necessary to intervene immediately without collecting baseline information or even retrospective baseline information. This design is weaker than the *AB* design because of the lack of preintervention comparison data. Nevertheless, it does provide information on client progress.

The *ABC* design can be used to evaluate additional interventions. This design is used when the first intervention is modified or does not appear to be working. A second intervention is added and monitored. Additional interventions are labeled *D, E,* and so forth.

Analysis of single-subject design data is derived from an examination of the data on line graphs. The data points are plotted and can be examined visually and statistically. In both methods, the baseline data points are compared with the intervention data points. Visual significance occurs when there is a distinct change in the pattern of the data points between the baseline and intervention phases. Statistical significance can be determined by the two standard deviation method.

The intervention and evaluation plan specifies what will be done by whom to achieve the identified goals as well as how progress on the goals will be evaluated. It is the contract between the worker and the client regarding the helping process. It is the plan of action that the social worker and client lay out in response to the client's problems and concerns. However, it should not be viewed as fixed once it has been developed. Priorities, goals, and plans often change and are modified as the helping process unfolds.

The following case study consists of an intervention and evaluation plan for Theodore J., who was introduced in Chapter 5. It was prepared by Denise Bubel when she was a first-year MSW student placed in an adult partial hospitalization program.

Mr. J.'s
Intervention and Evaluation Plan

Problem Situation and Case Assessment Summary

Theodore J. is an eighty-two-year-old Caucasian who lives with his eighty-year-old wife. He attends the adult partial hospitalization program five days a week. He has been diagnosed with irreversible dementia. He suffers from memory loss and cognitive decline, which cause him frustration and anxiety. He also has strong feelings of shame and embarrassment about his medical condition. Mrs. J. is very stressed and is having difficulty coping with the demands of her husband's care and his deteriorating health.

Change Goals

Goal 1 To have Mr. J. take more responsibility for himself.

Goal 2 To reduce Mr. J.'s feelings of shame and embarrassment about his incontinence.

Goal 3 To reduce Mrs. J.'s level of stress.

Goal-Intervention-Evaluation Worksheet (1)

Goal: To have Mr. J. take more responsibility for himself.

   Objective: Mr. J. will review his daily "to do" list every day before each meal by December 1.

   Objective: Mr. J. will take his medications every day at noon without being told to by his social worker or his wife by December 1.

Intervention Activities

Client: Mr. J. will meet with his social worker at least once a day during the week to identify and discuss strategies for helping him remember.

Worker:
1. Mr. J.'s social worker will meet with him daily to discuss strategies for helping him remember and to reinforce his taking responsibility for self-care.

2. The social worker will monitor Mr. J.'s compliance in reviewing his "to do" list before breakfast and lunch.

3. The social worker will monitor Mr. J.'s compliance in taking his medications before lunch.

4. The social worker will review with Mr. J. his progress at the end of each week.

Others:

1. Mrs. J. will monitor Mr. J.'s compliance in reviewing his "to do" list before his meals on the weekends.

2. Mrs. J. will monitor Mr. J.'s compliance in taking his medications before lunch on the weekends.

3. Mrs. J. will report Mr. J.'s weekend compliance to the social worker every Monday morning.

Evaluation and Measurement

At the end of each week, the social worker and Mr. J. will complete the two goal attainment scales.

Goal Attainment Scales

Level		Objective 1￼ Review "to do" list before each meal	Objective 2￼ Take noon medications every day
Most unfavorable	−2	0 to 20% of the time	never
Less than expected	−1	21% to 40% of the time	Remembers 1–2 days
Expected	0	41% to 60% of the time	Remembers 3–4 days
More than expected	+1	61% to 80% of the time	Remembers 4–5 days
Most favorable	+2	81% to 100% of the time	Remembers 6–7 days

Goal-Intervention-Evaluation Worksheet (2)

Goal: To reduce Mr. J.'s feelings of shame and embarrassment about his incontinence.

 Objective: Mr. J. will acknowledge his feelings of shame and embarrassment about his incontinence in his support group by October 1.

 Objective: Mr. J. will feel comfortable wearing undergarments designed for incontinence when he is in public places by November 1.

Intervention Activities
Client: Mr. J. will attend his daily support group at the adult partial hospitalization program. Mr. J. will meet with his social worker once a day to discuss his feelings about his incontinence.
Worker: 1. The social worker will provide individual counseling to Mr. J. on a daily basis. 2. The social worker will monitor Mr. J.'s participation in his support group. 3. The social worker will review with Mr. J. his progress at the end of each week.
Others: Mrs. J. will encourage Mr. J. to wear adult incontinence undergarments when they go out in public.

Evaluation and Measurement

The social worker will monitor Mr. J.'s participation in the support group and his willingness to discuss his concerns about his incontinence.

At the end of each week, the social worker and Mr. J. will complete the public comfort rating scale.

I am not comfortable going in public			I am somewhat comfortable going in public			I am comfortable going in public		
1	2	3	4	5	6	7	8	9

Goal-Intervention-Evaluation Worksheet (3)

Goal: To reduce Mrs. J.'s level of stress.

Objective: Mrs. J. will have a home health aide to help her care for her husband by October 1.

Objective: Mrs. J. will utilize relaxation techniques when she feels stressed by November 1.

Intervention Activities
Client: 1. Mrs. J. will apply for home health aide services. 2. Mrs. J. will learn and practice relaxation techniques.
Worker: 1. The social worker will provide Mrs. J. with a referral to a home health care agency. 2. The social worker will teach Mrs. J. relaxation techniques. 3. The social worker will meet with Mrs. J. once a month to review her situation.
Others:

Evaluation and Measurement

The social worker will monitor Mrs. J.'s referral for home health care.

Once a month, the social worker and Mrs. J. will meet to discuss the effectiveness of the relaxation techniques.

Once a month, Mrs. J. will complete the Index of Clinical Stress (Hudson & Abell, 1992).

DISCUSSION QUESTIONS

1. How realistic are the stated goals and objectives for Mr. and Mrs. J? Does the measurement and evaluation plan appear to be appropriate? How else might one assess progress on the goals? How would you proceed in evaluating progress?
2. Discuss the importance of developing goals and objectives in a variety of field placement settings. How has the process unfolded in different settings? In what types of settings does developing goals and objectives seem appropriate? Under what conditions does it not seem realistic?
3. Discuss the use of evaluation in your field placement. How is progress evaluated? What role do clients play in the process? How could you strengthen the evaluative component of the social work services provided by your field placement agency?
4. Discuss the strengths and limitations of the five types of measures commonly used in single-subject design evaluation. Under what conditions could you incorporate their use in your generalist practice? In what ways would you have difficulty using these types of measures in your practice?
5. Discuss the contracting process with group client systems. Compare the process with that for individual client systems. How does the process of developing goals, objectives, measures, and action and evaluation plans differ when working with groups rather than individual clients? How is the process similar?
6. Discuss possible ways of introducing clients to the idea of using a single-subject evaluation design. List the major points you would cover, and identify possible concerns clients might have about measurement and graphing.

REFERENCES

Applegate, J. (1992). The impact of subjective measures on nonbehavioral practice research: Outcome vs. process. *Families in Society, 73,* 100–108.

Barlow, D., Hayes, S., & Nelson, R. (1984). *The scientist practitioner.* New York: Pergamon Press.

Berlin, S., & Marsh, J. (1993). *Informing practice decisions.* New York: Macmillan. From S. Berlin and J. Marsh, *Informing Practice Decisions.* Copyright © 1993 by Allyn & Bacon. Reprinted/adapted by permission.

Bloom, M., Fischer, J., & Orme, J. (1995). *Evaluating practice: Guidelines for the accountable professional* (2nd ed.). Boston: Allyn and Bacon.

Bloom, M., Fischer, J., & Orme, J. (1999). *Evaluating practice: Guidelines for the accountable professional* (3rd ed.). Boston: Allyn and Bacon.

Campbell, J. (1988). Client acceptance of single-system evaluation procedures. *Social Work Research and Abstracts, 24,* 21–22.

Campbell, J. (1990). Ability of practitioners to estimate client acceptance of single-subject evaluation procedures. *Social Work, 35,* 9–14.

Corcoran, K. (1992). Practice evaluation: Setting goals, measuring and assessing change. In K. Corcoran (Ed.), *Structuring change: Effective practice for common client problems* (pp. 28–47). Chicago: Lyceum.

Coulton, C. J., & Solomon, P. L. (1977). Measuring outcomes of intervention. *Social Work Research and Abstracts, 13,* 3–9.

Fischer, J., and Corcoran, K. (1994). *Measures for clinical practice: A sourcebook* (Volumes 1–2, 2nd ed.). New York: Free Press.

Franklin, C., & Jordan, C. (1992). Teaching students to perform assessment. *The Journal of Social Work Education, 28,* 222–241.

Gabor, P. A., Unrau, Y. A., & Grinnell, R. M. (1998). *Evaluation for social workers: A quality improvement approach for the social services.* Boston: Allyn and Bacon.

Gingerich, W. (1979). Procedure for evaluating clinical practice. *Health and Social Work, 4,* 104–130.

Goldstein, H. (1973). *Social work practice: A unitary approach.* Columbia, SC: University of South Carolina Press.

Gottman, J. M., & Leiblum, S. R. (1974). *How to do psychotherapy and how to evaluate it.* New York: Holt, Rinehart & Winston.

Haynes, S. N. (1978). *Principles of behavioral assessment.* New York: Gardner.

Hepworth, D., Rooney, R., & Larsen, J. (1997). *Direct social work practice: Theory and skills* (5th ed.). Pacific Grove, CA: Brooks/Cole.

Hudson, W. (1982). *The clinical measurement package: A field manual.* Homewood, IL: Dorsey Press.

Hudson, W., & Abell, N. (1992). *Index of clinical stress (ICS).* Tallahassee, FL: WALMYR Publishing Co.

Jongsma, A., & Peterson, L. M. (1995). *The complete psychotherapy treatment planner.* New York: Wiley.

Jordan, C. & Franklin, C. (1995). *Clinical assessment for social workers: Quantitative and qualitative methods.* Chicago: Lyceum.

Kirst-Ashman, K., & Hull, G. (1993). *Understanding generalist practice.* Chicago: Nelson-Hall.

Krishef, C. H. (1991). *Fundamental approaches to single subject design and analysis.* Malabar, FL: Krieger Publishing Company. Reprinted by permission.

Kyte, N. S., & Bostwick, G. (1997). Measuring variables. In R. M. Grinnell, Jr. (Ed.), *Social work research and evaluation: Quantitative and qualitative approaches* (5th ed., pp. 161–183). Itasca, IL: Peacock.

Locke, B., Garrison, R., & Winship, J. (1998). *Generalist social work practice: Context, story, and partnerships.* Pacific Grove, CA: Brooks/Cole.

Mager, R. (1972). *Goal analysis.* Belmont, CA: Fearon.

Maluccio, A., & Marlow, W. (1974). The case for contract. *Social Work, 19,* 28–35.

Marlow, C. (1998). *Research methods for generalist social work* (2nd ed.). Pacific Grove, CA: Brooks/Cole.

Miley, K. K., O'Melia, M., & DuBois, B. L. (1998). *Generalist social work practice: An empowering approach* (2nd ed.). Boston: Allyn and Bacon.

National Association of Social Workers (1997). *Code of ethics.* Washington, DC: Author.

Nugent, W. R. (1992). Psychometric characteristics of self-anchored scales in clinical application. *Journal of Social Service Research, 3,* 137–152.

Poulin, J., & Young, T. (1997). Development of a helping relationship inventory for social work practice. *Research on Social Work Practice, 7,* 463–489.

Reid, W. (1970). Implications of research for the goals of casework. *Smith College Studies in Social Work, 40,* 140–154.

Robinson, J. P., Shaver, P., and Wrightsman, L. S. (1991). *Measures of personality and social psychological attitudes.* San Diego, CA: Academic Press.

Rosen, A. (1993). Systematic planned practice. *Social Service Review, 67,* 84–100.

Royse, D., & Thyer, B. (1996). *Program evaluation: An introduction.* Chicago: Nelson-Hall.

Seaburg, J. R., & Gillespie, D. F. (1977). Goal attainment scaling: A critique. *Social Work Research and Abstracts, 13,* 43–56.

Seabury, B. (1976). The contract uses, abuses, and limitations. *Social Work, 21,* 16–21.

Sheafor, B., Horejsi, C., & Horejsi, G. (1994). *Techniques and guidelines for social work practice* (5th ed.). Boston: Allyn and Bacon.

Shewart, W. A. (1931). *Economic control of quality of manufactured products.* New York: Van Nostrand Reinhold.

Siporin, M. (1975). *Introduction to social work practice.* New York: Macmillan.

Tripodi, T. (1994). *A primer on single-subject design for clinical social workers.* Washington, DC: NASW Press.

WALMYR Publishing Co., P.O. Box 12217, Tallahassee, FL 32317-12217, (850) 383-0045. Internet: www.syspac.com/~walmyr/wpchome.htm.

Witkin, S. (1991). Empirical clinical practice: A critical analysis. *Social Work, 36,* 158–163.

Young, T., & Poulin, J. (1998). The helping relationship inventory: A clinical appraisal. *Families in Society, 79,* 123–133.

APPENDIX 6.1
Intervention and Evaluation Planner

Client: _____   Worker: _____   Date: _____

Case Assessment Summary

Problem Situation (Provide a brief summary of the problem situation being addressed, and describe client system strengths and obstacles related to the problem situation)

Change Goals (State each goal in terms of desired outcomes)

Goal 1 _____

Goal 2 _____

Goal 3 _____

Goal-Intervention-Evaluation Worksheet

Complete one worksheet for each goal identified in the Case Assessment Summary. For each goal: (1) state the goal; (2) list the objectives related to the goal; (3) specify the intervention activities to be completed by the client, by the social worker, and by any other persons involved in the intervention; and (4) describe how progress on the goal is going to be evaluated, including any measures that will be used.

Goal _____

    Objective _____

    Objective _____

    Objective _____

Intervention Activities

Client:

1. _____ To be completed by _____

2. _____ To be completed by _____

3. _____ To be completed by _____

Worker:

1. _____ To be completed by _____

2. _____ To be completed by _____

3. _____ To be completed by _____

Others (Specify _____):

1. _____ To be completed by _____

2. _____ To be completed by _____

3. _____ To be completed by _____

Goal Evaluation and Measurement Plan

CHAPTER 7

Intervention and Termination

obin P. was a first-year MSW student with a field placement in a public child welfare agency. She was assigned to a unit that provides case management services to adolescents placed in foster care, their birth parents, and their foster parents. In her role as a case manager Robin monitored clients' service plan, provided supportive counseling to the adolescents, helped link clients to other services and resources, and advocated for clients' needs with the various systems and organizations involved in their lives.

Robin was pleased with her field placement in that she was getting experience in working with individual clients and with families. However, since the first-year placement was supposed to be a generalist one, Robin was concerned that all of her tasks were micro practice activities. She decided to talk to Mary C., her field instructor, about adding some macro practice activities to her placement responsibilities.

In preparing for her meeting with Beth, Robin realized that she was not clear about what constitutes macro practice. What do generalist social workers do that is considered macro practice? How do they work with an organization or community client system? What functions do generalist social workers perform at the organizational or community level? What is the purpose of the helping relationship with organizations and communities? How do macro practice activities differ from micro practice activities? How are they similar?

Interventions are the actions you and the client take to address the identified target problem or concern. You collaborated with the client to develop an intervention plan during the contracting phase, developing action strategies in conjunction with goals and objectives. Implementing these strategies is the heart of the action phase of the helping relationship.

The first section of this chapter presents a conceptualization and discussion of generalist social work practice interventions with individual, family, group, organization, and community client systems. This is followed by a discussion of the termination stage of the helping relationship. By the end of this chapter, you should be able to help Robin

1. Understand the purpose of the helping relationship in working with individual, family, group, organization, and community client systems
2. Identify micro-level generalist interventions
3. Understand the role the use of self plays in generalist social work practice
4. Identify macro-level generalist interventions

5. Describe the purpose of termination in generalist practice
6. Describe the termination process with micro and macro client systems.

TYPES OF GENERALIST SOCIAL WORK INTERVENTIONS

The action phase may also be called the intervention phase (Compton & Galaway, 1994), the change-oriented phase (Hepworth, Rooney, & Larsen, 1997), or the developmental phase (Miley, O'Melia, & DuBois, 1998), but regardless of the label used, it is the process of putting the plan you and your client developed into action. In it, you implement the activities and processes identified as potential strategies to help the client change and achieve the desired outcomes.

A classification of generalist social work practice interventions is shown in Figure 7.1. In this conceptualization, intervention tasks are categorized by system level (individual, family, group, organization, and community). Generalist practice often requires simultaneous interventions on multiple levels. In any given case situation, you and your client might be involved in a number of individual, family, group, organization, and/or community change activities.

As Figure 7.1 indicates, generalist social work practice entails micro-level and macro-level work. *Micro* social work practice is social work interventions with individuals, couples and families (Hepworth, Rooney, & Larsen, 1997). Practice with these client systems is also often referred to as direct practice or interpersonal practice (Garvin & Seabury, 1997). Some authors classify social work practice with small groups as a mezzo-level intervention (Miley, O'Melia, & DuBois, 1998) and others as micro-level direct practice (Hepworth, Rooney, & Larsen, 1997; Pinderhughes, 1995; Shulman, 1999). Because helping relationships with individual, family, and small group client systems share common purposes, this book treats social work practice with small groups as a form of micro practice. Regardless of the client system, the purpose of micro-level practice is to enhance functioning and empower the client. These two related purposes apply to work with individual clients, couples, families, and small groups.

Macro-level interventions focus on organizational and community change. Some authors include societal change as part of macro practice and place organizational change at the mezzo level (Miley, O'Melia, & DuBois, 1998). The more restricted definition of macro practice as work with community groups and organizations, program planning and development, and the implementation, administration, and evaluation of programs (Connaway & Gentry, 1988; Kirst-Ashman & Hull, 1993; Specht, 1988) more realistically fits with what most generalist social workers do in practice.

Typical client systems at the organizational level are agency task forces and agency committees. Organizational change usually occurs through participation in formally organized work groups. Thus, a generalist social worker seeking to change an organization would view the committee or task force as the client system. At the organizational level, the purpose of macro-level practice is to improve the functioning of the organization, improve services and service delivery, and/or develop new services. All three purposes focus on changing the organization or agency. Generalist social workers tend to be agency-based and to work within an organizational framework.

FIGURE 7.1. Client Systems, Purpose, and Intervention Tasks by System Level

System Level	Client Systems	Purpose of Helping Relationship	Intervention Tasks	
			Use of Self	System Change Activities
Micro				
Individual	Individual Persons	Enhance Functioning Empowerment	Provide Support Increase Motivation	Supportive Counseling Service Linkage
Family	Couples Families		Foster Hope Strengthen Commitment	Service Coordination Service Negotiation
Group	Small Groups		Mobilize Energy Increase Understanding Facilitate Communication	Resource Mobilization Client Advocacy Education and Training
Macro				
Organization	Agency Task Forces Agency Committees	Improve Organization Improve Services Develop Services		Education and Training Program Planning Community Development
Community	Professional Task Forces Community Coalitions Neighborhood Groups	Improve Conditions Empower Residents Develop Resources Increase Awareness Mobilize Citizens		

This does not mean that organizational change from outside the system is impossible (Chavis, Florin, & Felix, 1993). Social work has a long-standing tradition, of working for change from the outside, dating back to the early days of social work and the social reformers of the Progressive Era (Haynes & Mickelson, 1991; Reeser & Epstein, 1990). However, most organizational change can be classified under community practice. For the most part, social workers do not attempt to change organizations individually. They tend to work through formal mechanisms, such as agency committees or task forces.

Typical client systems at the community level are professional task forces, community coalitions, and neighborhood/community citizens' groups. Often the purpose of community practice is to improve community or neighborhood conditions, empower residents, develop resources, increase community awareness of social and economic problems, and mobilize the community to advocate for needed resources and changes. Generalist social workers engaged in community change usually work with some type of professional and/or community group. Some groups are composed of both professional and citizen representatives. Social workers engaged in community practice view the group they are working with as their client system. In other words, the client system is the professional task force, the neighborhood group, or the community coalition that is seeking to change or improve the community.

MICRO-LEVEL INTERVENTIONS

Figure 7.1 shows two major categories of intervention tasks: use of self and system change activities. Work with all client systems involves various combinations of activities from both categories.

Use of Self

Use of self refers to the social worker's interpersonal skills and interaction with the client system (Goldstein, 1995; Northen, 1995). Social workers intervene by means of the helping relationship to assist client systems in achieving identified change goals. Research studies have consistently found that the strongest predictor of client change is the helping relationship (Marziali & Alexander, 1991; Russell, 1990). It is through the helping relationship that change takes place. When the social worker interacts with the client system, the quality of the interaction causes client change. The social worker uses himself or herself to

- Provide support
- Increase the client's motivation to work toward change
- Strengthen the client's resolve
- Foster hope
- Mobilize energy
- Increase understanding
- Facilitate the communication process.

Use of self is traditionally associated with micro-level practice, the social worker's interactions with individual, couple, family, and group client systems. However, the characteristics described above also apply to work at the macro level. As a generalist social worker, you can provide support, foster hope, and increase motivation in your interactions at the organizational level with agency task forces and committees and at the community level with professional tasks forces, community coalitions, and neighborhood groups. Carrying out the various intervention tasks encompasses your use of self and system change activities. You must be skilled in the use of self regardless of the system level of the intervention. The ability to support, motivate, foster hope, strengthen commitment, mobilize energy, increase understanding, and facilitate communication is critical for all types of generalist practice interventions. Effective interpersonal skills are needed to cause change at the individual, family, group, organization, and community levels of generalist social work practice.

System Change Activities

System change activities are usually done in collaboration with the client system, or the social worker does them on behalf of the client system. As Figure 7.1 shows, there are seven system change activities that may take place when working with individuals, couples, families, and small group client systems. These interventions are supportive counseling, service linkage, service coordination, service negotiation, resource mobilization, client advocacy, and education and training.

Supportive Counseling. Supportive counseling is a traditional direct service intervention (Pinderhughes, 1995). In supportive counseling, the social worker takes the enabler role in the helping relationship (Hepworth, Rooney, & Larsen, 1997). The social worker and client agree to meet for a specified time period and engage in a collaborative therapeutic or counseling process. The purpose of the intervention is to help the client resolve concerns and challenges, enhance coping, and/or improve functioning. The following case example illustrates the supportive counseling intervention.

Jim L. is a fifteen-year-old sophomore previously diagnosed as having a moderate learning disability. He takes regular college preparation courses and has managed to maintain a B average. He receives tutoring in math and science and uses the writing center at the school to help him write all of his papers. Although he struggles academically, he has been relatively successful in school.

Jim has no close friends and very few friendly acquaintances. His peers view him as odd and as a "loser." His attempts to fit in and make friends have met with rejection and ridicule, and he has withdrawn socially and makes no attempt to interact with classmates. Jim spends all of his free time at home watching television and playing computer games.

While at home, Jim appears to take out his frustration on his family. He is very demanding of his parents and causes many disturbances within the family. He gets angry quickly and lashes out at his parents over little things. He constantly picks on his younger sister, puts her down in front of her friends, criticizes her looks and abilities, and treats her with general disrespect. When Jim gets into "one of his moods" or is "on the warpath," the tension in the family gets very high. During these times, everyone seems to be mad at everyone else. His parents start fighting, and the general mood in the family is tense and hostile.

Jim's parents are concerned about his lack of peer relationships and his behavior at home. They contacted the school social worker to inquire about help for their son. To his family's surprise, Jim agreed to meet regularly with the school social worker, and together they developed an intervention plan.

In this case example, supportive counseling was one of the agreed-on interventions. Jim recognized his difficulties with peer and family relationships, and he wanted to do something to improve the situation. Jim and the school social worker met once a week to help him improve his relationships. The social worker provided supportive counseling to help Jim gain insight into the problem and to help him develop coping strategies that would increase his effectiveness with peers and family members. He also used the counseling sessions to deal with his feelings of low self-worth and the hurt and anger he felt toward his classmates.

Service Linkage.   Service linkage is another traditional direct service function performed by social workers (Garvin & Seabury, 1997). The social worker takes the broker role in the helping relationship (Hepworth, Rooney, & Larsen, 1997), referring a client system to another agency for service. The process is more than just making a referral; service linkage is the process of creating a new link between the client system and an existing service. This is a major function of generalist social workers, especially since many clients who are referred to agencies for service do not follow through on the referral or, if they do, are not accepted for service (Lantz & Lenahan, 1976).

"One important aspect of successful referrals is the worker's ability to develop contacts and cultivate relationships with other workers and professionals in community resources" (Garvin & Seabury, 1997, p. 318). Having relationships with key contact people throughout the professional community will help you get your client accepted for service. Often, the client does not exactly fit the eligibility criteria, or there may be a limited number of service slots available. In these situations, your relationship with the agency contact person can help smooth the way so that the client is accepted for service (Garvin & Seabury, 1997). The importance of knowing someone in the system cannot be overstated. Becoming familiar with existing services within the community as well as developing relationships with professional colleagues is an important aspect of the broker role in generalist social work practice.

You also need to make an effort to support and strengthen the linkage. Weissman (1976) identified five strategies to help ensure a successful referral: checkback, haunting, sandwiching, alternating, and individualizing. Collectively, they are referred to as *cementing strategies.* The first four strategies involve following up with the client. The checkback strategy requires the client to call the worker to report on how the referral went. In haunting, the worker assumes responsibility for the follow-up contact. Sandwiching is scheduling a follow-up interview with the client to review the referral process and develop other linkage strategies as needed. Alternating involves planning a series of interviews following each contact with the referral source. The fifth strategy, individualizing, refers to the worker's efforts to improve the match between client needs and agency requirements (Garvin & Seabury, 1997). Thus, service linkage involves a concentrated and sustained collaborative effort to help the client make a successful connection with a needed resource.

In the case example about Jim, service linkage was one of the agreed-on interventions. Jim and his social worker, in consultation with Jim's parents, decided that a referral to an agency that provides family treatment was appropriate. The school social worker acknowledged that she had limited training and experience in family therapy and that family relationship problems could be more effectively addressed by a social worker who specialized in family treatment. The social worker also referred Jim to the social worker at the neighborhood teen center in an effort to get him involved in after-school activities with other teenagers. Both referrals and her follow-up efforts were part of a service linkage intervention.

Service Coordination.   Service coordination involves the use of the coordinator role in the helping relationship (Woodside & McClam, 1998). Clients have multiple problems and often need more than one service. In service coordination, the social worker coordinates the various services and professionals to ensure that they are integrated and working toward common goals. This involves monitoring the current status of the client, the services delivered, and the client's progress (Woodside & McClam, 1998).

Service coordination is sometimes referred to as case management (Dorfman, 1996). However, case management generally involves a broader set of roles and responsibilities than service coordination (Moxley, 1997; Rothman & Sager, 1998; Woodside & McClam, 1998). In fact, the diverse roles and functions of case management are similar to all of generalist social work.

In the earlier case example about Jim, a service coordination intervention was not employed. Although the social worker stayed in contact with the social worker providing family therapy and the worker at the teen center, she did not coordinate the unrelated services. No effort was made to ensure that the services were integrated. If Jim's social worker and the family therapist had developed an integrated treatment plan for Jim and the family, and if Jim's social worker had assumed responsibility for coordinating their efforts, a service coordination type of intervention would have taken place.

Service Negotiation.   Service negotiation involves helping individuals and families overcome difficulties they have encountered with service delivery systems. This function is also referred to as mediation (Garvin & Seabury, 1997) and the expediter role (Woodside & McClam, 1998). Service negotiation focuses on helping the client resolve problems and difficulties with existing service linkages. The social worker takes a position between the client and the service provider to improve linkage and resolve conflicts. The worker helps the client negotiate with system providers to address duplication of service, ineligibility, and poor service quality (Woodside & McClam, 1998). The worker's primary task is to facilitate communication between the client and service representatives so that they can reach an agreement (Garvin & Seabury, 1997). The social worker does not advocate for the client directly: instead, he or she helps mediate conflicts.

Service negotiation was not used in the case example. However, later in her work with Jim, the social worker helped the family negotiate with the school system. Jim's parents asked the school to run a full battery of psychological and diagnostic tests on Jim to assess his learning difficulties. The school system's first response was that he could not be tested until the start of the following school year, a delay of more than nine months. Jim's parents asked the school social worker to intervene. She helped the family negotiate a much earlier testing date by assisting them in presenting relevant information on Jim's functioning at home and his social isolation at school at a meeting she set up with the school psychologist. Thus the school social worker provided a service negotiation intervention for the family by facilitating better communication between the school psychologist and the family.

The following case example, written by Kathleen McCabe when she was a first-year MSW student illustrates the use of service negotiation in working with a dialysis patient.

My Doctors Are Not Talking to Each Other   *Kathleen McCabe*

Jerome E. is a forty-five-year-old African-American male diagnosed with end-stage renal disease. He has been coming to the dialysis unit for hemodialysis for less than a year. Both of his kidneys were removed due to the onset of cancer, which makes him ineligible to be evaluated for a kidney transplant for two years. Mr. E. also has hypertension that is kept under control with medication.

His medical condition has challenged him to adjust to a different lifestyle. Mr. E. can no longer perform the physical activities he performed prior to his operation for cancer. Personal relationships with the opposite sex are no longer a priority for him at this time. Mr. E. pays child support to two former wives for three children with the Social Security disability income he receives. He has frequent contact with two daughters from his first marriage, and has a good relationship with them and with his first wife. He has not seen much of his third child, a son from his second marriage, because his second wife, with whom he has a strained relationship will not allow him to visit. She feels he is not paying enough child support. Mr. E. would like to develop a relationship with his son. He is not sure how to approach the issue, and he is concerned about having to go to court because of his financial situation.

As a result of his medical condition, Mr. E. lost his last job as a corrections officer at a prison and has been unable to seek alternative employment. He can no longer perform physical activities that he could prior to his diagnosis. His blood pressure fluctuates, which leaves him feeling weak and light-headed at times. The doctors have not found the right combination of blood pressure medication and fluid removal during dialysis. Mr. E. is concerned that his renal doctor and the doctor who is treating his blood pressure seem to be unable to coordinate treatments or even to communicate with each other. They seem to dislike each other and have some sort of personal conflict. Mr. E. feels that his well-being is at risk because of his doctors' inability to communicate.

When Mr. E.'s treatments are correctly adjusted, he would like to find a part-time job. His treatment schedule complicates this. Dialysis treatments take up about six hours three times a week, and they leave him feeling tired and weak. The challenge is to find a part-time job with flexible hours in a work environment that is not physically demanding.

Mr. E. is also troubled and concerned about not being able to see his young son. He feels he is missing out on the quality time that is important to have with a child. He very much wants to resume visiting his son. Mr. E. realizes that for this to happen, he must reconcile his differences with his ex-wife.

Goals

Mr. E. agreed to the following goals:

1. To have his renal and blood pressure doctors coordinate his medical care
2. To have regular visits with his son
3. To find a flexible part-time job that is not too physically demanding.

Intervention

With Mr. E.'s permission and in consultation with her supervisor, I spoke to each of his doctors about the possible communication problem. I felt that it was my ethical responsibility to try to make sure my client received the best medical care possible. Neither doctor appeared receptive to what I had to say, and each indicated that it was not a problem. Mr. E. and I also role-played his speaking to the doctors about their apparent lack of communication and coordination. He did not need to confront the doctors; their communication problem disappeared before he had a chance to put his role-play into action.

Mr. E. and I also discussed possible ways to pursue the second goal, that of regular visits with his son. Mr. E. was tired of contacting his ex-wife, and he felt that their history of disagreements would interfere with their ability to communicate. I offered to meet with his ex-wife and explain the current situation to her. He agreed, and I set up an appointment. Mr. E.'s ex-wife was somewhat sympathetic and agreed to a trial visitation period of three weeks.

To help Mr. E. find an appropriate part-time job, I met with him to discuss his options and identify the type of work he would like to pursue. I helped Mr. E. decide that he was not ready to take on part-time work. We agreed to put the job goal on hold until Mr. E.'s treatments were better coordinated and he felt better physically.

Resource Mobilization.   At the micro level, resource mobilization involves helping the client obtain needed resources, such as housing, clothing, food, furniture, financial support, or health care (Hepworth, Rooney, & Larsen, 1997). The distinction between resource mobilization and service linkage at this level is minimal. Resource mobilization is the acquisition of needed services, while service linkage is helping clients obtain such services. Both are concerned with helping the client system gain access to needed services; both require knowledge of service networks; and both involve a referral process. The difference lies in the type of service. Resource mobilization focuses on helping clients obtain resources needed to meet basic human needs. Service linkage, on the other hand, focuses on obtaining social, psychological, and health care services. The following case illustrates a resource mobilization type of intervention by a generalist social worker.

Joanne R. is a first-year MSW student with a field placement at Catholic Social Services (CSS), where she is assigned to a case management unit that works primarily with low-income mothers who receive public assistance. One of her clients is a twenty-year-old mother, Nicole B., who was referred to CSS by her welfare case worker. Nicole had been evicted from her apartment and had no food for her two children, no money, and very few clothes for herself and her children suitable for the approaching winter. Joanne met with her client to assess her needs. Together they developed a list of Nicole's short-term and long-term resource needs.

Joanne helped her client locate an emergency shelter in which she could live until she found an apartment, obtained clothing from the Salvation Army, and secured a one-time emergency cash payment of $100 from her own agency. Joanne continued to work with Nicole during her stay in the shelter. Together they found a one-bedroom apartment, modestly furnished it, and filled the pantry with nonperishable food. After Nicole moved into the apartment, Joanne helped her learn to budget, and to increase her knowledge of child development and parenting as well as to enroll in a GED program.

Client Advocacy.   "Advocacy is speaking on behalf of clients when they are unable to do so, or when they speak and no one listens" (Woodside & McClam, 1998, p. 63). There are two types of client advocacy. In *case advocacy,* the client system is an individual, family, or group (Garvin & Seabury, 1997; Rothman & Sager, 1998). In *class advocacy*, the client system is a large collective or group of people defined by some demographic characteristic (Barber, 1995). Class advocacy is also referred to as cause advocacy (Miley, O'Melia, & DuBois, 1998).

Advocacy has a long tradition in social work and is defined as a professional responsibility of social workers (NASW, 1996). Ezell (1994) found that 90 percent of the social workers surveyed did case advocacy on a regular basis. Unlike the interventions described earlier, client advocacy requires the social worker to take a strong position on behalf of the client system (Garvin & Seabury, 1997).

Empowering practice involves the client system in the advocacy process. It is generally better to work with clients to advocate for rights, services, and/or resources than to advocate on their behalf without their participation in the process. Client advocacy involves educating clients about their rights, teaching advocacy skills to clients, and applying pressure to make agencies and resources respond to client needs. The following case illustrates the use of client advocacy.

Tracy D. is the social worker at the Mission House, a shelter for homeless families. One of her primary tasks is to help families make successful linkages with social service agencies in the community. Families use the shelter for short-term emergency housing and must begin developing alternative arrangements on entering the shelter. Most of the families need a wide range of social services beyond housing. Tracy helps shelter residents identify needs and develop action plans to improve their situations.

Elaine T. is thirty-six years old and has two children, ages ten and twelve. Her husband had deserted the family four years earlier, and she had a job with a cleaning service to support her family. Two years ago, she lost her job and was unable to secure another that paid enough to cover her modest living expenses. She managed on welfare payments until she was terminated in October. Unable to pay her rent, she was evicted in December. She entered the shelter with no money, few possessions, and little hope.

Tracy referred Mrs. T. to the community action agency for enrollment in a job-training program that taught basic computer skills. But Mrs. T. was not accepted into the job training program because she did not have a high school diploma. The worker at the community action agency recommended that Mrs. T. enroll in their GED program. Mrs. T. was not in favor of this option since completing the GED would take a fairly long time and on completion she still would not be prepared for a specific job.

Tracy and Mrs. T. decided to appeal the negative decision by the community action agency. First they worked together to compose a letter to the program coordinator requesting a reversal of the decision and, indicating that if a reversal was not granted, she would appeal the decision. Tracy also worked with Mrs. T. to teach her how to approach her appeal and how to present herself in the meeting. Together they outlined several reasons why Mrs. T. should be allowed to participate in the job training program. They role-played the appeal interview to help Mrs. T. become comfortable with the formal nature of the process. Tracy also called the job training coordinator and argued Mrs. T.'s case. Tracy accompanied Mrs. T. to the appeal meeting and spoke on her behalf.

> The appeal was turned down. Tracy and Mrs. T. began searching for alternative job training programs and other employment opportunities within the community.

Education and Training.   Education is a major function of generalist social work (DuBois & Miley, 1999). At the micro level, it involves helping individuals, families, and groups learn new concepts and skills. Many clients do not have the skills needed to meet the demands and expectations of their environment (Garvin & Seabury, 1997). Generalist social workers empower their clients through an exchange of information. This occurs as a normal part of most social work interventions. However, when it is a primary goal of the interaction, it becomes an intervention.

When functioning as an educator or trainer with any client, especially with disadvantaged and oppressed clients, it is important to be mindful of the discrepancy in power between you and your clients. You have the knowledge and power, and it is easy to assume the role of expert. Minimize the power differential by taking an empowering approach. Use a strengths approach, and begin with the capacities of your clients (Freud, 1987). Have them share their knowledge of the topic. Create a learning partnership in which you and the client are co-learners (DuBois & Miley, 1999). Engage in an educational dialogue as opposed to a one-way conveying of information (Freire, 1990).

An educational intervention may involve helping clients learn such new skills as parenting, disciplining children, life-care, budgeting, time management, and shopping. Skills training can take place with individual clients and families or in group settings. Groups that have an educational function are common in social work (Middleman & Wood, 1990). The following example illustrates an educational intervention.

> Time Out for Tots is a parenting program for teenage mothers that consists of fifteen two-hour sessions. The young mothers attend a weekly mother-only group session during which information on child development and parenting is presented by the social worker. Group members also share their personal experiences and challenges. The second component of the program involves both the mothers and the children in a weekly group play session. During this portion of the program, the social worker models appropriate parent-child interaction and supports the mothers' use of the concepts and techniques covered in the group sessions.

MACRO-LEVEL INTERVENTIONS

There are three major system change activities that generalist social workers engage in when working with organization and community client systems: education and training, program planning, and community development. The purposes of macro-level interventions at the organizational level are to improve the functioning of organizations, to improve the delivery of existing services, and to develop new services. The purposes of macro-level interventions at the community level are to improve community conditions, empower residents, develop community resources, increase citizen awareness of community issues, and mobilize citizens to work for change.

Education and Training

Education and training are major functions of macro-level generalist practice. At the organizational level, they occur primarily through staff development and continuing education aimed at improving the quality of services and service delivery to clients. At the community level, educational activities are used to increase community awareness and understanding of social issues and community problems (Miley, O'Melia, & DuBois, 1998). The social worker can make formal presentations at community meetings, serve as a panelist at a public forum, and/or conduct community workshops. The following case illustrates an educational intervention aimed at increasing community awareness of substance abuse problems.

> Sam W. is the social worker with the Community Prevention Coalition (CPC) a grant-funded drug and alcohol prevention program. CPC is a community-based program that seeks to empower the residents of an economically disadvantaged community that has high rates of poverty, crime, substance use, and other social ills.
>
> One of the objectives of the program is to increase awareness about social problems in the community. Education is the primary intervention Sam uses to achieve this objective. He began by organizing a series of presentations for all the churches in the community. His talks focused on the magnitude of the drug and alcohol problem in the community and the long-term effects it has on quality of life. Sam also spoke about the possibilities of change and how the community can take positive actions to improve conditions and address the various social problems.

Program Planning

Program planning, which is also known as social planning (Kurzman, 1985; Lauffer, 1978), is the development, expansion, and coordination of social services and social policies (Lauffer, 1981). It involves activities that "address the development and coordination of community agencies and services to meet community functions and responsibilities and to provide for its members" (Hardcastle, Wenocur, & Powers, 1997, p. 2). Program planning can be conducted at the individual agency level, by a consortium of human service agencies, or by regional or state human service planning agencies (Weil & Gamble, 1995). Generalist social workers typically become involved in program planning activities that seek to improve the operation of existing services and programs and to develop new services and programs at the agency and community level by working with agency task forces, professional task forces, and/or community coalitions.

As part of the planning process, generalist social workers may evaluate existing programs and services, conduct need assessments, identify funding sources, prepare grant proposals, or engage in public relations activities to build program support. To be effective in carrying out these tasks, the generalist social worker needs to be skilled in social work research methods and have well-developed writing and presentation skills. The following case illustrates the use of program planning as a macro-level intervention.

In his role as generalist social worker with the Community Prevention Coalition, Sam W. was assigned to represent the agency on a professional task force organized by the local United Way. The task force was composed of professional representatives from most of the community's human service agencies as well as representatives from several community and neighborhood groups. The task force was charged with identifying community needs and developing appropriate programs and services to address the needs.

At the initial organizational meeting, the members of the task force were assigned to various subcommittees, each of which was to assess needs related to a specific community problem or service area. Sam volunteered for the substance abuse subcommittee. Sam and the other subcommittee members designed and carried out a needs assessment focusing on the community's drug and alcohol problem, services and resources that were available, and the need for additional services and resources. Subcommittee members designed questionnaires, interviewed a sample of community residents and service professionals, conducted focus groups with the key informants, and presented the task force with a comprehensive report describing their findings and preliminary recommendations.

Community Development

Community development refers to interventions aimed at improving community conditions and empowering residents to seek community change. Community development also has a social action component—activities aimed at challenging inequalities, confronting decision makers, and empowering people to change unjust conditions (Rubin & Rubin, 1992). The focus is on social, political, and economic justice for the disadvantaged and disenfranchised (Weil & Gamble, 1995). Thus, community practice is the "development, redistribution, and control of community statuses and resources, including social power, and the alteration of community relations and behavior patterns to promote the development or redistribution of community resources" (Hardcastle, Wenocur, & Powers, 1997, p. 2).

Community development is used as an intervention strategy when disadvantaged populations have been excluded from the decision-making process and when the prevailing power structure does not appear to be responsive to the community as a whole or its representatives (Staples, 1990). Community development strategies seek to improve community conditions, empower residents, develop resources, and mobilize citizen groups. To achieve these purposes, the generalist social worker organizes constituent groups, builds community coalitions, conducts community needs assessments, lobbies political and government leaders, and advocates on behalf of constituent groups.

Social workers involved in organizing constituent groups often take responsibility for convening and facilitating meetings. They do the planning and the legwork to get participants to attend. This requires skill in managing groups and conducting meetings. An empowering approach to the process focuses on having community residents assume control and leadership of the development effort. The social worker helps get the process going, but ultimate responsibility for the effort rests with participants and indigenous leadership.

Coalition-building occurs when representatives of diverse community groups join forces to influence external institutions on one or more issues affecting their constituencies (Mizrahi & Rosenthal, 1993). The goal is to build a power base sufficient to influence decision making and allocation of resources (Weil & Gamble, 1995). Often, there is inherent tension between the coalition members' interest in maintaining the autonomy and power of their constituent groups and the need to share power and resources to make the coalition successful. Social workers need well-developed mediation and negotiation skills to effectively build coalitions, as well as skills in interorganizational relations and planning (Weil & Gamble, 1995).

Class advocacy involves organizing oppressed and disadvantaged groups to exercise their influence to correct inequality. This requires the active participation of citizens who are vulnerable or disenfranchised (Miley, O'Melia, & DuBois, 1998), and it provides an opportunity for whole groups of people to assume responsible participation in the social or public realm (Lewis, 1991). The social worker's role involves informing groups of disadvantaged people of their rights and entitlements, mobilizing citizen groups, and bringing pressure to bear on organizational decision makers, government officials, and political leaders. The following case illustrates a community development intervention.

Steve K. is a social worker in an economically disadvantaged city of about 50,000 people. The majority of the population is minority, with a large proportion on public assistance. The community is located in a county that is composed primarily of affluent suburban communities. The county government funds most of the services that are provided to the residents of the city. The community action agency has been seeking additional monies from the county to fund community-based programs, but their funding requests have regularly been turned down.

The residents of the city believe that their needs are being neglected by the county commissioners, who are predominately white and from the more affluent communities in the county. City dwellers feel that the level of funding is far below what is needed given the magnitude of the problems they are facing.

For years, the various community groups in the city have been distrustful of one another and have refused to unite to seek funding. To address this problem, Steve began to meet with various neighborhood and community groups. His expressed purpose was to explore the possibility of creating a coalition of community groups. He convened a series of meetings in which the indigenous leaders of the various groups discussed the advantages and disadvantages of working together to improve community conditions. Steve's role in the process was to organize and mobilize citizen support for the coalition, to facilitate communication among participants, to provide information about the planning process, and to help the group prepare formal requests for community development projects.

TERMINATION

In many respects, how you end with your client systems is as important as how you begin. During the termination phase, you and your client review, evaluate, and consolidate the work; process feelings and experiences; and plan ways to maintain the beneficial changes that have occurred (Fortune, 1995; Garvin & Seabury, 1997). Most of the research conducted on endings has focused on the ending process at the micro level (Fortune, 1987; Fortune, Pearlingi, & Rochelle, 1992). Very little research has been undertaken on terminating the helping relationship with organizational- and community-level client systems. Nevertheless, many aspects of the ending process are similar for all client system levels. For example, the tasks of assessing progress, stabilizing gains, preparing for the transition, and planning for the future are addressed with all client systems. However, termination with agency and professional task forces involves substantially less emphasis on sharing of feelings and the emotional component of termination than does termination with other client systems.

Types of Termination

There are five common reasons for ending the helping relationship: planned ending, time-limited service, ending open-ended service by mutual agreement, ending open-ended service for unanticipated reasons, transfer to another social worker, and dropping out (Fortune, 1995). Regardless of the reason, appropriate termination helps clients solidify the gains made and prepares them for the ending of the helping relationship.

Planned Endings. There are two types of planned endings. The first is the ending that was planned from the beginning of the service and that takes place after a specified amount of time. Managed-care companies typically require fixed time limits on social work services. As managed care becomes the norm, the occurrence of planned endings with time-limited services will increase. Because the ending is determined at the beginning of the service, the process is usually easier than in open-ended service (Fortune, 1995).

The second type of planned ending occurs when the service contract is open-ended (that is, there are no fixed time limits) and the social worker and client agree that the helping relationship does not need to continue. This usually occurs when the client has achieved the identified goals or has made sufficient progress on them and feels that other areas of concern can be handled outside the helping relationship.

In collaborative generalist practice, the client determines when to terminate the helping relationship. If the client feels ready to proceed without the help of a social worker, he or she should be given the opportunity to do so even if the social worker believes otherwise. Support the client's judgment and desire to function independently—but provide the option of returning if the need arises.

The ultimate goal of collaborative generalist social work practice is to empower clients and encourage their independent functioning. Long-term reliance on a helping relationship fosters dependency. If a client does not want to end a relationship that you believe should end, you need to communicate this to the client. One possible way of handling the situation is to revise the intervention and evaluation plan to set time limits and to identify goals related to termination. This way, the client is given a voice in the termination process and a set time frame for a successful, mutually agreed-on ending.

Another important reason to end the helping relationship is lack of success (Fortune, Pearlingi, & Rochelle, 1992). If progress is not being made, or if you agree that the chances of making progress are minimal, it is in your client's best interest to terminate service. Of course, this should be done only after an open and honest evaluation of your relationship and the reasons for the lack of success. If you have continually monitored progress and have adjusted the interventions in response to the lack of progress, a consideration of termination is warranted.

Unanticipated Endings.   There are a multitude of reasons for unplanned endings. A common type of unanticipated ending is transfer to another social worker. The social worker must terminate the helping relationship because he or she is leaving the agency, or the client has been reassigned to another worker or to another service agency. Termination under these conditions is difficult because the client has a continuing need for service and has to establish a relationship with the new worker. The primary tasks associated with this type of ending are to process the client's feelings about the change of workers and help the client prepare to transfer to the new worker or agency.

Another form of unanticipated ending, one that unfortunately is all too common in the human service field, is dropping out. The client simply does not return and does not inform the social worker. The primary drawback is that clients who drop out do not have opportunities to access the helping process, make plans to maintain gains achieved, or plan for continued growth.

Between 40 and 60 percent of cases end because of situational factors (DeBerry & Baskin, 1989; Fortune, 1995; Hynan, 1990). Thus, for approximately half of all clients, service ends without achieving the desired goals or without mutual agreement. The probability of achieving positive outcomes in these situations is small. Additionally, clients might experience disappointment, frustration, or anger over the disruption of service.

Clients' Reactions to Termination

Separation is inherent in ending a helping relationship. It is common to have mixed feelings about any type of separation. The intensity of feelings about termination vary depending on the amount of success achieved, the strength of the relationship, the type of termination, and the client's previous experiences with terminating professional and personal relationships.

Several factors influence clients' reactions to termination. The most important is the reason for termination. Planned, agreed-on terminations tend to be viewed as positive experiences. Unexpected terminations are more likely to result in negative feelings. Feelings of anger, disappointment, and a sense of unfinished business are common reactions to an unplanned termination (Fortune, 1995).

Not long ago, research on termination characterized the process in primarily negative terms. The emphasis was on sadness, loss, denial, depression, and other negative reactions (Fortune, 1995; Hepworth, Rooney, & Larsen, 1997). Recent research findings indicate that most clients react to termination in a more positive than negative way (Fortune, 1987; Fortune, Pearlingi, & Rochelle, 1992). The benefits gained from a positive helping relationship outweigh the loss associated with ending (Hepworth, Rooney, & Larsen, 1997). Positive feelings of accomplishment, positive feelings about the helping relationship, and increased self-worth are usually associated with planned terminations (Gutheil, 1993).

Although positive reactions appear to outweigh negative reactions, mixed feelings are the norm. Most clients' experience some negative feelings about ending. Fortune (1987) found that negative reactions to termination occur more frequently in open-ended, psychosocial treatment. A common negative reaction to termination is to cling to therapy and the practitioner (Hepworth, Rooney, & Larsen, 1997). Some clients use the helping process as a substitute for interpersonal relationships. In these situations, giving up a long and meaningful relationship with the social worker is especially hard. In a sense, the client has become dependent on the relationship with the social worker. Hepworth, Rooney, and Larsen (1997) point out that it is important to stress the goal of independence within the shortest possible time frame throughout the helping relationship. If most of your clients have great difficulty ending the relationship, it is important to examine the extent to which you are fostering dependency by emphasizing weaknesses, deficiencies, and pathology rather than strengths and opportunities for growth (Hepworth, Rooney, & Larsen, 1997).

Another common negative reaction to termination is reporting recurrence of old problems (Hepworth, Rooney, & Larsen, 1997). This is sometimes referred to as regression. The client feels anxious about ending the relationship and wants to keep it going so old problems reappear as areas of concern. A variation of regression is when the client shows deterioration in terms of current problems or concerns. Instead of getting better and maintaining improvement, the client appears to be getting worse. Hepworth, Rooney, and Larsen (1997) suggest that, when this occurs, it is important to focus on the client's fears about termination and the ending process rather than on the problems that have reappeared.

Sometimes new problems are introduced as the termination date draws near. This is often a ploy to continue the relationship. Although you have to be sensitive to the possibility of real problems that require attention, it is important to explore the client's feelings about termination before turning to these new issues (Hepworth, Rooney, & Larsen, 1997). Often, the new issues disappear once an open discussion about the fears and uncertainty of termination has taken place.

The Termination Process

Some researchers view termination as an intervention (Fortune, 1995), and others view it as a component of the helping process or as the final stage of the helping relationship (Hess & Hess, 1994). According to Fortune (1995), termination interventions are designed to

- Assess client progress and treatment process
- Generalize gains to other settings and situations
- Develop skills and strategies to maintain gains
- Assist in the transition to no service or to another service
- Deal with emotional reactions to ending treatment.

Other researchers have developed similar conceptualizations of the tasks that need to be completed during the termination phase (Garvin and Seabury, 1997; Miley, O'Melia, & DuBois, 1998).

The tasks involved in the termination process are highly interrelated. In actual practice, it is difficult to clearly separate the various components. From a process perspective, the three major purposes of the termination phase of the helping relationship are (1) reviewing client progress and goal outcome; (2) reviewing the helping relationship and the helping process; and (3) planning for the future.

Reviewing Progress and Outcomes.   The first major task to be accomplished during the termination phase is to evaluate progress related to the identified client concerns and challenges. Collaborative generalist social work practice entails specifying target problems, setting realistic outcome goals and objectives, developing an intervention and evaluation plan, and implementing the plan. Evaluation is an ongoing process carried out throughout the intervention phase. Deciding to terminate the helping relationship is an evaluative act. In planned terminations, you and the client have agreed to end the helping relationship. In unexpected terminations, there has not been agreement to ending the helping relationship. Under both conditions, a comprehensive review of progress during the termination phase is needed.

A final comprehensive review can confirm or disconfirm the decision to terminate (Fortune, 1995). Is termination appropriate? Is the helping relationship no longer needed? Is the client ready to move on without service or move to a new service? Based on the outcome criteria you and your client established earlier, has sufficient progress been made? What issues have been resolved? What still needs to be done?

Another reason for reviewing progress during termination is that it provides the opportunity to acknowledge the client's work, effort, and strengths. Termination brings mixed feelings. The client usually feels some degree of apprehension. Emphasizing client strengths and achievement is especially important when the client is feeling anxious and vulnerable. At this stage, one of your key tasks is to support the client and foster belief in himself or herself. Helping clients see how much they have accomplished and how they have successfully coped with their problems and challenges is critical.

A third reason for reviewing progress is that it is the first step in planning for the future. A comprehensive assessment of where the client currently is needs to occur before plans for future actions can be formulated.

Reviewing the Helping Relationship.   The helping relationship is the heart of collaborative generalist social work practice. It is through the helping relationship that clients address their concerns and challenges. During termination, it is critical for you and the client to explore each others' experiences and perceptions about your work together. This helps clients articulate what they liked and disliked in the helping relationship. Being aware of their feelings will make them better consumers of future relationships with helping processionals. In a concrete sense, an open and candid discussion of your helping relationship will begin preparing clients for possible future service episodes.

A second reason for reviewing your helping relationship is that it will give you and the client an opportunity to share feelings about working together. It is critical in a collaborative relationship for both you and the client to share what the relationship has meant to you and the joys and frustrations of working together. This is not a one-way street; both you and the client are expected to be open about the relationship.

A third reason for the review is that it provides an opportunity to explore the client's feelings about ending. Clients will have mixed feelings about terminating the helping relationship. There will be feelings of joy, excitement, and pride about accomplishments as well as feelings of anticipation, sadness, and loss. The intensity of clients' reactions to ending is influenced in part by their prior experiences with separation and ending relationships and in part by the type of termination and the progress they have made. Acknowledging the mixed feelings helps make them acceptable, validates the client's experiences, and allows a discussion to occur (Fortune, 1995). Clients with strong negative reactions will need more time to process their feelings about ending. They may be experiencing intense mourning and grief reactions and should have an opportunity to work through the grieving process as they would with any other significant loss.

At the other extreme are clients who deny having any feelings about ending. One possibility is that the client is responding as if there will be no ending (Garvin & Seabury, 1997). This may occur even if the client has agreed to termination. The client may have cognitively accepted the appropriateness of ending the helping relationship but has not accepted it emotionally. In this situation, sharing your feelings about ending may help the client become aware of his or her own feelings and confront and accept the impending separation (Hess & Hess, 1994).

Use the Helping Relationship Inventory (HRI) presented in Chapter 2 as a starting point for your discussion with the client. It covers the major components of the helping relationship. Comparing your responses with the client's responses is instructive. It will help you ensure that you engage in a comprehensive review of the structural and interpersonal aspects of the helping relationship.

Planning for the Future.   The third major task to be accomplished during termination is to help your clients plan for the future. This involves helping them make the transition to no service or to another service and solidify the gains made during the helping relationship. Fortune (1995) suggests that increasing the sense of mastery through realistic praise and highlighting the client's role in creating and maintaining change will help ensure gains after service ends.

Whether the client is ending the process or being transferred to another service, the social worker needs to ease the transition by making the new situation real (Fortune, 1995). Events that are distant, unspecified, and abstract are less real than events that are close at hand, specific, and concrete. Your task is to make the pending change in circumstances as concrete as possible. Be specific about the future. Have the client visualize what his or her life will be like outside the helping relationship or what will need to be done to begin a new helping relationship. If the client is being transferred elsewhere, link the client with the new service, visit the new agency, and engage in other activities that promote the connection so as to help smooth the transition. If service is ending, link the client to a support network and engage in activities that will support the transition to nonservice. In both situations, explore the client's feelings and expectations and make plans for following up and checking back.

Solidifying or maintaining the gains made through the helping relationship is another task that needs to be addressed during termination. "Workers cannot assume that beneficial changes the clients have attained will continue" (Garvin & Seabury, 1997, p. 428). One common reason is that the client's environment may not be supportive of the changes. The client may not have a support network that will bolster his or her new ways of coping. The kind of support the client received in the helping relationship may not be available. In fact, the client's environment may undermine the gains made.

During termination, the client and worker must develop a plan that specifies how change will be maintained. This plan should lay out strategies that the client can use to avoid future difficulties and respond to challenging situations as well as proactive strategies and activities aimed at preventing the reoccurrence of problems. Strategies that can be used for these purposes are overlearning, problem solving, and network interventions (Garvin & Seabury, 1997).

Overlearning focuses on helping clients practice new ways of coping after the initial learning. The key is to have the client practice the new skill or coping strategy in as many different situations as possible. Through role-playing and discussion the client is prepared to respond appropriately to a variety of anticipated challenging situations.

The second strategy is to help the client strengthen his or her problem-solving skills. Help your client predict problems that might be encountered in his or her environment, and brainstorm ways to effectively respond to each problem situation. Role-play different strategies and approaches. The goal is to have the client develop problem-solving skills directly related to potential environmental challenges following termination.

The third strategy is network intervention. This entails strengthening the client's support network. The plan is to intervene in the client's environment, based on the premise that others in the environment may also require professional help (Garvin & Seabury, 1997). Network intervention requires the participation of members of the client's social support system and environment. They have to agree to support the client and to become involved in the change effort. Involvement of the support network should begin prior to the termination phase and increase as the client moves closer to ending.

SUMMARY

Generalist social work practice involves a wide range of practice skills and interventions. It entails micro-level and macro-level work. Micro interventions focus on individuals, couples, families, and small groups. Macro interventions focus on agency task forces, agency committees, professional task forces, community coalitions, and neighborhood groups.

The helping relationship in micro interventions is directed toward the enhanced functioning and empowerment of the client systems. The helping relationship in macro interventions at the organizational level focuses on improving organizations and their services as well as developing new services. At the community level, the focus is on improving community conditions, empowering residents, developing resources, increasing awareness and mobilizing citizens.

Generalist social workers must be skilled in the use of self regardless of the system level of the intervention. The use of self to help individuals, families, and small groups is widely regarded a fundamental part of direct (micro) practice. It is also a critical component of macro practice. The ability to provide support, increase motivation, foster hope, strengthen commitment, mobilize energy, increase understanding, and facilitate communication are important skills regardless of the size of the client system. The helping process with individuals, families, groups, organizations, and communities all require generalist social workers who can effectively use themselves to help achieve the identified changes.

Generalist social workers must also be skilled in a variety of system change activities. At the micro level, generalist social workers engage in supportive counseling, service linkage, service coordination, resource mobilization, client advocacy, and education and training activities. At the macro level, they engage in education and training, program planning, and community development activities.

The termination phase of the helping relationship needs the same amount of attention as the other phases of the helping process. It is during the termination phase that the gains made during the intervention phase are solidified and future plans for maintaining the gains are developed. To simply end with clients without attention to the various components and issues of termination is a disservice.

The tasks outlined in this chapter regarding termination are applicable to client systems of all levels. Termination with individual, couple, family, small groups, and neighborhood and community citizen groups involves all of the issues and activities discussed above.

CASE EXAMPLE

The final case in this chapter was written by Leslie Freas, a first-year MSW student placed in an adult partial hospitalization program. The case illustrates the termination process with an individual client who did not want to end the relationship.

But I'm Not Ready to Leave   *Leslie Freas*

The senior care center is a sixteen-week partial hospitalization program for individuals aged sixty-five and over who are experiencing a mental illness. The majority of clients are experiencing depression, often following the onset of a medical condition, such as Parkinson's disease, cancer, or a stroke, and/or following the loss of a spouse or loved one. Some clients have a long history of mental illness, including major depression, bipolar disorder, and schizophrenia. Many of the clients are either coming out of psychiatric hospitalization or are placed in this program to prevent hospitalization. Others are referred by their outpatient psychiatrist or primary physician or make a self-referral.

The senior care center provides individual and group therapy. Different groups engage in psychoeducation, music and art therapy, discharge planning, relapse prevention, and more intense psychotherapy. Clients also meet weekly with a social worker for supportive counseling. In addition, the social worker oversees the treatment plan and is responsible for developing the discharge plan.

Sarah K. is a seventy-seven-year-old Caucasian woman with a forty-three-year history of depressive episodes who has been diagnosed with both major depressive disorder and bipolar disorder. In late 1994, Mrs. K. was diagnosed with Parkinson's disease. Shortly after, she was admitted to the hospital's inpatient psychiatric ward, where she received electroconvulsive therapy. Following her discharge from the hospital, Mrs. K. was referred to the senior care center for continued mental health treatment and therapy.

After attending the center for more than three years, Mrs. K. was told several weeks ago that she will be discharged at the end of March. When she entered the program, there was no set time limit on how long a client could stay. Recently the center was informed by the managed care company that the maximum length of stay would be approximately sixteen weeks per client.

Mrs. K.'s biggest obstacle is her physical health. Parkinson's has limited her ability to function independently, and it has also started to impair her cognitive abilities, including her memory. In addition, she is suffering from depression. With her medication and the benefits of the senior care center, Mrs. K. has been coping with depression very well. The concern is that she will fall back into depression once she is no longer attending the center.

Mrs. K. still needs to improve her ability to be assertive about her needs and wishes. She acknowledges this in her individual sessions with me, and she realizes that she especially needs to work on this before her discharge.

Mrs. K., also has many strengths. She is a genuinely caring and optimistic person. She is intelligent and has a wonderful sense of humor. In addition, Mrs. K. is determined to stay active and fight the effects of Parkinson's disease. She rarely misses her scheduled days at the center and states that she cannot sit around the house and do nothing. Mrs. K.'s husband and son are caring and supportive.

Given her current level of functioning and the new reimbursement guidelines and policies, the treatment team does not feel that her continued participation in the program is justified. Mrs. K., her husband, and their son are upset about her pending discharge. They all feel that she benefits from the treatment she receives at the center and that the center has become an important part of her life.

I explored her feelings about termination with Mrs. K. She was very clear that she did not want to stop coming to the center every day. She was afraid she would get depressed again and that her health would deteriorate. I acknowledged her feelings about the termination. Although I could not justify keeping Mrs. K. in the program based on the new guidelines, I felt that she needed the support and stability the program offered. Together we developed the following termination plan:

- Mrs. K. will enroll in the aftercare group at the hospital and attend outpatient therapy at the center
- I will investigate the possibility of Mrs. K.'s receiving physical and/or occupational therapy for Parkinson's through the hospital
- Mrs. K. will begin attending a senior activities center once a week
- Mrs. K. will continue to verbalize her feelings about being discharged during individual counseling with me and at home with her family
- Mrs. K. will verbalize her needs and wishes regarding discharge to the center staff and family members.

DISCUSSION QUESTIONS

1. Describe possible ethical issues that Leslie faced regarding the termination of Mrs. K. What values were in conflict? Discuss ways Leslie could have resolved any possible ethical dilemmas.
2. Discuss ways Leslie could deal with Mrs. K.'s upset and unhappiness about her pending discharge from the program.
3. Discuss whether the treatment team should have made an exception in Mrs. K.'s case and let her stay indefinitely, assuming managed care allowed it? What benefits do you see in having Mrs. K. stay in the program? What are the benefits of termination? What are the negatives of staying and leaving? What would you recommend if you were Leslie? What would you recommend if you were the managed care representative?
4. List the types of activities you perform in your field placement. For each activity, identify the client system level and client systems. Assess the extent to which your field placement provides micro and macro practice experiences.
5. How do the purpose of the helping relationship, the use of self, and the system change activities vary between micro and macro interventions? In what ways are micro interventions similar to macro interventions? In what ways are they different?
6. Discuss the termination phase of generalist practice. What needs to be accomplished during termination? How does termination vary depending on the type of client system?
7. Describe the various intervention activities the hospital social worker used with Mr. E., the dialysis patient. What is your reaction to the way she handled the communication problem between the two doctors? What could she have done differently? What about the intervention she used with Mr. E.'s ex-wife? Do you agree or disagree with the approach she used? In what alternative ways could she have addressed the patient's concerns?

REFERENCES

Barber, J. G. (1995). Politically progressive casework. *Families in Society, 76,* 30–37.

Chavis, D. M., Florin, P., & Felix, M. R. J. (1993). Nurturing grassroots initiatives for community development: The role of enabling systems. In T. Mizrahi & J. D. Morrison (Eds.), *Community organization and social administration* (pp. 41–67). New York: Haworth Press.

Compton, B. R., & Galaway, B. (1994). *Social work processes* (5th ed.). Pacific Grove, CA: Brooks/Cole.

Connaway, R., & Gentry, M. (1988). *Social work practice.* Englewood Cliffs, NJ: Prentice-Hall.

DeBerry, S., & Baskin, D. (1989). Termination criteria in psychotherapy: A comparison of private and public practice. *American Journal of Psychotherapy, 43,* 43–53.

Dorfman, R. (1996). *Clinical social work: Definition, practice, and vision.* New York: Brunner/Mazel.

DuBois, B., & Miley, K. K. (1999). *Social work: An empowering profession* (3rd ed.). Boston: Allyn and Bacon.

Ezell, M. (1994). Advocacy practice of social workers. *Families in Society, 75,* 36–46.

Fortune, A. E. (1987). Grief only? Client and social work reactions to termination. *Clinical Social Work Journal, 15,* 159–171.

Fortune, A. E. (1995). Termination in direct practice. In R. Edwards (Ed.), *Encyclopedia of social work* (19th ed.). Silver Spring, MD: NASW Press.

Fortune, A. E., Pearlingi, B., & Rochelle, C. (1992). Reactions to termination of individual treatment. *Social Work, 37,* 171–178.

Freire, P. (1990). *Pedagogy of the oppressed.* New York: Continuum.

Freud, S. (1987). Social workers as community educators: A new identity for the profession. *Journal of Teaching in Social Work, 1,* 111–126.

Garvin, C. D., & Seabury, B. A. (1997). *Interpersonal practice in social work: Promoting competence and social justice* (2nd ed.). Boston: Allyn and Bacon.

Goldstein, E. (1995). *Ego psychology and social work practice* (2nd ed.). New York: Free Press.

Gutheil, I. A. (1993). Rituals and termination procedures. *Smith College Studies in Social Work, 63,* 163–176.

Hardcastle, D. A., Wenocur, S., & Powers, P. R. (1997). *Community practice: Theories and skills for social workers.* New York: Oxford University Press.

Haynes, K. S., & Mickelson, J. S. (1991). *Affecting change: Social workers in the political arena* (2nd ed.). New York: Longman.

Hepworth, D., Rooney, R., & Larsen, J. (1997). *Direct social work practice: Theory and skills* (5th ed.). Pacific Grove, CA: Brooks/Cole.

Hess, H., & Hess, P. M. (1994). Termination in context. In B. R. Compton & B. Galaway, *Social work processes* (2nd. ed., pp. 529–539). Pacific Grove, CA: Brooks/Cole.

Hynan, D. J. (1990). Client reasons and experiences in treatment that influence termination of psychotherapy. *Journal of Clinical Psychology, 46,* 891–895.

Kirst-Ashman, K., & Hull, G. (1993). *Understanding generalist practice.* Chicago: Nelson-Hall.

Kurzman, P. (1985). Program development and service coordination as components of community practice. In S. H. Taylor & R. W. Roberts (Eds.), *Theory and practice of community social work* (pp. 59–94). New York: Columbia University Press.

Lantz, J., & Lenahan, B. (1976). Referral fatigue therapy. *Social Work, 12,* 239–240.

Lauffer, A. (1978). *Social planning at the community level.* Englewood Cliffs, NJ: Prentice-Hall.

Lauffer, A. (1981). The practice of social planning. In N. Gilbert & H. Specht (Eds.), *Handbook of the social services* (pp. 583–597). Englewood Cliffs, NJ: Prentice-Hall.

Lewis, E. (1991). Social change and citizen action: A philosophical exploration for modern social group work. *Social Work with Groups, 14,* 23–34.

Marziali, E., & Alexander, L. (1991). The power of the therapeutic relationship. *American Journal of Orthopsychiatry, 61,* 383–391.

Middleman, R., & Wood, G. (1990). From social group work to social work with groups. *Social Work with Groups, 13,* 3–20.

Miley, K., O'Melia, M., & DuBois, B. L. (1998). *Generalist social work practice: An empowering approach* (2nd ed.). Boston: Allyn and Bacon.

Mizrahi, T., & Rosenthal, B. (1993). Managing dynamic tensions in social change coalitions. In T. Mizrahi & J. D. Morrison (Eds.), *Community organization and social administration* (pp. 11–40). New York: Haworth.

Moxley, D. P. (1997). *Case management by design: Reflections on principles and practices.* Chicago: Nelson-Hall.

National Association of Social Workers (1996). *Code of ethics.* Silver Spring, MD: Author.

Northen, H. (1995). *Clinical social work* (2nd ed.). New York: Columbia University Press.

Pinderhughes, E. (1995). Direct practice overview. In R. Edwards (Ed.), *Encyclopedia of social work* (19th ed.). Silver Spring, MD: NASW Press.

Reeser, L. C., & Epstein, I. (1990). *Professionalism and activism in social work: The sixties, the eighties, and the future.* New York: Columbia University Press.

Rothman, J., & Sager, J. S. (1998). *Case management: Integrating individual and community practice* (2nd ed.). Boston: Allyn and Bacon.

Rubin, H. J., & Rubin, I. S. (1992). *Community organizing and development* (2nd ed.). New York: Macmillan.

Russell, M. (1990). *Clinical social work: Research and practice.* Newbury Park, CA: Sage.

Shulman, L. (1999). *The skills of helping individuals, families, groups and organizations* (4th ed.). Itasca, IL: Peacock.

Specht, H. (1988). *New directions for social work.* Englewood Cliffs, NJ: Prentice-Hall.

Staples, L. (1990). Powerful ideas about empowerment. *Administration in Social Work, 14,* 29–42.

Weil, M. O., & Gamble, D. N. (1995). Community practice models. In R. Edwards (Ed.), *Encyclopedia of social work* (19th ed.). Silver Spring, MD: NASW Press.

Weissman, A. (1976). Industrial social service: Linkage technology, *Social Casework, 57,* 50–54.

Woodside, M., & McClam, T. (1998). *Generalist case management: A method of human service delivery.* Pacific Grove, CA: Brooks/Cole.

CHAPTER 8

Generalist Practice with Economically Disadvantaged Clients and Communities

Stephen E. Kauffman

Kelly K. is a first-year MSW student placed in a community-based program that provides consultation services to grassroots human service programs in an economically disadvantaged community with numerous social problems. The agency's mission is to increase the number of services available to community residents as well as to strengthen the capacities of the local service organizations. Kelly is developing a collaborative program with the local legal-aid clinic. The clinic provides legal services to the low-income residents, many of whom also need social work and case management services. The objective is to develop a program that will provide social work and case management services to the legal-aid clients.

Kelly is excited and overwhelmed about helping develop a new service for the residents that would also strengthen an existing community agency. She knows that her first step is to learn all she can about the community and the experiences of the low-income residents who will use the new program. What is it like to be a member of a disadvantaged community? What is it like to be poor? What kinds of services and assistance do the potential clients need? How is working with disadvantaged communities and citizens different than working with other client populations? In what ways is it similar? What professional and community groups need to be involved in the planning process?

Poverty is without question the most ubiquitous, complex, and intractable of all social problems. It is a worldwide issue of concern, and it affects individuals and families in rich and poor nations alike. Poverty is often associated with a wide variety of other social problems, including substance abuse, domestic violence, disease, and environmental degradation. As a result, understanding poverty and developing skills for working with the poor are critical elements of effective generalist social work practice.

Social work owes its existence to the problem of poverty. The very first social workers, the Charity Organization Society and the settlement house volunteers, were driven by a concern for the poor. From these two groups of early social workers evolved the basic micro and macro practice approaches that are the core of the profession today. Such contemporary practice methods as case management, advocacy, community organization, and policy development all are linked to the historical relationship between the profession and the problem of poverty.

Although social work practice areas today are often diverse and the populations that social workers serve demonstrate a range of problems and economic classes, the issue of poverty is as important today as it was a hundred years ago. Many of the principles of social work practice and the values of the profession are defined by the relationship of the profession to the poor. The concept of empowerment, for example, comes in part from a recognition that discrimination and oppression are among poverty's most important causes. Empowering individuals and communities is therefore a significant tool for remediating these problems. Similarly, much of the curriculum in social work education is oriented toward educating students to understand the problem of poverty and develop skills to work with the poor.

In light of the critical necessity for social workers to understand poverty, this chapter examines the issues associated with generalist practice with the poor. The goals of the chapter are to provide an understanding of poverty and to equip you with some essential tools for effective interventions with economically disadvantaged clients. The chapter discusses the size and scope of the problem, macro policy issues, micro and macro practice issues, including various theories about the causes of poverty, and issues related to human behavior and social environment, including the consequences of poverty on individuals, families, and communities. The chapter also examines practice issues for social workers who engage in generalist practice with economically distressed clients and communities. By the end of this chapter, you should be able to help Kelly

1. Describe and critique the way poverty is measured in the United States
2. Understand the individual and social causes of poverty
3. Examine the economic and political factors that contribute to community poverty
4. Describe the consequences of poverty for individuals, families, and communities
5. Articulate the various micro and macro strategies a generalist social worker would adopt in working with economically disadvantaged clients and communities.

THE PROBLEM OF POVERTY

Poverty knows no boundaries. Approximately a third of the world's population, or about 1.5 billion people, live in extreme poverty (United Nations Development Program, 1997). While extreme poverty is rare in the United States, over 34 million individuals—about 12.7 percent of the U.S. population—are poor (Delaker, 1999). Certain subgroups in the United States, including children, African-Americans, and Latinos, have substantially higher poverty rates (Weinberg, 1998).

Many others are near the poverty threshold—almost 36 percent of households in the United States earn less than $25,000 and are considered poor or near-poor.

Poverty has a profound effect on the American economy. Federal, state, and local expenditures for social welfare comprised 21.1 percent of the Gross Domestic Product (GDP) in 1993, and the total dollar cost for all public social welfare activities, was $1.363 trillion (U.S. Department of Health and Human Services, 1997). These figures include all social welfare activities, including education, which is the largest single category of expenditures. Excluding education, more than $221 billion in public funds were spent on aid to the poor in 1993 alone.

The number of individuals receiving public assistance is large. Medicaid, the primary governmental medical assistance program for the poor, served more than 37 million Americans in 1996. The largest income support program for the poor, known as Temporary Assistance for Needy Families (TANF), currently serves more than 3 million recipients (U.S. Department of Health and Human Services, 1998), with an annual program cost of more than $16 billion.

In terms of indirect costs, which are costs to the economy beyond dollars spent by federal, state, and local programs, the figures are equally staggering. Looking at childhood poverty alone, the Children's Defense Fund has estimated that for every year that 14.5 million American children continue to experience poverty, their lifetime contribution to the economy will decline by approximately $130 billion. This is because poor children grow up to be less educated and less productive workers (Children's Defense Fund, 1998).

Poverty may even be more pervasive than the official statistics suggest. The number of people classified as poor depends on the way *poverty* is defined. Although defining *poverty* may seem to be a simple task, it is in fact a complex problem. Definitions differ according to what is being measured.

The official U.S. definition of poverty is an absolute income level based on family size that changes from year to year as a result of changes in the cost of living. This income figure was initially computed using American family spending patterns, food costs, and family size of the 1950s. It used an estimate of the cost of food an individual would need for short-term survival multiplied by three to account for other living expenses (Fisher, 1992). The underlying assumption was that spending patterns for all Americans were similar. Since the average American family of the time spent about one-third of its income on food and two-thirds on the remainder of expenses, the pattern was assumed to also apply to the poor. Using this measure, the poverty level is currently $16,660 for a family of four, with $2,800 added for each additional person in the family (Delaker, 1999).

There are questions about the adequacy of this measure (Citro & Micheal, 1995). The measure, for example, does not take into account changes in average income created by noninflationary factors such as worker productivity, which is the output of a worker per unit of work. Increased worker productivity has resulted in wage increases over the past forty years at a pace greater than inflation. This means that the average poor person today is "poorer" relative to the average worker than a poor person thirty years ago. Nor has the official poverty measure been adjusted for changes in spending patterns over time. The cost of food is no longer as significant an expense as it was in the past. Generally, Americans now spend a lower percentage of their income on food and a higher percentage on housing and medical care than they did in the 1950s.

Moreover, wealth, assets, power, education, and other psychological and social quality-of-life variables are not addressed by the measure. Some of these other variables might be as important as income in determining an individual's status in the larger society. For example, there is evidence that the accumulation of wealth contributes to the development of behaviors and attitudes consistent with those of the dominant culture (Sherraden, 1991), and the effect of wealth might be more important on the development of these values and behaviors than income (Yamada & Sherraden, 1997). Measures of wealth indicate vast differences between the poor and other groups in the society. Median household wealth in 1993 for the poorest 20 percent of all Americans was $4,249, which compares unfavorably to the average wealth of all American households, which was $37,587 (U.S. Bureau of the Census, 1995a). By focusing on income alone, the absolute measure of poverty misses important differences between the poor and the "typical" American.

Nevertheless, the absolute poverty measure has value. It sets the income thresholds for determining benefit eligibility for many government antipoverty programs. It allows us to identify trends over time and to identify groups in the population that might require special attention. It also highlights certain risk factors for poverty that are important in the assessment process. Using this measure, the poverty rate of children is 18.9 percent, of African-Americans 26.1 percent, of Latinos 25.6 percent, and of households headed by women 29.9 percent (Delaker, 1999).

THE CAUSES AND CONSEQUENCES OF POVERTY

The large number of people who are poor and the costs to the economy associated with poverty result in significant attention by policymakers. Thousands of federal, state, and local policies have been enacted in the last century to deal with the problem of poverty. Why does the problem remain?

There are a large number of differing opinions about what causes poverty and, therefore, how to address the problem. Poverty is associated with almost every component of the human condition, including employment, health, values, ideology, social relations, psychological factors, and social and economic justice. Thus policymakers are confronted with an extremely complicated issue.

Among the many approaches to the problem of poverty that have been implemented are governmental employment programs, child-care assistance, cash assistance, tax-based approaches, education and training, entrepreneurship assistance, and asset development. Some argue that none of these approaches should be used, and in fact, the central policy thrust of recent years has been to decrease policy efforts to eradicate poverty. The idea has been to remove public assistance because it may itself perpetuate poverty. The results of this approach will strongly influence future policy choices.

Theories of Causation on the Micro Level

Perhaps the critical question affecting policy choices about poverty as well as the effectiveness of direct practice with the poor is "What causes poverty?" An important distinction has been drawn between those who are poor through no fault of their own, "the deserving poor," and those whose poverty is linked to some kind of failure of personal responsibility, "the undeserving poor" (Katz, 1989). The deserving poor are children, the elderly, women with young children, people who are sick, and people who are disabled. The capacity of these individuals to work is limited, and there is general agreement that the provision of assistance is both acceptable and necessary.

On the other hand, poverty among able-bodied men and women creates questions about the reasons for their poverty. It is about these individuals that theories about causality have been developed. In general, there are three types of theories that attempt to explain poverty causation: (1) theories that focus on individual deficits, (2) theories that focus on social and structural causes, and (3) theories that link the individual with the social environment. Although each model has serious limitations, they all offer some utility for understanding poverty.

Individual Deficits.   Theories of poverty that focus on individual deficits suggest that poverty results from one or more of a variety of biological, behavioral, or psychological deficits. These models suggest that the poor are poor because of genetic tendencies, such as low intelligence levels, that limit their ability to function in a modern, competitive capitalistic economy, or because of a psychological or behavioral limitation, such as laziness (Goodwin, 1983; Handler & Hasenfeld, 1991; Katz, 1989).

There is little doubt that such personal attributes as problem-solving ability and personal efforts affect the capacity to earn a living. The principal weakness of these theoretical perspectives, however, is that they do not take into account the role of the environment. Biological, behavioral, and psychological deficits may be caused by the environment or may result from the interaction of the environment and genetic factors. Inadequate nutrition, exposure to toxic substances such as lead, instability of social relationships, poor schools, few opportunities for steady employment, and many other similar factors have all been demonstrated to affect behavior and/or brain development and learning capacity (Bower, 1994).

Social and Structural Causes.   A second set of poverty theories focuses more on the consequences of social and environmental conditions than on individual deficits as the cause of poverty. According to these models, the larger society has failed to provide the opportunities necessary for personal success or has placed roadblocks in the way of the poor. Unjust occupational and merit structures, lack of power, the inaccessibility of high-wage employment (Danziger & Gottshalk, 1995; Wilson, 1987), poor schools and limited educational opportunities, and discrimination are all seen as social conditions that cause and perpetuate poverty.

Women, African-Americans, Latinos, and other minorities experienced legal, institutionalized discrimination in the past that limited their opportunities to move out of poverty (Polenberg, 1980). Though almost all forms of legal discrimination have now been eliminated, the legacy continues. Unintentional discriminatory acts rooted in the value systems of the past and even intentional illegal discrimination still affect employment patterns and living and social conditions.

In employment, for example, the upward mobility of women and minorities is slowed by a "glass ceiling" through which few pass. As a consequence, these groups tend to remain in lower paying jobs, earning significantly less on average than their white male colleagues. Moreover, since women are the primary caregivers for children, their special needs, such as child care or time off work for childbirth, affect their employment patterns.

Another structuralist perspective suggests that the foundations of poverty are deeply rooted in the social and economic organization of society. There has never been a time when poverty did not exist, and it is unclear whether, under the best of circumstances, the American economy can produce enough jobs or enough income for welfare recipients to escape poverty (Poole, 1995, 1997). Poverty, at least in terms of relative deprivation, will probably exist as long as our economy is structured as it is now.

The argument supporting this position is based in part on the perception that poverty is useful to the affluent in American society (Gans, 1976). Further, poverty is embedded in the goals, processes, and assumptions that guide the marketplace. A primary goal of a capitalistic free-market economy is efficiency in the distribution of goods and services. *Efficiency* here refers to the optimal or best price, which takes into account the demand for the product or service, competition between producers, and the cost of production. One of the predominant elements of the cost of production and, in turn, the ability of a producer to compete is the price of labor. There will always be a desire on the part of producers to find the lowest possible labor cost. One way to ensure low labor cost is to have a ready pool of the unemployed who are willing to work at low wages—what Marx (1867) referred to as the "industrial reserve army."

This ready pool of the unemployed also serves another function for the economy. If everyone were employed, employers would have a difficult time finding employees. Prospective employees would be able to demand higher wages, and employers would have little choice but to pay more or risk losing the employee. To ensure an adequate return on their investments, the employers would then have to charge higher prices to their customers. As all employers would presumably face the same wage pressures, the aggregate increase in costs would result in societywide inflation. As the cost of everything increased, workers would see their spending power decrease. To keep up with the increased cost of living, workers would demand higher wages, causing even more cost and wage increases. Thus, a pool of the unemployed improves the capacity of a producer to compete and serves to keep inflation low.

Other factors are also involved. Improvements in productivity can improve the ability of a producer to compete and keep inflation low. But such improvements may also serve to reduce the need for new workers. In addition, the globalization of the economy means that low labor costs and an even larger pool of the unemployed are available outside of the United States.

A second argument supports this assertion of inevitability. The central thesis is that as wealth accumulates, reasonable investments will generate new wealth. In other words, "the rich get richer." Those without a reserve supply of cash (wealth) may be forced into borrowing money for even small household emergencies such as car repair or a minor illness. Significant debt can accrue, and catching up may not be possible: "the poor get poorer." Wealth has been moving from the poor to the rich in recent decades (Center on Budget and Policy Priorities, 1997). This redistribution of wealth has been caused by changes in federal tax rates that have favored high-income individuals even as many benefit programs targeting the poor have been reduced or eliminated. This trend appears likely to continue (DiNitto, 1996; Murdock & Micheal, 1996).

Structuralist perspectives have limitations. The primary issue is that many of the preconditions of poverty have been addressed by the implementation of a variety of social policies. Most forms of discrimination, for example, were made illegal with such laws as the Civil Rights Act and Voting Rights Act of the early 1960s. Unemployment and higher educational access also have less effect because of legislative actions such as unemployment insurance and student aid programs. Further, focusing on social conditions ignores the fact that some individuals thrive and become wealthy under deplorable environmental constraints, and a substantial number of children who attend the poorest schools are able to escape poverty through personal efforts.

Individual-Social Linkages. A third set of theories examines the relationship between individual and social causes. Perhaps the best known of these theories are those collected in the category of "culture of poverty" (Lewis, 1959, 1961, 1966). According to these theories, people have historically suffered from social constraints such as low wages, legal discrimination, and limited educational opportunities. Individuals have adapted their behaviors to the conditions in order to survive. Antisocial behavior is one such adaptation, with crime, drug-dealing, and gambling as means of making a living. As families and communities adopt antisocial behaviors as means of survival, they develop a tolerance for the behaviors. The behaviors and tolerance of the behaviors are passed from one generation to the next, representing a change in what constitutes normative behavior (Banfield, 1968, 1974).

At this point, culture of poverty models diverge into a more conservative and a more liberal perspective. The more conservative perspective argues that the social conditions initially leading to the antisocial behaviors have been remedied by such social policies as the Civil Rights Act and unemployment compensation. At the same time, other social policies, such as Aid to Families with Dependent Children (AFDC) or programs put in place during the War on Poverty in the early 1960s, created another form of antisocial behavior: welfare dependency.

The argument is that welfare dependency becomes a barrier to mainstream American life because it destroys individual initiative and creativity (Bane & Ellwood, 1994; Mead, 1986, 1992): why work or even dream of a better life when all your needs are being met? Thus, according to this perspective, the solution to poverty is to eliminate (or at least severely restrict) welfare assistance and antipoverty programs (Gilder, 1981; Murray, 1984). This perspective has recently come to prominence and fits nicely with what have been identified as historical American beliefs about hard work and individualism (Katz, 1989).

The more liberal culture of poverty perspective, on the other hand, does not agree that the barriers of discrimination and limited opportunities were removed by the policies of the last few decades (Wilson, 1987). Although legal discrimination has been dismantled and greater educational and employment opportunities have been created, say proponents, less overt forms of discrimination continue to exist. Likewise, available employment is generally limited to low-wage occupations. The social policies put in place to help the poor are often so full of restrictions and disincentives that they help only a small percentage of those who need assistance. The policy implications of this perspective are not focused toward eliminating assistance, but rather toward expanding it to address ongoing barriers to mainstream life while vigorously attacking the continuing problems of subtle discrimination and a low-wage economy.

So what causes individual and family poverty? While the absence of money is the core problem, the reasons given for this deficit depend very much on the values and beliefs of the person asking the question. Clearly, poverty has both a personal and a social dimension. Individuals differ in their innate abilities, motivation, and physical capacity, all of which affect their income. But at the same time, the environment's ability to nurture and the capacity and will of the social, political, and economic systems to provide or limit opportunities also play a major role. Thus, effective social work practice with the poor requires careful attention to the attitudes, behaviors, and environmental situation of the client.

The Consequences of Poverty for Individuals and Families

There are numerous consequences of poverty for individuals and families, and the consequences are interrelated. The interrelationships make effective practice and the selection of interventions with the economically disadvantaged somewhat problematic. The consequences of poverty are often as serious to an individual and family or community as the lack of cash itself. Thus, it often makes sense to aim interventions at the secondary problem even though the root cause, poverty, continues unabated. For individuals and families, the consequences of poverty include hunger and poor nutrition, inadequate shelter, and other consequences.

The United States, as an advanced capitalist country, allows the marketplace to make many of its decisions about the production, distribution, and consumption of goods and services. Such decisions are generally expressed by the exchange of cash or credit for goods or services. Most people do not directly trade a good or service for some other good or service, nor do most people have the skills to produce all of the products necessary for survival. Instead, our economic system requires people to exchange some skill or form of labor for cash, which is then exchanged for the items that people need or desire.

Cash is necessary in order to purchase many of the products that are necessary for simple survival. This includes almost all of the resources needed for adequate biological functioning, such as food, water, clothing, and shelter. A lack of any of these resources can cause stress and can lead to illness and death. Hence, the most immediate consequence of poverty is its potential effect on the capacity of an individual to survive, let alone thrive. We exist within a fairly narrow set of biological imperatives, and if sufficient resources are not available, the consequences may be catastrophic.

Hunger and Nutrition.   The number of hungry people in the United States is open to some debate. The largest official estimate of hunger comes from a 1997 study that reported that 12 million American households experienced some food insecurity. Of these households, 4 million reported moderate or severe hunger; and half of these were families with children (Watkins, 1998a). As many as one in twelve American children under the age of twelve suffers from hunger (Hunger Action Coalition, n.d.).

Another measure of the size of the hunger problem in America comes from examining the utilization of services. At the federal level, fifteen food and nutrition programs administered by the U.S. Food and Nutrition Service assist one in six Americans. The federal Women, Infants, and Children (WIC) program alone serves almost 7.5 million people (Watkins, 1998b), and the largest program, the Food Stamps program, was estimated to serve almost 22.3 million individuals in fiscal year 1999, at a cost of $24.2 billion (U.S. Department of Agriculture, 1998).

A survey of twenty-nine cities by the U.S. Conference of Mayors (Brown & Waxman, 1996) found that requests for emergency food increased in 1996 by an average of 11 percent over 1995, with 62 percent of requests coming from families. The mayors also estimated that about 18 percent of the requests for emergency food were not met (Brown & Waxman, 1996). These percentage increases were lower than in previous years. Moreover, the percentages of both assistance requests and those turned away increased even more in 1997 and 1998 (U.S. Conference of Mayors, 1997, 1998).

The consequences of hunger and inadequate nutrition are substantial and far-reaching. Problems can range from inadequate physical and mental development to death. The problem is especially acute among children. The more severe the poverty a child experiences, the more likely nutritional deficits will exist (Brown & Pollitt, 1996). A list of the possible health consequences is presented in Table 8.1.

Shelter. Shelter is of equal importance to food and nutrition for survival. A steady income is necessary for adequate shelter, and the two most important variables are the availability of shelter and the quality of living conditions. Both may suffer when an adequate income is not available.

For most people, housing represents the largest ongoing expense. Only about 56 percent of American families could afford to purchase a home in 1995 (Savage, 1999) because of the down payment and mortgage requirements. The percentages are even lower for minority families. Likewise, the median monthly housing cost in America is $523. (U.S. Bureau of the Census, 1999a). The median percentage of income going to housing is 29 percent (U.S. Bureau of the Census, 1999a), but more than 5.3 million American households report that housing costs consume more than half of their total income (U.S. Department of Health & Human Services, 1999). With such high costs associated with shelter, it is not surprising that between 4.9 million and 9.32 million Americans are homeless (U.S. Department of Health and Human Services, 1994).

The living conditions in American housing are also problematic. A housing survey found that, in 1997, 20 percent of American homes had some visible external problems, and small but significant percentages of homes had incomplete kitchens (2.3 percent), plumbing problems (1.2 percent), and lacked access to a safe drinking water (10.4 percent). Almost 10 percent reported accumulations of trash, litter, or junk within three hundred feet of the property (U.S. Bureau of the Census, 1999b).

Among the more important problems facing those who live in older, substandard housing is lead poisoning. Lead was used extensively in the past in paints, plumbing fixtures, and gasoline. Thirty million homes in the United States contain lead-painted surfaces (*Congressional Quarterly Weekly Reports,* 1991), and more than 80 percent of all homes built before 1978 have lead-based paint in them (Centers for Disease Control and Prevention, n.d.). Lead poisoning can cause learning disabilities, behavioral problems, seizures, and death, and as many as one child in six has toxic levels of lead in his or her blood. More than 55 percent of African-American children living in poverty have toxic levels of lead in their blood (National Health/Education Consortium, 1991; Needleman, 1991).

While the severity of lead poisoning is recognized in the larger public health community, one recent study suggests that few social workers have been trained to recognize or act on the symptoms (Silver, Kauffman, & Soliman, 1998). It is

TABLE 8.1. Life-Cycle Stage and Effects of Malnutrition

Life-Cycle Stage	Malnutrition Effects
Prenatal and Neonatal	Low birth weight
	Brain damage
	Neural tube defect
	Still births
	Growth retardation
	Developmental retardation
	Brain damage
	Early anemia
	Continuing malnutrition
Young Children and Adolescents	Developmental retardation
	Increased risk of infection
	High risk of death
	Blindness
	Anemia
	Delayed growth spurt
	Stunted height
	Goiter
	Inadequate bone mineralization
Adults and the Elderly	Thinness
	Lethargy
	Obesity
	Heart disease
	Diabetes
	Hypertension/stroke
	Anemia
	Spine and hip fractures
	Accidents
	Heart disease
	Diabetes

Note: Data are from *Malnutrition Worldwide*, by World Health Organization, n.d. Available Internet: http:/www.who.int/nut/.

highly likely that a substantial number of children have behavioral problems that might best be addressed through lead treatment interventions.

Other Consequences.   There are many other undesirable consequences associated with poverty. These include

- Higher rates of diseases, including cancer
- Higher family stress levels (Brooks-Gunn, Klebanov, Liaw, & Duncan, 1995)
- Greater childhood abuse rates (U. S. Department of Health and Human Services, 1996)
- Lower levels of educational attainment
- Higher levels of mental illness

- A greater likelihood of crime victimization (U.S. Department of Justice, Bureau of Justice Statistics, n.d.)
- Reduced access to legal assistance and health insurance (U.S. Bureau of the Census, 1995b, 1996).

With such a vast array of problems, frustration and a form of learned helplessness may also appear. Most of these consequences are due to increased stresses on the individual and the family, which result from an ongoing attempt to adapt to their situation. The effect of these stresses and traumas may carry across generations (Cattell-Gordon, 1990).

Theories of Causation on the Macro Level

The factors affecting community poverty are slightly better understood and less controversial than those affecting individuals and families. A variety of interrelated factors limit the capacity of the environment to nurture. At the community level, poverty can often be traced to the interplay of two issues: economics and political power.

Economic Issues. Just as individuals do, communities require an adequate supply of income to pay for the services they provide. These services usually include public safety, education, infrastructure, and governance. The quality and quantity of these services are dictated, at least in part, by the tax base, the revenues generated by personal, property, and business taxes. Other revenue sources include fees charged by the community for various services, grants from the state or federal government, and credit obtained by public debt financing (loans to the community through financial instruments such as bond sales).

In a community populated by a large percentage of middle- and upper-income wage earners and/or characterized by a vibrant business and commercial sector, the taxes and fees generated will most likely be adequate to purchase and provide the desired services. Similarly, public debt financing is easier when the community is perceived as having adequate future revenues to make loan payments.

On the other hand, when a community is populated by a large percentage of low-income wage earners and/or characterized by a weak business sector, the taxes and fees generated may be inadequate. Under these conditions, very few options exist for the community, all of which will result in the same set of problems. First, the quality and quantity of needed services may be reduced in order to keep tax rates low. Second, the community may attempt to raise taxes or fees, but increased taxes often will drive taxpayers away to live or work in communities with lower tax rates. Third, the community will attempt to borrow money, but higher interest rates will be charged because the credit worthiness of the community is in question. This last option may lead to the need to raise taxes to pay the debt, or it may strap the community with a high future debt or reduced services (Karger, 1994), which may force the community to again raise taxes in the future. All three options almost inevitably result in service cutbacks, since they all depend on having a wage-earning or commercial population that can pay the taxes necessary to pay for the services.

Many communities lack a strong wage-earning or commercial sector for several reasons. One of the most important is that the American economy has undergone sweeping changes in the last thirty years. Many of the high-wage, low- to moderate-skill manufacturing jobs that were available from the 1940s to the 1970s have moved to areas where labor costs are much lower, such as Central America or Asia, in recent years. At the same time, job growth in this country has centered on two very different sets of skills. At one level, the high-technology and financial services sectors have expanded and have created a large number of high-paying jobs that require significant training and education. At another level, a large number of low-paying, low-skill jobs have been created in the service economy in areas such as retail commerce. Communities that have seen significant high-technology or finance job creation have done well in maintaining civic services, while communities that have not experienced such growth have suffered.

Political Power. To at least some degree, a community can overcome the lack of a strong tax base if community leaders can muster the political coordination to efficiently develop new resources, such as external grants or new businesses. Such efforts may succeed, but they often result in substantial tax giveaways by the community as incentives to business development. The degree to which these tax giveaways benefit the community and the poor is an open question (Vidal, 1995).

A far more common outcome is that communities are unable to muster sufficient political strength. Instead, political fragmentation and, occasionally, political corruption results. As a community begins to spiral downward, a form of competition emerges among various interests in the community to hold on to available resources. With mounting and diverse problems facing the community, interest groups may erect barriers to prohibit other interest groups from allocating scare resources differently. In light of diminishing external resources, this trend could get worse (Bailey & Koney, 1997).

The Consequences of Community Poverty

As a community spirals downward, a variety of social problems are likely to manifest themselves. These problems include increasing crime rates; higher rates of substance abuse; deteriorating schools, transportation, and recreational infrastructure; and a decline in the accessibility of high-quality medical care. The community simply does not have the money to provide the services that may stop the spread of problems.

Moreover, as city services deteriorate and taxes increase, individuals and families who can afford to move from the community often do so. This not only reduces the tax base even further; it also removes other valuable assets from the community, including the political strengths and knowledge of those who move and their function as role models for children. It has been argued, for example, that one of the principal reasons for the development of what has been called the "underclass" was the departure of the middle class and professionals from inner-city communities (Wilson, 1987). Many of the social programs of the last four decades helped those who were most able to be helped, primarily the better-educated middle class. These individuals moved to the suburbs or other affluent communities while the poor remained in areas characterized by inadequate services, high crime rates, and high unemployment.

Another consequence of poverty in poor and powerless communities, and also one little recognized by the social work profession, is the problem of environmental justice. Because there is a desperate need for employment and because of the intentional targeting of such communities for undesirable types of business (Kauffman, 1994; Rogge, 1993; 1994), poor communities are likely to be home to prisons, factories that discharge large amounts of pollutants, and waste management companies. The concentration of such businesses may result in a variety of negative social and health effects ranging from lowered property values and disagreeable odors to increased rates of respiratory diseases and cancer. One community has even noted an increase in prostitution to serve the truckers who bring garbage into several recently built trash incinerators (Resident of Chester, PA, personal communication, May 1997)!

DEVELOPING HELPING RELATIONSHIPS WITH ECONOMICALLY DISADVANTAGED CLIENTS AND COMMUNITIES

The complex, multidimensional aspects of poverty demand flexibility from the generalist social work practitioner. Individuals and communities will almost inevitably present a range of different problems, each requiring different skills and knowledge. Because of the scope of the problem, this section will not attempt to address all of the practice issues with these client groups, but instead will focus on a set of generalist concepts as they apply to this rewarding area of practice. These concepts include (1) the range of target problems and goal-setting, (2) the importance of research and planning, (3) collaboration, coalition-building, and the importance of relationships, and (4) effective interventions.

The Range of Target Problems and Goal-Setting

The essential starting point in generalist social work practice with economically disadvantaged clients and communities is determining the desired outcomes of the intervention. At least three types of goals apply to this area of practice:

1. Goals that seek improvements in intangible concepts, such as the distribution of rights or psychological status
2. Goals that seek improvements in processes
3. Goals that seek specific, measurable, targeted outcomes.

Table 8.2 links each goal to a partial list of potential target problems. This may serve to guide your thinking about where to focus your intervention. Specifically, after the identification of the target problem, the client, whether an individual, a family, or a community, may require assistance in determining where best to focus corrective efforts. Consider, for example, the problem of poor community planning. Here, the appropriate goal is improvement of the processes the city uses to make its decisions. This may then require interventions at the level of city government. On the other hand, violence within a family might be better addressed by direct practice with the family to improve its internal communication or problem-solving skills.

The process of selecting goals is as important as the goals themselves, if not more so. It is critical to work closely with the client system. You bring a level of expertise to the relationship, but it is the client who experiences the problems, and more often than not, it is the client who actually implements the intervention. This means, at the very least, that the client is ultimately responsible for the change.

TABLE 8.2. Possible Target Problems and Goal Types

Goals That Seek Improvements in Intangible Concepts		Goals That Seek Improvements in Processes		Goals That Seek Specific, Measureable, Targeted Outcomes	
Micro	Macro	Micro	Macro	Micro	Macro
Target Problems	*Target Problems*	*Target Problems*	*Target Problems*	*Target Problems*	*Target Problems*
Lack of empowerment	Enviromental racism	Low political participation	Low political participation	Unemployment	Unemployment rates
Lack of self-efficacy	Social injustice	Poor family communication	Poor community planning	Family violence	Crime rates
Resident apathy	Discrimination		Service availability	Substance abuse	Rates of family violence
	Community isolation			Mental illness	Substance abuse rates
				Literacy	Pollution rates
				Hunger	Cost/availability of housing

The goal when addressing poverty is empowerment. It does not matter if the target of change is the individual, the family, or the community. In all cases, improvements in the quality of life will be achieved through the desire and efforts of individuals, either alone or in groups, to bring about change. You will seek to assist individuals and communities to work for and advocate on their own behalf. It is a collaborative process. Empowerment comes about by helping individuals, families, and communities "take action to improve their situation" (Guiterrez, 1994, p. 202) through the development of "organized responses to circumstances that affect their lives" (Nystrom, 1989, p. 161).

Empowerment of clients who have a long history of powerlessness is not a fast process. Education and support of the clients' own problem-solving abilities are effective empowerment strategies (DuBois & Miley, 1996). Beyond this, collaboration, use of a strengths perspectives, and adopting a perspective that shows the client the relationship between personal problems and the social and structural causes of those problems all promote empowerment (Simon, 1994). Shared responsibility, mutual trust, and a track record of small successes are also important. Strategies that use community and/or small groups are also useful as tools of empowerment (Breton, 1994; Guiterrez, 1994; Hirayama & Hirayama, 1987).

The Importance of Assessment

The large number of varying consequences and the problems of unclear or different causality make practice with the economically disenfranchised both challenging and rewarding. Individuals, families, and communities differ in their unique circumstances. They also differ in the tools and resources available to them. Hence, a significant amount of time must be spent in assessing individual as well as community needs. Effective practice requires getting to know the community and having various members of the community articulate their concerns as well as their strengths. Only a well-developed familiarity with the community will prepare you for work with this population.

The values, cultural standards, and past history of interventions with the community also must be examined. Some poor communities have experienced a kind of roller-coaster effect. The community has often been promised the moon by social workers and others. Great expectations arise, only to be shattered as the scope of the problems overwhelms the process. Or, more likely, funding priorities change and monies available for even a promising and successful project dry up before the community is back on its feet. This roller-coaster effect, moreover, is the basis for some of the powerlessness felt by residents in the community.

On the other hand, it is a mistake to focus only on the problems the community faces. Using the strengths perspective articulated in earlier chapters avoids the tendency to focus on deficits (Saleeby, 1992). The reasons for bringing a strengths perspective to the relationship are both practical and conceptual. The resources of the individual or the community will be the available tools for change. Thus, knowing what these tools are is critical. But, in a larger sense, keeping your attention on the problems or deficits is disempowering to the client (Hepworth, Rooney, & Larson, 1997). The residents already know what the problems are. Constantly reminding them of problems may bring up feelings of powerlessness from the past. Moreover, focusing on problems or deficits can result in a "blaming the victim" perspective. Thus, you need to keep the focus on the possibilities for change and the means to achieve the desired outcomes.

Collaboration, Coalition-Building, and the Importance of Relationships

A collaborative partnership approach is effective with economically disadvantaged clients. First, as discussed above, empowerment is a central goal for this type of practice, and working collaboratively with the client is essential for meeting this desired outcome. Second, there is strength in numbers. Only in a few instances can an individual or single agency bring all of the resources and expertise necessary for correcting complex, multidimensional problems for a single client or an entire community. Developing coalitions brings together expertise from a variety of different areas, which may expand resources, better integrate existing services, and increase the likelihood of reaching the identified change goals (Alter & Hage, 1993).

A range of skills are essential for practice with poor individuals and families. The worker may be required to provide different services at different times, including advocacy, counseling, linkages with other services, information, and referrals. Further, the client will need multiple services from multiple providers, and the social worker provides a vital coordination role. In this context, the whole realm of micro practice skills outlined in Chapter 7 come into play. In fact, it would be difficult to find a social work practice domain where the range of generalist practice skills is more necessary than with this client population. Any individual client, particularly a long-term welare recipient, is likely to have a variety of different needs for a variety of different services. As a generalist social worker with low-income clients, you will see needs for employment, training, child care, transportation, health services, life skills, substance abuse or mental health counseling, and legal assistance, all in a single day. As such, collaborative service networks with the social worker and the client at the center are inevitable and necessary.

Collaborations and coalitions are equally necessary when working with communities. The same argument about strength in numbers applies, and you will need even more resources and technical skills. Increasingly, funding sources, such as foundations and governmental agencies, are demanding collaborative components. They recognize that single-focus community programming is not as effective in bringing about change as are multifocus coalitions and partnerships. If community development activities do not voluntarily organize, efforts to bring about coalitions will be facilitated by the demands of resource providers (Bailey & Koney, 1997).

Residents should be participants in the coalitions. Partnerships should create a meaningful role for citizens in voluntary community associations and other institutions (Florin & Wandersman, 1990). Citizen participants are likely to improve outcomes (Bendrick & Egan, 1995; Mier, 1994), and intentional efforts to involve citizens in community coalitions leads to stronger communities (Unger & Wandersman, 1983; Woodson, 1981) and increased feelings of personal and political efficacy (Cole, 1974; Cole & Caputo, 1984; Florin & Wandersman, 1984; Zimmerman & Rappaport, 1988).

There is a downside to casting a wide net. Coalitions and the involvement of citizens may slow down processes in at least two ways. First, planning is substantially more complicated as the number of participants increases. Setting priorities is more difficult. Competition for scarce resources may overwhelm the planning process. Second, as individuals move in and out of the coalition, substantial time may have to be spent educating new members about the processes and decisions already made. Skillful group facilitation can minimize these problems. Over the long term, the time spent in planning and educational efforts will pay off through a more cohesive and committed coalition membership.

In almost any social work context, relationships are critical to the helping process. When working with economically disadvantaged clients, relationships are of particular importance. Past encounters with other outsiders may have eroded trust. Poor individuals and poor communities may have a long history of problematic relationships with social workers, government officials, or other authoritative figures and agencies.

Besides collaboration, the best way to build trust and a positive relationship is to

- Move slowly
- Avoid making promises you can't keep
- Take time to educate clients about your actions
- Explain the limits of your programmatic efforts
- Avoid demanding more from clients than they can give.

In addition, don't be disappointed if your ideas and suggestions are not initially carried out or if you feel you are being tested by the community (Guiterrez, Alvarez, Nemon, & Lewis, 1997). Low-income clients face a variety of demands on their time and have scarce resources. To some degree, even with the best of intentions, social work interventions represent an imposition.

Research activities, for example, such as surveys or interviews, not only demand time but may also be perceived as a significant intrusion into the clients' personal lives. Some planning activities like public meetings, or interventions like social actions, may not be well attended, as people do not feel comfortable. The process of building trust and effective collaborative relationships take time.

Implementing Effective Interventions

Almost all generalist social work skills are potentially useful when working with economically disadvantaged clients. In a short time, you may see clients with problems as straightforward as needing assistance finding a job all the way to complex problematic familial and community relationships. It is important to be prepared for any and all eventualities.

It cannot be stressed enough that you must start where the client is. This means understanding the client's needs, strengths, and cultural perceptions. Most social workers do not work with people like themselves, and many of our assumptions are rooted in our cultural background. Avoid assuming that your client sees the world the same way you do. Assume that you are different, and find out the specifics of your differences. Keep up with the literature. The current welfare reform activities will soon begin to generate a large amount of research that will be useful for your practice. The more you know about current policies, practices, and your client population, the more effective you will be.

At the level of the community, a wide range of knowledge, skills, and activities are necessary and useful. These include the knowledge and practical application of different practice modes, such as locality development, which attempts to improve cooperative problem solving; social planning, which attempts to address concrete deficiencies; and social action, which attempts to force legislative or organizational change (Rothman, 1995). It also requires multicultural sensitivity (Guiterrez, Alvarez, Nemon, & Lewis, 1997). More specifically, skills include group problem solving, group and collaborative facilitation, research and analysis (McNeely, 1996), resource development (Rubin & Rubin, 1992), planning and organizing, and skills in dealing with conflict, such as active listening and consensus-building (Guiterrez, Alvarez, Nemon, & Lewis, 1997).

As may be clear, practice work with economically disadvantaged clients and communities is complex and challenging. It demands a range of skills and knowledge perhaps greater than any other form of social work practice. The rewards are great. The opportunities to work with a large number of committed and concerned individuals presents an experience rarely felt elsewhere. By engaging in this practice domain, you are working to correct the central problem of our society—poverty. Many, perhaps most, of our social problems are either caused by or closely connected to poverty. Finding solutions will improve the quality of life for many Americans.

SUMMARY

Poverty is a worldwide problem. In the United States, more than 34 million people representing 12.7 percent of the population are poor. The number of people classified as poor depends on the way poverty is defined. The accuracy and adequacy of the poverty threshold has been called into question.

Poverty has been a persistent social problem with multiple theories of causation and multiple consequences. Some theories focus on individual deficits, others attribute poverty to social and structural factors. A third set of theories examines the relationship between individual and social causes.

Factors affecting community poverty are better understood and less controversial. At the community level, poverty can often be traced to the interplay of economics and political power. Poor communities lack the economic base to pay for needed community services. These services include public safety, education, infrastructure, and governance. Most poor communities also lack political power. Political fragmentation and, occasionally, political corruption characterize poor communities. There often is completion for scarce resources, which further contributes to the downward spiral of economically disadvantaged communities.

The consequences of poverty for individuals and families are profound. The most immediate is its effect on an individual's capacity to survive. Hunger and poor nutrition are common. Inadequate housing, exposure to environmental risks, unsafe streets and neighborhoods, and increased health problems are all associated with poverty.

Generalist social work practice with this population focuses on individual and community empowerment. The goal is to empower the poor individually and collectively to improve the quality of life socially, physically, and economically. This entails developing collaborative helping relationships with individuals and families to facilitate and strengthen their capacities to cope with the challenges that come with being poor as well as building community-based coalitions that seek resources and solutions to the economic and political problems facing economically disadvantaged communities.

CASE EXAMPLE

The following case example illustrates generalist social work practice with a community client system. It describes the process I went through in helping a low income community develop and implement a community-based social service center.

The Chester Experience

Chester, Pennsylvania, presents a classic case of a distressed city in the United States. The city has a population of approximately forty-two thousand and is located one-half hour south of Philadelphia. Chester was once a thriving manufacturing center, producing ships, steel, iron, cloth, pottery, paper, and refined oil. But between the 1950s and the 1980s, the city lost 32 percent of its jobs, the economy collapsed, and much of the middle class moved away. The city's problems were compounded by several decades of corrupt political leadership.

Assessment
Economic changes and political inefficacy have created a number of socioeconomic problems for the community. Needs assessments demonstrated that unemployment, crime, housing, substance abuse, environmental pollution, truancy, and low adult educational attainment rates are all serious problems in Chester. In addition, a number of barriers made services to residents inaccessible. These included a poor transportation network, service fragmentation, and a lack of awareness of the services that were available.

Intervention

Recognizing the need for better coordination between services and the reduction of barriers to service, several agencies met in the summer of 1995 to discuss methods to overcome these problems. The meetings were called by an organization that had been contacted by the Ford Foundation about a new program initiative designed to develop collaborative relationships between service providers. I was invited to help develop the program proposal and to formulate a client assessment and program evaluation plan.

The Ford Foundation provided funds for a program in Chester, in 1996. Endless hours were spent on the telephone with organizations like the United Way and combing the telephone directory to generate an exhaustive list of agencies. Next, questions had to be resolved about which agencies should be members; was the organization to be open to social service agencies only, or should government agencies, church groups, and informal groups be invited as well? We decided to be as inclusive as possible, even inviting unaffiliated residents.

More than a hundred social service organizations banded together in a formal network. Their organization, which they named Communities That Care (CTC), began holding regular monthly meetings and planning new service initiatives. The focus of these meetings was to improve coordination, which, it was hoped, would not only improve client functioning, but would also facilitate dialogue among service providers and strengthen the process of community advocacy.

There were questions about how to organize the meetings. Should one agency take the lead in calling and coordinating the effort, or should the meetings be less structured and controlled? If one agency served as the leader, would other agencies be jealous and refuse to participate? We decided to utilize a formal structure, with the agency that had been approached by the Ford Foundation as the lead agency. The justification was that this agency would be the grant recipient and would therefore be accountable for the funding. Fortunately, our fears were unwarranted.

CTC meetings have since become forums for the exchange of information. Newsletters and information pamphlets inform clients and other providers of services offered at the various agencies. The meetings have also generated ideas that individual agencies and small groups of agencies have formalized into proposals and/or grants for new programs. In discussions at CTC meetings, for example, it was determined that a real need existed for some form of centralized social services facility in Chester. Centralized service provision could help ameliorate problems faced by clients in accessing services, such as transportation, lack of awareness about available services, and excessive time expenditures.

Fortunately, a facility became available immediately. One of Chester's two hospitals was acquired by the other, much larger hospital. The larger hospital was a member of CTC, and it decided to use the smaller hospital building for its social service programs, including inpatient and outpatient substance abuse and mental health treatment. Unused space was made available to other providers at low or, in some cases, no cost. The new facility, called the One-Stop Shop (OSS), opened in mid-1998. More than twenty public and private social service agencies are now located in the facility. Services available include job training and placement, domestic and family mediation, child care, counseling, computer skills training, and educational support. Because many clients failed to follow up on referrals from and to such public social services as Medical Assistance and Temporary Assistance for Needy Families, an on-site county assistance office was established at the OSS in the fall of 1998.

Another initiative of the CTC network has been the development and adoption of a standardized assessment and client service planning system to make practice and program evaluations easier. Prior to the implementation of this system, clients often underwent several different assessments by the different agencies helping them. At the request of several agencies, I formulated a plan to eliminate this burden on the clients, meeting frequently with the various providers to address issues of client confidentiality, agency needs, and the overall assessment process.

In addition, several initiatives focus on the development of community leadership skills. Several of the agencies using the One-Stop Shop are offering newly designed programs to strengthen client leadership skills and problem-solving capacity. These interventions not only empower clients to self-advocate; they also promote ownership of change efforts, thus avoiding the perception that change has been imposed by outsiders.

Finally, several of the agencies provide intensive case management to families and individuals. Case management enables service linkage and follow-up assistance. In two of the agencies, the case management system has undergone major expansion because of grants to enlarge their service scope.

Evaluation

It is too early to know whether the One-Stop Shop is having a significant effect on the community. There have been problems in implementation. CTC serves as a planning and information exchange body only. The success of the CTC network and the OSS depends on the efforts, skills, and initiatives of individual social service agencies; CTC does not have independent staff to write grants, develop proposals, or provide services. Many agencies have chosen not to participate in CTC, and in some cases, this is a problem. The agencies operated by the city of Chester, for example, have chosen not to join the group. Only a fewer residents are members of CTC. As a result, the planning of activities is slowed because agencies must spend time to gather the support of the residents.

Finally, in an impoverished community like Chester, job development is critical, and the One-Stop Shop does not address this need. My hope is that reducing barriers to service will assist clients in their attempt to have their immediate needs met, and as their capacity to self-advocate improves, real change will take place with the community as the change agent. Empowering the residents is an important by-product of several of the programs of the One-Stop Shop, and in time, I believe this will be the most beneficial outcome.

DISCUSSION QUESTIONS

1. What strategies could be used to address the multiple problems in a city like Chester? What role should the residents play?
2. Why would a community like Chester be selected for the development of new, environmentally unfriendly businesses, like hazardous waste incinerators?
3. Which, if any, social problems in the United States are caused by poverty? If a problem is caused by povetty, is it better to address that problem or to address poverty?
4. What is the role of the generalist social worker when working with a poor person and his or her family? In other words, assuming no other problems, such as substance abuse or domestic violence, what strategies would you use.
5. Is poverty the fault of the poor person? Is it the responsibility of the poor person to solve the problem?

REFERENCES

Alter, C., & Hage, J. (1993). *Organizations working together.* Newbury Park, CA: Sage.

Bailey, D., & Koney, K. (1997). Interorganizational community-based collaboratives: A strategic response to shape the social work agenda. In P. Ewalt, E. Freeman, S. Kirk, & D. Poole (Eds.), *Social policy: Reform, research and practice* (pp. 72–83). Washington: NASW Press.

Bane, M. J., & Ellwood, D. T. (1994). *Welfare realities: From rhetoric to reform.* Cambridge, MA: Harvard University Press.

Banfield, E. (1968). *The unheavenly city.* Boston: Little, Brown.

Banfield, E. (1974). *The unheavenly city revisited.* Boston: Little, Brown.

Bendrick, M., & Egan, M. L. (1995). Worker ownership and participation enhances economic development in low-opportunity communities. *Journal of Community Practice, 2,* 61–85.

Bower, B. (1994). Growing up poor. *Science News, 46,* (July 9), 24–25.

Breton, M. (1994). On the meaning of empowerment and empowerment-oriented social work practice. *Social Work with Groups, 17*(3), 23–37.

Brooks-Gunn, J., Klebanov, P., Liaw, F., & Duncan, G. (1995). Toward an understanding of the effects of poverty upon children. In H. E. Fitzgerald, B. M. Lester, & B. Zuckerman (Eds.), *Children of poverty: Research, health, and policy issues* (pp. 3–41). New York: Garland.

Brown, L., & Pollitt, E. (1996). Malnutrition, poverty and intellectual development. *Scientific American, 274*(2), 38–43.

Brown, M., & Waxman, L. (1996). *Continued growth in overall demand for emergency food and shelter: Some cities report progress in battle with hunger and homelessness.* Washington, DC: The U.S. Conference of Mayors.

Cattell-Gordon, D. (1990). The Appalachian inheritance: A culturally transmitted traumatic stress syndrome. *Journal of Progressive Human Services, 1*(1), 41–57.

Center on Budget and Policy Priorities (1997). *Poverty rate fails to decline as income growth in 1996 favors the affluent: Child health coverage erodes as Medicaid for children contracts.* Washington, DC: Author.

Centers for Disease Control and Prevention (n.d.). *What every parent should know about lead poisoning in children.* Atlanta: Author.

Children's Defense Fund (1998). *Poverty matters: The cost of child poverty in America.* Washington, DC: Author.

Citro, C., & Micheal, R. (1995). *Measuring poverty: A new approach.* Washington, DC: National Academy Press.

Cole, R. L. (1974). *Citizen participation and the urban policy process*. Lexington, MA: D. C. Health.

Cole, R. L., & Caputo, D. A. (1984). The public hearing as an effective citizen participation mechanism: A case study of the General Revenue Sharing Program. *American Political Science Review, 78,* 404–416.

Congressional Quarterly Weekly Reports (1991). Lead exposure bill stalls in markup. *Congressional Quarterly Weekly Reports, 49,* 3206.

Danziger, S., & Gottshalk, P. (1995). *America unequal.* Cambridge, MA: Russell Sage Foundation and Harvard University Press.

Delaker, J. (1999). *Poverty in the United States: 1998* (U.S. Census Bureau, Current Population Reports, Series P60–207). Washington, DC: U.S. Government Printing Office.

DiNitto, D. (1996). The future of social welfare policy. In P. Raffoul & A. McNeece (Eds.), *Future issues for social work practice* (pp. 254–265). Boston: Allyn & Bacon.

DuBois, B., & Miley, K. K. (1996). *Social work: An empowering profession* (2nd ed.). Boston: Allyn & Bacon.

Federal Register (1998). *Federal Register, 63*(36), 9235–9238.

Fisher, G. (1992). The development and history of the poverty thresholds. *Social Security Bulletin, 55*(4), 3–14.

Florin P. R., & Wandersman, A. (1984). Cognitive social learning and participation in community development. *American Journal of Community Psychology, 12*(6), 689–708.

Florin, P. R., & Wandersman, A. (1990). An introduction to citizen participation, voluntary organizations, and community development: Insights for empowerment through research. *American Journal of Community Psychology, 18*(1), 41–54.

Gans, H. (1976). The positive functions of poverty. *American Journal of Sociology, 78*(2), 275–289.

Gilder, G. (1981). *Wealth and poverty.* New York: Basic Books.

Goodwin, L. (1983). *Causes and cures of welfare: New evidence on the social psychology of the poor.* Lexington, MA: Lexington Books.

Guiterrez, L. (1994). Beyond coping: An empowerment perspective on stressful life events. *Journal of Sociology and Social Welfare, 21*(3), 201–219.

Guiterrez, L., Alvarez, A., Nemon, H., & Lewis, E. (1997). Multicultural community organizing: A strategy for change. In P. Ewalt, E. Freeman, S. Kirk, & D. Poole (Eds.), *Social policy: Reform, research and practice* (pp. 62–71). Washington, DC: NASW Press.

Handler, J., & Hasenfeld, Y. (1991). *The moral construction of poverty: American welfare reform.* Newbury Park, CA: Sage.

Hepworth, D., Rooney, R., & Larson, J. (1997). *Direct social work practice: Theory and skills* (5th ed.). Pacific Grove, CA: Brooks/Cole.

Hirayama, H., & Hirayama, K. (1987). Empowerment through group participation: Process and goal. *American Journal of Community Psychology, 15,* 353–371.

Hunger Action Coalition (n.d). *Factsheet.* http://comnet.org/hacmi/facts.htm.

Karger, H. (1994). Toward redefining social development in the global economy: Free markets, privatization, and the development of a welfare state in Eastern Europe. *Social Development Issues, 16*(3), 32–44.

Katz, M. (1989). *The undeserving poor: From the war on poverty to the war on welfare.* New York: Pantheon.

Kauffman, S. (1994). Citizen participation in environmental decisions: Policy, reality, and considerations for community organizing. In M. D. Hoff & J. G. McNutt (Eds.), *The global environmental crisis: Implications for social welfare and social work* (pp. 219–239). Brookfield, MA: Avebury Press.

Lewis, O. (1959). *Five families; Mexican case studies in the culture of poverty.* New York: Basic Books.

Lewis, O. (1961). *The children of Sanchez.* New York: Random House.

Lewis, O. (1966). *La Vida: A Puerto Rican family in the culture of poverty.* New York: Basic Books.

Marx, K. (1867). *Capital* (S. Moore & E. Averly, Trans.). Available Internet: http://www.marxists.org/archive/marx/works/1867-c1/index.htm.

McNeely, J. B. (1996). Where have all the flowers gone? In R. Stone (Ed.), *Core issues in comprehensive community building initiatives* (pp. 86–88). Chicago: Chapin Hall for Children.

Mead, L. M. (1986). *Beyond entitlement.* New York: Free Press.

Mead, L. M. (1992). *The new politics of poverty: The working poor in America.* New York: Free Press.

Mier, R. (1994). *Social justice and local development policy.* Newbury Park, CA: Sage.

Murdock, S., & Micheal, M. (1996). Future demographic changes: The demand for social welfare services in the 21st century. In P. Raffoul & A. McNeece (Eds.), *Future issues for social work practice* (pp. 3–18). Boston: Allyn & Bacon.

Murray, C. (1984). *Loosing ground: American social policy, 1950–1980.* New York: Basic Books.

National Health/Education Consortium (1991, January). Healthy brain development. *The National Health/Education Consortium Report,* pp. 4–5.

Needleman, H. L. (1991). Childhood lead poisoning: A disease for the history texts. *American Journal of Public Health, 81,* 685–687.

Nystrom, J.F. (1989). Empowerment model for delivery of social work services in public schools. *Journal of Social Work Education, 11,* 160–170.

Polenberg, R. (1980). *One nation divisible: Class, race, and ethnicity in the United States since 1938.* New York: Penguin.

Poole, D. (1995). Beyond the rhetoric: Shared responsibility versus the Contract with America. *Health and Social Work, 20,* 83–86.

Poole, D. (1997). Welfare reform: The bad, the ugly, and the maybe not too awful. In P. Ewalt, E. Freeman, S. Kirk, & D. Poole (Eds.), *Social policy: Reform, research and practice* (pp. 96–101). Washington: NASW Press.

Rogge, M. (1993). Social work, disenfranchised communities, and the natural environment: Field education opportunities. *Journal of Social Work Education, 29,* 111–120.

Rogge, M. (1994). Environmental injustice: Social welfare and toxic waste. In M. D. Hoff & J. G. McNutt (Eds.), *The global environmental crisis: Implications for social welfare and social work* (pp. 53–74). Brookfield, MA: Avebury Press.

Rothman, J. (1995). Approaches to community organization. In J. Rothman, J. Erlich, & J. Tropman (Eds.), *Strategies of community intervention* (5th ed., pp. 23–63). Itasca, IL: Peacock.

Rubin, H. J., & Rubin, L. S. (1992). *Community organizing and development* (2nd ed.). New York: Macmillan.

Saleeby, A. C. (1992). *The strengths perspective in social work practice.* New York: Longman.

Savage, H. (1999). Who could afford to buy a house in 1995? Washington, DC: U.S. Bureau of the Census.

Sherraden, M. (1991). *Assets and the poor: A new American welfare policy.* New York: M. E. Sharpe.

Silver, P., Kauffman, S., & Soliman, H. (1998). *Environmental hazards: Social worker practices and attitudes.* Unpublished manuscript.

Simon, B. L. (1994). *The empowerment tradition in American social work: A history.* New York: Columbia University Press.

Unger, D. G., & Wandersman, A. (1983). Neighboring and its role in block organizations: An exploratory report. *American Journal of Community Psychology, 11,* 291–300.

United Nations Development Program (1997). *Reports: Income poverty.* http://www.undp.org.in/report/hdr97/hdrincme.htm.

U.S. Bureau of the Census (1995a). *Asset ownership of households: 1993.* Washington, DC: Author.

U.S. Bureau of the Census (1995b). *Health insurance coverage: 1995: Who goes without health insurance?* Washington, DC: Author.

U.S. Bureau of the Census (1996). *March 1996 current population survey.* Washington, DC: Author.

U.S. Bureau of the Census (1997a). *March 1997 current population survey.* Washington, DC: Author.

U.S. Bureau of the Census (1997b). *1993 American housing survey.* Washington, DC: Author.

U.S. Bureau of the Census (1999a). *Frequently asked questions.* Available Internet: http://www.census.gov/hhes/housing/ahs/ahsfaq.html.

U.S. Bureau of the Census (1999b). *American housing survey of the United States, 1997.* Washington, DC: Author.

U.S. Conference of Mayors (1997). *Summary: Hunger and homelessness report, 1997.* Washington, DC: Author.

U.S. Conference of Mayors (1998). *Summary: Hunger and homelessness report, 1998.* Washington, DC: Author.

U.S. Department of Agriculture (1998). *U.S. Department of Agriculture: 1999 budget summary.* Washington, DC: Author.

U.S. Department of Health and Human Services (1994). *Priority home! The federal plan to break the cycle of homelessness.* (HUD-1454-CPD). Washington, DC: Author.

U.S. Department of Health and Human Services, National Center on Child Abuse and Neglect (1996). *Third national incidence study of child abuse and neglect: Final report* (NIS-3). Washington, DC: Author.

U.S. Department of Health and Human Services, Social Security Administration (1997). *Social security programs in the United States, July 1997, 13–11758.* Washington, DC: Author. Available Internet: http://www.ssa.gov/statistics/sspus.html

U.S. Department of Health and Human Services (1998). *Change in welfare caseloads since enactment of the new welfare law.* Washington, DC: Author.

U.S. Department of Health and Human Services (1999). *The state of the cities, 1999.* Washington, DC: Author.

U.S. Department of Justice, Bureau of Justice Statistics (n.d.). *Victim characteristics.*http://www.ojp.usdoj.gov/bjs/cvict_v.htm.

Vidal, A. (1995). Reintegrating disadvantaged communities into the fabric of urban life: The role of community development. *Housing Policy Debate, 6,* 169–230.

Watkins, S. (1998a, March 13). *Come to the table: Sharing North Carolina's harvest.* Paper presented at the State Summit on Food Recovery, Raleigh, NC.

Watkins, S. (1998b, March 23). *Nutrition programs in the 105th Congress.* Paper presented at the Food Research and Action Center, Spring Policy Conference, Washington, DC.

Weinberg, D. (1998). *Press briefing on 1997 poverty and income estimates.* Available Internet: http://www.census.gov/hhes/income/income97/prs98asc.html

Wilson, W. J. (1987). *The truly disadvantaged: The inner city, the underclass and public polity.* Chicago: University of Chicago.

Woodson, R. L. (1981). *A summons to life: Mediating structures and prevention of youth crime.* Washington, DC: American Enterprise Institute.

Yamada, G., & Sherraden, M. (1997). Effects of assets on attitudes and behaviors: Advance test of a social policy proposal. In P. Ewalt, E. Freeman, S. Kirk, & D. Poole (Eds.), *Social policy: Reform, research and practice* (pp. 193–205). Washington, DC: NASW Press.

Zimmerman, M. A., & Rappaport, J. (1988). Citizen participation, perceived control, and psychological empowerment. *American Journal of Community Psychology, 16,* 725–750.

CHAPTER 9

Generalist Practice with Persons with Serious and Persistent Mental Illness

W. Patrick Sullivan

Sue L. is a first-year MSW student placed in a partial hospitalization program for people with mental illnesses. The program serves adults who have recently been discharged from inpatient psychiatric hospitalizations and are now in community-based living arrangements. It provides fifteen weeks of individual and group treatment to help participants successfully adapt to community-based living and prevent rehospitalization.

By the end of her first month of placement, Sue had noticed that most of her clients had been in the program before. They all had a cycle of hospitalization, discharge to some type of partial program, independent living, and rehospitalization. None of them seemed to be able to make it on his or her own. Much of the individual and group treatment provided to the participants focused on the individuals' problems and the importance of taking their medications. Very little attention was being given to their strengths or to their life outside the partial hospital program. Sue wondered whether the medical model was really appropriate in dealing with these clients and what aspects of her social work training were relevant to this placement.

More than 2 million people in the United States have serious and persistent mental illnesses such as schizophrenia, bipolar disorder, and major depression (Gerhart, 1990). It is widely agreed that these conditions are biologically based. There are no cures or effective prevention for most major mental illnesses. However, the course and outcome of these illnesses can, in many cases be effectively controlled. For example, although certain individuals are genetically vulnerable to schizophrenia, it is only through the particular interaction of individual and environmental stresses that illness, symptom exacerbation, or recovery is manifested (Liberman, Wallace, Blackwell, Eckman, Vaccaro, & Kuehnel, 1993; Nuechterlein, Dawson, Gitlin, Ventura, Goldstein, Snyder, Yee, & Mintz, 1992).

It is useful to distinguish between disease and illness (Kleinman, 1980). *Disease* is the underlying pathology that accounts for the disorder. Serious and persistent mental illnesses are often referred to as neurobiological diseases. *Illness,* on the other hand, involves psychosocial processes that reflect individual, social, and cultural responses to a disease. Social workers most often deal with illness and its consequences. The same individual and environmental factors that shape illness can also be modified to help the recovery process.

Social workers in mental health settings often serve people with the most severe forms of mental illness. Two decades ago, community mental health centers and other specialty mental health providers offered limited services to individuals who suffered from serious and persistent mental illness. Today, as a result of moral and fiscal concerns, many state mental health authorities have given priority to serving this vulnerable population in community-based programs. Social workers play key roles in the development of community-based programs and in the delivery of mental health services.

This chapter provides an overview and description of serious and persistent mental illness. It highlights the personal experiences of those who struggle to surmount the challenges of mental illness. It is designed to guide professionals who are committed to helping individuals with severe and persistent mental illness and their families through the recovery process. The concept of recovery can set the mission and vision for mental health services and establish a framework for generalist social work practice with this client population. Finally, the chapter looks at the strengths-based approach to the assessment, intervention, and termination phases of generalist social work practice. By the end of the chapter, you should be able to help Sue

1. Understand the nature of mental illness and the stigma that has been associated with the disease
2. Appreciate changes that have occurred in the provision of services to people with serious and persistent mental illnesses
3. Summarize the major policy issues affecting the provision of mental health services
4. Describe the concept of recovery as it applies to people with mental illnesses
5. Conceptualize the role social niches play in the recovery process
6. Describe the major factors that potentially affect the recovery process
7. Incorporate strengths and recovery principles in generalist practice with clients facing the challenge of serious and persistent mental illness.

UNDERSTANDING SERIOUS AND PERSISTENT MENTAL ILLNESS

Serious and persistent mental illness often disrupts all aspects of an individual's life. Schizophrenia, for example, affects a person's thoughts, moods, behavior, and ability to perform normal and expected social roles. The label *serious and persistent mental illness* reflects a biopsychosocial orientation highlighted by the three Ds: diagnosis, duration, and disability. Generally, illnesses that are neurobiological in nature may be diagnosed as serious. Duration refers to the length of time the condition has been present. If the troubling condition has extended for at least six months or has repeatedly interfered with an individual's functioning over a number of years, it is considered persistent. Disability is the extent to which areas of personal functioning have been negatively affected or restricted.

Many of the activities that others take for granted are denied those with serious and persistent mental illnesses. These illnesses have a devastating effect on individual functioning and the ability to work and live independently. They also carry a stigma and result in discrimination. Many people with serious mental illnesses lead lonely lives. Their social networks often shrink with each hospitalization. Their ability to form personal friendships and romantic relationships are stymied by the presence of symptoms.

Over time, the combination of personal and environmental insults can result in a cycle of disorientation and neglect of self, which ultimately leads to hospitalization or social marginalization. When this becomes a recurring process, the individual and his or her family and friends often feel resignation or hopelessness. It can also result in a profound sense of pessimism among professionals. Ultimately, all those involved may accept the current state of affairs as a predictable and constant feature of their lives. From this point forward, the individual, family, friends, and clinicians view the person as forever changed:

> Nothing remains behind the dull facade of the person. Gone are the thoughts, feelings, and intentions that we most often personally identify with who we are as individuals. Gone is the capacity both to suffer and to hope; a capacity we consider to be basic to our nature as human beings. In these ways a person *as a person*—as a feeling, thinking, and intending subject— is thought no longer to be home. The person having become victim to the illness, all that remains is an empty husk that can be bandied about by the winds and tides of the external environment, and which otherwise remains passive, withdrawn and inert. (Davidson & Stayner, 1997, p. 4)

Serious mental illnesses can create difficulties in a person's thoughts, attention, and ability to communicate that impede the ability to interact effectively with others. In fact, one of the struggles faced by those with severe and persistent mental illness is the frustration of trying to communicate their thoughts and feelings. This is caused, in part, by the illness. It is also caused by the unwillingness of others to listen (Davidson & Stayner, 1997; Sullivan, 1994b). In Western cultures, serious mental illness often becomes synonymous with the individual: one not only suffers from schizophrenia, one becomes a schizophrenic (Estroff, 1989).

People with serious mental illness recognize when they are being treated solely as mental patients and rightly view it as dehumanizing. Over time, however, they tend to accept and internalize this perception and view themselves as mental patients rather than as human beings. Their segregation in specialized programs and their lack of participation in the world of work further isolates them from contact with mainstream society. Isolated, impoverished, disaffiliated, and labeled, they are trapped in a prison from which there is no apparent escape (Davidson & Stayner, 1997; Sullivan, 1997; Taylor, 1997).

It is important for community mental health services to alter this state of affairs. Today, the language used about mental health reflects a more optimistic view of people with severe and persistent mental illness and of their prospects in life. In the past, these individuals were referred to as the "chronically mentally ill" or the "chronics." Obviously, this language does not project a positive or hopeful view of individual potential. Within this context, people receiving services were viewed as patients and were expected to play a passive and/or submissive role in the care process. Today, individuals are commonly referred to as "consumers"—an empowering term that affirms their rights as citizens. This trend reflects a sharp departure from the view of people with mental illness as chronic schizophrenics inhabiting the back wards of state hospitals.

Policy Issues

Health care, including mental health services, is in a state of rapid flux. Efforts to control health care costs and to ensure quality of care have resulted in a plethora of new organizational models, payment schemes, and license requirements. The rise of proprietary mental health and managed care organizations has created a new wave of challenges and opportunities for social workers. Professionals who advocate for individuals with severe and persistent mental illnesses observe such trends with a suspicious eye.

Some trends in mental health financing can positively affect mental health services. Flexibility in state Medicaid plans, often accomplished through waivers or rehabilitation options, can create a source of funding for community-based services that are not solely based on the medical model. Blended funding and even plans with capitation rates can be less restrictive than fee-for-service arrangements that preclude payment for critical community-based interventions. Managed care can also create a positive context for good community care, especially when managed care plans seek out services that have equal value but are less intensive, restrictive, and expensive. Good rehabilitation programs and assertive community treatment are far less expensive in human and economic terms than unnecessary inpatient hospitalization.

However, managed care can become managed cost. Efforts to control health care costs can result in stringent and narrow definitions of medical necessity and reduce or eliminate coverage for community care. Similarly, short-term help, which may have great utility and effectiveness in many instances, cannot be the only treatment offered to people with severe and persistent mental illness.

Generalist social workers must be cognizant of changes in mental health policy and health care financing and policy. To ensure that public policy supports efforts to help those facing serious and persistent mental illness, professionals must take an active role in the policy arena. If, for example, case management services are not reimbursable, mental health centers will probably not offer such services. If there are disincentives to entering the work force, such as loss of medical benefits, clients and professional social workers will remain reluctant to pursue employment goals.

It is of particular significance that the locus of care for people with serious mental illnesses has shifted from the hospital to the community. Public policy, key legal decisions, and the expansion of community-based services have helped ensure that those with mental illnesses are no longer out of sight, out of mind. Many who would have spent a significant portion of their lives in institutions have successfully adjusted to community life. Without question, some individuals have surmounted the potentially catastrophic effect of mental illness and are leading satisfying lives. This fact alone has helped shape a new mission for mental health services and a vision for those struggling daily— recovery.

The Ecological Perspective

The concept of recovery has been introduced as a viable vision for people with serious mental illness and as an organizing mission for mental health services (Anthony, 1993; Sullivan, 1994b). Recovery is "a deeply personal, unique process of changing one's attitudes, values, feelings, goals, skills, and/or roles. It is a way of living a satisfying, hopeful, and contributing life even with the limitations caused by illness" (Anthony, 1993, p. 15).

Social workers can play vital helping roles with those struggling through the difficult and painful recovery process. People with serious and persistent mental illness must overcome many obstacles before they can become fully participating members of society. Some of the obstacles, such as the stigma attached to mental illness, are socially constructed. Other obstacles, such as delusional and confused thinking, are inherent to the disease itself. Some people have spent days, months, and even years in psychiatric hospitals—days that are dark memories because the confusion that resulted in hospitalization makes it difficult to reconstruct the experience. The illness and the medications given to help often create a profound sense of lethargy, making it difficult to sleep at night and even more difficult to arise in the morning. It is against these seemingly long odds that those with serious and persistent mental illnesses struggle.

The ecological perspective has long guided social work practice approaches. Taylor (1997) extended the scope of the person-in-environment perspective by introducing the concept of the social niche. A *social niche* is "the environmental habitat of a category of persons, including the resources they utilize and the other categories of persons they associate with" (Taylor, 1997, p. 219). For example, many people with mental illnesses share a similar social niche or have similar person-in-environment interactions. This concept captures the interdependence of people with others and with their environment. It makes clear the fact that resources in human systems do not have to be tangible, but can also be intangible, such as support and the acquisition of a range of social skills. The acquisition of skills, knowledge, and social competence will ultimately dictate the degree of influence and options people can exercise (White, 1959).

The lack or loss of skills and support, the denial of real opportunities, and the clear challenges presented by serious illnesses restrict the options and influence of people with mental illness. Such individuals suffer from niche entrapment (Taylor, 1997). Entrapping niches have the following characteristics:

- "They are highly stigmatized; people caught in them are commonly treated as outcasts by others;
- "People caught in an entrapping niche tend to turn only to 'their own kind' for association, so that their social world becomes restricted and limited;
- "People caught in an entrapping niche are totally defined by their social category. The possibility that they may have aspirations and attributes apart from their category is not ordinarily considered. To outsiders, the person is 'just' a 'bag lady,' a 'junkie,' an 'ex-con,' a 'crazy' . . . and nothing else;
- "In the entrapping niche, there are no gradations of reward and status. One cannot be certified as a 'Master Bag Lady,' or work up to the position

of 'Head Parolee.' Thus, there are few expectations of personal progress within such niches;

- "In the entrapping niche, there are few incentives to set realistic longer-term goals or to work towards such goals;
- "In the entrapping niche, there is little reality feedback; that is, there are few natural processes that lead people to recognize and correct their own unrealistic perceptions or interpretations;
- "In the entrapping niche, there is little chance to learn the skills and expectations that would facilitate escape. This is especially true when the entrapping niche is free from the usual norms of work and self-discipline, and no demands arise for the clear structuring of time and effort; and
- "In the entrapping niche, economic resources are sparse. This in itself may lead to unproductive stress and cause some people to seek reinstitutionalization (in hospital or prison) for economic reasons." (Taylor, 1997, p. 221)

The characteristics of entrapping niches correspond to the challenges people with serious and persistent mental illnesses often face. The key word in this discussion is *entrapment*. In the absence of any discernible change or action, the individual may be relegated to an isolated and segregated life dominated by contacts with mental health professionals and committed family. Ultimately, he or she may begin to lose the most important commodity in the recovery process—hope.

Unfortunately, isolation and poverty are so common among people with mental illness that they have been seen as causal factors in schizophrenia (Faris & Dunham, 1939; Jaco, 1954). Poverty and isolation, or niche entrapment, do not cause schizophrenia. They are the consequences of the expression and course of the illness.

The mirror image of the entrapping niche is the enabling niche:

- "People in enabling niches are not stigmatized, not treated as outcasts;
- "People in enabling niches will tend to 'turn to their own kind' for association, support, and self-validation. But the enabling niche gives them access to others who bring a different perspective, so that their social world becomes less restricted;
- "People in enabling niches are not totally defined by their social category; they are accepted as having valid aspirations and attributes apart from that category;
- "In the enabling niche, there are clear, earned gradations of reward and status. People can work up to better positions. Thus there are strong expectations of change or personal progress within such niches;
- "In the enabling niche, there are many incentives to set realistic longer-term goals for oneself and to work towards such goals;
- "In the enabling niche, there is good reality feedback; that is, there are many natural processes that lead people to recognize and correct unrealistic perceptions or interpretations;
- "The enabling niche provides opportunities to learn the skills and expectations that would aid movement to other niches. This is especially true when the enabling niche pushes toward reasonable work habits and reasonable self-discipline and expects that the use of time will be clearly structured; and

- "In the enabling niche, economic resources are adequate, and competence and quality are rewarded. This reduces economic stress and creates strong motives for avoiding institutionalization." (Taylor, 1997, p. 223)

Key aspects of the entrapping niche are intrinsic to the design and functions of institutional and community treatment programs. There is a dearth of stimulating activities, much unstructured time, little expectation of work, and, beyond the heroic efforts of some staff, little reality feedback. The constant focus is on the management of the illness, and individual goals are based on medically oriented treatment plans.

One could reasonably argue that persons inhabit entrapping niches because of individual pathology and personality deficits, while those in better circumstances have prospered because of their abilities and skills. Few people wholly subscribe to this deterministic viewpoint. Most agree that opportunity, encouragement, and access to resources help sharpen, enlarge, and build on inherent competencies. Therefore, while entrapping niches may not cause pathology, it is not inconceivable to imagine that enabling niches can influence recovery (Sullivan, 1994a; Taylor, 1997).

THE RECOVERY PROCESS

Several factors are associated with the recovery process of current and former mental health services consumers (Sullivan, 1994b). These include use of appropriate medications, community support services, exercising willpower, work activity, and spirituality. In many respects, these factors correspond with a holistic view of mental illness and recovery. There is acknowledgment of the biophysical nature of the illnesses as well as the positive and negative influences of the external environment, including professional mental health services.

Medication

New psychotropic medications are being developed at a rapid pace. Increasingly, these medications produce improved symptom relief with reduced negative side effects. Some of them are effective with people previously considered untreatable. It is extremely important for social workers to keep abreast of developments in pharmacology and understand the role medications play in mental health treatment (Libassi, 1995).

Failure to comply with medication regimens is a common source of frustration for professionals and family members. However, medications may not be taken if the individual finds the side effects too disagreeable or feels that the medication does not work (Goldstein, 1992). Professionals may be too quick to blame noncompliance for lack of progress when in fact the medications may simply be ineffective for a given individual (Ruscher, de Wit, & Mazmanian, 1997). Experimentation may be necessary, and families should be consulted about what has and has not worked in the past.

It is also necessary to be sensitive to the emotional component of taking psychotropic medications. Individuals must accept that they are dealing with mental illness before they will commit to taking their medications. Belief in self-reliance is strong in our culture, and many people believe that they can simply tough out difficult times. Young people are especially susceptible to uneven compliance, particularly if they have not accepted their diagnosis and/or if taking medications requires alterations in their lifestyle.

Like many other factors in the recovery process, medication compliance is synonymous with maturity. Once individuals understand their illness and the adjustments needed in their lifestyles to recover, medication often becomes a key ingredient of success. As one respondent noted: "When I started taking the medications again it was like night and day for me. I felt different. I felt happy. I didn't feel like people were setting me up" (Sullivan, 1994b, p. 21).

Community Support Services

Community support services were a midcourse correction in the direction of mental health services. By the late 1970s, it was clear that people with the most severe mental illnesses were poorly served by existing community-based services. New models of care were developed to rectify this state of affairs. Skills training programs, partial hospital services, and case management were the forerunners of the wide array of specialized programs now available. These include consumer-based self-help programs, job clubs, and advocacy programs that recognize the strengths and potential of people with mental illnesses. The availability of these types of services and support have benefited many consumers and their families.

First-person accounts underscore that a key aspect of effective mental health and social work practice, regardless of the technology employed, is the nature of the professional relationship. Consumers see case managers as people who look after them and treat them with respect and dignity. Agencies are lauded for being safe places where consumers feel welcome. Tangible aid and services are particularly important. Such services include helping consumers secure furniture, set up an apartment, or organize and pay bills. In many agencies and among professional peers, the provision of concrete services is seen as the purview of paraprofessionals and subservient to mainstream clinical interventions. This view is counterproductive and minimizes the importance of the helping relationship as well as the delivery of needed and valued services. Services should be assessed on the basis of one key criterion, whether the client benefits.

Self-Will and Self-Monitoring

The acceptance of the biophysical roots of serious and persistent mental illness has been liberating as well as enslaving for affected individuals and their families. It has been liberating to the degree that the general public better understands mental illness and is less prone to blame the individual or family for the illness. Additional benefits have been the enactment of public policies that protect the rights of people with disabilities and increased availability of medical insurance and other essential financial and supportive assistance.

On the other hand, recognizing the biophysical nature of mental illness reduces the role of self in the recovery process. Family, friends, and professionals may fail to offer helpful feedback or encourage the individual to take the risks necessary to improve. In much mental health treatment—be it hospitalization, seclusion, restraint, medication, or even the importance ascribed to structured time—a key aspect of helping is the external control of behavior. While interventions can be helpful, they work via an outside agent and do not empower the individual.

The willpower of an individual who is working to recover from mental illness is a potent force. Many such people display a firm resolve to develop personally. They learn about their illness, recognize important signs of impending trouble, take beneficial actions, and alter their behavior to avert potential relapses (Breier & Strauss, 1983; Leete, 1989).

As interest in the process of recovery has gained momentum, the role of the self has emerged as a key factor. Many people who have successfully surmounted the effect of serious mental illness feel that exercising willpower, recognizing signs of increasing stress or illness, and making alterations in their behavior contributed to their successful recovery. These individuals engage in constant reality-testing and self-feedback as a way of coping with confusion and delusions. Some literally talk back to the voices, while others play music or pray (Romme & Escher, 1989).

The ability to recognize a functional sense of self is critical to the recovery process (Davidson & Strauss, 1992). A sense of self-efficacy and an internal locus of control can encourage coping behaviors. Success in dealing with aspects of the illness or stressful life events increases self-confidence and self-efficacy. Some people resort to coping strategies that are appropriate for any type of serious illness, including altering diets, getting more rest and exercise, and monitoring and managing stress. Others turn to traditional sources of help, including mental health professionals: "I start feeling like—perceptions, sensitivity to stuff . . . So I know I had better talk to somebody" (Sullivan, 1994b, p.22).

Social workers can support the growing competency of individuals in recovery by learning their idiosyncratic warning signs and effective coping responses. Similar conversations with key family members can also provide important information. Efforts to cope with difficult situations should be celebrated—whether successful or not. A range of supportive options should be considered in crisis situations. Options include intensive case management, respite care and other supportive services.

Vocational Activity

Work, in one form or another, has been central to mental health treatment for the most seriously ill for decades. The reasons for including work in treatment programs range from wanting people to earn their keep to providing structure in the day. Work strengthens the sense of self and self-worth and allows individuals to make contributions to society. Waters poignantly describes the importance of work for those with serious mental illnesses:

> Work puts us in a unique relationship with other human beings so that the opportunity to form meaningful relationships is readily available to us. Work also allows us to feel a common bond with larger community and gives us a better picture of what our lives will be in the future. All people benefit from work . . . but in many ways, given the confusion that so often accompanies mental illness, people with psychiatric disorders may benefit most of all. (1992, p. 40)

Unfortunately, the reality is that few persons with serious and persistent mental illnesses have been able to successfully compete for work in the marketplace.

Instead, treatment has focused on the inability of those with mental illness to adapt to their surroundings. The desire of people with serious and persistent mental illness to participate in work has been historically dismissed or ignored. Contemporary thinking, reinforced by the Americans with Disabilities Act, recognizes that appropriate modifications in the work environment and necessary supports must be available. When this is the case, people with mental illness can make important contributions in the world of work.

The prognosis for those with serious mental illness is much better in the developing world than it is in Western industrialized nations (Sullivan, 1994a). One plausible explanation for this finding is that opportunities to sustain work activity are readily available in developing countries. Indeed, those who have successfully adapted to community life agree that work provides needed structure in their lives and can distract them from their private troubles. The ability to work and/or continue in an educational program also motivates them to struggle forward:

> When I got that chance to be stable and grab a few classes, getting the grades—it wasn't too long before I wanted to do that rather than go manic. (Sullivan, 1994b, p. 22)

> Well I guess I sort of feel like you can accomplish something and get your work done and if you have troubles your mind doesn't dwell on them so much. So at least you're successful in one thing so you're not such a terrible or dumb or lazy person. (Sullivan, 1994b, p. 23)

Spirituality

Mental illness is a major life crisis that creates a range of emotions in the affected person. There is fear, anger, confusion, and at its worst despair about prospects for an enjoyable and productive life. The importance of emotional and tangible support is well recognized. Beyond the purely medical aspects of disease management through medication, much of the thrust of current mental health care focuses on the creation and maintenance of ongoing support networks.

Spirituality is a common source of support. It may or may not involve participation in organized religion. For persons with mental illness, like most other people, spirituality is a personal matter that is practiced in a manner consistent with individual beliefs and comfort levels.

Speaking of spirituality and mental illness together conjures up negative images for many. Religious preoccupation is often a companion of mental illness and can be seen as consistent with delusional belief structures. Given the personal nature of religion and spirituality, it remains a murky netherworld for many professionals, who may view it as a dangerous and forbidden area to explore. Nonetheless, if spirituality is deemed important by the client system, it needs to be acknowledged and recognized.

Given the challenge presented by serious and persistent mental illness, spirituality can be a buffer from negative life events and an important method of coping and solving problems (Pargament, Ensing, Falgout, Olsen, Reilly, Van Haitsma, & Warren, 1990; Sullivan, 1993). When troubled by their symptoms or the hassles of life, many turn to their spirituality for comfort and guidance: "You can't do it on your own, but if you give it to Him, He can take the burden off your shoulders and make it light" (Sullivan, 1993, p. 128). Calling on spiritual resources may be most common when things are the most bleak:

> I knew that there was a way out and that God was always watching or taking care of me and that in the end result he had it in control—and I didn't have to do anything stupid or desperate . . . I might go through heck but he wasn't going to let me go to the bottom. (Sullivan, 1993, p. 129)

If the sense of a competent self is a bedrock principle in the recovery process, spirituality seems to create an important emotional foundation for some consumers to take the risks necessary to improve their position in life. Spirituality provides an essential sense of security and support.

Organized religion offers the more tangible and instrumental support of a congregation. Religious institutions provide a connection to the larger community in much the same way as work. They provide opportunities to participate in activities, and they offer a source of reality feedback important to niche enlargement. They also provide access to a set of shared assumptions and world beliefs that connect individuals not only to a larger collective but also to a source of solutions to life problems. With the support and consent of a divine being, individuals can feel better able to manage and control life events (Pollner, 1989).

Spirituality may also counter despair by offering an explanatory framework that gives meaning to life and the experience of illness. Spirituality and faith may offer a sense of hope that can help minimize the negative effect of mental illness and the social response to it: "My faith in God and a higher power . . . has taught me that there are lots of good things in store for me" (Sullivan, 1993, p. 131). As a coping device, a source of support, and an organizing framework to explain one's current situation and possibilities, spirituality can have a unifying effect on the individual: "It's a big deal for me. It helps me to be a whole person" (Sullivan, 1993, p. 131).

Although the factors described above are more speculative than definitive, they have been repeatedly identified by consumers and confirmed in practice and empirical studies. They set forth a direction for mental health services and social work practice that strives to support the recovery process.

THE ROLE OF THE ENVIRONMENT IN THE HELPING PROCESS

People move through a variety of settings in a given day. Each of these settings invites and supports some behaviors and discourages and penalizes others. Some settings make taxing demands on the individual, while others are inherently more relaxing and pleasing. Physical, intellectual, social, and emotional development is affected by interactions with various environments.

In the late 1800s, during the early days of the asylum movement, it was believed that the pace and demands of urban life were key factors in the development of mental illness. Given this perspective, the natural solution was to remove the person from the source of stress to an asylum or state hospital (Rothman, 1971). Because family relationships, particularly between parents and children, have historically been implicated in the formation of mental illness, the impulse has been to remove or sequester the person with mental illness from the problematic family environment.

Rarely has the external environment been perceived as a source of support or opportunities that can contribute to the recovery process. Even less explored is the role of the environment in the development of resilience. Instead, the prevailing logic has been to create specialized services and programs that compensate for disabilities. Within these environments, people with mental illness interact only with "their own kind" and become totally defined by their social category. In other words, they become entrapped.

People with mental illness, like most people, require external support to succeed. Community mental health services and concerned professionals, vocational activities, consumer groups, and involved family and significant others are important sources of external support.

Further study is needed to ascertain the effects of external support on the course and prognosis of serious mental illness. Recent studies suggest a higher risk for schizophrenia among those born and reared in urban environments (Torrey & Yolken, 1998). Research points to a relationship between home atmosphere and relapse (Lefley, 1992). More studies are examining the atmosphere of treatment settings (Davidson, Tebes, Rakfeldt, & Sledge, 1996; Melle, Friis, Hauff, Island, Lorentzen, & Vaglum, 1996). Examination of environmental contributions to the expression and course of mental illness does not negate or discount the evidence of biophysical research. But as we strive to develop effective treatments and programs, the role of environmental contingencies must be examined.

Cultural Factors

We know very little about mental illnesses, and future research may nullify apparent cross-cultural disparities. With this caveat in place, it appears that people with mental illnesses have brighter prospects in the developing world than in the industrialized world.

Most developing countries can be characterized as sociocentric in orientation: Social cohesiveness is valued and affirmed via rules, norms, and customs. In theory, few people are excluded from social intercourse in spite of obvious disabilities or differences. In such settings, recovery is "very much a communal phenomenon, tending not only to reintegrate the deviant individual into the group but also to reaffirm the solidarity of the community" (Warner, 1983, p. 209).

In much of the developed world, particularly the West, the dominant cultural orientation is egocentric. There are firm boundaries between self and others. Illness in this setting is a personal phenomenon and, in some cases, a source of shame. In the absence of group solidarity and support, the person can be cut off from social processes, which further exacerbates the problem. It is not surprising that much modern mental health care is designed to create and develop social support networks and that the goals for treatment emphasize independence.

Work. One of the most important activities that connect an individual to the community is work. In the developed world, vocational rehabilitation is often the first order of business in mental health treatment (Asuni, 1988). In the developing world, by contrast, social rehabilitation is far more crucial, and it is assumed that a person's cognizance of social obligations is adequate motivation to return to work. Because work is often of the nonwage subsistence variety, there is always an opportunity to participate and be appreciated.

In the West, social attitudes and social policies create barriers and disincentives for those with psychiatric disabilities to work. The nature of securing work is vastly different than in the developing world. In this country, people must conduct a job search and win a position in a competitive marketplace. The structure of the world of work in the developed world matches poorly with the realities of serious mental illness. The unpredictable nature of the illness, the social deficits, and the information-processing challenges that must be surmounted require flexibility in the workplace. Until quite recently, such flexibility was nearly impossible to find.

Family. The pain and confusion that comes with suffering from a serious mental illness and the resulting social rejection is often simultaneously experienced by family members. What complicates matters further is that professionals have often blamed family members for the illness of their loved one. Families have often had to navigate a fragmented system of care on their own, or they have had to create some semblance of a system where none existed (Hatfield & Lefley, 1987). It is fair to suggest that families are often the original case managers. Unfortunately, many families have turned to professionals for support and have only found rejection and blame.

Previous theories cast a critical eye toward family interaction and in particular the relationship between a child and his or her mother. Not surprisingly, psychotherapy and family therapy were treatment staples, and the identified patient was often kept in isolation from the family to ensure that care was not compromised. Additionally, mental illness was touted in some circles as a myth, the product of a disordered society, or an expression of individuality (Laing, 1967; Szasz, 1970). This combination of factors left families isolated, embittered, and at times confused. Some parents of children with serious mental illness have spoken out about their treatment by professionals and the lack of adequate mental health services. Siblings have often been left in the shadows, and the recognition that siblings also need support and attention has been slow in coming.

The growing recognition and acceptance of the biophysical nature of serious mental illness has altered the perceptions of professional helpers and has diminished, to some degree, the stigma faced by families of the seriously mentally ill. Yet, vestiges of the past still remain, and it behooves beginning professionals to be sensitive to a family's previous involvement with professional helpers.

In the developing world, cultural beliefs help families cope with a seriously mentally ill member. A sociocentric society is often characterized by an extended family structure and/or one where fictive kin extend the boundaries of the family. There is a built-in source of emotional and instrumental support for families caring for a member with mental illness. Such buffers are absent in much of the developed world, where the increased geographic mobility of the population has reduced the role of the extended family and fictive kin. Families must create or secure their own support structures and networks. When supports are unavailable to families dealing with an ill member, the burden on them is great. Families under great duress turn to professionals and specialized services for help.

Despite the misunderstanding and stigma that continue to surround mental illness in the United States, many families have developed strategies that have helped them survive and thrive. In recent years, they also have found support and solidarity from others in like circumstances. There are significant differences between the perspectives of professionals and of families who are successfully coping with the chronic condition faced by a loved one (Robinson, 1993). The families construct a normalization story that focuses on strengths and wellness rather than deficits and disease. Professionals, on the other hand, offer a problem-saturated perspective and insist on "servicing the illness" instead of offering the help an individual needs for "getting on with [his or her] life" (Robinson, 1993, p. 20). Today, more professionals understand the nature of mental illness and respond to the needs of families in a more helpful fashion. Support organizations like the Alliance for the Mentally Ill have also become important advocates for people with mental illness and their families.

The Self.   Differences in the conceptualization of the self also affect the cultural and familial response to serious mental illness (Kleinman, 1980). In the West, beliefs about the importance of autonomy, freedom, permanence, and an internal locus of control are consistent with an egocentric orientation. The firm boundaries between self and others in Western societies make illness an individual event. In the case of serious and chronic conditions, the person is seen as forever altered and, in many ways, flawed. It is not surprising that negative labels and stigma are attached to serious mental illness and that the medical and disease perspective is pervasive.

In much of the developing world, the self is seen as permeable and subject to influence from external events, including the spirit world. In this context, mental illness is viewed as transitory. The person is not changed forever. Treating the person as a unique individual and recognizing his or her strengths and special challenges instead of labeling and classifying the individual as a disease type can help the individual and family cope with a troubling situation, reduce stigma, and achieve an optimistic view of the future (Guarnaccia, Parra, Deschamps, Milstein, & Argiles, 1992; Swerdlow, 1992).

Culture and Treatment.   The cross-cultural perspective provides important insights about the recovery process. The cultural and environmental context shape the definition and understanding of mental illness and the way in which individuals, families, and societies address the problem. The task before us is to fashion service systems and programs that capture the best of modern mental health treatment and incorporate an environmental context that promotes recovery—a context where mental illness is not stigmatized and the affected individuals are routinely included and supported in normal and expected community discourse.

Much of the history of mental health services for the seriously and persistently mentally ill in the United States has been the opposite of the process described above. Neglect, stigma, discrimination, and poverty have been the norm. Policies and programs—hospitals, residential treatment, partial hospitals, and the like—have been specialized environments outside of mainstream social processes.

A return to a vibrant extended family structure and a cohesive community united by deep personal ties is unlikely. In fact, advances in communication and computer technology have created virtual communities and support networks, which engender new opportunities and problems. So if the natural order of modern society is antagonistic to assimilating people with serious and persistent mental illnesses in daily discourse, the task before professionals, consumers, and advocates is to find a way to do so.

Mutual Support

Through involvement in support groups, individuals can learn new skills, gain new perspectives, and develop the confidence necessary to recover. In a study of consumers' perspectives on recovery, many informants resided in a community mental health center apartment program. The residents developed their own system of support much like that found among any group of friends. They called each other regularly; they checked on each other; and they monitored friends who were struggling (Sullivan, 1994b).

Support groups are effective because the members, through their own personal experiences, have an understanding and appreciation of the individual's experience. People feel heard and understood without having to continually explain what they really mean. The comfort one feels with peers may be the sole haven for a person with serious mental illness.

Rappaport, Reischel, and Zimmerman (1992) have studied the empowerment mechanisms in mutual support groups. A key finding is the effectiveness of what the researchers labeled *underpopulation.* In underpopulated settings, there are more roles to be filled than there are people available to fill them. Thus, for the group to function, some people must perform multiple tasks or tasks that they might not ordinarily be asked to perform. In mutual support groups, people suffering from mental illness must serve as group leaders or organize a social function—challenges or opportunities withheld from them in other settings. The support offered by the group creates a context in which success can be experienced. This in turn enhances the person's self-confidence and increases the likelihood that the person will take on challenging roles in the future. This and similar research points to the fact that people facing some of life's greatest challenges, whether physical or emotional, can succeed if given both the opportunity and the necessary supports. Strengths-based practice and mental health programs based on similar values can enhance the recovery process of people facing serious and persistent mental illness.

DEVELOPING HELPING RELATIONSHIPS WITH PERSONS WITH SERIOUS AND PERSISTENT MENTAL ILLNESS

The basic tenets and values of the strengths perspective are consistent with the core values of social work. The challenge is putting such values to work with client systems. Almost by definition, social workers deal with individuals who face serious and complex problems that have overwhelmed them and those who care about them. At times, these individuals come to the attention of social workers because family, friends, and the conventional system of services and supports are insufficient to meet their needs. However, implementing the strengths model is not difficult only because individuals with serious and persistent mental illness present complex problems; it is difficult because it runs counter to mainstream models of care.

Mental health programs and professionals aid the recovery process by helping people capitalize and build on personal and environmental strengths. Utilizing a strengths approach helps promote movement from entrapping niches to enabling niches. Figure 9.1 provides a visual illustration of the forces that influence what kind of niche a person occupies. The various individual and environmental factors can be either positive or negative. Stigma and discrimination, a lack of goals and self-confidence, and the absence of essential supports ultimately lead to niche entrapment. In contrast, positive achievements in any of the same

FIGURE 9.1. The Creation of Niches

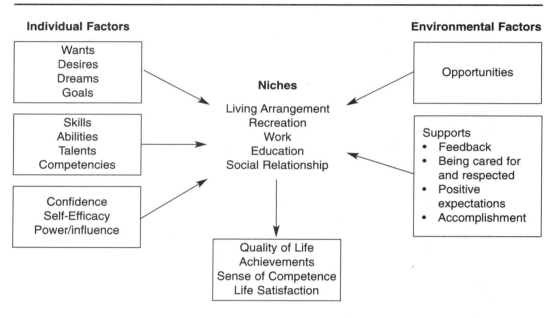

Note: From "Breaking Away: The Potential and Promise of a Strengths-Based Approach to Social Work Practice," by W. P. Sullivan and C. Rapp, 1994, in R. Meinert, J. T. Pardeck, and W. P. Sullivan (Eds.). *Issues in Social Work: A Critical Analysis* (p. 101), Westport, CT: Auburn House. Reproduced with permission of Greenwich Publishing Group, Inc., Westport, CT.

dimensions can move the consumer toward an enabling niche and recovery. These positive steps need not be dramatic. They can be as basic as the accomplishment of a simple goal, such as participating in a support group or becoming involved in a supported employment program. To outsiders, the day-to-day realities of community-based generalist practice may not appear complicated or sophisticated. Nevertheless, to be effective with this client population, you must be well versed in the full range of generalist practice skills. The following case example illustrates the opportunities and obstacles inherent in using a strengths approach with persons facing serious and persistent mental illness.

Juan H. is thirty years old and lives with his parents and a younger sister. Juan's childhood was unremarkable. He had several good friends and played on his high school basketball team. Near the end of his senior year, he became very interested in religion and decided to enter the seminary. While there, he became preoccupied with sin and the devil. He was hospitalized for two weeks and diagnosed with schizophrenia. Since then, he has been hospitalized on six occasions, three of them in a state psychiatric hospital for stays that exceeded one year. Juan has attempted to live independently and to hold a job, but he always begins neglecting his care, fails to take his medication, and returns home. His parents try to provide for him at home, but over time his delusions and deteriorating condition force them to seek inpatient treatment.

Juan's story is not unusual. Individuals with mental illness, their families, and mental health professionals face similar situations daily. Cyclic illness and treatment episodes are typical, and there is no cure for illnesses like schizophrenia. Periodic hospitalizations or restrictive treatments seem inevitable. Or is it better to keep Juan institutionalized and make his hospital stay as comfortable and satisfying as possible? This solution is costly, can be viewed as immoral, and would likely violate his civil rights.

Community-based models of care merge fiscal and practical considerations; affirm key social work values that respect diversity, individual worth, and dignity; and reflect a focus on maximum personal development. Professionals who work from the strengths perspective recognize that people affected by serious and persistent mental illness have limitations and deficits and face stern challenges in their lives. The mission is to help these individuals overcome the challenges. In so doing, a strengths-based approach can make a positive contribution.

From a traditional perspective, Juan's issues are commonplace. Closer supervision, better medication compliance, and more structure in his day-to-day life might be able to increase his tenure in the community. His problems are an obvious result of a serious medical condition, and a range of specialized services and personnel must be employed. The focus here is squarely on the illness that defines his existence. This traditional model of helping has been inadequate on its own. Persistent episodic mental illness is not merely the result of individual pathology; it is also the product of an insufficient system of care.

Social work, with expertise in environment-person transactions and a tradition of working with vulnerable populations, is well suited to play a major role in recovery from serious mental illness. Strengths-based generalist social work practice is predicated on the ability of the professional to collaboratively identify, develop, and match individual and environmental assets. Like all social work practice, the establishment of a helping relationship is essential. Given the nature of serious mental illness, the professional must possess a wide range of knowledge and skills. To advance recovery, the practitioner must be versed in the tenets of good interpersonal practice, be cognizant of community resources, and be an effective advocate.

Generalist social work practice with those facing serious and persistent mental illness is not for everyone. The work can be challenging and rewarding. It requires patience and a healthy dose of creativity. The effective practitioner begins with a profound respect for people who are facing challenging circumstances and through words and deeds conveys a sense of hope and the expectation that recovery is possible.

Assessment

The medical model still dominates mental health services, starting the moment consumers and families first seek help. Social workers are not immune to the medicalization of human problems, for "deficit, disease, and dysfunction metaphors are deeply rooted in social work, and the emphasis of assessment has continued to be the diagnosis of abnormal and pathological conditions" (Cowger, 1997, p. 59).

To help Juan recover, however, it is important to know more than the nature of his illness. The simple vignette reveals a number of strengths. Juan has an involved family; he has tried repeatedly to live in the community and hold a job;

he has excelled in athletics and has made friends; and there may be a faith community available to him. Adopting a strengths approach is not simply a matter of reframing troubling situations into positive statements. It means viewing the challenges and solutions in an entirely different light. People who are successful in life have identified and built on those things they do well and enjoy. Rarely does simply ameliorating deficits and weaknesses lead to positive personal and social development.

People with serious and persistent mental illness lack resources and power. They are rarely actors and are often acted on. They regularly face restrictions in life activities that most people take for granted, things as basic as freedom of movement. Most initial helping encounters do little to alter their life experiences. They may be asked a series of questions that seem incongruous with their current concerns, or they may be subjected to a battery of tests that are equally confusing. In the end they may be offered a verdict, the name of an illness, perhaps schizophrenia or bipolar or schizoaffective disorder, and a number assigned to the name. This kind of diagnostic procedure, guided by the *DSM*, has practical utility, and social work professionals should become proficient in such assessments. The difficulty arises when the diagnosis becomes the final word. Furthermore, in this process, the consumer is relatively passive, and the end result is a treatment plan that sets forth activities and interventions designed to achieve the goals established by experts.

A strengths assessment, in contrast, "provides structure and content for an examination of realizable alternatives, for the mobilization of competencies that can make things different, and for the building of self-confidence that stimulates hope" (Cowger, 1997, p. 63). The stimulation of hope can begin with the first helping encounter. The initial meeting should instill a belief in the possibility of change and a successful recovery.

The interest in assessing consumer and environmental strengths has resulted in a number of different instruments that a professional can chose from (for example, see Cowger, 1997; McQuaide & Ehrenreich, 1997; Rapp, 1998, and Chapter 5, "Assessment Tools"). The assessment should occur in the consumers' environment of choice when possible. This may be in the individual's home, at a restaurant, or in an office. From the beginning, make clear that this is an equal partnership. Conduct the assessment in a conversational style, and be sure to use language the consumer understands (Cowger, 1997; Rapp, 1998). Given the information-processing difficulties that some individuals face, you should be very concrete and establish a pace that is comfortable for the individual.

The potential power of the strengths assessment is its ability to highlight the individuality and uniqueness of the person and to use this information to mutually tailor a strategy to advance recovery. The process of assessing individual and environmental strengths should result in more than a plan to address an immediate problem or goal. The long-range purpose is to help consumers recognize and draw on their own competencies to surmount future challenges and work toward cherished goals.

To affirm uniqueness, assessment must be also culturally sensitive. The understanding of life events, the appraisal of these events, and the actions taken in response to them are shaped by the cultural context:

> Culture provides an all-encompassing, pervasive context that infuses meaning to behavior. Because human behavior is expressed in a context, diagnostic practices that

focus solely on individual and biologic forces are constricted. Relational variables such as family, group, community, minority group membership, and sociopolitical realities are central to the lives of many people of color. (Comas-Diaz, 1996, p. 163).

When the professional fails to consider contextual factors, an assessment may merely reflect his or her cultural background and bias. For example, a family's use of prayer could be viewed as an indication of denial, lack of education, or naïveté. But in fact, this response might be culturally appropriate, a source of comfort and relief, and consequently an important individual and environmental resource.

Thus, consideration of individual and family strength must be done within a cultural context. As McQuaide and Ehrenreich note, "strength is not a culture-free concept" (1997, p. 204). The stigma and social rejection experienced by people with serious mental illness is compounded if the person is also a member of a disenfranchised group. Such individuals struggle to survive in a number of cultural contexts and rarely encounter treatment environments that are culturally sensitive to their needs. Instead, most mental health services reflect the characteristics of dominant culture. Survival in such an inhospitable world is evidence that many persons with serious and persistent mental illness are amazingly resilient.

After the family had contacted the mental health center about Juan, a social worker, Rick C., was assigned. Juan and Rick agreed to meet the next afternoon at the home of his parents. When Rick arrived, Juan, his parents, his sister, and their next-door neighbor, a long-time friend of the family, were waiting to meet him. He spent time interacting with all present and accepted a drink and a snack. He asked Juan if he was comfortable sharing his situation at this time and Juan said he was. Rick listened to Juan's story and then to the family's story. They told Rick how they had cared for Juan for a number of years and how they recognized that things were going askew. They also discussed their conversations with their priest and their prayers for Juan's improvement. During this meeting, Rick spent most of his time listening and asked for specific information as a normal part of the conversation.

Devote the necessary time to listen to the problems and fears of individuals and those concerned about them. Issues of confidentiality must be respected, but when permission is given, family and friends can be a wealth of information. This is particularly true when working with people with serious mental illness. At the first contact, communication may be difficult because of the confusion and disorientation that can come with the neurobiological disorders, and the individual may feel wary of professional intervention. Patience is required. The simple act of spending time with the person is critical to the success of future work. Avoid rushing headlong into the process of assessment if the key actors have not had the chance to tell their stories. If you do not allow the stories to emerge, you may be perceived as insensitive (De Jong & Miller, 1995; McQuaide & Ehrenreich, 1997).

The completion of the individual assessment and care plan can take on many forms, depending on the style and structure of an agency. In some cases, specialized personnel and/or teams are assigned all assessment and referral duties. In other settings, the initial phase of the helping process is done by a multidisciplinary team in which each professional brings a unique perspective to the assessment process. In still other instances, professionals conduct assessments autonomously. Given the challenge of serious mental illness, it is likely that a wide range of professionals will be involved, making communication and coordination a necessity.

In some managed mental health care settings, a specialist will determine a care plan based on the diagnosis, best practice or clinical pathway information, and fiscal considerations. This is becoming increasingly common in behavioral health care. In community mental health care settings, it is still most common for an individual practitioner or team to work with an individual or family to establish a plan of action. In settings that serve people with serious and persistent mental illness, a wide range of services may be necessary and appropriate. Medication management, individual or group therapy, day treatment, and skills training may be utilized. In recent years, there has been more of a focus on independent living, work and education opportunities, and leisure time pursuits.

Intervention and Evaluation

Social workers often make their contribution to the recovery process in the general area of activities of daily living. That is, they help the consumer learn skills, acquire resources, and accomplish goals germane to living successfully in the community. In some settings, these activities are erroneously perceived to be ancillary to mainstream treatment. In fact, they are central to the recovery process.

Rick, the social worker, began an initial exploration of Juan's goals and interests. He explained how the role of case manager was similar to and different from the roles of other professionals Juan had encountered. Rick spent a great deal of time exploring interests and activities that Juan enjoyed now or in the past. He often asked Juan if he would be interested in doing a particular activity at this time. When Juan mentioned that he would like to live on his own, Rick asked what would be needed for him to meet this goal and what obstacles he felt he would face. Throughout the interview, Rick was encouraging and took the time to praise Juan for the successes he had experienced.

From the first encounter, you should convey the expectation of success and action. In order to facilitate change, Rick and Juan worked together to establish an initial goal that had a high probability of success. To be effective, goals should be mutually developed, concrete and specific, proactive and positive, achievable, and challenging (De Jong & Miller, 1995; Rapp, 1998).

A well-developed action plan focuses on a select set of goals; identifies the resources needed for goal attainment, and specifies what the key actors will do to achieve the goals. The effective social worker understands that major goals are accomplished by first addressing much smaller goals, even those that appear on the surface to be unrelated.

In his discussions with Juan and his family, Rick explored Juan's previous attempts to live independently. Rick learned that Juan eventually became isolated, which ultimately triggered a downward spiral marked by neglect and relapse. While mental health services, including case management, were available, these services alone were inadequate. Finally, Juan would return home or enter a more restrictive treatment setting.

One of the key principles of the strengths perspective is that behavior is shaped by the resources available to people (Davidson & Rapp, 1976; Rapp & Chamberlain, 1985; Sullivan, 1997). The focus is not on Juan's inability to live independently, and the goal is not to place him in a specialized living program to compensate for his deficits. A strengths approach focuses attention on the necessary resources and supports that will allow Juan to live in the environment of his choice.

It is critical to affirm Juan's stated goal of living independently and not to dismiss it as unrealistic. Professional attitudes and appraisals affect the confidence and esteem of vulnerable people (Davidson & Strauss, 1992). Time after time, clients note the importance of those professionals who believed in them. Professionals who belittle the hopes and aspirations of others undermine their confidence and self-esteem (Orrin, 1994).

Major goals, such as Juan's goal to live independently, are accomplished by completing a series of small, incremental steps or objectives. An initial objective may simply involve exploring possible living arrangements. This may entail reading the housing advertisements in the paper each morning or agreeing to visit a specific apartment complex. While some individuals may be ready to take more dramatic steps in the early phases of helping, this is the exception rather than the rule.

Recovery is a process with internal as well as external dimensions. Putting the "self into action" is a critical stage in recovery for persons with serious and persistent mental illness (Davidson & Strauss, 1992). Seemingly small steps like reading the newspaper are vitally important to the individual's future success. It is important to start somewhere (Orrin, 1994).

Rick and Juan began to establish plans for the next two weeks. Rick, felt confident that Juan would be able to live independently, but he was concerned about the potential for isolation. Exploring further, he learned that the one aspect of hospitalization Juan enjoyed was using the gym. In particular, he enjoyed shooting baskets and participating in basketball games. When asked if he would still like to play basketball, he readily said he would but that he didn't know where and with whom he could play.

With some help from the family as well as Juan, Rick located some of Juan's old friends and basketball teammates. Most were aware of Juan's difficulties and were glad to know that he was back with his family. Some of them would informally gather at the church gym on Sunday night and play a pick-up basketball game. While Juan was interested in joining them, he was afraid that he had lost the skills necessary to play. Therefore, Rick agreed to accompany Juan to a nearby YMCA where he could begin shooting baskets and get back into shape.

Playing basketball accomplishes several important objectives. First, it helps establish a working relationship between Juan and Rick. Second, it is action-oriented; Juan is proactive and begins to put the "self into action." Third, the activity is pleasurable and provides ready opportunities for increasing self-esteem. As Juan improves his skills, his confidence will grow. Finally, Rick is helping Juan establish a network of friends who can provide support, lessen the burden on his parents and family, and reduce his isolation. Each of these factors contributed to Juan's previous inability to live independently. Therefore, although on the surface playing basketball has little to do with independent living, in fact it is an important step in the overall process of community integration.

> Over the next few weeks, Juan and Rick visited the gym. At the gym, they reviewed his days between visits and discussed future goals. Juan wanted to go to the gym more often, but he could not afford a membership and Rick could not always accompany him. Together, they approached the facility manager, who agreed to exchange access to the gym for some volunteer work. Juan began doing minor cleanup and odd jobs at the facility. He was asked to notify the staff when he would not be able to come in.

Skillful helpers immediately seize opportunities to find other individuals or activities that can replace the direct service they are providing. In this case, Juan has the opportunity to act on his own and take steps to engage in everyday activities. With each step, a foundation is created for the next phase of recovery. If the tasks become overwhelming, a step back to a previous level of activity is appropriate. In such a situation, the professionals must work with the consumer to reinforce the gains that have been made and to assure the consumer of support when he or she is ready to take another risk. Persons with serious and persistent mental illness are amazingly resilient, and like all people, they have the right to take on challenges even if they might fail. Recovery is not a linear process, and relapse is part of the journey for those with serious mental illness. Social work practice is also rarely linear. The steps described so far may take months or even years. For some, getting to the point described thus far is a major accomplishment.

In this example, a natural community resource was essential to Juan's success. Forces of fear, stigma, and exclusion often work against recovery. Often, the professional must advocate in a persistent manner to gain access to a resource like the YMCA.

> Gaining confidence, Juan began to join some of his old friends on Sunday evenings for basketball. He saw that people of all ability joined in and that the atmosphere was relaxed. After working at the YMCA for some time, he felt ready to explore possible living arrangements. He wanted to remain close to his friends and activities, and he liked being in proximity to his family. The mental health center had a supported-living program at several neighboring apartment complexes. Juan felt most comfortable in a setting with on-site staff. Rick and Juan developed a transition plan leading to his move to the apartment.

Persons with serious and persistent mental illness can work, live, play, and learn in the environments of their choice if the necessary supports are in place to help them succeed (Anthony & Blanch, 1988). These supports can come from friends, family, job coaches, neighbors, employers, and clergy.

Throughout this time, Juan was actively involved with other mental health professionals. He regularly met with a psychiatrist who monitored his medication use, and he attended a support group for people with serious and persistent mental illness. In addition, he made occasional use of a drop-in center where other consumers socialized, ate lunch, and planned trips into the community. At other times, he attended group meetings or skills training sessions. Learning new skills became increasingly important to him as he became more confident about returning to work.

There were also times when he felt vulnerable and that he was becoming disorganized. At these times, he would call Rick or a twenty-four hour crisis line. Shortly after taking the job at the YMCA, he went through a predictably difficult time and spent three days at the respite program—a homelike setting with staff close by. Here he was praised for his effort to gain control, and Rick noted that in the past he would have likely been rehospitalized for an extended stay.

Sixteen months after the initial appointment, Juan was living in his own apartment and working at the YMCA three days a week. He met weekly with Rick and monthly with the psychiatrist. He remained in close contact with his family, joining them for dinner twice a week and at church on Sundays. Over time, he learned to monitor his stress level and to recognize signs of impending trouble. While there is no guarantee that he will avoid future hospitalization, crisis and respite services have sufficed thus far. He has rekindled old friendships and made new ones at the gym and on the job. His life may have taken a different course if the illness were not present, but by any yardstick he is in the process of recovery.

Termination

The outcomes for people like Juan are varied. Some fully recover, while others have persistent difficulty throughout their lives. Most will need some level of professional support and service for years. All should be afforded every opportunity to live productive and enjoyable lives. For many, a cornerstone of their success is a professional helper or service system that believes in them.

Termination usually occurs when professional services are no longer necessary and the consumer-professional relationship draws to a conclusion. For people with serious and persistent mental illness, termination has different connotations. Given the nature of serious mental illness and the realities of mental health services, it is likely that persons with serious and persistent mental illness will encounter scores of professionals over their lives. When dealing with a condition that can fragment the personality and result in chaotic thoughts and emotions, permanence and predictability are critical components of effective services. All transitions, whether a move to a new housing program or a change of professional helpers, must be handled skillfully. While no organization can control the departure and movement of staff, mental health consumers should be prepared well in advance of any change. Termination must commence at the earliest possible date, and new staff should work alongside familiar workers to the extent possible. Teams and support groups can help create a supportive organizational context that reduces the trauma that staff changes have on persons with serious and persistent mental illness.

SUMMARY

Serious and persistent mental illness disrupts all aspects of an individual's life. The ability to perform normal and expected roles is diminished, and interpersonal relationships with family members, friends, and peers become strained. The combination of personal and environmental insults can result in a cycle of disorientation and self-neglect, which ultimately leads to hospitalization or social marginalization. People with serious mental illness become stigmatized and are often labeled in negative ways. Over time, they tend to accept and internalize these negative perceptions and view themselves as mental patients rather than as human beings.

Mental health services and programs are in a state of rapid flux. Professionals who advocate for individuals with severe and persistent mental illnesses view many of the recent organizational and financing changes that are taking place in the field with suspicion. The primary concern is that managed care may become managed cost. Efforts to control costs can result in stringent and narrow definitions that can reduce or eliminate coverage for persons with serious and persistent mental illnesses. There is no cure for mental illnesses; at best, they can be managed over the long term.

The concept of recovery is a relatively new vision for people with mental illnesses and for the provision of service to this population. Generalist social workers can play a vital role in helping those struggling through the difficult and painful process of recovery. Incorporating an ecological perspective and the concept of the social niche is critical in helping people articulate the strengths and resources needed for a successful recovery. Social workers can help persons with mental illnesses reduce entrapping aspects of their environment while strengthening the enabling components.

A number of factors can aid the recovery process. New medications are improving symptom relief for people previously considered untreatable. The increased availability of community-based services is also aiding the recovery process. The community for people with mental illnesses is more widely available than in the past. The willpower of the individual is another key factor in the recovery process, as is the availability of meaningful vocational activities. Spirituality can also be a major force in the recovery process for many people with serious and persistent mental illnesses. Environmental and community factors also contribute to recovery.

CASE EXAMPLE

The following case example illustrates the experiences many people with serious and persistent mental illness have in their lives. It also illustrates the nature of generalist social work practice with this client population.

Get Me Out of This Place

Mary S. is a forty-two-year-old woman who has been recently discharged from a state psychiatric hospital. She has been hospitalized on three previous occasions, the last time for nine months. Mary was first hospitalized during her senior year of high school and has usually been diagnosed as suffering from severe depression. In the years following her initial hospitalization, Mary was able to complete high school and married when she was in her early twenties. It was the breakup of her short marriage that led to a suicide attempt and a hospitalization that lasted more than three years.

Since her graduation from high school, Mary has had a number of jobs that usually last for less than six months. She has periodically lived with her parents, but in recent years she has lived in boarding homes and congregate living facilities. The most recent hospitalization, the first in nearly a decade, came after an unsuccessful attempt to live on her own. After quitting her job at a local convenience store, Mary secluded herself in her apartment and neglected her care. Concerned neighbors were able to contact Mary's parents, who found her in a disheveled state. She had not taken her psychotropic medication for some time. After her hospital stay, she was placed in a nearby group home.

Assessment

Kristin P., the social worker assigned to Mary, began seeing her prior to discharge. While this early contact helped establish a relationship, Mary was still reticent. Kristin was involved with the hospital team during the discharge planning meetings and accompanied Mary on her first visit to the group home. Kristin felt that it was important to get Mary working on some simple goals.

The standard assessment data germane to psychiatric care had already been compiled. The next step was to gain information and insights that could help Mary in the process of recovery. While a standard strengths assessment would eventually be completed, the early assessment work was in the form of a conversation. During the first meeting at the group home, questions focused on activities for that day or the day after. Later, more attention was devoted to long-range goals. Mary was quick to say that her long-term goal was to "get out of this place." When pressed for specifics, Mary said that she was uncomfortable living with others and wanted a place of her own. Instead of dismissing this goal as unreasonable, Kristin began exploring with Mary the tasks and behaviors that would enable her to live independently. Over several visits, a range of important issues were discussed, including medication management, avoiding isolation, and employment. Several short-term and long-term goals were developed, along with an action plan to complete these tasks.

Intervention

In an approach that may seem counterintuitive, Kristin and Mary discussed those months when things appeared to be going well. Mary had lived independently for long periods of time. Mary noted that she saw her psychiatrist regularly, that a medication was found that seemed to work well for her, and that she took it as prescribed. Kristin helped Mary develop a simple list of things to do that was placed by her bedside, and an appointment was set up with a psychiatrist at the community mental health center to discuss medication options.

Mary had made some good friends while working and had enjoyed doing things socially outside of work. She knew that keeping active was important and that when she was alone the depression deepened. At first, Kristin encouraged Mary to participate in activities and outings at the group home. Later, Kristin and Mary tried to find some of the friends Mary had previously worked with. One of these old friends was now the general manager of a pet store. Mary began volunteering some time at the shop and eventually agreed to work there two mornings a week. To ease the transition, Kristin joined Mary for an hour or two, serving as an informal job coach. She also obtained permission to contact Mary's employer to check on any early signs of difficulty.

Over several months, Mary became more active and continued with her part-time job. She had adjusted well in the group home, but she was still interested in greater privacy. In evaluating the range of options available to her, Mary did not feel that she could live on her own at this time. Her level of work and activity seemed right for her, but although she was doing well, it was easy to slip back into solitude when her depression seemed unbearable.

Kristin began working with other staff to arrange for Mary to participate in a new apartment program. Other consumers and on-site staff members were available for support, but Mary would have the privacy she desired. Kristin helped Mary set up her apartment and secure necessary utilities. Mary's parents provided some furniture and other household necessities. Kristin helped Mary get acclimated to her new home and surroundings and visited Mary at the home twice a week. New goals were established as Mary continued the process of recovery.

Termination

Recovery is a process, not an end point. All people adjust their goals and aspirations during their lives. The life that Mary leads now may not be the one she dreamed about as a youth, but she is surmounting the challenges presented by serious mental illness. For those facing such illnesses, there may or may not be a termination from professional helpers. Good social work practice requires consumers to be encouraged to maximize their potential. In Mary's case, Kristin began scaling back her appointments, at times substituting a telephone call for a personal visit. It is hoped that others in the environment, such as neighbors and friends, can become the support networks that were once saturated with professional helpers. It is likely that Mary will continue to struggle with depression, but good social work practice will help develop an extensive range of options that will allow her to continue to live in the environment of her choice and participate in those activities that are most satisfying.

DISCUSSION QUESTIONS

1. In reviewing the case example, what are some of Mary's strengths?
2. What strengths and supports are available in the social environment?
3. How could Mary's previous hospitalizations have been avoided? What can be learned to prevent future hospitalizations?
4. How does the concept of recovery shape social work practice with those challenged by serious and persistent mental illness?
5. How does the assessment process and product differ from other assessment procedures you have used? Why is this style important in working with people with serious mental illnesses?
6. How is the role of the social worker different than in other case examples presented in this book?
7. Discuss the threats to the continued improvement in mental health services. What are social, political, and economic obstacles to the development of a strengths-based approach to mental health services? What strategies can generalist social workers utilize to improve services for this population?

REFERENCES

Anthony, W. (1993). Recovery from mental illness: The guiding vision of the mental health system in the 1990s. *Psychosocial Rehabilitation Journal, 16*(4), 11–23.

Anthony, W., & Blanch, A. (1988). Supported employment for persons who are psychiatrically disabled: An historical and conceptual perspective. *Psychosocial Rehabilitation Journal, 11*(2), 5–23.

Asuni, T. (1988). Sociocultural and economic determinants of rehabilitation. *International Journal of Mental Health, 17*(2), 8–14.

Breier, A., & Strauss, J. (1983). Self-control in psychotic disorders. *Archives of General Psychiatry, 40,* 1141–1145.

Comas-Diaz, L. (1996). Cultural considerations in diagnosis. In F. K. Kaslow (Ed.), *Handbook of relational diagnosis and dysfunctional family patterns* (pp. 152–168). New York: Wiley.

Cowger, C. (1997). Assessing client strengths: Assessment for client empowerment. In D. Saleebey (Ed.), *The strengths perspective in social work practice* (2nd ed. pp. 59–73). New York: Longman.

Davidson, L., & Stayner, D. (1997). Loss, loneliness, and the desire for love: Perspectives on the social lives of people with schizophrenia. *Psychiatric Rehabilitation Journal, 20*(3), 3–12.

Davidson, L., & Strauss, J. (1992). Sense of self in recovery from severe mental illness. *British Journal of Medical Psychology, 65,* 131–145.

Davidson, L., Tebes, J., Rakfeldt, J., & Sledge, W. (1996). Differences in social environment between inpatient and day hospital-crisis respite settings. *Psychiatric Services, 47*(7), 721–726.

Davidson, W. S., & Rapp, C. (1976). Child advocacy in the justice system. *Social Work, 21*(3), 225–232.

De Jong, P., & Miller, S. (1995). How to interview for client strengths. *Social Work, 40*(6), 729–736.

Estroff, S. (1989). Self, identity, and subjective experiences of schizophrenia: In search of the subject. *Schizophrenia Bulletin, 15*(2), 189–196.

Faris, R., & Dunham, H. W. (1939). *Mental disorders in urban areas.* Chicago: University of Chicago Press.

Gerhart, U. (1990). *Caring for the chronic mentally ill.* Itasca, IL: Peacock.

Goldstein, M. (1992). Psychosocial strategies for maximizing the effects of psychotropic medications for schizophrenia and mood disorder. *Psychopharmacology Bulletin, 28*(3), 237–240.

Guarnaccia, P., Parra, P., Deschamps, A., Milstein, G., & Argiles, N. (1992). Si Dios Quiere: Hispanic families' experience of caring for a seriously mentally ill member. *Culture, Medicine, and Psychiatry, 16*(2), 187–215.

Hatfield, A., & Lefley, H. (Eds.) (1987). *Families of the mental ill.* New York: Guilford.

Jaco, E. G. (1954). The social isolation hypothesis and schizophrenia. *American Sociological Review, 19,* 567–577.

Kleinman, A. (1980). *Patients and healers in the context of culture.* Berkeley, CA: University of California Press.

Laing, R. D. (1967). *The politics of experience.* New York: Ballantine.

Leete, E. (1989). How I perceive and manage my illness. *Schizophrenia Bulletin, 15*(2), 197–200.

Lefley, H. (1992). Expressed emotion: Conceptual, clinical, and social policy issues. *Hospital and Community Psychiatry, 43*(6), 591–598.

Libassi, M. (1995). Psychotropic medications. In R. Edwards (Ed.), *Encyclopedia of social work* (19th ed., pp. 1961–1966).

Liberman, R., Wallace, C., Blackwell, G., Eckman, T., Vaccaro, V., & Kuehnel, T. (1993). Innovations in skills training for people with serious mental illness: The UCLA social and independent living skills modules. *Innovations and Research, 2*(2), 43–59.

McQuaide, S., & Ehrenreich, J. H. (1997). Assessing client strengths. *Families in Society, 78*(2), 201–212.

Melle, I., Friis, S., Hauff, E., Island, T., Lorentzen, S., & Vaglum, P. (1996). The importance of ward atmosphere in inpatient treatment of schizophrenia on short-term units. *Psychiatric Services, 47*(7), 721–726.

Nuechterlein, K., Dawson, M., Gitlin, M., Ventura, J., Goldstein, M., Snyder, K., Yee, C., & Mintz, J. (1992). Developmental processes in schizophrenic disorders: Longitudinal studies of vulnerability and stress. *Schizophrenia Bulletin, 18*(2), 387–425.

Orrin, D. (1994). Past the struggles of mental illness: Toward the development of quality lives. *Innovations and Research, 3*(3), 41–45.

Pargament, K., Ensing, D., Falgout, K., Olsen, H., Reilly, B., Van Haitsma, K., & Warren, W. (1990). God help me: Religious and coping efforts as predictors of good outcome to significant life events. *American Journal of Community Psychology, 18*(6), 793–824.

Pollner, M. (1989). Divine relations, social relations, and well-being. *Journal of Health and Social Behavior, 30,* 92–104.

Rapp, C. (1998). *The strengths model.* New York: Oxford University Press.

Rapp, C., & Chamberlain, R. (1985). Case management services to the chronically mentally ill. *Social Work, 30*(5), 417–422.

Rappaport, J., Reischel, T., & Zimmerman, M. (1992). Mutual help mechanisms in the empowerment of former mental patients. In D. Saleebey (Ed.), *The strengths perspective in social work* (pp. 84–97). New York: Longman.

Robinson, C. (1993). Managing life with a chronic condition: The story of normalization. *Qualitative Health Research, 3*(1), 6–28.

Romme, M., & Escher, A. (1989). Hearing voices. *Schizophrenia Bulletin, 15*(2), 209–216.

Rothman, D. (1971). *The discovery of the asylum.* Boston: Little, Brown.

Ruscher, S., de Wit, R., & Mazmanian, D. (1997). Psychiatric patients' attitude about medication and factors affecting noncompliance. *Psychiatric Services, 48*(1), 82–85.

Strauss, J. (1989). Subjective experiences of schizophrenia: Toward a new dynamic psychiatry: II. *Schizophrenia Bulletin, 15*(2), 179–187.

Sullivan, W. P. (1993). "It helps me to be a whole person": The role of spirituality among the mentally challenged. *Psychosocial Rehabilitation Journal, 16*(3), 125–134.

Sullivan, W. P. (1994a). Recovery from schizophrenia: What we can learn from the developing nations. *Innovations and Research, 3*(2), 7–15.

Sullivan, W. P. (1994b). A long and winding road: The process of recovery from severe mental illness. *Innovations and Research, 3*(3), 19–27.

Sullivan, W. P. (1997). On strengths, niches, and recovery from serious mental illness. In D. Saleebey (Ed.), *The strengths perspective in social work practice* (2nd ed., pp. 183–197). New York: Longman.

Swerdlow, M. (1992). "Chronicity," "nervios," and community care: A case study of Puerto Rican psychiatric patients in New York City. *Cultural, Medicine, and Psychiatry, 16*(2), 217–235.

Szasz, T. (1970). *Ideology and insanity.* Garden City, NY: Anchor.

Taylor, J. (1997). Niches and practice: Extending the ecological perspective. In D. Saleebey (Ed.), *The strengths perspective in social work practice* (2nd ed., pp. 217–227). New York: Longman.

Torrey, E. F., & Yolken, R. (1998). Is household crowding a risk factor for schizophrenia and bipolar disorder? *Schizophrenia Bulletin, 24*(3), 321–324.

Warner, R. (1983). Recovery from schizophrenia in the third world. *Psychiatry, 46*(3), 197–212.

Waters, B. (1992). The work unit: The heart of the clubhouse. *Psychosocial Rehabilitation Journal, 16*(2), 41–48.

White, R. (1959). Motivation reconsidered: The concept of competence. *Psychological Review, 66*(5), 297–333.

CHAPTER 10

Generalist Practice with Older People

Norma D. Thomas

ohn L. is an MSW student with a first-year field placement with an Area Agency on Aging. As part of his placement duties, John makes home visits to his elderly clients to coordinate the various services they receive and to provide supportive counseling if needed. Prior to this field placement, John had had little contact with elderly people.

John's first client was Mrs. P., an eighty-year-old widow who lives alone in a dangerous part of the city. In the past, her son, who lives nearby and is a cocaine addict, abused her. John's field instructor asked John to assess the appropriateness of her living situation. Before meeting Mrs. P., John pictured her as a helpless old woman trapped in an unsafe neighborhood who needed help finding a safer place to live. What John found was a strong-willed woman who knew what she wanted and what she did not want and who had no intention of letting some young social worker tell her what was best for her. After his first meeting with Mrs. P., John realized that he was going to learn a lot from his elderly clients. He also wondered if they would all be so independent.

The United States, like most of the developed world, is experiencing a dramatic increase in the numbers of people we call "senior citizens" (or "seasoned citizens," a term that is gaining in popularity). In 1990, there were 31.6 million Americans aged sixty-five and older. By the year 2050, there will be 78.9 million, who will comprise 22 percent of the total population (U.S. Bureau of the Census, 1989, 1996). The fastest growing population segment in this country is people aged eighty-five and older. By the year 2050, there will be 19 million people over the age of eighty-five (U.S. Bureau of the Census, 1992a). The need for generalist social workers to work with the elderly has never been greater, and it will continue to increase as the population of older adults increases.

This chapter provides information on generalist practice with elderly clients. The chapter begins with a description of the demographic characteristics of the elderly. This is followed by a discussion of policy issues and micro and macro

TABLE 10.1. Projected Growth of Sixty-five and Older Population in the United States

Year	Total Numbers (Millions)	Caucasian Total Numbers (Millions)	Percent	Nonwhite Total Numbers (Millions)	Percent
2000	34.7	28.8	83%	5.9	14%
2030	69.4	50.7	73%	18.7	27%
2050	78.9	51.3	65%	27.6	35%

Note: From "Population Projections of the U.S. by Age, Sex, Race, and Hispanic Origin Data," U.S. Bureau of the Census, 1996, *Current Population Reports* (p. 25, No. 1130). Washington, DC: U.S. Government Printing Office.

practice issues. The chapter then covers developing helping relationships with older adults. By the end of the chapter, you should be able to help John

1. Appreciate the size and heterogeneity of the elderly population in the U.S.
2. Understand the major social and economic policy issues affecting the elderly and the delivery of services to elderly clients
3. Identify interview techniques that are appropriate for professional inter-actions with elderly clients
4. Identify content areas that should be included in a social work assess-ment of elderly clients
5. Describe the major generalist practice issues that need to be taken into consideration in working with older individuals, families, and groups.

The older adult population is not only increasing in numbers at a rapid pace but also in terms of its racial and ethnic diversity. From 1990 to the year 2050, the sixty-five and older population is projected to increase from 31.6 million to 78.9 million people (U.S. Bureau of the Census, 1996). As shown in Table 10.1, during that same period, the percentage of nonwhite elderly is expected to increase from 14 percent of the elderly population to 35 percent.

THE DEMOGRAPHICS OF AGING

The average life expectancy in 1990, was 75.4 years; 71.8 years for men, and 78.8 years for women (Atchley, 1997). There are ethnic and racial variations in life expectancy. For example, African-American women have an average life expectancy of 73.6 years, compared to 64.5 years for African-American males (National Center for Health Statistics, 1995). Life expectancy at birth for Native Americans is sixty-five years (Hooyman & Kiyak, 1999). Overall, the average life expectancy is expected to increase to 77.6 years by the year 2005 (U.S. Bureau of the Census, 1996).

Although women live longer, they do not necessarily live better. Women suf-fer disproportionately from chronic illnesses as they age. This is due in part to their living longer than men. Also, women tend to neglect their own health while caring for their families. Women make up the majority of residents in nursing homes that provide long-term care. They also experience higher rates of poverty. Nearly 16 percent of elderly women live in poverty, compared to 9 percent of men over the age of sixty-five (Hooyman & Kiyak, 1999).

In terms of income, 35 percent of Native American elderly live in poverty, compared to 30 percent of African-American elderly, 22 percent of Latino elderly,

14 percent of Asians and Pacific Islander elderly, and 10.5 percent of Caucasian elderly (Hobbs & Damon, 1996). Lower income contributes to other differences between minority and Caucasian elderly. Minority elderly have less formal education, diminished overall health, and decreased access to health and social services than their Caucasian peers.

There are so many myths about aging that it is impossible to explode them all in one brief section. One popular myth is that most older people live in nursing homes. However, only about 5.1 percent of older people are in long-term-care facilities at any one time (U.S. Bureau of the Census, 1993). Similarly, it is not true that most old people have multiple chronic illness and are dependent on others for their care. The majority of older people live independently with some degree of chronic illness that may require some minimal assistance. Dependency does increase with age, and people aged eighty-five and older need assistance with at least one activity of daily living. They also suffer disproportionately from Alzheimer's disease (Cox, 1993; Leon & Lair, 1990). Families provide upwards of 70 or 80 percent of care needed by older people with chronic illness (National Alliance for Caregiving and AARP, 1997).

Another set of myths is centered around mental and personality characteristics of older persons. For example, it is widely believed that older people can not learn new things. In fact, older people do learn new things, even though the way they learn may change. Older people are constantly adapting and keeping up with societal changes along with everyone else. Older people are also said to be grouchy and set in their ways and to have no interest in sex. Personality does not change because of age, but rather because of some physical or psychological disorder. Sex and affection are important parts of life as people get older. What is often missing is a partner, especially for women, because they have outlived the men. Barring any physiological or psychological disorder, older people can and do remain sexually active throughout life. Statistics are hard to come by. However, the Centers for Disease Control has reported a 94 percent increase in the number of older men infected with the HIV virus due to heterosexual sex and a 106 percent in the number of older women (CDC, 1998).

POLICY ISSUES

With the exception of the Social Security Act of 1935, social policy as it pertains to older adults is a product of the decades that began with the 1960s. Up until this point in history, older people did not have the numbers or the political power to significantly effect social service provision.

Ageism

American society values youth over old age. Ageism, the general collective stereotypes that depict older people as less productive, less attractive, resource-draining, asexual, or mentally deficient, is pervasive in our culture (Comfort, 1976):

> Despite our increase in knowledge about aging, there is still a persistent belief that the aged are less capable—and less important—than other people. Ageism can be a barrier to obtaining quality services. If service providers believe that the aged are less valuable

than other members of society are, they may render a lower quality of service. Beyond that, older people are well aware of the way others feel, so that the fact of ageism's existence has a negative effect on the mental and emotional health of older people. (Roff & Atherton, 1989, p. 94)

Ageism also has an enormous effect on income potential. While 62 percent of U.S. corporations encourage early retirement, only 4 percent offer retraining for persons who might want to return to the workforce (Hooyman & Kiyak, 1999; Ramirez, 1989). Despite the Age Discrimination in Employment Act of 1987, litigation because of alleged age discrimination is on the rise (Hooyman & Kiyak, 1999; Quadagno & Hardy, 1996).

Ageism also affects the provision of social services. For example, mental health care for senior citizens has always lagged behind the need. The 1995 White House Conference on Aging identified significant unmet needs for mental health services for seniors in nursing homes and in the community (Rosen & Persky, 1997). This is due in part to ageist beliefs that older people who exhibit psychiatric symptoms are suffering from organic disease rather than from a treatable mental health problem.

Social Services

The first White House Conference on Aging in 1961 was the catalyst for the creation of a system to provide services for persons when they reach old age. The resultant policy, the Older American's Act of 1965, called for the establishment of the Administration on Aging in the Department of Health and Human Services. The act provided funds for the development of Area Agencies on Aging to coordinate the delivery of services to older Americans. It also provided funding for an expanded research effort on the service needs of the elderly. The broad-ranged goals under Title I of the act were to ensure that all elderly had

- Adequate incomes
- The best possible physical and mental health care
- Suitable housing
- Full restorative services for those requiring care in an institution as well as comprehensive community-based long-term care services
- Opportunity for employment without age discrimination
- The ability to retire in health, honor, and dignity
- Opportunity to pursue meaningful activities
- Efficient community services when needed
- Immediate benefit from proven research knowledge
- Freedom, independence, and the free exercise of individual initiative (Butler, 1975; Gelfand, 1993).

The OAA established a continuum of services for the elderly. These include transportation for medical appointments and grocery shopping, home health and homemaker services, senior centers, home and congregate meal programs, educational opportunities, information and referral, and adult day care.

In 1973, the minimum age for services was established as sixty. Over time, the original goals of OAA have been expanded and altered in response to the changing needs of the older population. Recent technological advances, for example, have made it possible for many medical treatments to be provided in the home by skilled nursing professionals or, in some cases, by family members. Some medical tests, such as blood work and X rays, can also be done in the older person's own home.

The current system is not adequate to keep up with the rapidly growing older population. This is especially true for those living in rural areas where medical care, community-based in-home services, and access services, such as transportation, are not available. Urban elderly who live in high-crime areas also find it difficult to access in-home services because care providers are afraid to go to their homes (Thomas, 1998). Thus, minority elderly, who tend to live in low-income urban areas, are less likely to have access to formal services than Caucasian elderly (National Association of Area Agencies on Aging, 1992).

The demands for aging services have increased in proportion to the increase in the number of older persons. Waiting lists for services are common. The shortage of services for the elderly is exacerbated by the increasing percentage of women in the work force who can no longer care for elderly parents. The increased mobility of children also contributes to the increased demand for services. More adult children no longer live near their parents. This creates additional demand for support services for the elderly.

In many areas of the country, clients can wait for months and years if their service needs are deemed a low priority. Persons with higher incomes are able to obtain services privately, but older people with lower and more moderate incomes must wait for assistance from the public sector. The service shortage also has a negative effect on care providers. Their inability to help clients obtain necessary resources and services contributes to burnout among geriatric social workers (Poulin & Thomas, 1998).

Concurrent with the service shortage has been a shift in the ideological stance towards older people in this country (Atchley, 1997). There is concern that older people are benefiting disproportionately from the government's social welfare system to the detriment of younger people. The Older Americans Act has not been reauthorized since 1992. It is being attacked by its critics for targeting provisions to those in greatest social and economic need, for its method of administering employment services, for funding such advocacy programs as legal assistance, and for its research component. There is fear that if the Older Americans Act is not reauthorized, the system of service provision in this country will change to the detriment of older people.

Economic Security

Economic security is more than income; it is the ability to command goods and services to meet one's needs. A number of factors, such as accessible and affordable health care, adequate housing, and formal and informal service assistance, must be taken into consideration along with income levels to comprehensively assess economic security. In addition, economic security or its lack must be viewed from a life course perspective. During a lifetime, assets and resources are accumulated or lost, determining economic security in old age (Chen, 1991).

The Social Security Act of 1935, which established the Social Security program, provides a measure of income security to people who worked and contributed to the system. In 1990, 36 percent of the income of persons aged sixty-five and older was from Social Security (Social Security Administration, 1992). By 1996 this had risen to 40 percent (Social Security Administration, 1998). Dependence on Social Security has gone up while other resources such as pension and investment income, have decreased. Given the current employment trend toward downsizing and the decreased time that employees stay in jobs, fewer retirees can be expected to have access to pension income. Social Security was never intended to provide the sole income of the elderly, but about 16 percent of people over the age of sixty-five rely exclusively on income from it (Social Security Administration, 1996).

Since 1974, Supplemental Security Income (SSI) has been available to low-income individuals who need assistance because of age or disability. The amount of money varies from state to state, but generally it is at or near the poverty level. African-American elderly rely disproportionately on SSI; it is the primary source of income for one in five African-American's aged sixty-five and over (Kilkenny, 1990).

Older women who rely on Social Security as their primary source of income face diminished income security. Women live longer than men and often leave the workforce for long periods of time to care for young children and older relatives. Some of the issues affecting women are

- Equity and adequacy of spouse and survivor benefits
- Fairness of coverage of one-earner versus two-earner couples
- The nature of coverage for homemakers and divorced persons (Schulz, 1995).

Concerns about Social Security have reached crisis proportions because of fear that the aging of the baby boomers will bankrupt the system. Proposals to deal with the pending crisis range from increasing payroll taxes, to raising the age at which benefits can be collected, to privatizing the system. None of the proposals has widespread support. Americans generally resist tax increases. Raising the benefit age has potential adverse effects on women and minority group members. Privatizing the system would require financial sophistication on the part of American workers in order to guarantee adequate income on retirement. Practitioners need to pay strict attention to all proposals to modify the Social Security system because of their possible effects on the elderly and on people of all ages.

People face increased out-of-pocket expenses for health care as they age. As an individual ages, the amount of money spent for community-based and long-term health care increases above available income (Atchley, 1997; Liu, Perozek, & Manton, 1993). In 1995, a person aged sixty-five or above who lived in the community paid, on average, $2,750 annually in out-of-pocket expenses for health care costs (Wiener & Illston, 1996). The lack of universal health care forces many older people to choose between medicine and food.

Older people on Medicare are being pressured into signing up for such managed care options as health maintenance organizations. Many do not understand HMO restrictions, such as controlled access to physician and other services through a primary physician referral system. Medicare expenses are estimated to increase sixfold in the last year of a beneficiary's life because of the increased rate of chronic disease (Kronenfeld, 1993). Since older people cost HMOs more money than younger people, some observers expect premiums to increase for the elderly and for elderly people to be dropped from plans because of profit issues.

Media coverage of the debate over welfare reform has focused on younger recipients. However, numerous seniors, especially those who are not citizens, have lost benefits. The Personal Responsibility and Work Opportunity Reconciliation Act of 1996 (PRWOR) barred immigrant seniors arriving in this country from receiving food stamps, Medicaid, SSI, and other services. It also stopped benefits for many legal immigrants already here. Original estimates were that PRWOR would save more than $54.2 billion, of which 44 percent ($23.8 billion) would result from cuts to legal immigrant benefits (Friedland & Pankaj, 1998). Although adjustments in 1997 restored SSI benefits to people who received them prior to PRWOR, the restoration of food stamps has been left to individual states. Confusion over this law has resulted in many older legal immigrant's losing their benefits. In 1997, four hundred thousand legal immigrants lost benefits, including sixty-five thousand residents of nursing homes who relied on Medicaid as payment (Keigher, 1997).

Housing

As the size of the older population increases, there will be a greater need for additional housing units as well as for creative housing options. Living with children or other relatives is not a viable alternative for many older persons who wish to remain independent and not be a burden to their children. Often, their children do not live nearby. Consequently, substantial numbers of older people "age in place": they stay in their own homes or apartments as they grow older. This can be positive if the home can safely accommodate the physical changes and functional ability of the older person and if the person has enough income to maintain the home. But for others, this phenomena has been referred to as "stuck in place" because the older person is unable to relocate (Skinner, 1992). Elderly African-Americans and other minority elders often have few housing options due to lifelong disadvantages (Skinner, 1992). Approximately, 80 percent of those aged fifty-six to sixty-four, 77 percent of those sixty-five to eighty-four, and 67 percent over the age of eighty-five own their own homes (Golant & La Greca, 1994; Hooyman & Kiyak, 1999; Pynoos & Golant, 1996). More than 50 percent of the elderly live in dwellings built before 1939, and fewer than 5 percent of elderly homeowners and 10 percent of elderly renters live in dwellings built after 1970. Large numbers of elderly persons are living in homes in need of repair and general maintenance. Indeed, some 244,000 older homeowners and 506,000 elderly renters are living in residences that have two or more structural deficiencies (Gillespie & Sloan, 1990).

For many seniors, making a home safe requires taking an environmental inventory. Removing throw rugs, increasing the lighting, moving electrical cords, and installing handrails and grab bars around the tub to help decrease the incidence of falls are safety modifications that can be easily made. Converting a room on the first floor to a bedroom and putting in a first-floor bathroom or using a portable commode will decrease the need to climb the stairs. If the stairway will accommodate modification, a chair glide could be installed. Emergency response systems placed in the home allow the older person to contact someone in case of an emergency. Occupational therapists can instruct older people and their families in the use of adaptive devices that increase the likelihood that they can remain at home in the community.

There are a number of housing alternatives for older people who do not need the skilled or intermediate-level supervision of a nursing home. Shared housing is an option in which an older person invites someone into his or her home or moves into the home of another. The other person can be unrelated or a family member. Multigenerational families living under the same roof are more common among minority groups. This is rooted in differences in value systems, the need to share resources, and blocked access to other housing options.

The board and care or personal care home, a form of assisted living, is one option used by the low-income elderly. Many individuals in these homes require greater supervision because of mental or physical challenges. Residents usually share their bedroom space. The quality of the activities, services, and supervision varies from facility to facility.

Assisted-living developments, which cater to seniors in the higher income brackets, have become increasingly popular. Generally, an individual receives some help with instrumental activities of daily living, such as group dining or minimal housekeeping. Most residents of more upscale assisted-living facilities are fairly independent in activities of daily living (bathing, dressing, eating, mobility, and medication management).

Retirement communities, which offer a continuum of care services, give an older person the security of levels of increased care in the same community. Generally, retirement communities are an option only for older people with very high incomes.

For older people who cannot remain in their own homes, and who require the most medical care and supervision, there are nursing homes. Although nursing homes are highly regulated, the quality varies greatly. Social workers assisting families in finding a nursing home need to consider the following factors:

- Appearance isn't everything but it is important. Is the facility clean and free of odors? Is the atmosphere like a home or hospital?
- How are visitors greeted? Are family members encouraged to stay involved with the older resident? Does the facility have programs to support the caregivers? How are the residents addressed by the staff?
- Are residents involved in activities or just sitting in the hallway; or are large numbers in bed?
- Does the facility appear to respect and acknowledge cultural differences among the residents?
- Are the patient's and family's rights clearly spelled out?
- Contact the state's Department of Health to verify the current licensure status of the facility. Also, ask questions about the medical staff in order to feel comfortable about the quality of medical care provided (Smith, 1992).

Unfortunately, many decisions about nursing home placement are made as a result of hospital policies and the availability of space. Often, the elderly person is placed in the first nursing home that has an available bed. Deciding to move an elderly person to a nursing home should be done only after careful consideration, and the older person and the family should be involved in the decision so as to reduce trauma and loss.

Economics are a prime consideration. Nursing home care is expensive. Even older people with considerable resources may run out of money within approximately two years. After they have exhausted their resources, and for those without assets or income, Medicaid pays for nursing home care. For economic reasons, most nursing homes prefer private-pay patients and there are fewer beds available for Medicaid patients. It is more difficult to find a nursing home for an elderly person with limited resources. Thus, minority group members are underrepresented in nursing homes. Collectively, they only make up about 12 percent of the nursing home population (Strahan, 1997).

There is a clear need for housing alternatives for older persons, especially those of low to moderate means, who cannot remain in their own residences. Unfortunately, the number of seniors who find themselves homeless is increasing. At any point in time, approximately one hundred thousand elders are homeless (Atchley, 1997). Deinstitutionalization, poverty, and inadequate housing options all contribute to the increase in homelessness among the elderly (Tully & Jacobson, 1994).

DEVELOPING HELPING RELATIONSHIPS WITH OLDER ADULT CLIENTS

In order to successfully engage with older people and develop positive helping relationships, social workers must overcome institutionalized ageism as well as face issues related to their own aging, family members' aging, and their own mortality (Greene, 1986; Poulin & Thomas, 1998; Schneider & Kropf, 1992). The negative image of aging in this country influences the choices that students entering social work school make in terms of placement experiences as well as course work. Many practitioners see aging as synonymous with death and dying, forgetting that all people ultimately die. Successful practice in this field requires a reversal of thinking so that we can help people live with the complications of aging.

Social work practice with older adult clients encompasses a variety of target problems. Much of the work with this population centers around connecting clients to needed formal resources and helping them develop and maintain informal support systems in order to prolong their ability to remain in the community with the highest possible quality of life. Social workers provide therapeutic interventions with persons who have mental health problems, such as depression. Generalist social workers also provide supportive counseling to elderly persons who have experienced multiple losses and help those needing assistance and support in caring for their grandchildren. Older people and their support systems may have the same problems as younger people. The major difference is that the elderly have had a longer time to accumulate them.

Holosko and Feit cite five intervention activities for social workers serving elderly clients identified by Tobin and Gustafson (1987):

Use of Touch: touch was used frequently with the elderly and reflected an active approach to meeting their needs (touch activity demonstrates caring and reassurance and is readily understandable where other techniques used by social workers may not be as easily understood by the older person);

Activities: which are perceived to be more typical include providing more concrete assistance, more reaching out to families and more talking by the worker in sessions;

Reminiscence: or the use of the past which helps clients to develop ego strength (by noting past coping) and adaptation capabilities, as well as helping to recapture and reaffirm the current self;

Transference: referring projections onto the worker of meaning, wishes and thoughts that are redirected from other persons; and

Countertransference: or specific concerns evoked by the worker to the client (e.g., dependency, helplessness, and death). (Holosko & Feit, 1991, p. 25)

Informality is an American trait that often extends into interactions with clients. Beginning social workers mistakenly think that addressing someone with an air of familiarity is the key to building a relationship. But for most ethnocultural groups, formality is the expectation, especially with older people, since veneration of elders is a key component of their value systems (Randall-David, 1989). In addition, older people believe that they have earned the right to be respected by those who come to provide them with assistance. The following communication guidelines are recommended for working with elderly clients, especially those who are members of racial and ethnic minority groups.

- Never address older people by their first names unless you have been given permission to do so. Do not ask them if it is all right to call them by their first names; because you are an authority figure, they will more than likely tell you it is fine even when they are offended. If people want to be addressed by their first names, they will tell you. Using surnames connotes respect.
- Older people usually enter service delivery systems because someone else suggested it; typically they are not self-referred. Understand that there is a great reluctance to enter helping relationships, and be willing to take the time in an initial visit to ease the discomfort of the potential client and the client system (Watt & Soifer, 1991).
- Much of the community-based service provided to older people is done in their homes. Food, which is important to many ethnocultural groups and may be the only thing someone has to offer in exchange for assistance, is very important to seniors when welcoming someone into their home. Do not offend the person offering the gift. In other words, be careful how you turn a gift down.
- Older people have lived a long time and have a story to tell. They resent attempts to structure their information into categories. Start conversations on less threatening subjects, and guide the older person into telling his or her own story. You will get all the information you need, but using a narrative approach will enhance the interaction.
- Non-verbal communication is critical in obtaining the trust of the elderly. Physical space, eye contact, greetings, and hand gestures, including shaking hands, have to be measured by culture as well as circumstance (NAAA, 1992, p. 34).

Assessment

Assessment of older people requires a comprehensive, broad-based ecological approach. Psychological, biological, and sociological factors become more complex and intertwined as people age (Kropf & Hutchison, 1992). Often, a physical disease may be the cause of serious psychiatric symptoms. Depression can result from later-life issues, such as grief over the loss of family members and friends, diminished physical capacity, or rapid role changes, or it may be a symptom of an underlying medical condition (Watt & Soifer, 1991). Social work practice with older people requires knowledge of pharmacology and disease processes and how they affect client functioning. In addition, you must be able to differentiate psychiatric problems that are treatable from problems that originate from an organic disease. Many factors must be included in a comprehensive assessment of an older person.

Depression.   The psychiatric problems that affect younger people are also present in older age groups. There is a high prevalence of depression among the elderly.

Approximately 15 percent to 22 percent of elderly community residents report symptoms of depression, with 10 percent to 15 percent requiring clinical intervention (Blazer & Williams, 1980). Even more nursing home residents suffer from depression. Between 12 percent and 25 percent of the aged living in institutional settings meet diagnostic criteria for major depression (LaRue, 1992).

Symptoms of depression among the elderly include

- Prolonged sadness
- Insomnia or excessive sleeping
- Loss of interest in things normally enjoyed
- Fatigue, constant tiredness
- Psychomotor retardation
- Significant weight gain or loss
- Guilt
- Anxiety
- Self-blame
- Helplessness and hopelessness
- Sexual dysfunction
- Agitation
- Real or perceived cognitive deficit
- Persistent pain, headache, or chest pain
- Thoughts about death
- Feeling about wanting to die (Philadelphia Corporation for Aging, 1995).

Because all of these symptoms could signal physical problems, it is important for older people to receive a comprehensive assessment by a multidisciplinary team in order to determine causation.

Associated with the high rates of depression among the elderly is a high rate of suicide. For persons sixty-five and over, the rate of suicide is 21.4 per 100 people, near double that of younger age groups (Turk-Charles, Rose, & Gatz, 1996). The oldest old, those over the age of eighty-five, have the highest suicide rates. The elderly are more successful in committing suicide than are their younger counterparts. If an older person talks about suicide, he or she must be taken seriously. Questions to ask elderly clients who are at risk of attempting suicide include:

- "Do you ever feel that life is not worth living?
- "Do you feel that your situation is hopeless?
- "Have you ever thought of really hurting yourself?
- "Have you been thinking about killing yourself?
- "Have you planned how you would do that?
- "What do you think you would do?
- "Do you have the means (pills, weapon, etc.) to carry out your plan?" (PCA, 1995, p. 9)

What Is Mother Trying to Do?

Senora R., a seventy-eight-year-old Latina, was referred to a local Area Agency on Aging because her daughter, Maria, was worried. Maria had recently visited her mother and found that she had lost thirty pounds in the last two months, was not taking her medication properly, rarely left the house, and seemed to have no interest in anything. Senora R. does have chronic illnesses: diabetes, high blood pressure, and an unspecified heart condition. Maria thought her mother was deliberately not eating or taking her medication in an attempt to end her life.

Rachel J., the social worker, scheduled an appointment the next day and talked to Senora R. The client described several losses in the last year, including her husband, two sisters, her best friend, and a neighbor. In addition, the neighborhood was changing around her. Drugs were being sold openly on the corners, and her house was next to one that had been abandoned. She did not want to move but was fearful of venturing out of her home even to buy groceries. She didn't want to carry much money, so she brought home only small quantities of food at a time. She had no one who would regularly go to the pharmacy for her, so she tried to stretch her medication, cutting down on the dosage. She was fully aware of the negative results that poor nutrition and medication mismanagement could produce, but she stated that she did not care. "What is there really to live for? I am still here but everyone around me has gone" she stated.

Rachel expressed to her the concern that Senora R. was not eating and not taking her medicine as a benign way to end her life. Senora R. did not confirm this, but she asked if the worker and daughter blamed her if it was true? Instead of trying to convince Senora R. of all she had to live for, Rachel asked her to describe what her life was like before the large number of losses occurred. She was devoted to her house and the care of her husband. She had not worked outside of the home but did volunteer for her church and at the children's school when they were young. Senora R. was a pianist and had taught local students.

With the assistance of Maria, Rachel convinced Senora R. to visit the local senior center. The staff members were all bilingual and bicultural, and most of the participants were Latino. The activity coordinator talked to Senora R. about help she could provide to the center—for example, she could assist with the choir and the intergenerational programs. The center had shopping assistance as well as an on-site nurse who could monitor Senora R.'s health and assist in obtaining prescriptions. The housing situation would need to be worked on over time. Senora R. did not want to give up her independence by moving in with her daughter, which would be another loss, but the neighborhood does pose a threat to her safety.

Memory.   If you are thirty and forget where you put your keys, it is assumed that you have too much to remember, are stressed, or are just absentminded. If you are eighty and do the same thing, you are assumed to have Alzheimer's disease. Decreasing ability to remember becomes a source of worry to people as they age and to those who care for them. As with symptoms of depression, memory problems require a comprehensive assessment to rule out causes that can be treated, such as a disease process, psychiatric disorder, nutrition, or a medication problem.

For most people, both long-term and short-term memory are well preserved into advanced old age (Albert, 1988). However, forgetting names or recent events is common and can be a source of frustration. It would seem logical that the longer one lives, the more information there is to remember and recall. Therefore, some of it will be lost or take longer to retrieve when an individual gets older. Providing cues, or other forms of recognition assistance, like pictures, helps to improve recall (Albert, 1988). Using lists, having a consistent place for keys and purse or wallet, writing down telephone numbers, and using message pads, voice recorders, medication organizers, and the like all aid memory and help the elderly keep information straight.

Some diseases produce reversible and/or irreversible declines in memory and physical functioning. These diseases are classified under the heading of dementia. Strokes account for 10 to 20 percent and Alzheimer's disease 50 to 60 percent of irreversible dementia (PCA, 1995). From 20 to 50 percent of people aged eighty-five and older have Alzheimer's disease (Evans, Funkenstein, & Albert, 1989; National Institute on Aging, 1996; Pennsylvania Care Management Institute, 1990).

Alzheimer's disease is marked by a slow decline in mental and physical ability over a period of two to twenty years (National Institute on Aging, 1996). The person progresses from not remembering how to do simple things to a total inability to even feed himself or herself. This disease places a tremendous burden on caregivers and is one of the leading reasons for placement of an older person in a nursing facility.

The Alzheimer's Association provides a list of ten warning signs that should prompt older persons and their families or caregivers to seek an evaluation:

1. "Recent memory loss that affects job skills
2. "Difficulty performing familiar tasks
3. "Problems with language
4. "Disorientation of time and place
5. "Poor or decreased judgment
6. "Problems with abstract thinking
7. "Misplacing things
8. "Changes in mood or behavior
9. "Changes in personality
10. "Loss of initiative." (Alzheimer's Association, n. d.)

There is still no cure for Alzheimer's disease. Environmental (Harvard Medical School, 1992) and genetic links (Mayeux, Sano, Chen, Tatemichi, & Stern, 1991) are under intense study to determine predictors of the disease. Treatment often involves medication to control behavior problems, a change in the environment to reduce overstimulating the person, a routine that is followed every day, behavioral management exercises, and reminiscence therapy that seeks to retrieve long-term memory. Drug therapies that have received recent FDA approval are aimed at improving or slowing the decline of cognitive functioning. These drugs have met with mixed results (Youngjohn & Crook, 1996).

Cats, Cats, and More Cats

Mr. M., a Caucasian is an eighty-four-year-old former teacher. He was referred to a local Area Agency on Aging because the neighbors were complaining about odors coming from his home. His wife had died early in the marriage, and there were no children. Mr. M. never remarried and was estranged from his siblings. On investigation, the social worker, June P., discovered a gracious man who lived alone except for a large number of cats that freely roamed inside and outside a large split-level home.

Mr. M. did not receive Social Security because he never applied for it. He was from a well-known family in the area. Neighbors and his estranged family believed that he had sufficient assets to take care of his needs. He drove his car to the bank daily, and he regularly visited a niece, Sara G., who lived one hour from his residence. It was clear that his cognition and judgment were impaired. As a simple test, June asked him for directions to his niece's home, which he could not provide. She also asked him to add simple figures, which he also could not do.

Mr. M. refused to allow the SPCA to take the cats, which were his only companions. When June called the SPCA, she learned they had previously removed the cats from the home, and Mr. M. retrieved them and paid all associated fees.

The home was filled with antiques, which had been ruined by cat urine, droppings, and scratches. The client, however, was in good physical health, which was verified by a nursing assessment. He shopped for food for himself and the cats, and all his bills had been paid at the time of the initial visits. The neighbors reported that the situation had been deteriorating for years and described him as "eccentric."

Mr. M. consented to and underwent a complete physical and psychological assessment, which found him to be in good physical health with severe cognitive deficits, probably of the Alzheimer's type. The task of all agencies now involved was to visit frequently and watch for signs that this fragile situation was changing for the worse.

A neighbor took it upon himself to disable Mr. M's car by removing the distributor cap, since the local and state police would not stop him from driving. Since Mr. M. then stopped visiting his niece, Sara visited him. She was appalled at the living conditions and vowed to take a more active role in planning for her uncle's care.

Mr. M. began to deteriorate. Although he could still get food delivered to the home for himself and the cats, he began to neglect the cats. It was then possible for the Humane Society, in cooperation with the SPCA, to remove the cats from the home. They removed around eighty cats. His physical condition eventually required hospitalization. Sara pursued legal guardianship in order to have his affairs taken care of, since he did have a vast estate. Mr. M. was eventually placed in a nursing home (Thomas, 1997 p. 50).

Capacity.   The term *capacity* refers to the ability of an older person to make reasonable decisions and to understand the consequences of those decisions. All of us, regardless of age, have used poor judgement, at one time or another. Older people are presumed to have the capacity to make decisions for themselves until it is demonstrated that their actions endanger themselves and/or others.

The question of competency often arises in cases that are referred for older adult protective services, especially when the referral is for self-neglect. In states that have an elder abuse law, the highest percentages of protective service referrals are for self-neglect (Salend, Kane, Satz, & Pynoos, 1984). The question often raised is whether the protective service agency is violating an individual's right to live the way he or she wishes to live. Intervention is justified if the person no longer has the ability to make informed decisions and the quality of life deteriorates.

An assessment of an elderly person's capacity or competence should include

- "Evaluating the patient's orientation to person, place, time and situation;
- "Testing of recent and remote memory and logical sequencing;
- "Assessing intellectual capacity including the ability to comprehend abstract ideas and to make a reasoned judgment based on that ability;
- "Assessing mood and affect, noting any suicidal ideations;
- "Examining the content of thought and perception for delusions, illusions, and hallucinations;
- "Inspecting visible behavior, noting agitation and anxiety as well as appetite, eating habits and sleeping patterns; and
- "Reviewing past history for evidence of psychiatric disturbance that might affect the patient's current judgment." (Knapp, 1996, p. 183)

Courts are often called upon to declare an older person incompetent if he or she will not accept assistance on a voluntary basis. Social workers who handle issues of guardianship often find themselves in the uncomfortable role of advocating against the client's wishes in order to have someone appointed to safeguard the client's interests.

Alzheimer's

Ms. B was sixty-nine and lived in a small apartment. A referral to the Protective Service Agency was made by the landlord, who liked the resident but considered evicting her because her apartment was cluttered with trash, and infested with bugs, and the neighbors were complaining. Since Ms. B. lived in a first-floor apartment, which opened to the trash area, no one could understand why she was so "lazy" that she would not even throw the trash into the bins.

A social history revealed that, until approximately two years before the referral, Ms. B. had worked and was meticulous. After a comprehensive assessment was completed, Ms. B. was diagnosed with Alzheimer's disease and eventually moved to a long-term care facility. Unfortunately, Ms. B. received this evaluation only after she was hospitalized through an involuntary commitment. She was not willing to voluntarily receive treatment, and the landlord served her with an eviction notice, to which she reacted so violently that commitment to a psychiatric facility for evaluation was necessary (Thomas, 1997, p. 52).

Addiction. Social workers often bypass discussions of addiction when doing assessments of the elderly. It is hard to believe that someone's grandmother or grandfather could possibly have an addiction to prescription or nonprescription drugs or to alcohol. In fact, it is the reverse of the stereotype of older people.

The extent of alcohol and drug abuse among the elderly is difficult to measure. Estimates range from around 5 percent (Maddox, 1988) to 10 percent

(Pennsylvania Care Management Institute, 1990). Approximately 20 percent of admissions of elderly people to hospitals are related to the abuse of alcohol (Pennsylvania Care Management Institute, 1990).

Older people turn to alcohol to handle the many losses in their lives. They use alcohol to mask the pain of day-to-day existence. This includes isolation due to loss of family and friends and, for some, chronic physical pain. The use of alcohol in combination with prescription drugs taken by older persons can have deadly consequences. Do not be afraid to ask questions about alcohol use, including

- Do you drink alcohol?
- How much do you drink at one time?
- When do you drink?
- What kind of alcohol do you drink?

These questions must be asked if a person is having blackouts, frequent falls, and or memory loss. The same treatment interventions that work for younger people are also appropriate for older people.

Other Considerations.   Assessment is also complicated by the fact that older people are not socialized to accept assistance from social workers and formal social service agencies:

> Elderly persons often believe that problem solving is a matter of honor, something one does on one's own; and the concept of asking strangers for help is viewed as an abrogation of responsibility by many. Similarly, the elderly commonly view professionals as possessing authoritative knowledge—"the truth"—and thus may feel obligated to follow the "prescription" even if the options presented are not viewed as necessary or desirable. Self-determination, a cherished social work value, can easily be set aside in such situations. (Watt & Soifer, 1991, p. 38)

Before data gathering and assessment take place, establish the reason that the client or the client's support system is requesting assistance, and overcome any discrepancies between the two. Most older people are not self-referred, and it is not uncommon for clients to deny that they need assistance. Your first contact is a critical point at which trust may or may not begin to be established.

A holistic assessment should be based on the client's self-report, so long as the older person has capacity as well as from information from significant others in the person's network and professional service providers. Collect information on the level of service being provided by the support network, both formal and informal, along with information on unmet social, psychological, and environmental challenges and strengths. This information will provide the basis for a comprehensive assessment and the development of an intervention plan (Kropf & Hutchison, 1992).

Intervention

Generalist social workers in the field of gerontology work in a variety of settings with a variety of client systems that deal with a variety of micro and macro practice issues. This area of generalist social work requires a range of practice skills as well as the ability to understand and function on an interdisciplinary team. Social workers need to recognize that differences in culture, history, geographical location, gender, religion, sexual identity, and age all effect the helping process with this population.

Generalist social work with older people is an exciting and dynamic field of practice. Where else can one provide assistance while at the same time learn from people who have a wealth of experience? Given the dramatic increase in the number of people over the age of sixty, many who enter social work in other areas of practice will eventually find that their employment includes service to senior citizens. Our goal should be to advocate for the increased quality of life of senior citizens in the hope that, if we live long enough, we personally will benefit from those efforts.

Case Management.   Case management is the model of practice most often used with senior citizens and their families (Morrow-Howell, 1992; Soares & Rose, 1994). Most of the services available to older people are funded by the Older Americans Act and provided through the national system of Area Agencies on Aging (AAA), usually through a case management model. Case management encompasses assessing the strengths and needs of older clients from an ecological systems perspective and linking the client to those services, formal and or informal, that can meet the person's needs (Frankel & Gelman, 1998). Case managers sometimes monitor the cost of service provision as well as service quantity (Frankel & Gelman, 1998; Moxley, 1997). Clients needing case management usually have complex multifaceted needs that cannot be met by simple information and referral programs.

Case management requires workers to develop high-level skills in collaborating with professionals from other disciplines. Case managers should take an interdisciplinary approach to providing services to elderly clients and coordinate the intervention with formal and informal service providers. It is necessary to learn the language of medical practitioners, mental health professionals, financial planners, managed care counselors, religious leaders, and informal gatekeepers. The following case example illustrates why social workers and other people from disciplines—in this case, financial planners—must work together to develop the best possible care plan.

A Place of My Own

Lenora G., aged seventy-eight, is a retired teacher. A few years before she retired at age sixty-three, she sold her home and moved into a rent-controlled apartment. About ten years after she retired, she had a mild heart attack, and she moved to New Mexico to live with her son.

For the past five years, Mrs. G. has lived a moderately active and fairly independent life. She has what amounts to a small apartment in her son's home, with her own bedroom, bathroom, kitchenette, and entrance. Her rooms adjoin the family room, so she is integrated into the household but also perceives herself as independent. Her son is fifty-four years old and unmarried. He is a sales representative for a middle-sized computer hardware manufacturer and has responsibility for the Southwest region of the United States. Although he has some control over his travel schedule, he often has to be away from home for days at a time.

Mrs. G.'s daughter, a housewife, lives in Texas with her husband, a policeman, and their two college-age children. Mrs. G. and her daughter are estranged and have not spoken to each other in more than fourteen years.

Mrs. G. receives $16,000 annually from her teacher's retirement fund, but this pension does not include cost-of-living adjustments. She receives $8,000 a year from Social Security. In addition, she has financial assets of about $130,000, which are invested conservatively. She is a member of a health maintenance organization and is covered by Medicare, but she has no long-term-care insurance.

Mrs. G. complains a lot about being sick, although her physical health is reasonably good. In addition to her cardiac history, her chronic problems include high blood pressure and late-onset diabetes. All of these problems were controlled by a complex pharmaceutical regimen until recently. For the past two years, Mrs. G. has exhibited symptoms of depression. Five times in the last six months, she completely confused her medication schedule and had to be taken to the emergency room by ambulance. Her son thought her complaints about depression and her failure to properly comply with her pharmaceutical schedule were a ploy for attention because of his difficult travel schedule, but it has become increasingly apparent that Mrs. G.'s memory and cognitive capacities are declining rapidly (Tacchino & Thomas, 1997, p. 41–42).

The case manager approached the situation by completing a comprehensive biopsychosocial assessment with Mrs. G. As part of the assessment process, Mrs. G. discussed her future plans with her son. This was done even though she is currently exhibiting cognitive impairment. Finances, which are part of the overall assessment, were evaluated in terms of the options available to the family. The financial planner assumed that, despite what the client and family may want, it is the resources that dictate Mrs. G.'s options. The financial planner felt that the client should sign a durable power of attorney, a living will, and a will while the she has capacity. In addition, the financial planner recommended maximizing Mrs. G.'s current assets in order to provide for her during her projected life span.

A cooperative, interdisciplinary approach ensures that all aspects of a client's life are handled by the people who have the most expertise in each area. Instead of adversarial relationships, practitioners can cooperate if they understand the basic values of their respective professions, understand each other's professional language, and are willing to listen and respect each other's expertise.

Issues in Working with Older Individuals.   Generalist social work practice with older individuals necessitates recognizing each person as a unique individual and not part of a homogeneous group of people. Unless they are hampered by some form of dementia, seniors can take an active role in determining their treatment plan goals and objectives. Someone who is over the age of sixty has the right to make decisions, even if a social worker does not always agree with the decisions.

Allowing older people the time to tell their stories is not only the best way to gather necessary information for an assessment; it is also a form of intervention that works well with older people. Reminiscent approaches to practice have been associated with Robert Butler's research and development of life review therapy, which in essence allows people to reevaluate, resolve, and ultimately integrate the past with the present (Butler, 1980–1981). From a strengths-based perspective, reminiscence encourages people to apply coping strategies that previously worked to current situations. It also allows people to gain satisfaction from successes, as well as to resolve past difficulties in order to live better in the present (Silver, 1995).

Allowing older people to tell their many stories helps them develop a positive identity. Their life and their experiences are validated. A narrative approach provides the elderly with guidance and helps them create order out of chaos in their day-to-day existence. It also gives the storyteller a sense of power that he or she might not normally feel (Viney, 1993).

Practical issues must be taken into consideration when working with older people. For example, hearing loss is a significant problem as one ages. Around 30 percent of persons aged sixty-five to seventy-four and 50 percent of people aged seventy-five and older have some hearing loss (Roff & Atherton, 1989). If interviews take place in hospital rooms, in office cubicles, or in the home where there are loud noises and other distractions, the older person may have difficulty understanding what you are saying. Medication, illness, stress, and exhaustion also affect an older person's ability to hear and understand verbal communication. Guidelines for working with hearing impaired elderly include the following:

- Face the hearing impaired person directly and on the same level whenever possible.
- Remember that your speech will be hard to understand if you are eating, chewing, or smoking while talking.
- Keep your hands away from your face when talking.
- Get the person's attention before you begin speaking.
- Don't talk with your back turned or attempt to talk from another room.
- Reduce background noises such as the radio, stereo, or television.
- Don't shout. Speak in a normal fashion.
- Find different media for communicating if the older person does not understand you, like writing out the message (Kropf & Hutchison, 1992; Schneider & Kropf, 1987).

Although the median educational level of people over the age of sixty-five is about 12.2 years (U.S. Bureau of the Census, 1992b), this figure varies based on gender, race, ethnicity, and region of the country. Bear this in mind when giving printed information to older clients. Do not assume that a client can read and understand consent forms, medical instructions, medication regimens, special diets, or other written communication. You should also avoid using professional jargon when interviewing older adults. One way to ensure that a client understands your intended communication is to have him or her repeat it.

Everything Has Changed

Mr. Z. is a seventy-six-year-old first-generation Italian man who lives alone in an inner-city neighborhood. His wife died several years ago, and his children no longer live in the same city. He was recently hospitalized due to complications related to diabetes. His vision and hearing are both impaired, but he refuses to wear glasses or a hearing aid, saying that they will make him "look old."

The hospital social worker, Amy L., was asked to talk to Mr. Z. about the need to follow his diet and medication regimen and the complications that could result if he does not. She was also asked to determine what other supports could help Mr. Z. comply with his medical program. The attending physician had also ordered a psychiatric consult in order to see if the noncompliance was related to a cognitive impairment.

Amy introduced herself to Mr. Z. and explained why she was asked to meet with him. She asked him how long he had been in United States, what type of work he did, and about his family. His command of English was limited even though he had been in this country for more than sixty years. He has always lived and worked in the same close-knit Italian-speaking neighborhood and had not needed to learn English. It was evident that Mr. Z. did not understand the written instructions provided by his physicians and home health nurse. Mr. Z., was a man of great pride and would not ask for assistance in reading the material.

Amy also discussed with Mr. Z. his refusal to wear glasses and use a hearing aid. The issues were his self-image and lack of information about hearing aids that were virtually undetectable and glasses that were attractive. The worker found someone in the hospital who could write out instructions in Italian and arrange for hearing and vision evaluations on Mr. Z.'s return to the community. The social worker found no evidence of cognitive impairment.

Issues in Working with Older Families.   Because people are living longer, there are more people aged eighty-five and older who are living with or receiving care from children who are themselves senior citizens. They in turn may still have responsibility for their children or their grandchildren. Daughters provide 70 percent of the care to chronically ill elders (Pavalko & Artis, 1997). This responsibility, combined with the need to interrupt employment and the stress that this produces, may have future health and economic implications for women and their families (Robison, Moen, & Dempster-McClain, 1995). Caregivers rarely receive any outside support:

> One-third of the caregivers of the frail are themselves over sixty-five. As might be anticipated, husbands are the oldest group, and half of these male caregivers receive no informal or formal assistance in their caregiving tasks. Twenty percent of caregivers have children at home, and almost half of the adult daughters providing care are employed full time. With the needs that these families and their frail relatives are likely to have, it is startling to note that less than 10 percent receive assistance from any formal services. (Cox, 1993, p. 108)

Multigenerational households are more common for African-American, Asian and Pacific Island, Latino, and Native American families. The living arrangements of these ethnocultural groups reflect cultural values that emphasize concern for the collective as well as veneration of elders. This does not mean, however, that such living arrangements come without stress. Indeed, caring for an elderly family member places strain on the time, resources, and privacy of the caregiver and family.

The phenomenon of second-time-around parenting is increasing in this country. Approximately 3.7 million children live with their grandparents, and the number of grandparents with permanent custody of their grandchildren has doubled in the last decade (Hooyman & Kiyak, 1999). It has always been common for African American grandparents to take care of their grandchildren or other people's children (Hill,

1981, Kennedy, 1978). The difference now is the permanency of the arrangements. Because of AIDS, addiction problems, unemployment, and the young age of many parents, grandparents are taking on roles that have traditionally been assumed by much younger people. Parenting grandchildren produces physical, emotional, and economic stress. It is important to provide support and education to older people who are trying to cope with generational differences and their own needs as well.

I Can't Take Care of Mom, Too

When she was fifty-three and recuperating from injuries and other side effects of an automobile accident, Ms. J., an African American, was called on to care for her seventy-two-year-old mother Mrs. P., who had a stroke. Ms. J. was already caring for two grandchildren whose mother, a drug addict, died the previous year from AIDS. The children were eight and nine. Ms. J.'s mother moved into her home.

Until the accident, Ms. J. worked full-time. Eventually, her own health problems, the demands of caretaking, and the strain on the family income contributed to Ms. J.'s having a heart attack. She was hospitalized, and Mrs. P. was placed in a nursing home for a temporary stay; she died shortly after admission. Ms. J. is slowly recovering, but she feels guilty and blames herself for her mother's death. She is having difficulty coping with the care of the grandchildren, and her employer is pressuring her to return to work.

Ms. J. could benefit from a host of support and or therapeutic groups for grief and loss issues, second-time-around parenthood, and her own physical problems and chronic illness. The children also need support; they have their own issues of grief and loss, fear of abandonment, and stresses in this household. It is important to take a holistic approach when there is an older person in the family. While the older person may be the focus, everyone has to be included. In the family in the above case example, even when the older person is no longer there, there is still a great deal of work that needs to be done. This family, like so many, could have used intervention much sooner, which may have prevented some of the stresses that were allowed to build to the breaking point.

Resist the current practice of working only with the older person and not the whole family. In most service delivery systems, one worker may deal with the person over sixty, someone else with the children, another will find a support group for the caretaker, and someone else may help with health and disability issues. In order to empower older people and their families, recognize that multiple systems are involved and be able to work in a collaborative, interagency, and interdisciplinary environment.

Are We in This Together?

The H. family is the classic example of too many social workers trying to deal with all the issues of one family. Muriel H. is sixty-five and bedridden but is alert. She was referred to the social work agency because the family was being evicted for nonpayment of rent. Mrs. H. received home delivered meals and personal care service, and a nurse visited weekly.

When the worker, Josephine S. went to the home for the assessment, she found a daughter, Lisa H., and her two children, John and Carrie, living there. Lisa and her children were involved with the local child protection agency because of allegations of neglect. The house was dirty and infested with vermin. The school social worker was also involved because of the children's poor attendance and poor grades at school.

On investigation, it was learned that John and Carrie were required to stay home to help care for Mrs. H. if Lisa had to leave the home for any reason. Lisa, who was the primary caretaker for the young children and the older woman, had a caseworker from public assistance who was pushing her toward employment. Legal aid was involved in order to stop the eviction, as were a host of other social service agencies that Josephine would find out about when she would bump into them going to or coming from the home. Mrs. H. was skillful in negotiating the system and had a wide variety of formal and informal resources. She was mistrustful of formal agencies and only reluctantly gave out information.

Josephine called a meeting of all the social workers she knew of in this case, to review the various goals and objectives for this family, to determine where resources could best be consolidated, to eliminate duplication, and to fill in the gaps. In frustration, she exclaimed that if all the money that was being spent on all the social workers was just given to the family, they could probably solve their own problems.

Josephine was successful in developing a tight, coordinated plan of care and took the responsibility to follow up with all those involved, keeping everyone informed. She was able to work with legal aid to resolve the most pressing crisis which was the eviction. Through the relationship she developed with Mrs. H., Josephine was able to get a clear picture of all the formal and informal assistance received by the family in order to help the family help themselves.

Issues in Group Work with Older Adults.   Support groups, education, advocacy, and therapeutic groups are all beneficial to people as they age. Working with a frail elderly population, however, requires different practice approaches. A sensory orientation group can be very beneficial to persons with cognitive deficits (Bowlby, 1993; Burnside & Schmidt, 1994; Corey & Corey, 1997; Ott, 1993; Thomas & Coleman, 1998). Such groups utilized in settings where some sensory deprivation can occur, like long-term care facilities—concentrate on increasing cognition by stimulating the senses. These groups can not only help increase the elderly person's awareness to person, place, and time; they can also assist with the development of peer relationships, provide emotional support and much needed stimulation (especially in institutional settings), and help in identity formation and in maintaining whatever level of social functioning the person has remaining (Rice, 1997; Thomas & Coleman, 1998; Toseland, 1995). A recent study found that sensory orientation groups helped residents of a skilled care unit maintain their level of cognitive functioning, especially if the individual's level of cognitive functioning had not deteriorated too far (Thomas & Coleman, 1998).

Group activity provides an outlet for older persons who may have lost their natural support network and need to develop new relationships to avoid being isolated. You can be instrumental in helping older persons begin to relearn socialization and relationship-building skills. Group activities provide older people with the opportunity to practice having meaningful conversations with people they do not know. "Get to know you" group exercises can be used in senior citizen centers or similar settings. In these exercises the group is divided into dyads. Each person asks the other questions and listens to and records the responses in order to report to a larger group. "Get to know you" questions include:

- Where was the best place you ever lived? What made that place so special?
- What is your favorite season of the year, and why?
- Name and describe one of the most beautiful things you have ever seen.
- Where is the farthest place you have ever traveled?
- What is the most exiting thing you have ever done? Why was it so exciting?
- What do you think was good about the "good old days"?
- What is good about the time in which we live now?
- What is the best advice you ever gave anyone?
- Do you have a favorite quote (or Bible verse or other religious teaching)?
- What is your most prized possession?
- If you could have lunch with someone, living or deceased, who would that someone be?
- What is the secret to having a happy life?

These questions help the older person feel comfortable asking for information beyond a yes or no response. It also allows them to practice listening skills. You and the members of the group will learn a great deal about one another. You will discover commonalties and begin to see others in a different light.

SUMMARY

The elderly population in the United States is expanding rapidly. The most dramatic increases in the United States are in the number of people aged eighty-five and older and in elderly members of minority groups. Social workers and policymakers must work together to effectively plan for the changing face of the older population.

Not only must there be increased community-based and long-term care services for people who need assistance, but better housing options and a plan to insure future economic security are also needed. Issues surrounding health care are critical for the entire population. However, for older people on fixed incomes who must pay disproportionately for medical expenses, health care concerns have reached a crisis point.

In addition, older people have a wealth of knowledge, skills, and talent that is underutilized. Social workers can be instrumental in better utilizing senior citizens as a resource.

Social work with older people requires continued training from a multidisciplinary perspective. Knowledge of the biological, psychological, and sociological aspects of aging is critical in holistic assessment and intervention with older people. This is a field of practice that allows the social worker to use a wide range of therapeutic approaches.

CASE EXAMPLE

This final case example illustrates the range of generalist practice skills that are required in working with elderly persons and their families or caretakers. The case is based on a client of a protective service worker I supervised at an Area Agency on Aging.

Bedridden and Alone

Assessment

Mr. W., a sixty-two-year-old African-American, was referred to the county Area Agency on Aging by a neighbor who was concerned that he was often left alone in a basement apartment. He was bedridden and would not be able to exit the apartment in case of an emergency.

A protective service social worker was asked to make an emergency home visit. On arrival, Paul R., the social worker discovered that the door was locked and that the caregiver, the son Leon W., was not at home. Paul could observe and talk to the client through an open window with bars. Mr. W. stated adamantly that he was well taken care of, did not wish to change the situation, and only wanted to remain with his son. He further stated that Leon was running some errands and never left him alone for long periods of time. Paul's assessment was that the client was alert to person, time, and place, and knew the consequences of his decision. Therefore, Paul decided against petitioning to have the client removed from the home against his wishes. Since this home had no telephone, Mr. W. was asked to inform Leon that Paul would return in the morning.

The next day, Paul returned and met with Leon, a man in his late thirties, who was hostile and demanded to know who had called the agency. Paul let Leon vent his anger and explained that the agency was concerned with the client's well-being. After Leon calmed down, he, Mr. W. and Paul were able to have a conversation.

Mr. W. was terminally ill with colorectal cancer, and the family was receiving assistance from a local nursing agency. Leon stated that they were in danger of being evicted because of nonpayment of rent. The apartment was filthy, although the area around the client was kept clean.

Paul knew that if he did not gain the trust of the son, he would not be able to improve the situation for the client. He therefore asked Leon and Mr. W. how he could best help them. The most immediate problems they indicated were the eviction and the need for transportation to medical appointments. In exchange for his assistance, Paul asked the family's permission to list Mr. W. with the local police and fire stations so that if a call came in from this address, emergency personnel would know that an incapacitated older person lived there.

Leon explained that he sometimes had to leave his father alone in order to take care of errands, because there was no one else to assist. He had to lock the doors because they lived in a high-crime area. Paul was also able to determine that there were other children and several other siblings of the client's who lived in the area. The client and his son would not, however, divulge names or contact information. Paul decided that the family was in need of ongoing, long-term assistance, not just emergency protective services.

Intervention

Paul contacted an agency that provides legal assistance to low-income families to assist with delaying the eviction proceedings. He also contacted the local nursing agency. Their perception of Leon was that he was difficult to work with, often did not get his father to medical appointments, and did not follow the prescribed medication regimen for Mr. W. They had the names of and contact information for a few of the relatives and provided this information to Paul.

During the next visit, Paul decided to try to gain Leon's trust by being empathic. Paul tried to convey that he understood how difficult Leon's caretaking role must be for him, especially without the assistance of the other relatives. Paul began to realize that Leon was bitter about having to care for his father but also felt obligated to do so.

When Paul shared some of the concerns expressed by the nursing agency, Leon and Mr. W. stated that they did not understand the regimen and what the medicine was supposed to do. Neither trusted doctors and nurses and believed more in natural healing remedies. In addition, the nursing agency never helped Leon arrange for ambulance transportation to get Mr. W. to clinic appointments. Leon did not drive, and Mr. W. could not go in a regular van. This time, Paul was given permission to contact other family members.

Paul's hidden agenda was to make the family members feel guilty about not assisting Leon. He determined that there were two other older children and nine brothers and sisters of the client all living in the area. The family did not like the choice of Leon as the caregiver. The consensus was that Leon had a "difficult" personality, and they were estranged from him because of his past lifestyle. It was easier to just stay away. They were unaware of the current living situation, the terminal diagnosis, and the pending eviction.

It was clear to Paul that his own biases about how a family should respond had to be kept in check. He organized a family meeting in order to enable family members to talk about their deep-rooted issues and come together to work on the immediate situation. As a result, the mutual decision was that Mr. W. would move to the home of an older sibling who had the space, resources, and supports to provide the care needed. The nursing agency continued to medically monitor Mr. W. and agreed to provide reeducation on the medication regimen and to assist with better transportation arrangements.

Termination

Once Mr. W. was placed with the family member and the goals of the care plan were being met, Paul terminated official involvement with the family. Through follow-up, he learned that the son was eventually evicted from the

> sibling's home but was able to find his own apartment. Mr. W. died at home, thereby avoiding going to a nursing home. This was his ultimate goal during the whole process.

DISCUSSION QUESTIONS

1. What would you have done on the initial visit to Mr. W.'s home? Discuss the pros and cons of the social worker's leaving a bedridden client in a locked apartment.
2. Mr. W. did not want to be placed in a nursing home and was willing to endure less than ideal conditions. Discuss this from a micro and macro level. What could the social worker have done to ease the client's fears? What is needed on a macro level to provide a range of services to older persons in this situation?
3. Discuss some of the ethnocultural beliefs that might be part of the W. family dynamic. How are these beliefs a source of strength? How might they present obstacles?
4. The social worker decided that the way to help Mr. W. was to gain the trust of his son, the caregiver. Would you have done anything differently? How might the situation have changed if the worker focused his initial attention on the client?
5. From a strength's perspective, what are the positive attributes of this case situation?
6. What effect will the predicted demographic changes in the elderly population have on the delivery of social services in the year 2050? How will the changing demographic profile in the U.S. affect the training of future social workers?
7. What is the key to developing helping relationships with elderly clients? What practice guideline would you focus on in working with an elderly client?
8. What makes assessment of elderly clients challenging? What special factors need to be taken into consideration? How would you conduct an assessment with an elderly client?

REFERENCES

Albert, M. S. (1988). General issues in geriatric neuropsychology. In M. S. Albert & M. B. Moss (Eds.), *Geriatric neuropsychology* (pp. 3–10). New York: Guilford.

Alzheimer's Association (n.d.). *Is it Alzheimer's? Warning signs you should know.* Chicago, IL.

Atchley, R. C. (1997). *Social forces and aging: An introduction to social gerontology* (8th ed.). Belmont: Wadsworth.

Blazer, D., & Williams, C. (1980). Epidemiology of dysphoria and depression in an elderly population. *American Journal of Psychiatry, 137,* 430–444.

Bowlby, C. (1993). *Therapeutic activities with persons disabled by Alzheimer's disease and related disorders.* Gaithersburg, MD: Aspen.

Burnside, I., & Schmidt, M. (1994). *Working with older adults: Group processes and techniques.* Boston: Jones and Bartlette.

Butler, R. (1975). *Why survive? Being old in America.* New York: Harper and Row.

Butler, R. (1980–1981). The life review: An unrecognized bonanza. *International Journal of Aging and Human Development, 12,* 35–38.

Centers for Disease Control and Prevention. (1998, January 23). *Morbidity and mortality weekly report: AIDS among persons aged ≥ 50 years.* Rockville, MD: CDC National AIDS Clearinghouse.

Chen, Y. (1991). Improving the economic security of minority persons as they enter old age. In The Gerontological Society of America, *Minority elders: Longevity, economics, and health: Building a public policy base* (pp. 14–23). Washington, DC: The Gerontological Society of America.

Comfort, A. (1976). Age prejudice in America. *Social Policy 7* (3), 3–8.

Corey, M., & Corey, G. (1997). *Groups: Process and practice* (5th ed.). Pacific Grove, CA: Brooks/Cole.

Cox, C. (1993). *The frail elderly: Problems, needs, and community responses.* Westport, CT: Auburn House.

Evans, D. A., Funkenstein, H. H., & Albert, M. S. (1989). Prevalence of Alzheimer's disease in a community population of older persons. *JAMA, 262,* 2551–2556.

Frankel, A., & Gelman, S. (1998). *Case management: An introduction to concepts and skills.* Chicago: Lyceum.

Friedland, R. B., & Pankaj, V. (1998, January/February). Most-vulnerable older immigrants hit by welfare reform. *Aging Today,* p. 4.

Gelfand, D. E. (1993). *The aging network: Programs and services* (4th ed.). New York: Springer.

Gillespie, A. E., & Sloan, K. (1990). *Housing options and services for older adults: Choices and challenges.* Santa Barbara, CA: ABC-CLIO.

Golant, S. M., & La Greca, A. J. (1994). City-suburban, metro-nonmetro, and regional differences in housing quality of U.S. elderly households. *Research on Aging, 16,* 322–346.

Greene, R. (1986). Countertransference issues in social work with the aged. *Journal of Gerontological Social Work, 9*(3), 79–88.

Harvard Medical School (1992, August). Alzheimer's disease part I. *The Harvard Mental Health Letter, 9*(2), 1–4.

Hill, R. B. (1981). *Economic policies and black progress: Myths and realities.* Washington, DC: National Urban League.

Hobbs, F., & Damon, B. L. (1996). *65+ in the United States.* Washington, DC: U.S. Department of Commerce, Bureau of the Census.

Holosko, M. J., & Feit, M. D. (1991). *Social work practice with the elderly.* Toronto: Canadian Scholars' Press.

Hooyman, N., & Kiyak, H. A. (1999). *Social gerontology: A multidisciplinary perspective* (5th ed.). Boston: Allyn and Bacon.

Keigher, S. M. (1997). America's most cruel xenophobia. *Health and Social Work, 22*(3), 232–237.

Kennedy, C. E. (1978). *Human development: The adult years and aging.* New York: Macmillan.

Kilkenny, W. (1990). Toward empowering the black elderly: Alternatives and solutions. In *Aging and old age in diverse populations: Research papers presented at minority affairs initiative empowerment conferences* (pp. 121–134). Washington, DC: American Association of Retired Persons.

Knapp, M. (1996). Assessment of competence to make medical decisions. In L. Carstensen, B. Edelstein, & L. Dornbrand (Eds.), *The practical handbook of clinical gerontology* (pp. 174-187). Thousand Oaks, CA: Sage.

Kronenfeld, J. J. (1993). *Controversial issues in health care policy.* Newbury Park, CA: Sage.

Kropf, N. P., & Hutchison, E. D. (1992). Effective practice with elderly clients. In R. L. Schneider & N. P. Kropf (Eds.), *Gerontological social work: Knowledge, service settings, and special populations* (pp. 3–28). Chicago: Nelson-Hall.

LaRue, A. (1992). *Aging and neuropsychological assessment.* New York: Plenum.

Leon, J., & Lair, T. (1990). *Functional status of the noninstitutionalized elderly: Estimates of ADL and IADL difficulties, research findings 4.* (DHHS Publication No. PHS 90-3462). Rockville, MD: Public Health Service.

Liu, K., Perozek, M., & Manton, K. (1993). Catastrophic acute and long-term care costs: Risks faced by disabled elderly persons. *The Gerontologist 33*(3), 299–307.

Maddox, G. L. (1988). The future of gerontology in higher education: Continuing to open the American mind about aging. *The Gerontologist 28*(6), 748–752.

Mayeux, R., Sano, M., Chen, J., Tatemichi, T., & Stern, Y. (1991). Risk of dementia in first-degree relatives of patients with Alzheimer's disease and related disorders. *Archives of Neurology, 48,* 269–273.

Morrow-Howell, N. (1992). Clinical case management: The hallmark of gerontological social work. *Journal of Gerontological Social Work, 18*(3/4), 119–131.

Moxley, D. P. (1997). *Case management by design: Reflections on principles and practices.* Chicago: Nelson-Hall.

National Alliance for Caregiving and American Association of Retired Persons (1997, June). *Family caregiving in the U.S.: Findings from a national survey.* Washington, DC: Author.

National Association of Area Agencies on Aging (1992). *Choosing to meet the need: A guide to improve targeting of Title III services to low-income minority elderly* (Grant No. 90-AM-0392). Washington, DC: U.S. Administration on Aging, Department of Health and Human Services.

National Center for Health Statistics (1995). *Vital statistics of the United States, 1990: Volume II—mortality, part A.* Washington, DC: U.S. Government Printing Office.

National Institute on Aging (1996). *Progress report on Alzheimer's disease* (Publication No. 96-4137). Washington, DC: U. S. Department of Health and Human Services.

Ott, R. L. (1993). Enhancing validation through milestoning with sensory reminiscence. *Journal of Gerontological Social Work, 20*(1/2), 147–159.

Pavalko, E. K., & Artis, J. E. (1997). Women's caregiving and paid work: Causal relationships in late midlife. *Journals of Gerontology, 52B,* S170–179.

Pennsylvania Care Management Institute (1990). *Care management orientation manual.* Philadelphia, PA: PCMI.

Philadelphia Corporation for Aging (1995). *Clinical protocol series for care managers in community based long-term care: Depression* (Grant #90-AM-0688). Washington, DC: Administration on Aging, Department of Health and Human Services.

Poulin, J., & Thomas, N. D. (1998). Burnout and the geriatric care manager. *Geriatric Care Management Journal, 8*(1), 25–29.

Pynoos, J., & Golant, S. M. (1996). Housing and living arrangements for the elderly. In R. H. Binstock & L. K. George (Eds.), *Handbook of aging and the social sciences* (4th ed., pp. 303–324). San Diego, CA: Academic Press.

Quadagno, J., & Hardy, M. (1996). Work and retirement. In R. H. Binstock & L. K. George (Eds.), *Handbook of aging and the social sciences* (4th ed., pp. 325–345). San Diego, CA: Academic Press.

Ramirez, A. (1989, January). Making better use of older workers. *Fortune,* pp. 179–182.

Randall-David, E. (1989). *Strategies for working with culturally diverse communities and clients.* Washington, DC: Association for the Care of Children's Health.

Rice, S. (1997). Group work with elderly persons. In G. G. Greif & P. H. Ephross (Eds.), *Group work with populations at risk* (pp. 105–120). New York: Oxford University Press.

Robison, J., Moen, P., & Dempster-McClain, D. (1995). Women's caregiving: Changing profiles and pathways. *Journals of Gerontology, 50B,* S362-373.

Roff, L. L., & Atherton, C. R. (1989). *Promoting successful aging.* Chicago: Nelson-Hall.

Rosen, A. L., & Persky, T. (1997). Meeting mental health needs of older people: Policy and practice issues for social work. *Journal of Gerontological Social Work, 27*(3), 45–54.

Salend, E., Kane, R. A., Satz, M., & Pynoos, J. (1984). Elder abuse reporting: Limitations of statutes. *The Gerontologist, 24*(1), 61–69.

Schneider, R. I., & Kropf, N. P. (1987). *Virginia ombudsman program: Professional certification curriculum.* Richmond: Virginia Department for the Aging.

Schneider, R. I., & Kropf, N. P. (Eds.). (1992). *Gerontological social work: Knowledge, service settings, and special populations.* Chicago: Nelson-Hall.

Schulz, J. H. (1995). Economic security policies. In R. H. Binstock & L. K. George (Eds.), *Handbook of aging and the social sciences* (4th ed., pp. 410–426). San Diego, CA: Academic Press.

Silver, M. H. (1995). Memories and meaning: Life review in old age. *Journal of Geriatric Psychiatry, 28*(1), 57–74.

Skinner, J. H. (1992). Aging in place: The experience of African American and other minority elders. *Generations, 16*(2), 49-52.

Smith, L. (1992). *Right choices: Handle with care.* Lafayette, IN: Lynn Smith Enterprises.

Soares, H., & Rose, M. (1994). Clinical aspects of case management with the elderly. *Journal of Gerontological Social Work, 22*(3/4), 143–156.

Social Security Administration (1992). *Income of the aged, chartbook, 1990.* Washington, DC: U.S. Government Printing Office.

Social Security Administration (1996). *Fast facts and figures about Social Security.* Washington, DC: U.S. Government Printing Office.

Social Security Administration. (1998). *Income of the aged chartbook, 1996.* Washington, DC: Office of Research, Evaluation, and Statistics.

Strahan, G. (1997). An overview of nursing homes and their current residents: Data from the 1995 national nursing home survey. *Vital and Health Statistics. No. 280.* Hyattsville, MD: National Center for Health Statistics.

Tacchino, K., & Thomas, N. (1997). Why financial practitioners and geriatric care managers must talk to each other. *Generations, 21*(2), 41–44.

Thomas, N. (1997). Hoarding: Eccentricity or pathology: When to intervene? *Journal of Gerontological Social Work, 29*(1), 45–55.

Thomas, N. (1998). Case management from urban and suburban perspectives. *Journal of Case Management, 7*(4), 139–146.

Thomas, N., & Coleman, S. (1998). Using the sensory orientation group with a frail elderly population. *Groupwork, 10*(2), 95–106.

Tobin, S., & Gustafson, J. (1987). What do we do differently with elderly clients? *Journal of Gerontological Social Work, 10*(3/4), 107–120.

Toseland, R. W. (1995). *Group work with the elderly and family caregivers.* New York: Springer.

Tully, C. T., & Jacobson, S. (1994). The homeless elderly: America's forgotten populations. *Journal of Gerontological Social Work, 22*(3/4), 61–81.

Turk-Charles, S., Rose, T., & Gatz, M. (1996). The significance of gender in the treatment of older adults. In L. Carstensen, B. Edelstein & L. Dornbrand (Eds.), *The practical handbook of clinical gerontology* (pp. 107–128). Thousand Oaks, CA: Sage.

U.S. Bureau of the Census (1989). Middle series projections. *Current Population Reports.* (P-25, No. 1018). Washington, DC: U.S. Government Printing Office.

U.S. Bureau of the Census. (1992a). Population projections of the United States by age, sex, race and Hispanic origins: 1992–2050. *Current Population Reports* (P-25, No. 1092). Washington, DC: U.S. Government Printing Office.

U.S. Bureau of the Census. (1992b). Educational attainment in the United States: March 1991 and 1990. *Current Population Reports* (P-20, No. 462). Washington, DC: U.S. Government Printing Office.

U.S. Bureau of the Census. (1993). *Nursing home population: 1990.* Washington, DC: U.S. Government Printing Office.

U.S. Bureau of the Census. (1996). Population projections of the U.S., by age, sex, race, and Hispanic origin data: 1995–2050. *Current Population Reports* (P-25, No. 1130). Washington, DC: U.S. Government Printing Office.

Viney, L. (1993). *Life stories: Personal construct therapy with the elderly.* New York: Wiley.

Watt, S., & Soifer, A. (1991). Conducting psycho-social assessments with the elderly. In M. J. Holosko & M. D. Feit (Eds.), *Social work practice with the elderly* (pp. 31–46). Toronto: Canadian Scholar's Press.

Wiener, J. M., & Illston, L. H. (1996). Financing and organization of health care. In R. H. Binstock & L. K. George (Eds.), *Handbook of aging and the social sciences* (4th ed., pp. 427–445). San Diego, CA: Academic Press.

Youngjohn, J. R., & Crook, III, T. H. (1996). Dementia. In L. L. Carstensen, B. Edelstein, & L. Dornbrand (Eds.), *The practical handbook of clinical gerontology* (pp. 239–254). Thousand Oaks, CA: Sage.

CHAPTER 11

Generalist Practice with People of Color

Norma D. Thomas

Donna J. is an MSW student with a first-year field placement at an inner-city Head Start program. The program serves predominantly low-income children of color. Donna is in her early twenties and comes from a middle-class suburban family. Prior to her field placement, Donna had had almost no contact with low-income inner-city people of color.

Donna enjoys her interactions with the children she works with in the program. Her contacts with the children's parents, however, have been less positive. She cannot understand why they seem either hostile or indifferent to her attempts to help them with their children's behavior at school and in the home. Donna wonders what she is doing wrong and why she is having such a difficult time developing trust with the children's parents.

People of color are the fastest growing population groups in the United States. In 1992, there were 32 million African-Americans, 24 million Latinos, 8 million Asians and Pacific Islanders, and 2 million Native Americans, including the Eskimo and Aleut, living in the United States (U.S. Bureau of the Census, 1994). By the year 2010, these numbers will have grown to 40 million African-Americans, 39 million Latinos, 17 million Asians and Pacific Islanders, and 2.8 million Native Americans (U.S. Bureau of the Census, 1990).

Social work has traditionally served disadvantaged populations (Trattner, 1999). As shown in Table 11.1, people of color are disproportionately represented among the nations poor. In the years between 1990 and 1994, the percentages of African-Americans living in poverty ranged from 30.6 percent to 33.4 percent. Latino populations are also overrepresented among the poor, with the percentages living in poverty ranging from 28.1 percent to 30.7 percent. As minority populations grow the numbers of economically disadvantaged individuals and families will probably also grow. Consequently, we will find that more and more of our clients are people of color.

TABLE 11.1. Numbers (Millions) and Percentages in Poverty by Race and Year

	All Persons		Whites		African-Americans		Latinos	
	Number	%	Number	%	Number	%	Number	%
1994	38.1	14.5	25.4	11.7	10.2	30.6	8.4	30.7
1993	39.3	15.1	26.2	12.2	10.9	33.1	8.1	30.6
1992	38.0	14.8	25.2	11.9	10.8	33.4	7.6	29.6
1991	35.7	14.2	23.7	11.3	10.2	32.7	6.3	28.7
1990	33.6	13.5	22.3	10.7	9.8	31.9	6.0	28.1

Note: From *Social Welfare Policy, Programs and Practice* (p. 82), by E. Segal and S. Brzuzy, 1998, Itasca, IL: Peacock. Based on data from *Poverty and Income Trends: 1994,* Center on Budget and Policy Priorities, 1996, Washington, DC: Author; and *Statistical Abstract of the United States: 1996,* U.S. Bureau of the Census, 1996, Washington, DC: U.S. Government Printing Office.

We will also find ourselves working with more people who do not speak English as their primary language. These clients will need assistance in creating a bridge between their native culture and the American culture. This is as true for people of color born in this country and as for those born elsewhere. In addition, class differences between people of color and social workers can create barriers to building a working relationship.

Acquiring cross-cultural understanding requires us to go inside our own selves to explore what makes us unique and what has influenced our behavior. In other words, we need to discover how our culture has influenced who we are before we can understand why culture is so important to those to whom we are providing assistance (Devore & Schlesinger, 1996; Pinderhughes, 1989).

This chapter describes various approaches and guidelines for working with people of color. It provides information on the major racial groups in this country in terms of differences in culture and communication style and explores value differences between majority workers and minority clients that, if not understood, can have a negative effect on relationship-building. The chapter also presents a model for the assessment of people of color and their environment, and discusses the effect of racism on micro and macro practice. By the end of this chapter, you should be able to help Donna

1. Summarize the social work profession's history in working with people of color
2. Describe the major macro policy issues affecting people of color in this country
3. Identify the major micro practice issues in working with people of color
4. Describe differences in communication styles of various groups of people of color and the majority population
5. Describe the major values of the different groups of people of color and compare them with the values of the dominant society
6. Describe the major generalist practice issues that need to be taken into consideration in working with individuals, families, and groups of color.

HISTORY OF SOCIAL WORK WITH PEOPLE OF COLOR

Historically, the field of social work has responded to people of color by not acknowledging their cultural differences and by assuming that they were responsible for their own plight in life and were therefore undeserving. Social welfare was denied from the beginning:

> There was little social welfare for Native Americans during the colonial period—or later on, for that matter; most of those who survived were forced onto the nation's worst lands where, out of sight, they were either ignored despite their poor plight or placed on federal reservations administered by corrupt and uncaring officials.
>
> Then there were blacks, who were also viewed by most colonists as uncivilized and permanently inferior—children of Satan not entitled to the same rights as white people and hence excluded from the social welfare system. Black slaves were the responsibility of their masters and were prohibited from receiving aid under most of the poor laws; free blacks, for the most part, were simply denied assistance and forced to develop their own informal self-help mechanisms. (Trattner, 1999, pp. 23–24)

Because of their own cultural traditions and because they were excluded from majority institutions, members of racial and ethnic groups formed their own social welfare institutions. For example, Chinese immigrants brought their own systems of mutual aid, which included trade associations, formal lending institutions, and informal loan mechanisms (Day, 1989). This practice is still used by ethnocultural groups that cannot obtain loans from formal lending institutions.

Social work has often followed the policies espoused by the broader society and has therefore not been immune to discriminatory practices. Some workers in the early social work movement provided services to people of color and were instrumental in the development of social change organizations like the National Association for the Advancement of Colored People. Nevertheless, racism among social workers is well documented (Trattner, 1999). *Social Work*, the journal of the National Association of Social Workers, had only two articles on the civil rights movement before 1963 (Ehrenreich, 1985). The National Association of Black Social Workers was formed in 1968 in response to the belief that NASW was not addressing issues related to African-Americans.

Social work students are often taught generic practice models that are supposed to fit all population groups. The assumption is that ignoring differences will reduce conflict. However, the more common result is misunderstanding and stereotyping (Pinderhughes, 1989). Even within ethnic and racial groups, one approach does not fit all (Hardy, 1989). Color-blind and culture-neutral approaches attempt to remove barriers from social work practice by pretending that no differences exist among peoples:

> [T]he system and its agencies provide services with the express philosophy of being unbiased. They function with the belief that color or culture makes no difference and that all people are the same. Culturally-blind agencies are characterized by the belief that helping approaches traditionally used by the dominant culture are universally applicable; if the system worked as it should, all people— regardless of race or culture—would be served with equal effectiveness. . . . The consequences of such a belief are to make services so ethnocentric as to render them virtually useless to all but the most assimilated people of color. (Cross, Bazron, Dennis, & Isaacs, 1989, p. 15)

To develop competency in working with people of color, generalist social workers must first suspend the notion that everyone is the same. All people have the basic needs of food, clothing, and shelter and share most of the goals outlined in Maslow's hierarchy of needs (1968), but the way people achieve these goals may depend on culture and history. Needs are also shaped by socioeconomic status, gender, sexual identity, physical and mental abilities, and religious factors (Harper & Lantz, 1996; Lum, 1996).

MACRO POLICY ISSUES

Racism is the biggest issue facing people of color and their communities. The legacy of slavery and the genocide of Native Americans has left a permanent scar on the nation. For people of color, issues related to race have more of an effect than issues related to gender, sexual identity, and age (Lorde, 1995). People of color often do not believe majority workers who state that they do not see color when they look at them. The fact of the matter is that ours is a very color-conscious society.

Race and racism are often conceptualized as a black and white issue. However, racism is also experienced by other groups, as this discussion of the reluctance of Asian-Americans to seek mental health services indicates:

> Cultural differences and minority group experiences must be jointly examined if one is to fully understand Asian Americans. The reluctance of Asian Americans to utilize mental health services may be due to different cultural values or attitudes toward mental health or toward services. Another plausible explanation for this phenomenon is that some Asian Americans, experiencing racial prejudice or discrimination, may avoid services because of distrust or suspiciousness. Minority group experiences do affect mental health. (Sue & Morishima, 1982, p. 8)

Racism is the root cause of generational poverty, diminished self-esteem that promotes community violence, self-medicating through drugs and alcohol, and disproportional involvement in the criminal justice system.

If social workers believe that everyone in America is equal and continue to blame the victims, social work practice will be a frustrating experience (Ryan, 1976). It is difficult to work with people who have been so beaten down by issues out of their control that they can't put their lives together to get back up. Since many of us who enter the profession are of different races and social classes than the people with whom we work, it is hard for us to see the world from the viewpoint of those who have not had the benefits we take for granted.

Communities of color are currently facing a backlash in this country. Policymakers and much of the American public assume that people of color, especially African-Americans, now have the same opportunities as white Americans. Programs directed toward correcting past injustices are viewed as reverse discrimination against the white majority, especially white males. These beliefs have fueled a push to dismantle procedures and policies that promote affirmative action:

> Almost any set of data that is examined shows the subordinate position of women and of people of color in our economy. Wages, incomes, promotion rates, middle management, top management, number of contractors, number of independent manufacturing firms: The numbers all tell the same story. Women and minorities suffer their gender and their race severely. And yet there is a growing series of objections from white men who claim to have suffered because of affirmative action programs. (Axinn & Levin, 1997, p. 320)

The perception that white males are the victims of affirmative action is fairly widespread even though reverse discrimination occurs infrequently. A survey conducted by the National Opinion Research Center found that 70 percent of the American public believed that whites were being hurt by affirmative action policies, but that only 7 percent reported experience with reverse discrimination (Patterson, 1995).

The backlash against communities of color is also being manifested in legislation. In California, Proposition 187, passed in 1994, terminated all public social services to persons who could not document their legal status in this country, while Proposition 209, passed in 1996, prohibits preferences based on race and gender in public education, employment, and state contracting (Karger & Stoesz, 1998). In Texas in 1996, the Fifth Circuit Court of Appeals ruled in *Cheryl J. Hopwood v. State of Texas* that neither race nor ethnicity could be used in admission decisions by the University of Texas Law School. These laws and cases have led to the perception of a more hostile environment for persons from underrepresented minority groups. The Association of American Medical Colleges reported a 17 percent drop in minority applications to medical schools in 1997 in California, Texas, Louisiana, and Mississippi. There has also been a 27 percent decrease in the number of all students enrolled in colleges (Hawkins, 1997). African-American, Latino, and Native American freshman enrollment declined the year after Proposition 209 was passed in California, and so too did enrollment of Caucasians and Asians. This is generally attributed to the increase in the number of students who refuse to list their race on college applications (Locke, 1998).

Although discrimination based on race is illegal, it is still prevalent, and it is the basis of all macro issues that negatively affect people of color. Social work practitioners must guard against perpetuating institutionalized practices of agencies that promote unequal treatment of communities of color. We can debate the merits of many programs that grew out of the civil rights movement, but the problems that they were attempting to rectify still exist.

MICRO PRACTICE ISSUES

Social work practitioners must investigate and utilize practice approaches that are suited to work with multicultural groups. Working effectively with people of color requires an approach that builds on the capacities of people to overcome difficulties:

> Focusing exclusively on problems, including racism, ethnocentrism, or classism, makes the problems more important than the [people]. Focusing exclusively on problems minimizes the celebration of what is human in those we serve, especially the resourceful, creative, joyful power of the human spirit. (Baker and Steiner, 1996, p. 302)

Strengths-based social work practice focuses on helping client systems tap the strengths within them (Saleebey, 1992). Potential strengths include cultural values and traditions, resources, coping strategies, family, friends, and community support networks. Past successful experiences need to be linked to solving current problems (deShazer, 1985, 1988). The client is the expert in identifying past success and in developing solutions based on past experiences. Focusing on concrete tasks and objectives (Reid, 1986; Reid & Epstein, 1972) works better for people of color than more abstract methods (Devore & Schlesinger, 1996; Freeman, 1990; See, 1998).

The identification of strengths takes place during the interview process. One way of identifying strengths is to help clients and client systems reconnect with their cultural and geographic roots. This helps African-Americans and other displaced people of color develop a sense of belonging (De Jong & Miller, 1995; Saleebey, 1992).

Reconnecting people with their cultural and geographic roots is a core tenet of Afrocentric social work practice. Afrocentric practice recognizes that African-American history began before Africans were brought to America as slaves and that the African experience must be included in understanding and working with African-American people (Asante, 1987; See, 1998). Afrocentric practice incorporates the concept of the collective—the individual, the family, and the community—while acknowledging that African-American culture has connections to both African and Western cultures (Harvey, 1997). The term *Maafa*, a Swahili word meaning disaster, calamity, damage, injustice, or catastrophe, has been applied to the long-term effect of slavery on African people, and the continuing psychological trauma, as well as the miracle of survival (Marimba, 1994; Roberson, 1995). *Maafa*-based practice focuses on helping practitioners and clients recognize their recent history, get in touch with their ancient cultural history, and use those strengths to cope with the present.

To help people of color determine the problem for which they seek social work intervention, whether at the micro or macro level, we must allow clients to tell their stories in their own way and to construct their own versions of reality (Saleebey, 1994). We must therefore be active listeners, use our skills to guide clients in telling their stories, and use techniques that help them construct their reality.

Storytelling, which is the way history was passed on by many peoples of color, especially those of African and Native American descent, is a natural way to develop the helping relationship. It allows for the incorporation of cultural references because the story is told from the person's perspective. This is not a one-way interaction. You will need to also use a storytelling approach to interpret the story to the client and to relate it to current issues. Sometimes, you can use metaphor, which is a powerful tool for building relationships with people of color because it allows for the influence of culture to emerge (Baker & Steiner, 1996; Barker, 1985; Baynes, 1967; O'Hanlon & Weiner-Davis, 1989; Whan, 1979). A simple example of the use of metaphor is the following:

An African-American woman in her fifties has come to a career-counseling center for assistance in finding a job. She was recently laid off from a factory where she had worked for a number of years, and she knew that the prospects of being rehired were bleak. Her self-esteem was at a low point.

The counselor could have asked her a series of set application questions to ascertain her skill level and employability. Instead, he asked her to talk about her early life before coming to work at this factory. He also asked her to describe obstacles she had overcome as well as opportunities she was given.

The woman described going to segregated schools in the rural South, working long, hard hours as part of a sharecropping family, and her eventual move to the North. She raised a large family, and all of her children were in college or had graduated from college. The counselor utilized her description of preparing the soil for seed, providing the young plants with the right amount of water, and harvesting the crops at the right moment as a metaphor for how she now had to begin again and prepare herself for a new career. The counselor was able to help her list her strengths and her skills from listening to her tell her story and to build on them to make a plan for additional education and training that would enable her to find new employment.

The use of narrative allows clients to tell their stories from the beginning or to start with the end of the story and work backwards. In telling the story, clients' conception of self, relationships, and life experiences take shape and provide meaning and purpose (Goldstein, 1990). The following case example illustrates the narrative approach.

I'm Not Possessed

Tamika C., a young teenager born in this country whose parents are from Haiti, was encouraged to talk to the school social worker by her teachers, who were concerned about Tamika's repeated crying episodes in the classroom. Tamika had not experienced previous emotional problems and is an exceptional student. She did not talk about these crying spells with her family because she was convinced they would believe she was "possessed."

At the beginning of the session, Shirley W., the social worker, asked Tamika to describe the events that led up to these episodes. Tamika described seemingly disconnected recollections of various discussions with teachers or other students that made her sad and want to cry. Mrs. W. began to realize that these descriptions were metaphors. When Tamika was asked to talk about other times she had these feelings, she described the death of her uncle, with whom she was close, six months earlier. Her family would not discuss the death; apparently there are mysteries surrounding it.

Being able to finally tell the story, to relate current experiences to a past one, and to have her expressions of grief validated, allowed Tamika to express her grief and begin the healing process. She was encouraged to talk to her family about their religious beliefs so that she could better understand their reasons for not wanting to discuss the death of her uncle. Her parents raised her as a Catholic and sent her to Catholic schools in order to promote her assimilation into American culture, but they themselves still hold on to the cultural and religious beliefs of Haiti.

This case did not necessitate a long assessment period gathering scientific data, but rather the ability of the social worker to actively listen in a nonjudgmental way. The intervention also required some knowledge of how the religious practices of Haiti, influenced by African and European religions, affected this young woman's reluctance to appear to be "possessed" (Bibb & Casimir, 1996; Brandon, 1997; Charles, 1986). Tamika struggled between two cultures, and the social worker recognized her dilemma.

The concept of culture is key to effective practice with people of color. Culture is a set of unified values, ideas, beliefs, and standards of behavior shared by a group of people; it is the way a person accepts, orders, interprets, and understands experiences (Saleebey, 1994; Thomas & Hayman-El, in press; Velasquez, Vigil, & Benavides, 1989). Culture is also an unconscious phenomenon; people do not necessarily think about it even though it influences day-to-day behavior. It is transmitted from generation to generation, influenced by current conditions as well as history, and carried forth in unconscious group memories (Brandon, 1997; Roberts, 1964):

> Social groups help individuals remember. Society tests our memory for personal information, for cognitive data, and places demands on our skills, but it also provides help for us when we cannot recall something. Other people often help us reconstitute our own past experiences, and our own experience comes to encompass images of the experiences of other people which they have conveyed to us from their memories. Collective memory is part of a group's way of managing and storing its own information. The idea of an individual memory totally separate from social memory is an abstraction almost devoid of meaning. Individuals' memories exist and are maintained in a social and cultural context. Every recollection, however personal it may be, exists in relationship with the whole material and moral life of the societies of which we are part (or of which we have been part) and with ideas which many other people around us also hold. Through membership in a social group-particularly kinship, religious, and class affiliations—individuals are able to acquire, to localize and to recall their memories. (Brandon, 1997, p. 132)

The concept of collective memory is instrumental in understanding why culturally competent practice requires abandoning the notion that people of color will adapt to Eurocentric models of practice. Culture is an integral component of a healthy identity, a healthy family, and ultimately a healthy community. Understanding the cultures of the people to whom we provide service is mandatory.

Determining a client's level of acculturation is an important part of understanding their culture (Atkinson, Thomson, & Grant 1993; Pinderhughes, 1982; 1989). Standardized instruments that help determine the degree of acculturation are the Acculturation Rating Scale for Mexican Americans (Cuellar, Harris, & Jasso, 1980), the Suinn-Lew Asian Self-Identity Acculturation Scale (Suinn, Rickard-Figuerora, Lew, & Vigil, 1987), and the Black Identification Scale (Whittler, Calantone, & Young, 1990).

An understanding of clients' culture can also be achieved through the interview process. The following open-ended questions can gather relevant information about the importance of culture in the life of the client and client system:

- "Do you (or members of your immediate family) speak a language other than English?
- "How would you describe your racial/cultural/ethnic heritage?
- "To whom do you (or members of your immediate family) go to when you are sick or in pain?
- "Does your view of the world differ from the majority culture?
- "What is your cultural heritage?

- "Describe your religious/spiritual beliefs?
- "Who makes the decisions in your household?" (Thomas & Hayman-El, in press)

Another set of questions helps clarify the importance of culture in the lives of the people with whom clients interact:

1. "What values do you see as of great importance in your culture?
2. "How are the values of the mainstream U.S. culture different from those of your own culture? Would you share conflicts or stress that this has caused you?
3. "What is the relative importance of self and your family or other groups in decision making in your culture? Are decisions made on a collective or on an individual basis?
4. "How important is the role of history in your culture and in your family?
5. "When people in your culture have problems, where do they go for help?
6. "What kind of help would they be looking for when they go for help?
7. "What kind of personal qualities would the people of your culture expect in the person they go to for help?
8. "How might religious beliefs influence the helping process in your culture?
9. "How much is it of concern to your family if you go for help outside of the family?
10. "Have you served as a helper in your culture? If so, describe what you did?
11. "What other things do you think I need to know about your culture so that I can be a better helper?" (Wehrly, 1995, p. 150)

DEVELOPING HELPING RELATIONSHIPS WITH PEOPLE OF COLOR

People of color have the same problems and concerns as Caucasians. Racism, oppression, and blocked opportunities compound their problems. People of color come to formal services reluctantly, often when they have exhausted all other family and community resources. Therefore, the first contact with a social worker not only determines whether an individual will engage in a helping relationship but also whether other members of the community will use that agency system. A first step in building relationships with people of color is understanding differences in communication and values.

Communication Differences

Even when we are talking the same language, our perceptions of the interaction are culturally influenced (Samovar & Porter, 1994). Different groups of people translate nonverbal communication such as spatial observance, handshaking, and eye contact, in different ways (Samovar & Porter, 1994; Sue & Sue, 1990). Mastering cross-cultural communication is the key to effective practice with individuals, families, groups, and communities of color. This requires sharpening observation and listening skills as well as learning about clients' cultural beliefs and traditions.

I Didn't Mean to Be Disrespectful

Dorothy M., a social worker, went to the home of an African-American family composed of a middle-aged woman, Mrs. L., who works full-time, her terminally ill mother, Mrs. T., for whom she is primary caretaker, and her two small children, Terry and Tina. Dorothy, who correctly recognized the stress on Mrs. L., suggested to Mrs. T., without prior consultation with Mrs. L., that she should consider going to a nursing home to relieve her daughter of this stress. Although everyone was polite to Dorothy, after she left Mrs. L. called the agency to request that this worker never again return to her home. When asked to explain, Mrs. L. stated that the worker had talked to her mother alone about the option of a nursing home instead of discussing this with both of them. She had no intention of ever placing her mother in a nursing home because it was against everything in her experience. She had called the agency for assistance, not for someone to destroy her household. When Dorothy was told about this complaint, she could not remember anything in the tone of voice or the body language of Mrs. L. or Mrs. T. that would have indicated that they were offended by her suggestion.

Because social workers are seen as experts and authority figures and represent agencies from which clients are sometimes required to receive service involuntarily, clients and their networks are often reluctant to tell us that our service does not meet their needs. However, 50 percent of people of color quit therapy after the first interview even if they came to treatment voluntarily (Ivey, 1981; see also Boyd-Franklin, 1989; Marin & Marin, 1991; Sue and Sue, 1990; Wilkinson & Spurlock, 1986; Yamamoto, 1986). Beginning social workers often make the mistake of taking everything said at face value. For example, metaphors, riddles, and proverbs are interspersed in the speech of Native Americans (Sutton & Broken Nose, 1996) and African-Americans (Weber, 1994). Their use can be very confusing to white Americans:

Proverbial wisdom can be found on every socioeconomic level in the black community, and it is transmitted from generation to generation. Listening to speech that is peppered with proverbial sayings might seem strange to nonblacks. But, because proverbial sayings are generally accepted as "truths" because they are taught to children at a very early age, they effectively sum up events and predict outcome. (Weber, 1994, p. 224)

Being of the same race and ethnicity as the client can assist the worker in terms of relationship-building, but it does not automatically eliminate barriers. Most schools of social work teach from a Eurocentric perspective. For example, the traditional problem-solving approach (Perlman, 1957) assumes that if a logical rational progression is followed, the desired outcome will occur. Since ways of thinking are shaped by culture and experience, what is logical thinking to the worker may not be logical thinking to the client. In such cases, the client is considered to be the problem. The result is that clients and their support systems are negatively labeled based on cultural differences. The social worker can similarly face negative labeling based on the past experiences of the client and client system. For example, a social worker may view the client as resistant and dysfunctional, while the client views the social worker as judgmental, remote, and unconcerned.

Minority and white clients sometimes feel that a worker of color is less effective than a white worker because they assume that the worker's training must have been inferior (Proctor & Davis, 1994). Therefore, minority workers often have to prove themselves to their clients:

> Social workers may wish that clients came to helping situations already accepting their competence. Yet workers may have to deliberately work toward a perception of their competence, particularly when perceptions are affected by societal based racial biases. (Proctor and Davis, 1994, p. 320)

Communication barriers are sometimes created because we are unaware of group differences in verbal and nonverbal communication. The following subsections provide illustrations of different communication patterns of people of color. These generalizations do not apply to all of the people all of the time, but rather illustrate some of the common patterns that are often labeled as "pathology" rather than as cultural differences.

African-Americans.   Even though English is the spoken language of most African-Americans, there are differences in use of words, meanings, pronunciation, interpretation, and the thought processes between people of African descent and white Americans. Since most African-Americans are educated in Eurocentric schools, they tend to be bicultural. Most European Americans are not. They do not have to understand the African-American community or any other community of color unless they choose to.

The African-American communication style is based primarily on West African communication patterns. West Africa is where much of the slave trade originated. However, there are also influences from East Africa and other parts of the continent. Call and response (in which a speaker calls out to the audience, which responds in unison), the use of the verb *to be*, riddles, and expressive verbal and nonverbal language are typical (Asante, 1990; Kochman, 1981; Sue & Sue, 1990; Weber, 1994). Examples of expressive language are boasting, bragging, and "playing the dozens" (repeated teasing put-downs about family and heritage) :

> That something of the African backgrounds of Black Americans survived in their speech is not difficult to argue despite the intense efforts to prove that Blacks were incapable of cultural retention because of slavery. However, no displaced people ever completely loses the forms of their previous culture. . . . It is in this sense that language in Afro-America is uniquely more African than European, other factors aside. (Asante, 1990, pp. 235–236)

African-Americans often have trouble with work relationships because white workers feel threatened by their expressive manner of speech (Foreman & Pressley, 1987; Kochman, 1981). For example, an African American male social worker was trying to get his point across to a white female supervisor. As his voice got louder and he increasingly used hand gestures to emphasize his point, the supervisor felt more threatened. Neither really heard the other. She ended up documenting the interaction to demonstrate the worker's instability. He ended up believing that his supervisor had not listened to him and had acted in a discriminatory manner because of his race. Differences in expression were interpreted as aggression rather than communication style. If differences are not understood between peers, they are unlikely to be understood between workers and clients.

African-American clients are often viewed as unresponsive if they do not look a worker directly in the eye when the worker is speaking. Even worse, clients are sometimes labeled as dishonest, deceitful, or having something to hide. The African-American style of eye contact conflicts with the Eurocentric expectation that people should look other people directly in the eye (Thomas & Hayman-El, in press).

Native Americans.   The Native American population is very diverse, with more than five hundred officially recognized tribes living on and off the reservations (Sutton & Broken Nose, 1996). Many of the Native Americans not living on reservations live in urban centers. Because there is so much diversity in terms of language, traditions, lifestyles, and treatment by the government, Native Americans are not really a single population group. Nevertheless, there are a few communication characteristics that are, for the most part, common to Native Americans.

The Native American communication style is characterized by a more indirect, softer speech pattern than that of clients of European heritage. Native Americans are less likely to use interjections and to initiate conversation and tend to use longer periods of silence than most other population groups (Sue & Sue, 1990; Sutton & Broken Nose, 1996). They consider it impolite to look a speaker directly in the eye, especially an authority figure (Lewis & Ho, 1994).

Social workers are likely to seat themselves facing the client. They look a client straight in the eye and expect the client to look them in the eye. This can get in the way of developing a helping relationship:

> A Native American considers such behavior—covert or overt—to be rude and intimidating; contrary to the white man, he shows respect by not staring directly at others. Similarly, a worker who is excessively concerned with facilitating the display of inner feelings on the part of the client should be aware of another trait. A Native American client will not immediately wish to discuss other members of his family or talk about topics that he finds sensitive or distressing. . . the client—particularly the Native American—will test the worker by bringing up peripheral matters. He does this in the hope of getting a better picture of how sincere, interested and trustworthy the worker actually is. (Lewis & Ho, 1994, p. 169)

Many of the questions social workers ask during initial interviews create barriers to developing helping relationships. Native Americans may be offended by questions about their personal lives before a sense of trust has been established, and they may see the questioning as a sign of disrespect (Harper & Lantz, 1996). It is better to ease into interviews with general conversation and allow Native Americans to construct their stories their own way, rather than to ask direct questions.

Latino Americans.   Latino groups include Mexicans, Cubans, Puerto Ricans, Central and South Americans, and Dominicans. The communication styles of these various groups differ, and it is imperative to understand the unique attribute of each group. Latino communication patterns are also influenced by whether the person was born in this country or migrated here from another country (Garcia-Preto, 1996).

In general, Latino groups approach interviews with social workers in a low-keyed manner, especially when dealing with authority figures. They are generally respectful of authority, which they show by the absence of eye contact, and they tend to respond to conversation rather than to initiate it (Sue & Sue, 1990). However, when communicating in their first language in situations they find comfortable, they can appear quite animated (Morales & Sheafor, 1995).

The concept of *personalismo* or interpersonal relationships is important in Latino culture. *Personalismo* is a preference for face-to-face contact or a sense of personal attention. Latinos do not like feeling absorbed by bureaucratic institutions or being treated as cases or numbers.

The New Worker

> When Ms. K. began working in a primarily Latino community center, she posted her hours of availability on the office door, had the information posted in the newsletter, and informed the center participants she met about her hours and the need to make appointments. She was annoyed when people stopped her in the hall, dropped by her office outside of the posted times and expected her to be available to them. Although bilingual, Mrs. K. was not bicultural and did not understand that the concepts of time and *personalismo*, were different for this population group. It took socialization and the patience of the center members before she was able to abandon her notions of proper client-worker interactions and boundaries, and build trust.

This case points to the fact that we must be flexible in applying our training in cross-cultural situations. If something does not work in a particular situation, we must be willing to try something different and to follow the lead of the client and client system.

Asian-Americans. The Asian and Pacific Island population is the fastest growing minority group in this country. This diverse group includes people who are Chinese, Japanese, Filipino, Pacific Islanders, Vietnamese, Korean, Cambodian, Laotian, Hmong, Indian, Nepalese, and Tibetan, among other nationalities. It is important to learn about the individual group with whom you are interacting.

The communication styles of Asian-Americans are in many ways very similar to those of Native Americans and Latino Americans (Sue & Sue, 1990). Often Asian-Americans and Pacific Islanders are labeled "passive." Asian cultures emphasize the virtues of conforming and following rules. There is a strong belief that playing by the rules will lead to success. Even though this stereotype is positive, it often causes the exclusion of Asian-Americans from special programming because they are viewed as not needing assistance (Sue & Morishima, 1992).

Members of Asian and Pacific Island groups often view needing assistance as shameful (Sue & Morishima, 1992). It is important to understand the reluctance of this population to participate in the helping relationship and to reframe issues in a positive way to help the client and family save "face" (Harper & Lantz, 1996).

Our Worst Fears

Mr. N. is a sixty-five-year-old Vietnamese refugee. He escaped with his wife and two oldest children through the jungle, avoided land mines, and made it to a refugee camp in Thailand at the end of the Vietnamese war. There, the family experienced brutal treatment. After six months, they were sent to the Philippines, where they were taught English by persons whose primary languages were Spanish and Filipino dialects. The family's education about the United States came from the media, which provided them with a distorted view of Americans—African-Americans in particular, whom they learned to fear.

The family eventually came to the United States and settled in a black neighborhood in a Southern city. They were assigned by the refugee resettlement agency to an African-American worker. The family could not understand the English spoken in this city and were afraid of the neighborhood and the caseworker.

Mr. S., the caseworker, approached this new situation with trepidation; he did not speak Vietnamese and knew nothing about the culture. In fact, he asked to be reassigned, but his request was not granted because the agency had no one who was any more knowledgeable than he. Before scheduling his first visit, Mr. S. found someone who could interpret the language and instruct him about acceptable behavior. The Vietnamese interpreter also connected the family with places to shop for Vietnamese food and a Buddhist Temple for worship. Mr. S. introduced the family to people in the neighborhood whom they came to rely on for many basic necessities.

Much later in the relationship, the younger family members shared with Mr. S. their fears of African-Americans, the reasons for their difficulty understanding the English that was being spoken around them, and their experience in coming to America. This helped the worker better understand the trauma that the family had faced and their resiliency in being able to survive.

Value Differences

People of color and the majority population have different values and belief systems. In many ways, ethnocultural groups are more similar to each other than they are to the majority culture in the United States. Although people who are born and educated here learn Euro-American values, they also retain the values of their particular ethnic groups. Culture is ancient and lasting. Despite attempts at acculturation and assimilation, it does not disappear. It adapts to fit the circumstances in which groups of people find themselves (Brandon, 1997). Table 11.2 compares the values of the majority culture with those of other ethnocultural groups. These are generalizations, and all group members do not necessarily espouse these beliefs.

Table 11.2 compares the values of the majority culture with those of other ethnocultural groups. These are generalizations, and all group members do not necessarily espouse these beliefs.

Pinderhughes (1982) contrasted American and West African values. She noted sharp contrasts in beliefs about

TABLE 11.2. Values Comparisons Between Euro-American and other Ethnocultural Groups

Euro-American Values	Values of Other Ethnocultural Groups
Mastery over Nature	Harmony with Nature
Personal Control Over the Environment	Fate
Doing—Activity	Being
Time Dominates	Personal Interaction Dominates
Human Equality	Hierarchy/Rank/Status
Individualism/Privacy	Group Welfare
Youth	Elders
Self-Help	Birthright Inheritance
Competition	Cooperation
Future Orientation	Past or Present Orientation
Informality	Formality
Directness/Openness/Honesty	Indirectness/Ritual/"Face"
Practicality/Efficiency	Idealism
Materialism	Spiritualism

Note: From *Towards a Culturally Competent System of Care* (Vol. II, p. 12), by M. R. Isaacs and M. P. Benjamin, 1991, Washington, DC: CAASP Technical Assistance Center— Center for Child Health and Mental Health Policy; based on *Strategies for Working with Culturally Diverse Communities and Clients,* by E. Randall-David, 1989, Washington, DC: Association for the Care of Children's Health.

- Individualism versus collectivity
- Ownership versus sharing
- Power versus obedience to authority
- Mastery of the environment versus spiritual commune with the environment
- Efficiency versus acceptance of fate
- Emphasis on youth, the future, and progress versus the past.

Common values that hold Asian and Pacific Island groups together include group orientation encompassing family and family relationships, filial piety, respect for authority, self-control, and an emphasis on educational achievement. Asian peoples also have a strong tradition of using shame to control behavior as well as a belief in the wisdom of the middle position (Chung, 1991; Min, 1995; Ross-Sheriff, 1991).

Latinos generally share a belief in fate, the importance of the family, and respect for age. They also show respect for socio-economic position and authority and a preference for *personalismo* (Morales & Sheafor, 1995).

Native Americans are also oriented to the family and tribe. They value humility and modesty, have a nonmaterialistic view of the world, and hold values similar to Latinos concerning personal interaction (Attneave, 1969; Everett, Proctor, & Cartnell, 1983; Harper & Lantz, 1996; Jilek, 1982).

All of the different groups of color venerate elders. This contrasts sharply with the youth orientation of American society. Respect is demonstrated through formal boundary systems. It is not acceptable to call adult clients by their first names unless given permission to do so. This is contrary to the American belief that to be informal shows that one is friendly. For people of color, not using titles and surnames is a sign of disrespect. To call an African-Americans only by first name is viewed as a remnant of slavery.

Spirituality.   The concept of spirituality goes beyond being religious or part of an organized religion, and even the belief in a higher being. It is a part of the every-day life of many people of color. Spirituality is reflected in practices such as bless-ing food and calling on ancestors for guidance. Spiritual beliefs help people garner the strength needed to overcome adversity. People who have maintained a connection to their spiritual beliefs tend to be more satisfied with their lives than those who do not believe in a higher power (Coke, 1992; Martinez, 1988; Red Horse, 1982; Tooles-Walls & Zarit, 1991). When assessing the strengths and coping strategies of people of color, it is important to inquire about their spiritual beliefs, their involvement with religion, and whether they belong to an organized reli-gion. This provides information not only about the source of their strength and guidance, but also about informal support that might be available to them.

We also need a basic understanding of the religious practices of people of color with whom we interact and how these practices influence our clients' behav-ior. For example, people of African descent may practice Christian religions but add African spiritual worship, such as Santeria, Voodoo, and other Yoruba-based religions (Black, 1996). Santeria and Espiritualism are also practiced on Cuba, Puerto Rico, and other islands with African, Spanish, and Indian influences (Brandon, 1997).

Many African and Asian people practice various forms of Islam. Islam is simi-lar to Judeo-Christian religions in that it sees the individual as unique and respon-sible for his or her own actions (Smith, 1991). Confucianism plays a major role in the day-to-day lives of many Asian-Americans of ethnic Chinese descent. Confucianism governs behavior, demands respect for authority, and teaches that the good of the whole is more important than personal beliefs (Philips, 1996; Smith, 1991). Hinduism has two basic tenets: karma (as you sow, so shall you reap) and reincarnation. The caste system is also a component of the Hindu way of life, but there have been attempts to end this system in India (Almeida, 1996; Smith, 1991). Buddhism is widely practiced by Asian-Americans. Buddhists believe that an indi-vidual should seek nirvana or the highest point a human spirit can strive to attain (Smith, 1991). Taoism is noted for its emphasis on balance to enhance spiritual well-being. Practices such as acupuncture, herbal medicine, and the concepts of yin and yang emanate from Taoist beliefs (Philips, 1996; Smith, 1991).

You are not expected to learn all the tenets of each religious system. However, you must understand how religion and spirituality are intertwined with behavior, patterns of seeking help, health care, and family practices of clients. You are oblig-ated to find out as much as possible about the religion or spiritual beliefs of clients. If your own beliefs were shaped by Judeo-Christian religions, you must be able to accept other beliefs that run counter to your religious upbringing.

Acceptance of Fate.   Practitioners often have a hard time accepting clients who do not act to improve their situation because they have accepted their fate. The American values of taking charge of one's life and individual responsibility run counter to the beliefs of many ethnocultural groups. Moving someone towards an action takes time, patience, and the development of trust. This is especially true in situations that have taken a long time to get to the point where social work inter-vention is needed.

The patience of Native Americans can be interpreted as lack of motivation and laziness. Their seeming inactivity contrasts with the "doing" nature of the

American value system (Lewis & Ho, 1994). African-Americans use phrases like "Lord willing," "If God wanted me to do this," and "God only gives us as much as we can bear" to demonstrate their belief that their current situation will change when God is ready to change it. Sometimes practitioners can help people who believe in fate to understand that the actions they do or do not take in this life will affect the next life (Karnik & Suri, 1995; Philips, 1996).

Taking initiative and functioning autonomously are values of general American society. If they are not part of a client's belief system, negative labels often find their way into the assessment. Social work practice in a managed care environment requires practitioners to demonstrate their effectiveness in increasingly shorter time periods. Culturally competent practice, however, requires the opposite—slowing down and listening to the client's story to understand his or her perception of reality.

Time. In America, everything is fast. The world operates by appointments. This linear time runs counter to the concept of time used by people of color. People of color are often more focused on the present and the past than on the future. In some cultural groups, time is characterized as circular or tied to natural phenomena (Lewis & Ho, 1994). Social workers often resent people who show up late for appointments or are not home at a scheduled time. Clients and families do not like the fact that they cannot see workers whenever they wish, or that they have to plan their day around the time the worker wants to visit. The following case example illustrates the conflict between different concepts of time.

They Are Never There

Emily D., the social worker from a sectarian social service agency, had scheduled several appointments for the T. family, immigrants from Southeast Asia, to come to the office and discuss their need for alternate housing. The apartment building in which they lived was being sold, and they had to relocate. The family had arrived late to each appointment, and Emily had other appointments and did not see them. She scheduled a visit to their home, but when she arrived, they were out. Emily felt that she had given her best effort. She recommended closure, saying the family was "resistant to assistance." She felt that when the eviction was closer, they would be willing to accept help. The family, on the other hand, did not understand why they were not being helped. They have come to the agency several times, and no one has met with them. From their viewpoint, the agency and worker were not helpful, and the family did not know where to turn for help.

In the above case, the agency wanted to help and the family wanted help. The barrier was the different values placed on time. Agencies and workers who wish to achieve a high level of cultural competency in a multicultural practice environment must be willing to expand their concept of time. Although agencies need to have set hours of operation, they must be flexible enough to respond to clients' time perceptions. Not doing so can be a major barrier to the delivery of services.

All communities of color have insider jokes about their concept of time and how it clashes with the dominant American culture. Time is another concept about which communities of color are more similar to each other than they are to the majority culture. Social work practitioners who set long-range goals for their clients, instead of setting short-range attainable goals, will become frustrated in their attempts to push clients toward a future orientation.

WORKING WITH INDIVIDUALS AND FAMILIES OF COLOR

In working with people of color, if you are not a member of the group, you have a barrier to overcome. Because of the country's history of racism, the immigration experience of people of color, and the clash in cultures, practitioners and clients must educate one another and build a relationship before collaborative work can begin. U.S. history provides numerous examples of abuses of power, including the internment of the Japanese during World War II, the long history of African-American slavery, and the genocide of Native Americans and their subsequent segregation on reservations, so mistrust of authority by people of color should come as no surprise.

Although individuals of color do receive assistance through social work intervention, it is best to conceptualize practice with people of color from a collective rather than an individual perspective. The focus should be not only on the individual but also on the family systems, including extended family, immediate family, kinship networks, fictive kin (people considered nonblood relatives), and community organizations. The family has a major influence on whether an individual client will stay with the process. For example, many ethnocultural societies are patrimonial. A worker may encourage a Latina client to be more assertive with her husband about her educational and work goals. But if the husband is not involved and does not support the wife's goals, the wife, may feel torn between two cultures and leave treatment.

Families of people of color often are multigenerational, with extended family members living in the same household or nearby. Since elder veneration is a value of every group of color in this country, elders have a great deal of influence over the middle and younger generations. This can cause tension in initial relationships and may cause some couples to seek social work help.

A Conflict of Roles

The P. family, who immigrated to the United States from India, have requested marital therapy. The family consists of a husband, wife, and a son and a daughter, both of whom attend private school. The husband is a physician; the wife, a college professor. They are Hindu and of the Brahmin caste.

The husband's mother lives with the family and exerts a great deal of influence in the household. Although the daughter-in-law has tried to keep the peace by following the dictates of her husband's mother, she is having difficulty meeting everyone's expectations while still maintaining her own career. She helps with her husband's practice while also caring for her children and her mother-in-law. The wife has insisted that they seek outside help, but the husband was reluctant to participate. He expressed shame about talking to an outsider about issues that should remain in the family. They have not discussed this with the mother-in-law.

In this case, the worker must begin by learning about Indian culture. Some time needs to be spent allowing the wife to express her feelings of being trapped and to discuss the role conflict between where she has prestige and feels valued, and at home, where she does not feel valued by her husband and mother-in-law. The husband needs to be encouraged to discuss his feelings so as not to discourage him from coming to subsequent sessions. At some point, there will need to be a discussion with the mother-in-law; she is key to the situation and must take part in family therapy for it to be effective. Involving the mother-in-law will take time, patience, and understanding of the cultural aspects of the situation.

My Home Is with My Family

Senora C. was born in Puerto Rico but has lived in the United States for forty years. She lives in an urban area and speaks very little English. Her four children accompany her to places like the Social Security office and the bank to help her transact business. She lives in a house with two of her children, their spouses, and five grandchildren. This home has only one bathroom and three bedrooms and belongs to one of the children. Senora C. sleeps on a sofa bed in the living room.

The social worker has suggested relocating to senior citizen housing, but although Senora C. describes her situation as being "homeless with a home," she is reluctant to make changes. She is afraid that the family will abandon her if she leaves. She also fears that the family will suffer because she is the caretaker for the grandchildren after school and the family cannot afford to have a different adult member leave a job to care for them.

As social workers, we might push Senora C. to think of her own needs. But it is obvious that she cannot do so and that she will need time to weigh the positives and negatives of moving. Talking to the family to get their views and to gain their trust will be critical. Locating her as close to the family as possible is one solution. Another is helping the rest of the family work out alternative arrangements for child care and reviewing family income and expenses to determine whether they can afford to pay for child care. This case illustrates the importance of working with the entire family system instead of concentrating on the needs of the individual client.

In African-American, Asian, Latino, and Native American cultures, life revolves around the family. People seek the guidance of their family before making major decisions. When help is needed, the family provides it. Families need to be helped to deal with the shame and guilt that is generated when they cannot provide needed assistance. The following guidelines, which were developed to use with Asian families, can be applied to work with other ethnic groups of color:

- "When assessing Asian American families, practitioners should gather information regarding specific families' ethnic backgrounds, languages, immigration and refugee experiences, acculturation levels, and community support systems.
- "Attempt to maintain and, if appropriate, reestablish traditional family structures according to cultural norms. Respect the family hierarchy.
- "Use extended family members for support systems; lines between nuclear families and extended families are not as rigid in Asian families as they are in Western culture.
- "Allow families and their individual members opportunities to save face whenever possible.
- "Avoid creating situations that may lead to conflict and confrontation. Rather, use indirect methods of communication, when appropriate, to make a point.
- "Because Asians prefer to keep problems within the family, maintaining confidentiality is critical. Families must be assured that their problems will not become public knowledge.
- "Service providers must be active and offer tangible interventions for Asian Americans. Passivity in the worker may be viewed as lack of expertise and authority. Many Asian American families are seeking concrete, tangible solutions to their problems and are uncomfortable with process- and insight-oriented strategies." (Philips, 1996, p. 2)

The model shown in Figure 11.1 illustrates assessment as a combination of inputs from the informal environment that affect individual factors that in turn result in a response from formal systems. Informal inputs include the family and fictive kin or nonblood relatives as well as neighbors, friends, and community organizations such as religious institutions. These people and groups have their own knowledge and perceptions of formal services, and their views will influence whether individuals and their family systems engage in the helping process. Informal inputs have an affect on individual characteristics, which are shaped by such experiences as racism, immigration, and other biopsychosocial factors. The output is the formal response, which can be formal assistance the client is already using. The client may need to be connected to additional services or resources, or we may need to engage in resource mobilization to meet the identified needs. Many factors must be considered in conducting a comprehensive assessment of individuals and families of color.

GROUP WORK WITH PEOPLE OF COLOR

Although people of color are generally group-centered, they are often reluctant to engage in therapeutic and support groups because they feel shame and do not want to talk to outsiders about problems. They are reluctant to trust the information they receive from social workers and may not readily understand the benefits of group approaches.

FIGURE 11.1. Holistic Assessment

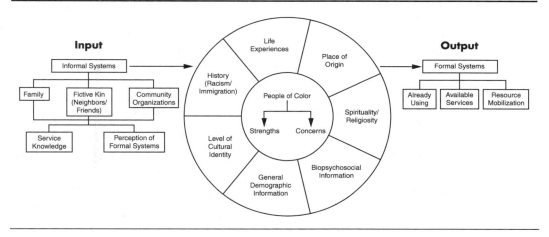

Group leaders should pay particular attention to the demographic composition of a group. Although there are no rules about how many people of color to have in a group, having only one category of persons (whether based on gender, age, race, or physical ability) is not a good idea.

People of color often cannot divorce themselves from the issue of race and racism. Therefore, the group leader, regardless of the purpose of the group, should raise the issue. Discussing race and racism may be initially difficult because of the volatility of such discussions (Davis, 1984). However, it is necessary for trust to develop and for the members to come together as a group.

Group leaders who work with groups of people of color must be willing to be active participants and to provide some information about themselves. The following are some suggestions for working with groups of African-American youth:

- Groups should not have a psychotherapeutic focus but rather should focus on the improvement of skills so members can function in society; in other words, groups should use action-oriented, not insight-oriented, techniques.
- Behavior in the group should be examined in terms of members' experiences in American society.
- Group leaders have to learn to deal with anger as well as be comfortable with the possibility that they may have to confront group members.
- Group leaders must be willing to self-disclose as well as understand the culture of members.
- The group leader is a role model who provides guidance and direction but should avoid telling people what to do.
- The group leader needs to be aware of nonverbal behavior as a component of communication patterns, including physical contact.
- Group workers must be prepared to be challenged before a relationship is established. (Brown, 1984, pp. 121–123)

The incorporation of culturally sensitive material as an integral part of the group process serves to help people of color recapture their past strengths and apply them to future situations (Harvey, 1997; Kunjufu, 1985). Groups that take members through rites of passage have helped African-Americans of all ages gain a sense of self-esteem.

Group leaders can facilitate the success of groups with Latinos by understanding the natural support networks of the members and by being bilingual, if necessary, and bicultural (Delgado & Humm-Delgado, 1984). Being focused on the present rather than the past or the future and paying attention to location and access issues increase the likelihood that Latino clients will participate in the group. It is important to socialize the members about group rules, behavior, and self-disclosure.

In discussing group work with Native Americans, Lewis and Ho (1994) emphasize the need for the leader to be bilingual and bicultural. They are pessimistic about obtaining positive results with Native Americans in heterogeneous groups. Actions by the leader that call attention to lateness or silence may result in members' dropping out. Contrary to what was recommended for other groups of people of color, action-oriented steps are not a good idea.

You May Be Black, but You're from a Different World

Ms. J., an African-American, had never worked with high school students when she was assigned to work with a group of freshmen that would meet every week. The goal of the group was to prevent dropping out of school. At least 40 percent of freshmen did not complete high school. The group, made up entirely of African-Americans, decided what areas they wanted to focus on. Since this was a morning group, breakfast food was provided as an incentive to attend meetings.

These students described gang violence, police brutality, and sexual experiences that shocked Ms. J. whose life experiences were very different. When the students challenged her about her background and the expressions on her face when they talked about events in their lives, Ms. J. felt free to talk about her own growing up, the generational differences between them, her feelings of being overwhelmed by their experiences, and her admiration of their strength in surmounting the obstacles.

Ms. J.'s self-disclosure provided the students with a view of the world that went beyond their neighborhoods. They learned that all African-Americans are not the same, do not all live in the inner city, and have the power to achieve. Ms. J. was then able to establish trust and serve as a role model for the young people in the group. All the group members finished high school, and one went on to a community college.

The worker in this case was not careful about her nonverbal behavior, and group members picked up on her discomfort about their self-disclosure and stories. As young people often will, they challenged her to engage them in a discussion about her own experiences. Once she did so, they were able to relate to and to trust her.

COMMUNITY WORK WITH PEOPLE OF COLOR

In order to work with a community with which you are unfamiliar the first thing you and/or your organization needs to do is to become known. This takes time. Joining community groups as a member of an advisory committee or board member, going to community or public affairs meetings, meeting public officials, and volunteering for service all help you become known and trusted. Following through on your promises and commitments is necessary in building community relationships.

Doing outreach and program development in communities of color means being prepared to stay involved for a long period of time. Communities of color have been repeatedly studied and used for pilot programs, so much so that a great deal of distrust has developed among the residents of many communities. You need to be in it for the long run and have patience to engage in community work.

A Latino research center and a community mental health center designed an outreach project with the goal of increasing the use of mental health services by Puerto Rican clients. After three-years, the use of outpatient mental health services increased, and hospitalizations decreased. The outreach efforts had overcome cultural barriers to mental health service utilization (Vazquez, 1994). This experience emphasizes the need for long-term commitment. Programs that in the short run are viewed as failures may prove to be successful when measured over a long period of time. Another example is the Head Start program, which is one of the few surviving programs developed during the War On Poverty in the 1960s. Children participating in the program did benefit over time, even though initial program evaluations found no significant improvements (Johnson, 1998; Segal & Brzuzy, 1998).

In many ways, communities of color organize themselves to take care of their own needs because they are unable to access mainstream organizations and services. Communities of color have organized around societal injustice, such as inequality, economic and environmental injustice, community violence, and the current HIV and AIDS crises (Gutierrez, Alvarez, Nemon, & Lewis, 1996).

To understand the functioning of a community and its support networks, you will need to become aware of community-based services provided by churches, indigenous health care providers, and private organizations. Outsiders involved in organizing a community must be bicultural and bilingual or obtain the assistance of someone who can relate on a primary level to the members of the community (Rivera & Erlich, 1998). In order to avoid the mistakes made in the past, do not assume that all communities of color are identical and do not apply the same techniques to every community. The unique attributes of each population group and each community must be recognized and taken into consideration.

No One Came

A local mental health agency wants to increase the numbers of Asian-Americans who utilize its services. The Asian population has grown rapidly, but the agency still serves very few Asians. The first idea was to post flyers in the community to advertise the services. This did not get results, probably because the flyers were in English.

> The program manager of the agency decided to put together a focus group and hold a meeting. Flyers were sent out to Asian community organizations that the agency had identified, but no one showed up the day of the meeting.
>
> The program manager then contacted an Asian service provider who arranged the location of the meeting, printed signs in Chinese, and called everyone who had indicated they would come to remind them of the meeting. The service provider also lined up several people to provide interpretation, since the ethnic Chinese participants spoke different languages and dialects. On the day of the meeting, the provider met the focus group at the bus stop, provided Chinese pastries, and arranged for the agency to give each participant a small gift and monetary compensation. Although an agency official welcomed and thanked everyone for coming, the Asian community leader ran the focus group meeting. The agency expected the meeting to result in a list of issues to address, but the focus group participants' number one concern was learning English as a second language.

If this agency is able to begin where the community is it will honor their request for assistance. Once community members trust the agency, they may seek assistance in working on issues that are traditionally viewed as mental health. However, relieving the stress caused by not knowing English is the residents' primary concern.

Organization in communities of color requires getting to know key gatekeepers. These are people who can give legitimacy to your efforts or can put up roadblocks. Learning who has the power in the community and including those people in the process is critical for a community effort to succeed. To work effectively with communities, you must do the same things you do when working with smaller client systems. You must be patient and respectful, have some understanding of the culture, approach the work from a strengths perspective, enter the relationship as a partner, and remember that trust is earned, not automatically bestowed (Gutierrez, Alvarez, Nemon, & Lewis, 1996).

SUMMARY

All of us gravitate to people who we believe share something in common with us. It could be language, culture, field of employment, geographic origins, or other experiences. Likewise, people of color would like the social worker who engages with them to have a real understanding of their culture and experiences to increase the chances that a good relationship will develop. The reality is that most clients and workers are dissimilar in many ways, such as race, ethnicity, gender, sexual orientation, religion, age, and social class. In order for work to begin and progress, a relationship must develop that transcends differences. Unfortunately, barriers are all too often created in the initial meeting, and the result is that clients do not return to complete the social work process.

When social workers work with individuals, families, groups, or communities with which they are unfamiliar, it is incumbent on them to learn as much as possible about the values, beliefs, and cultural traditions of the client system. We must suspend the notion that it is the client who has to adapt to the agency's method of providing service. Rather, we must learn to be flexible in our service delivery so that it fits the needs of the client group we are trying to engage.

In addition, we must continually explore who we are as cultural beings. We must learn our own history and culture in order to understand the importance of history and culture to others. It is very hard to walk in someone else's shoes unless we feel comfortable walking in our own shoes. As social workers, we must be open to the idea that each community of color has a uniqueness that cannot be ignored. The concept of the melting pot in America has never accurately depicted what happens to people who have come to this country.

Learning how to successfully work with people who are different from us takes considerable time and energy. It is not mastered by one or two training sessions or by reading existing literature. It is a continuous learning process that, with commitment, can reap tremendous benefits for the clients, their community, and the social worker.

CASE EXAMPLE

The final case example in this chapter is based on a case that one of my caseworkers had at an Area Agency on Aging. It illustrates culturally sensitive generalist practice and the importance of taking a client system's values and beliefs into consideration.

We Take Care of Our Own

Mrs. F. is sixty-five years of age and lives with her daughter, Miriam S. She came to this country from Cuba twenty years ago, on a makeshift raft with her husband, her twenty-year-old son, and her eighteen-year-old daughter. During the voyage, the raft capsized, and the son was lost at sea. Mrs. F.'s parents and siblings still reside in Cuba, and she has not seen them since she left. The F. family came to the United States because Mr. F. faced imprisonment because of his political views.

Assessment

Mr. and Mrs. F. became U.S. citizens and owned a grocery store in a Cuban neighborhood in a large metropolitan area. The business was successful but it closed when Mr. F. died of a heart attack two years ago when he was sixty-eight. He had no pension or life insurance. The proceeds from the sale were invested in order to give Mrs. F. some financial security. Her only other income is from her husband's Social Security benefits.

Daughter Miriam persuaded Mrs. F. to sell her home and move in with her and her two daughters so that Mrs. F. would not be lonely and could stretch out her resources as long as possible. Mrs. F. went from a bustling urban Cuban neighborhood, to a suburban area with no other Cuban families. The move was stressful for both mother and daughter. For Mrs. F., it represented loss of independence, community, friends, and status. Miriam felt obligated to take her mother in, but at the same time was resentful.

Miriam is raising two children on her own. She was divorced right before her father's death. As devout Catholics, the parents fought bitterly with their daughter about the divorce and the shame it would bring to the family. Miriam harbors guilt that she may have caused her father's heart attack.

The two granddaughters resent Mrs. F.'s coming to their home. They now have to share a bedroom. They see Grandma as overbearing and old-fashioned. She speaks to them in Spanish, a language they do not under-stand. They were not consulted about this change in living arrangements. They love and respect their grandmother but are embarrassed to introduce her to their friends, who are Caucasian and were born in this country.

Mrs. F. has chronic health problems for which she receives medical attention and takes medication. Her overall health is good, and she cares for herself with little assistance. Miriam describes her as having mood fluctua-tions from marked irritability to melancholia. Sometimes Mrs. F. will not accept telephone calls from her friends, who now live forty-five minutes away. She does not go to church on a daily basis like she used to, even though the church is within walking distance. Mrs. F.'s own parents are in failing health in Cuba, and she sends money to help support them.

Miriam has talked about her home situation to her best friend who is concerned that she is being pulled in too many directions and needs guid-ance. Miriam very reluctantly went to a family service agency to discuss her situation with a social worker.

Intervention

At the initial meeting, the social worker let the daughter express her frustra-tion about being the one in the middle and feeling guilty about her less-than-positive attitude about caring for her mother. The social worker was concerned about Miriam's level of stress. The worker convinced Miriam that the first course of action was to have an open discussion with all the house-hold members to determine their views of the current living situation. Miriam wanted the meeting to take place in her home because she was convinced that her mother would never come to the agency, and the worker agreed.

It took several sessions before Mrs. F. and the children felt comfortable enough to express their honest feelings about the current living situation. Mrs. F. was feeling profound loss not only because of the move, but because she had not let herself grieve for the loss of her husband and because of her inability to care for her own parents. She no longer had access to the neighborhood support system that could relate to her past and present experiences. Miriam had her own guilt about her role as a parent and as a daughter. The teenage girls are experiencing their own issues of trying to fit in with their peers.

It was eventually decided that Mrs. F. would move to a small apartment in her old neighborhood. Miriam and the granddaughters would visit a few times a month, or more often if needed. Miriam and her children continued in therapy in order to help them adjust to the divorce and their own grief issues. Mrs. F. was reconnected with her church and community, and her spirits lifted.

Termination

The worker terminated involvement with Mrs. F. after three months, when relocation was achieved and she was reestablished in her old community. The remaining family members stayed in therapy an additional three months. Miriam and her children attend different support groups around the issues of divorce and grief.

DISCUSSION QUESTIONS

1. Since Miriam S. has come to the agency reluctantly, what should the social worker do to develop the initial relationship? Assuming that the worker is not Cuban, what might he or she do before the interview to prepare for working with someone from another culture?
2. What additional historical information would the social worker need in order to understand this family?
3. Miriam is sandwiched between two generations. How can the social worker help her discuss options within the cultural context of family obligation?
4. The family has experienced much grief and loss. What cultural strengths and coping skills might the social worker help Miriam and the rest of the family draw on?
5. What additional community resources might the social worker seek to provide the family with a support network? What additional options would you suggest for this family?
6. How has social work's approach to working with people of color changed over the history of the profession? In what ways has social work's approach mirrored the prevailing societal values?
7. How has racism affected people of color and their communities? How are racist beliefs institutionalized? How might generalist social workers combat institutional racism?
8. In what ways is the strengths model of practice similar to Afrocentric social work practice? In what ways is it different?
9. What are the major communication style and value differences between African-Americans, Native Americans, Latino Americans, Asian-Americans, and Caucasian Americans?

REFERENCES

Almeida, R. (1996). Hindu, Christian, and Muslim families. In M. McGoldrick, J. Giordano, & J. Pearce (Eds.) *Ethnicity and family therapy* (2nd ed., pp. 395–423). New York: Guilford.

Asante, M. (1987). *The Afrocentric idea*. Philadelphia: Temple University Press.

Asante, M.,(1990). The African essence in African-American language. In M. Asante & K. Asante (1990). *African culture: The rhythms of unity* (pp. 233–252). Trenton, NJ: Africa World Press.

Atkinson, D. R. Thomson, C. E., & Grant, S. K. (1993). A three-dimensional model for counseling racial/ethnic minorities. *The Counseling Psychologist, 21,* 257–277.

Attneave, C. (1969). Therapy in tribal settings and urban network intervention. *Family Process, 8,* 192–210.

Axinn, J., & Levin, H. (1997). *Social welfare: A history of the American response to need* (4th ed.). New York: Longman.

Baker, M. R., & Steiner, J. R. (1996). Solution-focused social work: Metamessages to students in higher education opportunity programs. In P. L. Ewalt, E. M. Freeman, S. A. Kirk, & D. L. Poole (Eds.). *Multicultural issues in social work* (pp. 295–309). Washington, DC: NASW Press.

Barker, P. (1985). *Using metaphors in psychotherapy.* New York: Brunner Mazel.

Baynes, C. F. (Trans.). (1967). *I Ching.* Princeton, NJ: Princeton University Press.

Bibb, A., & Casimir, G. J. (1996). Haitian families. In M. McGoldrick, J. Giordano, & J. Pearce (Eds.), *Ethnicity and family therapy* (2nd ed., pp. 97–112). New York: Guilford.

Black, L. (1996). Families of African origin: An overview. In M. McGoldrick, J. Giordano, & J. Pearce (Eds.), *Ethnicity and family therapy* (2nd ed., pp. 57–65). New York: Guilford.

Boyd-Franklin, N. (1989). *Black families in therapy: A multisystems approach.* New York: Guilford.

Brandon, G. (1997). *Santeria from Africa to the New World: The dead sell memories.* Bloomington: Indiana University Press.

Brown, J. A. (1984). Group work with low-income black youths. *Social Work with Groups, 7*(3), 111–124.

Center on Budget and Policy Priorities. (1996). *Poverty and income trends: 1994.* Washington, DC: Author.

Chan, S. (1991). *Asian Americans: An interpretive history.* Boston: Twayne.

Charles, C. (1986). Mental health services for Haitians. In H. P. Lefley & P. B. Pederson (Eds.), *Cross-cultural training for mental health professionals* (pp. 183–198). Springfield, IL: Thomas.

Coke, M. (1992). Correlates of life satisfaction among elderly African-Americans. *Journal of Gerontology, 47*(5), 316–320.

Chung, D. (1991). Asian cultural commonalties: A comparison with mainstream American culture. In S. Furuto, R. Biswas, D. Chung, & F. Ross-Sheriff (Eds.), *Social work practice with Asian Americans* (pp. 27–44). Newbury Park, CA: Sage.

Cross, T. L., Bazron, B. J., Dennis, K. W., & Isaacs, M. R. (1989). *Towards a culturally competent system of care: A monograph on effective services for minority children who are severely emotionally disturbed* (Volume 1). Washington, DC: Georgetown University Child Development Center, CAASP Technical Assistance Center.

Cuellar, I., Harris, L. C., & Jasso, R. (1980). An acculturation scale for Mexican American normal and clinical populations. *Hispanic Journal of Behavior Sciences, 2,* 199–217.

Davis, L. E. (1984). Essential components of group work with black Americans. *Social Work with Groups, 7*(3), 97–109.

Day, P. J. (1989). *A new history of social welfare.* Englewood Cliffs, NJ: Prentice-Hall.

Delgado, M., & Humm-Delgado, D. (1984). Hispanics and group work: A review of the literature. *Social Work with Groups, 7*(3), 85–95.

De Jong , P., & Miller, S. (1995). How to interview for client strengths. *Social Work, 40*(6), 729–736.

de Shazer, S. (1985). *Keys to solution in brief therapy.* New York: Norton.

de Shazer, S. (1988). *Clues: Investigating solutions in brief therapy.* New York: Norton.

Devore, W., & Schlesinger, E. G. (1996). *Ethnic-sensitive social work practice* (4th ed.). Boston: Allyn & Bacon.

Ehrenreich, J. H. (1985). *The altruistic imagination: A history of social work and social policy in the United States.* Ithaca: Cornell University Press.

Everett, F., Proctor, N., & Cartnell, B. (1983). Providing psychological services to American Indian children and families. *Professional Psychology, 14,* 588–603.

Fong, R., & Mokuau, N. (1996). Not simply "Asian Americans": Periodical literature on Asians and Pacific Islanders. In P. Ewalt, E. Freeman, S. Kirk, & D. Poole (Eds.), *Multicultural issues in social work* (pp. 269–281). Washington, DC: NASW Press.

Foreman, A. K., & Pressley, G. (1987). Ethnic culture and corporate culture: Using black styles in organizations. *Communication Quarterly, 35*(4), 293–307.

Freeman, E. (1990) Theoretical perspectives for practice with black families. In Logan, S., Freeman, E., & McRoy, R. *Social work practice with black families: A culturally specific perspective* (pp. 38–52). White Plains, NY: Longman.

Garcia-Preto, N. (1996). Latino families: An overview. In M. McGoldrick, J. Giordano, & J. Pearce (Eds.), *Ethnicity and family therapy* (2nd ed., 141–154). New York: Guilford.

Goldstein, H. (1990). The knowledge base of social work practice: Theory, wisdom, analogue, or art? *Families in Society: The Journal of Contemporary Human Services, 71*(1), 32–43.

Gutierrez, L., Alvarez, A., Nemon, H., & Lewis, E. A. (1996). Multicultural community organizing: A strategy for change. *Social Work, 41*(5), 501–507.

Hardy, K. V. (1989). The theoretical myth of sameness: A critical issue in family therapy training and treatment. In G. E. Saba, B. M. Karrer, & K. V. Hardy (Eds.), *Minorities and family therapy* (pp. 17–33). New York: Haworth.

Harper, K. V., & Lantz, J. (1996). *Cross-cultural practice: Social work with diverse populations.* Chicago: Lyceum.

Harvey, A. (1997). Group work with African-American youth in the criminal justice system: A culturally competent model. In G. Grief & P. Ephross (1997). *Group work with populations at risk* (pp. 160–174). New York: Oxford University Press.

Hawkins, B. D. (1997). "Hostile environments": Reducing applications to medical schools nationwide. *Black Issues in Higher Education, 14*(20), 18–20.

Ivey, A. (1981). Counseling and psychotherapy: Toward a new perspective. In A. J. Marsella & P. Pedersen (Eds.), *Cross-cultural counseling and psychotherapy* (pp. 279-311). New York: Pergamon.

Jilek, W. (1982). *Indian healing: Shamanic ceremonialism in the Pacific Northwest today.* Laine: Hancock House.

Johnson, H. (1998). Public welfare and income maintenance. In H. Johnson (Ed.), *The social services: An introduction* (5th ed., pp. 45–74). Itasca, IL: Peacock.

Karger, J., & Stoesz, D. (1998). American social welfare policy: A pluralist approach (3rd ed.). New York: Longman.

Karnik, S., & Suri, K. (1995). The law of karma and social work considerations. *International Social Work, 38,* 365–377.

Kochman, T. (1981). *Black and white styles in conflict.* Chicago: University of Chicago Press.

Kunjufu, J. (1985). *Countering the conspiracy to destroy black boys* (Vol. II). Chicago: African-American Images.

Lewis, R. G., & Ho, M. K. (1994). Social work with Native Americans. In B. Compton & B. Galaway, *Social work processes* (pp. 167–172). Pacific Grove, CA: Brooks/Cole.

Locke, M. (1998, April). California's Proposition 209 takes effect: Minority admissions plummet. The Associated Press News Service.

Lorde, A. (1995). Age, race, class and sex: Women redefining difference. In M. Andersen & P. Collins (Eds.), *Race, class, and gender: An anthology* (2nd ed., pp. 532–540). Belmont, CA: Wadsworth.

Lum, D. (1996). *Social work practice and people of color: A process-stage approach.* Pacific Grove, CA: Brooks/Cole.

Marimba, A. (1994). *Yorugu: An Afrocentric critique of European cultural thought and behavior.* Trenton, NJ: Africa Free World Press.

Marin, G., & Marin, B. (1991). *Research with Hispanic populations.* Newbury Park, CA: Sage.

Martinez, C. (1988). Mexican-Americans. In L. Comas-Diaz & E. E. H. Griffith (Eds.), *Clinical guidelines in cross-cultural mental health* (pp. 182–203). New York: Wiley.

Maslow, A. H. (1968). *Toward a psychology of being.* New York: Van Nostrand.

Min, P. G. (Ed.). (1995). *Asian Americans: Contemporary trends and issues.* Thousand Oaks, CA: Sage.

Morales, A. T., & Sheafor, B. W. (1995). *Social work: A profession of many faces* (7th ed.). Boston: Allyn & Bacon.

O'Hanlon, W. H., & Weiner-Davis, M. (1989). *In search of solutions: A new direction in psychotherapy*. New York: Norton.

Patterson, O. (1995, August 9). Affirmative action on the merit system. *New York Times*, p. 13.

Perlman, H. (1957). *Social casework: A problem solving process*. Chicago: University of Chicago Press.

Philips, W. (1996). Understanding Asian family values. *Children's Voice—Child Welfare League of America*, 6(2), 1–2.

Pinderhughes, E. (1982). Family functioning of Afro-Americans. *Social Work*, 27(1), 91–98.

Pinderhughes, E. (1989). *Understanding race, ethnicity, and power: The key to efficacy in clinical practice*. New York: Free Press.

Proctor, E. K., & Davis, L. E. (1994). The challenge of racial difference: Skills for clinical practice. *Social Work*, 39(3), 314–323.

Red Horse, J. (1982). Clinical strategies for American Indian families in crisis. *Urban and Social Change Review*, 15(2), 17–19.

Reid, W. J. (1986). Task-centered social work. In F. J. Turner (Ed.), *Social work treatment* (3rd ed., pp. 267–295). New York: The Free Press..

Reid, W. J., & Epstein, L. (1972). *Task-centered casework*. New York: Columbia University Press.

Rivera, F. G., & Erlich, J. L. (1998). *Community organizing in a diverse society* (3rd ed.). Boston: Allyn & Bacon.

Roberson, E. (1995). *The Maafa and beyond: Remembrance, ancestral connectedness and nation building for the African global community*. Columbia, MD: Kujichagulia Press.

Roberts, J. M. (1964). The self-management of cultures. In W. H. Goodenough (Ed.), *Explorations in cultural anthropology* (pp. 433–54). New York: McGraw Hill.

Ross-Sheriff, F. (1991). Adaptation and integration into American society: Major issues affecting Asian Americans. In S. M. Furoto, R. Biswas, D. K. Chung, K. Murase, F. Ross-Sheriff (Eds.), *Social work practice with Asian Americans* (pp. 45–64). Newbury Park, CA: Sage.

Ryan, W. (1976). *Blaming the victim*. New York: Vintage.

Saleebey, D. (1992). Introduction: Power in the people. In D. Saleebey (Ed.), *The strengths perspective in social work practice*. New York: Longman.

Saleebey, D. (1994). Culture, theory, and narrative: The intersection of meanings in practice. *Social Work*, 39(4), 352–361.

Samovar, L. A., & Porter, R. E. (1994). Intercultural communication: An introduction. In L. A. Samovar & R. E. Porter (Eds.), *Intercultural communication: A reader* (7th ed., pp. 4–36). Belmont: Wadsworth.

See, L. A. (Ed.). (1998). *Human behavior in the social environment from an African-American perspective*. New York: Haworth.

Segal, E., & Brzuzy, S. (1998). *Social welfare policy, programs and practice*. Itasca, IL: Peacock.

Smith, J. (1991). *The world's religions*. San Francisco: Harper.

Sue, D. W., & Sue, D. (1990). *Counseling the culturally different: Theory and practice* (2nd ed.). New York: Wiley.

Sue, S., & Morishima, J. K. (1992). *The mental health of Asian Americans*. San Francisco: Jossey-Bass.

Suinn, R. M., Rickard-Figuerora, D., Lew, S., & Vigil, P. (1987). The Suinn-Lew Asian self-identity acculturation scale: An initial report. *Educational and Psychological Measurement*, 7, 401–417.

Sutton, C. T., & Broken Nose, M. A. (1996). American Indian families: An overview. In M. McGoldrick, J. Giordano, & J. Pearce (Eds.), *Ethnicity and family therapy* (2nd ed., pp. 31–44). New York: Guilford.

Thomas, N., & Hayman-El, L. (in press). Cultural identity and African-American elderly: Implications for practice. Unpublished manuscript.

Tooles-Walls, C., & Zarit, S. (1991). Informal support from black churches and the well-being of elderly blacks. *The Gerontologist, 31*(4), 490–495.

Trattner, W. I. (1999). *From poor law to welfare state: A history of social welfare in America* (6th ed.). New York: Free Press.

U.S. Bureau of the Census. (1990). *Population estimates and projections* (Series P-25, 1053). Washington, DC: U.S. Department of Commerce.

U.S. Bureau of the Census. (1994, March). *Current population reports: Population estimates and projection* (P25–1114). Washington, DC: U.S. Department of Commerce.

U.S. Bureau of the Census. (1996D). *Statistical abstract of the United States: 1996.* Washington, DC: U.S. Government Printing Office.

Vazquez, R. G. (1994). *A study of program efforts to facilitate access and increase the utilization of community mental health services by Puerto Rican/Hispanic clients.* Unpublished doctoral dissertation, Hunter College.

Velasquez, J., Vigil, M., & Benavides, E. (1994). A framework for establishing social work relationships across racial/ethnic lines. In B. Compton & B. Galaway (Eds.), *Social work processes* (pp. 172–176). Pacific Grove, CA: Brooks/Cole.

Weber, S. N. (1994). The need to be: The socio-cultural significance of black language. In L. A. Samovar & R. E. Porter (Eds.), *Intercultural communication: A reader* (7th ed., pp. 221–225). Belmont, CA: Wadsworth.

Wehrly, B. (1995). *Pathways to multicultural counseling competence: A developmental journey.* Pacific Grove, CA: Brooks/Cole.

Whan, M.W. (1979). Accounts, narrative, and case history. *British Journal of Social Work, 9,* 489–499.

Whittler, T. E. Calantone, R. J., & Young, M. R. (1990). Strength of ethnic affiliation: Examining black identification with black culture. *The Journal of Social Psychology, 131*(4), 461–467.

Wilkinson, C. B., & Spurlock, J. (1986). The mental health of black Americans: Psychiatric diagnosis and treatment. In C. B. Wilkinson (Ed.). *Ethnic psychiatry* (pp. 13–59). New York: Plenum.

Yamamoto, J. (1986). Therapy for Asian Americans and Pacific Islanders. In C.B. Wilkinson (Ed.), *Ethnic psychiatry* (pp. 89–141). New York: Plenum.

CHAPTER 12

Generalist Practice with Abused and Neglected Children and Their Families

Martha Morrison Dore and Nancy Feldman

Ricki M. is a senior BSW student who has a field placement with the county child protective services agency. Ricki is assigned to the unit that provides children and families with services in their own homes, the SCOH unit. SCOH services are designed to keep families together and to prevent the placement of children into foster care. Ricki is nervous about having to visit families in their own homes and about being able to develop helping relationships with involuntary clients. Her first visit is scheduled with Ms. J. and her ten-year-old daughter, Shanai, both of whom have diabetes. SCOH services are involved because of Ms. J.'s neglect of Shanai's medical condition.

In preparing for the home visit, Ricki researched diabetes. She also reviewed the family's case record and found that other workers had been relatively unsuccessful in getting Ms. J. to recognize the seriousness of the disease and to follow the recommendations for the care of her daughter. Ms. J. continually failed to keep Shanai's medical appointments, to follow up on scheduled tests, and to get Shanai to follow the prescribed diet. Ricki was perplexed. Why was Ms. J. unconcerned about her own and her daughter's health? Why was she unwilling to do what was expected of her in terms of caring for Shanai? Ricki wondered how to approach her work with Ms. J. What could she do that might be more effective? How could she develop a helping relationship with Ms. J?

Child maltreatment is a pervasive social problem in this country. Each year, three million reports of suspected child abuse or neglect are filed with state and county child protective services (CPS). About half of these reports are for neglect, a quarter are for physical abuse, and the other quarter are for sexual, psychological , and other forms of abuse. Reports of suspected child maltreatment have tripled in the last twenty years, primarily because of better systems of reporting (Center for the Future of Children, 1998).

What makes parents and other caregivers abuse and neglect the children they are supposed to love and cherish? That question has been studied by generations of thoughtful people committed to the health and well-being of children. Not so long ago, it was believed that such behavior occurred only in immigrant families and among the poor. We know now that the maltreatment of children occurs at all levels of society and among all ethnic and racial groups. Certain factors make the risk of child abuse and neglect more likely, though not inevitable. These risk factors include poverty, unemployment, single parenthood, adolescent parenthood, parental mental illness, parental substance abuse, and low educational attainment by parents, and they combine to heighten stress in families. These stressors may push parents or caregivers into acting in ways that are characterized by society and experienced by children as abusive and neglectful.

This chapter presents information that a generalist practitioner needs to know to work effectively with families and children where there are issues of abuse and neglect. We first present an overview of the history of care for abused and neglected children in the United States, followed by a review of current public policy issues that define the delivery of services to this population. Next we discuss the causes of child abuse and neglect and the effect on the psychosocial functioning of the child. We also look briefly at the long-term effects of childhood abuse and its implications for perpetuating an intergenerational cycle of child maltreatment. The remainder of the chapter focuses on practice with families with issues of child abuse and neglect. We discuss developing a helping relationship with such families, particularly with parents who are often frightened and unresponsive to the offer of help from the generalist social worker. By becoming informed about the multiple factors that contribute to the maltreatment of children and the variety of effective interventions with such families and children, generalist social workers who find themselves confronted with these vulnerable families can see their strengths and build on them for the safety and benefit of the children. By the end of this chapter, you should be able to help Ricki

- Describe how the response to child abuse and neglect have changed over time
- Identify the current policy issues related to the prevention of child maltreatment and the care of abused and neglected children
- Understand the causes and consequences of child maltreatment
- Identify special issues in developing helping relationships with abusive and neglectful families
- Describe the types of interventions available for families dealing with child abuse and neglect.

SOCIAL RESPONSES TO CHILD MALTREATMENT

As our beliefs about child development and our understanding of the role of children in society have changed, so too has our definition of and response to child abuse and neglect. Prior to the late 1800s, community authorities were primarily concerned with child neglect. Abuse of children was not an issue of social concern until the latter part of the nineteenth century.

Caring for Neglected Children

In the earliest years of this country's settlement, all hands were needed to ensure the survival of the family and the community. Children were expected to contribute in concrete ways and from the time they were very young. Few families could afford to educate their children or otherwise provide them with the kind of freedom from work and want that many children today experience. In most families, a child of six or seven was expected to work alongside his or her parent of the same sex, farming, engaging in a trade, or maintaining the household. Families could little afford special activities to ensure optimal growth and development. The early colonial settlers were primarily Protestants whose religious beliefs viewed children as fundamentally flawed from birth and held parents responsible for breaking children's will through severe discipline and hard work.

In colonial times, when parents abandoned a child or when death or disability meant they were unable to adequately care for a child, community elders stepped in without hesitation. Children were most often placed with another family who would agree to care for the child in return for the child's labor. Occasionally, in the best of situations, the new family would agree to teach the child a trade. These placements were not monitored, and no thought was given to the emotional or developmental needs of the child, only to providing for his or her survival. Alternatively, some communities built almshouses or workhouses that housed all indigent people, including those who were mentally ill or mentally retarded as well as the indigent aged and children without resources. These facilities usually included a work program, often a farm, where children as young as four years of age labored for their keep.

As population increased, particularly in larger cities, it became difficult to place in families all of the children who were without adequate support. During the late 1700s and early 1800s, concerned individuals of economic means founded orphanages to care for such children. Parents who could not afford to care for their children could place them in these institutions, or the authorities might determine that a child was neglected. There was a similar trend toward institutional care in Europe during this time, sparked by the work of Catholic nuns who often cared for dependent children in their convents. Indeed, the first children's institution in this country was founded by Catholic nuns in New Orleans in 1727 to care for children orphaned in an epidemic.

Most children's institutions founded in the beginning half of the nineteenth century were either secular or Protestant in origin. It wasn't until the first large wave of Irish immigrants began arriving at midcentury that Catholic institutions began appearing in any numbers. This reflected a growing concern among Catholics that Protestant child rescue organizations were taking in large numbers of Catholic children and converting them. Similarly, Jewish children's homes were established in large cities after the Civil War. By 1880, there were more than six hundred orphanages nationally caring for more than fifty thousand children. Thirty years later, the number of children's institutions as well as the number of residents had nearly doubled (Smith, 1995).

The popular term for children living in orphanages and other children's homes during this period was "dependent and neglected." Most were not really orphans. The typical resident had one living parent who was unable to care for the child financially and so placed the child in the care of others, contributing a small amount weekly to the child's upkeep. These were usually widowed or abandoned mothers for whom gainful employment was limited and day care nonexistent. In a 1902 book entitled *The Care of Destitute, Dependent, and Delinquent Children*, Homer Folks described conditions in orphanages as ranging from adequate to deplorable. He was particularly hard on communities that placed children in almshouses, painting a grim picture of life among adults with psychotic disorders, mental disabilities, severe physical impairments, and other debilitating conditions.

Although care for dependent and neglected children in congregate institutions became widespread in the second half of the nineteenth century, placement of children in the homes of unrelated families was still the preferred form of care in some communities. The Boston Children's Aid Society championed the use of substitute family care for children whose parents were unable to care for them, and its director was an outspoken opponent of institutional placement of children. Massachusetts agencies began experimenting with paying foster families in the late 1880s, thereby insuring that the younger children would not have to work for their keep (Tyor & Zainaldin, 1979).

One noteworthy program was that of the Children's Aid Society of New York, whose director argued that institutional care could not adequately prepare children to fulfill their social and community roles (Brace, 1880). Instead, he advocated putting children from the streets of New York aboard trains headed west and placing them in rural homes along the way:

> Children chosen to be placed out were considered orphaned, homeless, abandoned, dependent, or neglected. In reality, only a few were orphans, and many others had at least one living parent and housing of some sort. Unless children were actual orphans, parents were required to give their permission for the child's participation in the placement program. Children who were thought to be incorrigible, who appeared to be sickly, or who were physically or mentally handicapped were generally not accepted for participation. (Cook, 1995, p. 183)

As the orphan trains wended their way west, crowds would gather at each station stop along the way in response to advance notices posted by Children's Aid Society agents. The children were arrayed along the train platform, and farmers who wanted an extra hand in the fields or their wives who needed help in the kitchen would step forward to claim an appropriate candidate (Wheeler, 1983). Approximately 150,000 dependent and neglected children were placed this way between 1854 and 1930 (Cook, 1995).

Services to children of color were provided outside mainstream child welfare practice. As with other social services for African-Americans, services to dependent and neglected African-American children were provided by churches and other voluntary and benevolent associations, particularly those organized by women of color (Billingsley & Giovannoni, 1972). The National Association of Colored Women, founded in 1896 and representing African-American clubwomen nationally, led the way in calling for its member organizations to respond to the needs of vulnerable children. One response was the Virginia Industrial School for Girls, founded by the Virginia Federation of Colored Women's Clubs in 1915 to care for dependent and delinquent African-American girls (Peebles-Wilkins, 1995). Other responses were more personal. For example, Carrie Steele Pitts, a woman of color who worked as a maid at the

Atlanta Railroad Station, founded an institution in 1888 to care for the infants and young children she found abandoned there (Peebles-Wilkins, 1995).

The Discovery of Child Abuse

It wasn't until the second half of the nineteenth century that child abuse was widely recognized as a separate issue that warranted active intervention in the private lives of families (Hacsi, 1995). Until this time, children did not have rights separate from those of their parents—actually, those of their fathers, since women had few legal rights independent of their husbands and fathers. Children were the property of their fathers and a father could treat a child just about any way he wanted without fear of community intervention. There was more public concern about cruelty to animals than about cruelty to children.

In 1885, the American Humane Association (AHA), which had been founded as a federation of animal rescue groups, took on the cause of child rescue as well. Children were snatched from situations determined to be dangerous to their well-being and placed in institutions or foster homes. The New York Society for the Prevention of Cruelty to Children was the first separate organization for child protection. By the early twentieth century, there were more than three hundred Societies for the Prevention of Cruelty to Children across the United States, all under the purview of the AHA (Schene, 1998). These anticruelty societies acted as private policing agencies with little regard for or interest in understanding family circumstances or dynamics; neither did they provide services to preserve families. Needless to say, they were viewed suspiciously and with some disdain by those in the newly emerging social work profession who were involved in child-helping, as child welfare work was called in its early years.

Efforts to integrate child rescue with other approaches to child-helping were met with intractable resistance by members of the AHA. Eventually, some progressive AHA member agencies split off from the organization and joined with other child-helping agencies to form the Child Welfare League of America (CWLA) in 1921. Its membership primarily included orphanages, child-placing agencies, and industrial schools (Anderson, 1989). These agencies viewed their work as child protection, rather than child rescue. They defined child protection as a range of activities designed to prevent child from all forms of maltreatment:

> Child protection is a specialized service in the field of child welfare on behalf of children suffering from cruelty or abuse; or whose physical, mental or moral welfare is endangered through the neglect of their parents or custodians; or whose rights or welfare are violated or threatened. (Theodore Lothrop, quoted in Anderson, 1989, p. 231)

The difference between child rescue and child protection was more in quality than in kind. Those in the child protection movement identified less as policemen and more as social workers. Although they did remove children from situations of abuse and neglect, they often tried to work preventively with families to address problems that led to maltreatment of children. These usually had to do with poverty and unemployment or with alcoholism. Those in the child protection movement also gave more thought to the needs of the child and tried to find the most suitable placement, rather than the most expedient. Most believed that the birth family was really the best place for a child.

Child Protection in the Twentieth Century

The Social Security Act of 1935 provided grants to rural communities that lacked privately funded children's services to establish public child welfare services, including child protection. Before public child welfare agencies were established under the Social Security Act, child protection was mostly in the hands of private child welfare agencies and the police. There was little public or legal oversight. By the 1940s, several states were using public child welfare agencies to provide child protection. However, it wasn't until 1956, when Congress passed the Home Life Amendment to the Social Security Act, that federal funding became available to establish public child protective services in all communities, rural and urban.

The 1935 Social Security Act also had a significant effect on the use of large congregate institutions for caring for dependent and neglected children. By providing universal entitlement to Aid to Dependent Children (later renamed Aid to Families with Dependent Children, or AFDC), the law allowed single parents who previously might have placed their children in care because they were unable to support them financially to now receive public assistance to care for them at home. States expanded their use of foster homes as the preferred method of out-of-home care for children who could not remain with their biological families (Hacsi, 1995).

In the 1950s, radiologists who looked at X-rays of children's bones began to notice a pattern of numerous poorly mended fractures in some children. In discussing this phenomenon at professional meetings, these doctors realized they were seeing evidence of ongoing physical abuse of children. A widely noticed article published in 1962 in the *Journal of the American Medical Association* exposed these findings (Kempe, Silverman, Steele, Droegemueller, & Silver, 1962) and heightened awareness of the prevalence of child abuse. The result was the passage in all states of laws requiring the mandatory reporting of child abuse by physicians and medical personnel as well as teachers, social workers, and other professionals who became aware of possible maltreatment of children by their parents or caretakers.

The 1950s and 1960s also saw a movement to close large congregate care facilities of all types and to substitute community-based care. This movement, which began in the field of institutional care for adults with mental illness and mental retardation, eventually resulted in the closing of many large congregate care institutions for children and adolescents as well.

In 1974, Congress passed the Child Abuse Prevention and Treatment Act (CAPTA) providing federal funds to states to treat families identified as abusive and neglectful toward their children. It was the first federal recognition of the pervasive national problem of child abuse. It grew directly out of efforts by the American Humane Association and other advocates for maltreated children. CAPTA provided support for state reporting systems and increased the funds available to states for treating victims of child abuse and neglect.

Recognition of child maltreatment as an issue of national significance has led to a call for more attention to prevention. In 1991, the U.S. Advisory Board on Child Abuse and Neglect recommended implementation of a national program of home visits to families of newborns to educate parents about infant care and to identify and target potentially vulnerable families for ongoing services (U.S. Advisory Board on Child Abuse and Neglect, 1991). Hawaii's successful Healthy Start program was the model for this initiative. The following year, the National Committee to Prevent Child Abuse began a nationwide campaign to develop prevention and early intervention services in all states. By 1996, 150 programs in which nurses, teachers, and/or social workers make home visits were in operation in twenty-eight states and seem likely to reduce the incidence of child maltreatment (Guterman, 1997).

Between 1974 and 1978, a subcommittee of the U.S. Senate held a series of hearings regarding placement of Native American children in families of other ethnocultural groups for foster care and adoption. In response to this committee's findings, Congress passed the Indian Child Welfare Act, which granted decision-making powers on child welfare issues to tribal authorities (Mannes, 1995). The act represents an important recognition of the hegemony of a minority group over the welfare of its own members.

Studies of foster care carried out in the 1960s and 1970s highlighted the lack of attention paid to planning for permanent futures for children in placement (Fanshel, 1971; Fanshel & Shinn, 1976). Many children seemed to drift for years in foster care, lost in a system that could only react to the next crisis. Little effort was made to ensure that families remained connected with their children and that they were working to address the problems that contributed to the removal of their children from home (Jenkins & Norman, 1975).

The publication in 1973 of *Beyond the Best Interests of the Child* (Goldstein, Solnit, & Freud) called public attention to the significance of psychological parenting in a child's life, that is, the importance of primary attachment. The primary attachment figure is usually a birth parent but may also be a grandparent, older sibling, foster parent, or adoptive parent. Goldstein and his colleagues stressed the importance of preserving these relational ties and called attention to the fact that a brief period of time in an adult's life is an essential period in a child's developmental time. So, for example, a child who is placed in foster care for six months or a year has often begun to form strong attachments to his or her foster parents. To move the child to a series of foster homes inhibits the formation of these important ties and may make it impossible for the child to form lasting attachments. Goldstein and his colleagues, all psychotherapists, were responding to a child welfare system that placed children in out-of-home care with little thought to the importance of psychological parenting. The effect of *Beyond the Best Interests of the Child* on child welfare policy was significant, particularly with regard to providing a theoretical basis for permanency planning.

The Adoption Assistance and Child Welfare Act of 1980, or P.L. 96-272 as it was popularly known, called on state and local child welfare agencies to review the status of all children in out-of-home care every eighteen months and to make reasonable plans for permanency for each child. Permanency options, in order of preference, included

1. Returning the child to his or her birth or extended family
2. Terminating parental rights and placing the child for adoption
3. Establishing guardianship with relatives or others
4. Making a specific plan for long-term foster care.

The law required the use of the least restrictive, most homelike setting possible for every child. It was an attempt to shift public policy away from breaking up families and placing children. Not only did it emphasize timely reunification or the development of alternative plans for permanency for the child; it also called on public child welfare agencies to act to prevent "the unnecessary separation of children from their families by identifying family problems, assisting families in resolving their problems, and preventing the breakup of the family where the prevention of child removal is desirable and possible" (Samantrai, 1992). Initially, P.L. 96-272 appeared to be effective in reducing the number of children entering the foster care system, with a nearly 50 percent reduction between 1977 and 1983.

One effect of the emphasis on permanency planning has been a substantial increase in kinship care, the placement of children with relatives. By 1991, nearly a third of children removed from their birth parents were placed with kin (Berrick, 1998). A number of factors have contributed to growth in the use of kinship care. One is the shrinking supply of foster homes. Another is the increased demand for out-of-home placements for children due to the drug epidemic, AIDS, and homelessness (Dubowitz et al., 1994). There has also been increased recognition of the importance of cultural ties and kinship support networks, particularly among minority families (Hornby, Zeller, & Karraker, 1996). Some practitioners feel that adjustment is easier and the psychological trauma of separation and placement is greatly reduced when a child is placed with a relative. Some also believe that relatives have a special commitment to the children of kin. Kinship care may facilitate ongoing contact between children and their birth parents (Dubowitz, Feigelman, & Zuravin, 1993). Kinship placements are also more stable and less apt to break down than other forms of foster care (Casey Family Program, 1994).

Kinship care is not without controversy, however. There is some evidence that child welfare authorities are less careful in screening kinship care families for conditions that might present a threat to the child's safety or well-being. There is also likely to be less supervision by the child welfare agency of the child's ongoing adjustment in a kinship placement (Dubowitz, Feigelman, & Zuravin, 1993). These families are given fewer supports and services in managing the care of the children, even when the children have special needs. Many relatives who provide kinship care are elderly grandparents and great-grandparents with few resources for caring for additional family members. They may also lack the energy required to care for active young children. A number of recent studies have highlighted the need for more training and support of kinship caregivers (Berrick, 1998; Dubowitz et al., 1994).

Another result of P.L. 96-272, was the development of family preservation programs to prevent family breakup and child placement (Edna McConnell Clark Foundation, 1985). One such program is the HomeBuilders™ model, developed in Tacoma, Washington, by clinicians at Catholic Family Services and described later in this chapter. In the early 1990s, a number of states passed legislation specifically calling for HomeBuilders-type family preservation services aimed at families with children at imminent risk of foster home placement. This activity culminated in a 1993 amendment to the Social Security Act entitled the Family Preservation and Support Services Program. This amendment provided federal funds to state child welfare agencies to develop family preservation and family support services nationwide (Early & Hawkins, 1994).

Current Policy Issues

At the same time child welfare advocates were calling for increased attention to preventing family breakup and out-of-home placement of children, a new threat to family stability and child safety was appearing on city streets and in suburban neighborhoods: crack cocaine. This inexpensive form of cocaine made its debut in the drug culture in the mid-1980s, and within a few years the number of children entering foster care increased dramatically, despite a decade of family preservation programs and policies. In some communities, testing positive for cocaine at birth was deemed sufficient evidence of neglect to remove an infant from its mother. In others, crack-addicted mothers, unable to provide even minimal parenting, lost their children to the foster care system. The number of infants and young children entering foster care skyrocketed, placing new demands on an already overburdened child welfare system. By 1989, there were 360,000 children in foster care nationally, up from 262,000 at the end of 1982 (Pelton, 1989). By the mid-1990s, this number had reached half a million.

Horror stories of crack-addicted mothers leaving young children alone for hours, even days, at a time as they pursued their drugs filled the media. Instances of severe maltreatment and even death of children at the hands of parents high on drugs made banner headlines across the country. Few drug treatment centers were equipped to treat women with children, and programs that accepted pregnant drug-involved women were rarer still. Thus, even parents who wanted help with their drug problems were hard-pressed to find it. By the mid-1990s, between 40 and 60 percent of children in foster care had parents who were involved with drugs or alcohol (Dore & Doris, 1997).

Drug-abusing parents were difficult to reach. Family preservation programs like HomeBuilders were seldom successful in ameliorating their problems (Dore, 1993). Even parents who sought and received treatment often relapsed, thereby extending the stay of their children in foster care or requiring new placement of those already reunified. The length of time children spent in foster care once again increased as addicted parents struggled to rebuild their lives.

In response to this shifting child welfare environment, Congress passed the Adoption and Safe Families Act, P.L. 105-89, in 1997. This legislation requires timely review of foster care cases and severance of parental rights of parents who fail to actively move toward reunification with their children. It requires permanency-planning hearings for children within twelve months of entry into out-of-home care. It also gives states the right to require even shorter periods for case review for children under three years of age. The law also stipulates that authorities may act within thirty days to terminate parental rights in certain circumstances, such as when the parent's rights to a child's sibling have been terminated, when the parent has assaulted the child or a sibling, or when the child has been subjected to "aggravated circumstances" as defined by state law (Child Welfare League of America, 1998). Termination must be initiated for a child in the care of state child welfare authorities for fifteen out of the most recent twenty-two months.

The Adoption and Safe Families Act of 1997 also places greater emphasis on adoption as an alternative to family reunification than did previous child welfare policies. States are required to document efforts to place children for adoption and are given bonus payments for exceeding previously established base levels of adoption of children in foster care.

Many concerns have been raised about the effect of this legislation in conjunction with the potential effects of abolishing AFDC. The Personal Responsibility and Reform Act of 1996 replaced AFDC with Temporary Assistance to Needy Families (TANF), which requires adults who receive public assistance to participate in some form of work or work-related activity. Adults may collect TANF for no longer than five years over their lifetimes, according to federal guidelines. Some states have reduced the eligibility period even more. Opponents fear that poor and minority families, who are most vulnerable to changes in the economy and instability in the labor market are disproportionately affected by the provisions of TANF. They are quickly using up their lifetime eligibility for assistance and are forced to place their children in foster care because they cannot support them. Or, being forced to take jobs, these parents are unable to afford, or even find, appropriate child care, and their children are being neglected or placed in dangerous situations.

There is also concern that the many families affected by substance abuse and the lack of adequate treatment resources will be greatly disadvantaged under the Adoption and Safe Families Act (Courtney, 1998). Parents struggling to rebuild their lives can leave their children in foster care for no longer than fifteen months within a twenty-two month period before their parental rights are terminated. Given the limited resources devoted to supporting reunified families, there are grave concerns about the vulnerability of this particular group to termination of parental rights.

There are also fears that adoption resources are woefully inadequate for all the children who may be released for adoption under this bill's provisions. Further, many children who come into foster care have been emotionally damaged by their experiences of abuse and neglect. It is far from clear that the child welfare system will be able to find adoptive homes for children with emotional and behavioral problems and whether it will provide ongoing services and supports to families that do adopt these children.

CAUSES AND EFFECTS OF CHILD MALTREATMENT

Why do some parents abuse and neglect their children? What effects does maltreatment have on children? Do these effects last into adulthood?

Causes of Maltreatment

Generally, parents who harm their children do so because of a combination of factors (Belsky, 1984; Belsky, 1993). These factors include the parents' own personal characteristics, social factors such as a culture's belief in the use of corporal punishment, and child factors such as difficult temperament. The personal characteristics associated with abusive and neglectful behavior include clinical levels of depression, alcoholism, and drug addiction; 50 percent or more of parents whose children come to the attention of child welfare authorities have substance abuse problems. Mothers who maltreat their children are significantly more likely to demonstrate symptoms of posttraumatic stress disorder (PTSD) than other mothers (Famularo, Kinshcherff, & Fenton, 1992). There are associations between PTSD symptoms and physical and sexual abuse in both children and adults (Carlson, Furby, Armstrong, & Shlaes, 1997), and the presence of this disorder in maltreating parents indicates that many parents who abuse and neglect their children may themselves have been abused and neglected in childhood (Kaufman & Zigler, 1987; Widom, 1989). There is also an association between childhood abuse, particularly sexual abuse, and symptoms of borderline personality disorder in women, a disorder that has been associated with maltreating behavior (Taylor et al., 1991).

About one-third of individuals who have been abused and neglected are likely to grow up to abuse and neglect their own children (Malinosky-Rummell & Hansen, 1993; Oliver, 1993). Another third are at heightened risk for maltreating their children and can be pushed into such behavior by high levels of environmental stress. The final third of such persons grow up to be competent parents who nurture and care for their children appropriately.

Among the child-related factors that appear to place children at higher risk of maltreatment are premature birth, being the first born, being male, having a physical disability, being under age six, and having a difficult temperament, including being difficult to soothe, restless, fussy, colicky, and a poor eater. One of these characteristics alone does not heighten the risk of maltreatment, but when several occur in combination, particularly when a parent is vulnerable or the environmental stressors are great, the probability of abuse or neglect greatly increases.

Environmental stressors include events or conditions that adversely affect the parent's functioning in his or her multiple roles. For example, unemployment or underemployment and the resulting poverty place stress on families when they are unable to meet daily living expenses. Increased hostility and conflict among family members often follow job loss and a subsequent decline in family income (Conger, Ge, Elder, Lorenz, & Simons, 1994; McLoyd, Jayaratne, Ceballo, & Borquez, 1994). Poverty is related to severe forms of violence against children when children are preschool age, the caretaker is under twenty-five years old, and the caretaker is a single parent (Gelles, 1992). This constellation of factors suggests a highly stressful environment interacting with a parent with few personal or interpersonal resources for coping.

Garbarino and Sherman (1980) studied community environments as factors in child maltreatment. They compared two inner-city neighborhoods that were equally economically depressed. One neighborhood had relatively low rates of child maltreatment, and the other had high rates. In the neighborhood with low rates of child maltreatment, there was a strong sense of community despite the poverty, residents knew one another, and most residents had lived there for several years. In the neighborhood with high rates of maltreatment, residents were isolated from one other even in the same building, there was no sense of community, and people moved in and out all the time.

This study highlights an important factor repeatedly observed in the environments of maltreating families: they are often socially isolated and have few social networks to offer them support in times of high stress. While this isolation is frequently attributed to deficits in the family's ability to interact socially with others, it may also be a function of living in an environment that does not support the universal need of families and children for ongoing social supports. Families living in high-rise apartment buildings and surrounded by street violence are unlikely to feel safe enough to reach out to neighbors or make new acquaintances at the community playground. Alex Kotlowitz compellingly documents the fear and social isolation found in such communities in his book *There Are No Children Here* (1991).

Effects of Maltreatment in Childhood

Although the physical effects of child abuse and neglect are most immediately apparent in bruises, broken bones, and failure to thrive, all forms of child maltreatment have serious adverse consequences for social and emotional development. Babies who are abused or neglected by their primary caregivers have difficulties forming the secure attachments to others that predict positive social and emotional functioning throughout childhood and into adulthood. Maltreated infants are often disorganized in their responses to their caregivers after a brief separation from them (Carlson, Cicchetti, Barnett, & Braunwald, 1989; Lyons-Ruth, Connell, & Zoll, 1989). They are highly distressed during the separation and appear to want to establish physical contact with the returning caregiver, just like children who have not been maltreated. However, unlike most distressed infants, who go directly to their caregiver to be comforted, the maltreated children appear anxious about what to do and generally avoid contact with the caregiver. Crittenden and Ainsworth (1989), who have conducted much of the research on attachment in abused and neglected children, attribute this response to the insensitivity to their children's affective state often observed in maltreating mothers. Harsh, controlling, interfering, and negative interactions with infants and children mark this maternal insensitivity (Fagan & Dore, 1993; Pianta, Egeland, & Erickson, 1989).

A child who has experienced harsh treatment from a parent or other caregiver often treats others harshly in return. Preschool children who have been physically abused are less able to initiate positive interactions with peers than other children and, at the same time, more likely to use aggression against others in their play (Haskett & Kistner, 1991; Muller & Silverman, 1989).

As maltreated children enter the school years, their difficulties in learning become apparent. Physically abused children display "pervasive and severe academic and socio-emotional problems," while neglected children are similar to their nonmaltreated peers in social and emotional functioning but learn more slowly and are at high risk of school failure (Kurtz, Gaudin, Howing, & Wodarski, 1993, p. 100). Stress in the family may not only contribute to child abuse and neglect, but may also have an independent effect on the child's social, emotional, and academic functioning (Kurtz, Gaudin, Howing, & Wodarski, 1993). For example, parents of neglected children have high rates of marital conflict and interpersonal problems, both of which affect children's functioning even when there is no evidence of maltreatment (Fincham, 1994; Kashani, Daniel, Dandoy, & Holcomb, 1992). Substance abuse is also common in these families, another factor that independently places children at high risk of poor developmental outcomes (Dore, Nelson-Zlupko, & Kauffman, 1996).

Maltreated school-aged children also have high rates of depression (Kaufman, 1991; Kazdin, Moser, Colbus, & Bell, 1985; Toth, Manly, & Cicchetti, 1992). This depression may be a consequence of the disrupted attachments experienced by maltreated children. Abused and neglected children may see themselves as unloved and unlovable, which in turn leads to pervasive feelings of sadness and hopelessness (Cummings & Cicchetti, 1990).

Child maltreatment is generally classified into five subtypes: physical abuse, sexual abuse, physical neglect, psychological maltreatment, and educational neglect (Wells & Tracy, 1996). Researchers have asked whether child neglect has a different effect on a child's psychosocial development than physical or sexual abuse. There is some evidence, that neglect has particularly dire effects on academic performance (Kurtz, Gaudin, Howing, & Wodarski, 1993). Emotional or psychological abuse, on the other hand, seems to be detrimental to a child's developing self-esteem and is closely associated with depression (Crittenden,

Claussen, & Sugarman, 1994). However, most forms of child maltreatment occur in combination; one study found that a single form of abuse or neglect occurs in isolation only 5 percent of the time, so it is difficult to determine differential effects (Ney, Fung, & Wickett, 1994).

A study found that physical abuse and verbal abuse are frequently associated, as are physical neglect and sexual abuse (Ney, Fung, & Wickett, 1994). This study also found a correlation between frequency of maltreatment and its severity. In addition, the earlier in the child's life the maltreatment began, the greater its severity and frequency. Physical neglect was a precursor to abuse in many instances. These researchers determined that, from the child's perspective, physical neglect, physical abuse, emotional neglect, and verbal abuse have the greatest negative effect on the child's view of himself or herself and the world (p. 710).

Another study found that frequency of abuse was highly correlated with child functioning on a variety of dimensions that included social competence and behavior problems (Manly, Cicchetti, & Barnett, 1994). The more frequent the abuse, the more impaired the child's functioning became. However, frequency and severity were interrelated, and if maltreatment was severe enough, its frequency did not matter. Even a relatively few instances of severe maltreatment could result in great damage to a child's psychosocial functioning. As in the study described above, the presence of physical neglect was key in determining the effect of other forms of maltreatment.

Children who were sexually abused but did not experience any other form of maltreatment functioned at a much higher level than other maltreated children and were indistinguishable from the children in the comparison group who had not been maltreated (Manly, Cicchetti, & Barnett, 1994). It may be that children that are sexually abused are more likely to receive counseling and other services than other maltreated children. Sexually abused children may experience serious impairments at later stages of psychosocial development, such as when they begin forming intimate relationships.

Effects in Adulthood

Child abuse and neglect may negatively affect all aspects of a child's life, including emotional and psychological functioning, relationships with peers and adults, behavioral functioning, and capacity for learning. Some children are more resilient than others, but it is unlikely that any child escapes totally unscathed (Farber & Egeland, 1987). Even children who function well despite being maltreated are likely to experience latent effects that can inhibit adjustment in adulthood, particularly interpersonal relationships (Luthar, 1993). There is increasing evidence of a long-term negative effect on adult functioning.

There is an association between childhood maltreatment and antisocial behavior in men. One study found that 55 percent of a group of men who had been maltreated as youngsters forty years earlier had a criminal record, were alcoholic or mentally ill, or had died before the age of thirty-five (McCord, 1983). A study of men incarcerated for violent crimes found that 41 percent had been physically or sexually abused or severely neglected in childhood (Dutton & Hart, 1992).

Most men appear to externalize their responses to childhood abuse and neglect, engaging in aggressive and violent behavior against others. Women, on the other hand, tend to internalize their responses, which are manifested in major depression, suicidal behaviors, self-mutilation, eating disorders, dissociation, and psychosis. Studies have consistently found rates of depression that far exceed those for women who were not sexually abused (Carlson, Furby, Armstrong, & Shales, 1997). Women with a borderline personality and disassociative and other disorders have higher than expected rates of childhood physical and sexual abuse (Herman, Perry, & van der Kolk, 1989; Weaver & Clum, 1993). Women who were abused as children often turn to drugs or alcohol to cope with the effects of the trauma (Briere & Zaidi, 1989; Pribor & Dinwiddie, 1992). Because depression, personality disorders, and substance abuse are also associated with parenting behaviors that are abusive and neglectful, it is not hard to see how the maltreatment of children is transferred from one generation to the next.

DEVELOPING A HELPING RELATIONSHIP WITH MALTREATING PARENTS AND THEIR CHILDREN

In most states, child and protective service (CPS) investigators use specific criteria to assess whether abuse or neglect has taken place and whether there is a risk of future maltreatment. Often these criteria are contained in a standardized rating scale. There are seven primary areas of assessment (McDonald & Marks, 1991):

1. Characteristics of the child
2. Characteristics of the primary caretaker
3. Environmental factors
4. Characteristics of the maltreatment
5. The alleged perpetrator's access to the child
6. Family characteristics
7. Parent-child interaction.

Assessment of the child includes age, capacity for self-protection, developmental status (physical and social functioning relative to age), physical appearance, and reactions to caretaker. The physical and mental health of the caretaker are assessed, along with any history of criminal behavior or substance abuse. The CPS worker also notes how the caretaker responds to the investigation. Is the caretaker aware of any problems? How motivated is the caretaker to solve the problems? How cooperative is the caretaker with the investigation? Environmental factors include the cleanliness, safety, and security of the general living environment and the presence or absence of social supports. The type, severity, and frequency of the alleged maltreatment would also be considered.

Family characteristics considered in a CPS investigation include whether there is an adult male present in the household and his relationship to the child. Unrelated adult males, such as the mother's boyfriend, are responsible for a high proportion of child deaths from physical abuse. Sexual abuse of young girls is also more often perpetrated by males with frequent access to the child, such as an uncle or a stepfather. A history of family violence is also considered. Clinicians in battered women's shelters have long observed a relationship between spousal abuse and child abuse. Research is beginning to document this relationship as well.

Evidence is found to substantiate the reported abuse or neglect in about a third of cases, meaning that parents or other caregivers have clearly violated state laws defining child abuse or neglect. Definitions of the various forms of child maltreatment are established in each state, and while there are similarities, there are also differences. Some states have established very narrow standards for abuse, often requiring physical evidence of maltreatment. Other states have broader standards that include less obvious forms of mistreatment, such as psychological abuse.

Once a CPS investigation has substantiated child maltreatment, child welfare authorities must decide whether to leave the child in the situation without additional services, to provide services to the entire family, or to remove the child from the home. Children are removed from their homes and placed in foster care in about one case in ten. In 25 percent of substantiated cases, no services are provided to the family at all. In the remaining 65 percent of cases, child welfare agencies either provide services themselves or, more often, refer the family to a community agency for family counseling, parenting education, individual therapy, or other appropriate services (Center for the Future of Children, 1998). In many communities, a type of program called intensive family preservation services would be mandated to try to prevent family breakup and out-of-home placement of the maltreated child. When the CPS investigation is complete, and abuse or neglect has been substantiated, the generalist social worker often becomes involved.

Target Problems

Target problems related to abuse and neglect include

- Inadequate parenting skills
- Lack of effective strategies for problem-solving
- Limited ability to cope with stress
- Mental health issues such as depression, anxiety, and substance abuse
- Difficulties in interpersonal relationships
- Lack of material resources.

A parent's own history of abuse or neglect and/or unmet nurturance needs may come into play as well. Difficulties with court, school, hospital, or child welfare personnel may also require intervention. Equally as important is responding directly to the child, who may be experiencing emotional and/or behavioral difficulties related to an insufficiently stable and nurturing environment. If the child has been placed out of the home, the trauma of separation and placement, fears of becoming attached to foster parents, and feelings of disloyalty to the birth family need to be addressed (Dore & Eisner, 1993).

Types of Interventions

A variety of direct interventions are available for families dealing with child abuse or neglect. These include

1. Individual play therapy with the maltreated child
2. Family therapy for the entire family
3. Family groups in which several maltreating families participate
4. Group psychotherapy for parents or children
5. Parent support or mutual aid groups

6. Assistance in creating or enhancing support networks
7. Parent training or education on child management issues
8. Assistance for parents to make the home safe
9. Support for parents and children in school meetings, court proceedings, medical appointments, supervised foster care visits, and so on
10. Work with the child and teacher in the school setting.

Indirect interventions may include referrals to after school programs, supplementary or remedial education programs, recreation programs, camps, respite care, substance abuse treatment programs, income maintenance, and other concrete services; and advocating for, or creating, more or different services according to need.

In many communities, there are two primary types of agencies potentially involved with families dealing with child abuse or neglect. One is the preventive services agency, which may contract with the public child welfare agency to provide preplacement services to families and children to attempt to preserve the family, prevent further maltreatment, and keep the child out of the foster care system. The other is the agency that provides foster care, adoption, and reunification services to families whose children have been removed from the home by child welfare authorities after a protective services investigation.

A preventive services agency may serve families for as little as four to six weeks or as long as several years. One example of a short-term treatment model of preventive services is the HomeBuilders™ model, which has a well-developed treatment approach based on crisis intervention and cognitive-behavioral theories (Kinney, Haapala, & Booth, 1991). The practitioner works with one or two families at a time, for from four to eight weeks and is available on call to the family twenty-four hours a day, seven days a week. Most of the work is done in the family home with both the parents and the children. It includes basic environmental interventions, such as helping the family replace broken windows or plaster and paint walls in order to bring the housing up to code. The family preservation workers, as they are called, also teach parents new behavior management techniques, such as using behavior charts and time-outs. The HomeBuilders approach is holistic; intervention includes whatever it takes to stabilize the family and prevent out-of-home placement. It has proven effective with certain types of families, particularly those with some personal and social resources who are committed to making the changes necessary to keep their children at home. It appears to be less effective with parents who are unable to follow through with the specific techniques they are taught, whether because of limited education or cognitive ability or mental health issues, such as severe depression or substance abuse. It also seems to be less effective with very poor families and with single-parent families, who may require longer-term, more extensive support services.

Another model of preplacement family preservation service is the family-based treatment model based on family systems theory (Lindblad-Goldberg, Dore, & Stern, 1998). Programs using this model usually last for three to six months or even longer. Services are delivered primarily in the family's home, and clinicians are on twenty-four-hour-a-day call. Unlike the HomeBuilders-type models, which are based on cognitive and behavioral psychology, family-based models use family systems theories and techniques. They look beyond the family to its relationships with other social systems, such as the neighborhood and larger community. Treatment is not confined to the family; instead there is active intervention in the family's social network to identify and develop resources that can alleviate stress and enhance the family's ability to cope. Attention is also paid to intergenerational processes at work in the family. Genograms and ecomaps are used to help families identify patterns of relationships that may positively or negatively affect functioning (see Lindblad-Goldberg, Dore, & Stern, 1998, for a complete discussion of the family-based model).

Services for families whose children are in foster care focus primarily on addressing the factors contributing to the abuse or neglect with the goal of reunification—or of making a determination that reunification is not possible and that termination of parental rights is necessary. Securing adequate housing is often a prevailing issue, particularly for families who have been homeless or who are living in housing hazardous to the health and well-being of the child. Unfortunately, many children are removed from the care and custody of their parents simply because their living environment is unsuitable. Severe federal cutbacks in funding for public housing programs have left many poor families homeless.

Substance abuse and spouse abuse frequently confront the generalist practitioner working with families in the child welfare system (Dore, Doris, & Wright, 1995). These are particularly difficult issues because of the lack of treatments available in most communities and the time constraints imposed by the Adoption and Safe Families Act of 1997. You will need to know how to do a substance abuse assessment with a parent and how to assess for spousal violence. Motivational interviewing techniques have proved to be effective in helping individuals with substance abuse problems accept treatment. (See Hohman, 1998, for an excellent discussion of the use of motivational interviewing with child welfare clients.) It is also important to know the treatment resources available in the community and the criteria for referral and admission to these programs. There is nothing more detrimental to substance-abusing parents who have acknowledged the need for treatment than to be referred to a program that is unable to accept them because of funding constraints or admission criteria. Achieving sobriety is a long and arduous process requiring a great deal of support and encouragement. Most people do not achieve sobriety on the first or even second try. Maintaining hope and a belief in the parent's ability to succeed is an important part of your role.

You also need to be familiar with shelters for battered women and to provide the mother with information on how to keep herself and her child safe in violent situations. Helping a woman recognize that she has options and developing a concrete plan to deal with violence are essential first steps in helping her move out of a violent relationship. Battered women's support groups can be valuable resources in treatment planning for mothers in abusive relationships.

Another type of intervention often used with parents who are working toward reunification is developing a network of social supports that are available on an ongoing basis. Do not overlook the role of religious institutions in this network; they can provide a community of warmth and acceptance for isolated parents and children. Many parents who have maltreated their children feel deeply ashamed of their behavior, particularly if it is associated with a substance-abusing lifestyle. Religious institutions can help these parents forgive themselves and find meaning in their lives.

Reconnecting parents with extended family members may also be a part of developing a social network. Often, maltreating parents, have worn out their family relationships, particularly if they have had substance-abuse problems or have difficulty in interpersonal relationships. Helping them learn how to establish and maintain ongoing interpersonal relationships may be an important aspect of the intervention process. Mutual aid and support groups can be effective ways for parents to learn new social skills (Otto, 1990). A recent approach has been to develop multifamily groups that include maltreating parents and their children (Meezan, O'Keefe, & Zarianai, 1997).

Parenting programs are frequently used with parents who have abused or neglected their children; but they need to be used with caution (Dore & Lee, 1999). Maltreating parents usually have other problems in addition to their lack of awareness of child management techniques, and parent programs that focus on teaching specific parenting skills, such as use of time-outs and positive reinforcements, are not effective with parents with multiple problems. Parenting programs should be part of an array of treatment activities and services, not the sole approach.

Children who have been maltreated by a parent or other caregiver have treatment needs as well. Individual play therapy is the traditional approach to addressing problems experienced by these children (Mann & McDermott, 1983). Some children who have been victims of abuse suffer from post-traumatic stress disorder. Play therapy can help these children work through and eventually gain some sense of control over stressful events. Play therapy can also serve to explore attachment issues, externalize fear, and widen the emotional and behavioral repertoire of maltreated children. (See Gil, 1991, and Webb, 1991, for further discussion of the use of play therapy with traumatized and maltreated children.) Therapeutic nurseries and play groups have been established to provide treatment for very young children (Oates & Bross, 1995). Group treatment is seen by some as the intervention of choice for children of school age or even younger (Steward, Farquahar, Dicharry, Glick, & Martin, 1986). Group treatment often helps children overcome shame and self-blame by exposing them to other children's similar experiences. It also provides an opportunity to develop and expand interpersonal skills, including nonaggressive ways to express anger and upset.

Special Issues in Working with Abusive or Neglectful Families

There are numerous challenges in developing collaborative relationships with clients where child abuse and neglect is involved. Poor parents and parents of color have been particularly vulnerable to intrusion by a child welfare system in which inadequate attention has been paid to bolstering a family's ability to function as a unit (Pelton, 1989). Historically, children in these families have been more likely to be removed from their homes and the rights of their parents more readily terminated (Stehno, 1982). Families have less frequently been offered supports and services designed to enable them to resume caring for their children (Jones, 1993). Understandably, attempts to help are often perceived as investigatory and are met with mistrust and defensiveness.

Mistrust and suspicion is also exacerbated by the social worker's role as mandated reporter, someone who is required by law to report any suspicion of child abuse or neglect to a central state registry or hotline. Creating an effective helping relationship in this context demands forthrightness about the responsibility to provide services to the child and family while ensuring the safety and well-being of the child. Be clear with parents at the beginning of the work together that you are required by law to report possible abuse or neglect. If such a report becomes necessary, first inform the parent that it must be made and discuss the reasons for your concerns.

Practitioners are often fearful that making a report will severely damage the fragile trust built with maltreating families. The worker, often correctly, believes that the parent will end the relationship and that no further productive work can be done. There is no choice, however, but to make the report. Parents can be helped to understand this. If there is a positive working relationship, help the parent work through the feelings of anger, fear, and humiliation that present barriers to further work. If CPS investigators can be assured that the family is actively working to address the situation, continued services to the family without child placement may be recommended. If CPS makes a decision to place a child as a result of the report, the worker may have an opportunity to work with the family toward reunification or an extended kinship placement, or to help parents make a decision about terminating their rights and freeing the child for adoption.

Social workers working with families in which there are abuse or neglect issues are vulnerable to siding with the child to the detriment of the helping process. Children are vulnerable and need protection. However, attempts to support children by siding with them against their parents usually makes it impossible to engage parents in meaningful change. It may be hard to feel empathy for a hostile parent whose defense against the fear of being judged inadequate is to attack the worker's ability to help the family. However, joining with the entire family system helps protect fragile family bonds, which, while perhaps far from ideal, are usually important to the child. Further, engaging the parents in the process of change is essential to keeping the child out of an already overburdened foster care system.

Another potential barrier to developing a helping relationship with parents is raised by a client's questions about the social worker's own parenting status. "Do you have kids?" is a question that can be experienced as an attack, especially by a worker who is childless. And sometimes it is an attack, a defensive maneuver designed to convey the message "You can't help me." But just as often, the parent is asking for reassurance that he or she will not be judged harshly as an inadequate parent. The supposition is that another parent can better understand the difficulties of being a parent. Or, the parent may simply want to know more about who the worker is. If that is the case, an answer is conveyed not only by the content of the response, but also by the manner. A matter-of-fact, open, and honest response can reassure the parent that you are respectful of his or her concerns. Regardless of the parent's intent, a nondefensive, nonreactive posture goes far in establishing a productive worker-client relationship.

Parenting practices acceptable in some cultures may be considered abusive under current laws in the United States. This is particularly true for some forms of child discipline. For example, switching or striking a child with branches, is a common practice in some cultures, but CPS workers may see it as abusive, particularly if it leaves welts. In communities with a large immigrant population or diverse cultural or ethnic groups, it is important to learn about the particular customs and practices of the various groups. Sources of information include professional literature, supervision, and formal immigrant organizations.

Some immigrant groups experience difficulty coming from an environment in which children are raised communally to one society in which nonfamily involvement in child-rearing is seen as intrusion into family privacy. This may result in loneliness, isolation, and despair for immigrant families accustomed to receiving support from a large extended kinship system or a whole village.

Beware of feelings of urgency to respond to situations that appear to involve abuse or neglect. Sensationalist media coverage of previous cases may encourage impulsive and otherwise reactive responses, making it difficult to weigh both confirming and contradictory evidence about what has occurred and what action is in the best interests of the child. Don't let fear of leaving a child in a potentially dangerous situation lead you to overestimate the threat to the child's safety and to remove the child from the family without considering less drastic measures. Removing a child from familiar surroundings always has the potential for traumatizing the child, no matter how unsatisfactory those surroundings may appear to an adult. It is only when the risk to the child of remaining in the situation clearly outweighs the risk of damage from removal that such a step should be considered.

The current child welfare system has great potential for reabusing and neglecting already vulnerable children and families. Despite laws that mandate the use of methods to assess imminent danger and future risk of abuse and neglect, many child protective workers "remove first and ask questions later" because of pressures from sensationalist media coverage of tragic events or from child welfare administrators who implicitly or explicitly convey that this is good practice. There are also fiscal incentives for retaining children in foster care longer than may be necessary. In some states, the contract agencies that provide placement prevention services also provide foster care services. They get paid at a higher rate for the latter than the former, providing an incentive to place children away from their families and to keep them in placement.

Child abuse and neglect also occur in foster homes. It is not just biological parents who maltreat children. Low boarding payments, inadequate screening of foster parents, lack of training in meeting the special emotional needs of foster children, and lack of supportive services, including frequent, routine home visits, all contribute to the potential for abuse and neglect by foster parents. It's a sad irony that children who are removed from their biological families because of maltreatment may be placed in substitute homes that are equally as abusive or neglectful, or more so.

Awareness of the potential for abuses in the child welfare system causes some social workers to avoid making use of the system even when it is necessary and appropriate. Concerns about the system's present inadequacies and history of racism and antipoor attitudes may cloud our judgment. We may hesitate to remove children from situations that are clearly detrimental to their well-being because we are worried about how they will be treated by the system. Those who have such concerns must ask ourselves what we are doing to advocate for changes in the system. We must clearly document instances of maltreatment perpetrated by the child welfare system and educate the community and lawmakers about these abuses. We should not wait until a child dies in foster care to speak out about the failures of the child welfare system and to propose changes that can make it more responsive to the needs of troubled families and their children.

SUMMARY

The abuse and neglect of children is a significant social problem that appears to be growing, as indicated by the increasing number of reports to child protection agencies. At last count, at least half a million children were in out-of-home care in the child welfare system because of maltreatment by parents or other caregivers.

The response in the United States to child abuse and neglect has changed over time. In this country's earliest years, neglect drew greater attention than abuse. Town fathers did not hesitate to step in and remove children from families that were judged inadequate to care for them. Placing such children as unpaid laborers with other families in the community was the common response. As cities and towns grew larger and less able to manage all the children in their care, congregate care institutions were built to house them. These facilities were often constructed by religious groups to care for children of their faith. Most dependent and neglected children were cared for in this way, although there were also agencies that continued to place children with foster families, especially very young children. In the twentieth century, institutional care for children fell out of favor, and efforts were increasingly made to help families provide care to their own children. Throughout the twentieth century, public awareness of the existence and extent of child abuse has grown, particularly with the invention of the X-ray, which allowed doctors to see long-standing patterns of abuse.

Social concern with child maltreatment has led to varied public policy responses on the federal level. The first response was to fund public agencies to handle child protection and care. Federal legislative initiatives have funded programs of foster care, particularly for children living below the poverty level. In the 1970s, identification and reporting of child abuse and neglect was the predominant policy concern. Then, as the number of children entering out-of-home care soared, legislation was enacted to fund programs to preserve families and keep children in their own homes. As the drug epidemic in the 1980s began to affect families and the care of their children, the policy pendulum swung back again. Family preservation took a back seat to child protection. At the same time, however, Congress enacted legislation to limit the length of time a child could be in foster care without a permanent home. Concurrent planning, a mechanism whereby a permanent plan for a child is made at the time he or she enters care in the event that family reunification is not possible, is the focus of child welfare policy at the present time.

In the last fifty years, researchers and others concerned about the maltreatment of children have sought to develop an understanding of why some parents and caregivers abuse and neglect children in their care. The reasons seem to be complex and varied, having to do with the child, the family, and the social environment. Some children, such as those with disabilities, are particularly vulnerable to abuse. And some families, particularly those who are stressed by poverty, unemployment, racism and oppression, mental illness, and substance abuse, are more likely than others to maltreat their children. Some communities have unusually high rates of child abuse and neglect. These seem to be communities with transient populations and few social connections among inhabitants.

Child abuse and neglect raise intense reactions in almost everyone. Generalist social workers who work with maltreating families, or with families at high risk of child maltreatment, must be aware not only of the dynamics of abusive and neglectful families but also of the effects of the child welfare system on families as well. It is essential to base practice with these families on a thorough assessment of each situation without a rush to judgment. Most parents want to do right by their children but may be unable to for a variety of reasons, often having to do with their own unmet needs for nurturing, difficulties in psychosocial function-ing, or both. To identify and build on a family's strengths so that it can better cope with the stress of nurturing its children is at once more challenging and more gratifying for all concerned than severing a family's affectional ties and offering a child an unknown future.

CASE EXAMPLE

The following case example shows how one generalist social worker addressed the problems of a family experiencing many of the stressors found in families at high risk for child maltreatment. This case illustrates the kind of family situation that often results in intervention by child welfare authorities: a minority family, struggling financially, with many children and overworked, isolated, and depressed parents who have relinquished some of their authority to a child or children in the family. It also demonstrates how the generalist practitioner works with multiple systems in such cases and maintains a presence in the community and in the family home.

A Vulnerable Family

Manuel R., age thirty-four, and his wife Maria, twenty-eight, had five children: Yvette, nine; Manuel Jr., eight; Carlos, seven; Connie, four; and Angelique, one. The R. family was referred to a family service agency for counseling by Maria R.'s physician. Maria was suffering from high blood pressure and anemia and reported feeling overwhelmed by her family responsibilities. Her husband had been working two jobs to make ends meet and did not have much time to spend with Maria and the children. In addition to meeting the daily needs of five children under the age of ten, Maria was dealing with school behavior problems that Yvette, age nine, had begun to exhibit. At the time of referral, Yvette was being recommended for special education. This disturbed Manuel and Maria, for they had always thought of her as a bright child, and they feared that special education would limit her opportunities to learn and develop.

At intake, members of the R. family appeared caring toward each other, but highly stressed. Yvette often stepped in when one of the younger children approached Maria for attention or help. Manuel seemed uncomfortable, but he was able to speak openly about needing outside help, stating: "Our pastor has always been able to help us. This time it is different." He spoke softly about his concern about his wife's health. Manuel said that his worries distracted him at work and made him snap at his young children at home. Maria said little during the session, responding only in monosyllables when addressed, She appeared to be sad and withdrawn. She cradled her youngest child, Angelique, in her lap, holding her tenderly but not interacting with her. The other children played with a Lego set in a corner of the room.

In the first session, Jane F., the social worker, learned that the R. fam-ily's support network consisted of their church and extended families. The support was mainly spiritual and emotional and was extremely important to the family. However, concrete support, in the form of respite for Maria, for example, was not forthcoming, since church and extended family members were also overburdened. Jane also determined that Maria had received prenatal care for all of her pregnancies and that the children had developed within normal range in all areas (motor, cognitive, physical, and socioemotional).

Assessment

Jane assessed the R. family as having many strengths. The parents were deeply committed to each other and to their children. The children were healthy and developing well physically. The family had strong spiritual values and beliefs and a network of supportive individuals. However, the family was currently experiencing a great deal of stress. Maria was overwhelmed with the responsibility of caring for five active young children alone. She had few social contacts with other mothers and little support in her parenting role from family and friends. There were few Latino families in the neighborhood, and their church was located several miles away, in their old neighborhood. Maria felt shy around the other young mothers in her building who gathered at the playground to chat while their children played.

Manuel tried to help out with the children when he could, but his work demands were great. The oldest daughter, nine-year-old Yvette, tried to alleviate some of the pressures on her mother by acting as a surrogate mother with the youngest children. But her anxieties about her mother and the family situation were being expressed in behavior problems in the classroom. This bright, formerly high-achieving girl was being labeled as a problem child by school authorities and was about to be tracked into special education classes for children with learning and behavior difficulties.

Intervention

Jane's initial interventions focused on reducing stress in the family. She invited Maria to a women's support group in which most of the women were mothers and several were Latina. The three older children began attending a neighborhood program after school five days a week. Connie, the four-year-old, was put on a waiting list for Head Start. In family counseling sessions, efforts were made to strengthen the parental unit and remove Yvette from the parenting role. Jane also assisted the family with Yvette's school problems. She attended a school-based support team meeting with Mr. and Mrs. R., in which the plan to put Yvette in special education was discussed. When Jane suggested ways to include Yvette in classroom activities without overly focusing on her problem behavior, she was invited to work with Yvette's fourth grade class.

Jane, along with her supervisor, Carol W., focused on helping the children and teachers create a productive learning environment through the use of improvisational drama and games. For example, when two youngsters began to fight while Jane and Carol were working with the class, they were asked to create and direct a play about fighting. The two children became so engrossed in producing their play that their interactions with one another improved dramatically. Although Yvette was not in any way identified as the focus of attention for her problem behavior, her school behavior problems ceased after only a few weeks of participating in classroom activities with Jane and Carol.

However, during this period, the state hotline received an anonymous report claiming that Maria was abusing Angelique and that burns were seen on the baby's arms and hands. When questioned by a child protective service (CPS) caseworker, Maria asserted that Angelique had been playing close to the radiator and that she hadn't realized how hot it was until Angelique screamed after having been burned. When asked why she had not taken Angelique to the doctor, Maria replied that she was afraid they would blame her and take her baby away from her. Maria also stated that she knew how to take care of burns and that Angelique's burns were healing well, which was, in fact, the case.

Nevertheless, the CPS worker perceived that Angelique and four-year-old Connie were in immediate danger of serious harm because there was no daily community oversight of them (that is, they were not in day care or school). The worker believed that Maria was covering up her actions. Maria's openness about the stress she had been feeling and the family's involvement with the family service agency backfired. The worker took it as evidence that Maria was a troubled woman and could not be trusted with the care of her youngest children. Without interviewing Manuel, the neighbors, Jane, or anyone else involved with the family, the CPS worker immediately removed Angelique and Connie from their family and placed them in separate foster homes.

Over the next several weeks, Jane helped the family negotiate a reunification plan with the CPS worker and foster care agency personnel and prepare for an upcoming court date. She educated Manuel and Maria about the hearing process and spoke to the court-appointed lawyer on their behalf. Maria plunged into a deep depression and Yvette and Carlos began exhibiting behavioral difficulties in school. Manuel Jr. started having nightmares. The family system was under enormous stress. In family therapy sessions, the children talked about what the removal of their younger siblings meant for them and for the absent children. In individual sessions, Maria began to explore her emotional pain, including the frustration and despair from feeling and being powerless against the child welfare system and from seeing herself as a failure as a wife and mother. Jane continued to support Manuel in his increasingly active role as father.

Support from the women's group, the family and individual therapy sessions, and a series of successful visits with Connie and Angelique at the foster care agency helped Maria feel less depressed and more hopeful. She became more actively involved in meeting the court's requirements. She had to complete a parent training program, and although she continued to feel that she had been wrongly accused of hurting her child, Maria was able to use the parent training sessions to learn alternative methods of disciplining and stress management techniques. After hearing the positive testimony of both Jane and the foster care worker, the judge in charge of the case ordered the return of the two youngest R. children to the home. The child welfare agency was to supervise the family for six months, at which time another decision would be made about the agency's involvement with the family.

The three older children continued attending the after-school program, and Connie began a full-day Head Start program. Maria and Angelique joined a mother-child play group that was initiated and organized by the women's support group. With support and encouragement from Jane, Maria made friends with one of the young mothers in her building, who then introduced Maria to the other mothers at the playground. At Jane's suggestion, Maria and her new friend, Elise C., began exchanging child-care duties so that each mother had one free afternoon a week. Maria usually used her afternoon to shop for groceries at a big discount supermarket several bus transfers away, a trip that would have been stressful and exhausting with several children in tow.

While Manuel continued to be absent for many hours because of his heavy work schedule, the time he spent with the family was qualitatively different than it had been before. Maria had previously served as a barrier between Manuel and the children in an attempt to "protect" the little time he had to relax. Now he played and talked with the children . The various school and sleep problems experienced by the children decreased, then disappeared, as the family system became more stable. Family members were able to recognize ways they had grown individually and as a family.

Termination

A year and a half after beginning at the family service agency, Maria and Manuel initiated termination. Maria's physical health had improved considerably; she was no longer anemic, and her blood pressure had returned to normal range. Her depression had lifted, and her affect was brighter and more lively. Manuel commented that she seemed more like the young woman he had courted. Maria was also more responsive to the children in family sessions and during Jane's home visits. The children were doing well in school and at home, and they seemed to be in agreement that it was time for family sessions to end. The family's support network had been greatly enlarged with the addition of mothers from the women's support group, neighbors, parents from the Head Start program, and school personnel who had become allies when they realized how committed the R. parents were to the education of their children.

In addition to reviewing the work they had done together, Jane reassured the family that they could always come back if they needed to and that the older children's participation in the after-school program and Connie's participation in Head Start would not be affected by termination of counseling. Maria continued to participate in the women's support group.

DISCUSSION QUESTIONS

1. How would you discuss your role as a mandated reporter with the R. family in order to help them continue the helping relationship?
2. What are the strengths in the R. family, and how does Jane, the social worker, build on these in her work with the family?
3. What are some other ways, Jane could have created or expanded social supports for the R. family?

4. How might the R. family's experiences have been different if they had not been working with Jane at the time Maria was reported for child abuse?
5. How can a family's spiritual values be identified and incorporated into treatment planning?
6. What have been the changes in response to child abuse and neglect over time in the United States? What caused these changes?
7. How have changes in public policy regarding child maltreatment reflected events in the larger society?
8. What effect might physical and emotional neglect have on an infant? On a three-year-old? On a school-age child? On an adolescent?
9. What does it mean to say that child abuse is multiply determined?

REFERENCES

Anderson, P. G. (1989). The origin, emergence, and professional recognition of child protection. *Social Service Review, 63,* 222–244.

Belsky, J. (1984). The determinants of parenting: A process model. *Child Development, 55,* 83–96.

Belsky, J. (1993). Etiology of child maltreatment: A developmental-ecological analysis. *Psychological Bulletin, 114,* 413–434.

Berrick, J. D. (1998). When children cannot return home: Foster family care and kinship care. *Futures for Children, 8*(1), 72–87.

Billingsley, A., & Giovannoni, J. M. (1972). *Children of the storm: Black children and American child welfare.* New York: Harcourt.

Brace, C. L. (1880). *The dangerous classes of New York, and twenty years' work among them* (3rd ed.). New York: Wynkoop & Hallenbeck.

Briere, J., & Zaidi, L. Y. (1989). Sexual abuse histories and sequelae in female psychiatric emergency patients. *American Journal of Psychiatry, 144,* 1426–1430.

Carlson, E. B., Furby, L., Armstrong, J., & Shales, J. (1997). A conceptual framework for the long-term psychological effects of traumatic child abuse. *Child Maltreatment, 2,* 272–295.

Carlson, V., Cicchetti, D., Barnett, D., & Braunwald, K. (1989). Disorganized/disoriented attachment relationships in maltreated infants. *Developmental Psychology, 25,* 525–531.

Casey Family Program (1994, October). National study documents the value of relative foster care. *News Release.* Seattle, WA: Author.

Center for the Future of Children. (1998). Protecting children from abuse and neglect: Analysis. *The Future of Children, 8*(1), 1–3.

Child Welfare League of America. (1998). The Adoption and Safe Families Act of 1997 (P.L. 105-89). Available Internet: http://www.childrensdefens.org/safestart_pass3.html.

Conger, R. D., Ge, X., Elder, G. H., Lorenz, F. O., & Simons, R. L. (1994). Economic stress, coercive family process, and developmental problems of adolescence. *Child Development, 65,* 541–561.

Cook, J. F. (1995). A history of placing-out: The orphan trains. *Child Welfare, 74,* 181-197.

Courtney, M. E. (1998). The costs of child protection in the context of welfare reform. *The Future of Children, 8*(1), 88–103.

Crittenden, P. M., & Ainsworth, M. (1989). Child maltreatment and attachment theory. In D. Cicchetti & V. Carlson (Eds.), *Child maltreatment* (pp. 432–463). New York: Cambridge University Press.

Crittenden, P. M., Claussen, A. H., & Sugarman, D. B. (1994). Physical and psychological maltreatment in middle childhood and adolescence. *Development and Psychopathology, 6,* 145–164.

Cummings, E. M., & Cicchetti, D. (1990). Attachment, depression, and the transmission of depression. In M. T. Greenberg, D. Cicchetti, & E. M. Cummings (Eds.), *Attachment during the pre-school years* (pp. 339–372). Chicago: University of Chicago Press.

Dore, M. M. (1993). Family preservation and poor families: When "homebuilding" is not enough. *Families in Society, 74*, 545–556.

Dore, M. M., & Doris, J. M. (1997). Preventing child placement in substance-abusing families: Research-informed practice. *Child Welfare, 77*(4), 407–426.

Dore, M. M., Doris, J., & Wright, P. (1995). Identifying substance abuse in maltreating families: A child welfare challenge. *Child Abuse and Neglect: The International Journal, 19*, 531–543.

Dore, M. M., & Eisner, E. (1993). Child-related dimensions of placement stability in treatment foster care. *Child and Adolescent Social Work Journal, 10*, 301–317.

Dore, M. M., & Lee, J. W. (1999). The role of parent training with abusive and neglectful parents. *Family Relations, 48*, 1–13.

Dore, M. M., Nelson-Zlupko, L., & Kauffman, E. (1996). Psychosocial functioning and treatment needs of latency-aged children from drug-involved families. *Social Work, 44*, 179–190.

Dubowitz, H., Feigelman, S., Harrington, D., Starr, R., Zuravin, S., & Sawyer, R. (1994). Children in kinship care: How do they fare? *Children and Youth Services Review, 16*(1/2), 85–106.

Dubowitz, H., Feigelman, S., & Zuravin, S. (1993). A profile of kinship care. *Child Welfare, 72*(2), 153–169.

Dutton, D. G., & Hart, S. D. (1992). Evidence for long-term, specific effects of child abuse and neglect on criminal behavior in men. *International Journal of Offender Therapy and Comparative Criminology, 36*, 129–137.

Early, B. P., & Hawkins, M. J. (1994). Opportunity and risks in emerging family policy: An analysis of family preservation legislation. *Children and Youth Services Review, 16*(5/6), 309–318.

Edna McConnell Clark Foundation (1985). *Keeping families together: The case for family preservation*. New York: Author.

Fagan, J., & Dore, M. M. (1993). Mother-child play interactions in neglecting and non-neglecting mothers. *Early Child Development and Care, 87*, 59–68.

Famularo, R., Kinscherff, R., & Fenton, T. (1992). Psychiatric diagnoses of abusive mothers: A preliminary report. *The Journal of Nervous and Mental Disease, 180*, 658–661.

Fanshel, D. (1971). The exit of children from foster care: An interim research report. *Child Welfare, 50*(2), 65–81.

Fanshel, D., & Shinn, E. (1976). *Children in foster care*. New York: Columbia University Press.

Farber, E. A., & Egeland, B. (1987). Invulnerability among abused and neglected children. In E. J. Anthony & B. J. Cohler (Eds.), *The invulnerable child* (pp. 253–288). New York: Guilford.

Fincham, F. D. (1994). Understanding the association between marital conflict and child adjustment: Overview. *Journal of Family Psychology, 8*, 123–127.

Folks, H. (1902). *The care of destitute, neglected, and delinquent children*. New York: Macmillan.

Garbarino, J., & Sherman, D. (1980). High-risk neighborhoods and high-risk families: The human ecology of child maltreatment. *Child Development, 51*, 188–198.

Gelles, R. J. (1992). Poverty and violence toward children. *American Behavioral Scientist, 35*, 258–274.

Gil, E. (1991). *The healing power of play*. New York: Guilford.

Goldstein, J., Solnit, A., & Freud, A. (1973). *Beyond the best interests of the child*. New York: Free Press.

Guterman, N. B. (1997). Early prevention of physical child abuse and neglect: Existing evidence and future directions. *Child Maltreatment, 2*(1), 12–34.

Hacsi, T. (1995). From indenture to foster family care: A brief history of child placing. *Child Welfare, 74*, 162–180.

Haskett, M. E., & Kistner, J. A. (1991). Social interactions and peer perceptions of young physically abused children. *Child Development, 62*, 979–990.

Herman, J. L., Perry, J. C., & van der Kolk, B. A. (1989). Childhood trauma in borderline personality disorder. *American Journal of Psychiatry, 146*, 490–495.

Hohman, M. M. (1998). Motivational interviewing: An intervention tool for child welfare case workers working with substance-abusing parents. *Child Welfare, 77*(3), 275–290.

Hornby, H., Zeller, D., & Karraker, D. (1996). Kinship care in America: What outcomes should policy seek? *Child Welfare, 75*(5), 397–417.

Jenkins, S., & Norman, E. (1975). *Beyond placement: Mothers view foster care.* New York: Columbia University Press.

Jones, L. (1993). Decision making in child welfare: A critical review of the literature. *Child and Adolescent Social Work Journal, 10*(3), 241–262.

Kashani, J. H., Daniel, A. E., Dandoy, A. C., & Holcomb, W. R. (1992). Family violence: Impact on children. *Journal of the American Academy of Child and Adolescent Psychiatry, 31*, 181–189.

Kaufman, J. (1991). Depressive disorders in maltreated children. *Journal of the American Academy of Child and Adolescent Psychiatry, 30*, 257–265.

Kaufman, J., & Zigler, E. (1987). Do abused children become abusive parents? *American Journal of Orthopsychiatry, 57*, 186–192.

Kazdin, A. E., Moser, J., Colbus, D., & Bell, R. (1985). Depressive symptoms among physically abused and psychiatrically disturbed children. *Journal of Abnormal Psychology, 94*, 298–307.

Kempe, C. H., Silverman, F. N., Steele, B. F., Droegemueller, W., & Silver, H. K. (1962). The battered child syndrome. *Journal of the American Medical Association, 181*, 17–24.

Kinney, J., Haapala, D., & Booth, C. (1991). *Keeping families together: The homebuilders model.* New York: Aldine de Gruyter.

Kotlowitz, A. (1991). *There are no children here: The story of two boys growing up in the other America.* New York: Doubleday.

Kurtz, P. D., Gaudin, J. M., Howing, P. T., & Wodarski, J. S. (1993). The consequences of physical abuse and neglect on the school age child: Mediating factors. *Child and Youth Services Review, 15*, 85–104.

Lindblad-Goldberg, M., Dore, M. M., & Stern, L. (1998). *Creating competence from chaos: A comprehensive guide to home based services for children with serious emotional disturbances and their families.* New York: Norton.

Luthar, S. S. (1993). Annotation: Methodological and conceptual issues in research on childhood resilience. *Journal of Child Psychology and Psychiatry, 34*, 441–453.

Lyons-Ruth, K., Connell, D. B., & Zoll, D. (1989). Patterns of maternal behavior among infants at risk for abuse: Relations with infant attachment behavior and infant development at 12 months of age. In D. Cicchetti & V. Carlson (Eds.), *Child Maltreatment* (pp. 464–493). New York: Cambridge University Press.

Malinosky-Rummell, R., & Hansen, D. J. (1993). Long-term consequences of childhood physical abuse. *Psychological Bulletin, 114*, 68–79.

Manly, J. T., Cicchetti, D., & Barnett, D. (1994). The impact of subtype, frequency, chronicity, and severity of child maltreatment on social competence and behavior problems. *Development and Psychopathology, 6*, 121–143.

Mann, E., & McDermott, J. F. (1983). Play therapy for victims of child abuse and neglect. In C. E. Schaefer & K. J. O'Connor (Eds.), *Handbook of play therapy* (pp. 134–168). New York: Wiley.

Mannes, M. (1995). Factors and events leading to the passage of the Indian Child Welfare Act. *Child Welfare, 74*(1), 264–282.

McCord, J. (1983). A forty-year perspective on effects of child abuse and neglect. *Child Abuse & Neglect, 1*, 265–270.

McDonald, T., & Marks, J. (1991). A review of risk factors assessed in child protective services. *Social Service Review, 65*, 112–132.

McLoyd, V. C., Jayaratne, T. E., Ceballo, R., & Borquez, J. (1994). Unemployment and work interruption among African American single mothers: Effects on parenting and adolescent socioemotional functioning. *Child Development, 65*, 562–589.

Meezan, W., O'Keefe, M., & Zariani, M. (1997). A model of multi-family group therapy for abusive and neglectful parents and their children. *Social Work with Groups, 20*(2), 71–88.

Mueller, N., & Silverman, N. (1989). Peer relations in maltreated children. In D. Cicchetti & V. Carlson (Eds.), *Handbook of child maltreatment* (pp. 529–578). New York: Cambridge University Press.

Ney, P. G., Fung, T., & Wickett, A. R. (1994). The worst combinations of child abuse and neglect. *Child Abuse and Neglect, 18*, 705–714.

Oates, R. K., & Bross, D. C. (1995). What have we learned about treating child physical abuse? A literature review of the last decade. *Child Abuse and Neglect, 19*(4), 463–473.

Oliver, J. E. (1993). Intergenerational transmission of child abuse: Rates, research, and clinical implications. *American Journal of Psychiatry, 150*, 1315–1324.

Otto, M. L. (1990). Treating abusive parents in outpatient settings. *Journal of Offender Counseling, Services, and Rehabilitation, 15*, 57–64.

Peebles-Wilkins, W. (1995). Janie Porter Barrett and the Virginia Industrial School for Colored Girls: Community response to the needs of African American children. *Child Welfare, 74*(1), 143–161.

Pelton, L. (1989). *For reasons of poverty: A critique of the child welfare system in the United States.* New York: Praeger.

Pianta, R., Egeland, B., & Erikson, M. F. (1989). The antecedents of maltreatment: Results of the Mother-Child Interaction Research Project. In D. Cicchetti & V. Carlson (Eds.), *Child maltreatment* (pp. 203-253). New York: Cambridge University Press.

Pribor, E. F., & Dinwiddie, S. H. (1992). Psychiatric correlates of incest in childhood. *American Journal of Psychiatry, 149*, 52–56.

Samantrai, K. (1992). To prevent unnecessary separation of children and families: Public Law 96-272—policy and practice. *Social Work, 37*(4), 295–302.

Schene, P. A. (1998). Past, present, and future roles of child protective services. *The Future of Children, 8*(1), 23–38.

Smith, E. P. (1995). Bring back the orphanages: What policymakers today can learn from the past. *Child Welfare, 74*, 115–142.

Stehno, S. (1982). Differential treatment of minority children. *Social Work, 27*(1), 39–46.

Steward, M. S., Farquhar, L. C., Dicharry, D. C., Glick, D. R., & Martin, P. W. (1986). Group therapy: A treatment of choice for young victims of child abuse. *International Journal of Group Psychotherapy, 36*(2), 261–277.

Taylor, C. G., Norman, D. K., Murphy, J. M., Jellinek, M., Quinn, D., Poitrast, F. G., & Goshko, M. (1991). Diagnosed intellectual and emotional impairment among parents who seriously mistreat their children: Prevalence, type, and outcome in a court sample. *Child Abuse and Neglect, 15*, 389–401.

Toth, S. L., Manly, J. T., & Cicchetti, D. (1992). Child maltreatment and vulnerability to depression. *Development and Psychopathology, 4*, 97–112.

Tyor, P. L., & Zainaldin, J. S. (1979). Asylum and society: An approach to institutional change. *Journal of Social History, 13*, 23–48.

U.S. Advisory Board on Child Abuse and Neglect. (1991). *Creating caring communities: Blueprint for an effective federal policy on child abuse and neglect.* Washington, DC: U.S. Government Printing Office.

Weaver, T. L., & Clum, G. A. (1993). Early family environments and traumatic experiences associated with borderline personality disorder. *Journal of Counseling and Clinical Psychology, 61*, 1068–1075.

Webb, N. B. (1991). *Play therapy with children in crisis.* New York: Guilford.

Wells, K., & Tracy, E. (1996). Reorienting intensive family preservation services in relation to public child welfare practice. *Child Welfare, 75*(6), 667–692.

Wheeler, L. (1983). The orphan trains. *American History Illustrated, 18*, 10–23.

Widom, C. (1989). Does violence beget violence? A critical examination of the literature. *Psychological Bulletin, 106*, 3–28.

CHAPTER 13

Generalist Practice with Gay and Lesbian Clients

Frann S. Anderson

Nichole B. is a part-time MSW student in her second year of a three-year program. Her foundation field placement is with a high school located in a working-class community. In her placement, Nichole provides individual counseling services to teenagers who are having academic and/or social problems in the school. As a school social worker, Nichole is also expected to work with the student's families.

Tom H, a sixteen-year-old junior, dropped by Nichole's office just after the holiday break. Tom appeared nervous and was hesitant to tell Nichole what was on his mind. Finally, he told Nichole a story about a friend who was gay and who was struggling with the decision about coming out. The friend was worried about how his parents would react and about the lack of tolerance for minorities among his peers. Nichole asked Tom to return the next day so they could explore his friend's situation in more detail.

After Tom left, Nichole was uncomfortable about the interaction. She was not sure why. Was it how she had handled his unexpected visit? Did she really understand what Tom was telling her? Was it the seriousness of the decision to come out? Was it her level of comfort with the topic? Was it her feelings of being over her head and not really knowing much about homosexuality or the coming out process? Was it Tom? Was it the topic? Was it her?

As recently as 1973, homosexuality was widely accepted as an Axis I mental illness in the *Diagnostic and Statistical Manual (DSM)* (Maylon, 1981). It was also—and in many cases still is—condemned by many religious groups as an evil perversion. (For information on specific religious groups, see Hellman, Green, Gray, & Williams, 1981; Hetrick & Martin, 1987; Jonsen & Stryker, 1993; Lauritsen, 1993; Panem, 1988; Patton, 1986; Pierce & VanDeVeer, 1988.) Social stigma, vernacular stereotypes and myths, and religious condemnation of homosexuality continue to permeate society (Maylon, 1981). Bigotry and discrimination against gays and lesbians present the generalist social worker with many personal and cultural challenges.

This chapter examines the current cultural roadblocks to providing social work services to gay and lesbian clients. It covers the dynamics of homophobia and heterosexism as they relate to the perpetuation of stereotypes about homosexuals and the way these stereotypes affect the helping relationship. The chapter presents real experiences of gay men, lesbian women, and gay and lesbian youth and explains how to tailor social work practice to meet the special needs of this minority. Macro practice issues related to current civil rights issues are presented and discussed in terms of the responsibilities generalist social workers encounter as advocates for sexual minorities. By the end of the chapter, you should be able to help Nichole

1. Describe the social and psychological ramifications of homophobic and heterosexist attitudes on gay men and lesbian women
2. Identify the major policy issues affecting the gay and lesbian community
3. Understand the complexity of the coming out process for gay and lesbian clients
4. Understand the role of the social worker in helping gay and lesbian clients through the coming-out process
5. Describe the special needs of gay and lesbian teenagers and elderly persons
6. Describe the special needs of children with gay and lesbian parents.

GAYS AND LESBIANS AS A SPECIAL POPULATION

For some time, the gay and lesbian population has been a hidden minority, and little attention has been paid to their needs in the community (Fassinger, 1991). However, gay men and lesbian women living in the United States are becoming more and more visible, and it is likely that more will seek the services of social workers or other mental health practitioners. When working with gay or lesbian clients, it is important to understand the effect of homophobia on their lives. Even more important is the need for the practitioner to understand his or her own attitudes towards gays and lesbians so as not to add to their problems by unconscious homophobic responses (Mackelprang, Ray, & Hernandez-Peck, 1996). If social workers approach the helping relationship with homophobic attitudes, inaccurate beliefs and stereotypes, and limited knowledge about the special needs of their gay and lesbian clients, they run the risk of alienating gay and lesbian clients and intensifying their clients' internalized homophobic response.

Homophobia

Homophobia has been defined as "dread of being in close quarters with homosexuals" (Weinberg, 1972, p. 4), "explicit hostility or prejudice toward gay men and lesbian women" (Herek, 1986, p. 563), and "a negative or fearful reaction to homosexuals" (Neisen, 1990, p. 22). Homophobia has been attributed to people's attempts to deny homosexual feelings in themselves (Maier, 1984) and to the belief that homophobia may "keep men within the boundaries of traditional sex roles" (Neisen, 1990, p. 23). The later belief suggests that all men—gay and straight—are victims of homophobic stereotyping that forces them to conform to particular sex roles.

It was once believed that homophobia was more common among heterosexual men than heterosexual women (Ernulf & Innala, 1987; Millham, San Miguel, & Kellog, 1976; Mosher & O'Grady, 1979; Weinberg, 1972). However, more recent studies suggest that there is no significant gender difference in homophobic responses to homosexuals (Simon, 1995; Van de Ven, 1994; Van de Ven, Bornholt, & Baily, 1996). Large numbers of men and women are homophobic.

The manifestation of homophobia ranges from less destructive acts, such as name-calling (Zastrow & Kirst-Ashman, 1990), to more violent acts, such as assault and murder (Bohn, 1984; Britton, 1990; Clift, 1988; Herek, 1989; Herek & Berrill, 1990; Lance, 1987; Stevenson, 1988). Homophobia permeates our culture and influences not only how heterosexual individuals perceive homosexuals, but also how homosexuals perceive themselves (Neisen, 1990; Neisen, 1993; Sophie, 1987; Zastrow & Kirst-Ashman, 1990). Negative and destructive behaviors directed at homosexuals can result in damaging internalized messages about their self-worth, self-acceptance, and overall value as human beings. Gays and lesbians are susceptible to internalized homophobia: "an internalization of negative attitudes and assumptions . . . expressed by others in the individual's environment, from her immediate friends and family to the institutions of the church, school, and mass media" (Sophie, 1987, pp. 53–54).

Heterosexism

Homophobia is not the only force that leads to internalized, negative messages about sexual orientation. The oppression of sexual minorities is perpetuated by basic societal beliefs that heterosexuals are "better" than homosexuals and that heterosexuality is the only acceptable form of sexual expression (Neisen, 1990; 1993; Spaulding, 1993). The term *heterosexism* refers to the social construct that supports these beliefs and continues to fuel prejudice and discrimination toward sexual minorities.

Neisen likens heterosexism to racism and indicates that the same power structures that support discrimination based on race also support discrimination based on sexual orientation:

> Heterosexism manifests itself in subtle but not necessarily less obvious forms of exclusion or lack of acknowledgment of gay/lesbian/bisexual lifestyles. For example, heterosexism is manifest when individuals refuse to rent to gays/lesbians/bisexuals, when the military discharges or imprisons someone for homosexual behavior or mere suspicion of being homosexual, and when governments prohibit gays and lesbians to legally marry. (1990, p. 25)

Other examples of heterosexism include gay bashing, gay or lesbian teenagers being thrown out of their homes when they reveal their sexual orientation, employers terminating gay and lesbian employees based on their homosexuality, and parents forbidding their gay and lesbian children to bring their partners to family gatherings. Heterosexism is very much a part of the daily life of gay and lesbian individuals.

Women are victimized by heterosexist beliefs that define them "in terms of men, or not at all" (Spaulding, 1993, p. 233). Lesbian women are perceived to be heterosexuals who are unable to have the "right" kind of sexual experience with men (Spaulding, 1993). Heterosexism also defines men according to rigid sex roles. Gay men are perceived to be heterosexual men who are unable to have the

TABLE 13.1. Sexual/Physical Victimization and Heterosexism

Effects of Sexual/Physical Victimization	Effects of Heterosexism
Blame of Self "I deserve to be abused." "It's my own fault."	**Blame of Self** "Maybe gay people are sick and I deserve to be put down, beat up, etc."
Shame/Negative Self-Concept "I'm dirty for participating in the sexual acts." "I'm bad, otherwise I wouldn't have gotten hit." "No one will love me because I'm damaged/used."	**Shame/Negative Self-Concept** "I'm going to hell for being gay." "I'm bad for acting on my homosexual desires." "No one will love me because I'm gay . . . especially my friends and family."
Anger Directed Toward Self "I'm going to kill myself." "I'll drink/do drugs so I can forget what happened." "I'm going to go out and do to someone else what happened to me."	**Anger Directed Toward Self** "I'm going to kill myself." "I'll drink/do drugs to forget about being sexual with someone of the same sex." "I'll drink/do drugs to cover up my thoughts about being gay and to cover up my attraction to other people of the same sex." "I'm going to have as much sex as I can."
Victim Mentality "I feel helpless/powerless." "Other people are in control of my body." "I can't tell anyone what happened." "I don't trust anyone." "I'm going to protect myself by staying alone."	**Victim Mentality** "I feel helpless/powerless. "I can't come out." "I can't be what I am." "There is no one I can tell I'm gay" "I'm not going to let any of the neighbors know I have a lover . . . I'll just say he is my friend."

Source: Adapted from J. H. Neisen, 1993, The Haworth Press.

"right" kind of sexual experience with women. In other words, heterosexism defines the homosexual's love relationship in terms of failure to attract members of the opposite sex. For instance, in the heterosexual construct, lesbian women are believed to be women who hate men, rather than women who love women.

Heterosexism can damage the psyche of the homosexual client. Internalized shame stunts emotional growth and contributes to a devaluing of self (Neisen, 1990). Like other victimized groups, gays and lesbians internalize a multitude of attitudes and beliefs that they incorrectly attribute to their homosexuality, when in fact they are responses to the abusive nature of heterosexism. Table 13.1 illustrates how heterosexism perpetuates the same sense of victimization experienced by victims of sexual and physical abuse.

In later stages of the coming out process, it is helpful for gay and lesbian clients to understand shame as an introject of heterosexism in order to move to more self-affirming behaviors and internalized messages. Table 13.2 illustrates the recovery process for gays and lesbians as it parallels the recovery process for victims of abuse.

When conducting coming-out groups for lesbians, Morrow (1996) dedicates one session to discussing heterosexism and homophobia. She encourages group

TABLE 13.2. The Healing Process from Sexual/Physical Victimization and Heterosexism

Recovery from Sexual/Physical Abuse	Recovery from Heterosexism
Breaking the Silence	**Breaking the Silence**
"I have been abused."	"Mom, I'm gay."
	"Beth, I've really struggled with my sexual feelings, and I think I'm lesbian."
Establishing Perpetrator Responsibility	**Establishing Perpetrator Responsibility**
"I didn't ask to be sexually abused."	"I didn't do anything to be harassed."
"I didn't deserve to be abused."	"I don't deserve to be harassed for being gay . . .
"(Name) abused me."	for being myself."
	"(Name of individual/institution) who abused me because of my homosexuality."
Reclaiming Personal Power	**Reclaiming Personal Power**
"I'm okay."	"I'm okay."
"I am lovable."	"I am lovable."
"I set my own boundaries regarding my sexual	"I am proud to be gay."
behavior/physical space."	"My God loves and accepts me as a lesbian."
"I celebrate myself."	"I decide whom I come out to and how much about my personal life I will share."

Source: Adapted from J. H. Neisen, 1993, The Haworth Press.

members to recall instances of both in their daily lives and to consider the influence of external forces on decisions about coming out. This helps group participants see how societal views about homosexuality directly influence their thoughts, feelings, and behaviors and contribute to the sense of oppression experienced by sexual minorities.

Heterosexism can invade relationships between heterosexual individuals and homosexual individuals even when the heterosexual in the relationship does not consciously embrace the heterosexist construct. The following case example illustrates this point.

What Did I Say?

As a second-year MSW student, Melissa T. was "out" to most of the faculty and students at her school. It was common knowledge that Melissa and her partner of ten years were lesbian mothers raising their seven-year-old daughter together and struggling openly with the challenges facing gays and lesbians in the late 1990s.

When Melissa began her second year practice class, the students took turns introducing themselves and sharing important facts about themselves. Melissa once again shared her sexual minority status and her status as a lesbian mother. The instructor, Mr. S., was a licensed social worker who taught at the school as an adjunct faculty member. As a part-time faculty member, Mr. S. spent little time on campus and knew very few students. Mr. S. was impressed by Melissa's candor. He thanked her for being so open about her minority status and noted that she would add a new dimension to class discussions about macro practice and social work with oppressed groups. Mr. S. and Melissa talked about the struggles facing gays and lesbians and about the special challenges to same-sex families as the media drew more attention to gay and lesbian parenting.

Anyone eavesdropping on the conversation would have thought Mr. S. was open and accepting of gay and lesbian parents—until his covert heterosexist beliefs emerged. "Tell me, Melissa," Mr. S. inquired, "what does your daughter's father think about your being lesbian?" To the heterosexual listener, this may have seemed like an innocent question. But to a lesbian mother whose child was conceived by donor insemination, the question reeked of heterosexism.

Mr. S.'s belief that all children are conceived through heterosexual sex and that all families are composed of a mother and father is an example of how heterosexism can make itself known even when supportive heterosexual allies are unaware of their own heterosexist beliefs.

It is a common myth that, in gay and lesbian relationships, one member of the couple chooses a masculine, dominant role and the other a feminine, submissive role. While this may be true of some gay and lesbian couples, it is not the norm for the majority (Jay & Young, 1979; Peplau, 1981). Not all gay men behave in an effeminate manner (the *queen* or *swish*), and not all lesbian women behave in a masculine manner (the *butch* or *dyke*). While a small number of gay men and lesbian women identify strongly with the opposite sex and dress accordingly, the majority of gay and lesbian individuals do not differ in dress from their heterosexual counterparts (Zastrow & Kirst-Ashman, 1990).

To better equip social work students to work with clients of various sexual orientations, the Council on Social Work Education (CSWE) included sexual minorities in their 1993 curriculum policy statement, mandating inclusion of educational material on diverse populations. With the inclusion of educational content on gays and lesbians in social work curricula, CSWE addressed sexual discrimination, oppression, and homophobia within institutions of social work education (Mackelprang, Ray, & Hernandez-Peck, 1996).

Policy Issues

The civil rights of sexual minorities are regularly violated in the areas of housing, employment, and education. Homosexuals are legally prohibited from marrying their life partners. On the federal level, civil rights laws do not provide for the fair treatment of sexual minorities. State civil rights laws are being fought for, one right at a time. Opponents attempt to overturn laws that protect the civil rights of sexual minorities as soon as they are passed. While the civil rights of sexual minorities are better protected than in the past, the political arena remains a place of hostility and discouragement for gay men, lesbians, and their families.

Gay men and lesbian women take responsibility for most of the organizing and political activism on behalf of sexual minorities. But the rights of minorities will not be realized until the majority seeks justice for oppressed groups as well. Social workers can lobby for civil rights issues when they are being voted on in state legislatures. Generalist social workers must remain up to date on legislative proceedings as they occur in their state and on the federal level. This is true for all legislative activity that affects disenfranchised populations.

Many of the issues that prevent sexual minorities from realizing civil rights are directly related to homophobia and heterosexist ideologies. Educating heterosexual individuals about the real lives of gay men and lesbian women can diminish homophobic attitudes and broaden the heterosexual viewpoint to include same-gender partnership. Since social workers are found in diverse settings, the opportunity to educate diverse groups of people about sexual minorities is readily available. It is not only important to speak up for the rights of gay men and lesbians, it is equally important to look for opportunities to educate clients, coworkers, and others about homophobia and heterosexism. The more that heterosexual individuals receive accurate information about sexual minorities, the more they will support gay and lesbian rights (Bohan, 1997). Social workers can fill the important role of educator in addressing discrimination against sexual minorities.

Many people continue to reject sexual minorities on the basis of religious convictions. Many religious denominations are struggling with the issue of homosexuality and deciding whether and how to incorporate or oppose gays and lesbians in their church families. It is a difficult issue with no easy answers. However, the issue of civil rights for sexual minorities is about justice for all. Religious diversity needs to be respected and revered, but civil rights issues cannot be determined according to the dogma of one particular denomination or religious group.

MICRO PRACTICE ISSUES

Traditionally, research on homosexuality has been conducted in large part with gay men rather than lesbian women, and the findings were generalized to lesbian women (de Monteflores & Schultz, 1978; Kaplan, 1974; Klein & Wolf, 1985; Leiblum & Rosen, 1989; Masters & Johnson, 1970; Minton & McDonald, 1983/1984). However, while gay men and lesbian women have many issues in common, gay men's experiences are very different from those of lesbian women (Behrendt & George, 1995; Buhrke, 1989; Cox & Gallois, 1996; de Monteflores & Schultz, 1978; Lipton, 1996).

The Gay Male Experience

Society's stereotype of men as strong, unemotional, and competitive has led gay men to feel confusion and inner turmoil when they recognize that they are attracted to other men (Behrendt & George, 1995; Green, 1987; Herek, 1986; Zilbergeld, 1992). Men cannot show feminine traits lest they be considered "sissies." Although it can be endearing for a girl to be called a "tomboy," a sissy is ostracized and degraded (Green, 1987). Boys in our culture carry a greater burden to be "manly" than do girls to be "womanly," regardless of sexual orientation.

Since most gay men have been socialized in a heterosexist society, they too grow up believing in stereotypical gender roles. Gay men enter adulthood believing that being a man is directly related to mastering masculine behaviors (competition, emotional detachment, pursuit of female sex partners), rejecting feminine behaviors (being tender, seeking emotional support from others, submission to men), and, most importantly, never acknowledging same-sex feelings or attractions (Behrendt & George, 1995; Herek, 1986; MacDonald, 1976; Morin & Garfinkle, 1978; Nungesser, 1983). The gay male who is beginning to become aware of his same-sex attraction becomes anxious about his identity as a man. Gay men may also feel confused about who initiates relationships and sex (men are expected to be in control), what it means when one man allows another to initiate contact (only women are submissive), and how a relationship can thrive when both partners are expected to be emotionally distant (Behrendt & George, 1995). This affects not only gay male relationships but also how gay men perceive themselves. As products of a heterosexist society, many gay men question their value and, in turn, experience shame and guilt.

HIV/AIDS.   The social stigmatization of homosexuality has been firmly in place for many years. Attacks on gay men, however, have never been as blatant or malicious as they became in the early 1980s with the AIDS epidemic and its initial connection to the gay community. It sparked an unnerving response from the government and from religious and right-wing political groups whose insistence that AIDS was unique to homosexuals set back research and treatment by ten years (Brandt, 1988; Jonsen & Stryker, 1993; Lauritsen, 1993; Panem, 1988; Patton, 1986; Peck & Bezold, 1992; Pierce & VanDeVeer, 1988; Shilts, 1987). The portrayal of AIDS as a disease contracted through immoral acts by immoral individuals strengthened bigotry and prejudice against gays (Shilts, 1987; Stine, 1993; Zastrow & Kirst-Ashman, 1990).

Attitudes about homosexuality are correlated with attitudes about AIDS (Price & Hsu, 1992). Public policy formation in the 1980s was directly influenced by the perception of gays as AIDS carriers and by calls for mandatory testing and quarantining of gays (Pierce & VanDeVeer, 1988). Because of the focus on AIDS as a gay man's disease, mental health programs for gay men have focused on AIDS rather than on mental health issues and other issues associated with their sexual orientation (Lipton, 1996).

Fear of AIDS and HIV infection are common concerns of gay men seeking counseling related to their homosexuality (Harowski, 1988; Lipton, 1996). Harowski coined the term "worried well" to describe members of the gay male community who are not infected with the HIV virus but have "increased general anxiety, some decrease in sexual desire, and over-concern with health and bodily functioning" (1988, p. 303).

Generalist social workers are likely to come in contact with gay men who are living with AIDS and who have a host of other problems or concerns:

> Any social worker who works with a gay or lesbian client needs to be aware of the ramifications and emotional impacts AIDS has had . . . These include not only serious illness, but poverty when their resources have been depleted, social isolation, insurance and public assistance problems, and problems getting medication. (Zastrow & Kirst-Ashman, 1990, p. 559)

To effectively advocate for the gay man with AIDS, it is important to know what services are available and how to obtain them. The social service system and medical system can be cumbersome so it is necessary to be prepared to help clients navigate these systems when their energy and spirits are depleted.

Most adult gay males have personally experienced the effect of AIDS through the loss of a partner, lover, or friend. Many others are living with HIV or AIDS themselves or are offering support to partners, lovers, or friends who are HIV positive or living with AIDS. When young heterosexual adults are beginning relationships, careers, and families, most gay and lesbian adults have buried the young members of their community who have fallen to AIDS. People often experience death for the first time when elderly members of the family die (Germain, 1991), but AIDS has forced gay men to deal with the loss of loved ones much earlier in their lives than is normally expected. It is likely that issues of loss and grief will need to be addressed in the helping relationship with gay men.

Gay Men as Fathers.   In the heterosexual world, few people think of gay men as fathers. However, many gay men come to terms with their sexual orientation only after entering into a heterosexual relationship and fathering children. Approximately 25 percent or more of gay men have been heterosexually married (Dunne, 1988).

Gay men marry for many reasons. Some men do not acknowledge their same-sex attractions until after engaging in a heterosexual relationship. Others marry to fit in and avoid the social ostracism associated with being gay. Some hope their same-sex attraction will disappear once they engage in a heterosexual marriage. Others desire a family and want to father children (Coleman, 1981/1982; McDonald & Steinhorn, 1990).

Gay men perceive their sexual orientation as potentially harmful to their children and as having a potentially negative influence on the children's own development of sexual identity (Coleman, 1981/1982; Dunne, 1988; McDonald & Steinhorn, 1990). Because of this, gay men are more likely than lesbian women to keep their sexual orientation a secret from their children. Only 46 percent of gay fathers revealed their homosexuality to their children, compared to 94 percent of lesbian mothers (Wyers, 1987). This statistic suggests that gay fathers are greatly affected by internalized homophobia and the shame imposed by heterosexist beliefs.

Other gay fathers keep their orientation secret in order to gain custody and visitation rights after a divorce. The judicial system tends to grant custody rights to heterosexual parents over gay parents even when there is evidence that the heterosexual parent may not be the best caretaker (Germain, 1991).

While the majority of gay fathers have children in heterosexual relationships, many are finding other ways to become parents. Gay men become fathers through adoption and foster parenting. Female friends or a partner's female family members have become impregnated with their sperm and have carried their biological children. Others have fathered children with lesbian women who share the responsibilities of parenting much like heterosexual couples who live apart. As the number of gay fathers increases, social workers will need to develop services and interventions that address the needs of families headed by gay men.

The Lesbian Experience

Although gay men and lesbian women experience the same kinds of prejudice and discrimination by virtue of their sexual minority status, lesbian women must deal with additional societal pressures (Morgan, 1997; Simon, 1995; Smalley, 1988; Spaulding, 1993). Homosexual women are forced by a heterosexist society to grapple not only with their status as a sexual minority, but also with their status as women in a male-dominated society (Morgan, 1997; Riddle & Sang, 1978; Spaulding, 1993).

Just as boys are socialized to engage in male-related behaviors, so too are girls socialized to engage in female behaviors. These gender roles generally begin to take shape during childhood (Riddle & Sang, 1978). When boys are learning to be competitive and emotionally distant, girls are learning to be sensitive, nurturing, supportive, and noncompetitive. Girls also learn that these traits rank them as subordinate, ineffectual, and less valued than males (Herek, 1986; Morgan, 1997; Riddle & Sang, 1978; Spaulding, 1993).

Like gay men, lesbians experience rejection, self-loathing, anxiety, worry, shame, and ostracism related to their status as homosexuals. However, these issues tend to be entangled with equally damaging messages women receive about being female. Lesbians must deal with sexual harassment and unwanted sexual advances by men who believe that lesbians are waiting for men to "turn them straight." Gay men do not experience this aspect of heterosexism as frequently as lesbians do. It puts lesbians at risk for both physical and sexual violence, while gay men tend to be victims of physical violence only (Spaulding, 1993).

Women face discrimination in employment and are less likely than men to be granted career advancement. Heterosexual women benefit from their relationships with male spouses who receive financial and career advances with regularity. Because both partners in a lesbian relationship are likely to face discrimination on the job, lesbians tend to be disadvantaged financially compared to their gay male and heterosexual peers (Riddle & Sang, 1978). Further, the social pressures placed on lesbians to socialize with business acquaintances puts them at a disadvantage when they feel that they must hide their sexual orientation and find male escorts to attend business functions.

While gay men struggle to learn ways to be emotionally close, lesbian relationships are often emotionally intense because both partners have been socialized to be sensitive, nurturing caretakers. Lesbians encounter problems when a relationship becomes intensely close (Roth, 1985). Overcloseness, or "fusion," interferes with the couple's ability to develop separate senses of self and heightens the amount of stress the couple experiences. Typical behaviors include the following:

- "one partner may begin to distance in an effort to establish separateness, or each partner may distance in an alternating fashion;
- "conflicts may become open and intense possibly leading to violence;
- "one of the partners may involve a third element to reduce the intensity (a child, a romantic involvement); and
- "the couple may engage in repeated cycles of fusion and unrelatedness." (Roth, 1985, p. 288)

To meet the needs of lesbian women, it is important to understand the realities of heterosexist oppression. Lesbian couples often need help sorting through relationship issues and discovering healthy ways to be in a relationship. The notion that emotional intensity in a lesbian couple is inherently pathological must be put aside. The helping process entails educating lesbian partners about boundaries, autonomy, and healthy relationship formation (Roth, 1985; Smalley, 1988).

It is also important to offer affirmation to the lesbian couple and support the relationship as one that has been able to endure despite many obstacles, including the weight of oppression. Many heterosexual relationships would have difficulty withstanding the civil injustices and prejudices lesbian couples face on a daily basis. The strengths of such a union should be respected, acknowledged, and regarded as a positive aspect of the relationship.

Because many lesbian women have been victimized by men, it is important to understand the dynamics of abuse and the complicated nature of being twice victimized—as a female, and as a sexual minority. When addressing victimization with lesbian women, do not make the mistake of attempting to find the cause of a lesbian's attraction to women (Riddle & Sang, 1978). This can be tempting when a lesbian client is a survivor of sexual abuse. Lesbian identity development needs to be understood as separate from abuse experiences. Affirm a lesbian client's identity as a gay woman with a history of trauma, not as a woman who is gay because of a history of trauma.

HIV/AIDS. During the early years of the AIDS epidemic, the U.S. government turned a deaf ear to doctors who were treating gay men with AIDS, and there was a widespread belief that gay men deserved to die a horrid death because of their "immoral lifestyle" (Lauritsen, 1993; Patton, 1986; Shilts, 1987; Stine, 1993; Zastrow & Kirst-Ashman, 1990). When the government finally did respond, it was in the form of policy debates about mandatory testing, quarantining, tattooing, and other methods of branding persons suspected of having AIDS. Policies were being developed with homosexuals in mind, sometimes as a means of singling gays and lesbians out in visible ways (Pierce & VanDeVeer, 1988; Shilts, 1987). As a result, discrimination toward homosexuals—gay men and lesbians—was being condoned and supported by the government, some of whose members were content to let the homosexual population die off from this dreadful illness.

The general assumption in the U.S. was that being homosexual made an individual susceptible to AIDS. Lesbians were included in attempts to limit the activities of homosexuals, using AIDS as the rationale for differential treatment. Lesbian women were not contracting the disease—a fact that should have dispelled the idea that being homosexual was a precursor to becoming infected with the AIDS virus. Nevertheless, discrimination against homosexuals intensified, and lesbian women bore the burden of hate directed toward all gays.

Before the AIDS crisis, gay men and lesbian women rarely socialized. Believing the heterosexist myths about gay men and women, lesbians assumed that gay men hated women, and gay men assumed that lesbians hated men. The two groups had little or no interest in each other. But by 1980, it was clear that the government had no interest in the health crisis that was sweeping through urban gay communities. Homosexuals had no other choice but to tend to gay AIDS patients themselves. Gay and lesbian doctors, nurses, and social workers began to band together to offer services on a volunteer basis, since federal monies were being withheld. Grassroots organizations formed to offer gay men dying of AIDS a safe place to meet and receive the few available services. Lesbian women nursed dying gay men and offered companionship and support to those who were HIV-positive. In the midst of death, discrimination, and homophobic panic, lesbian women and gay men embraced each other as family.

Like gay men, lesbian women have had to deal with loss and grief as they nursed and buried young friends dying of the disease. With great compassion, lesbian women working with gay men established comprehensive social services programs for people living with AIDS. Acknowledgment of their contribution is long overdue.

Lesbian-Headed Families.   Lesbian women become parents in various ways. Like gay fathers, a small number of women marry and have children within the context of a heterosexual relationship (Kirkpatrick, 1988). Other lesbian women adopt children or become foster mothers. More and more lesbian women are turning to donor insemination to conceive and give birth to their own biological children. Because women tend to win custody of their children more frequently than men, some lesbian women become mothers when they meet and commit to a partner who is rearing children (Pies, 1988).

Perhaps the biggest issue facing lesbian mothers is the homophobic belief that lesbians are unfit mothers and that a female-headed household will damage the child (Faria, 1994; Fraser, Fish, & Mackenzie, 1995; Hare, 1994; Levy, 1992; Zastrow & Kirst-Ashman, 1990). Because of this stigma, some lesbian mothers may attempt to pass as heterosexual to avoid losing a job or housing (Zastrow & Kirst-Ashman, 1990). Women who have had children in heterosexual relationships may hide their sexual orientation because they fear they will lose custody of their children if it is discovered that they are lesbian. Lesbian mothers who are open about their sexual orientation tend to form supportive relationships with other gay-headed or lesbian-headed families, or gay-friendly heterosexual couples. Thus, they find support within their own community (Levy, 1992; Pies, 1988).

Many lesbian women lack the traditional support systems that are available to heterosexual women, and those who hide their sexual orientation to protect their families may be adding further stress to internal family functioning as the weight of the secret takes its toll (Hare, 1994). Lesbian women obtain less support from their birth families than heterosexual women (Levy, 1992). Consequently, they create support systems with other lesbian mothers or lesbian friends to help cope with the stresses of parenting.

When lesbian mothers decide to parent together, complicated issues can arise. In many states, only one mother can claim legal custody of a child. The nonbiological mother may participate equally in the daily care of the child, but cannot legally claim the child as her own. Society may not acknowledge the nonbiological mother as a parent and therefore withholds recognition (Pies, 1988). The following case example illustrates how nonbiological mothers are disregarded by social systems.

I'm Her Parent, Too!

Mary A. and Emily L. have been together as a couple for eight years. Early in their relationship, they decided they wanted to have children. Since Emily had medical problems that prohibited her from carrying a child, Mary became pregnant through anonymous donor insemination and bore two children. When their daughter was four and their son two, Emily decided to become a "stay-at-home mom" so that the couple could save on day-care expenses. Since the children called Emily "Mama," Emily's status as their mother was never questioned.

When Mary and Emily's daughter, Alexis, was hit by a car and rushed to the hospital, Emily sat with her in the ambulance and held her hand. At the hospital, the medical team discovered that Alexis's wrist and hand were fractured. Halfway through the examination, a nurse in the emergency room noticed that Emily's last name was different than Alexis's. She asked Emily why the two did not share the same name. Without giving it much thought, Emily explained that she was Alexis's nonbiological mother and that her partner was Alexis's birth mother. The hospital staff then questioned Emily's authority to give permission to treat Alexis and insisted that she contact Mary before they would proceed. Because Alexis's injuries were not life-threatening, the hospital staff would not provide further treatment until Mary gave legal consent to give Alexis something to relieve the pain. Since Emily had contacted Mary immediately when Alexis had been injured, Mary was on her way to the hospital and could not be reached. Emily helplessly held the little girl's hand while Alexis pleaded with her to stop the pain. They waited for thirty agonizing minutes for Mary to arrive at the hospital.

This is one example of how nonbiological lesbian mothers are disregarded by various systems in society. Other institutions that need to serve nonbiological mothers and their children include schools, churches, scout troops, and sports teams. Disregard can add more stress to emotionally overburdened relationships and can affect the couple's relationship with each other and their children.

DEVELOPING HELPING RELATIONSHIPS WITH GAY AND LESBIAN CLIENTS

The term *coming out,* or *coming out of the closet,* describes the process in which gay men and lesbian women acknowledge and come to terms with their sexual orientation. The process has been described in different ways (Coleman, 1981/1982; de Monteflores & Schultz, 1978; Hanley-Hackenbruck, 1989; McDonald & Steinhorn, 1990; Morrow, 1996; Moses & Hawkins, 1982; Sophie, 1986), but it has three specific phases: the awareness phase, the acceptance phase, and the integration phase.

During the awareness phase, gay and lesbian individuals begin to acknowledge for the first time that they are experiencing homosexual feelings. These feelings may be as simple as a thought or a fantasy (Coleman, 1981/1982). During this stage, homosexual individuals begin to realize that there is something different about them compared to the heterosexual individuals they identified with (Cass, 1979). This first realization of same-sex attraction or this awareness of difference often manifests itself as confusion, isolation, and anxiety as the gay or lesbian person becomes consciously aware that his or her feelings are in direct conflict with prevailing societal expectations.

During the acceptance phase of coming out, individuals begin to grapple with their identity as gay or lesbian people. *Acceptance* means the person's acceptance of sexual orientation, not that the person becomes settled with this identity. In this phase, homosexual individuals begin to explore their feelings by experimenting with same-sex relationships (Coleman, 1981/1982) or associating with other gay and lesbian individuals or groups. The person begins to identify himself or herself as gay or lesbian rather than heterosexual (Moses & Hawkins, 1982). The person may also disclose sexual minority status to family members and friends. This can be the most difficult phase in the coming out process. The homosexual person will generally experience the most severe attacks to self-esteem and self-identity as others voice their disdain of gays and lesbians in direct ways (de Monteflores & Schultz, 1978). Because of rejection, persons in this phase may oscillate between heterosexual and homosexual relationships as they attempt to resolve their own internalized homophobia and heterosexism (Moses & Hawkins, 1982).

In the integration phase of coming out, gay or lesbian individuals begin to integrate more positive beliefs about themselves and embrace their homosexuality (Cass, 1979; Coleman, 1982; de Monteflores & Schultz, 1978; Hanley-Hackenbruck, 1988; Moses & Hawkins, 1982). They are able to acknowledge their status as a sexual minority and experience a sense of pride and connectedness to the gay and lesbian community. Once an individual has entered the integration stage, she or he may be more likely to publicly acknowledge her or his status as a lesbian woman or gay man (Moses & Hawkins, 1982) and no longer feels compelled to keep feelings and relationships a secret.

These phases may seem fairly straightforwarded and appear to progress in a linear fashion. However, the process of coming out is fraught with complicated issues that must be negotiated by gay and lesbian persons and those engaged in a helping relationship with them. Not every gay and lesbian person will come out of the closet. Many people become stuck in the earlier stage of awareness and invest their energies in denial of their same-sex attractions. Others may acknowledge their status as gay men or lesbian women during the acceptance stage, but continue to live double lives, posing as heterosexuals in public and engaging in same-sex relationships in private. A gay or lesbian parent may choose to remain in the closet in order to protect his or her rights to children. Because of the social stigma that is still associated with homosexuality, coming out is not always a safe choice, depending on family, employment, and community circumstances.

There has been a great deal of debate about the necessity of coming out. One camp supports an individual's right to choose whether to come out of the closet, citing discrimination and victimization as real concerns. The other camp takes the position that living in secrecy and denying one's true self can be psychologically damaging (Zastrow & Kirst-Ashman, 1990). Gay and lesbian clients may seek professional help to address the decision to come out. There are no easy answers. Information on the positive and negative aspects will help gay and lesbian clients weigh the advantages and disadvantages within the context of their own lives and make choices that best support their personal development.

While the successful integration of a gay or lesbian identity may seem like the final stage of the coming-out process, even after successful integration occurs, coming out is a life-long process. Gay and lesbian people who are out are faced with decisions about whether to disclose their sexual minority status on a daily basis. Each new situation—meeting new employers, coworkers, neighbors, business associates, classmates, or teachers—means making another decision about whether to come out.

The decision is complicated by the fact that the federal government does not offer legal protections to sexual minorities. Discrimination against gay men and lesbians is legal and widely practiced. This is a unique stress that heterosexual individuals do not experience. Do not underestimate the effect of discrimination on homosexual clients.

The helping process for gay men and lesbian women should incorporate work around externalizing introjected shame and guilt. In order for the work to be beneficial, you need to be aware of your own heterosexist beliefs and remain open to accepting the diverse experiences of gay men and lesbians without imposing personal opinions (Lipton, 1996).

Lesbian mothers need support with coming out issues addressing both internalized and societal homophobia and self-esteem (Levy, 1992). Support for lesbian mothers and gay fathers must extend beyond emotional support. To fully meet the needs of homosexual parents, you need to understand such legal issues as power of attorney, joint custody when there are minor children, and partnership agreements.

Gay and Lesbian Adolescents

Adolescence can be a trying time. Developmentally, it is a period of separation and individuation from the family and establishment of membership and connection with peer groups (Newman & Newman, 1995). Because of the conflict between individuality and group membership, teens ask themselves "who am I?" and "where do I fit in?" A teen who answers the first question "gay or lesbian" soon discovers that the answer to the second question is "nowhere."

Gay and lesbian teens are victims of the same homophobic and heterosexist biases as their adult counterparts. The fragile nature of the adolescent ego makes adolescent children even more vulnerable to stigmatization. The cultural ethos that perpetuates hate toward same-sex love also erodes the adolescent's main source of support, role modeling, and sense of identity, the family (Cates, 1987; Herdt & Boxer, 1993; Hetrick & Martin, 1987; Maylon, 1981; Morrow, 1993; Saltzburg, 1996; Telljohann & Price, 1993, Unks, 1995). Indoctrinated into heterosexist, stigmatizing beliefs about homosexuality, the parents of gay and lesbian youth often feel the same fear, hate, and disgust as the general culture (Telljohann & Price, 1993).

Gay and lesbian youth face social discrimination as they attempt to assimilate themselves into a minority group that is foreign even to their parents. However, homosexual youth must face the stark reality that their families cannot offer the same support or guidance as parents of other minority children because they do not understand the experience of being homosexual. This dynamic often intensifies the homophobic response that the gay and lesbian teen experiences in the family.

A common coping strategy is for the family to reject the gay or lesbian child's sexuality and, very often, the child as well. This can make existence for a gay or lesbian adolescent uncomfortable at best, and violent and abusive at worse (Herdt & Boxer, 1993; Kruks, 1991; Malyon, 1981; Telljohann & Price, 1993; Unks, 1995). The gay or lesbian teen may be faced with a decision about whether to remain in a hostile family environment or leave home for a life on the streets.

It is estimated that gay and lesbian youth make up approximately one-quarter of all homeless youth in the United States (Unks, 1995). Male gay children are at greater risk for being violently thrown out of their homes, while lesbian children are more likely to suffer physical, verbal, and sexual abuse at home (Hetrick & Martin, 1987). Homelessness and victimization related to their sexual orientation put gay and lesbian youth at greater risk for drug and alcohol dependence (Seattle Commission on Children and Youth, 1998). Substance abuse is a coping strategy gay and lesbian youth use to deal with feelings about being rejected by family and feelings about their own homosexuality (Hetrick & Martin, 1987; Seattle Commission on Children & Youth, 1988).

The school setting plays a pivotal role in adolescent development. Within the context of peer relationships, teens experience the social pressures of conforming to societal norms. Since adolescence is a time of group identification, the gay and lesbian teen experiences great stress related to rejection by peers and the education system as a whole. Many gay and lesbian teens drop out of school as a means of coping with homophobic harassment and violence directed toward them by peers (Morrow, 1993). Educational systems do little to address the harassment of homosexual youth. The schools are not a source of support for gay and lesbian students (Morrow, 1993). Burdened by the social stigma of being homosexual, many gay and lesbian youth take their own lives before they reach adulthood. The Department of Health and Human Services estimated that one-third of all successful teen suicides are committed by gay or lesbian youth (Unks, 1995).

When working with family members of gay and lesbian youth, understand that when a child chooses to come out of the closet, the family often goes into the closet. Saltzburg (1996) has had success working with the families of gay and lesbian youth in family therapy interventions. She has found that helping parents know and embrace the total identity of their homosexual adolescent can help the parents accept their gay and lesbian teen. Challenging stereotypes about gays and lesbians and teaching parents of gay and lesbian teens about the positive aspects of being gay will ensure parental involvement in their children's lives into adulthood.

An important function of social work practice is "active advocacy and intervention on behalf of gay and lesbian adolescents" (Morrow, 1993, p. 659). Social workers can play a key role in introducing support groups for gay and lesbian teens and their families. Such youth groups as Project 10 (Uribe, 1995), Gay/Straight Alliance (Blumenfeld, 1995), and OutRight! (Singerline, 1995) offer supportive and safe environments for gay and lesbian youth and their families. The group format can also be used to educate heterosexual youth about homosexuality as a means of addressing homophobia and dispelling the myths that stigmatize gay and lesbian youth.

Gay and lesbian teens need healthy role models to help acclimate them to the gay and lesbian community and validate their identities as sexual minorities. Heterosexual parents usually cannot provide this type of support. Therefore, it is important for gay and lesbian adults to offer guidance to the children in their community. Social workers can ask gay and lesbian adults to act as mentors to homosexual youth and their families. By directly addressing the isolation that gay and lesbian youth experience because of their sexual minority status, Social workers can help gay and lesbian teens feel less hopeless and preclude their acting out their despair in self-destructive ways.

Gay and Lesbian Elders

Research about elderly gays and lesbians is limited and is for the most part dominated by studies of gay males (Friend, 1988). These studies show that heterosexism continues to adversely affect gay men and lesbian women during the later stages of the life-cycle (Friend, 1988).

Because homosexual partners do not enjoy the legal protections of marriage, many gay and lesbian elders find themselves left out of important decision making on behalf of a sick or dying partner (Berger, 1982a, 1982b). Grief over the loss of a spouse is often compounded by feelings of anger about being left out of important decisions about medical treatment and the estates of partners (Friend, 1988). A will may be called into question by the deceased partner's family, jeopardizing the financial security of the surviving partner who may have owned property jointly with the spouse or established a joint bank account during their lives together. A heterosexual spouse rarely faces these problems and inherits the estate and holds onto the possessions that were accumulated through the years.

Older lesbians and gay men are a diverse group with diverse lifestyles (McDonald & Steinhorn, 1990). Some are parents or grandparents; some live in committed relationships with life partners; and some remain single. Many older gay men and lesbian women are better equipped to deal with the stigma and problems of aging because they have dealt with the stigma and problems of being homosexual (Friend, 1988; Moses & Hawkins, 1982; McDonald & Steinhorn, 1990):

> Older gays and lesbians have been forced to look to their own resources as an individual; this is not true for older heterosexuals who have most likely been able to look to their families of origin and their families of procreation for the support they need. When that support is lost to them, heterosexuals often do not have a supportive friendship network to fall back on, as lesbians and gay men do. Lesbians and gay men, who have not tended to form traditional family groups, have most often had to learn how to depend on themselves. This is an important attribute that is not always developed in our society, even though it may be given lip service. (McDonald & Steinhorn, 1990, p. 110)

In other words, heterosexual women have learned to rely on their husbands and families for a great deal of financial and emotional support and often find themselves in financial crisis when they are widowed or divorced and feel displaced when their children leave home. This is not true for older lesbians, who have most likely been on their own since coming out. Many heterosexual men have spent their lives being cared for by women, while their gay counterparts have spent most of their lives tending to their own needs—cooking, cleaning, doing laundry, shopping, and making social arrangements.

Older lesbians and gay men face the same life-cycle issues as older heterosexuals—financial security, health, loss of friends and spouses, and acceptance (Germain, 1991). Because of the coping styles they were required to develop as sexual minorities, older lesbians and gay men seem to be better equipped to address old age. They continue to enjoy many of the same activities they participated in as younger men and women (Moses & Hawkins, 1982). In working with older lesbians and gay men, remember that life-cycle issues related to the loss of a spouse and financial security may be of greater concern to clients than the stigma of aging. Be careful to not impose your beliefs about ageism on older lesbians and gay men, but rather support the strengths that these individuals bring to the elderly community.

Children of Gays and Lesbians

Heterosexual society has three fears about gay men and lesbians raising children:

1. That children raised in same-sex households will be sexually abused by their homosexual parent or their parent's partner
2. That the children of gay men and lesbians will be coaxed into a same-sex sexual orientation by their fathers or mothers
3. That children of gay men and lesbians will be ostracized and humiliated by peers because of their parent's sexual orientation and therefore are likely to be psychologically damaged (Germain, 1991).

The myth that homosexuals are child molesters continues to be perpetuated by society. While a small percentage of child molesters are homosexual, 80 percent to 97 percent of adults who sexually abuse children are heterosexual men who prey on young girls (Moses & Hawkins, 1982; Newton, 1978). There is no support for the notion that the children of gay men and lesbians are more likely than the children of heterosexual parents to be molested by their parents.

It is also a myth that the children of gay men and lesbians will be coaxed into a same-sex orientation by their fathers or mothers. If it were true that parents determined their children's sexual orientation, all children raised in heterosexual households would be heterosexual. We know it is not true because the majority of gay men and lesbians were raised in heterosexual families and nonetheless grew up to be gay men and lesbians (Golombok, Spence & Rutter, 1983; Moses & Hawkins, 1982; Pies, 1988; Tasker & Golombok, 1995). The children of lesbians and gay men are no more likely to be gay or lesbian than the children of heterosexuals. It is interesting to note that children raised in gay and lesbian households who self-identify as gay or lesbian tend to make a better adjustment to their sexual minority status as teens or young adults. Gay and lesbian children raised in heterosexual households tend to keep their sexual orientation a secret longer and do not act on their feelings until adulthood (Tasker & Golombok, 1995).

The third fear, that children of gay men and lesbians will be ostracized and humiliated by peers and are more likely to be psychologically damaged, also turns out to be a myth. Children belonging to other minority groups, such as those with handicapped parents and those from other nontraditional family units, are also ostracized by peers. They find ways to cope with the unique aspects of their family, and there is no reason to expect that the children of gay men and lesbians will not do the same (Moses & Hawkins, 1982). Many children from lesbian households have been teased by peers and have not experienced this teasing as any different from, say, being teased about wearing glasses (Tasker & Golombok, 1995).

As children enter adolescence, they become less open about their parents' sexual orientation and may even feel embarrassed by it (Kirkpatrick, 1988; Lewis, 1990; McDonald & Steinhorn, 1990). However, lesbian mothers have been able to help their children see themselves as separate from their parents and as having a sexual orientation of their own by allowing the children to express their anger and confusion about their parent's sexual orientation. When the children externalized their feelings about having a lesbian mother, they became more accepting of their mother's sexual orientation (Lewis, 1990). It is important to note that studies have been conducted with children conceived within heterosexual relationships whose parents struggled with their own homosexuality. Since there are no studies on children who have been raised from birth by gay men or lesbian women, these findings cannot be generalized to all children of gay men and lesbian women.

In school settings, the children of gay and lesbian parents go virtually unnoticed. Because of the general assumption that all children come from heterosexual relationships, children from same-sex families seem invisible when units on family issues are presented. It must be stressful for the children of gay men and lesbians to spend their school years never having their unique and special families acknowledged. Nonetheless, children from same-sex households tend to be as well-adjusted as children from heterosexual households (Hare, 1994; Kirkpatrick, 1988; Levy, 1992; McDonald & Steinhorn, 1990; Pies, 1988; Tasker & Golombok, 1995). This suggests that children of gay men and lesbians receive support and love from their families to help them negotiate larger heterosexist institutions such as schools.

Do not assume that the problems bringing the children of gay and lesbian parents to treatment are related to their parent's sexual orientation (Hare, 1994). Adults working in educational systems should acknowledge the partners of the children's parents as adults living within the home and carrying the same responsibility for the children as biological parents. This will strengthen the child's sense of family and lessen the burden of having to keep a parent's relationship with a partner a secret.

The best way for social workers to help gay men, lesbians, and their children adjust in a heterosexual world is to make a commitment to educate the general public on issues related to homosexuality (Levy, 1992). When homophobia is diminished in society, gay men and lesbian parents can spend more of their time and energy tending to the needs of their children. This is the best support any family can receive.

SUMMARY

The gay and lesbian population in the United States is much less a hidden minority than in the past. Gay men and lesbian women are becoming more visible, and it is likely that more will seek the services of social workers or other mental health practitioners. If social workers approach the helping relationship with homophobic attitudes, inaccurate beliefs and stereotypes, and limited knowledge about the special needs of gay and lesbian clients, they run the risk of alienating their clients and intensifying their clients' internalized homophobic response.

Homophobia is the dread of being in close quarters with homosexuals. It is common among heterosexual men and women. Homophobia permeates our culture and influences not only how heterosexuals perceive homosexuals, but also how homosexuals perceive themselves.

Heterosexism is the oppression of sexual minorities that is perpetuated by the societal beliefs that heterosexuals are better than homosexuals and that heterosexuality is the only form of sexual expression. It is a social construction that supports these beliefs and sustains prejudice and discrimination toward sexual minorities.

The civil rights of homosexuals are regularly violated in the areas of housing, employment, and education. Federal laws do not provide for the fair treatment of sexual minorities, and few states have laws protecting their rights. The lack of civil rights protection is directly related to homophobic and heterosexist ideologies.

Coming out is the process in which gay men and lesbian women acknowledge and come to terms with their sexual orientation. It consists of three phases—

awareness, acceptance, and integration. Coming out is a complicated issue and complex process. Generalist social workers can aid this process by helping individuals weigh the positive and negative aspects of coming out within the context of their own life. The goal is to help gay and lesbian clients make choices that best support their personal development.

Gay and lesbian teens are victims of the same homophobic and heterosexist biases as their adult counterparts. However, the fragile nature of the adolescent ego makes adolescent children even more vulnerable to stigmatization and internalized negative self-perceptions. Rejection by family members and peers may force the homosexual adolescent to leave home for a life on the streets.

Gay and lesbian elderly are a diverse group with diverse lifestyles. Many have learned to cope with the stigma of being homosexual. Their concerns are similar to those of elderly heterosexuals. They tend to be more concerned about finances, partnership relationships, loss of friends and partners, and health issues than about the stigma of aging or minority sexual orientation.

The children of gays and lesbians face special challenges and are also victims of homophobic prejudices and beliefs. Our heterosexual society views having children raised by gay or lesbian parents with trepidation. There is a fear that they will be sexually abused by the homosexual parent or partner, that they will be converted to same-sex sexual orientation, and that they will be psychologically damaged by social rejection by their peers.

There are many obstacles to providing good social services to sexual minorities. Homophobia, heterosexism, and ignorance about the lives of gay and lesbian people are just a few. As social workers, it is important to investigate our own biases and beliefs about this special population and take personal responsibility for working through our own misinformation about homosexuality. A good understanding of our own belief system and a willingness to accept our gay and lesbian clients as healthy, valuable members of society can make a vast difference in the helping relationship. Once we succeed in this endeavor, we can begin to tackle the daunting task of becoming advocates for this minority group as it struggles for justice.

CASE EXAMPLE

The final case in this chapter illustrates the complexity of the coming-out process. It highlights the difficulties gay and lesbians have with family and professional relationships. It also brings home the internal struggle homosexuals go through regarding their sexual identity.

I Feel Shame

Michael C. was a twenty-six-year-old Caucasian male who sought help with issues related to his sexual orientation. Although he had dated women off and on since he was sixteen, he was concerned about his fantasies about being with men. He had never pursued a physical relationship with a man, but he believed that over the past several years he had been in love with at least two male friends.

Assessment

During the course of the assessment, Michael revealed that he had never discussed his homosexuality with anyone. He was anxious about his feelings and experienced shame and guilt whenever he allowed himself to fantasize about men. He was raised with strong Christian morals and believed that homosexuality was dirty and sinful. He used alcohol to deal with his anxiety and often drank to excess to avoid intense self-loathing. Michael also reported bouts of depression during which he actively planned his death. He admitted to two suicide attempts, one of which resulted in a two-week hospitalization. Both attempts involved overdoses of amphetamines and alcohol. The last attempt was six months prior to the assessment.

At the time he sought help, Michael reported increased bouts of depression that were interfering with his ability to perform his job. As a young attorney, he had demanding responsibilities. He wanted desperately to get rid of the feelings of hopelessness that intensified with each passing day and made it more and more difficult to concentrate on work. He hoped that discussing his feelings about his sexual orientation would end the depression once and for all.

In the early weeks of treatment, Michael discussed his fears about what it meant to be gay. He had worked hard to become involved in "masculine" activities so as not to be identified as a "queer" or "fag" by his friends and associates. He was goalie of a local ice hockey team, and he always accepted invitations to dinner when friends "fixed him up" with women. Michael feared that accepting himself as a gay man meant that he would have to become more feminine in order to be attractive to other gay men. Once this transformation occurred, he was fairly certain that he would lose his job and his family's love and support. The fear of contracting AIDS lay heavy on his mind. He associated gay sex with AIDS and seemed fairly certain that accepting himself as a gay man also meant accepting that he would die of AIDS. Addressing these fears became the starting point for Michael's treatment.

Intervention

I began educating Michael on the damage that homophobia and heterosexism can cause to self-esteem. Once Michael understood that his fears were directly related to his own internalized homophobia and heterosexism, he was able to freely explore his desire to establish meaningful romantic relationships with men. With my support, Michael began to attend events sponsored by gay and lesbian organizations in neighboring cities. He socialized with other gay and lesbian people at "gay bingo" (bingo for gays and lesbians) and at coffeehouses where gay men and lesbians performed. Michael began to meet men who shared his interest in sports and began to develop a social network of gay men. He enjoyed their company and found that very few fit the stereotype of the "swish" he had feared he would become. As he became more acclimated to gay culture, his depression began to lift, and his alcohol abuse greatly decreased.

Four months into the helping process, Michael decided to come out to his brother and his best friend from college. Both had supported him during his bouts of depression and showed genuine concern for his well-being. Michael's college friend took the news better than his brother did. Michael asked his brother to join him in family sessions with me. Working together, Michael and I were able to lay his brother's homophobic and heterosexist beliefs aside. Michael was then able to reconnect with his brother. Once the secret of his sexuality was revealed, Michael's relationship with his brother and best friend grew closer.

Michael struggled with telling his parents. He was certain that coming out at work would cost him his job. He discussed this issue extensively in treatment and decided that he wanted to come out to his parents before becoming involved in a relationship. The work issue was more complicated. He knew that coming out could cost him his livelihood. In therapy sessions, Michael examined how the secret of his sexuality would require ongoing deception. Michael believed that he could not shed the shame he associated with his sexuality until he was able to bring his secret into the open. He decided to speak with his parents first, then decide how to handle work and other relationships.

At my suggestion, Michael asked his brother to go with him as a support the day he told his parents that he was gay. They took the news badly and asked him to leave the house. Michael initially had difficulty with the rejection, but he was able to use the helping process to better understand his coming out as part of his individuation from his parents. Michael continued to keep in touch with his parents, giving them time to come to terms with his status as their adult gay son. He reasoned that it would take time for them to come to terms with something that took him years to accept.

Evaluation and Termination

Eight months after beginning his work with me, Michael reported feeling less depressed and free of the feelings of shame and hopelessness that had consumed him. He became more confident in his identity as a gay man and his anxiety about others discovering his sexuality was greatly reduced. Michael met two colleagues from work at a Gay Pride Parade, and they introduced him to a support group for gay and lesbian attorneys. Through this group, Michael began volunteering his legal services to the gay and lesbian community, working on civil rights legislation for sexual minorities. He began dating and occasionally introduced his gay dates and friends to his parents. He had also found a church that was affirming of sexual minorities and had begun to attend services regularly. Michael and I agreed that he had made significant progress during our eight months together and that Michael was ready to leave treatment. Michael left my office with the understanding that he should return whenever he felt the need to do so.

DISCUSSION QUESTIONS

1. Gay men and lesbian women may experience life-cycle issues differently than their heterosexual counterparts. In the case of Michael, coming out complicated his becoming autonomous from his family. What other life-cycle issues can become complicated

for gay men and lesbian women? Are there life-cycle issues that become complicated for the families of gays and lesbians? If so, what are they?

2. If you were treating Michael's parents, how would you approach the treatment? What would be your goals in treatment? Do you think that the issues for Michael's parents would be vastly different from the issues that Michael addressed in treatment? Do you think that there would be issues that are unique to the parents of gay and lesbian clients? If so, what are some of these issues?

3. What macro issues does the social work practitioner need to be aware of when treating gay and lesbian clients? Are there macro issues that affect the treatment on a micro level? Using the case example of Michael, discuss macro issues that affected him as an individual.

4. Are you aware of any current legislative measures that directly affect gays and lesbians? If so, what are the issues? What is your stance on these issues? If not, are there current problems that directly affect gays and lesbians that you would consider taking to the legislature? If so, what issues? How would you present your case to the legislators?

5. Do you think a gay or lesbian therapist can work more effectively with gay or lesbian clients? What might be issues for the heterosexual therapist working with gay and lesbian clients? What might be issues for the gay or lesbian therapist working with gay and lesbian clients?

6. If you worked in a school setting, what kind of curriculum would you develop to educate staff and faculty about gay and lesbian families? How would you educate parents and students about this subject? How would you educate employers and employees in the work setting?

REFERENCES

Behrendt, A. E., & George, K. (1995). Sex therapy for gay and bisexual men. In L. Diamant & R. D. McNaulty (Eds.), *The psychology of sexual orientation, Behavior and identity* (pp. 220–236). Connecticut: Greenwood.

Berger, R. M. (1982a). The unseen minority: Older gays and lesbians. *Social Work, 27,* 236–242.

Berger, R. M. (1982b). *Gay and gray.* Urbana, IL: University of Illinois Press.

Blumenfeld, W. J. (1995). Gay/straight alliance: Transforming pain to pride. In G. Unks (Ed.), *The gay teen* (pp. 211–224). New York: Routledge.

Bohan, J. S. (1997) Teaching on the edge: The psychology of sexual orientation. *Teaching of Psychology,* 24(1), 27–31.

Bohn, T. R. (1984). Homophobic violence: Implications for social work practice. *Journal of Social Work and Human Sexuality,* 2(2/3), 91–112.

Brandt, A. M. (1988). AIDS in historical perspective: Four lessons from the history of sexually transmitted diseases. *American Journal of Public Health, 78,* 367–371.

Britton, D. M. (1990). Homophobia and homosociality: An analysis of boundary maintenance. *Sociology Quarterly, 31,* 423–439.

Buhrke, R. A. (1989). Lesbian related issues in counseling supervision. *Women and Counseling,* 8(1/2), 195–206.

Cass, B. C. (1979). Homosexuality identity formation: A theoretical model. *Journal of Homosexuality, 4,* 219–235.

Cates, J. A. (1987). Adolescent sexuality: Gay and lesbian issues. *Child Welfare,* 66(4), 353–364.

Clift, S. M. (1988). Lesbian and gay issues in education: A study of the attitudes of first year students in a college of higher education. *British Education Research Journal, 14,* 31–50.

Coleman, E. (1981/1982). Developmental stages of the coming out process. *Journal of Homosexuality, 7*(2/3), 31–43.

Council on Social Work Education, Commission on Accreditation. (1993). *Handbook of accreditation standards and procedures.* Washington, DC: Author.

Cox, S. & Gallois, C. (1996). Gay and lesbian identity development: A social identity perspective. *Journal of Homosexuality, 30*(4), 1–30.

de Monteflores, C., & Schultz, S. J. (1978). Coming out: Similarities and differences for lesbians and gay men. *Journal of Social Issues, 34*(3), 59–72.

Dunne, E. (1988). Helping gay fathers come out to their children. In E. Coleman (Ed.), *Psychotherapy with homosexual men and women* (pp. 213–222). New York: Haworth.

Ernulf, K. E., & Innala, S. M. (1987). The relationship between affective and cognitive components of homophobic reactions. *Archives of Sexual Behavior, 16,* 501–509.

Faria, G. (1994). Training for family preservation practice with lesbian families. *Families in Society: The Journal of Contemporary Human Services, 75*(7), 416–422.

Fassinger, R. E. (1991). The hidden minority: Issues and challenges in working with lesbians and gay men. *The Counseling Psychologist, 19,* 157–176.

Fraser, I. H., Fish, T. A., & Mackenzie, T. M. (1995). Reactions to child custody decisions involving homosexual and heterosexual parents. *Canadian Journal of Behavioral Science, 27*(1), 52–63.

Friend, R. A. (1988). The individual and social psychology of aging: Clinical implications for lesbians and gay men. In E. Coleman (Ed.), *Psychotherapy with homosexual men and women* (pp. 307–331). New York: Haworth.

Germain, C. B. (1991). *Human behavior in the social environment.* New York: Columbia University Press.

Golombok, S., Spence, A., & Rutter, M. (1983). Children in lesbian and single mother households: Psychosexual and psychiatric appraisal. *Journal of Child Psychology and Psychiatry, 24,* 551–572.

Green, R. (1987). *The "sissy boy syndrome" and the development of homosexuality.* New York: Yale University Press.

Hanley-Hackenbruck, P. (1989). Psychotherapy and the coming out process. *Journal of Gay and Lesbian Psychotherapy, 1,* 21–39.

Hare, J. (1994). Concerns and issues faced by families headed by a lesbian couple. *The Journal of Contemporary Human Services, 1,* 27–35.

Harowski, K. J. (1988). The worried well: Minimizing coping in the face of AIDS. In E. Coleman (Ed.), *Psychotherapy with homosexual men and women* (pp. 229–306). New York: Haworth.

Hellman, R. E., Green, R., Gray, J. L., & Williams, K. (1981). Childhood sexual identity, childhood religiosity and homophobia as influences in the development of transsexualism, homosexuality and heterosexuality. *Archives of General Psychiatry, 38,* 910–915.

Herdt, G., & Boxer, A. (1993). *Children of horizons.* Boston, MA: Beacon.

Herek, G. M. (1986). On heterosexual masculinity. *American Behavioral Scientist, 29*(5), 563–577.

Herek, G. M. (1989). Hate crimes against lesbians and gay men: Issues for research and policy. *American Psychologist, 44,* 948–955.

Herek, G. M. & Berrill, K. T. (1990). Anti-gay violence and mental health: Setting an agenda for research. *Journal of Interpersonal Violence, 5,* 414–423.

Hetrick, E. S., & Martin, A. D. (1987). Developmental issues and their resolution for gay and lesbian adolescents. *Journal of Homosexuality, 26*(1), 25–43.

Jay, K. & Young, A. (1979). *The gay report.* New York: Summit.

Jonsen, A. R., & Stryker, J. (Eds.). (1993). *The social impact of AIDS in the* United States. Washington, DC: National Academy Press.

Kaplan, H. S. (1974). *The new sex therapy: Active treatment of sexual dysfunction.* New York: Brunner/Mazel.

Kirkpatrick, M. (1988). Clinical implications of lesbian mothers studies. In E. Coleman (Ed.), *Psychotherapy with homosexual men and women* (pp. 201–211). New York: Haworth.

Klein, F., & Wolf, T. (1985). *Bisexualities: Theory and research.* New York: Haworth.

Kruks, G. (1991). Gay and lesbian homeless/street youth: Special issues and concerns. *Journal of Adolescent Health, 12,* 515–518.

Lance, L. M. (1987). The effects of interaction with gay person on attitudes towards homosexuality. *Human Relations, 4,* 329–336.

Lauritsen, J. (1993). *The AIDS war.* New York: Asklepios.

Leiblum, S., & Rosen, R. (1989). *Principles and practice of sex therapy* (2nd ed.). New York: Guilford.

Levy, E. F. (1992). Strengthening the coping resources of lesbian families. *Journal of Contemporary Human Services, 1,* 23–31.

Lewis, K. (1990). Children of lesbians: Their point of view. *Social Work, 25*(3), 203–214.

Lipton, B. (1996). Opening doors: Responding to the mental health needs of gay and bisexual college students. *Journal of Gay and Lesbian Social Services, 1*(2), 7–24.

MacDonald, A. (1976). Homophobia: Its roots and meanings. *Homosexual Counseling Journal, 3*(1), 23–33.

Mackelprang, R. W., Ray, J., & Hernandez-Peck, M. (1996). Social work education and sexual orientation: Faculty, student and curriculum issues. *Journal of Gay and Lesbian Social Services, 5*(4), 17–31.

Maier, R. A. (1984). *Human sexuality in perspective.* Chicago: Nelson Hall.

Masters, W. H. & Johnson, V. E. (1970). *Human sexual inadequacy.* Boston: Little, Brown.

Maylon, A. K. (1981). The homosexual adolescent: Developmental issues and social bias. *Child Welfare, 60*(5), 321–329.

McDonald, H. B., & Steinhorn, A. I. (1990). *Homosexuality.* New York: Continuum.

Millham, J., San Miguel, C. L., & Kellog, R. (1976). A factor analytic conceptualization of attitudes toward male and female homosexuals. *Journal of Homosexuality, 2,* 3–10.

Minton, H. L., & McDonald, G. J. (1983/1984). Homosexuality identity formation as a developmental process. *Journal of Homosexuality, 9*(2/3), 91–104.

Morgan, K. S. (1997). Why lesbians choose therapy: Presenting problems, attitudes and political concerns. *Journal of Gay and Lesbian Social Services, 6*(3), 57–75.

Morin, S., & Garfinkle, E. (1978). Male homophobia. *Journal of Social Issues, 34*(1), 29–47.

Morrow, D. F. (1993). Social work with gay and lesbian adolescents. *Social Work, 38*(5), 505–648.

Morrow, D. F. (1996). Coming-out issues for adult lesbians: A group intervention. *Social Work, 41*(6), 647–656.

Moses, A. E., & Hawkins, R. (1982). *Counseling lesbian women and gay men: A life issues approach.* St. Louis: Mosby.

Mosher, D. L., & O'Grady, K. E. (1979). Homosexual threat, negative attitudes toward masturbation, sex guilt, and males' sexual and affective reactions to explicit sexual films. *Journal of Consulting and Clinical Psychology, 47*(5), 860–873.

Neisen, J. H. (1990). "Heterosexism": Redefining homophobia for the 1990s. *Journal of Gay and Lesbian Psychotherapy, 1*(3), 21–35.

Neisen, J. H. (1993). Healing from cultural victimization: Recovery from shame due to heterosexism. *Journal of Gay and Lesbian Psychotherapy, 2*(1), 49–63.

Newman, B., & Newman, P. (1995). *Development through life: A psychosocial approach.* New York: Brooks/Cole.

Newton, D. E. (1978). Homosexual behavior and child molestation: A review of evidence. *Adolescence, 13,* 29–43.

Nungesser, L. (1983). *Homosexual acts, and identities.* New York: Praeger.

Panem, S. (1988). *The AIDS bureaucracy.* Cambridge, MA: Harvard University Press.

Patton, C. (1986). *Sex and germs: The politics of AIDS.* Buffalo, NY: Black Rose Books.

Peck, J., & Bezold, C. (1992, July). Health care and AIDS. *The Annals of the American Academy of Political and Social Science, 522,* 130–139.

Peplau, L. A. (1981). What homosexuals want in relationships. *Psychology Today, 15*(3), 28–38.

Pierce, C., & VanDeVeer, D. (1988). *AIDS: Ethics and public policy.* Belmont, CA: Wadsworth.

Pies, C. (1988). *Considering parenthood: A workbook for lesbians.* San Francisco: Spinster Ink.

Price, V., & Hsu, M. L. (1992). Public opinion about AIDS policies: The role of misinformation and attitudes toward homosexuals. *Public Opinion Quarterly, 56,* 29–52.

Riddle, D. I., & Sang, B. (1978). Psychotherapy with lesbians. *Journal of Social Issues, 34*(3), 84–100.

Roth, S. (1985). Psychotherapy with lesbian couples: Individual issues, female socialization and social context. *Journal of Marital and Family Therapy, 11*(3), 286–307.

Saltzburg, S. (1996). Family therapy and the disclosure of adolescent homosexuality. *Journal of Family Psychotherapy, 7*(4), 1–18.

Seattle Commission on Children and Youth. (1988). *Report on gay and lesbian youth in Seattle.* Seattle, Wash.: Author.

Shilts, R. (1987). *And the band played on.* New York: St. Martin's.

Simon, A. (1995). Some correlates of individuals' attitudes toward lesbians. *Journal of Homosexuality, 29*(1), 89–103.

Singerline, H. (1995). OutRight! Reflections on an out-of-school gay youth group. In G. Unks (Ed.), *The gay teen* (pp. 235–232). New York: Routledge.

Smalley, S. (1988). Dependency issues in lesbian relationships. In E. Coleman (Ed.), *Psychotherapy with homosexual men and women* (pp. 125–135). New York: Haworth.

Sophie, J. (1986). A critical examination of stage theories of lesbian identity-development. *Journal of Homosexuality, 12*(2), 39–51.

Sophie, J. (1987). Internalized homophobia and lesbian identity. *Journal of Homosexuality, 14*(1/2), 53–65.

Spaulding, E. C. (1993). Unconsciousness raising: Hidden dimensions of heterosexism in theory and practice with lesbians. *Smith College Studies in Social Work, 63*(3), 221–245.

Stevenson, M. R. (1988). Promoting tolerance of homosexuality: An evaluation of intervention strategies. *Journal of Sex Research, 25,* 500–511.

Stine, G. J. (1993). *Acquired immune deficiency syndrome: Biological, medical, social and legal issues.* New Jersey: Prentice-Hall.

Tasker, F., & Golombok, S. (1995). Adults raised as children in lesbian families. *American Journal of Orthopsychiatry, 65,* 203–215.

Telljohann, S. K., & Price, J. H. (1993). A qualitative examination of adolescent homosexuals' life experiences: Ramifications for secondary school personnel. *Journal of Homosexuality, 26*(1), 41–56.

Unks, G. (Ed.). (1995). *The gay teen.* New York: Routledge.

Uribe, V. (1995). Project 10: A school-based outreach to gay and lesbian youth. In G. Unks (Ed.), *The gay teen* (pp. 3–12). New York: Routledge.

Van de Ven, P. (1994). *Challenging homophobia in schools.* Unpublished doctoral thesis, University of Sydney.

Van de Ven, P., Bornholt, L., & Baily, M. (1996). Measuring cognitive, affective and behavioral components of homophobic reaction. *Archives of Sexual Behavior, 25*(2), 155–179.

Weinberg, G. (1972). *Society and the healthy homosexual.* New York: Doubleday Anchor.

Wells, J. W. (1991). The effects of homophobia and sexism on heterosexual sexual relationships. *Journal of Sex Education and Therapy, 17*(3), 185–195.

Wyers, N.L. (1987). Homosexuality in the family: Lesbian and gay spouses. *Social Work, 32*(2), 143–148.

Zastrow, C., & Kirst-Ashman, K. K. (1990). *Understanding human behavior and the social environment.* Chicago: Nelson Hall.

Zilbergeld, B. (1992). *The new male sexuality: The truth about me, sex and pleasure.* New York: Bantam.

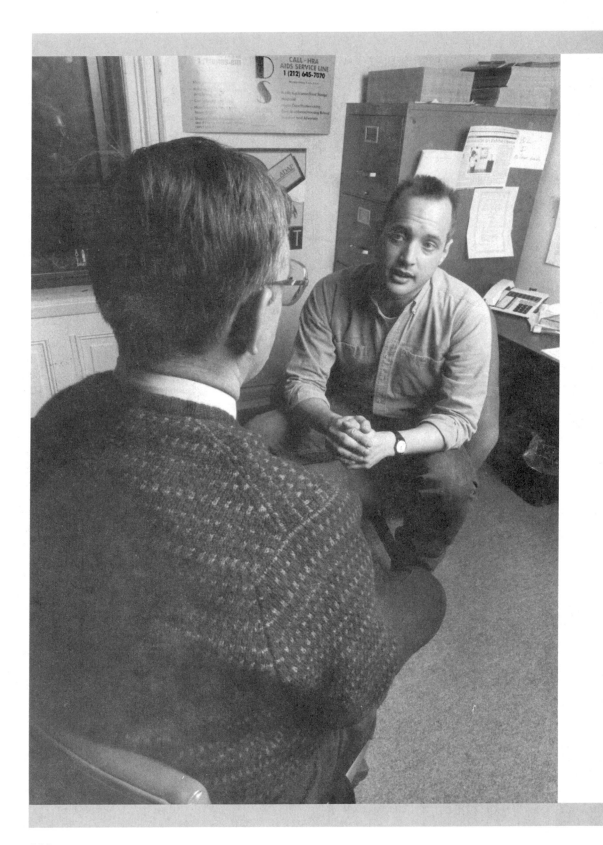

CHAPTER 14

Generalist Practice with People with HIV and AIDS

Brent Satterly

Vincent J. is a senior BSW student with a field placement at a community health clinic in an economically disadvantaged urban community. The clinic has a large HIV/AIDS patient population of infection drug users. Vincent provides case management and supportive counseling services to individual clinic patients who have tested positive for HIV and to patients with AIDS. Vincent also runs a support group for persons with AIDS and is involved in a community education program about the disease and its prevention.

Vincent's prior knowledge of AIDS and HIV was limited. His social work classes had not really spent much time discussing working with AIDS/HIV clients. Early in his field placement he realized that he needed to understand the disease and its process as well as how it socially and psychologically affects individuals and families. What was the course of the disease? What was the prognosis for his clients? Would he be able to focus on strengths with clients who are dying? Could he really help his clients? Was he prepared to handle the emotional stress of working with individuals suffering from AIDS?

In the early 1980s, physicians began reporting consistent occurrences of formerly rare diseases, such as Kaposi's sarcoma, a cancer of the blood cells, and Pneumocystis carinii pneumonia, a type of lung infection. Although these diseases were usually not dangerous, they were killing off scores of relatively healthy, young gay men because of an apparent suppression of their immune systems. Rumors of a "gay plague" or a "gay cancer" were officially confirmed by naming this disease gay-related immune deficiency. It soon became apparent that the disease was not limited to the gay community. Heterosexual men and women were being infected, as were drug users who injected their drugs. The disease was occurring among all racial and ethnic groups and spanning all socioeconomic levels. It was renamed AIDS (acquired immunodeficiency syndrome). In 1984, Robert Gallo of the National Institutes of Health and Luc Montagnier of the French Pasteur Institute simultaneously announced the discovery of the virus causing AIDS, which was named HIV (human immunodeficiency virus).

AIDS is a disease, not a type of person or groupings of people. To fully understand the complexities of working with clients infected with HIV or suffering from
AIDS, it is necessary to remember that the virus and the disease affect all types of
people across gender, race, sexual orientation, culture, age, religion, ability, and
class. They also affect people who are homeless, incarcerated, mentally ill, and
injection drug users. Given such varied populations, the psychosocial issues experienced by people living with or affected by HIV or AIDS are also varied.

The purpose of this chapter is to provide an understanding of the primary
issues affecting persons living with HIV or AIDS and their families and friends.
The chapter begins by describing the disease, its epidemiology (the tracking of an
epidemic), modes of transmission, and treatments. A discussion of the history of
social work practice with HIV and AIDS as well as significant policy and macro
practice issues follows. The chapter then explores the various concrete and psychosocial target problems for HIV-infected individuals and their families.
Pertinent cultural and micro practice issues are discussed in light of the helping
relationship. By the end of the chapter, you should be able to help Vincent

1. Describe the disease process for HIV infection and AIDS
2. Understand the modes of transmission of HIV infection
3. Summarize the federal government's responses to the AIDS crisis
4. Articulate the major HIV/AIDS policy issues
5. Apply a strengths perspective in working with HIV/AIDS clients and
   their families
6. Describe the special considerations associated in working with children
   and adolescents who are HIV-infected or who have AIDS
7. Understand the effect cultural differences have in generalist social work
   practice with HIV/AIDS clients from different ethnic and cultural backgrounds
8. Identify the micro practice issues in working with HIV/AIDS clients.

UNDERSTANDING HIV AND AIDS

AIDS is a cluster of symptoms caused by the human immunodeficiency virus
(HIV). HIV invades the body's immune system, our natural system of defense. The
immune system works by producing white blood cells that systematically destroy
hostile pathogens, such as bacteria, fungi, or viruses, expired body cells, or cancer-
ous cells by enveloping and killing them. These white blood cells distinguish
between hostile organisms and friendly ones on the basis of their surface frag-
ments, which are known as antigens. The body responds to the presence of antigens by producing a protein known as antibodies, which attaches itself to the
hostile agents, inactivating them and stamping them for eradication. Lymphocytes
are white blood cells that remember previous invaders and are utilized as a quick
response to future infections.

HIV attacks this system by destroying a certain type of lymphocyte called the
helper T-cell, that recognizes pathogens and tells the immune system to produce
antibodies to inactivate and mark the foreign invaders for destruction and also to
produce killer T-cells to destroy infected cells. HIV destroys the helper T-cells,
thereby weakening the immune system. The body normally has one thousand

T-cells per cubic millimeter of blood. As the T-cell count declines, the body is left with little ability to fight off infections and diseases. This lack of immunity to infections and diseases can ultimately lead to death (Gottlieb, 1991).

AIDS is diagnosed, according to the current Centers for Disease Control and Prevention (CDC) classification, when an individual's test results indicate the presence of HIV antibodies in the bloodstream and a T-cell count below two hundred. If the T-cell count is greater than two hundred, the individual must have one or more of the conditions associated with AIDS to be diagnosed with the disease. A person who does not meet these criteria is HIV-infected, not diagnosed with AIDS. A person with HIV can harbor the virus for years without developing AIDS as defined by the CDC.

Currently, the CDC lists twenty-seven clinical conditions used in diagnosing AIDS (CDC, 1996a). These include opportunistic infections, cancers, conditions specifically associated with AIDS, and conditions that might be diagnostic of AIDS (Strong, DeVault, & Sayad, 1998). Opportunistic infections are diseases that strike a compromised immune system, such as Pneumocystis carinii pneumonia and tuberculosis. Common types of cancers linked to HIV and AIDS are Kaposi's sarcoma, lymphoma, invasive cervical cancer. The specific conditions associated with AIDS are wasting syndrome and AIDS dementia. Conditions that might be diagnostic of AIDS include herpes simplex and candidiasis.

There are some common symptoms experienced by people with AIDS and HIV. Persons diagnosed with AIDS are more likely to experience some of these symptoms than those who are HIV-infected only. It is important to note that these symptoms are also associated with infections unrelated to HIV and AIDS. If an individual is experiencing these symptom on an ongoing basis, he or she should seek appropriate medical care. The symptoms include:

- Unexplained weight loss of ten pounds or more
- Recurring shortness of breath or dry cough
- Recurring diarrhea
- Unexplained fatigue
- Unexplained fever, chills, and night sweats over a period of weeks
- Swollen lymph nodes lasting two months.

Women may experience

- Abdominal cramping
- Recurring vaginal candidiasis (yeast infections)
- Abnormal pap smears (Strong, DeVault, & Sayad, 1998).

Epidemiology of HIV and AIDS

Nearly 665,000 people have been diagnosed with AIDS in the United States and an additional 98,900 have been diagnosed with HIV (CDC, 1998a). One death from AIDS occurs every nine minutes, and one new HIV infection occurs every fifty-four seconds (Dorgan, 1995). Newly diagnosed cases declined in 1997 by approximately 15 percent, primarily because of the efficacy of new therapies for HIV and AIDS.

These decreases in infection are *smallest* among women, African-Americans, and persons infected via heterosexual contact. Table 14.1 shows the significant increase in AIDS cases among racial and ethnic minorities. AIDS is increasing among people who do not have access to treatment, whose treat-

TABLE 14.1. Estimated Persons Living with AIDS, by Race and Ethnicity, 1992–1997, in the United States

Race or Ethnicity	1992	1993	1994	1995	1996	1997	Percentage Increase 1992–1997
Caucasian	68,606	80,605	86,907	91,843	98,705	107,807	57%
African-American	45,823	60,754	72,055	81,563	92,777	107,049	134%
Latino	23,760	31,121	36,446	41,036	46,255	52,735	122%
Asian-American and Pacific Islander	1,010	1,282	1,440	1,599	1,858	2,089	107%
Native American	459	552	644	695	778	875	91%
Total	139,853	174,532	197,770	217,113	240,873	271,246	94%

Note: Adapted from *HIV/AIDS Surveillance Report* (pp. 1–37), Centers for Disease Control and Prevention, 1998, *10*(1).

ment protocols have failed, and who were not diagnosed with HIV infection until they developed AIDS (CDC, 1998a). Injection drug users and their at-risk partners also continue to face increased rates of infection. Pediatric AIDS incidence, on the other hand, has consistently declined, reflecting the effective implementation of voluntary testing and drug treatment protocols during pregnancy (CDC, 1998a; Strong, Devault, & Sayad, 1999).

Modes of Transmission

AIDS is not a highly communicable disease. Only four body fluids contain sufficient amounts of HIV for transmission to occur. These fluids are blood, vaginal secretions, semen, and breast milk. The primary modes of transmission are having sex with an infected person, sharing a needle with someone who is infected (for example, shooting drugs), being born to an infected mother, or drinking the breast milk of an infected mother. Prior to April 1985, infected blood used in transfusions and organ transplants was also a possible mode of transmission. Currently, all blood is screened for HIV infection prior to use (Strong, DeVault, & Sayad, 1999).

The behaviors putting a person at risk for HIV transmission through sexual contact include anal sex, vaginal sex, oral sex, and other sexual behaviors that involve contact with bodily fluids of an infected person. HIV may enter the body through small cuts or sores, and the use of barriers, such as latex condoms, dental dams, and surgical gloves, can provide efficient protection when used consistently and correctly (Nevid, 1998; Strong, DeVault, & Sayad, 1999).

Sharing needles and other mechanisms to inject drugs is another mode of HIV transmission (CDC, 1996b). Half of new HIV infections are among injection drug and crack cocaine users (CDC, 1997). Alcohol and other drugs can also cause people to engage in other risk behaviors (Stein, 1992). Crack binges are frequently associated with hypersexuality, when a user may have sex with multiple partners to obtain crack or the money to acquire it (Kolata, 1995).

The transmission of HIV from mother to child often takes place prior to the onset of labor, perhaps as early as the second trimester, and accounts for 30 to 50 percent of mother-to-child transmission. Transmission during the birth process itself occurs when the infant is exposed to blood or mucus in the birth canal; 50 to 60 percent of pediatric HIV cases are attributed to this mode. The remainder of cases are a result of the ingestion of breast milk (Landers & Shannon, 1997). The use of volunteer testing and AZT (an AIDS drug) has reduced mother to child transmission to 2 percent of infected mothers (CDC, 1998b; Irvine, 1998).

The term *risk groups* was utilized early in the epidemic to describe groupings of persons, such as gay men, injection drug users, or hemophiliacs who were assumed to be likely to be infected with HIV. This phrase was discarded for its inaccuracy and its dangerous message of immunity to infection for those outside those groups. *Risk behaviors* is the current term used to refer to specific actions that increase the likelihood of infection. No one is immune to or exempt from HIV infection.

Antiviral Treatments

There is no cure for AIDS. Antiviral treatments can slow the virus, which also slows the damage to the infected person's immune system. Currently, eleven major AIDS drugs have been approved by the Food and Drug Administration. They fall into three categories: (1) infection treatments; (2) immune system treatments; and (3) antiretroviral treatments. Antibiotics and painkillers are among the most common types of drugs that treat infections and symptoms. Drugs to bolster the immune system are most effective when the virus has been detected early. The final type of drug attacks the virus itself by blocking the HIV genetic code (RNA) from converting to DNA, a necessary step in the HIV life-cycle, or by blocking HIV from maturing. The latter antiretroviral drugs are called protease inhibitors (New Mexico AIDS Education and Training Center, 1999).

Early and aggressive treatment using triple drug combinations, known as a drug cocktail, has been found to be most effective. The cocktail consists of two drugs that block the genetic conversion and one protease inhibitor. The use of three drugs helps prevent HIV from mutating and developing resistance to a drug (*San Francisco Chronicle*, 1998). Although the cocktail has provided significant hope to persons with AIDS and HIV, often allowing them to enjoy a better quality of life, it is by no means a cure.

HISTORY OF SOCIAL WORK WITH PERSONS LIVING WITH HIV OR AIDS

In the United States, social services are primarily provided by public and not-for-profit agencies. When services are provided some other way, it is generally because of the marginalization of the target group. This was the case with gay men in the early days of the AIDS epidemic. Social services were not being provided by social service agencies, the federal government had begun disassembling institutions focused on public health (Padgug & Oppenheimer, 1992; Shilts, 1987). Grassroots organizations staffed by gay men and lesbians, emerged to fill the void (Gamson, 1991; Stein, 1998). Some of the services provided included (1) hotlines and newsletters to distribute information about the disease and social services, (2) assistance with activities of daily living, (3) research, (4) advocacy and political activism, and (5) counseling (Stein, 1998).

Social service agencies began to step in to assist grassroots efforts in the organization, funding, and provision of social services to a rapidly growing population of persons infected with HIV or AIDS, especially those who were not members of the gay community. Unfortunately, people with HIV and AIDS often did not receive compassionate or quality treatment from social workers providing such services (Bayer, Fox, & Willis, 1986). In the late 1980s, a large proportion of social workers said that they would refuse to provide service to people with AIDS or HIV (Dhooper, Royse, & Tran, 1987). These attitudes can be attributed to fear of contagion and to homophobia, the irrational fear and/or hatred of gay people or those suspected of being gay (O'Hare, Williams, & Ezoviski, 1996; Weinberg, 1972). Because AIDS first appeared in the gay community in the United States, the disease was (and often still is) considered a "gay plague" and treated as a moral issue (O'Hare, Williams, & Ezoviski, 1996).

Resources

Today there is a complex, multifaceted, AIDS establishment characterized by increasing bureaucratization and professionalization. It includes AIDS service organizations, federal, state, and local government, social service agencies, hospitals, clinics, private institutions, and pharmaceutical companies. Because the system is large and complex, it is often necessary for a case manager to help an HIV-infected individual connect with and navigate through the bureaucracies to obtain help.

Financial assistance is primarily accessed through Social Security Disability Insurance (SSDI) and Supplemental Security Income (SSI). Both of these entitlement programs are administered by the Social Security Administration. They are designed to alleviate some of the financial burdens placed on persons with disabilities, which includes many individuals with AIDS and HIV (Stein, 1998).

The Housing Opportunities for Persons with AIDS Act is a federally funded program designed to increase access of persons with AIDS and HIV to adequate housing. Grants are given to the states to (1) organize efforts to expand current housing, (2) provide information about housing projects, (3) provide short-term housing, (4) lease, purchase, repair, or convert housing, (5) provide short-term financial assistance to pay rent for homeless persons, and (6) provide nutritional, day-care, substance-abuse treatment, health, and mental health services (Stein, 1998).

Food stamps, which an individual can trade for food products at a grocery store, is often an option. Low-income women who are pregnant or caring for young children can obtain free food and health care information from the Women, Infants and Children program (Feyler, Freedman, Egan, Hirsch, Landau, & Goldfein, 1997). Food warehouses and mobile food delivery organizations provide people with HIV or AIDS with hot and cold meals, generally through case management referrals.

Medicaid is a needs-based entitlement program intended to provide medical coverage for poor people who are eligible due to disability, age, or membership in a family with dependent children. This program is the single largest payer of medical expenses of people with HIV (Stein, 1998).

Services

A variety of organizations provide individuals with a multitude of other services. These include

- Legal services
- Hospice care
- Primary pediatric care
- Residential care for women and children
- Residential care for gay, lesbian, bisexual, or transgendered youth
- Counseling services for children whose parents are HIV-infected
- Temporary foster care for children whose parent is hospitalized
- Home-based services to enable children to remain in their own homes while their parents are in drug treatment.

Broader multiservice programs may provide

(1) case management services to help clients identify their needs, plan for meeting identified needs, and obtain assistance when services are not provided by the [multiservice] agency; (2) coordinating and monitoring services to avoid duplication and to ensure that client needs are being met; (3) information and referral services and education through community outreach programs; and (4) services to help women gain access to drug treatment programs and to relocate their families out of drug-intensive neighborhoods. (Stein, 1998, p. 54)

POLICY ISSUES

Two policy areas directly affect generalist social work practice with people with HIV and AIDS: policymaking and confidentiality, which includes partner notification and mandated reporting.

Policymaking and Service Use

The construction of policy for services to people with HIV and AIDS is affected by societal attitudes about HIV. The assignment of personal responsibility for HIV infection has contributed to the delay of policymaking and implementation throughout the history of the epidemic. It may also affect the use of services when they are available:

Social policies designed to afford a timely response to HIV infection may deter service utilization when the people to be served are concerned about the stigma of identification and the discrimination that may result. This outcome suggests that HIV-positive people may not take advantage of services when they perceive that they will be judged to be responsible for their HIV-positive status. (McDonell, 1993, p. 408)

Such fears are not without merit. In today's political climate, there is a drive to incorporate behavior change into policy. This results in the rewarding of benefits to those who engage in behavior change and the withholding of specific financial and medical benefits from individuals participating in nonconforming behavior (Stein, 1998). Policies designed to counter this trend include, the Ryan White CARE Act, the American Disabilities Act (ADA), and the Vocational

Rehabilitation Act (VRA), all of which ensure nondiscriminatory access to health care and social services (Stein, 1998).

Confidentiality

According to the NASW *Code of Ethics* (1996), confidentiality is a primary ethical mandate of the social work profession. Confidentiality is especially important when working with people with HIV and AIDS. To deliver effective social services with professional integrity and confidence while protecting ourselves from the risk of civil liability, we need to be aware of the limits of confidentiality as well as the legal implications of and statutes affecting generalist social work with people with HIV and AIDS.

Two concepts relevant to social work policy are mandatory reporting and partner notification. Mandatory reporting requires a physician to report a diagnosis of HIV to the state health department for the purposes of statistical compilation. Partner notification is a physician's legal option or mandate to warn an infected person's spouse or partner he or she may be at risk of infection (Reamer, 1993). In the 1976 landmark case *Tarasoff v. the Regents of the University of California*, the California Supreme Court ruled that a mental health professional has the legal duty to warn an intended victim when a client poses a threat of violence (Yu & O'Neal, 1992). The question of whether this ruling is applicable to HIV infection has been hotly debated. Some argue that HIV is not a deadly weapon, such as a knife or handgun, and that sexual transmission or needle-sharing is a "passive mutual consensual behavior instead of a deliberate taking of another person's life" (Yu & O'Neal, 1992, p. 424). Others state that an uninformed sexual partner is placed in danger, which embraces the spirit of *Tarasoff*.

The AIDS epidemic has complicated issues of confidentiality, resulting in a struggle between public health and individual rights. Does the public's interest supplant the client's liberties in order to prevent infection of an uninformed partner? Would disclosure to a third party represent a failure to abide by the *Code of Ethics*? Could disclosure severely damage the helping relationship? Should the social worker protect the individual client, the uninformed partner, or society (Yu & O'Neal, 1992; see also the discussion of ethical dilemmas in Chapter 1)? The answers to these questions are not easily arrived at:

> Too often, the HIV policy debate is characterized as an inevitable conflict between public health and individual rights. Policies that infringe individual rights, such as forcible HIV testing or detention, are defended on the basis of an overriding need to protect public health. But an effective response to the epidemic demands a more complex understanding. This is not to say that there will never be conflicting values or interests because many of the necessary measures may represent profound challenges to prevailing cultural beliefs and practices. However, an effective response to the HIV epidemic requires, above all, a recognition by all individuals, the infected and the uninfected, and by communities and governments that they have a common interest in working together to do whatever is necessary. . . to contain the spread of HIV in order to ensure the survival of families and societies. The emphasis in our response to the epidemic must be on this community of interest rather than on the potential conflicts. (Hamblin, 1992, pp. 4–5)

MACRO PRACTICE ISSUES

Macro practice issues should not be ignored or go unaddressed in the field (Long & Holle, 1997). The macro practice issues related to working with people with HIV and AIDS include worker education and training, funding, and socioeconomic vulnerabilities.

Worker Education and Training

As mentioned earlier in this chapter, social workers and social work students have demonstrated a low level of empathy and compassion for people with AIDS and HIV, partly due to homophobia and AIDS-related social stigma (O'Hare, Williams, & Ezoviski, 1996). Social workers and social work students also lack accurate knowledge about HIV and AIDS (Peterson, 1991; Yu & O'Neal, 1992). Forty percent of masters of social work programs offer no training in human sexuality and primary prevention, and 20 to 30 percent offer little to no training about AIDS and HIV (Diaz & Kelly, 1991). However, regardless of practice area, social workers are likely to encounter people with HIV and AIDS (O'Hare, Williams, & Ezoviski, 1996), so negative attitudes, inadequate or inaccurate knowledge, and lack of training will, likely have a negative effect on the quality of social work practice with clients with HIV and AIDS.

Social work education and continuing professional education must include HIV/AIDS education in the training curricula for social workers. O'Hare, Williams, and Ezoviski (1996) recommend the use of more assertive methodologies for the desensitization of social workers inhibitions. This can include role-playing and exposure to people with HIV and AIDS. HIV-infected professionals as well as professionals from the gay community can serve as valuable resources for social workers and social work students.

Funding

The Ryan White Comprehensive AIDS Resources Emergency (CARE) Act, P.L. 101-381, enacted by Congress in 1990 and reauthorized in 1996, authorizes the largest federal investment in services to persons living with HIV or AIDS. It provides direct assistance to the following:

- Eligible metropolitan areas that report the largest numbers of reported cases of AIDS, in order to meet emergency needs
- States, in order to improve the availability, quality, and organization of health care and support services for people with AIDS and HIV and their families
- Public and nonprofit organizations, to provide support for early intervention services
- Clinical research on treatments for children and pregnant women with HIV or AIDS as well as health care for their families
- AIDS education and training centers, special projects of national significance, and dental reimbursement (Health Resources and Services Administration, 1997).

Funds provided by the act have enabled practical approaches to the management of HIV services and the delivery of care to people living with HIV and AIDS. By the end of fiscal year 1991, sixteen metropolitan areas had received $86 million collectively. Just six years later, forty-nine metropolitan areas had received $429 million. In addition, significant increases occurred for AIDS drug-assistance programs (Health Resources and Services Administration, 1997).

Socioeconomic Vulnerabilities to Infection

Although significant federal funds are being allocated, financial constraints and access to social and medical services remain primary barriers to reducing infection and providing proper health care among many groups of Americans. HIV infection is preventable, and individuals who have access to appropriate preventative measures and the ability to implement the measures effectively have a greater likelihood of protecting themselves from infection. Socioeconomic causes of vulnerability to HIV infection contribute to complex clinical issues as they appear in generalist social work practice. Among the variables that contribute to vulnerability are poverty, inadequate health care and health education, and geographic isolation (Hamblin, 1992). These factors exaggerate the negative effect of the target problems often associated with HIV and AIDS. The populations social workers encounter often struggle with these life situations.

DEVELOPING HELPING RELATIONSHIPS WITH PERSONS WITH AIDS OR HIV

A social worker can play various roles to assist clients and their families in coping with the multitude of problems that often accompany HIV infection. Among these roles, case manager, advocate, and counselor are the most pertinent to generalist social work practice.

In order to navigate the complex system of social services for people with HIV or AIDS, a social worker must often assume the role of a case manager. Case management incorporates the provision of advice, therapy, or counseling services to specific communities and networking and linking clients with specific services and formal and informal helping networks (Rothman, 1991). It is often directed at empowering clients to alleviate concrete needs.

Advocacy also plays a significant role in social work with people infected with HIV and AIDS. Because of AIDS-related stigma, a social worker often finds himself or herself confronting social inequities and discrimination within the social system on behalf of clients.

The role of the social worker as counselor is different from that of case manager and advocate. A counselor assists clients by helping them meet psychosocial needs rather than concrete needs presented by HIV infection. These roles may overlap depending on individual situations and the outcome of assessment.

Target Problems

Many of the people who contract HIV and AIDS are poor. Even for those who are not, treatment is extremely expensive, costing $20,000 annually. Besides the costs of medication, treatment costs include regular doctor's visits, the use of special-ists, medical testing, and alternative treatment, such as acupuncture, acupressure, massage, and herbal therapies. As a result, people with AIDS or HIV often strug-gle with financial hardships. They may be unable to work because of poor health or AIDS discrimination. Thus they lose their employer-provided medical insur-ance and may be unable to pay for necessary treatments as well as for food, shel-ter, child care, and so on.

The newest and generally most effective antiretroviral drug treatments are promising, but many obstacles accompany their utilization. Treatment regimens can involve the ingestion of massive doses of medications multiple times daily. Potent and psychologically negative side effects such as vomiting, fatigue, disfig-urement, and flu-like symptoms, are likely. Strict adherence to treatment regi-mens is difficult for many HIV-infected individuals who are concerned with day-to-day survival and the immediate business of life. Unfortunately, missing doses can lead to the development of resistance, making the medications ineffec-tive (*San Francisco Chronicle*, 1998).

Becoming a participant in experimental procedures or clinical trials is one way people with HIV or AIDS access new medications. Women and children are less likely to have access to experimental trials than adult men:

> [Data] support the suggestion that poor women and their children do not have rou-tine access to advanced treatments, and in comparison to individuals who have access to experienced primary care physicians and facilities, those who must rely on alterna-tive sources of care may experience worse health, an increase in hospitalizations, and earlier death. (Stein, 1998, p. 62)

Furthermore, individuals who do participate in these experiments may receive the nonactive agent, rather than the anti-HIV experimental drug.

HIV infection has been increasing at a remarkable rate among people who find themselves homeless. Homeless people may be infected as a result of engag-ing in sex for money, shelter or drugs, or their infection may be a result of sexual assault, or substance abuse. Homeless people with severe mental illness and those who abuse alcohol or drugs may engage in behaviors that put them at risk of contracting HIV and AIDS (Somlai, Kelly, Wagstaff, & Whitson, 1998). People who are homeless, especially women with children are unlikely to have money or access to treatment for HIV or AIDS.

Homelessness and HIV

Paul G. is a middle-aged Caucasian male who identifies himself as a hetero-sexual. He sought individual outpatient treatment to help him cope with a diagnosis of HIV infection. Earlier in the year, he lost his job due to discrim-ination against people with HIV and AIDS. He was actively engaged in a lawsuit to rectify that situation at the onset of therapy. Early treatment focused on developing a helping relationship as well as providing accurate information and education about HIV and AIDS.

Paul had been living with his brother, who forced him to move because of his fear of contagion for his children. Paul refused to go to a shelter, and he found himself homeless. Paul, his therapist, and his case manager attempted to access permanent housing through a housing program funded by the Housing Opportunities for Persons with AIDS Act.

While he was waiting for permanent housing, Paul lived out of his truck. He no longer attended therapy sessions regularly and started missing doses of his medications. After numerous unsuccessful attempts to contact Paul, his case manager and therapist learned through his ex-wife that Paul had been attacked while living on the street. He died two days after the attack. His family did not hold funeral services.

People with HIV or AIDS often find themselves facing legal difficulties caused by fear of AIDS, bureaucracy, and a lack of accurate knowledge about HIV and AIDS. These include job and housing discrimination, illegal denial of dental or medical care, loss of insurance, unfair denial of government benefits, or refusal of service in a restaurant or store. Other legal needs that accompany HIV infection include writing a will, planning for custody for children, and assigning power of attorney to another person. People with HIV and AIDS also require legal assistance to steer through complex regulations to access services and benefits (AIDS Law Project of Pennsylvania, 1998; Reamer, 1993).

Psychosocial Problems

Most people with HIV and AIDS are affected by such psychosocial issues as social stigmatization; personal, familial, and societal rejection; isolation; multiple losses; mental health issues, such as depression, adjustment reactions, anxiety, and thoughts of suicide; and drug and alcohol abuse (Harvard Mental Health Letter, 1994a, 1994b; Mancoske, Wadsworth, Dugas, & Hasney, 1995; McDonell, 1993; O'Hare, Williams, & Ezoviski, 1996; Ostrow, 1998; Stein, 1998).

The Infected Individual.   Social stigmatization is a significant aspect of being infected with HIV or having AIDS. The dominating societal attitude toward people with AIDS and HIV is hostility. This AIDS-related stigma results from the fact that AIDS is incurable and contagious and is associated with groups of people who are already oppressed and stigmatized, such as gay and bisexual men, injection drug users, and people of color (Herek & Glunt, 1988; McDonell, 1993; O'Hare, Williams, & Ezoviski, 1996; Ostrow, 1998). Indeed, AIDS is viewed as indicative of moral failure (Sontag, 1988).

With stigmatization comes rejection and isolation. Due partly to fear of contagion, societal blame, and homophobia, family, friends, coworkers, and acquaintances maintain social distance from the person with HIV or AIDS (McDonell, 1993). The infected individual may lose his or her income, job, housing, family, religious community, and friends (Ostrow, 1998). Or the infected person may chose to isolate himself or herself because of fear of such rejection.

Mental health issues, such as difficulty adjusting, depression, anxiety, and suicides, to name a few, affect those living with HIV or AIDS as well as their families and friends. The disease progresses from exposure to diagnosis of HIV infection, symptoms, diagnosis of AIDS, terminal stage, and death. As the disease

TABLE 14.2. Psychosocial Issues and Possible Accompanying Strengths of People with HIV or AIDS

Stage of HIV Infection	Individual Psychosocial Issues	Strengths and Interventions
Exposure	High-risk behaviors: Denial, fear	
HIV-Positive Test Result	Crisis reaction: Shock, denial, depression, suicidality, guilt, anger, relief Disclosure: Fear, shame, guilt	Alter risk behavior; seek and utilize social support system; demonstrate courage to disclose to others; gather accurate information; devise a plan of action
Symptom-Free Period	Stability: Fear of symptom appearance	Adopt a fighting spirit; view stress as growth potential; seek a sense of stability; search for meaning; regain control; restore self esteem; increase involvement in HIV/AIDS community
Symptoms	Loss of control/independence: Guilt, anger, depression, suicidality, treatment decisions, possible disfigurement	Seek and utilize social support system; make treatment decisions; explore sense of own mortality
AIDS Diagnosis	Grief, relief, depression	Gain access to AIDS diagnosis-only benefits
Terminal Stage	Preparation for death: Depression, acceptance, assisted suicide	Make treatment decisions; plan funeral arrangements

Note: Adapted from "Disease, Disease Course, and Psychiatric Manifestations of HIV" by D. G. Ostrow, 1998, in M. F. O'Conner & I. D. Yalom (Eds.), *Treating the Psychological Consequences of HIV* (pp. 33–71). San Francisco, CA: Jossey-Bass Publishers; and "Coping with the Threat of AIDS: The Role of Social Support," by J. Leserman, D. O. Perkins, and D. L. Evans, 1992, *American Journal of Psychiatry, 149*(11), 1514–1520.

progresses through these stages, individuals progress through various mental health reactions (see Table 14.2).

Upon exposure and/or diagnosis of HIV infection, an infected person may manifest depression, anxiety, thoughts of suicide, somatic preoccupation (physical symptoms not fully explained by a general medical condition), shock, guilt, denial, anger, fear, substance abuse, isolation, and even relief. Many of these reactions are thought to dissipate with time, although maladaptive coping mechanisms, such as substance abuse, may continue or recur (*Harvard Mental Health Letter*, 1994a, 1994b; Mancoske, Wadsworth, Dugas, & Hasney, 1995; Ostrow, 1998). Accompanying strengths vary from person to person. Individuals may alter risk behaviors, seek out and utilize social support systems, gather accurate information about HIV and AIDS, and demonstrate the courage to disclose their HIV status in the face of stigma, rejection and isolation (Forstein, 1994).

On the other hand, the individual may be secretive and fearful of rejection. When disclosing to a former or current sexual partner or an individual who has engaged in any risk behavior(s) with the infected person, disclosure may involve shame, guilt, and fear of having infected another person as well as the recommendation that the partner at risk get tested for HIV.

During the symptom-free period, an infected person may fear symptom appearance and experience a generalized feeling of uncertainty. The person might also attempt to re-establish a sense of equilibrium. This can take the form of searching for meaning, restoring self-esteem, regaining a sense of control, assuming a level of altruistic ambition, and increasing one's involvement in the AIDS community.

As symptoms appear, guilt, anger, thoughts of suicide, and depression, may resurface. This stage also includes loss of independence and control, possible disfigurement resulting from treatments or such illnesses as Kaposi's sarcoma, a cancer that causes purple lesions on the skin, and the need for treatment decisions.

When AIDS is diagnosed, grief, depression, and even relief may occur. The individual will gain access to benefits allotted only to people with an AIDS diagnosis, such as experimental drug treatments and financial assistance.

As the terminal stage and death approach, an infected person may be depressed, seek assisted suicide, or display acceptance (Ostrow, 1998). Constructing a will, planning funeral arrangements, and making final treatment decisions can also be a part of this process.

Drug and alcohol abuse may be used as coping mechanisms at any time as individuals seek to numb the pain of social stigmatization, isolation, rejection, and mental health reactions. The use of mood-altering substances can contribute to the progression of the disease, since some drugs have immune-suppressing qualities. It may also increase viral replication and vulnerability to opportunistic infections linked with HIV (Batki, 1990). Drugs may also interact with cocktail medications, which may result in resistance to the medications.

The Family System.   For the purposes of this chapter, a friend, partner, parent, child, grandparent, or even a collateral contact such as a professional is considered to be family for an individual with HIV or AIDS. AIDS-related stigma profoundly affects the family system of an infected person. The stigma may contribute to an AIDS-phobic reaction on the part of family members (*Harvard Mental Health Letter*, 1994b). Family members may feel afraid for the infected person and for themselves. They may experience societal and community rejection and isolation from their social support systems.

As shown in Table 14.3, families and friends also move through stages and experience similar and different mental health reactions (Ostrow, 1998). An HIV diagnosis may confirm a long-held suspicion about the infected person's HIV status or overall health (Land, 1992) . If the infected person is gay, the disclosure of HIV infection may be the first time the family member learns about his sexual orientation, exaggerating the effect of the disclosure (*Harvard Mental Health Letter*, 1994b). Shock, uncertainty, depression, fear, guilt and shame may be felt. Family members may also deny that AIDS is incurable in order to maintain their own emotional and psychological well-being, which may motivate them to seek out and utilize social support systems and gather accurate information about HIV and AIDS.

During the symptom-free period, family members might experience uncertainty about the future, but also adopt a positive view of life, as reinforced by social supports. Witnessing the struggle and effective coping with HIV may be a

TABLE 14.3. Psychosocial Issues and Possible Accompanying Strengths of Families of People with HIV or AIDS

Stage of HIV Infection	Familial Psychosocial Issues	Strengths and Interventions
Exposure (0 Years)	Denial, secrecy, fear, concern	
HIV-Positive Test Result	Crisis reaction: Shock, denial, uncertainty, depression Disclosure: Fear, shame, guilt	Use denial as healthy coping skill; seek and utilize social support system; gather accurate information; devise a course of action
Symptom-Free Period	Stability: Uncertainty	Search for meaning; engage in introspection; adopt a positive view of life; increase involvement in AIDS community; view stress as growth potential
Symptoms	Caregiving: Fear, exhaustion, caregiver burnout	Support reciprocity; make treatment decisions; seek and utilize social support system; experience greater intimacy with family and individual
AIDS Diagnosis	Anticipatory grief, depression	Seek and utilize social support system
Terminal Stage	Preparation for death: Anticipatory grief; caregiver burnout; final treatment decisions; depression; acceptance; suicide assistance	Participate in planning funeral arrangements; seek and utilize social support system; experience greater intimacy with family and individual
Death	Grief process and bereavement recovery	Nurture self; seek and utilize social support system

Note: Adapted from "Disease, Disease Course, and Psychiatric Manifestations of HIV," by D. G. Ostrow, 1998, in M. F. O'Conner & I. D. Yalom (Eds.), *Treating the Psychological Consequences of HIV* (pp. 33–71). San Francisco, CA: Jossey-Bass Publishers; and "Coping with the Threat of AIDS: The Role of Social Support," by J. Leserman, D. O. Perkins, and D. L. Evans, 1992, *American Journal of Psychiatry, 149*(11), 1514–1520.

life-affirming event for them, leading them to engage in introspection and a search for meaning. They may get involved in the AIDS community.

When symptoms do occur, fear of the future, exhaustion, and caregiver burnout may result. On the other hand, the infected person and the family may experience greater intimacy with one another. Supporting the infected person, participating in treatment decisions, and taking advantage of social support systems is important when symptoms are present.

An AIDS diagnosis might trigger anticipatory grief and depressive reactions (Ostrow, 1998). As the terminal stage approaches, caregiver burnout may be experienced more acutely as might depression and anticipatory grief. In this stage, family members may be faced with the decision about whether to assist with the infected person's suicide. Potent decisions involving quality of life are not to be taken lightly. The revitalization of inner strengths and resources are critical here, especially when attempts to alter the situation and reframe its meaning fail to reduce stress levels and despair. Participating in planning funeral arrangements, continued development of intimacy with other family members and the infected person, and social supports can help family members learn to accept (Ostrow, 1998).

When death does occur, grief and bereavement are complicated by social stigmatization, multiple losses from within the AIDS community, and possibly posttraumatic stress reactions. Nurturing oneself and gathering strength from social supports can contribute to effective coping with the loss (Bidgood, 1992; Shelby, 1994).

The stress and emotional difficulty of dealing with a family member's HIV or AIDS may lead to the implementation of maladaptive coping mechanisms, including drug and alcohol abuse. The dysfunctional dynamics of chemically addicted family systems compound the effect of psychosocial factors (Stein, 1992).

The efficacy of drug cocktails has altered the life-cycle of HIV and its psychosocial stages. For example, if the drug cocktail is effective after AIDS has been diagnosed, the individual and family may feel hope for a future and a cure, fear of false hope, or fear of running out of money if assets were liquidated in preparation for death. On the other hand, the cost of these medications preclude some from gaining access to them, causing depression, anxiety, and anger.

Children, Adolescents, and HIV

The infection of children and adolescents is a particularly challenging aspect of the HIV epidemic for social workers. The stress of learning that children or adolescents are infected with HIV can contribute to parental substance abuse, abandonment by a spouse or partner, psychological turmoil, and dissolution of a family system (Lewert, 1992).

Generally, parents or guardians don't tell children under the age of four that they have been diagnosed with HIV or AIDS because they are not developmentally capable of understanding the implications of such a disclosure. Parents or guardians usually tell adolescents aged fourteen and older about the diagnosis because of their sexual maturity and potential public health risks (Lipson, 1993). The problem is what to tell children between four and fourteen. How does a parent or guardian decide to tell a child about his or her infection status? What prevents some parents from doing so? As social workers, we need to be able to assist clients in answering such questions.

Parents and guardians often want to delay disclosure, while professionals want to hasten it. Disclosure to children means admitting the presence of the illness, which parents or guardians may be psychologically suppressing. They may fear their children's questions about the nature of transmission, feeling ashamed of their high-risk behavior and not wanting to hear blame and anger from the children. They may also wish to shield the children from the rejection and isolation that often accompany HIV infection. In addition, parents or guardians may fear that their children will disclose their HIV status or ask their parents about the prognosis (Lipson, 1993).

Disclosure should be viewed in terms of process—that is, involving children in a continual cognitive involvement with their illness and its effects.

Shifting from a one-time developmental moment in which children understand HIV to ongoing and flexible conversations about children's health, relationships, and events helps parents or guardians and their children adjust to living with HIV infection.

Another distinctive issue related to HIV infection of children and adolescents is foster care. Foster care may be needed because of abuse, neglect, or abandonment or because of the death of an HIV-infected biological parent. Foster parents who care for HIV-infected children and adolescents often develop strong emotional connections with the foster children. They "assume all the pain and anguish of a biological parent, without being accorded the same rights and privileges. Many treatment decisions, including the enrollment of their foster child in a clinical treatment trial, may not be theirs to make" (Lewert, 1992, p. 164). They often require the same social work services as biological parents.

Because adolescent development often includes such high-risk behaviors as sexual exploration and experimentation with drugs, HIV infection among adolescents is on the rise. An HIV diagnosis can severely interrupt adolescent psychological development. It can make formation of sexual identity, separation and individuation, and planning for the future difficult. It can lead to maladaptive coping behaviors such as substance abuse, high-risk sexual activity, running away, and suicide. Social work services and interventions must be developmentally appropriate and comprehensive. It is necessary to address the basic needs for shelter, food, and medical care, to provide emotional support, to discourage suicide, substance abuse, pregnancy, and other risks, and to provide accurate information about sexual development and behavior in working with HIV-infected adolescents (Pennbridge, Belzer, Schiner, & MacKenzie, 1992).

Pregnancy and HIV

HIV infection is increasing rapidly among women and is often complicated by the possibility of pregnancy. When called to assist clients in making difficult reproductive decisions, social workers need to understand the social, political, and personal issues involved.

HIV-infected women who are pregnant or are thinking about becoming pregnant are viewed as "vectors of transmission" of disease. They are perceived as selfish, immoral, and irresponsible. Currently, they are being blamed for sustaining and perpetuating the AIDS epidemic just as gay males were blamed for initiating it. Gender-based discrimination is exaggerated for HIV-infected women, who must often also endure inadequate child care, poverty, lack of housing and health care, poor employment prospects, violence, and other forms of oppression and prejudice (Boston Women's Health Book Collective, 1992; Bradley-Springer, 1994; Stutzner-Gibson, 1991).

Given this political and social backdrop, the decision-making process is often individualistic and filled with uncertainty.

> In situations of uncertainty, such as risk of contracting or transmitting HIV, probabilistic reasoning is essential. Yet probabilistic reasoning—the weighing of risks and benefits, the ability to conceive of abstract harm, and the skill of distinguishing between likely and unlikely future consequences—is difficult for almost everyone. (Levine & Dubler, 1990, p. 342)

Generally, knowledge of HIV infection is not a major determinant in reproductive choice. HIV infection alone is not seen by women as sufficient reason to terminate a wanted pregnancy. Ironically, the pending loss of child-bearing potential and the limits placed on a woman's life by HIV infection often lead to an accelerated reproduction rate (Almond & Ulanowsky, 1990; Bernstein, MacKenzie, Oleska, & Pizzo, 1989; Stutzner-Gibson, 1991).

Pregnancy can serve as a symbol of love of a partner. It can represent the development of a new relationship and role fulfillment as a mother. It can also confer status and demonstrate a commitment to the future. In spite of possible condemnation for placing children at risk for HIV infection, pursuing or continuing a pregnancy "may be the most reasonable and available choice, a natural outcome of all the forces in their lives, in which avenues for self-definition and expression other than mothering are largely absent" (Levine & Dubler, 1990, p. 323).

The reduction of the incidence of pediatric AIDS resulting from voluntary testing and the use of antiviral treatments during pregnancy has been one of the brightest spots in AIDS research and treatment throughout the epidemic (CDC, 1998a; Strong, Devault, & Sayad, 1999). Such advances, however, further contribute to the complexities of reproductive choice for HIV-infected women. Accurate information on risks and safeguarded procedures is needed to help HIV-infected women make appropriate treatment decisions and referrals.

Cultural Considerations

In order to develop a helping relationship with members of racial, ethnic, and sexual minority groups, it is important to understand aspects of their histories and culture. These groups may be diverse within themselves. For example, the cultural group called "Asian-Americans and Pacific Islanders" is composed of at least thirty-two different ethnic and racial clusters and languages, each with variations based on what generation an individual is part of, whether the person is native to the country, and the level of acculturation of family members (Wade, Watts, & Mo, 1991). To get an accurate and sensitive assessment, a social worker must ask:

1. Are members ascribing to traditional cultural values?
2. Are there differing or conflicting values among members of the same family?
3. Do any intergenerational cultural strains exist?
4. To what extent do families rely on external support systems?
5. What types of support systems are utilized?
6. What are appropriate resources for social workers to access or refer?

African-Americans.   The CDC (1998a) reports that 107,000 African-Americans are currently diagnosed with AIDS. Among men, 60 percent of those reported as infected with HIV in 1997 were African-American or Latino. Among women, African-Americans or Latinas accounted for 78 percent of reported cases. Although the majority of people with AIDS and HIV are Caucasian, African-Americans are being infected in far greater numbers than their relative percentage in the population. They represent one of the fastest growing segments of HIV infection (CDC, 1998a; see also Table 14.1).

The African-American community has significant reasons to mistrust social service and/or government efforts to address HIV and AIDS. African-Americans have a history of ill-treatment in the United States. "We must be cognizant that our history of slavery and racism has contributed to the social environment in which those blacks at greatest risk of HIV infection are also among the most disadvantaged members of our society" (Thomas & Quinn, 1993, p. 321). The infamous Tuskegee syphilis study contributes to the belief among African-Americans that AIDS is a form of racial genocide. In 1932, the U.S. Public Health Service, in conjunction with the Tuskegee Institute, a reputable black college, recruited six hundred African-American men to participate in an experiment on the untreated effects and symptoms of syphilis (Strong, DeVault, & Sayad, 1999; Thomas & Quinn, 1991). The study was intended to last from six to nine months, but "the drive to satisfy scientific curiosity resulted in a forty year experiment that followed the men to 'end-point' (autopsy)" (Thomas & Quinn, 1991, p. 1500). The Tuskegee syphilis study ended in 1972, just one decade before the appearance of AIDS, and its legacy is suspicion and fear. We must respect such beliefs and experiences in the development of the helping relationship.

Two significant strengths of African-American culture are family and religion. The nuclear and extended family, neighbors, friends, and religious organizations play a role in the development and support of members (Wade, Watts, & Mo, 1991). The African-American family contributes to a sense of coherence and stability in the environment. Since people with a strong sense of family are more likely to frame an event as less stressful than those with a weak sense of family, and since women with a strong sense of coherence report fewer high-risk behaviors than those with a weak sense of coherence, it can be theorized that the African-American family can help prevent HIV infection (Sweet-Jemmott, Catan, Nyamathi, & Anastasia, 1995).

Historically, religion has played a profound role in sustaining African-Americans in the face of adverse social situations. It has also been a source of societal change and influence. Whole neighborhoods access support, education, and services emanating from a local religious institution (Wade, Watts, & Mo, 1991). The Black Coalition Caucus, an organization focused on examination of HIV, AIDS, and genocide, has resolved "to look to our black clergy and church for absolute assurance that CDC AIDS testing and counseling initiatives are not just another Tuskegee tragedy being perpetrated on the Black race" (Department of Health and Human Services, 1989, p. 6). The importance of religion in the African-American community should not be underestimated.

Latinos.   The CDC (1998a) reports that 52,700 Latinos are currently diagnosed with AIDS. The current rate of HIV infection among Latinos underlines the urgency of addressing HIV and AIDS within this community (CDC, 1998a). Language, family, gender roles, and religion are relevant to Latino culture and AIDS. *Confianza*, the breaking down of barriers and the formation of trust, cannot be established in Latino communities without breaching the language barrier. Discussion of HIV, which may include conversations about sexuality, must be handled respectfully, since sexuality is one of the least discussed topics in Latino culture (Medina, 1987).

The family provides support in Latino culture and can incorporate nuclear and extended families, communities, friends, and religious organizations.

Generally speaking, Latinos are not accustomed to external support or involvement from outside the family system. Members rely on internal familial support.

Gender roles have a profound effect on the interrelationships within the Latino family. Three *traditional roles* are *machismo*, *etiqueta*, and *marianismo*. *Machismo*, male pride, incorporates an exaggerated importance of being male. Boys are socialized to be independent and dominant in their relationships with women. It also encourages respect of the maternal figure and responsibility for the older adults in the family. *Etiquita* is the process whereby little girls are socialized to be quiet and respectful. They are adorned with feminine outfits and jewelry. Their virtue and virginity are strictly supervised by older members of the family. They are consistently told of their inferiority to men, submissiveness, and physical beauty. *Marianismo* is the role of the obedient and submissive woman. Expression of sensuality is considered self-indulgent and suggests a lack of virtue. Sex is *for procreative purposes* only. The woman's role is primarily centered around her husband and children (Medina, 1987).

Approximately 85 percent of Latinos are Catholic, and religious influences reinforce these familial roles. Religious and familial socialization can contribute to HIV infection. For example, *machismo* and *marianismo* might discourage use of the barrier method to prevent HIV infection, since couples are expected to bear children. Understanding these roles is important for developing relationships in Latino communities.

Asian-Americans and Pacific Islanders. Asian-Americans and Pacific Islanders account for less than 1 percent of AIDS incidence (CDC, 1998a). Traditional Asian culture is interdependent within its immediate community. Individualism is generally not tolerated. Family members are expected to ensure the continuity of the family name and legacy. Children are expected to marry, to have children, and to care for the elders of the family (Wade, Watts, & Mo, 1991). HIV infection can interrupt this cycle, jeopardizing the family's standing in the community.

Racial and Ethnic Minority Gays, Lesbians, and Bisexuals. Gays, lesbians, and bisexuals who are members of racial or ethnic minority groups face special difficulties. Organizations that have traditionally provided support to their racial or ethnic group will refuse to support members with nontraditional sexual orientations. For example, the black church is a source of strength for many African-Americans, but gay, lesbian, and bisexual members who acknowledge their sexual orientations face the loss of both family and church. This can contribute to the use of maladaptive coping mechanisms, such as drug and alcohol use and high-risk sexual behavior, leading to HIV infection. Meanwhile, gay, lesbian, or bisexual African-Americans may experience overt and covert racism and discrimination from the gay, lesbian, and bisexual community.

In Latino culture, homosexuality is generally viewed as a threat to *machismo* and male sexual identity. There are also religious taboos to be dealt with. In the Latino and Asian-American cultures, being gay, lesbian, or bisexual means losing status and dishonoring the family name. The cultures tend to lack knowledge about AIDS and HIV and to ridicule people who are infected. As a result, HIV education efforts and reductions in HIV infection have met with little success (Medina, 1987; Wade, Watts, & Mo, 1991).

African-American Culture and HIV

Lamont R. is an HIV-infected, middle-aged African-American, gay male. His presenting problems consisted of anxiety, self-loathing, and relationship difficulties with his family of origin around his sexual orientation and religious affiliations. Outpatient treatment focused on familial assessment and the development and implementation of intervention strategies. Lamont and his social worker use progressive relaxation techniques and role-playing conversations about sexuality, religion, and cultural issues to reduce anxiety. Lamont adamantly refused to discuss religious and sexuality issues with certain family members, fearing rejection. Lamont did talk to family members he deemed "safe," and he reported positive and low-anxiety conversations with them. As a result of one of these conversations, one of his brothers came out to him as a bisexual, thereby ending the isolation and increasing social supports for both men. Lamont was also referred to a gay-affirming and culturally sensitive religious organization through professional networks.

Rural Communities.   HIV and AIDS have traditionally been associated with urban populations in the United States. In rural communities, HIV presents unique challenges to social work practice. Urban settings often have involved community leaders, broad-based media coverage, qualified and knowledgeable mental health providers, alternative and mainstream medical treatment options, and shrewd political health advocates to help create sophisticated approaches to HIV and AIDS. In rural communities, infected individuals face social isolation and stigmatization, lack of information, transportation difficulties, and fear of unwanted disclosure. Social workers who work with HIV-infected clients or their families may become outcasts. HIV-infected individuals may lie about their illness in order to preserve their and their family's standing in the community (Heckman, Kelly, Somlai, Kalichman, & Heckman, 1999; O'Rourke & Sutherland, 1994). Social workers need to be prepared to deal with these as well as with inadequate social service systems.

Micro Practice Considerations

The helping relationship involves deep emotion, and the micro practice issues involved are intensely personal. The use of self, in which workers themselves become therapeutic tools, can be especially effective in working with clients with HIV and AIDS. Use of self is "an overarching process whereby clinicians use their own life experiences, their intellectual and emotional understanding of inner and outer reality, their understanding of human development, their understanding of their patient's lives, their feelings in session, and the process of empathy in working with their patients" (Frost, 1998, p. 5).

Self-Disclosure.   Self-disclosure is "an interaction in which the therapist reveals personal information about him or herself, and/or reveals reactions and responses to the client as they arise in the session" (Knox, Hess, Peterson, & Hill, 1997, p. 275). Self-disclosure can involve informing the client of the HIV status of the social worker or the worker's feelings about HIV policy and politics.

A client may ask, "Do you have AIDS?" If the social worker is HIV-infected, the revelation of his or her HIV status has benefits and risks. Disclosure may make it possible to explore issues of death and dying, losses, the meanings of those losses, and, the meaning of the therapeutic relationship with the social worker. On the other hand, clients may feel that their issues are being minimized. The worker and client may feel uncomfortable about the worker's self-exposure or loss of composure and grief. The worker may feel guilty about withholding the information, if this occurred (Philip, 1994). An HIV-infected gay therapist described his decision to self-disclose as clouded:

> It is difficult even in hindsight for me to say with any certainty that the best time for disclosure of my own illness to patients would have been after some reasonable lapse of time following diagnosis—enough time to process the shock, assess the damage, think through the needs of self and patients, and so forth. (Philips, 1994, p. 538)

For social workers who are not infected, what appears to be an easy answer to the question of HIV status can open other issues. Some clients may feel that HIV-negative social workers do not understand the experience of living with HIV infection. They may expect to encounter prejudice and discrimination from the worker once disclosure has occurred. Consultation with colleagues, supervisors, and peers can help a social worker determine the best course of action (Philip, 1994).

The Strengths Perspective. Many social work interventions in the area of HIV and AIDS adopt a deficit approach:

> The vastly disproportionate focus of the existing literature on negative aspects of HIV, with only a few more recent studies on coping, is unjustified. By failing to recognize the growth some [individuals] with HIV have created in themselves, social work professionals can inadvertently minimize the personal strengths and power of their clients. This mindset tends to keep these clients in simple categories (for example, victim) and may impede ethical social work practice, which includes primacy of clients' interests, rights, and prerogatives. (Dunbar, Mueller, Medina, & Wolf, 1998, p. 145)

People with HIV and AIDS can adapt to and cope effectively with the multiple stressors involved in living with HIV. Successful strategies include

- Adopting a fighting spirit
- Reframing stress to increase personal growth
- Planning a course of action
- Seeking and utilizing a social support system.

People who utilize such techniques are less likely to feel unwell, to have low self-esteem, and to feel angry and helpless than those who do not engage such coping mechanisms (Leserman, Perkins, & Evans, 1992). Additionally, women who utilize active coping strategies, as opposed to avoidance, are less likely to engage in HIV risk behaviors (Nyamathi & Lewis, 1991).

Six strengths-based interventions are of clinical import to social work practice (Dunbar, Mueller, Medina, & Wolf, 1998). First, anticipate, recognize, and encourage growth in order to validate feelings and experiences as well as to develop appropriate clinical interventions. Allowing individuals to develop their own agendas and the subsequent skills for achieving productive growth is empowering. This does not mean denying painful issues but rather determining an appropriate time in the helping process to raise them (Dunbar, Mueller, Medina, & Wolf, 1998).

Second, assist clients with issues of death and dying and help them grieve for their multiple losses. Anticipating death and gaining a sense of survival by living with HIV can allow clients to explore and accept their own mortality, which is often something a worker has not examined.

Third, help clients affirm life. Assist them in establishing realistic plans for the future based on both the long and short terms. Empower clients to engage in this process by using their own strengths as motivators.

Fourth, a genuine, committed helping relationship between you and your clients can encourage self-evaluation, self-affirmation, and self-care as part of the helping process. Clear self-evaluation and introspection can lead clients to a sense of resolution with themselves. Self-affirmation and self-care are the logical next step so you should monitor clients' progress and assist them at any point.

Fifth, the evaluation of relationships, facilitation of relationship resolutions, and development of new relationships creates a sense of empowerment and a sense of wholeness. This may require helping clients develop skills to get concrete and psychological needs met in order to improve or end difficult relationships.

Finally, keep biases in check. Be introspective and honest, and utilize supervision to work through any negative feelings or judgments about clients.

SUMMARY

This chapter has examined the multifaceted issues related to HIV and AIDS. Understanding the disease, modes of transmission, epidemiology, treatments, and how the disease manifests itself in this varied population is necessary for effective generalist social work practice. A grasp of the history of social work in light of this epidemic can give social workers a profound respect for the ability of grassroots efforts to create change. Being knowledgeable about the current policies, funding, and micro and macro practice issues is equally important. The target problems, cross-cultural components, and psychosocial issues affecting the infected individual and his or her family systems is especially relevant to the development of the helping relationship.

Conducting generalist social work practice in the field of HIV and AIDS is a challenging and rewarding endeavor. Since there is no cure for AIDS, social workers have a continuing obligation and opportunity to provide services to people with HIV and AIDS and their families. Engaging individuals in the context of a committed, genuine helping relationship is the essence of the longstanding social work mission of seeking individual well-being, empowerment, and social justice.

CASE EXAMPLE

The following case example is representative of some of the complexities involved in working with people infected with HIV or AIDS and their families. It depicts specific aspects of the helping relationship as well as multiple levels of care and collaborative efforts.

Emotional Expression and HIV

Rob W. was referred for individual therapy as a result of his case manager's recommendation to work on "some of his emotional issues." His presenting problems consisted of major depression, an inability to express emotion, and familial conflicts.

Assessment

Rob is a thirty-one-year-old, gay Caucasian who was infected with HIV in the mid-1980s. He reportedly engaged in high-risk sexual behavior as a maladaptive means of coping when a relationship ended. Rob's life was very secretive because of his fear of familial rejection over his sexuality. When he was twenty-four, he left Pennsylvania and moved to Washington to flee such fears. He moved back to his family's home in Pennsylvania when he became too ill to care for himself.

Rob came out to his family as gay at the age of twenty-eight when he disclosed his HIV status. This multiple disclosure shocked his family. They had little opportunity to process their feelings, however, because Rob's rapidly failing health meant that he needed care.

Rob's strengths were numerous. He was bright and insightful and was able to benefit from his insights. Rob had worked as a clerk in law offices in Pennsylvania and Washington. He had hoped to seek further education and possibly enter law school. His social support system was extensive and spanned the country. His family rallied around him emotionally, physically, and financially. His many friends from Washington often traveled to his home to visit him, as did some of his local school friends. Their visits provided him with a sense of community and hope outside of his overwhelmed immediate family. In addition, his sense of spirituality was powerful.

Intervention and Evaluation

Rob spoke of "emotional numbness" or a "block." Therapy focused on examining how to express his emotional wants and needs, as well as how to cope with the slow loss of the use of his left arm. He reported that therapy and case management helped him develop an internal resolve that he had not experienced previously. His willingness and motivation to actively participate in treatment contributed to this level of acceptance.

Rob attended therapy until his health deteriorated and mobility became problematic. The social worker began conducting in-home visits. Rob began feeling and expressing grief about his situation. A hospice nurse began to help with Rob's care. When Rob questioned her, this nurse disclosed her role as a hospice nurse and explained that hospice care is pain-management care given to those who are dying. Apparently, three months before, when Rob was in the hospital, he was diagnosed with progressive multifocal leukoencephalopathy (PML), a neurologic infection. The diagnosis explained the increasing weakness of his limbs. He had approximately six months to live. Reportedly, this was not discussed with Rob or the family, nor did he or the family ask what the diagnosis meant. So when the hospice nurse casually disclosed her role, it communicated to Rob for the first time that he was dying. He had a panic attack as a result and quickly contacted his social worker.

The social worker collaborated with Rob's case manager, case management assistant, and a social work colleague to provide additional social and professional supports and services to him and his family in the home. Rob's mother and father began seeing another social worker in outpatient treatment for issues of grief, loss, and anger. The case manager provided in-home social supports and delivery of services to Rob. The case manager and the social worker designed a family intervention where Rob could express his wishes for his memorial services and his grief and loss over his pending death. Unfortunately, Rob's throat swelled significantly due to a side effect of medication, making breathing difficult, so Rob, who had struggled to express his emotions because of psychological blocks, was now physically blocked from having a good cry. The family session allowed everyone to express pain and grief, while individual work focused on helping Rob express grief in different ways than potent crying spells.

Termination

Paradoxically, the tragic way Rob discovered his prognosis allowed for a significant emotional and spiritual breakthrough. While discussing the family session, he disclosed to the social worker that he "never really felt like I belonged on this planet." He described a sense of "not fitting in" here and needing to "move on." He reported a spiritual sense of peace around death. More than a dozen social service staff attended the funeral to mourn the loss of this courageous young man. Aftercare services are still in place for the family for bereavement counseling and support.

DISCUSSION QUESTIONS

1. How might you develop a helping relationship with Rob and his family?
2. What other areas of intervention might have been effective for Rob? What other resources could have been accessed to provide more comprehensive care?
3. What feelings or emotions might working with Bob raise? How would you care for yourself as a worker in this case?
4. What are some of the psychosocial issues and possible strengths affecting an individual infected with HIV or diagnosed with AIDS? The family of an infected person?
5. What are some of the important cultural considerations to keep in mind when working with African-Americans, Latinos, Asian-Americans, or Pacific Islanders?
6. How might you use strengths to help a person affected by HIV or AIDS?

REFERENCES

AIDS Law Project of Pennsylvania. (1993, July). Act 148: The confidentiality of HIV-related information act. *Pennsylvania AIDS Law Report, 1*, 1–11.

AIDS Law Project of Pennsylvania. (1998). *AIDS and the law: Your rights in Pennsylvania* (3rd ed.). Philadelphia: AIDS Law Project.

Almond, B., & Ulanowsky, C. (1990). HIV and pregnancy. *Hastings Center Report, 20*(2), 16–21.

Batki, S. (1990). Substance abuse and AIDS: The need for mental health services. *New Directions for Mental Health Services, 48*, 55–56.

Bayer, R., Fox, D. M., & Willis, D. P. (Eds.). (1986). AIDS: The public context of an epidemic [Special issue]. *Milbank Quarterly, 64*(1).

Bernstein, L. J., MacKenzie, R. G., Oleska, J. M., & Pizzo, P. A. (1989). AIDS in children and adolescents. *Patient Care, 23*(18), 80–99.

Bidgood, R. (1992). Coping with the trauma of AIDS losses. In H. Land (Ed.), *A complete guide to psychosocial intervention* (pp. 239–251). Milwaukee, WI: Family Service of America.

Boston Women's Health Book Collective. (1992). *The new our bodies, our selves: a book by and for women.* New York: Simon & Schuster.

Bradley-Springer, L. A. (1994). Human immunodeficiency virus infection in the health-care worker. *Journal of the Association of Nurses in AIDS Care, 4*(1), 37–47.

Cadwell, S. A. (1994). Twice removed: The stigma suffered by gay men with AIDS. In S. A. Cadwell, R. A. Burnham, & M. Forstein (Eds.), *Therapists on the front line: Psychotherapy with gay men in the age of AIDS* (pp. 3–24). Washington, DC: American Psychiatric Press.

Cadwell, S. A. (1998). Transference and countertransference. In M. F. O'Conner & I. D. Yalom (Eds.), *Treating the psychological consequences of HIV* (pp. 1–32). San Francisco: Jossey-Bass.

Centers for Disease Control and Prevention. (1996a). *HIV/AIDS surveillance report, 7*(2), 1–10.

Centers for Disease Control and Prevention. (1996b). AIDS associated with injection drug use: United States, 1995. *Morbidity and Mortality Weekly Report, 45*, 392–398.

Centers for Disease Control and Prevention. (1997). *HIV/AIDS surveillance report, 9*(2), 1–44.

Centers for Disease Control and Prevention. (1998a). *HIV/AIDS surveillance report, 10*(1), 1–37.

Centers for Disease Control and Prevention. (1998b). 1998 guidelines for treatments of STD's. *Morbidity and Mortality Weekly Report, 47*, (RR-1).

Department of Health and Human Services. (1989). Prevention and beyond: A framework for collective action. In *Program supplement for the National Conference on HIV Infection and AIDS Among Racial and Ethnic Populations.* Washington, DC: Department of Health and Human Services.

Dhooper, S. S., Royse, D. D., & Tran, T. V. (1987). Social work practitioners' attitudes toward AIDS victims. *Journal of Applied Social Sciences, 12*, 108–123.

Diaz, Y. E., & Kelly, J. A. (1991). AIDS-related training in U.S. schools of social work. *Social Work, 36*, 38–42.

Dorgan, C. A. (1995). *Statistical record of health and medicine.* New York: Gale Research.

Dunbar, H. T., Mueller, C. W., Medina, C., & Wolf, T. (1998). Psychological and spiritual growth in women living with HIV. *Social Work, 43*(2), 144–154.

Feyler, N., Freedman, D., Egan, P., Hirsch, A., Landau, R., & Goldfein, R. (1997). *AIDS Law Project of Pennsylvania: HIV/AIDS legal advocacy manual.* Philadelphia: AIDS Law Project.

Forstein, M. (1994). Testing for HIV: Psychological and psychotherapeutic considerations. In S. A. Cadwell, R. A. Burnham, & M. Forstein (Eds.), *Therapists on the front line: Psychotherapy with gay men in the age of AIDS* (pp. 185–202). Washington, DC: American Psychiatric Press.

Frost, J. C. (1998). Countertransference considerations for the gay male when leading psychotherapy groups for gay men. *International Journal of Group Psychotherapy, 48*(1), 3–24.

Gamson, J. (1991). Silence, death, and the invisible enemy: AIDS activism and social movement newness. In M. Buraway, A. Burton, A. A. Ferguson, K. J. Fox, J. Gamson, N. Gartrell, L. Hurst, C. Kurzman, L. Salizinger, J. Schiffman, & S. Ui (Eds.), *Ethnography unbound: Power and resistance in modern metropolis* (pp. 35–57). Berkeley, CA: University of California Press.

Gottlieb, M. S. (1991, June 5). AIDS—the second decade: Leadership is lacking. *The New York Times*, p. A29.

Hamblin, J. (1992). People living with HIV: The law, ethics and discrimination. *HIV and Development Programme, UNDP, 4*, 1–9.

Harvard Mental Health Letter, (1994a). *Lester Grinspoon, 10*(7), 1–4.

Harvard Mental Health Letter, (1994b). *Lester Grinspoon, 10*(8), 1–4.

Heckman, T. G., Kelly, J. A., Somlai, A. M., Kalichman, S. C., & Heckman, B. D. (1999). High-risk sexual behavior among persons living with HIV disease in small towns and rural areas. *Journal of Sex Education and Therapy, 24*(1&2), 29–36.

Herek, G. M., & Glunt, E. K. (1988). An epidemic of stigma: Public reactions to AIDS. *American Psychologist, 43*, 886–891.

Health Resources and Services Administration. (1997). *Ryan White CARE Act: Title I manual*. Washington, D.C.: Department of Health and Human Services.

Irvine, J. (1998, June 28). Studies say c-sections can fight AIDS. *Monterey Herald*, p. A-7.

Knox, S., Hess, S. A., Petersen, D. A., & Hill, C. E. (1997). A qualitative analysis of client perceptions of the effects of helpful therapist self-disclosure in long-term therapy. *Journal of Counseling Psychology, 44*(3), 274–283.

Kolata, G. (1995, February 28). New picture of who will get AIDS is dominated by addicts. *The New York Times*, pp. 1, 3.

Land, H. (1992). Stress and coping in AIDS caregivers: Partners, friends and family members. In H. Land (Ed.), *A complete guide to psychosocial intervention* (pp. 199-214). Milwaukee, WI: Family Service of America.

Landers, D. V., & Shannon, M. T. (1997). Management of pregnant women with HIV infection. In P. A. Volderding & M. A. Sande (Eds.), *The medical management of AIDS* (5th ed., pp. 459–468). Philadelphia: Saunders.

Leserman, J., Perkins, D. O., & Evans, D. L. (1992). Coping with the threat of AIDS: The role of social support. *American Journal of Psychiatry, 149*(11), 1514–1520.

Levine, C., & Dubler, N. N. (1990). Uncertain risks and bitter realities: The reproductive choices of HIV-infected women. *The Milbank Quarterly, 68*(3), 321–351.

Lewert, G. (1992). Children and AIDS. In H. Land (Ed.), *A complete guide to psychosocial intervention* (pp. 153–168). Milwaukee, WI: Family Service of America.

Lipson, M. (1993). What do you say to a child with AIDS? *Hastings Center Report, 23*(2), 6–12.

Long, D. D., & Holle, M. C. (1997). *Macro systems in the social environment*. Itasca, IL: Peacock.

Mancoske, R. J., Wadsworth, C. M., Dugas, D. S., & Hasney, J. A. (1995). Suicide risk among people living with AIDS. *Social Work, 40*(6), 783–787.

McDonell, J. R. (1993). Judgments of personal responsibility for HIV infection: An attributional analysis. *Social Work, 38*(4), 403–410.

Medina, C. (1987). Latino culture and sex education. *SIECUS Report, 15*(3), 1–4.

National Association of Social Workers. (1996). *Code of Ethics*. Washington, DC: NASW Press.

Nevid, J. S. (1998). *Choices: Sex in the age of STD's* (2nd ed.). Boston: Allyn & Bacon.

New Mexico AIDS Education and Training Center. (1999, April 17). Antiviral therapy. *New Mexico AIDS InfoNet Fact Sheet, 410*. [On-line]. Available Internet: http://nmia.com/~hivcc/410-antiviral-therapy.html.

Nyamathi, A., & Lewis, C. (1991). Coping of African American women at risk for AIDS. *Women's Health Issues, 1*, 53–62.

O'Hare, T., Williams, C. L., & Ezoviski, A. (1996). Fear of AIDS and homophobia: Implications for direct practice and advocacy. *Social Work, 41*(1), 51–58.

O'Rourke, J. K., & Sutherland, P. S. (1994). Negotiating HIV infection in rural America: Breaking through the isolation. In S. A. Cadwell, R. A. Burnham, & M. Forstein (Eds.), *Therapists on the front line: Psychotherapy with gay men in the age of AIDS* (pp. 363–378). Washington, DC: American Psychiatric Press.

Ostrow, D. G. (1998). Disease, disease course, and psychiatric manifestations of HIV. In M. F. O'Conner & I. D. Yalom (Eds.), *Treating the psychological consequences of HIV* (pp. 33–71). San Francisco: Jossey-Bass.

Padgug, R. A., & Oppenheimer, G. M. (1992). Riding the tiger: AIDS and the gay community. In E. Fee & D. M. Fox (Eds.), *AIDS: The making of a chronic disease* (pp. 245–278). Berkeley, CA: University of California Press.

Pennbridge, J. N., Belzer, M., Schiner, A., & MacKenzie, R. G. (1992). Adolescents, HIV, and AIDS. In H. Land (Ed.), *A complete guide to psychosocial intervention* (pp. 169–186). Milwaukee, WI: Family Service of America.

Peterson, K. J. (1991). Social workers knowledge about AIDS: A national survey. *Social Work, 36*(1), 31–37.

Philip, C. E. (1994). Necessary and unnecessary disclosure: A therapist's life-threatening illness. In S. A. Cadwell, R. A. Burnham, & M. Forstein (Eds.), *Therapists on the front line: Psychotherapy with gay men in the age of AIDS* (pp. 535–548). Washington, DC: American Psychiatric Press.

Reamer, F. G. (1993). AIDS and social work: The ethics and civil liberties agenda. *Social Work, 38*(4), 412–419.

Rothman, J. (1991). A model of case management: Toward empirically based practice. *Social Work, 36*(6), 520–528.

San Francisco Chronicle. (1998, June 1). Stanford AIDS study called discouraging, p. A-2.

Shelby, R. D. (1994). Mourning within a culture of mourning. In S. A., Cadwell, R. A., Burnham, & M. Forstein (Eds.), *Therapists on the front line: Psychotherapy with gay men in the age of AIDS* (pp. 185–202). Washington, DC: American Psychiatric Press.

Shilts, R. (1987). *And the band played on: Politics, people, and the AIDS epidemic.* NY: St. Martin's.

Somlai, A. M., Kelly, J. A., Wagstaff, D. A., & Whitson, D. P. (1998). Patterns, predictors, and situational contexts of HIV risk behaviors among homeless men and women. *Social Work, 43*(1), 7–20.

Sontag, S. (1988). *AIDS as metaphor.* New York: Farrar, Strauss & Giroux.

Stein, J. B. (1992). HIV disease and substance abuse: Twin epidemics, multiple needs. In H. Land, (Ed.), *A complete guide to psychosocial intervention* (pp. 107–115). Milwaukee, WI: Family Service of America.

Stein, T. J. (1998). *The social welfare of women and children with HIV and AIDS: Legal protection, policy, and programs.* New York: Oxford University Press.

Strong, B., DeVault, C. & Sayad, B. (1999). *Human sexuality: Diversity in contemporary America* (3rd ed.). Mountain View, CA: Mayfield Publishing.

Stutzner-Gibson, D. (1991). Women and HIV disease: An emerging social crisis. *Social Work, 36*(1), 22–28.

Sweet-Jemmott, L., Catan, V., Nyamathi, A., & Anastasia, J. (1995). African-American women and HIV-risk-reduction issues. In A. O'Leary & L. Sweet-Jemmott (Eds.), *Women at risk: Issues in the primary prevention of AIDS* (pp. 131–157). New York: Plenum.

Thomas, S. B., & Quinn, S. C. (1991). The Tuskegee syphilis study, 1932 to 1972: Implications for HIV education and AIDS risk educational programs in the black community. *American Journal of Public Health, 81*(11), 1498–1505.

Thomas, S. B., & Quinn, S. C. (1993). The burdens of race and history on black Americans' attitudes toward needle exchange policy to prevent HIV disease. *Journal of Public Health Policy, 14*(3), 320–347.

Wade, S., Watts, S. E., & Mo, B. (1991, Winter). Cultural expectations and experience: Three views. *Open Hands*, 8–9.

Weinberg, G. (1972). *Society and the healthy homosexual.* New York: St. Martin's.

Yu, M. M., & O'Neal, B. (1992). Issues of confidentiality when working with persons with AIDS. *Clinical Social Work Journal, 20*(4), 421–430.

CHAPTER 15

Generalist Practice with Survivors of Natural Disasters

Hussein Soliman

Norma D. is an MSW student with a second year placement in a family service agency in an urban community. Norma provides case management and supportive services to a primarily minority elderly client population. She enjoys working with the elderly and hearing their stories.

During her second month of placement, rains from a hurricane that hit North Carolina flooded the river that runs through the community. The rains were unusually heavy, and the river flooded for the first time in recent memory. The flood damage was limited to the streets relatively close to the river. Nevertheless, for those affected, the damage was extensive. Homes were flooded, cars floated down the street, and approximately two thousand people were displaced from their homes.

All agency personnel were dispatched to help the people affected by the flood. Norma was not prepared for the effect that the physical destruction of people's homes and distress it caused had on her. By natural disaster standards the flood was a relatively small-scale event, but Norma was overwhelmed by the magnitude of the damage and the suffering. She felt a sense of powerless in much the same way her clients did. Norma couldn't understand why her agency sent her out so completely unprepared. She also wondered why social work courses had not covered anything like what she was encountering.

Natural disasters can strike anywhere. They do not differentiate among poor, rich, rural, or urban communities. Population growth and metropolitan development are combining to create bigger and more vulnerable targets for disasters. Although urban areas may be better equipped to manage disasters than rural areas because of the resources and infrastructures available, dependence on the infrastructure is greater in urban areas. Thus, when disasters strike highly populated urban areas, more people are affected and the magnitude of disaster is potentially much greater than when a sparsely populated rural area is hit. Natural disasters have caused $500 billion in damage in the last twenty years (Jaffe, 1999). Disaster relief is one of the newest fields in generalist social work practice. To provide effective relief services to survivors of disasters, it is necessary to understand the multiple effects natural disasters have on individuals, families, and communities. The purpose of this chapter is to examine the nature of social work practice with survivors of natural disasters. The focus is on the specific knowledge, strategies, and skills needed in order to provide effective social work services to survivors of natural disasters. Information is provided on the nature of disasters, types of needs created by disasters, the role social workers play in disaster relief efforts, and strategies and techniques that generalist social workers can use in working with survivors and their communities. By the end of this chapter, you should be able to help Norma

1. Understand the difference between disaster survivors and other types of social service recipients
2. Describe the characteristics of natural disasters
3. Understand the social and psychological effect that massive natural disasters have on individuals, families, and communities
4. Describe the service needs of disaster survivors and the types of assistance they require
5. Articulate the interpersonal and organizational challenges associated with the delivery of crisis intervention services
6. Understand the effect of providing disaster services on those providing the services.

CHARACTERISTICS OF DISASTERS

All disasters cause physical destruction, physical injuries, anxiety, distress, mental anguish, and disruption of daily life. Each disaster also has unique characteristics. Five factors can help distinguish one disaster from another:

1. "Type of disaster (a natural event as compared to a disaster perpetuated by man)
2. "Duration of disaster
3. "Degree of personal impact
4. "Potential for occurrence (recurrence)
5. "Control over future impact." (Berren, Beigel, & Ghertner, 1980, p. 104)

Type of Disaster

Some disasters are caused by a natural phenomenon that human beings have no control over, while others are caused by human actions and presumably could have been avoided. Disasters caused by natural phenomena are referred to as "acts of God." Recent examples in the United States include hurricanes that devastated parts of North Carolina in 1989 and 1999 and Florida in 1992, the 1993 flood of the Mississippi River, earthquakes in San Francisco in 1989 and Los Angeles in 1994, and tornadoes that touched down in Florida in 1998 and Oklahoma and Kansas in 1999. A prime example of accidents and human acts that cause tremendous adversity is the 1986 nuclear power plant accident in Chernobyl, USSR, which is considered one of the worst technological disasters of all time. Other examples include the Three Mile Island nuclear power plant malfunction 1979 and the toxic waste contamination of the Love Canal in New York

State in 1976. People were not immediately aware of the actual occurrence of these disasters. Nevertheless, both generated considerable anxiety and fear among the people who lived nearby.

In some instances, a disaster may be caused by a combination of natural phenomena and human errors. The following case example illustrates such a situation.

God Didn't Do This

In 1960 the Buffalo Mining Company, owned by the Pittston Corporation, built a third impoundment in the Buffalo Creek hallow in West Virginia. The impoundments, called dams by the local residents, were used to dump coal-mining by-products. The water in the impoundments was mixed with slag, mine dust, shale, clay, low-quality coal, and other impurities. From 1957 to the winter of 1972, one thousand tons of water, on average, was dumped every day.

Three smaller creeks come together to form Buffalo Creek which is seventeen miles in length. Below the creek is a valley where five thousand people lived. Most of the people depended on coal mining for a living.

Prior to the incident, it rained for several days. As the level of the water rose in the dam, company officials became concerned about the ability of the structure to hold back the water. At eight o'clock on the morning of February 26, the dam collapsed, spilling more than 132 million gallons of water into the valley, to a depth of twenty or thirty feet. The water crushed homes, cars, trees, and many villages. People had little or no time to escape. One hundred and twenty-five persons died, and seven were missing. Most homes were destroyed, leaving four thousand homeless.

Residents experienced two kinds of trauma during and after the disaster. The first is individual trauma: "a blow to the psyche that breaks through one's defense so suddenly and with such brutal force that one cannot react to it effectively" (Erikson, 1976, p. 153). The Buffalo Creek survivors suffered from deep shock caused by their exposure to death and devastation. The second is collective trauma: "a blow to the basic tissue of social life that damages the bonds attaching people together and impairs the prevailing sense of community—a gradual realization that the community no longer exists as an effective source of support and that an important part of the self has disappeared" (Erikson, 1976, p. 154).

Survivors were disappointed in the way the Pittston Corporation treated them. One survivor stated, "I resent the fact that no one even bothered to come to see if we were well, needing anything, offered to help clean up, or seemed to care what happened to us" (Erikson, 1976, p. 182). In the process of establishing responsibility for the disaster, some company officials declared that the disaster was an act of God. The claim was not well received by the residents: "All I can say is that the disaster was murder. The coal company knew the dam was bad, but they did not tell the people. All they wanted was to make money. They did not care about the good people that lived up Buffalo Creek" (Erikson, 1976, p. 183). The claim added to the frustration and agony felt by the survivors: "The big shots want to call it an act of God. It's a lie. They've told a lie on God, and they shouldn't have done that. God didn't do this. He wouldn't do that" (Erikson, 1976, p. 178).

Duration of Disaster

Some disasters occur as a single episode and are labeled acute. Examples of acute disasters are tornadoes, which last only a few minutes, and floods. It can take up to ten months for floodwater to recede. Other disasters occur over a prolonged period of time, these are labeled chronic. An example of a chronic disaster is the sustained contamination of the Pigeon River in Tennessee (Soliman, 1996).

Another example of a chronic disaster is the Love Canal incident in Niagara Falls, New York, in the 1970s. People discovered chemicals in their homes and some residents experienced miscarriages, children born with birth defects, and respiratory ailments as a result of exposure to toxic chemicals. After seeking a cause for these problems, community members discovered toxic chemical contamination resulting from dumping of toxic materials by an electrochemical company (Levine, 1982).

Although acute disasters such as massive floods, hurricanes, or earthquakes may generate widespread destruction, a worker can easily identify the different elements that trigger social and psychological reactions. However, in the case of chronic technological disaster, such as toxic contamination or nuclear radiation incidents, the worker may experience difficulty in determining the magnitude of the disaster, so that identifying and responding to needs may be problematic.

Degree of Personal Impact

Some disasters cause tremendous damage to communities, destroying homes, schools, and community infrastructure. Other disasters, such as earthquakes, health epidemics, and famine, cause widespread injuries and death. World participation and support are necessary if the damages caused by the disaster exceed the country's capacities for recovery. This was the case when powerful earthquakes struck Turkey and Taiwan in 1999.

In more localized disasters, recovery efforts focus mainly on utilizing community resources and contributions of local agencies and organizations. In the United States, this generally includes the disaster management office in each county, volunteer groups, and support from neighboring counties. As the volume of destruction caused by a disaster increases, support from the state and federal governments and from other countries becomes imperative.

Potential for Occurrence

While some disasters have high potential of occurring, other disasters have a low level of probability. For example, people living on the Atlantic coast are more likely to experience hurricanes than people who live inland. People who live near a nuclear reactor may have a greater chance of experiencing radiation accidents than people who do not live within close proximity. Residents who live on the banks of rivers or in floodplains are more vulnerable to flooding than those who do not. Whether such people are more likely to be prepared for a disaster depends on their perception of risk, environmental awareness, educational level, and past experiences with disasters.

Control over Future Impact

In some cases, people may be able to prevent a disaster from happening or minimize its effects. For example, extra security measures may protect public places from attacks by terrorists. Examining a levee when the water level is high and strengthening the banks of a river during periods of continuous rains can prevent widespread damage. A warning system can alert people to the need to move quickly to safe areas and thus might minimize the number of fatalities caused by a tornado.

SOCIAL WORK AND DISASTER RELIEF

Unpredictability, destruction, and uncertainty characterize disasters. Natural disasters often strike without warning, causing individuals, families, and communities to face new situations and multiple losses. Survivors experience severe trauma and need multiple services. In recent years, there has been an increase in participation of social workers in disaster recovery activities. Disaster relief services need to deal with the social, psychological, and economic effects of disasters as well as to provide support and services to survivors (Muzekari, Lonigan, Bond, & Hiers, 1991; Soliman & Poulin, 1997).

Although disaster recovery is a new field of service, the social work profession has a longstanding tradition of helping people cope with environmental problems (Siporin, 1987; Speizman & Lloyd, 1965). For example, Hull House tried to improve the physical conditions of slum housing in early twentieth-century Chicago. The crusade against the use of lead-based paint also reflected social work's emphasis on the physical environment (Trattner, 1994).

Social workers help individuals and families affected by a disaster and provide services at the community and organizational level. Specifically, generalist social workers

1. Help alleviate the stress caused by the disaster
2. Help individuals and families identify their needs
3. Connect the survivors to existing resources
4. Provide information to survivors
5. Offer support to individuals and families
6. Work with agencies and organizations to coordinate service delivery
7. Participate in promoting and developing new services
8. Organize community recovery efforts.

To perform these tasks, generalist social workers need to collaborate with other disaster relief professionals and coordinate their efforts with the overall recovery program. They educate individuals and families about the different aspects of disaster, including the magnitude and the development of the disaster, types of services available, and the process of activating these services. The worker also educates survivors about the psychological effects of disasters and effective coping strategies. The worker takes an active part in organizing these activities and provides agencies with essential information on the survivors' needs. Moreover, coordination among the different entities that participate in recovery efforts is another important task that a social worker effectively assumes. To respond to survivors' needs, the worker may also act as a mediator between the survivors and the agencies and as an advocate for survivors' interests. Social workers have been invited to join relief teams because they have expertise in assessing individual, family, and community needs as well as in implementing interventions at both micro and macro levels.

Policy Issues

The major policy issue associated with disaster relief and recovery is the lack of coordination among the multitude of agencies and organizations involved. Regardless of the geographic location of the disaster or the type of catastrophe, a large number of agencies provide relief efforts. Typically, there is a wide array of federal, state, and local government agencies as well as a large number of nongovernmental agencies. Each agency fills a specialized role within the relief operation. For example, immediately following a disaster, the Red Cross and the Salvation Army provide shelter, clothing, and food to survivors. Volunteer organizations often participate in evacuation, cleanups, food distribution, and restoration. Local medical and mental health agencies provide treatment and crisis intervention for survivors. The state emergency management agency focuses on evacuation and relocation services. The Federal Emergency Management Agency (FEMA) focuses on damage assessment, compensation, provision of loans for reconstruction, and temporary housing. Figure 15.1 shows the multiple systems involved in disaster recovery operations.

Dealing with the processes and procedures of all these organizations can be time-consuming, disorienting, and frustrating. Typically, each agency has its own set of procedures and requirements. Completing the paperwork for each organization can be confusing and tedious. The survivor has to repeat the same information to representatives of each agency. Multiple application processes can cause a delay in obtaining needed services. In the end, the survivors are victimized not only by the disaster but also by the lack of organization and coordination among the relief agencies as well as the bureaucracy of these systems.

Micro Practice Issues

Disasters cause changes in the physical environment, disruption of social ties, psychological stress, and economic distress. Typically, people's responses to a major disaster reflect a normal reaction to an abnormal circumstance. "One of the most persistent myths about the reaction of people to a major disaster is that they disintegrate physically, mentally, and morally, and engage in panic reactions with irrational and antisocial acts" (Farberow, 1985, p. 45). Instead, responses vary from individual to individual, from family to family, and from community to community depending on the severity of the disaster, the magnitude of changes, the extent of loss, and the perceptions of the losses.

Floods, earthquakes, major tornadoes, and hurricanes cause massive damage. Homes, schools, stores, roads, medical facilities, transportation, communication equipment, and farmland are destroyed, drastically affecting survivors' daily activities. For example, when the Mississippi River overflowed its banks in 1993, roads and bridges were destroyed, making movement from place to place difficult and preventing relief workers from reaching survivors.

FIGURE 15.1. Systems and Services Involved with Flood Survivors

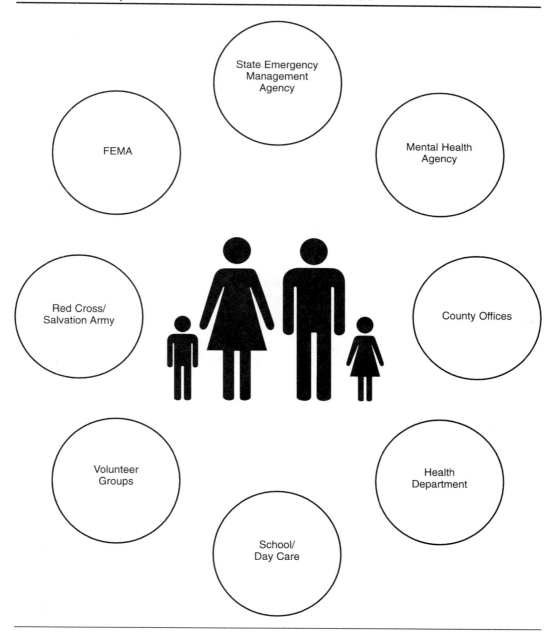

A major disaster interferes with people's ability to communicate and interact. Disasters interrupt social ties and interpersonal relationships among the survivors. For example, when people are evacuated from their homes before or after a disaster, they are no longer able to communicate with relatives, friends, neighbors, and significant others. If they are moved into public facilities, they lose their privacy and control over their daily schedule. In addition, they are unable to fulfill work responsibilities and other commitments. Figure 15.2 illustrates the psychosocial effect of a massive disaster.

Most of the time, a sudden disaster causes loss of resources, personal belongings, and income. Survivors are faced with tasks that need immediate attention, including evacuation, medical treatment, care for the elderly, contact with families and significant others, and salvaging valuable belongings. These tasks, along with the destruction of their homes, farms, and roads, and the need to care for injured family members prevent survivors from performing regular work activities.

Common psychological and psychiatric reactions to natural disasters include

- Depression
- Anxiety and somatic symptoms (Phifer, 1990)
- Generalized anxiety (Canino, Bravo, Rubio-Stipec, & Woodbury, 1990)
- Posttraumatic stress disorder (David, Mellman, Mendoza, & Kulick-Bell, 1996)
- Insomnia and apathy (Erikson, 1976).

Children are especially vulnerable following a disaster and may show evidence of posttraumatic stress disorder, changes in behavior, and resistance to social interaction (Belter, Dunn, & Jeney, 1991; Gammon, Daugherty, Finch, Belter, & Foster, 1993).

Multiple Needs

Massive natural disasters create a variety of needs for individuals, families, groups, and communities. Needs vary by the stage or phase of the disaster. One classification of the stages of disaster identifies three phases: pre-impact, impact, and post-impact (Farberow, 1985). The pre-impact phase includes the threat and warning period preceding the disaster. The impact phase occurs when the disaster strikes and immediate relief efforts are organized. During the post-impact phase, relief activities continue, individual needs are assessed, and actions to meet these needs take place.

Another classification focuses on the psychosocial effects of disasters (Duffy, 1978). A heroic phase immediately following the disaster is characterized by strong altruistic reactions to help the victims help themselves and others. This is followed by the honeymoon phase, which lasts from three to six months. During this phase, survivors are optimistic about reconstructing their lives; their optimism is based in part on promises from governmental and state organizations. The third phase is disillusionment. It can last from one month to two years. During the disillusionment phase, survivors try to deal with the frustration caused by unfilled promises and the barriers they face in rebuilding their lives. The final phase is reconstruction, in which survivors rely on their own resources and energy to achieve their goals and rebuild their communities.

In the period before an expected disaster, such as a hurricane, survivors need help finding safe places to move to. Most services involve collecting and protecting valuable items and providing transportation to safe areas. As survivors move to new areas or into temporary shelters, they need food, clothing, and information about the extent of the damage to their property and possessions. Evacuation services may also continue during the impact phase for survivors who have not participated in early evacuation efforts or if the disaster strikes without warning.

FIGURE 15.2. Psychosocial Effect on Families

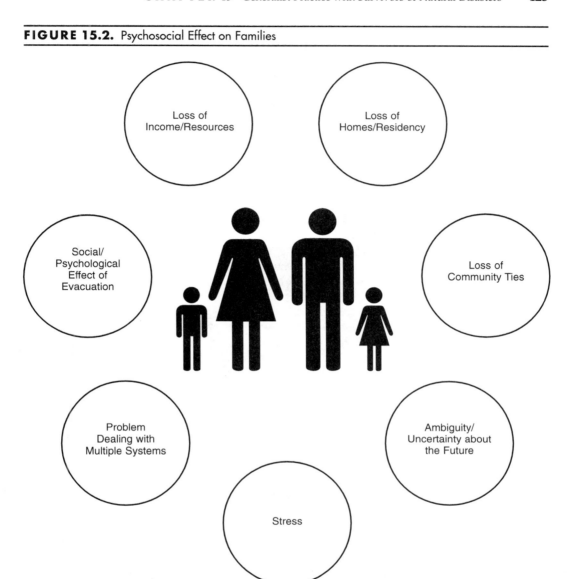

Most long-term emotional problems appear during the disillusionment and reconstruction phases (Farberow, 1985). Survivors become dissatisfied with the complicated process for obtaining compensation, loans, or grants. They may experience delays, inconsistent information, and/or excessive bureaucratic red tape that holds up approval for services and resources. For example, a survivor of the 1993 Mississippi River flood did not receive compensation for his losses because he could not present birth certificates or the title to his land. His account of watching his home float away, with all the documents inside, was not convincing enough for the official processing his application. Another survivor had to fill out a thirty-five page application form for a small loan. It was filled with unfamiliar terminology that was difficult to understand. He decided that the loan was not worth the time and effort.

Emotional and psychological reactions to disasters may require professional intervention. Children often react to massive disasters with difficult behavior, stress, and problems in social interaction (Belter, Dunn, & Jeney, 1991). Counseling and individual treatment may be needed. Survivors may also have difficulty adapting to the areas where they have been relocated and may experience such posttraumatic symptoms as nightmares, sleep problems, lack of interest, and emotional isolation. Assessing the psychological effects of a disaster on individuals and families is an important aspect of disaster relief services.

Two Million Homeless

In August 1992, Hurricane Andrew hit Florida and other southern states along the Gulf of Mexico. High winds toppled trees, knocked out electrical transformers, demolished homes, and sank boats. People were injured by fires, flying glass, metal, wood, and debris. An evacuation warning was issued, prior to the storm, but some people couldn't move quickly enough and others decided to stay.

Dade County, whose two million residents live in Miami and about thirty other municipalities, sustained most of the damage to homes, stores, streets, facilities, and infrastructure. Health officials expressed concerns about the spread of disease because of poor sanitation and lack of clean drinking water.

The damage inflicted on Florida by Hurricane Andrew was estimated to be about $30 billion, which makes it one of the most expensive natural disasters in U.S. history. Eighty-five thousand homes were damaged. Eighteen deaths were directly related to the storm, and twelve were indirectly related. Approximately 250,000 people became homeless. Of these, approximately 100,000 found temporary shelter with family or friends.

Emergency services and personnel were rushed to devastated communities to help provide food, water, shelter, and medical treatment. In one day, nearly a million prepackaged meals were served by the military, the American Red Cross, and Second Harvest Food Bank of Orlando. Eleven field kitchens, twelve tent cities, two field hospitals, and twelve county-organized food distribution centers were opened.

Insurance claims adjusters descended on Dade County trying to find homeowners who needed cash for emergency supplies and new housing. The conditions made it hard for adjusters and consumers to find each other. People stood in lines for hours to process applications for disaster assistance and insurance claims for damaged cars and homes and to apply for small business administration loans. Individuals who received immediate assistance had a difficult time cashing the checks because most of the banks were closed.

Many agencies worked at alleviating the psychological reactions caused by Andrew. Large numbers of children had nightmares and experienced lethargy, fear, and depression. Elderly survivors suffered from stress that triggered heart attacks. Experts reported an increase in marital conflicts and child abuse.

Because of the magnitude of the disaster, the federal government helped Florida and the other states affected by the hurricane. President Bush ordered the army to secure and provide services to the devastated communities. At his request, Congress supplied $7.6 billion to help survivors in Florida and Louisiana.

It took years for the stricken communities to recover from Hurricane Andrew. The process of delivering services was inadequate. Many organizations had to redefine their relief programs to provide better quality services, minimize delays, facilitate better communication with survivors, and improve the training of service providers to better enable them to handle the pressures caused by a widespread natural disaster.

Crisis Outreach Services

Survivors of massive natural disasters require a variety of services, including housing, medical care, material aid, and social services. When Hurricane Hugo hit Charleston, North Carolina, in 1989, residents received counseling, advocacy, needs assessment, information about food and supplies, manual labor, and emotional support services (Muzekari, Lonigan, Bond, & Hiers, 1991).

Crisis outreach services should be proactive in identifying survivors' needs and providing immediate services (Drum & Valdes, 1988). In other words, services should be provided within the shortest time possible in order to assure positive outcomes. Procedures for obtaining services need to be clear and simple. Survivors of massive disasters often lack experience in dealing with social service systems. Difficult and lengthy application forms that require extensive documentation create obstacles for survivors in obtaining the necessary services.

Survivors' evaluations of crisis services are influenced by how they are treated by agency representatives and professional staff. Service delivery must be sensitive to the survivors' self-sufficiency. The utilization of relief services depends, in part, on how well the services maintain survivors' dignity and respect (Muzekari, Lonigan, Bond, & Hiers, 1991).

Traditional office-based mental health services are not well suited for disaster situations because they lack the mobility and flexibility to meet the survivors' needs (Buckwalter, Smith, Zevenbergen, & Russell, 1991). Disaster relief services that reach out to survivors in their home environments are more effective than those that require the survivors to come to them (Kurpius & Rozecki, 1992; Muzekari, Lonigan, Bond, & Hiers, 1991; Phifer, 1990).

Following a massive natural disaster, mental health services are necessary to help survivors cope with their losses and psychological distress (Dufka, 1988; Summers & Cowan, 1991). The drastic and overwhelming demands of a disaster situation require highly motivated workers. Outreach workers connect survivors to service resources. The door-to-door approach utilized in recovery projects (Muzekari, Lonigan, Bond, & Hiers, 1991; Soliman, Raymond, & Lingle, 1996) gives workers the opportunity to visit survivors in their own homes, where they obtain firsthand knowledge of the changes and damages caused by the disaster.

Subsequent home visits communicate workers' willingness to help survivors adjust to the changes caused by the disaster.

Thirty-nine Illinois Counties Declared Disaster Areas

The 1993 flood caused tremendous problems for communities along the Mississippi River. Thirty-nine counties in Illinois were declared federal disaster areas. Damages caused by the flood included

- $47 million in housing damages
- Displacement of more than eighteen thousand people
- 884,000 acres of flooded cropland
- More than nine thousand lost jobs
- Fourteen hundred students displaced from their normal school buildings.

Following the flood, the Illinois Department of Mental Health and Developmental Disabilities (IDMHDD) received grants from FEMA totaling $3,732,448. Their mission was to provide crisis services to individuals and families to help alleviate the mental and emotional problems caused by the flood. The following goals were identified:

- Identify and respond to flood survivors at risk of emotional problems through active outreach
- Provide crisis counseling, information sessions, support groups, and referrals as needed
- Educate the general public about normal psychological stress reactions to disaster and recovery process
- Educate service providers about flood survivor's needs.

The IDMHDD was responsible for the overall administration of Project Recovery, as this effort was named. A core management group developed recommendations for the implementation of the project. The recommendations and guidelines were based primarily on input from twenty local mental health centers that were contracted to provide services to flood survivors.

Immediately after the flood hit, emergency centers were opened to register the survivors. FEMA asked outreach workers to initiate contacts with flood survivors whose names were on the FEMA list. Outreach workers used door-to-door contacts to identify survivors' needs and provide services. Workers also visited schools and worked with children.

Outreach services were provided from August 1993 to January 1995. Twenty agencies and more than a hundred supporting staff participated. They provided casefinding (identifying survivors, assessing their needs, and developing plans to respond to those needs), information and referral, public education, screening, individual and group counseling, mental health training, consultation, community organization, and advocacy services, including

- 40,341 individual crisis counseling contacts
- Community support to 7,701 persons in neighborhood groups
- 5,295 presentations to children in 225 classroom settings

- Information to 6,842 ministers and human service workers
- Public information and education materials such as brochures, coloring books, flood stress information cards, posters, and videotapes. (Soliman, Raymond, & Lingle, 1995)

DEVELOPING HELPING RELATIONSHIPS WITH SURVIVORS OF DISASTERS

Typically, survivors of disasters are ordinary people who have managed on their own throughout their lives, and who have overcome difficult situations by relying on their own resources, informal support systems, and previous life experiences. The primary characteristics of disaster survivors, especially those from rural or smaller communities, are

- "pride in independence and self sufficiency;
- "less acceptance of mental illness;
- "a general tendency to reject the unfamiliar and specialized;
- "greater numbers of the socially and economically disadvantaged;
- "the propensity when seeking help to go first to family, friends, doctors, and ministries
- "physical limitations of distance and transportation; and
- "shortage of professionals." (Farberow, 1985, p. 43)

In working with survivors of natural disasters, keep in mind that most probably have never received help from social service agencies. Some may refuse services or may accept help only reluctantly. The content and the process of service delivery to this population must be sensitive to the survivors' feelings of self-sufficiency and their general lack of experience with service agencies. In short, recovery programs should strive to maintain the survivors' dignity and respect.

Developing a helping relationship is vital in the provision of disaster-related services. Within short periods of time, people experience many losses and have to cope with many unexpected challenges. Having a clearly defined purpose promotes the development of a solid helping relationship. Discussing the collaborative nature of the relationship is imperative. Do not assume the role of expert; form partnerships with the survivors and assume the role of consultant, "Clients are usually the experts on their own situation, and we make a serious mistake when we subjugate their knowledge to official views" (Saleebey, 1992, p. 7).

Labeling people who experience disasters as victims is inconsistent with the strength perspective. The term *survivors* is preferred. Incorporating the strengths perspective is vital when working with this population. Focus on helping the survivors recognize and identify their own strengths.

While some survivors have been successful in dealing with life experiences, others may have had limited opportunities to deal with catastrophic situations or may have not dealt with them successfully. Therefore, it is important to look for strengths in all areas of survivors' lives, including successful work experiences, effective interpersonal relationships, and ability to handle personal responsibilities. Use your knowledge and skills to help survivors utilize their own strengths to face the demands posed by the disaster.

It is important to perceive survivors as individuals who understand the magnitude of their losses and have the best perspective on how to improve the situation. Relationship-building with survivors focuses on empowering them to make their own decisions based on their understanding of their needs, resources, and abilities. Engage the survivor in a meaningful dialogue and help the survivor assess the extent of the disaster, available resources, and the options available to begin the recovery process.

It may be necessary to help survivors overcome their own biases against asking for help. Encourage them to view their needs for services as a normal reaction to abnormal circumstances. An empowering and collaborative approach makes it much easier for survivors to accept help.

Recognition of survivors' strengths, identification of interpersonal resources, discussion of personal reactions to the disasters, and the provision of emotional support enhance the development of helping relationships. The negative portrayal of human service providers as professionals who seek to control people's lives may represent a barrier in initiating collaborative or positive relationships with survivors. Therefore, an emphasis on self-determination is required. Make it clear that your role is to present information about available services and resources and that they will select from the available alternatives to develop the preferred plan of action.

The basic values of social work that especially apply to working with survivors of disasters are respecting the survivor's situation, protecting the survivor's dignity, self-determination, and confidentiality. Although survivors of natural disasters may share similar experiences, in terms of type of material loss, fear, frustration, and victimization, there are personal differences among them. View each survivor as a unique individual with special abilities and needs.

Challenges in Developing Effective Relationships

Survivors of natural disasters often need multiple services to deal with the consequences of the disaster. Many services will not be available immediately. Most groups that respond to disasters require time to organize the logistical aspects of service delivery. Sometimes the delivery of services is delayed because of road and traffic conditions caused by the disaster or because of intense evacuation efforts. In such cases, relief workers and survivors may have to rely on local resources and informal support systems within the community. For example, following a massive earthquake in Turkey in 1999, residents had to rely on local construction companies to use their equipment to search for survivors under the debris. It took several days for international support to arrive and participate effectively in rescuing survivors.

Organizational barriers may also delay the delivery of needed services (Soliman, Lingle & Raymond, 1998). Organizational difficulties include duplication of services by other agencies, paperwork, caseload size, and lack of professional support. It may be difficult for workers to locate survivors, and it may be dangerous to provide services to survivors in their homes. For example, when the Mississippi River flooded in 1993, massive destruction of roads made it difficult for outreach workers to reach survivors in certain areas. Even where roads were not destroyed, driving on some roads was unsafe. Numerous visits may be required, or survivors may not be receptive to service. These organizational barriers negatively influence the development of helping relationships with survivors.

Numerous factors influence survivors' receptivity to services. These factors include their perceptions of mental health and the stigma attached to receiving therapy, lack of trust of outsider organizations, and past frustrations and unsuccessful experiences with relief organizations. Survivors may not want to rely on professionals to resolve problems but may instead want to rely on traditional support systems, such as family members, friends, neighbors, and coworkers. The negative stereotype attached to receiving services from professionals may prevent people—even those in drastic need of help—from asking for help or accepting it. An outreach worker who was unsuccessful in motivating survivors to ask for services put it this way: "The . . . flood survivors were accustomed to helping each other. . . . Unless we saw the need for assistance (food or clothing), these people would not ask. They were very proud and I found their determination enlightening" (Soliman, Lingle, & Raymond, 1998, p. 565).

Another reason survivors may not be receptive to help is that promised services were not forthcoming in the past, and they see no reason to believe that support will materialize in the current situation. As one worker stated, "At times, it's difficult to establish trusting relationships. Often survivors were wary of help from strangers and many had already had bad experiences with other government sponsored programs" (Soliman, Lingle, & Raymond, 1998, p. 565).

Client Assessment

The person-in-environment perspective requires an exploration of the interplay between survivors and their environments. This is especially important in disaster situations. The amount of loss, damage to the physical environment, and psychosocial reactions to the disaster need to be assessed at each stage.

Before an expected disaster strikes, assessment focuses on helping people determine their evacuation needs. The evacuation alert usually comes with short notice. People often do not have the time to move furniture, equipment, and other possessions to safety. In high-risk areas people may already have an evacuation plan and will thus have specified their expectations and preferences. For example, people who live in a floodplain may know where they prefer to go when a flood takes place. The type of resources available also affects the evacuation assessment. At this stage, the need for accurate information about the disaster and its potential effect is vital.

The disruption caused by disasters creates shock, disorientation, and loss of control. High winds, lightning, or other severe weather conditions often accompany disasters. These conditions may generate a considerable amount of anxiety and fear. The fear of injury or loss of life can last through the disaster episode and longer.

After the disaster, people assess the changes or damages that occurred in their close environment. They may be angry or sad or feel victimized when they observe damage in their own domains. Survivors then focus their attention on the devastation in their broader environment. Assessment of the immediate environment is vital to survivors even if it may put them in physical danger. Because homes have symbolic meaning to people, the need to visit the community after the disaster and survey the damage to their homes is psychologically overwhelming. Homes encompass most of peoples' material and social belongings, and the destruction of significant pieces of furniture or the disappearance of family photo albums may cause distress. Similarly, a child who loses a teddy bear or a doll may experience negative emotional reactions because of the symbolic meaning of the particular toy.

Psychological reactions to a disaster are greatest during the postdisaster stage (Farberow, 1985). Survivors with special vulnerabilities to stress, such as children and the elderly, are in greater need of mental health attention than other age groups (Summers & Cowan, 1991). Long-term psychological reactions are most common among survivors who had physical dependency, high need for outside support, and low tolerance for dislocation and loss of stability (Summers & Cowan, 1991, p. 31).

Worker Responses to Disaster Relief Work

Participation in disaster recovery efforts can result in psychological distress among workers (Bradfield, Wylie, & Echterling, 1989; Muzekari, Lonigan, Bond, & Hiers, 1991). Personal involvement in the lives of survivors and their destroyed environments as well as repeated exposure to multiple harmful stimuli may cause workers to experience intense emotional reactions and stress (Hodgkinson & Shepherd, 1994; Phifer, 1990). Workers may experience depression, grief, frustration, powerlessness, confusion, fearfulness, anxiety, poor concentration, nightmares, intrusive memories, physical illness, fatigue, accidents, and changes in sleeping, eating, smoking, and drinking patterns (Bradfield, Wylie, & Echterling, 1989; Hodgkinson & Shepherd, 1994; Karakashian, 1994; Muzekari, Lonigan, Bond, & Hiers, 1991; Tumelty, 1990). These conditions can severely disrupt workers' personal lives, including their interpersonal relationships (Bradfield, Wylie, & Echterling, 1989; Figley, 1984).

Participation in disaster relief work can also be a positive experience for relief workers (Soliman, Lingle, & Raymond, 1998). Hodgkinson and Shephard found that 85 percent of the social workers who participated in two major British disasters "believed that they had reaped personal and professional benefits from their involvement" (1994, p. 594). Personal gains from participating in disaster work include increased ability to understand self, to react logically in abnormal situations, and to sustain personal pressures. Professional gains include learning about different types of problems, communicating with clients with multiple losses, and the ability to assess and plan services quickly in an unstable work environment (Soliman, Lingle, & Raymond, 1998).

In general, training may help workers avoid overidentifying with survivors and lessen the resulting emotional stress. Professional support is important in helping workers deal with the frustration and stress associated with disaster relief work, as is holding regular debriefing sessions. Supporting the worker through the termination process and encouraging reflection about the helping process and the lessons learned can also alleviate worker stress and burnout.

SUMMARY

Social workers play positive and constructive roles in helping survivors of natural disasters. Considering the devastation caused by natural disasters every year, the opportunity for social workers to participate in disaster relief efforts is great. The magnitude of loss caused by disasters requires a clear understanding of the nature of disasters, their social, economic, and cultural effects, and the different strategies and techniques that can be used to help survivors adjust to these changes.

Social work practice with survivors of natural disasters involves a number of generalist social work practice roles, including facilitator, negotiator, enabler, collaborator, educator, organizer, mediator, and advocate. Social workers often perform these roles simultaneously in their work with individuals, families, groups, organizations, and communities. When a social worker becomes part of the relief effort, intervention involves working at the micro level with individuals and families and at the macro level with organizations and communities.

At the micro level, disaster relief workers assess individual and family needs, provide information, make referrals, link survivors with existing services, and provide supportive counseling. Connecting survivors to available organizations and agencies may also require explaining the nature of these services, their requirements, and the application process.

At the macro level, the worker needs to identify major community, state, and federal efforts to support survivors of disasters. Communicating with representatives of state and federal emergency management personnel and understanding both the planning and implementation phases of the relief effort are some of the challenging aspects of disaster relief work. On this level, intervention involves organizing meetings for the community and the various representatives, identifying unmet needs, and coordinating procedures and strategies among local, state, and federal participating organizations. It is critical to acquire valid information, understand policy and regulations, and use effective communication to help survivors articulate their needs as well as to advocate for quality services for individuals, families, and communities.

CASE EXAMPLE

The following case example illustrates the variety of roles generalist social workers assume in delivering relief services to survivors of natural disasters. It is based on a family's experiences during the flood of 1993.

We Lost Everything

The W. family was on the FEMA list of people to visit, and when my supervisor asked me to visit Gloria W., I drove to the community and discovered that the W. home was surrounded by water. A community resident took me there in his boat.

Gloria W. told me that she and her husband had not evacuated because her husband would not leave the home. He was staying in his room and refused to go to the city. In the four days since the flood began, Gloria had gone to the city two times with her son-in-law. She bought food and registered with FEMA. She told me that the water covered their small motel next door and that most of the furniture was destroyed.

The couple owns ten acres of land, and Henry W. plants crops. He rents motel rooms to people who come during hunting seasons every year. Gloria mentioned that Henry had just finished renovating the eight-room motel three weeks before. She indicated that her greatest concern was that they would not receive compensation from FEMA because they did not have flood insurance.

Gloria told me that she wanted to leave the house and move to the city camp like everybody else, but she didn't want to leave her husband alone. Since the flood, she had not seen her only sister, who lived nearby and had moved to live with her son in Georgia after the water ruined her small house. Her only daughter moved with her husband and two children to an apartment complex, and FEMA paid their rent. Her only son called some friends who were able to get his message to her. Gloria stated, "I know that my son will leave everything and come to see me." She worried because her son just started a new job in New York, and she didn't want him to risk losing it.

Gloria was extremely worried about her husband. He wasn't sleeping or eating. She thought he might be suicidal. "I sometimes want to go and apply for loans or emergency assistance like everybody else, but I'm also afraid that if I leave him he would hurt himself. I told him that we can't stay here by ourselves because we don't have a boat, and it does not seem that the water will go away soon." When I asked about her immediate need, she said, "I know we need food and stuff, but the most important thing is to leave and go where everybody is."

She felt that her husband was traumatized by the experience. He had fought in Vietnam and still had dreams about the war. Since the flood, he had refused to take his blood pressure medicine, and she saw him crying the other day. She added, "We had a similar experience in the sixties, but the water didn't destroy everything. We helped each other, and the water receded three days after the flood." When I asked her what she thought would help her this time, she said, "I know we live in a floodplain area. We didn't buy insurance because the county decided to withdraw from the plan, but we have our will and many people are helping us. The thing that is difficult to accept is the flood and try to work with the difficult circumstances, but my husband has a difficult time accepting that."

Assessment

Mr. and Mrs. W. had different perceptions of the situation. Henry was traumatized by the loss. Water covered their house, farm, and business. Henry felt isolated from his neighbors and immediate family. Gloria understood that living in a floodplain meant a high probability of flooding. She accepted the fact that the flood happened. Although she did not accept victimization, she struggled with their losses.

When I asked Gloria to assess the family's needs, she indicated that the most important thing was to move to temporary housing with the other survivors. She wanted to apply for assistance, communicate with people, and find out what resources were available. She also wanted to establish contact with her daughter, her son, and her sister. She asked for help in convincing her husband to leave and in getting him medical and professional assistance to help him deal with his feelings of loss and depression. By the end of the first interview, Gloria and I agreed on the following needs:

- Help Gloria convince her husband to move to a new place. She suggested asking Tom J., an old friend of her husband, to help convince Henry.
- Obtain information on possible places to move.

- Obtain copies of and review the application procedures of emergency relief programs and loans.
- Arrange for Henry to visit their family doctor.
- Make arrangements with someone who has a boat to take Gloria grocery shopping.

Gloria seemed highly motivated and willing to pursue solutions.

Intervention and Service Provision

I visited the W. family the next day. Prior to the visit, I had contacted Tom J., who agreed to go with me to see Henry. Tom said, "I know that Henry W. loves his place so much, but I think I will be able to talk with him and convince him to move. We have three apartments in this building, and it is only fifteen miles away from our community." I also spoke with two families who agreed to visit the W. family once a day to help them.

Gloria was pleased when she saw Tom. Tom went straight to Henry's room, and in fifteen minutes, Tom and Henry came out and joined the discussion.

I gave Gloria the application forms for compensation and emergency funds. Tom mentioned the difficulty that the survivors from this community are having with FEMA. Because the community had withdrawn from the flood insurance plan, residents were not eligible to receive compensation for their damaged homes. I told them that I would be meeting with a FEMA representative in three days and would share the results with them. Gloria was happy when I told her I had arranged a doctor's appointment for Henry and that that Bob P., her old neighbor, would take them to the appointment in his boat.

I talked about applications for emergency assistance and loans. Tom thought that some of the assistance applied to their situation, but that the compensation from FEMA wouldn't apply because of the insurance problem. By the end of the visit, Henry stated that he would like to move to where Tom lived. He also agreed to meet me in the emergency center to fill out the forms and applications.

When I met the couple at the center the next day, Henry looked better and engaged in conversation. I helped them fill out applications for small loans. I drove them to look at the apartment and visit with their daughter. Henry's spirit got a boost from visiting his daughter and seeing his grandchildren. The process of moving to the new place was easier than they thought it would be. Gloria was glad that the temporary apartment was close to her daughter's apartment.

Four days later, Gloria called me from their new apartment. She asked me to refer Henry to the community mental health center for help with his depression. I did so, and Henry had first counseling session with a mental health therapist the following week. The W.'s support network began to take shape. Their son came from New York and spent four days with his parents. Neighbors and friends surrounded the family. They began to attend church services.

I worked with FEMA, the county administrator, state emergency officials, and a state representative to set up a community meeting at which residents expressed their anger and frustration with the local community leaders who had withdrawn from the National Flood Insurance Program three years before. Following a heated discussion, a FEMA representative announced that FEMA would meet with survivors to discuss their requests for assistance.

Some of the needs were for food and furniture. I contacted the local church and helped open a food pantry there. I also found a way to transport food and supplies that were donated by people in other states.

Follow-Up

After six months in the temporary apartment, Henry and Gloria W. were able to move back to their house. The loan from FEMA helped them refurnish their small motel. Local volunteer groups painted their house and did construction work. Like other families, they experienced difficulty preparing their land for farming. The flood left more than three feet of sand on the land. The state provided a public assistance fund to remove the sand and prepare for planting.

DISCUSSION QUESTIONS

1. Describe the social worker's approach to working with the W. family. What did you like about his approach? What would you have done differently? What ethical issues were raised in the case example.
2. Identify Mr. and Mrs. W.'s strengths. What were the primary challenges they faced? In what ways did the social worker adopt a strengths perspective? In what ways did he adopt a deficit perspective?
3. Identify the different roles that the worker engaged in when he worked with the W. family. Provide examples of each role.
4. How does social work practice in disaster relief differ from generalist practice with other client populations? How is it the same?

REFERENCES

Belter, R., Dunn, S., & Jeney, P. (1991). The psychological impact of Hurricane Hugo on children: A needs assessment. *Advanced Behavior Research Therapy, 13,* 155–161.

Berren, M., Beigel, A., & Ghertner, S. (1980). A typology for the classification of disasters. *Community Mental Health Journal, 16*(2), 103–111.

Bradfield, C., Wylie, M., & Echterling, L. (1989). After the flood: The response of ministers to a natural disaster. *Sociological Analysis, 49,* 397–407.

Bravo, M., Rubio-Stipec, M., & Canino, G. (1990). Methodological aspects of disaster mental health research. *International Journal of Mental Health, 19,* 37–50.

Buckwalter, K., Smith, M., Zevenbergen, P., & Russell, D. (1991). Mental health services of the rural elderly outreach program. *Gerontologist, 31,* 408–412.

Canino, G., Bravo, M., Rubio-Stipec, M., & Woodbury, M. (1990). The impact of disaster on mental health: Prospective and retrospective analyses. *International Journal of Mental Health, 19*(1), 51–59.

David, D., Mellman, T., Mendoza, L., & Kulick-Bell, R. (1996). Psychiatric morbidity following Hurricane Andrew. *Journal of Traumatic Stress, 9*(3), 607–612.

Department of Mental Health and Developmental Disabilities. (1993). *Final report, project recovery: Regular service grant crisis counseling program* (IDMHDD-997-DR Crisis).

Drum, D., & Valdes, L. (1988). Advocacy and outreach: Application to college/university counseling centers. In D. Kurpius & D. Brown (Eds.), *Handbook of consultation: An interview for advocacy and outreach* (pp. 38-60). Alexandria, VA: American Association for Counseling and Development.

Duffy, J. (1988). The Porter Lecture: Common psychological themes in societies' reaction to terrorism and disasters. *Military Medicine, 153,* 387–390.

Dufka, C. (1988). The Mexico City earthquake disaster. Social Casework, *69,* 162–170.

Erikson, K. (1976). *Everything in its path: Destruction of community in the Buffalo Creek flood.* New York: Simon and Schuster.

Farberow, N. (1985). Mental health aspects of disaster in smaller communities. *The American Journal of Social Psychiatry, 4,* 43–55.

Figley, C. (1984). Role of the family: Both haven and headache. In *Role stressors and supports for emergency workers.* DHHS Pub. No [ADM] 85-1408). Rockville, MD: National Institute of Mental Health.

Gammon, J., Daugherty, T., Finch, A., Belter, R., & Foster, K. (1993). Children's coping styles and report of depressive symptoms following a natural disaster. *The Journal of Genetic Psychology, 154,* 259–267.

Hodgkinson, P., & Shepherd, M. (1994). Impact of disaster support work. *Journal of Traumatic Stress, 7,* 587–600.

Jaffe, M. (1999, May 23). More disasters? No, experts say, just more people in their way. *The Philadelphia Inquirer,* p. E4.

Karakashian, M. (1994). Countertransference issues in crisis work with natural disaster victims. *Psychotherapy, 31,* 334–341.

Kurpius, D., & Rozecki, T. (1992). Outreach, advocacy, and consultation: A framework for prevention and intervention. *Elementary School Guidance and Counseling, 26,* 176–189.

Levine, A. (1982). Love Canal: Science, politics, and people. Lexington, MA: Lexington Books.

Muzekari, L., Lonigan, C., Bond, F., & Hiers, T. (1991). *In the eye of the beholder: CMHC reactions to disaster.* Paper presented at the 99th annual convention of the American Psychological Association, San Francisco, CA (ERIC Document Reproduction Service No. ED 336 693).

Phifer, J. (1990). Psychological distress and somatic symptoms after natural disaster: Differential vulnerability among older adults. *Psychology and Aging, 5*(3), 412–420.

Saleebey, D. (1992). *The strength perspective in social work practice.* New York: Longman.

Siporin, M. (1987). Disasters and disaster aid. In A. Minahan (Ed.), *Encyclopedia of social work* (18th ed., pp. 438–449). Silver Spring, MD: National Association of Social Workers.

Soliman, H. (1996). Community responses to chronic technological disaster: The case of the Pigeon River. *Journal of Social Service Research, 22*(1-2), 89–107.

Soliman, H., Lingle, S., & Raymond, A. (1998). Perceptions of indigenous workers following participation in a disaster relief project. *Community Mental Health Journal, 34*(6), 557–568.

Soliman, H., & Poulin, J. (1997). Client satisfaction with crisis outreach services: The development of an index. *Journal of Social Service, 23*(2), 55–76.

Soliman, H., Raymond, A., & Lingle, S. (1996). An evaluation of community mental health services following a massive natural disaster. *Human Services in the Rural Environment, 20*(1), 8–13.

Speizman, M., & Lloyd, G. (1965). School responds to Betsy. *Postscripts: Alumni Bulletin Tulane University School of Social Work,* pp. 1–2.

Summers, M., & Cowan, M. (1991). Mental health issues related to the development of a national disaster response system. *Military Medicine, 156,* 30–32.

Trattner, W. (1994). From poor law to welfare state (5th ed.). New York: Free Press.

Tumelty, D. (1990). *Social work in the wake of disaster.* London: Jessica Kingsly Publishers.

Appendix

THE NATIONAL ASSOCIATION OF SOCIAL WORKERS
Code of Ethics

*(Adopted by the NASW Delegate Assembly,
August 1996, Washington, D.C.)*

OVERVIEW

The *NASW Code of Ethics* is intended to serve as a guide to the everyday professional conduct of social workers. The *Code* includes four sections. The first section, "Preamble," summarizes the social work profession's mission and core values. The second section, "Purpose of the *NASW Code of Ethics*," provides an overview of the *Code*'s main functions and a brief guide for dealing with ethical issues or dilemmas in social work practice. The third section, "Ethical Principles," presents broad ethical principles, based on social work's core values, that inform social work practice. The final section, "Ethical Standards," includes specific ethical standards to guide social workers' conduct and to provide a basis for adjudication.

PREAMBLE

The primary mission of the social work profession is to enhance human well-being and help meet the basic human needs of all people, with particular attention to the needs and empowerment of people who are vulnerable, oppressed, and living in poverty. A historic and defining feature of social work is the profession's focus on individual well-being in a social context and the well-being of society. Fundamental to social work is attention to the environmental forces that create, contribute to, and address problems in living.

Social workers promote social justice and social change with and on behalf of clients. "Clients" is used inclusively to refer to individuals, families, groups, organizations, and communities. Social workers are sensitive to cultural and ethnic diversity and strive to end discrimination, oppression, poverty, and other forms of social injustice. These activities may be in the form of direct practice, community organizing, supervision, consultation, administration, advocacy, social and political action, policy development and implementation, education, and research and evaluation. Social workers seek to enhance the capacity of people to address their own needs.

Social workers also seek to promote the responsiveness of organizations, communities, and other social institutions to individuals' needs and social problems.

The mission of the social work profession is rooted in a set of core values. These core values, embraced by social workers throughout the profession's history, are the foundation of social work's unique purpose and perspective:

- service
- social justice
- dignity and worth of the person
- importance of human relationships
- integrity
- competence.

This constellation of core values reflects what is unique to the social work profession. Core values, and the principles that flow from them, must be balanced within the context and complexity of the human experience.

PURPOSE OF THE *NASW CODE OF ETHICS*

Professional ethics are at the core of social work. The profession has an obligation to articulate its basic values, ethical principles, and ethical standards. The *NASW Code of Ethics* sets forth these values, principles, and standards to guide social workers' conduct. The *Code* is relevant to all social workers and social work students, regardless of their professional functions, the settings in which they work, or the population they serve.

The *NASW Code of Ethics* serves six purposes:

1. The *Code* identifies core values on which social work's mission is based.
2. The *Code* summarizes broad ethical principles that reflect the profession's core values and establishes a set of specific ethical standards that should be used to guide social work practice.
3. The *Code* is designed to help social workers identify relevant considerations when professional obligations conflict or ethical uncertainties arise.
4. The *Code* provides ethical standards to which the general public can hold the social work profession accountable.
5. The *Code* socializes practitioners new to the field to social work's mission, values, ethical principles, and ethical standards.
6. The *Code* articulates standards that the social work profession itself can use to assess whether social workers have engaged in unethical conduct. NASW has formal procedures to adjudicate ethics complaints filed against its members.[1] In subscribing to this code, social workers are required to cooperate in its implementation, participate in NASW adjudication proceedings, and abide by any NASW disciplinary rulings or sanctions based on it.

The *Code* offers a set of values, principles, and standards to guide decision making and conduct when ethical issues arise. It does not provide a set of rules that prescribe how social workers should act in all situations. Specific applications

---

[1] For information on NASW adjudication procedures, see *NASW Procedures for the Adjudication of Grievances.*

of the *Code* must take into account the context in which it is being considered and the possibility of conflicts among the *Code*'s values, principles, and standards. Ethical responsibilities flow from all human relationships, from the personal and familial to the social and professional.

Further, the *NASW Code of Ethics* does not specify which values, principles, and standards are most important and ought to outweigh others in instances when they conflict. Reasonable differences of opinion can and do exist among social workers with respect to the ways in which values, ethical principles, and ethical standards should be rank ordered when they conflict. Ethical decision making in a given situation must apply the informed judgment of the individual social worker and should also consider how the issues would be judged in a peer review process where the ethical standards of the profession would be applied.

Ethical decision making is a process. There are many instances in social work where simple answers are not available to resolve complex ethical issues. Social workers should take into consideration all the values, principles, and standards in this *Code* that are relevant to any situation in which ethical judgment is warranted. Social workers' decisions and actions should be consistent with the spirit as well as the letter of this *Code*.

In addition to this *Code*, there are many other sources of information about ethical thinking that may be useful. Social workers should consider ethical theory and principles generally, social work theory and research, laws, regulations, agency policies, and other relevant codes of ethics, recognizing that among codes of ethics social workers should consider the *NASW Code of Ethics* as their primary source. Social workers also should be aware of the impact on ethical decision making of their clients' and their own personal values and cultural and religious beliefs and practices. They should be aware of any conflicts between personal and professional values and deal with them responsibly. For additional guidance social workers should consult the relevant literature on professional ethics and ethical decision making and seek appropriate consultation when faced with ethical dilemmas. This may involve consultation with an agency-based or social work organization's ethics committee, a regulatory body, knowledgeable colleagues, supervisors, or legal counsel.

Instances may arise when social workers' ethical obligations conflict with agency policies or relevant laws or regulations. When such conflicts occur, social workers must make a responsible effort to resolve the conflict in a manner that is consistent with the values, principles, and standards expressed in this *Code*. If a reasonable resolution of the conflict does not appear possible, social workers should seek proper consultation before making a decision.

The *NASW Code of Ethics* is to be used by NASW and by individuals, agencies, organizations, and bodies (such as licensing and regulatory boards, professional liability insurance providers, courts of law, agency boards of directors, government agencies, and other professional groups) that choose to adopt it or use it as a frame of reference. Violation of standards in this *Code* does not automatically imply legal liability or violation of the law. Such determination can only be made in the context of legal and judicial proceedings. Alleged violations of the *Code* would be subject to a peer review process. Such processes are generally separate from legal or administrative procedures and insulated from legal review or proceedings to allow the profession to counsel and discipline its own members.

A code of ethics cannot guarantee ethical behavior. Moreover, a code of ethics cannot resolve all ethical issues or disputes or capture the richness and complexity involved in striving to make responsible choices within a moral community. Rather, a code of ethics sets forth values, ethical principles, and ethical standards to which professionals aspire and by which their actions can be judged. Social workers' ethical behavior should result from their personal commitment to engage in ethical practice. The *NASW Code of Ethics* reflects the commitment of all social workers to uphold the profession's values and to act ethically. Principles and standards must be applied by individuals of good character who discern moral questions and, in good faith, seek to make reliable ethical judgments.

ETHICAL PRINCIPLES

The following broad ethical principles are based on social work's core values of service, social justice, dignity and worth of the person, importance of human relationships, integrity, and competence. These principles set forth ideals to which all social workers should aspire.

Value: *Service*

Ethical Principle: *Social workers' primary goal is to help people in need and to address social problems.*

Social workers elevate service to others above self-interest. Social workers draw on their knowledge, values, and skills to help people in need and to address social problems. Social workers are encouraged to volunteer some portion of their professional skills with no expectation of significant financial return (pro bono service).

Value: *Social Justice*

Ethical Principle: *Social workers challenge social injustice.*

Social workers pursue social change, particularly with and on behalf of vulnerable and oppressed individuals and groups of people. Social workers' social change efforts are focused primarily on issues of poverty, unemployment, discrimination, and other forms of social injustice. These activities seek to promote sensitivity to and knowledge about oppression and cultural and ethnic diversity. Social workers strive to ensure access to needed information, services, and resources; equality of opportunity; and meaningful participation in decision making for all people.

Value: *Dignity and Worth of the Person*

Ethical Principle: *Social workers respect the inherent dignity and worth of the person.*

Social workers treat each person in a caring and respectful fashion, mindful of individual differences and cultural and ethnic diversity. Social workers promote clients' socially responsible self-determination. Social workers seek to enhance clients' capacity and opportunity to change and to address their own needs. Social workers are cognizant of their dual responsibility to clients and to the broader society. They seek to resolve conflicts between clients' interest and the broader society's interests in a socially responsible manner consistent with the values, ethical principles, and ethical standards of the profession.

Value: *Importance of Human Relationships*

Ethical Principle: *Social workers recognize the central importance of human relationships.*

Social workers understand that relationships between and among people are an important vehicle for change. Social workers engage people as partners in the helping process. Social workers seek to strengthen relationships among people in a purposeful effort to promote, restore, maintain, and enhance the well-being of individuals, families, social groups, organizations, and communities.

Value: *Integrity*

Ethical Principle: *Social workers behave in a trustworthy manner.*

Social workers are continually aware of the profession's mission, values, ethical principles, and ethical standards and practice in a manner consistent with them. Social workers act honestly and responsibly and promote ethical practices on the part of the organizations with which they are affiliated.

Value: *Competence*

Ethical Principle: *Social workers practice within their areas of competence and develop and enhance their professional expertise.*

Social workers continually strive to increase their professional knowledge and skills and to apply them in practice. Social workers should aspire to contribute to the knowledge base of the profession.

ETHICAL STANDARDS

The following ethical standards are relevant to the professional activities of all social workers. These standards concern (1) social workers' ethical responsibilities to clients, (2) social workers' ethical responsibilities to colleagues, (3) social workers' ethical responsibilities in practice settings, (4) social workers' ethical responsibilities as professionals, (5) social workers' ethical responsibilities to the social work profession, and (6) social workers' ethical responsibilities to the broader society.

Some of the standards that follow are enforceable guidelines for professional conduct, and some are aspirational. The extent to which each standard is enforceable is a matter of professional judgment to be exercised by those responsible for reviewing alleged violations of ethical standards.

1.   Social Workers' Ethical Responsibilities to Clients

1.01 Commitment to Clients

Social workers' primary responsibility is to promote the well-being of clients. In general, clients' interests are primary. However, social workers' responsibility to the larger society or specific legal obligations may on limited occasions supersede the loyalty owed clients, and clients should be so advised. (Examples include when a social worker is required by law to report that a client has abused a child or has threatened to harm self or others.)

1.02 Self-Determination

Social workers respect and promote the right of clients to self-determination and assist clients in their efforts to identify and clarify their goals. Social workers may limit clients' right to self-determination when, in the social workers' professional judgment, clients' actions or potential actions pose a serious, foreseeable, and imminent risk to themselves or others.

1.03   Informed Consent

(a)   Social workers should provide services to clients only in the context of a professional relationship based, when appropriate, on valid informed consent. Social workers should use clear and understandable language to inform clients of the purpose of the services, risks related to the services, limits to services because of the requirements of a third-party payer, relevant costs, reasonable alternatives, clients' right to refuse or withdraw consent, and the time frame covered by the consent. Social workers should provide clients with an opportunity to ask questions.

(b)   In instances when clients are not literate or have difficulty understanding the primary language used in the practice setting, social workers should take steps to ensure clients' comprehension. This may include providing clients with a detailed verbal explanation or arranging for a qualified interpreter or translator whenever possible.

(c)   In instances when clients lack the capacity to provide informed consent, social workers should protect clients' interests by seeking permission from an appropriate third party, informing clients consistent with the clients' level of understanding. In such instances social workers should seek to ensure that the third party acts in a manner consistent with clients' wishes and interests. Social workers should take reasonable steps to enhance such clients' ability to give informed consent.

(d)   In instances when clients are receiving services involuntarily, social workers should provide information about the nature and extent of services and about the extent of clients' right to refuse service.

(e)   Social workers who provide services via electronic media (such as computer, telephone, radio, and television) should inform recipients of the limitations and risks associated with such services.

(f)   Social workers should obtain clients' informed consent before audiotaping or videotaping clients or permitting observation of services to clients by a third party.

1.04   Competence

(a)   Social workers should provide services and represent themselves as competent only within the boundaries of their education, training, license, certification, consultation received, supervised experience, or other relevant professional experience.

(b)   Social workers should provide services in substantive areas or use intervention techniques or approaches that are new to them only after engaging in appropriate study, training, consultation, and supervision from people who are competent in those interventions or techniques.

(c)   When generally recognized standards do not exist with respect to an emerging area of practice, social workers should exercise careful judgment and take responsible steps—including appropriate education, research, training, consultation, and supervision—to ensure the competence of their work and to protect clients from harm.

1.05 Cultural Competence and Social Diversity

(a) Social workers should understand culture and its function in human behavior and society, recognizing the strengths that exist in all cultures.

(b) Social workers should have a knowledge base of their clients' cultures and be able to demonstrate competence in the provision of services that are sensitive to clients' cultures and to differences among people and cultural groups.

(c) Social workers should obtain education about and seek to understand the nature of social diversity and oppression with respect to race, ethnicity, national origin, color, sex, sexual orientation, age, marital status, political belief, religion, or mental or physical disability.

1.06 Conflicts of Interest

(a) Social workers should be alert to and avoid conflicts of interest that interfere with the exercise of professional discretion and impartial judgment. Social workers should inform clients when a real or potential conflict of interest arises and take reasonable steps to resolve the issue in a manner that makes the clients' interests primary and protects clients' interests to the greatest extent possible. In some cases, protecting clients' interests may require termination of the professional relationship with proper referral of the client.

(b) Social workers should not take unfair advantage of any professional relationship or exploit others to further their personal, religious, political, or business interests.

(c) Social workers should not engage in dual or multiple relationships with clients or former clients in which there is a risk of exploitation or potential harm to the client. In instances when dual or multiple relationships are unavoidable, social workers should take steps to protect clients and are responsible for setting clear, appropriate, and culturally sensitive boundaries. (Dual or multiple relationships occur when social workers relate to clients in more than one relationship, whether professional, social, or business. Dual or multiple relationships can occur simultaneously or consecutively.)

(d) When social workers provide services to two or more people who have a relationship with each other (for example, couples, family members), social workers should clarity with all parties which individuals will be considered clients and the nature of social workers' professional obligations to the various individuals who are receiving services. Social workers who anticipate a conflict of interest among the individuals receiving services or who anticipate having to perform in potentially conflicting roles (for example, when a social worker is asked to testify in a child custody dispute or divorce proceedings involving clients) should clarify their role with the parties involved and take appropriate action to minimize any conflict of interest.

1.07 Privacy and Confidentiality

(a) Social workers should respect clients' right to privacy. Social workers should not solicit private information from clients unless it is essential to providing services or conducting social work evaluation or research. Once private information is shared, standards of confidentiality apply.

(b) Social workers may disclose confidential information when appropriate with valid consent from a client, or a person legally authorized to consent on behalf of a client.

(c) Social workers should protect the confidentiality of all information obtained in the course of professional service, except for compelling professional reasons. The general expectation that social workers will keep information confidential does not apply when disclosure is necessary to prevent serious, foreseeable, and imminent harm to a client or other identifiable person or when laws or regulations require disclosure without a client's consent. In all instances, social workers should disclose the least amount of confidential information necessary to achieve the desired purpose; only information that is directly relevant to the purpose for which the disclosure is made should be revealed.

(d) Social workers should inform clients, to the extent possible, about the disclosure of confidential information and the potential consequences, when feasible before the disclosure is made. This applies whether social workers disclose confidential information on the basis of a legal requirement or client consent.

(e) Social workers should discuss with clients and other interested parties the nature of confidentiality and limitations of clients' right to confidentiality. Social workers should review with clients circumstances where confidential information may be requested and where disclosure of confidential information may be legally required. This discussion should occur as soon as possible in the social worker–client relationship and as needed throughout the course of the relationship.

(f) When social workers provide counseling services to families, couples, or groups, social workers should seek agreement among the parties involved concerning each individual's right to confidentiality and obligation to preserve the confidentiality of information shared by others. Social workers should inform participants in family, couples, or group counseling that social workers cannot guarantee that all participants will honor such agreements.

(g) Social workers should inform clients involved in family, couples, marital, or group counseling of the social worker's, employer's, and agency's policy concerning the social worker's disclosure of confidential information among the parties involved in the counseling.

(h) Social workers should not disclose confidential information to third-party payers unless clients have authorized such disclosure.

(i) Social workers should not discuss confidential information in any setting unless privacy can be ensured. Social workers should not discuss confidential information in public or semipublic areas such as hallways, waiting rooms, elevators, and restaurants.

(j) Social workers should protect the confidentiality of clients during legal proceedings to the extent permitted by law. When a court of law or other legally authorized body orders social workers to disclose confidential or privileged information without a client's consent and such disclosure could cause harm to the client, social workers should request that the court withdraw or limit the order as narrowly as possible or maintain the records under seal, unavailable for public inspection.

(k) Social workers should protect the confidentiality of clients when responding to requests from members of the media.

(l) Social workers should protect the confidentiality of clients' written and electronic records and other sensitive information. Social workers should take reasonable steps to ensure that clients' records are stored in a secure location and that clients' records are not available to others who are not authorized to have access.

(m) Social workers should take precautions to ensure and maintain the confidentiality of information transmitted to other parties through the use of computers, electronic mail, facsimile machines, telephones and telephone answering machines, and other electronic or computer technology. Disclosure of identifying information should be avoided whenever possible.

(n) Social workers should transfer or dispose of clients' records in a manner that protects clients' confidentiality and is consistent with state statutes governing records and social work licensure.

(o) Social workers should take reasonable precautions to protect client confidentiality in the event of the social worker's termination of practice, incapacitation, or death.

(p) Social workers should not disclose identifying information when discussing clients for teaching or training purposes unless the client has consented to disclosure of confidential information.

(q) Social workers should not disclose identifying information when discussing clients with consultants unless the client has consented to disclosure of confidential information or there is a compelling need for such disclosure.

(r) Social workers should protect the confidentiality of deceased clients consistent with the preceding standards.

1.08 Access to Records

(a) Social workers should provide clients with reasonable access to records concerning the clients. Social workers who are concerned that clients' access to their records could cause serious misunderstanding or harm to the client should provide assistance in interpreting the records and consultation with the client regarding the records. Social workers should limit clients' access to their records, or portions of their records, only in exceptional circumstances when there is compelling evidence that such access would cause serious harm to the client. Both clients' requests and the rationale for withholding some or all of the record should be documented in clients' files.

(b) When providing clients with access to their records, social workers should take steps to protect the confidentiality of other individuals identified or discussed in such records.

1.09 Sexual Relationships

(a) Social workers should under no circumstances engage in sexual activities or sexual contact with current clients, whether such contact is consensual or forced.

(b) Social workers should not engage in sexual activities or sexual contact with clients' relatives or other individuals with whom clients maintain a close personal relationship when there is a risk of exploitation or potential harm to the client. Sexual activity or sexual contact with clients' relatives or other individuals with whom clients maintain a personal relationship has the potential to be harmful to the client and may make it difficult for the social worker and client to maintain appropriate professional boundaries. Social workers—not their clients, their clients' relatives, or other individuals with whom the client maintains a personal relationship—assume the full burden for setting clear, appropriate, and culturally sensitive boundaries.

(c) Social workers should not engage in sexual activities or sexual contact with former clients because of the potential for harm to the client. If social workers engage in conduct contrary to this prohibition or claim that an exception to this prohibition is warranted due to extraordinary circumstances, it is social workers—not their clients—who assume the full burden of demonstrating that the former client has not been exploited, coerced, or manipulated, intentionally or unintentionally.

(d) Social workers should not provide clinical services to individuals with whom they have had a prior sexual relationship. Providing clinical services to a former sexual partner has the potential to be harmful to the individual and is likely to make it difficult for the social worker and individual to maintain appropriate professional boundaries.

1.10 Physical Contact

Social workers should not engage in physical contact with clients when there is a possibility of psychological harm to the client as a result of the contact (such as cradling or caressing clients). Social workers who engage in appropriate physical contact with clients are responsible for setting clear, appropriate, and culturally sensitive boundaries that govern such physical contact.

1.11 Sexual Harassment

Social workers should not sexually harass clients. Sexual harassment includes sexual advances, sexual solicitation, requests for sexual favors, and other verbal or physical conduct of a sexual nature.

1.12 Derogatory Language

Social workers should not use derogatory language in their written or verbal communications to or about clients. Social workers should use accurate and respectful language in all communications to and about clients.

1.13 Payment for Services

(a) When setting fees, social workers should ensure that the fees are fair, reasonable, and commensurate with the services performed. Consideration should be given to clients' ability to pay.

(b) Social workers should avoid accepting goods or services from clients as payment for professional services. Bartering arrangements, particularly involving services, create the potential for conflicts of interest, exploitation, and inappropriate boundaries in social workers' relationships with clients. Social workers should explore and may participate in bartering only in very limited circumstances when it can be demonstrated that such arrangements are an accepted practice among professionals in the local community, considered to be essential for the provision of services, negotiated without coercion, and entered into at the clients' initiative and with the client's informed consent. Social workers who accept goods or services from clients as payment for professional services assume the full burden of demonstrating that this arrangement will not be detrimental to the client or the professional relationship.

(c) Social workers should not solicit a private fee or other remuneration for providing services to clients who are entitled to such available services through the social workers' employer or agency.

1.14 Clients Who Lack Decision-Making Capacity

When social workers act on behalf of clients who lack the capacity to make informed decisions, social workers should take reasonable steps to safeguard the interests and rights of those clients.

1.15 Interruption of Services

Social workers should make reasonable efforts to ensure continuity of services in the event that services are interrupted by factors such as unavailability, relocation, illness, disability, or death.

1.16 Termination of Services

(a) Social workers should terminate services to clients and professional relationships with them when such services and relationships are no longer required or no longer serve the clients' needs or interests.

(b) Social workers should take reasonable steps to avoid abandoning clients who are still in need of services. Social workers should withdraw services precipitously only under unusual circumstances, giving careful consideration to all factors in the situation and taking care to minimize possible adverse effects. Social workers should assist in making appropriate arrangements for continuation of services when necessary.

(c) Social workers in fee-for-service settings may terminate services to clients who are not paying an overdue balance if the financial contractual arrangements have been made clear to the client, if the client does not pose an imminent danger to self or others, and if the clinical and other consequences of the current nonpayment have been addressed and discussed with the client.

(d) Social workers should not terminate services to pursue a social, financial, or sexual relationship with a client.

(e) Social workers who anticipate the termination or interruption of services to clients should notify clients promptly and seek the transfer, referral, or continuation of services in relation to the clients' needs and preferences.

(f) Social workers who are leaving an employment setting should inform clients of appropriate options for the continuation of services and of the benefits and risks of the options.

2. Social Workers' Ethical Responsibilities to Colleagues

2.01 Respect

(a) Social workers should treat colleagues with respect and should represent accurately and fairly the qualifications, views, and obligations of colleagues.

(b) Social workers should avoid unwarranted negative criticism of colleagues in communications with clients or with other professionals. Unwarranted negative criticism may include demeaning comments that refer to colleagues' level of competence or to individuals' attributes such as race, ethnicity, national origin, color, sex, sexual orientation, age, marital status, political belief, religion, or mental or physical disability.

(c) Social workers should cooperate with social work colleagues and with colleagues of other professions when such cooperation serves the well-being of clients.

2.02 Confidentiality

Social workers should respect confidential information shared by colleagues in the course of their professional relationships and transactions. Social workers should ensure that such colleagues understand social workers' obligation to respect confidentiality and any exceptions related to it.

2.03 Interdisciplinary Collaboration

(a) Social workers who are members of an interdisciplinary team should participate in and contribute to decisions that affect the well-being of clients by drawing on the perspectives, values, and experiences of the social work profession. Professional and ethical obligations of the interdisciplinary team as a whole and of its individual members should be clearly established.

(b) Social workers for whom a team decision raises ethical concerns should attempt to resolve the disagreement through appropriate channels. If the disagreement cannot be resolved, social workers should pursue other avenues to address their concerns consistent with client well-being.

2.04 Disputes Involving Colleagues

(a) Social workers should not take advantage of a dispute between a colleague and employer to obtain a position or otherwise advance the social workers' own interests.

(b) Social workers should not exploit clients in disputes with colleagues or engage clients in any inappropriate discussion of conflicts between social workers and their colleagues.

2.05 Consultation

(a) Social workers should seek the advice and counsel of colleagues whenever such consultation is in the best interests of clients.

(b) Social workers should keep themselves informed about colleagues' areas of expertise and competencies. Social workers should seek consultation only from colleagues who have demonstrated knowledge, expertise, and competence related to the subject of the consultation.

(c) When consulting with colleagues about clients, social workers should disclose the least amount of information necessary to achieve the purposes of the consultation.

2.06 Referral for Services

(a) Social workers should refer clients to other professionals when the other professionals' specialized knowledge or expertise is needed to serve clients fully or when social workers believe that they are not being effective or making reasonable progress with clients and that additional service is required.

(b) Social workers who refer clients to other professionals should take appropriate steps to facilitate an orderly transfer of responsibility. Social workers who refer clients to other professionals should disclose, with clients' consent, all pertinent information to the new service providers.

(c) Social workers are prohibited from giving or receiving payment for a referral when no professional service is provided by the referring social worker.

2.07 Sexual Relationships

(a) Social workers who function as supervisors or educators should not engage in sexual activities or contact with supervisees, students, trainees, or other colleagues over whom they exercise professional authority.

(b) Social workers should avoid engaging in sexual relationships with colleagues when there is potential for a conflict of interest. Social workers who become involved in, or anticipate becoming involved in, a sexual relationship with a colleague have a duty to transfer professional responsibilities, when necessary, in order to avoid a conflict of interest.

2.08 Sexual Harassment

Social workers should not sexually harass supervisees, students, trainees, or colleagues. Sexual harassment includes sexual advances, sexual solicitation, requests for sexual favors, and other verbal or physical conduct of a sexual nature.

2.09 Impairment of Colleagues

(a) Social workers who have direct knowledge of a social work colleague's impairment that is due to personal problems, psychosocial distress, substance abuse, or mental health difficulties and that interferes with practice effectiveness should consult with that colleague when feasible and assist the colleague in taking remedial action.

(b) Social workers who believe that a social work colleague's impairment interferes with practice effectiveness and that the colleague has not taken adequate steps to address the impairment should take action through appropriate channels established by employers, agencies, NASW, licensing and regulatory bodies, and other professional organizations.

2.10 Incompetence of Colleagues

(a) Social workers who have direct knowledge of a social work colleague's incompetence should consult with that colleague when feasible and assist the colleague in taking remedial action.

(b) Social workers who believe that a social work colleague is incompetent and has not taken adequate steps to address the incompetence should take action through appropriate channels established by employers, agencies, NASW, licensing and regulatory bodies, and other professional organizations.

2.11 Unethical Conduct of Colleagues

(a) Social workers should take adequate measures to discourage, prevent, expose, and correct the unethical conduct of colleagues.

(b) Social workers should be knowledgeable about established policies and procedures for handling concerns about colleagues' unethical behavior. Social workers should be familiar with national, state, and local procedures for handling ethics complaints. These include policies and procedures created by NASW, licensing and regulatory bodies, employers, agencies, and other professional organizations.

(c) Social workers who believe that a colleague has acted unethically should seek resolution by discussing their concerns with the colleague when feasible and when such discussion is likely to be productive.

(d) When necessary, social workers who believe that a colleague has acted unethically should take action through appropriate formal channels (such as contacting a state licensing board or regulatory body, an NASW committee on inquiry, or other professional ethics committees).

(e) Social workers should defend and assist colleagues who are unjustly charged with unethical conduct.

3. Social Workers' Ethical Responsibilities in Practice Settings

3.01 Supervision and Consultation

(a) Social workers who provide supervision or consultation should have the necessary knowledge and skill to supervise or consult appropriately and should do so only within their areas of knowledge and competence.

(b) Social workers who provide supervision or consultation are responsible for setting clear, appropriate, and culturally sensitive boundaries.

(c) Social workers should not engage in any dual or multiple relationships with supervisees in which there is a risk of exploitation of or potential harm to the supervisee.

(d) Social workers who provide supervision should evaluate supervisees' performance in a manner that is fair and respectful.

3.02 Education and Training

(a) Social workers who function as educators, field instructors for students, or trainers should provide instruction only within their areas of knowledge and competence and should provide instruction based on the most current information and knowledge available in the profession.

(b) Social workers who function as educators or field instructors for students should evaluate students' performance in a manner that is fair and respectful.

(c) Social workers who function as educators or field instructors for students should take reasonable steps to ensure that clients are routinely informed when services are being provided by students.

(d) Social workers who function as educators or field instructors for students should not engage in any dual or multiple relationships with students in which there is a risk of exploitation or potential harm to the student. Social work educators and field instructors are responsible for setting clear, appropriate, and culturally sensitive boundaries.

3.03 Performance Evaluation

Social workers who have responsibility for evaluating the performance of others should fulfill such responsibility in a fair and considerate manner and on the basis of clearly stated criteria.

3.04 Client Records

(a) Social workers should take reasonable steps to ensure that documentation in records is accurate and reflects the services provided.

(b) Social workers should include sufficient and timely documentation in records to facilitate the delivery of services and to ensure continuity of services provided to clients in the future.

(c) Social workers' documentation should protect clients' privacy to the extent that is possible and appropriate and should include only information that is directly relevant to the delivery of services.

(d) Social workers should store records following the termination of services to ensure reasonable future access. Records should be maintained for the number of years required by state statutes or relevant contracts.

3.05 Billing

Social workers should establish and maintain billing practices that accurately reflect the nature and extent of services provided and that identify who provided the service in the practice setting.

3.06 Client Transfer

(a) When an individual who is receiving services from another agency or colleague contacts a social worker for services, the social worker should carefully consider the client's needs before agreeing to provide services. In order to minimize possible confusion and conflict, social workers should discuss with potential clients the nature of the clients' current relationship with other service providers and the implications, including possible benefits or risks, of entering into a relationship with a new service provider.

(b) If a new client has been served by another agency or colleague, social workers should discuss with the client whether consultation with the previous service provider is in the client's best interest.

3.07 Administration

(a) Social work administrators should advocate within and outside their agencies for adequate resources to meet clients' needs.

(b) Social workers should advocate for resource allocation procedures that are open and fair. When not all clients' needs can be met, an allocation procedure should be developed that is nondiscriminatory and based on appropriate and consistently applied principles.

(c) Social workers who are administrators should take reasonable steps to ensure that adequate agency or organizational resources are available to provide appropriate staff supervision.

(d) Social work administrators should take reasonable steps to ensure that the working environment for which they are responsible is consistent with and encourages compliance with the *NASW Code of Ethics.* Social work administrators should take reasonable steps to eliminate any conditions in their organizations that violate, interfere with, or discourage compliance with the *Code.*

3.08 Continuing Education and Staff Development

Social work administrators and supervisors should take reasonable steps to provide or arrange for continuing education and staff development for all staff for whom they are responsible. Continuing education and staff development should address current knowledge and emerging developments related to social work practice and ethics.

3.09 Commitments to Employers

(a) Social workers generally should adhere to commitments made to employers and employing organizations.

(b) Social workers should work to improve employing agencies' policies and procedures and the efficiency and effectiveness of their services.

(c) Social workers should take reasonable steps to ensure that employers are aware of social workers' ethical obligations as set forth in the *NASW Code of Ethics* and of the implications of those obligations for social work practice.

(d) Social workers should not allow an employing organization's policies, procedures, regulations, or administrative orders to interfere with their ethical practice of social work. Social workers should take reasonable steps to ensure that their employing organizations' practices are consistent with the *NASW Code of Ethics.*

(e) Social workers should act to prevent and eliminate discrimination in the employing organization's work assignments and in its employment policies and practices.

(f) Social workers should accept employment or arrange student field placements only in organizations that exercise fair personnel practices.

(g) Social workers should be diligent stewards of the resources of their employing organizations, wisely conserving funds where appropriate and never misappropriating funds or using them for unintended purposes.

3.10 Labor–Management Disputes

(a) Social workers may engage in organized action, including the formation of and participation in labor unions, to improve services to clients and working conditions.

(b) The actions of social workers who are involved in labor–management disputes, job actions, or labor strikes should be guided by the profession's values, ethical principles, and ethical standards. Reasonable differences of opinion exist among social workers concerning their primary obligation as professionals during an actual or threatened labor strike or job action. Social workers should carefully examine relevant issues and their possible impact on clients before deciding on a course of action.

4. Social Workers' Ethical Responsibilities as Professionals

4.01 Competence

(a) Social workers should accept responsibility or employment only on the basis of existing competence or the intention to acquire the necessary competence.

(b) Social workers should strive to become and remain proficient in professional practice and the performance of professional functions. Social workers should critically examine and keep current with emerging knowledge relevant to social work. Social workers should routinely review the professional literature and participate in continuing education relevant to social work practice and social work ethics.

(c) Social workers should base practice on recognized knowledge, including empirically based knowledge, relevant to social work and social work ethics.

4.02 Discrimination

Social workers should not practice, condone, facilitate, or collaborate with any form of discrimination on the basis of race, ethnicity, national origin, color, sex, sexual orientation, age, marital status, political belief, religion, or mental or physical disability.

4.03 Private Conduct

Social workers should not permit their private conduct to interfere with their ability to fulfill their professional responsibilities.

4.04 Dishonesty, Fraud, and Deception

Social workers should not participate in, condone, or be associated with dishonesty, fraud, or deception.

4.05 Impairment

(a) Social workers should not allow their own personal problems, psychosocial distress, legal problems, substance abuse, or mental health difficulties to interfere with their professional judgment and performance or to jeopardize the best interests of people for whom they have a professional responsibility.

(b) Social workers whose personal problems, psychosocial distress, legal problems, substance abuse, or mental health difficulties interfere with their professional judgment and performance should immediately seek consultation and take appropriate remedial action by seeking professional help, making adjustments in workload, terminating practice, or taking any other steps necessary to protect clients and others.

4.06 Misrepresentation

(a) Social workers should make clear distinctions between statements made and actions engaged in as a private individual and as a representative of the social work profession, a professional social work organization, or the social worker's employing agency.

(b) Social workers who speak on behalf of professional social work organizations should accurately represent the official and authorized positions of the organizations.

(c) Social workers should ensure that their representations to clients, agencies, and the public of professional qualifications, credentials, education, competence, affiliations, services provided, or results to be achieved are accurate. Social workers should claim only those relevant professional credentials they actually possess and take steps to correct any inaccuracies or misrepresentations of their credentials by others.

4.07 Solicitations

(a) Social workers should not engage in uninvited solicitation of potential clients who, because of their circumstances, are vulnerable to undue influence, manipulation, or coercion.

(b) Social workers should not engage in solicitation of testimonial endorsements (including solicitation of consent to use a client's prior statement as a testimonial endorsement) from current clients or from other people who, because of their particular circumstances, are vulnerable to undue influence.

4.08 Acknowledging Credit

(a) Social workers should take responsibility and credit, including authorship credit, only for work they have actually performed and to which they have contributed.

(b) Social workers should honestly acknowledge the work of and the contributions made by others.

5.   Social Workers' Ethical Responsibilities to the Social Work Profession

5.01   Integrity of the Profession

(a) Social workers should work toward the maintenance and promotion of high standards of practice.

(b) Social workers should uphold and advance the values, ethics, knowledge, and mission of the profession. Social workers should protect, enhance, and improve the integrity of the profession through appropriate study and research, active discussion, and responsible criticism of the profession.

(c) Social workers should contribute time and professional expertise to activities that promote respect for the value, integrity, and competence of the social work profession. These activities may include teaching, research, consultation, service, legislative testimony, presentations in the community, and participation in their professional organizations.

(d) Social workers should contribute to the knowledge base of social work and share with colleagues their knowledge related to practice, research, and ethics. Social workers should seek to contribute to the profession's literature and to share their knowledge at professional meetings and conferences.

(e) Social workers should act to prevent the unauthorized and unqualified practice of social work.

5.02   Evaluation and Research

(a) Social workers should monitor and evaluate policies, the implementation of programs, and practice interventions.

(b) Social workers should promote and facilitate evaluation and research to contribute to the development of knowledge.

(c) Social workers should critically examine and keep current with emerging knowledge relevant to social work and fully use evaluation and research evidence in their professional practice.

(d) Social workers engaged in evaluation or research should carefully consider possible consequences and should follow guidelines developed for the protection of evaluation and research participants. Appropriate institutional review boards should be consulted.

(e) Social workers engaged in evaluation or research should obtain voluntary and written informed consent from participants, when appropriate, without any implied or actual deprivation or penalty for refusal to participate; without undue inducement to participate; and with due regard for participants' well-being, privacy, and dignity. Informed consent should include information about the nature, extent, and duration of the participation requested and disclosure of the risks and benefits of participation in the research.

(f) When evaluation or research participants are incapable of giving informed consent, social workers should provide an appropriate explanation to the participants, obtain the participants' assent to the extent they are able, and obtain written consent from an appropriate proxy.

(g) Social workers should never design or conduct evaluation or research that does not use consent procedures, such as certain forms of naturalistic observation and archival research, unless rigorous and responsible review of the research has found it to be justified because of its prospective scientific, educational, or applied value and unless equally effective alternative procedures that do not involve waiver of consent are not feasible.

(h) Social workers should inform participants of their right to withdraw from evaluation and research at any time without penalty.

(i) Social workers should take appropriate steps to ensure that participants in evaluation and research have access to appropriate supportive services.

(j) Social workers engaged in evaluation for research should protect participants from unwarranted physical or mental distress, harm, danger, or deprivation.

(k) Social workers engaged in the evaluation of services should discuss collected information only for professional purposes and only with people professionally concerned with this information.

(l) Social workers engaged in evaluation or research should ensure the anonymity or confidentiality of participants and of the data obtained from them. Social workers should inform participants of any limits of confidentiality, the measures that will be taken to ensure confidentiality, and when any records containing research data will be destroyed.

(m) Social workers who report evaluation and research results should protect participants' confidentiality by omitting identifying information unless proper consent has been obtained authorizing disclosure.

(n) Social workers should report evaluation and research findings accurately. They should not fabricate or falsify results and should take steps to correct any errors later found in published data using standard publication methods.

(o) Social workers engaged in evaluation or research should be alert to and avoid conflicts of interest and dual relationships with participants, should inform participants when a real or potential conflict of interest arises, and should take steps to resolve the issue in a manner that makes participants' interests primary.

(p) Social workers should educate themselves, their students, and their colleagues about responsible research practices.

6. Social Workers' Ethical Responsibilities to the Broader Society

6.01 Social Welfare

Social workers should promote the general welfare of society, from local to global levels, and the development of people, their communities, and their environments. Social workers should advocate for living conditions conducive to the fulfillment of basic human needs and should promote social, economic, political, and cultural values and institutions that are compatible with the realization of social justice.

6.02 Public Participation

Social workers should facilitate informed participation by the public in shaping social policies and institutions.

6.03 Public Emergencies

Social workers should provide appropriate professional services in public emergencies to the greatest extent possible.

6.04 Social and Political Action

(a) Social workers should engage in social and political action that seeks to ensure that all people have equal access to the resources, employment, services, and opportunities they require to meet their basic human needs and to develop fully. Social workers should be aware of the impact of the political arena on practice and should advocate for changes in policy and legislation to improve social conditions in order to meet basic human needs and promote social justice.

(b) Social workers should act to expand choice and opportunity for all people, with special regard for vulnerable, disadvantaged, oppressed, and exploited people and groups.

(c) Social workers should promote conditions that encourage respect for cultural and social diversity within the United States and globally. Social workers should promote policies and practices that demonstrate respect for difference, support the expansion of cultural knowledge and resources, advocate for programs and institutions that demonstrate cultural competence, and promote policies that safeguard the rights of and confirm equity and social justice for all people.

(d) Social workers should act to prevent and eliminate domination of, exploitation of, and discrimination against any person, group, or class on the basis of race, ethnicity, national origin, color, sex, sexual orientation, age, marital status, political belief, religion, or mental or physical disability.

Name Index

Subject Index

COLLABORATIVE SOCIAL WORK
Edited by Sybil Sosin
Picture research by Cheryl Kucharzak
Production supervision by Kim Vander Steen
Designed by Lucy Lesiak Design, Park Ridge, Illinois
Composition by Point West, Inc., Carol Stream, Illinois
Typefaces, Palatino, Futura, & Helvetica
Paper, Finch Opaque
Printed and bound by The P. A. Hutchison Company, Mayfield, Pennsylvania